Quantum Computing and Artificial Intelligence in Logistics and Supply Chain Management

This book discusses the transformative potential of quantum computing in reshaping the landscape of supply chain management. It bridges the gap between these two dynamic fields, offering a comprehensive guide to the application of quantum principles in supply chain operations. Through detailed examples and case studies, it highlights how quantum computing can tackle industry-specific issues, such as managing global supply chain disruptions, enhancing production schedules, and enabling real-time decision-making. This book is for researchers, professionals, and technologists interested in quantum computing and supply chain practices.

Features:

- Provides an in-depth analysis of quantum computing technologies and their capacity to solve complex optimization problems at scales unimaginable with traditional computing
- Examines the impact of quantum computing on manufacturing and logistics, with a focus on sectors such as automotive and aerospace
- Provides real-world scenarios illustrating how quantum solutions can streamline operations and drive efficiency
- Explores quantum algorithms and their use in addressing challenges like route optimization, inventory management, and demand forecasting, offering strategies to reduce costs and improve resilience
- Considers the current limitations, ethical implications, and the path to widespread adoption of quantum computing in supply chains, emphasizing the need for interdisciplinary collaboration

Advances in Digital Technologies for Smart Applications

Series Editor: Saad Motahhir

The *Advances in Digital Technologies for Smart Applications* series publishes leading-edge research on innovative digital technologies and their application in smart systems. Key topics include AI, IoT, blockchain, and their integration into various sectors, including finance, healthcare, and public governance.

Data Analytics for Finance Using Python
Nitin Jaglal Untwal, Utku Kose

Big Data and Blockchain Technology for Secure IoT Applications
Shitharth Selvarajan, Gouse Baig Mohammad, Sadda Bharath Reddy, Praveen Kumar Balachandran

Technology-Based Teaching and Learning in Pakistani English Language Classrooms
Muhammad Mooneeb Ali

Medical Knowledge Paradigms for Enabling the Digital Health Ecosystem
Usha Desai, Vivek P Chavda, Ankit Vijayvargiya, Ravichander Janapati

Soft Computing in Renewable Energy Technologies
Najib El Ouanjli, Mahmoud A. Mossa, Mariya Ouaissa, Sanjeevikumar Padmanaban, Said Mahfoud

Leveraging the Potential of Artificial Intelligence in the Real World: Smart Cities and Healthcare
Tien Anh Tran, Edeh Michael Onyema, Arij Naser Abougreen

eGovernment Whole-of-Government Approach for Good Governance: The Back-Office Integrated Management IT Systems
Said Azelmad

Advances in Digital Marketing in the Era of Artificial Intelligence: Case Studies and Data Analysis for Business Problem Solving
Moez Ltifi

Quantum Computing and Artificial Intelligence in Logistics and Supply Chain Management
Pushan Kumar Dutta, Pronaya Bhattacharya, Jai Prakash Verma, Ashok Chopra, Neel Kanth Kundu, Khursheed Aurangzeb

For more information about this series, please visit: https://www.routledge.com/Advances-in-Digital-Technologies-for-Smart-Applications/book-series/ADT

Quantum Computing and Artificial Intelligence in Logistics and Supply Chain Management

Edited by
Pushan Kumar Dutta, Pronaya Bhattacharya,
Jai Prakash Verma, Ashok Chopra,
Neel Kanth Kundu and Khursheed Aurangzeb

CRC Press
Taylor & Francis Group
Boca Raton London New York

CRC Press is an imprint of the
Taylor & Francis Group, an **informa** business
A CHAPMAN & HALL BOOK

Designed cover image: Shutterstock image ID: 2235023207

First edition published 2026
by CRC Press
2385 NW Executive Center Drive, Suite 320, Boca Raton FL 33431

and by CRC Press
4 Park Square, Milton Park, Abingdon, Oxon, OX14 4RN

CRC Press is an imprint of Taylor & Francis Group, LLC

ISBN: 978-1-032-79811-0 (hbk)
ISBN: 978-1-032-80729-4 (pbk)
ISBN: 978-1-003-49829-2 (ebk)

DOI: 10.1201/9781003498292

Typeset in Sabon
by Deanta Global Publishing Services, Chennai, India

Contents

Preface

The world of supply chain logistics is changing fast, driven by exciting new technologies like quantum computing and artificial intelligence (AI). These tools are helping make logistics smarter, safer, and more sustainable. This book, *Emerging Issues of Quantum Computing and Artificial Intelligence in Supply Chain Logistics*, is here to explain how these technologies are shaping the future of how goods are managed, moved, and delivered.

The logistics sector plays a key role in connecting people and businesses. But as supply chains get more complex, keeping them efficient and secure becomes a big challenge. Quantum computing brings powerful problem-solving abilities to this field, helping with scheduling, risk management, and predicting future needs. AI works alongside quantum computing to improve decision-making and make systems more flexible and reliable. Together, these technologies create solutions that are both smarter and more practical for the challenges of today and tomorrow.

The introduction provides a clear overview of the challenges facing supply chains today, like the need to cut costs, reduce environmental impact, and protect against cyberattacks. It also sets the stage for the rest of the book by explaining why quantum computing and AI are important tools for addressing these challenges. This section helps readers understand why now is the right time to focus on these technologies.

The first part of the book focuses on AI and its role in supply chain management. Topics include how AI can classify objects in real time, secure data communication, and create smarter strategies for meeting customer needs. By showing practical examples, this section makes it easy to see how AI is already helping logistics systems work better.

The second part moves into quantum computing. Here, readers learn how quantum systems are used to solve complex logistics problems, improve the movement of goods, and even help companies better predict what customers will want. Quantum computing's ability to process huge amounts of data quickly makes it a perfect fit for logistics tasks that need both speed and accuracy.

The final section ties everything together by focusing on how these technologies can make supply chains more sustainable and secure. Case studies show how Industry 4.0 technologies are helping companies meet sustainability goals. Other chapters explain how quantum computing can improve marketing, protect supply chain communication, and even help farmers work more efficiently.

The conclusion wraps up the key ideas from the book, showing how quantum computing and AI will continue to shape the future of supply chains. It also encourages readers to think about how these tools can help solve real-world problems and improve global trade.

This book is written for everyone—students, researchers, business leaders, or anyone curious about how modern technology is changing the world of logistics. We hope this book makes these complex topics simple and shows how they can make a big difference in everyday life. As you read through the chapters, you'll find real examples and practical ideas that can inspire new ways to think about logistics.

Editors

Pushan Kumar Dutta is an accomplished academic, researcher, and Assistant Professor Grade III Associate Professor at Amity University, Kolkata, with expertise in Electronics and Communication Engineering, AI, and digital transformation. With a prolific record in both research and academic publishing, Dr Dutta has edited over 30 books for prestigious publishers such as IGI Global, Springer, Elsevier, Taylor & Francis, and more, primarily focusing on emerging technologies and Industry 4.0/5.0 advancements. His areas of editorial expertise encompass AI and machine learning in healthcare and business, sustainable development, IoMT, quantum computing applications, and digital manufacturing.

In addition to his publishing achievements, Dr Dutta is Series Editor for *Sustainable Industrial Engineering Systems* with CRC Press. Recognized as a "Mentor of Change" by NITI Aayog, he is dedicated to guiding students, fostering innovative project development, and mentoring award-winning projects. His impactful contributions in predictive analytics, edge computing, and data mining, especially in smart healthcare and earthquake studies, highlight his commitment to applying AI for societal and industrial betterment. Dr Dutta is a recipient of the Venus International Faculty Award (2018) and is among the top three researchers at Amity University Kolkata by Scopus-listed publications. He holds two patents in advanced technological solutions, contributes to hackathon mentorship, and actively participates in sustainable engineering practices through design thinking. Dr Dutta's teaching encompasses Data Science, AI, Basic Electrical, and Digital Architecture, and he excels in research methodology, project ideation, and sustainable development coursework.

Pronaya Bhattacharya received his PhD from Dr. A.P.J. Abdul Kalam Technical University, Lucknow, Uttar Pradesh, India. He is currently Associate Professor in the Computer Science and Engineering Department, Amity School of Engineering and Technology, Amity University, Kolkata, India. He has over 10 years of teaching experience. He has authored or coauthored more than 140 research papers in leading SCI journals and top core IEEE COMSOC conferences. Some of his top-notch findings are published in reputed SCI journals, such as *IEEE JBHI, IEEE TVT, IEEE IoTJ, IEEE TNSE, IEEE TNSM, IEEE TCSS, IEEE TGCN, IEEE Internet of Things Magazine, IEEE Communication Standards Magazine, ETT* (Wiley), *Expert Systems* (Wiley), *CCPE* (Wiley), *FGCS* (Elsevier), *OQEL* (Springer), *WPC* (Springer), *ACM-MOBICOM, IEEE-INFOCOM, IEEE GLOBECOM, IEEE-ICC, IEEE-CITS, IEEE-ICIEM, IEEE-CCCI*, and *IEEE-ECAI*. He has an H-index of 33 and an i10-index of 71. He has edited five books and is currently editing eight books with renowned publishers like IGI Global, Elsevier, and Springer. His research interests include healthcare analytics, optical switching and networking, federated learning, blockchain, and the IoT. He is listed in the top 2% of scientists as per the list published by Stanford University. He has been appointed in the capacity of a keynote speaker, a technical committee member, and the session chair across the globe. He has won ten Best Paper Awards at Springer ICRIC-2019, IEEE-ICIEM-2021, IEEE-ECAI-2021, Springer COMS2-2021, and IEEE-ICIEM-2022. He is a reviewer of 40 reputed SCI journals, such as *IEEE IoTJ, IEEE TII, IEEE JBHI, IEEE Sensors, IEEE TVT, IEEE Network Magazine, ETT* (Wiley), *IJCS* (Wiley), *MTAP* (Springer), *OSN* (Elsevier), *WPC* (Springer), and others. Orcid ID: https://orcid.org/0000-0002-1206-2298

Jai Prakash Verma is working as Associate Professor in the Computer Science and Engineering Department, Institute of Technology, Nirma University. He has been associated with the department since July 2006. Dr Verma received his BSc (PCM) and MCA degrees from the University of Rajasthan, Jaipur, and his PhD from Charusat University, Changa. His PhD subject area was Text Data Summarization and Big Data Analytics. His research interests include data mining, big data analytics, and machine learning. He has contributed to the research in these domains with several international conferences and journal publications. He is a recognized PhD guide at Nirma University and currently guides three PhD scholars. He has also been working as the IQAC coordinator for the School of Technology at Nirma University and actively contributing to all ranking-related tasks for the institute, such as NAAC, NBA, NIRF, etc. He is actively involved in various training programs, such as customized training on big data analytics for naval officers at INS Valsura, Indian Navy, and SAC-ISRO scientists in Ahmedabad. Along with other faculty members in the department, he coordinates activities of CoE (Data Science) in collaboration with SUNY Binghamton, New York. Orcid ID: 0000-0001-6116-1383

Ashok Chopra is a highly skilled, accomplished, and experienced senior academician in teaching, training, and development, with a strong learning acumen. He is Registrar, Program Chair, PhD holder, Member of the University Research Committee at Amity University Dubai, and Associate Professor at Amity Business School. He has demonstrated research success with multiple published papers, articles, books, and chapters. He is an expert in creating stimulating environments for applied learning, accommodating students'/trainees' diverse cultural and educational backgrounds, experiences, and individual learning styles. With more than 25 years of international industry experience in senior and leadership positions, entrepreneurial expertise of more than 10 years, and more than 13 years of experience as an academician and corporate trainer, he is a perfect blend of academia, industry, and entrepreneurship.

He has to his credit 2 books, 14 book chapters and case studies, and more than 80 papers in international journals and conferences of repute; he is on the reviewing, editorial, and advisory boards of reputed journals, conferences, and institutions.

https://orcid.org/0000-0002-2863-8730, Scopus Author ID: 57208471138

He holds a PhD, MBA, and certifications such as Certified 6 Sigma Manager (Black Belt). He is also a postgraduate in Business, Administrative, and Marketing & Sales Management and Chartered Fellow CILT UK & Full Member CIPS UK.

He served as a consultant at FIATA/NAFL (International Federation of Freight Forwarders Associations), Switzerland, from Jan 2014 to Dec 2015. He has conducted over 300 corporate training programs through an entrepreneurial venture and has provided management consultancy to several organizations.

His core skills as an academician include ensuring program and course curricula are up to date, relevant, and reflective of best practices within a professional/program discipline. Further responsibilities include defining, evaluating, and validating learning outcomes for courses and programs, creating learning environments that accommodate students' diversity in cultures, education, experiences, and learning styles, and designing appropriate strategies and methods for facilitating and assessing student learning that are invitational and reflective of best practices in teaching. He has developed ways to evaluate student performance consistent with the course's learning outcomes and metrics that address multiple learning styles. He has produced multi-media materials, alternative delivery strategies, and incorporated various educational technologies into the learning process. Communicating, ensuring that students are aware of course, program learning outcomes, learning strategies, and evaluation techniques; providing individual tutoring and academic counseling as per student needs.

He has won one gold, three silver medals, and two cash prizes for topping among 26 centers in India during his postgraduation in Business Management and Marketing & Sales Management.

Neel Kanth Kundu received his B.Tech. degree in electrical engineering with a specialization in communication systems and networking from the Indian Institute of Technology Delhi, New Delhi, India, in 2018, and his

PhD degree in electronic and computer engineering (ECE) with a focus on scientific computation from The Hong Kong University of Science and Technology (HKUST), Clear Water Bay, Hong Kong, in 2022. From September 2022 to January 2023, he was Post-Doctoral Research Associate with the ECE Department, HKUST. From February 2023 to October 2023, he was Post-Doctoral Research Fellow with the Department of Electrical and Electronic Engineering, The University of Melbourne, Australia, where he holds an honorary fellow position. Since October 2023, he has been Assistant Professor with the Centre for Applied Research in Electronics, Indian Institute of Technology Delhi. He is currently a joint faculty member with the Bharti School of Telecommunication Technology and Management, Indian Institute of Technology Delhi. His research interests include signal processing for 6G wireless communications, quantum communications, and quantum information processing. He was a recipient of the INSPIRE Young Faculty Fellowship awarded by the Department of Science and Technology, Government of India. He was a recipient of the Hong Kong PhD Fellowship and the Overseas Research Award at HKUST. ORCID: https://orcid.org/0000-0002-6439-4024

Khursheed Aurangzeb (Senior Member IEEE) is Associate Professor in the Department of Computer Engineering, College of Computer and Information Sciences at King Saud University (KSU), Riyadh, Saudi Arabia. He received his PhD degree in Electronics Design from Mid Sweden University Sweden in June 2013, his MS degree in Electrical Engineering (System on Chip Design) from Linkoping University, Sweden, in 2009, and his BS degree in Computer Engineering from COMSATS Institute of Information Technology Abbottabad, Pakistan, in 2006. Dr Khursheed has authored and coauthored more than 90 publications including IEEE, ACM, Springer, Hindawi, MDPI journals, and flagship conference papers. He has obtained more than 17 years of excellent experience as an instructor and a researcher in data analytics, machine/deep learning, signal processing, electronics circuits/systems, and embedded systems. He has been involved in many research projects as a principal investigator and a co-principal investigator. His research interest is in the diverse fields of embedded systems, computer architecture, signal processing, wireless sensor networks, communication, and camera-based sensor networks, with an emphasis on big data and machine/deep learning with applications in smart grids, precision agriculture, and healthcare.

Contributors

Amir Abdelwahed
Computer Engineering and Systems
Faculty of Engineering
Ain Shams University
Cairo, Egypt

Khder Alakkari
Faculty of Economics
Tishreen University
Latakia, Syria

Hussein Alkattan
South Ural State University
Russia

Rishabh Anand
Google
Gurugram
India

Christo Ananth
Samarkhand State University
Uzbekistan

Amit Aylani
Vidyalankar Institute of Technology
Mumbai, India

Bunil Kumar Balabantaray
National Institute of Technology Meghalaya
Shillong, India

Amr Badr
Faculty of Science
School of Science and Technology
University of New England
Armidale, Australia

Purvee Bhardwaj
Rabindranath Tagore University
Bhopal, India

Ramakant Bhardwaj
Amity University
Kolkata, India

Pronaya Bhattacharya
Department of Computer Science Engineering
Amity University Kolkata
Kolkata, India

E. Bijolin Edwin
Division of Computer Science and Engineering
Karunya Institute of Technology and Sciences
Coimbatore, India

Jayanta Biswas
Amity University
Kolkata—CII School of Logistics
India

Akshat Bokdia
School of Computer Science and Engineering
Vellore Institute of Technology
Vellore, India

Rakhmanov Buribay
Samarkand State University (named after Sh. Rashidov)
Samarkand
Uzbekistan

Hoang Chi Cuong
Van Lang University
Ho Chi Minh City, Vietnam

Hamideza Rabiei Dastjerdi
Faculty of Humanities and Social Sciences
Dublin College University
Dublin, Ireland

Narayanage Jayantha Dewasiri
Faculty of Management Studies
Sabaragamuwa University of Sri Lanka
Sri Lanka

Pandya Dipali
Mechanical Engineering Program
Navrachana University
Vadodara, India

P. K. Dutta
Department of Electronics and Communication Engineering
Amity University Kolkata
Kolkata, India

V. Ebenezer
Division of Computer Science and Engineering
Karunya Institute of Technology and Sciences
Coimbatore, India

Laith Farhan
Manchester Metropolitan University
UK

Indrajit Ghosal
Brainware University
Kolkata, India

M. S. Gill
Gulzar Group of Institutions
Khanna, India

Sherif S. M. Ghoneim
Department of Electrical Engineering
College of Engineering
Taif University
Taif, Saudi Arabia

K. V. Haneefa
Christ University
Bengaluru, India

Bindiya Jain
Faculty of Computer Science and Engineering
Poornima University
Jaipur, India

M. Robinson Joel
Department of Information Technology
Kings Engineering College
Chennai, India

Seema Kaloria
Department of Computer Science & Engineering
Poornima University
Jaipur, India

Gurpreet Kaur
Chitkara Business School
Chitkara University
Punjab, India

Sudhakaru Komera
Department of Electronics and Communication Engineering
St. Johns College of Engineering and Technology
Yemmiganur, India

Lalitha Swamy Thayumanavar
National Institute of Technology Meghalaya
Shillong, India

Nitin Lodha
School of Computer Science and Engineering
Vellore Institute of Technology
Vellore, India

Suman Majumder
Nanyang Technological University
Singapore
and
Computer Science Engineering
Amity University
Kolkata, India

Udit Mamodiya
Faculty of Engineering and Technology
Poornima University
Jaipur, India

Geetha Manoharan
School of Business
SR University
Warangal, India

Purushottam Maramamula
Bharatiya Engineering Science & Technology Innovation University (BESTIU)
Andhra Pradesh, India

Maad M. Mijwil
Al-Iraqia University
Baghdad, Iraq

Madhusudan Narayan
Amity Business School
Amity University Jharkhand
Ranchi, India

Satyendra Narayan
Algoma University
Brampton, ON

Sukumar Nandi
Indian Institute of Technology Guwahati
Guwahati, India

Khoa Nguyen
Central Queensland University
Melbourne, Australia

Rachamalla Nikhitha
Department of Computer Science and Engineering
Vignana Bharathi Institute of Technology (Autonomous)
Hyderabad, India

Özen Özer
Department of Mathematics
Faculty of Science and Arts
Kırklareli University
Turkey

Dipali Pandya
Mechanical Engineering Program
Navrachana University
Vadodara, India

Viren Parikh
Mechanical Engineering Program
Navrachana University
Vadodara, India

Abhik Patra
Department of Mechanical and Automation Engineering
Amity University Kolkata
Kolkata, India

Imran Khan Patan
Department of Electronics and Communication Engineering
Jawaharlal Nehru Technological University Anantapur
Ananthapuramu, India

Abdul Razak
Entrepreneurship Development Institute of India
Ahmedabad, India

Álvaro Rocha
ISEG Lisbon School of Economics and Management
University of Lisbon
Portugal

Singla Ruchira
Department of Electrical and Electronics Engineering
Amity School of Engineering and Technology
Amity University Uttar Pradesh
India

Rahul Siripothula
Department of Computer Science and Engineering
Vignana Bharathi Institute of Technology (Autonomous)
Hyderabad, India

Rajesh Saturi
Department of Computer Science and Engineering
Vignana Bharathi Institute of Technology (Autonomous)
Hyderabad, India

Rashmi Singh
Amity Institute of Applied Sciences
Amity University
Uttar Pradesh, India

Kaloria Seema
Department of Computer Science & Engineering
Poornima University
Jaipur, India

S. M. Ghoneim Sherif
Department of Electrical Engineering
College of Engineering
Taif University
Taif, Saudi Arabia

Ashutosh Sharma
Amity Institute of Applied Sciences
Amity University Jharkhand
Ranchi, India

Amjan Shaik
BESTIU
India
and
St Peters Engineering College
Hyderabad, India

Mohammad Shahparan
Silk Road International University of Tourism and Cultural Heritage
Samarkand
Uzbekistan

Zuha Siddiqui
Department of Computer Science and Engineering
Vignana Bharathi Institute of Technology (Autonomous)
Hyderabad, India

Manisha Singh
CKMEM College
Satna, India

Arnav Sonavane
Vidyalankar Institute of Technology
Mumbai, India

Rahul Soni
Electrical and Electronics Engineering Program
School of Engineering & Technology
Navrachana University
Vadodara, India

Ashok Kumar Srivastava
Amity University Jharkhand
Ranchi, India

S. Stewart Kirubakaran
Division of Computer Science and Engineering
Karunya Institute of Technology and Sciences
Coimbatore, India

Nadir Subaşı
Department of Computer Programming
Kırklareli University
Turkey

Roshni Thanka
Division of Computer Science and Engineering
Karunya Institute of Technology and Sciences
Coimbatore, India

Emrehan Taşkin
Institute of Science (Department of Mathematics)
Kırklareli University
Kırklareli, Türkiye

Vasumathi A.
VIT Business School
Vellore, India

Vijayarajan V.
School of Computer Science and Engineering
Vellore Institute of Technology
Vellore, India

Vinh Thai
RMIT University
Melbourne, Australia

Chapter 1

Artificial intelligence in supply chain management

Vasumathi A., Abdul Razak, and Geetha Manoharan

1.1 INTRODUCTION

In the contemporary business landscape, the emergence of the information technology, financial globalization, and discriminating customer prospects have precipitated notable transformations in the realm of supply chain management (SCM) for industries (Perumal, K., et al., 2022; Lourens, M., et al., 2022). These changes underscore the significance of competition within supply chain management, rather than solely among individual organizations. Supply chain management (SCM) refers to the dynamic integration of various operations within a supply chain, spanning from the initial suppliers to the final end-users. The primary objective of SCM is to deliver services, products, and information that effectively enhance the value of the customer and facilitate the achievement of a sustainable competitive advantage (Durai, S., et al., 2024a). In the current era characterized by the prevalence of big data, process industries generate, gather, and store substantial volumes of interactive data. These data serve as a valuable resource for facilitating the procedure process, control, and planning. The judicious utilization of these facts and the mining of data and knowledge from them provide significant potential for advantageous outcomes. The significant increase in data volume from many areas of supply chain management has compelled firms to devise and execute novel technologies capable of efficiently and intelligently analyzing vast amounts of data. This is necessary since conventional decision support systems are inadequate in handling big data effectively. Therefore, within the context of the current era of big data, professionals in the domain of supply chain management are actively pursuing strategies (Blanchard, D., 2021) to effectively manage and utilize large volumes of data to achieve intelligent and efficient supply chain operations (Paksoy, T., et al., 2020).

An organization can take part and coordinate the full range of endwise procedures from procuring things or items, changing them into complete goods, to shipping them depending on supply chain excellence in an epoch of larger demand ambiguity, advanced supply risk, and growing viable intensity. The process involves transforming raw materials into final products

DOI: 10.1201/9781003498292-1

and subsequently distributing them to consumers. Since this capacity can be increased through enhanced transparency throughout the whole supply chain process (Almahairah, M. S. Z., et al., 2023), numerous progressive organizations have experienced heightened exposure.

Individuals have made efforts to enhance their sources of information and collaborate with their strategic communication partners by sharing up-to-date information.

Therefore, supply chain management (SCM) is increasingly reliant on data and has shifted its emphasis toward this aspect of focusing on the replacement of resources such as inventory, warehouses, and transportation apparatus.

Understanding the rising importance of information for SC accomplishment, SC professionals have extensively examined diverse approaches aimed at enhancing information management and utilizing it to generate significant benefits.

One potential method for enhancing the quality of commercial decision-making could involve the utilization of artificial intelligence (AI), which has been present for a considerable period, although its application in the domain of supply chain management has not been fully realized.

1.2 WHAT IS ARTIFICIAL INTELLIGENCE?

The term "artificial intelligence" has been subject to criticism for several decades. In the year 1955, John McCarthy introduced the phrase "artificial intelligence" to investigate the potential of machines to efficiently solve issues and employ language in a manner comparable to human beings. Artificial intelligence (AI) encompasses the creation and advancement of computer systems capable of executing activities that traditionally necessitate hominoid intelligence, such as learning, reasoning, problem-solving, and decision-making. To accomplish this objective, artificial intelligence (AI) is endowed with the ability to acquire knowledge and comprehend novel thoughts, assimilate information from past encounters, engage in logical thinking, make inferences, and interpret symbols within a given context. The aforementioned qualities have facilitated the effective use of AI in diverse domains, including game playing, human performance modeling, machine learning (ML), information mining, genetic algorithms, and expert systems (ESs).

Furthermore, artificial intelligence (AI) has been extensively employed in the domain of robotics (Rajchandar, K., et al., 2024b), facilitating the development of machines that possess the ability to execute hazardous or challenging jobs that surpass human capabilities (Durai, S., et al., 2024a). For example, artificial intelligence (AI)-enabled robotic systems have the potential to be employed across various domains, including manufacturing, health care, and research settings. These robots may effectively perform a range of activities such as information gathering, surveying, and health care. Through the use of artificial intelligence (AI), organizations can automate intricate operations, enhance operational effectiveness, and gain significant insights from their data. The ongoing advancement and enhancement of AI technology will likely result in further advancements and expanded utilization in the future. Indeed, the manufacturing sector (Manoharan, G., et al., 2024a) is currently reaping the benefits of artificial intelligence. The impact of AI on the sector is demonstrated by its ability to enhance productivity, lower expenses, and enhance decision-making processes Herbert Simon, an expert in the field, expressed his dissatisfaction with the extravagant connotations associated with the term. However, he acknowledged that "artificial intelligence" has become firmly established and predicted that, over time, it will become ingrained enough in language that would no longer be subject to superficial rhetoric. While it may be accurate in colloquial usage, in technical contexts where greater precision is desired, that assertion does not appear to hold.

The issue about the phrase lies not just in its grandiose nature, which establishes impractical expectations and suggests a greater level of capacity than has been previously observed. Furthermore, the aforementioned phenomenon is intricately linked to the dynamic evolution of technologies and their corresponding capacities across time (Chawla, P., et al., 2023). The development of tax-filing software and chess-playing computers, which were once considered important achievements in the field of artificial intelligence, can now be understood as gradual advancements toward the realization of more comprehensive and versatile forms of AI. The terminology used to describe these systems has shifted away from the term "artificial intelligence" in contemporary discourse. The aforementioned discrepancy is encapsulated within a widely acknowledged concept examined in the Defence Science Board's Summer Study on Autonomy in 2016. This definition posits that autonomy refers to the capacity of computer systems to execute tasks often reliant on human intelligence. According to the definition, when technology reaches a level of commonality where it can accomplish a task without the need for human intellect, it can no longer be classified as artificial intelligence (AI) and is applicable in various fields such as education (Kiran, G. R., et al., 2024), academic leadership (Manoharan, G. & Ashtikar, S. P., 2024b), natural disasters (Singh, C. R. & Manoharan, G., 2024), climate changes (Kumar, C. S., et al., 2024), and marketing (Tripathi, M. A., et al., 2023).

This statement elucidates the reasons behind the reclassification of formerly designated artificial intelligence (AI) systems as mere computing entities. Moreover, the utilization of the term "perform tasks" in a broad manner enables artificial intelligence (AI) to embrace a comprehensive spectrum of tasks that are capable of being executed (Al-Sartawi, M., 2021). This phenomenon is the reason behind assertions like "AI is the modern equivalent of electricity." However, it also elucidates the apprehension felt by numerous specialists when attempting to encapsulate AI within a succinct description that offers explanatory or classificatory significance.

On the contrary, individuals tend to discuss artificial intelligence (AI) by focusing on the practical uses it facilitates, which predominantly involve different manifestations of autonomous capabilities.

Given these factors, the definition provided by the Defence Science Board, which states that artificial intelligence (AI) refers to the ability of computer systems to carry out activities characteristically requiring human intelligence, is deemed suitable for the scope of this text when discussing AI in a broad sense. However, it is customary for us to discuss AI within the framework of particular applications, levels of autonomy, or categories of technology, as elucidated in the subsequent sections.

The concept of "human intelligence" AI, or artificial intelligence, is generally defined as the utilization of computer systems to engross in reasoning, pattern identifying, learning, and understanding of particular behaviors through experience. It involves the acquisition and refinement of different systems of implication to address decision-making scenarios where producing the best or precise solutions is either prohibitively costly or challenging. In essence, the main goals of artificial intelligence (AI) encompass realizing the details of human intelligence and emerging computer structures proficient in emulating human behavioral forms and creating issue-solving-oriented knowledge. Therefore, artificial intelligence (AI) must possess the dimensions to obtain and understand new concepts, learn autonomously, engage in rational thinking, make interpretations, allocate significance, and understand symbols within their particular circumstances (Thavamani, S., et al., 2022).

An area of AI's possible application remains underexplored in the emerging field of supply chain management (SCM). SCM necessitates a deep understanding of intricate and unified decision-making procedures as well as the progress of intelligent knowledge bases that are vital for collaborative problem-solving. An instance of this can be observed in the case of Eastman Kodak, where the cognitive processes of skilled order pickers were organized and subsequently utilized to create a rule-based expert system. This system was designed to determine the most efficient path for order picking within a warehouse. It is an agent-based forecasting system that aims to synchronize various stages of joint demand planning and forecasting processes within the supply chain (SC). The system is designed to facilitate the prediction of final customer demand by enabling data exchange among various SC partners and leveraging previous predictive experience (Lourens, M., et al., 2023; Bhavya, K. R., et al., 2023). The examples provided demonstrate the utility of certain subfields within the area of artificial intelligence, such as expert systems and agent-based systems, in addressing many facets of the supply chain, including warehousing, combined demand preparation, and inventory control. With the aforementioned example taken into consideration, the primary aims are as follows:

(1) To ascertain the subfields of artificial intelligence (AI) that are greatest appropriate for supply chain management (SCM) applications, and subsequently, to delineate these subdomains with respect to their efficacy in enhancing supply chain efficiency (Kshetri, N., 2021; Shameem, A., et al., 2023).
(2) To consolidate the current body of literature relating to the utilization of artificial intelligence (AI) in supply chain management (SCM), focusing on its practical implications and technological advantages.

To organize the current literature on artificial intelligence (AI) systematically, a hierarchical taxonomy will be developed. This taxonomy will categorize the literature based on its application areas within supply chain management (SCM), problem scope, and the techniques employed (Al-Turjman, F., 2019).

In this inquiry, the objective is to provide a condensed overview of current trends in artificial intelligence (AI) research and to identify prospective areas of application within supply chain management (SCM) that have yet to be investigated.

This study will also explore prospective developments in artificial intelligence by extending the domain of artificial intelligence (AI) literature and address unexplored research issues about supply chain management (SCM).

1.3 TAXONOMY OF AI

The term "AI" typically refers to a broad array of technologies that exhibit differing levels of complexity and sophistication. In the initial stages of AI development, researchers focused on creating automated systems that can execute predetermined tasks by predefined sets of rules. These approaches continue to be utilized to a certain degree; but, in recent decades, there has been a shift toward employing more advanced systems that possess the ability to engage in machine learning. However, the implementation of artificial intelligence (AI) remains constrained in comparison to several other sectors. The utilization of artificial intelligence (AI) technologies, including expert systems (ESs), machine learning (ML), artificial neural networks, and genetic algorithms (GA), is progressively gaining prominence across many applications such as transportation (Shiva, C. K., et al., 2024) within the industrial business.

1.3.1 Expert systems

Expert systems are widely recognized as a crucial domain within the domain of artificial intelligence. In the domain of expert systems, answers are sought by leveraging the knowledge and skills of individuals who possess specialized knowledge in a specific topic. These systems can be conceptualized as computer-organized counseling systems. Expert systems are utilized in applications that necessitate the involvement of both machines and humans (Gutta et al., 2024).

The utilization of expert systems (ESs) is regarded as a pivotal technique in the implementation of artificial intelligence (AI) in the industrial sector. The term "ES" denotes computer programs that possess autonomous decision-making capabilities for solving a particular problem. Expert systems (ESs) play a significant role in preserving the essential knowledge required for enhancing manufacturing competitiveness (Gupta et al., 2024). In organizational settings, they are frequently employed to facilitate a wide range of knowledge and for training. Expert systems (ESs) facilitate streamlined dissemination of knowledge, leading to reduced expenses (Manoharan, G., et al., 2024b). Within the realm of the manufacturing business, the utilization of expert systems (ESs) has proven to help facilitate decision-making processes about quality, process control, and scheduling. An illustration of the utilization of an expert system (ES) is its utilization in the identification of flaws in products during the manufacturing process, subsequently providing operators with recommendations for repair measures. Expert systems (ESs) can also contribute to the optimization of production schedules through the investigation of production information and the provision of suggestions for process improvements.

Acquiring optimal manufacturing resources via the supply chain is a fundamental method for meeting the exigent demands of the market and attaining cost reduction objectives. Nevertheless, in the current manufacturing paradigm, the quality of a product is frequently compromised as the supply chain becomes more extensive and complex, particularly when multiple layers of suppliers are engaged in the production of parts and components. Frequently, the linkage between product standards tends to be disrupted presently, resulting in the omission of the technical requirements. Moreover, the acceptance criteria established by the demand side may exhibit ambiguity or exceed the defined requirement specification toward the conclusion of the supply chain. Hence, it is imperative to implement an expert system that can effectively disseminate and enforce the standards devised and employed by the demand side across all pertinent elements and constituents. This will ensure that all suppliers are compelled to adhere to the prescribed standards.

To address quality control issues in the supply chain process, experts have shifted their focus from internal quality management within individual enterprises to examining each node within the supply chain network. This shift aims to investigate the mechanisms of network transmission and coordination. The use of information technology tools and the utilization and dissemination of product quality data analysis play a significant role in determining the quality status. The execution of an expert system for quality evaluation enables the generation of novel findings through the processes of induction and reasoning. Knowledge is stored using various methods such as text files, programs, or databases.

1.3.2 Artificial neural network

Artificial neural networks are computational models that intend to emulate the structure and learning mechanisms observed in the *human* brain, which is composed of interconnected neurons.

The foundational principles of artificial neural networks may be traced back to the efforts of psychologists and neuropsychologists during the 19th century when they sought to comprehend the intricacies of the human brain. However, the initial scholarly investigations on these topics were initiated by McCulloch and W. Pitts. Artificial neural networks are founded upon the emulation of a rudimentary model of neuronal functioning within the human brain. The process of learning occurs with the network acquired through this method. Artificial neural networks find use in various domains, including control and system identification, image and sound recognition, estimate and prediction, failure analysis, medical, communication, traffic management, and production management. Artificial neural networks, with a particular emphasis on the process of learning, are employed in the analysis of nonlinear systems or systems characterized by incomplete and erroneous information (Kumari, S, et al., 2023). One significant drawback associated with artificial neural networks is the challenges that arise when attempting to transfer preexisting expert knowledge for the sake of problem-solving.

Over the last decade, notable transformations have occurred in supplier management within the realm of business, resulting in an increased level of corporate reliance on suppliers (Kersten, W., et al., 2019). Meanwhile, organizations encounter several goods that require procurement and a wide range of possible providers. Moreover, considering the diverse array of prerequisites, it appears impractical to apply the same policies for selecting different vendors. The necessity for supplementary policies arises from the requirement for a diverse range of shopping items and suppliers. The categorization of providers enables the differentiation of suppliers to allocate orders. The neural network model classifies suppliers into three distinct categories, namely desirable, average, and undesirable.

The supply chain refers to a complex interconnected network comprising several organizations and sectors. Within this network, the acquisition and processing of materials occur, resulting in the production of intermediate or final goods. Subsequently, these finished products are dispatched to the respective customers. Hence, it can be observed as a comprehensive hierarchical structure, encompassing many stages such as manufacturing, distribution, retail, and other related industries. Supply chain management refers to the strategic management approach that involves the design, planning, and control of several interconnected elements within a supply chain, including transportation, data flow, and investment flow. The primary objective of this approach is to establish a harmonious equilibrium between the supply and demand dynamics, leading to enhanced customer satisfaction and a reduction in the overall operational expenses associated with the supply chain (Gulati, N., et al., 2022). Constructed on the aforementioned attributes, neural networks are being utilized within the domain of supply chain management, primarily in three key domains: optimization, prediction, and decision support.

1.3.2.1 Optimization

The utilization of neural networks has become widely prevalent in addressing optimization challenges, rendering it the most prominent computing technique in this domain. The subject matter holds significant importance within the domain of supply chain management. The submission of neural networks in addressing optimization problems within supply chain management, such as shop scheduling, warehouse management, and transportation path selection, has been the subject of current research. Several of these issues are fundamental challenges in constructing the logistics data system for the organization. Furthermore, when compared to other knowhows, neural networks have robust adaptability, allowing them to rapidly assess and adjust to developing restrictions through their actual processing competencies.

1.3.2.2 Forecasting

Uncertainty has increased and has been seen as a significant impediment for decision-makers within companies. The primary sources of uncertainty in supply chain management arise from fluctuations in goods demand, postponements in delivery, and machine-driven malfunctions. Due to the lack of precision in predicting the limited components of the supply chain, there will be significant fluctuations in the overall supply chain, and this volatility is expected to gradually increase.

Therefore, enhancing the precision of forecasting and reducing the level of uncertainty in supply chain management has emerged as a central concern. It is widely recognized that the available information for decision-making is often inadequate, posing significant challenges for various forecasting techniques like expert systems, statistical tools, and forecasting analysis. Moreover, the utilization of the black box purpose in neural networks can effectively overcome this challenge and yield a more desirable outcome in terms of forecasting. Moreover, it can be argued that the neural network can be characterized as a nonlinear system. A significant proportion of supply chain forecasting problems exhibit complexity and nonlinearity, rendering linear forecasting technologies ineffective. In contrast, neural networks offer a more viable solution to address these challenges.

1.3.2.3 Decision support

When managers engage in the decision-making process, they encounter two distinct challenges. There are two primary concerns regarding decision-making information: its excessive volume and its incompleteness. As previously stated, expert systems and statistical approaches encounter significant obstacles. On the other hand, the neural network emulates the cognitive processes of the human brain. To a certain degree, the capacity for "creativity" enables individuals to arrive at more logical and well-informed choices, even when faced with little information. Currently, the majority of research about decision support systems primarily concentrates on the organization and investigation of data utilized in the decision-making process. The neural network's distinctive dimensions for identification, information classification, and self-organization position it as an optimal technology for data search within the domain of supply chain management. A neural network-based process has been developed to identify probable customers throughout the sales process. One of the key challenges encountered by the decision support system is the identification of the inherent correlation among the vast dataset. The self-organization and generality abilities exhibited by neural networks have proven to be a highly effective method for addressing this particular issue.

1.3.3 Machine learning (ML) technique

Machine learning is a subfield of artificial intelligence that permits machines to autonomously analyze and interpret datasets without explicit programming. The utilization of machine learning techniques enables businesses to make well-informed decisions by leveraging data analytics through the application of algorithms and statistical models (Manoharan, G., et al., 2023, Kaswan, K. S., 2024). Enterprises are making significant investments in machine learning to capitalize on its potential applications across various domains. The integration of machine learning techniques is crucial for health care and the medical profession to effectively evaluate patient data, enabling accurate disease prediction and efficient treatment strategies. The utilization of machine learning in the banking (Makkar, S., et al., 2022) and financial industry is imperative for customer data analysis (Jaichandran, R., et al., 2023), enabling the identification and recommendation of investment possibilities to clients as well as facilitating risk mitigation and fraud protection measures (Al-Safi, J. K. S., et al., 2023). Retailers employ machine learning techniques to forecast evolving client preferences and analyze consumer behavior through the examination of customer data.

Machine learning techniques are employed to instruct machines on the automated and efficient handling of substantial amounts of data. Conventional methods often fail to extract patterns or derive meaningful information from vast amounts of data [15]. The proliferation of datasets has led to an increasing need for machine-learning methodologies. Machine learning (ML) techniques are extensively utilized across several industries, ranging from the medical field to the military sector, to ascertain and extract valuable knowledge and information from vast datasets. Numerous investigations have been conducted by mathematicians and programmers, leading to the advancement of diverse machine-learning algorithms. This study examines the utilization of machine learning (ML) in supply chain management (SCM). Numerous studies have shown the benefits associated with the utilization of ML techniques in several domains such as demand and sales estimates, transportation and distribution, production, inventory management, supplier selection, and segmentation, among others.

These systems can enhance their performance over time by identifying patterns in extensive datasets and implementing corrective measures to enhance their ability to classify future patterns, without requiring explicit programming for such tasks. A more advanced category of machine learning systems demonstrates the utilization of deep learning techniques (Ashiq, V. M., et al., 2023). In the subsequent analysis, we will examine the recent advancements in computer vision and image recognition systems that have been made possible by the utilization of deep neural networks in deep learning (Kaswan, K. S., 2024).

Many organizations have frequently utilized machine learning (ML) techniques, namely verdict tree (DT) and support vector machine (SVM) techniques as administered learning approaches as shown in Figure 1.1 as well as the Q-learning methodology as a reinforcement learning (RL) approach, to address the supplier selection problem (Sehrawat, S. K., et al., 2024).

In the domain of supply chain management (SCM), the process of planning is predicated upon the estimation of sales and demand. The utilization of machine learning techniques has facilitated the accurate prediction and forecasting of demand, sales, and inventory by including nonlinear analysis. Consequently, this has led to the maximization of supply chain performance. The implementation of an intelligent forecasting process has been shown to lead to performance optimization, cost reduction, and the augmentation of sales and profit. In this particular scenario, there is a necessity to establish a connection between the parameters linked to several descriptive variables and their respective dependent variables in a significantly nonlinear fashion (Manoharan, G., et al., 2022). ML techniques are distinct from conventional methods such as exponential smoothing, moving average, trend analysis, time-series method, and Box-Jenkins method. Unlike these traditional methods, ML techniques are not heavily dependent on the accuracy of past information. Consequently, ML techniques have

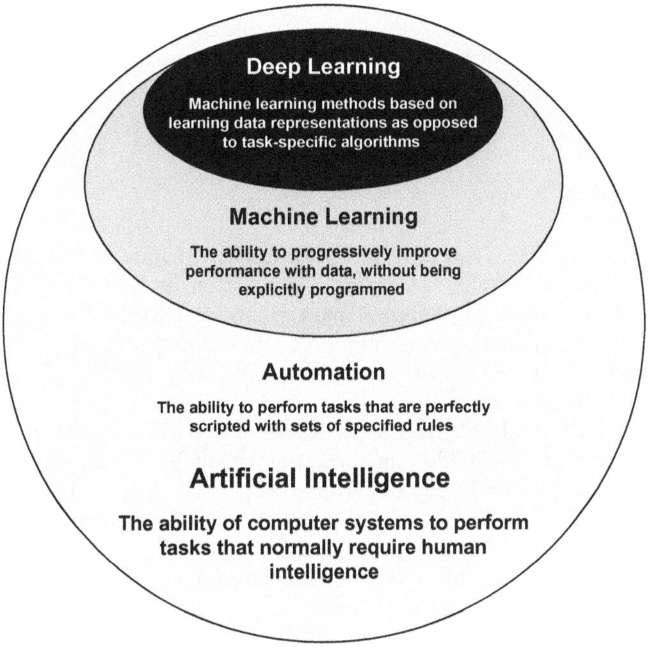

Figure 1.1 The core areas for future taxonomy for Artificial Intelligence algorithms.

gained recognition as viable substitutes for demand prediction and planning in supply chain management (SCM) (Manoharan, G., et al., 2022; 2023d).

1.4 CONCLUSION

Due to the need to understand intricate and interconnected decision-making procedures and establish intelligent knowledge bases crucial for collaborative problem-solving, supply chain management (SCM) has transformed into a discipline closely aligned with knowledge management. In essence, there is an increasing need for supply chain partners to obtain knowledge from expanded sources and apply automation in their decision-making procedures (Deviprasad, S., et al., 2023). Artificial intelligence (AI) has been proposed as an important tool for decision support, enabling firms to establish connections between their customers, suppliers, and supply chain (SC) partners. This is achieved by facilitating the exchange of information among different entities within the business network. Additionally, AI has the potential to replace physical assets such as inventory, facilities, and transportation kit with digital data (Manoharan, G., & Narayanan, S., 2021). Despite the existence of artificial intelligence (AI) for the past 50 years and its recent use in supply chain management (SCM), the full probable of AI has not been fully utilized to address supply chain (SC) challenges that are either cost-prohibitive or challenging to solve owing to their inherent complexity and lack of well-defined structure.

REFERENCES

Almahairah, M. S. Z., Goswami, S., Karri, P. N., Krishna, I. M., Aarif, M., & Manoharan, G. (2023, December). Application of Internet of Things and Big Data in Improving Supply Chain Financial Risk Management System. In *2023 10th IEEE Uttar Pradesh Section International Conference on Electrical, Electronics and Computer Engineering (UPCON)* (Vol. 10, pp. 276–280). IEEE.

Al-Safi, J. K. S., Bansal, A., Aarif, M., Almahairah, M. S. Z., Manoharan, G., & Alotoum, F. J. (2023, January). Assessment Based on IoT for Efficient Information Surveillance Regarding Harmful Strikes Upon Financial Collection. In *2023 International Conference on Computer Communication and Informatics (ICCCI)* (pp. 1–5). IEEE.

Al-Sartawi, M. (2021). *Big Data-Driven Digital Economy: Artificial and Computational Intelligence*. Springer.

Al-Turjman, F. (Ed.). (2019). *Artificial intelligence in IoT*. Springer. https://link.springer.com/book/10.1007/978-3-030-04110-6

Ashiq, V. M., Fredrik, E. T., Kumar, N. K., Torres-Cruz, F., Colque, J. P. B., & Manoharan, G. (2023, September). A Deep Learning Approaches for Natural Language Processing and Sentiment Analysis in Social Media. In *2023 6th International Conference on Contemporary Computing and Informatics (IC3I)* (Vol. 6, pp. 1746–1750). IEEE.

Bhavya, K. R., Dharmaraj, A., Pareek, P., Sathe, M. A., Tiwari, M., & Manoharan, G. (2023, September). Application of Soft Computing Techniques for Predictive Analytics in Financial Markets. In *2023 6th International Conference on Contemporary Computing and Informatics (IC3I)* (Vol. 6, pp. 1756–1760). IEEE.

Blanchard, D. (2021). *Supply chain management best practices*. John Wiley & Sons.

Chawla, P., Kumar, A., Nayyar, A., & Naved, M. (Eds.). (2023). *Blockchain, IoT, and AI Technologies for Supply Chain Management*. CRC Press.

Deviprasad, S., Madhumithaa, N., Vikas, I. W., Yadav, A., & Manoharan, G. (2023). The Machine Learning-Based Task Automation Framework for Human Resource Management in MNC Companies. *Engineering Proceedings*, 59(1), 63.

Durai, S., Manoharan, G., & Ashtikar, S. P. (2024a). Harnessing Artificial Intelligence: Pioneering Sustainable Solutions for a Greener Future. In A. Derbali (Ed.), *Social and Ethical Implications of AI in Finance for Sustainability* (pp. 89–117). IGI Global. https://doi.org/10.4018/979-8-3693-2881-1.ch003.

Durai, S., Manoharan, G., Priya, T. S., Jayanthi, R., Razak, A., & Ashtikar, S. P. (2024b). Quantifying the Impacts of Artificial Intelligence Implementations in Marketing. In H. Irani & H. Nozari (Eds.), *Smart and Sustainable Interactive Marketing* (pp. 120–144). IGI Global. https://doi.org/10.4018/979-8-3693-1339-8.ch008.

Gupta, S., Dutta, P. K., Roy, S., Bhaduri, A., Maji, K., Choudhary, A., & Sarkar, A. (2024). Evaluating Waterfall vs. Agile Models in Software Development for Efficiency and Adaptability. In *Practical Approaches to Agile Project Management* (p. 7). IGI Global. https://doi.org/10.4018/979-8-3693-3318-1.ch008.

Gutta, L. M., Dhamodharan, B., Dutta, P. K., & Whig, P. (2024). AI-infused Quantum Machine Learning for Enhanced Supply Chain Forecasting. In *Quantum Computing and Supply Chain Management: A New Era of Optimization* (pp. 21–26). IGI Global. https://doi.org/10.4018/979-8-3693-4107-0.ch003.

Jaichandran, R., Krishna, S. H., Madhavi, G. M., Mohammed, S., Raj, K. B., & Manoharan, G. (2023, January). Fuzzy Evaluation Method on the Financing Efficiency of Small and Medium-Sized Enterprises. In *2023 International Conference on Artificial Intelligence and Knowledge Discovery in Concurrent Engineering (ICECONF)* (pp. 1–7). IEEE.

Kaswan, K. S. (2024). Quantum Computing for Supply Chain Optimization. In *Quantum Computing and Supply Chain Management: A New Era of Optimization* (pp. 32–33). IGI Global. https://doi.org/10.4018/979-8-3693-4107-0.ch001.

Kersten, W., Blecker, T., & Ringle, C. M. (2019). *Artificial Intelligence and Digital Transformation in Supply Chain Management: Innovative Approaches for Supply Chains.* Neopubli GmbH.

Kiran, G. R., Manoharan, G., Durai, S., Ashtikar, S. P., & Kunchala, R. (2024). Higher Education in India and the Influence of Online Certification Programs. In A. Naim, A. Saklani, S. Khan, & P. Malik (Eds.), *Evaluating Global Accreditation Standards for Higher Education* (pp. 149–163). IGI Global. https://doi.org/10.4018/979-8-3693-1698-6.ch010.

Kshetri, N. (2021). *Blockchain and Supply Chain Management.* Elsevier.

Kumar, C. S., Vani, D. P., Damodar, K., Manoharan, G., & Veerapaga, N. (2024). Climate Change Mitigation Through AI Solutions. In S. Bhartiya, V. Bhatt, & A. Jimenez Ruiz (Eds.), *Gastronomic Sustainability Solutions for Community and Tourism Resilience* (pp. 37–59). IGI Global. https://doi.org/10.4018/979-8-3693-4135-3.ch003.

Kumari, S., Kumar, V., Sharmila, A., Murthy, C. R., Ahlawat, N., & Manoharan, G. (2023, August). Blockchain Based E-Analysis of Social Media Forums for Crypto Currency Phase Shifts. In *2023 5th International Conference on Inventive Research in Computing Applications (ICIRCA)* (pp. 1222–1225). IEEE.

Lourens, M., Raman, R., Vanitha, P., Singh, R., Manoharan, G., & Tiwari, M. (2022, December). Agile Technology and Artificial Intelligent Systems in Business Development. In *2022 5th International Conference on Contemporary Computing and Informatics (IC3I)* (pp. 1602–1607). IEEE.

Lourens, M., Sharma, S., Pulugu, R., Gehlot, A., Manoharan, G., & Kapila, D. (2023, May). Machine Learning-Based Predictive Analytics and Big Data in the Automotive Sector. In *2023 3rd International Conference on Advance Computing and Innovative Technologies in Engineering (ICACITE)* (pp. 1043–1048). IEEE.

Makkar, S., Bajpai, T., Bhola, M., Mahesh, D., & Manoharan, G. (2022, May). Blockchain Disruption in Banking Sector. In *AIP Conference Proceedings* (Vol. 2418, No. 1). AIP Publishing.

Manoharan, G. & Ashtikar, S. P. (2024a). A Theoretical Framework for Emotional Intelligence in Academic Leadership in Higher Education. In S. Saluja, J. Kukreja, & S. Sharma (Eds.), *Building Organizational Resilience with Neuroleadership* (pp. 96–112). IGI Global. https://doi.org/10.4018/979-8-3693-1785-3.ch007.

Manoharan, G. & Ashtikar, S. P. (2024b). Nexus Between Leadership and Effective Communication: Implications for Educational Institutions. In J. Kukreja, S. Saluja, & S. Sharma (Eds.), *Neuroleadership Development and Effective Communication in Modern Business* (pp. 274–291). IGI Global. https://doi.org/10.4018/979-8-3693-4350-0.ch015.

Manoharan, G., & Narayanan, S. (2021). A research study to investigate the feasibility of digital marketing strategies in advertising. *PalArch's Journal of Archaeology of Egypt/Egyptology*, 18(09), 450–456.

Manoharan, G., Ashtikar, S. P., & Nivedha, M. (2024a). Harnessing the Power of Artificial Intelligence in Reinventing the Manufacturing Sector. In D. Satishkumar & M. Sivaraja (Eds.), *Using Real-Time Data and AI for Thrust Manufacturing* (pp. 113–137). IGI Global. https://doi.org/10.4018/979-8-3693-2615-2.ch007.

Manoharan, G., Ashtikar, S. P., & Nivedha, M. (2024b). Integrating Artificial Intelligence in Library Management: An Emerging Trend. In K. Senthilkumar (Ed.), *AI-Assisted Library Reconstruction* (pp. 144–157). IGI Global. https://doi.org/10.4018/979-8-3693-2782-1.ch008.

Manoharan, G., Durai, S., & Rajesh, G. A. (2022, May). Identifying Performance Indicators and Metrics for Performance Measurement of the Workforce is the Need of the Hour: A Case of a Retail Garment Store in Coimbatore. In *AIP Conference Proceedings* (Vol. 2418, No. 1). AIP Publishing.

Manoharan, G., Durai, S., Rajesh, G. A., & Ashtikar, S. P. (2023). Sentiment Analysis of Customer Reviews for Online Stores That Support Customer Buying Decisions. In K. Hiran, K. Hemachandran, A. Pise, & B. Rabi (Eds.), *Handbook of Research on AI and Knowledge Engineering for Real-Time Business Intelligence* (pp. 234–242). IGI Global. https://doi.org/10.4018/978-1-6684-6519-6.ch015.

Manoharan, G., Sharma, V. K., Lourens, M., Kumar, A., Nayak, B. B., & Hinge, P. (2023d, September). Design and Empirical Analysis of a Artificial Intelligence-Based Human Resource Management Processing Systems for Detecting Personal Stress. In *2023 6th International Conference on Contemporary Computing and Informatics (IC3I)* (Vol. 6, pp. 2421–2426). IEEE.

Paksoy, T., Kochan, C. G., & Ali, S. S. (Eds.). (2020). *Logistics 4.0: Digital Transformation of Supply Chain Management*. CRC Press.

Perumal, K., Chowdhary, C. L., & Chella, L. (2022). *Innovative Supply Chain Management via Digitalization and Artificial Intelligence*. Springer.

Rajchandar, K., Kothandaraman, D., Manoharan, G., & Kabanda, G. (2024a). Robotics and its Navigation Techniques: The Present and Future Revelations. In *Handbook of Artificial Intelligence and Wearables* (pp. 189–204).

Sehrawat, S. K., Dutta, P. K., Bhatia, A. B., & Whig, P. (2024). Predicting Demand in Supply Chain Networks With Quantum Machine Learning Approach. In *Quantum Computing and Supply Chain Management: A New Era of Optimization* (pp. 15–20). IGI Global. https://doi.org/10.4018/979-8-3693-4107-0.ch002.

Shameem, A., Ramachandran, K. K., Sharma, A., Singh, R., Selvaraj, F. J., & Manoharan, G. (2023, May). The Rising Importance of AI in Boosting the Efficiency of Online Advertising in Developing Countries. In *2023 3rd International Conference on Advance Computing and Innovative Technologies in Engineering (ICACITE)* (pp. 1762–1766). IEEE.

Shiva, C. K., Vedik, B., & Manoharan, G. (2024). Sustainable Smart Transportation: Technologies, Benefits, Challenges to Urbanisation Concept. In S. Singh, S. Tanwar, R. Jadeja, S. Singh, & Z. Polkowski (Eds.), *Secure and Intelligent IoT-Enabled Smart Cities* (pp. 355–370). IGI Global. https://doi.org/10.4018/979-8-3693-2373-1.ch017.

Singh, C. R. & Manoharan, G. (2024). Strengthening Resilience: AI and Machine Learning in Emergency Decision-Making for Natural Disasters. In D. Satishkumar & M. Sivaraja (Eds.), *Internet of Things and AI for Natural Disaster Management and Prediction* (pp. 249–278). IGI Global. https://doi.org/10.4018/979-8-3693-4284-8.ch012.

Thavamani, S., Mahesh, D., Sinthuja, U., & Manoharan, G. (2022, May). Crucial Attacks in Internet of Things via Artificial Intelligence Techniques: The Security Survey. In *AIP Conference Proceedings (Vol. 2418, No. 1)*. AIP Publishing.

Tripathi, M. A., Tripathi, R., Effendy, F., Manoharasn, G., Paul, M. J., & Aarif, M. (2023, January). An In-Depth Analysis of the Role That ML and Big Data Play in Driving Digital Marketing's Paradigm Shift. In *2023 International Conference on Computer Communication and Informatics (ICCCI)* (pp. 1–6). IEEE.

Chapter 2

3D object classification in digital supply chains

Lalitha Swamy Thayumanavar, Sukumar Nandi, and Bunil Kumar Balabantaray

2.1 INTRODUCTION

Fast recognition of 3D objects is a challenging task in computer vision, and it can be applied in numerous fields such as automated driving, robotic systems, pattern recognition, and more [1]. For 3D recognition, researchers employ diverse methods to represent 3D models, such as mesh, voxel grid, point cloud, or view-based forms. Early 3D model retrieval algorithms [2, 3] predominantly relied on model-based feature representation. However, acquiring model-based features is not always straightforward, and not all real-life 3D models can be effectively represented using such features.

Machine learning algorithms find applications in numerous domains and are capable of handling a wide range of tasks, ranging from simple activities like food ordering to complex endeavors such as understanding the intricacies of celestial bodies [4]. It has rapidly evolved as a cutting-edge technology, emulating the way humans learn but in a significantly faster manner. Machine learning is an empirical method in which parameters are adjusted (i.e., learned) on a training dataset to optimize a predefined loss or cost function [5]. The increasing demands of modern lifestyles and remarkable advancements in machine learning techniques have propelled this field into a new era of endless possibilities.

Numerous researchers have explored the application of various machine learning algorithms for view-based object recognition, as mentioned in [6–8] The view-based representations refer to the visual depictions of an object that are obtained by rendering the object from multiple angles [9]. These representations capture the appearance and characteristics of the object from different viewpoints. By capturing the object's visual information from various angles, these view-based representations provide a comprehensive and detailed understanding of the object's shape, texture, and other visual features. Such representations are valuable in tasks such as object recognition, classification, and 3D shape analysis, as they enable a holistic view of the object from different perspectives and can be applied in tasks, as mentioned in [10–13].

 DOI: 10.1201/9781003498292-2

However, to the best of our knowledge, there is a lack of comprehensive comparative studies on view-based object classification using machine learning techniques. Understanding the performance of machine learning in 3D model retrieval and conducting thorough assessments of each algorithm, along with their respective strengths and weaknesses, hold significant importance for the advancement of 3D model retrieval.

The chapter presents several key contributions, summarized as follows:

1. Experimental evaluation of traditional machine learning algorithms: This study thoroughly examines the performance of traditional machine learning algorithms, providing insights into their strengths and limitations.
2. Comparison of back-propagation with back-propagation-free algorithms: To analyze the effectiveness of back-propagation in 3D object classification, we conducted a comparison between feed-forward networks with the back-propagation algorithm and feed-forward networks without back-propagation.
3. Exploring the efficiency of convolutional-based frameworks: To analyze the performance of convolutional neural networks (CNNs) by proposing the fine-tuning of the VGG19 model.
4. Comparative analysis of the algorithms: The chapter provides an in-depth analysis and comparison of both the aforementioned algorithms and state-of-the-art methods.

Through the evaluation of their performance, strengths, and weaknesses, this research enables a comprehensive understanding of the capabilities of these algorithms and their suitability for various applications.

2.2 RELATED WORK

Machine learning algorithms have become increasingly popular in addressing computer vision challenges, particularly in the domain of 3D shape representation. This surge in interest has spurred the development of numerous algorithms, which adopt both model-based and view-based approaches to effectively represent and analyze 3D shapes through machine learning techniques.

Model-based methods leverage native 3D shape representations such as volumetric grids [14, 15], polygon meshes [16], and point clouds [17, 18] to characterize 3D models. For instance, VoxNet [18] combines a supervised 3D CNN with a volumetric occupancy grid representation for object class detection in 3D point-cloud data. 3D ShapeNets [19] employs a convolutional deep belief network to model geometric 3D shapes as probabilistic distributions on a voxel grid. Recent advancements include the introduction of 3D generative-adversarial networks [24] and octree-generating networks [20], which further enhance shape classification capabilities.

View-based recognition methods, on the other hand, describe 3D models using collections of 2D projections. Early approaches relied on "handcrafted" descriptors, such as Fisher vectors [21] and light field descriptors [22], to represent shapes from different viewpoints. More recently, deep learning approaches such as convolutional neural networks (CNNs) [23, 24] have gained prominence. These methods efficiently integrate information from multiple views by employing unified CNN architectures with view-pooling layers.

Support vector machines have also demonstrated effectiveness in 3D object recognition [25–27], particularly when limited views are available. Additionally, random forest methodologies have shown versatility across various domains, including image recognition, 3D object recognition, and bioinformatics [28]. Furthermore, extreme learning machines (ELMs) have emerged as intelligent techniques with promising outcomes in terms of computational efficiency and accuracy [29].

In [30–32], deep learning approaches, namely convolutional neural networks (CNNs) and pre-trained models, are employed. These approaches aim to efficiently integrate information from multiple views by incorporating a unified CNN architecture with a view-pooling layer.

In our experiments, we have chosen five classical methods of machine learning algorithms to conduct experiments and evaluate the performance of machine learning techniques.

2.3 METHODOLOGY

2.3.1 Machine learning

In the machine learning domain, algorithms are broadly classified into several categories, encompassing supervised, unsupervised, semi-supervised, and reinforcement learning. This work primarily focuses on the supervised learning category.

Supervised machine learning algorithms necessitate external guidance to formulate predictions or classifications. Typically, the input dataset is partitioned into training and test sets, with the training data incorporating the output variable to be predicted or classified. These algorithms glean patterns from the training data and subsequently apply them to the test set to formulate predictions or classifications. The workflow of supervised machine learning algorithms is depicted in Figure 2.1. We further segmented the supervised algorithms into two groups: traditional and neural network-based.

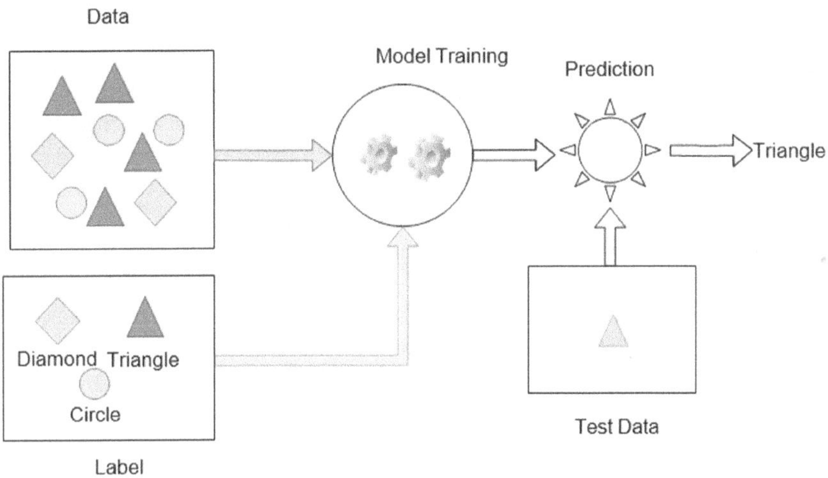

Figure 2.1 Workflow of machine learning.

2.3.2 Traditional learning

Traditional learning, also known as the conventional approaches in machine learning, involves the development of algorithms based on explicit rules and predefined features. These methods typically rely on manually engineered features and require extensive domain knowledge. Traditional learning algorithms encompass a wide range of techniques such as decision trees, support vector machines, and linear regression, among others. For this work, we consider support vector machine (SVM) and random forest (RF).

2.3.3 Neural network

Neural networks, a subset of artificial intelligence, emulate the structure and operations of biological neural networks. These computational models comprise interconnected artificial neurons arranged in layers. Each neuron processes inputs, conducts computations through weighted connections, and generates an output. The training of neural networks involves adjusting weights between neurons to discern patterns within data, facilitating accurate predictions. Neural networks have shown remarkable capabilities in tasks such as image recognition, natural language processing, and speech synthesis.

Classified into two main categories, neural networks are distinguished as feed-forward networks and feed-back networks. In this research, we focus on feed-forward networks. The subsequent section provides a succinct overview of feed-forward network architectures and their relevance in the context of the study.

General architecture of feed-forward networks:

1. Input layer: The model takes a set of input data, represented as feature vectors, and maps them to the input layer of the neural network. Each feature in the input vector corresponds to a neuron in the input layer.
2. Hidden layer: Hidden layers are intermediate layers between the input and output layers. The number of hidden layers and the number of nodes in each hidden layer are hyperparameters that can be adjusted based on the complexity of the problem.
3. Activation function: Activation functions introduce nonlinearity into the network, allowing it to learn complex patterns. Each neuron in the hidden layer applies an activation function to the weighted sum of its input data. Common activation functions used are sigmoid, ReLU (Rectified Linear Unit), or tanh functions.
4. Output layer: The output layer of the model produces the final predictions. For binary classification problems, there is a single output neuron with a sigmoid activation function to produce a probability value between 0 and 1. For multiclass classification, multiple output neurons are used, and the SoftMax function is applied to obtain normalized class probabilities.

Multilayer perceptron (MLP): The multilayer perceptron (MLP) is a prominent and robust type of artificial neural network (ANN) characterized by a layered feed-forward structure. In this architecture, information progresses unidirectionally from the input layer to the output layer, traversing through intermediate hidden layers. Employing a supervised training procedure, the MLP generates a nonlinear function model, enabling the prediction of output data based on input data.

The MLP is organized as a graph devoid of cycles, where units are arranged into layers, and each layer contains a specific number of identical units [33]. This fully connected network ensures that every unit in one layer is linked to every other unit through assigned weights. The training process involves the correction of weights (using optimization algorithms like gradient descent) by propagating errors from layer to layer. This process begins at the output layer and proceeds backward, a mechanism known as back-propagation.

Extreme learning machine: Introduced by Huang et al., extreme learning machine (ELM) stands as a robust and efficient algorithm, also known as feedforward back-propagation free method. In comparison to multilayer perceptron (MLP), ELM shares a similar architecture. However, a distinctive feature lies in ELM's elimination of iterative training, specifically the absence of back-propagation for tuning network parameters. This unique characteristic significantly reduces the computational demand during the network training process due to this reason applied in various research areas, including pattern recognition, image processing, time-series analysis, and big data analytics. Notably, a key aspect of ELM involves the random assignment of weights connecting the input and hidden layers. These weights, generated randomly before training, remain constant throughout the process.

The training methodology of ELM involves a single-step process utilizing the Moore–Penrose pseudoinverse, a mathematical technique for solving linear systems, thus termed the "batch training" phase. Throughout the training, hidden layer weights are initialized randomly and kept fixed, while output layer weights are calculated using the pseudoinverse to minimize the mean squared error between predicted and actual outputs.

A standard single-hidden layer feed-forward network (SLFN) with N hidden neurons and an activation function $g(x)$ can be mathematically represented as follows:

$$\sum_{i-1}^{n} \beta_i g(w_i.x_j + b_j) = O_i, \quad j = 1\ldots N \tag{2.1}$$

In each term represents the output O_i for a given input sample x_j. The weight vector w_i connects the input layer to the ith hidden layer, and β_i represents the weight vector between the ith hidden layer and the output layer.

2.3.4 Deep neural network

Deep neural networks (DNNs) are characterized by their incorporation of multiple hidden layers between input and output layers. These intermediary layers play a pivotal role in acquiring hierarchical representations from data, enabling DNNs to comprehend intricate relationships and extract complex features.

Transfer learning: In computer vision, transfer learning is a popular method and is usually expressed through the use of pre-trained models. A pre-trained model is a deep neural network that has been trained on a large-scale dataset, typically using a task such as image classification as a pre-training objective. These models leverage the knowledge learned from this initial training to solve related tasks without starting from scratch. By utilizing pre-trained models, researchers can benefit from the learned representations and save significant computational resources and time. Fine-tuning or transfer learning can be performed on pre-trained models to adapt them to specific tasks or datasets, further enhancing their performance and efficiency.

In this study, we employed VGG19, a renowned pre-trained model, for object classification. Proposed by Simonyan and Zisserman [34], VGG19 is a convolutional neural network with 19 layers, trained on the ImageNet database containing one million images across 1000 categories. Notably, VGG19 employs multiple 3 × 3 convolutional filters in each convolutional layer. The architecture, detailed in Figure 2.2, utilizes 16 layers for feature

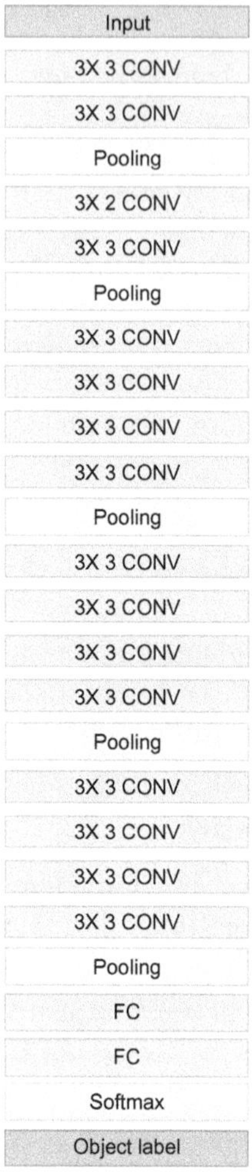

Figure 2.2 Architecture of fine-tuned model VGG19.

extraction and the subsequent 3 layers for classification. The feature extraction layers are grouped into five, each followed by a max-pooling layer, while fully connected layers facilitate final predictions by mapping features to object categories.

To adapt pre-trained models for our work, the last three layers are modified by removing the fully connected, softmax, and classification layers specific to the original dataset. Instead, three fully connected layers with ten outputs matching the new dataset's classes are introduced. This modified network, termed the fine- tuned model, is trained using a new dataset comprising 2D images of objects. Inputting a 224 × 224 image into this model yields the object label as the output.

2.4 EXPERIMENTAL ENVIRONMENT

All the experiments are performed on the Linux environment, using Python language. Computer hardware environment configuration: Intel(R) Xeon(R) Silver 4216 CPU @ 2.10 GHz, 128 GB RAM memory, and one NVIDIA GPU with TITAN RTX.

2.5 DATASETS

The Princeton ModelNet hosts an extensive collection of 127,915 CAD models spanning 662 categories. Our experimental focus narrows down to its meticulously annotated subset, ModelNet10, readily accessible on the Princeton ModelNet website. In order to compare the performance of the five machine algorithms, this paper tests from two different sample sizes of ModelNet10. In both cases, we considered 12 rendered views of each model, as described in [33].

1. Case 1 (ModelNet10): For this category, we used the training and test split of the dataset as described in [34]. We employed 3991 models for training and 908 for testing, totaling 4899 models in all.
2. Case 2 (Sample set of ModelNet10): In this category, we utilized a small sample size of ModelNet10, comprising a total of 100 models. Of these, 80 were employed for training, while the remaining 20 were used for testing.

2.6 RESULTS AND DISCUSSION

2.6.1 Performance of algorithms

To evaluate the efficacy of each algorithm, we employ two dataset scenarios: one with a large sample size and another with a small sample size. We maintain consistent procedures for both categories.

We started our experiment with the SVM algorithm, involving evaluations with varying kernels: Radial Basis Function (RBF), Polynomial (Poly), and Linear. The outcomes of these experiments are depicted in Figure 2.3, which illustrates the performance comparison of different support vector classifier (SVC) configurations. From this figure, we can clearly see that the RBF kernel performs well among all.

From the experimental result, it was observed that the random forest with 500 estimators yielded the best results for both flavors of the dataset (Figure 2.4).

In the case of feed-forward algorithms MLP and ELM, we varied the number of hidden nodes and presented the validation accuracy along with

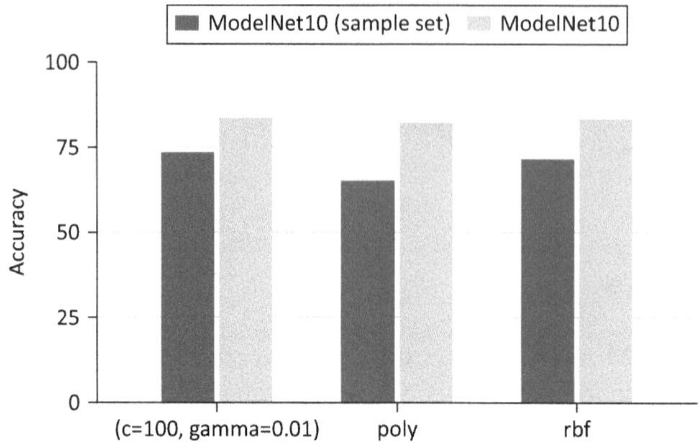

Figure 2.3 Performance of SVM.

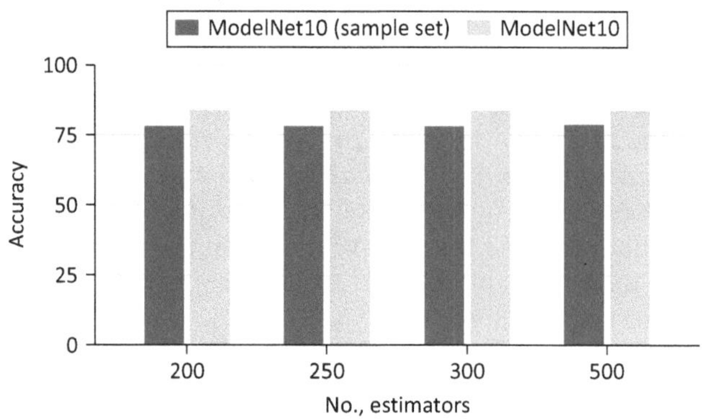

Figure 2.4 Performance of RF.

the hidden nodes in Figures 2.5 and 2.6. It is worth noting that the ELM method has drawn attention due to its significant increase in accuracy when using a large sample dataset.

For the deep learning framework CNN, we executed the model for 50 epochs. We varied the layers at the top of the model, and the accuracy variation with the epochs is shown in Figure 2.7.

2.6.2 Discussion

The obtained results using the sample set of ModelNet10 are presented in Table 2.1. From this table, we can observe that among traditional methods, RF performs well. When compared with fine-tuned CNN, the latter outperforms all other methods.

The results presented in Table 2.2 show the performance of the experimented algorithms using ModelNet10. Although all the methods show a

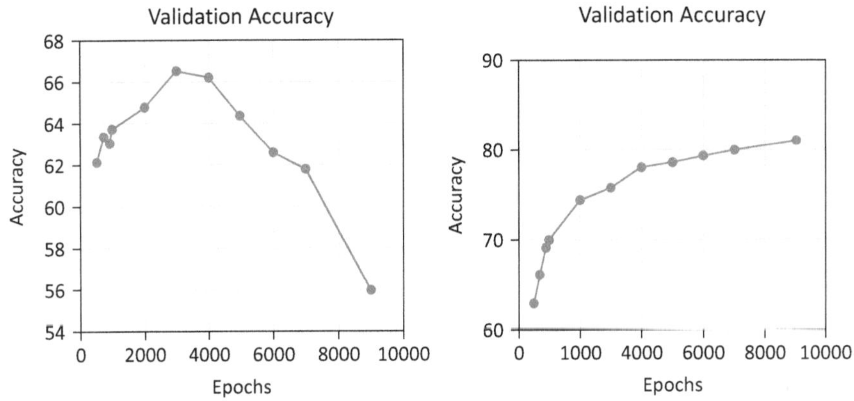

Figure 2.5 Validation accuracy of ELM: ModelNet10 (sample aet) and ModelNet10.

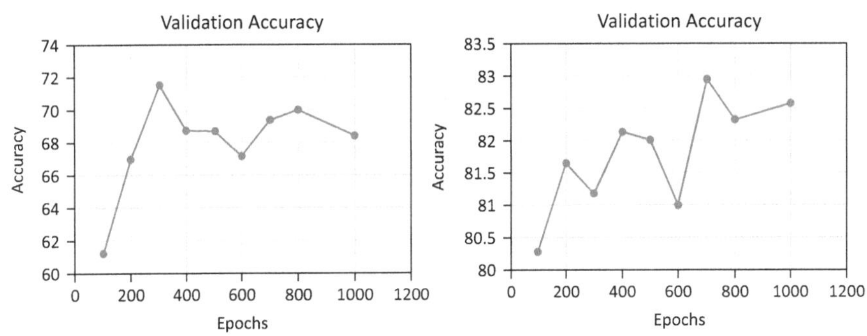

Figure 2.6 Validation accuracy of MLP: ModelNet10 (sample set) and ModelNet10.

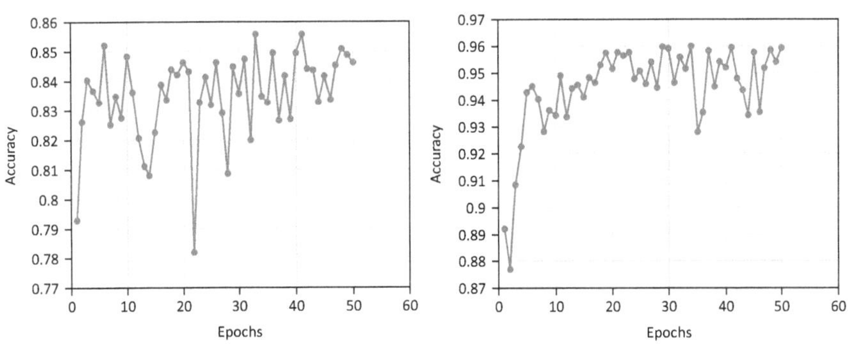

Figure 2.7 Validation accuracy of CNN: ModelNet (sample set) and ModelNet10.

Table 2.1 Accuracy of ML algorithms using ModelNet10 (sample set)

Model	*Accuracy (in %)*	*Training Time (in seconds)*
ELM	66.59	6.49
MLP	68.71	326.290
SVM	74.54	3.44
RF	79.66	63.05
Fine-tuned CNN	87.12	3964.80

Table 2.2 Comparison of machine learning algorithms using ModelNet10

Model	*Accuracy (in %)*	*Training Time (in seconds)*
ELM	81.01	255.201
MLP	82.08	399.66
SVM	84.32	40.07
RF	84.63	195.81
Fine-tuned CNN	95.89	19921.93

positive response with an increase of the sample dataset, ELM achieves a significant increase of 14.42% and RF shows a smaller increase of 4.97%. While comparing ELM with MLP, it is evident that MLP's performance is slightly better, attributable to the utilization of back-propagation.

When we compare traditional methods, considering only accuracy, random forest (RF) emerges as the winner with a slight increase in accuracy. However, if we take into account the training time, the support vector machine (SVM) is the clear winner, achieving almost the same accuracy as RF.

The random forest (RF) algorithm demonstrates strong performance across both datasets. When comparing traditional methods with deep neural frameworks, the latter consistently outperforms others by a notable margin of 10%, as depicted in Figure 2.8. Additionally, it is noteworthy that RF excels with smaller datasets, whereas support vector machines (SVM) exhibit superior performance with larger datasets.

Furthermore, we assessed the effectiveness of our experimental algorithms by comparing them with state-of-the-art methods sourced from public repositories, as outlined in Table 2.3.

The table underscores the superiority of our fine-tuned CNN, surpassing not only the other experimental methods but also the existing state-of-the-art approaches in terms of performance. Additionally, it is evident from the table that the RF and SVM algorithms outperform the method proposed by Patra and Dutta [35] and perform comparably well to the approach introduced by Rao et al. [36].

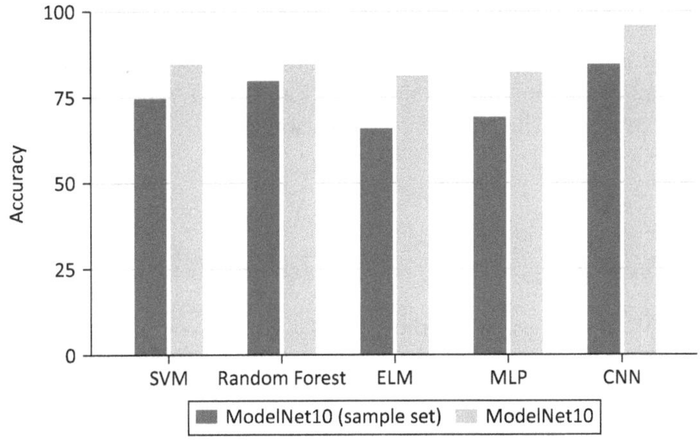

Figure 2.8 Performance of machine algorithms using larger-size and smaller-size datasets.

Table 2.3 Performance comparison with state-of-the-art methods

Model	*Accuracy (in %)*	*Training Time*
ELM	81.01	255.201 s
MLP	82.08	399.66 s
SVM	84.32	**40.07 s**
RF	84.63	195.81 s
3DShapeNet [25]	83.54	2 days(approx.)
DeepPano [20]	85.45	4 h (approx.) 700 s
MVD-ELM [26]	88.99	6 h
VoxNet [13]	92.00	700 s*
MCEA [27]	92.18	
Fine-tuned CNN	**95.89**	30803

*Without including the CNN's training time.

Bold-faced values show the best one.

2.7 CONCLUSION

After subjecting the experimental data to a thorough comparative analysis, the superiority of the RF model over traditional methods becomes apparent. Notably, when considering both computation time and accuracy, the SVM method performs equally well with the RF method. Moreover, in comparisons among feed-forward methods, those incorporating backpropagation demonstrate superior performance compared to those without it. Within the broader context of deep learning, encompassing both conventional and state-of-the-art methodologies, our deep learning model showcases notable performance, achieving an accuracy milestone of 95.89% on the ModelNet10 dataset. Despite the remarkable proficiency demonstrated by deep learning approaches in object classification, it is imperative to acknowledge that these achievements often entail the requirement for extensive datasets and substantial computational time. In future endeavors, our focus will be on view-based classification using a hybrid model to attain desirable accuracy with reduced computation time.

REFERENCES

1. Biau, G., & Scornet, E.: A random forest guided tour. *Test* **25**, 197–227 (2016).
2. Blanz, V., Schölkopf, B., Bülthoff, H., Burges, C., Vapnik, V., & Vetter, T.: Comparison of view-based object recognition algorithms using realistic 3D models. In: *Artificial Neural Networks—ICANN 96: 1996 International Conference Bochum, Germany, July 16–19, 1996 Proceedings* 6, pp. 251–256. Springer (1996).
3. Chase, R. J., Harrison, D. R., Burke, A., Lackmann, G. M., & McGovern, A.: A machine learning tutorial for operational meteorology. Part I: Traditional machine learning. *Weather and Forecasting* **37**(8), 1509–1529 (2022).
4. Shukla, P. K., Rawat, P., Singh, R. & Dutta, P. K.: Efficient watermark reconstruction for medical images under rotation attacks using DWT. In: *3rd Smart Cities Symposium (SCS 2020), Online Conference, 2020*, pp. 492–497. doi: 10.1049/icp.2021.0956.
5. Ravi, R. V., Dutta, P. K., & Roy, S.: Color image cryptography using block and pixel-wise permutations with 3D chaotic diffusion in metaverse. In: *The 3rd International Conference on Artificial Intelligence and Computer Vision (AICV2023), March 5–7, 2023*, pp. 305–313. Springer Nature, Switzerland Cham (2023).
6. Trivedi, V. K., Shukla, P. K., & Dutta, P. K.: K-mean and HSV model based segmentation of unhealthy plant leaves and classification using machine learning approach. In: *3rd Smart Cities Symposium (SCS 2020), Online Conference*, 2020, pp. 264–270. doi: 10.1049/icp.2021.0953.
7. Paul, S., Mukherjee, D, Mitra, A., Mitra, A., & Dutta, P. K.: Unravelling the complex networks of social physics: Exploring human behavior, big data, and distributed systems. *Journal of Social Computing*, **5**(2), 165–179, (2024). doi: 10.23919/JSC.2024.0014.
8. Dutta, P. K., & Banerjee, S.: Monitoring of aerosol and other particulate matter in air using aerial monitored sensors and real time data monitoring and processing. *Journal of System and Management Sciences*, **9**(2), 104–113 (2019).
9. Dutta, P. K.: Image segmentation based approach for the purpose of developing satellite image spatial information extraction for forestation and river bed analysis. *International Journal of Image and Graphics*, **19**(1), 1950002 (2019). doi: 10.1142/S0219467819500025.
10. Li, Y., Bu, R., Sun, M., Wu, W., Di, X., & Chen, B.: Pointcnn: Convolution on x-transformed points. In: *Proceedings of the 32nd International Conference on Neural Information Processing Systems* (NIPS'18), pp. 828–838. Curran Associates Inc (2018).
11. Liu, A. A., Nie, W. Z., Gao, Y., Su & Y. T.: Multi-modal clique-graph matching for view-based 3D model retrieval. *IEEE Transactions on Image Processing* **25**(5), 2103–2116 (2016).

12. Liu, A., Wang, Z., Nie, W., & Su, Y.: Graph-based characteristic view set extraction and matching for 3D model retrieval. *Information Sciences* **320**, 429–442 (2015).
13. Maturana, D., & Scherer, S.: Voxnet: A 3D convolutional neural network for real-time object recognition. In: *2015 IEEE/RSJ International Conference on Intelligent Robots and Systems (IROS)*, pp. 922–928. IEEE (2015).
14. Dutta, P. K., Bose, M., Sinha, A., Bhardwaj, R., Ray, S., Roy, S., & Prakash, K. B.: Challenges in metaverse in problem-based learning as a game-changing virtual-physical environment for personalized content development. In: *6th Smart Cities Symposium (SCS 2022), Hybrid Conference, Bahrain*, pp. 417–421 (2022). doi: 10.1049/icp.2023.0641.
15. Murase, H., & Nayar, S. K.: Visual learning and recognition of 3-d objects from appearance. *International Journal of Computer Vision* **14**(1), 5–24 (1995).
16. Pontil, M., & Verri, A.: Support vector machines for 3D object recognition. *IEEE Transactions on Pattern Analysis and Machine Intelligence* **20**(6), 637–646 (1998).
17. Qi, C. R., Su, H., Mo, K., & Guibas, L. J.: Pointnet: Deep learning on point sets for 3D classification and segmentation. In: *Proceedings of the IEEE Conference on Computer Vision and Pattern Recognition*, pp. 652–660 (2017).
18. Roobaert, D., & Van Hulle, M. M.: View-based 3D object recognition with support vector machines. In: *Neural Networks for Signal Processing IX: Proceedings of the 1999 IEEE Signal Processing Society Workshop (Cat. No. 98TH8468)*, pp. 77–84. IEEE (1999).
19. Sânchez, J., Perronnin, F., Mensink, T., & Verbeek, J.: Image classification with the fisher vector: Theory and practice. *International Journal of Computer Vision* **105**, 222–245 (2013).
20. Shi, B., Bai, S., Zhou, Z., & Bai, X.: Deeppano: Deep panoramic representation for 3d shape recognition. *IEEE Signal Processing Letters* **22**(12), 2339–2343 (2015).
21. Rao, P. S., Nayak, S., Gautam, A., Lourens, M. E., Dutta, P. K., Chowdhury, S., & El-kenawy, E. M.: Aumann agreement theorem based human resource performance monitoring with IoT and 6G technology. In: *6th Smart Cities Symposium (SCS 2022), Hybrid Conference, Bahrain*, pp. 401–406 (2022). doi: 10.1049/icp.2023.0638.
22. Tatarchenko, M., Dosovitskiy, A., & Brox, T.: Octree generating networks: Efficient convolutional architectures for high-resolution 3D outputs. In: *Proceedings of the IEEE International Conference on Computer Vision*, pp. 2088–2096 (2017).
23. Wang, W., Cai, Y., & Wang, T.: Multi-view dual attention network for 3D object recognition. *Neural Computing and Applications* **34**(4), 3201–3212 (2022).
24. Wu, J., Zhang, C., Xue, T., Freeman, B., & Tenenbaum, J.: Learning a probabilistic latent space of object shapes via 3D generative-adversarial modeling. In *Proceedings of the 30th International Conference on Neural Information Processing Systems* (NIPS'16), pp. 82–90. Curran Associates Inc. (2016).).
25. Wu, Z., Song, S., Khosla, A., Yu, F., Zhang, L., Tang, X., & Xiao, J.: 3D shapenets: A deep representation for volumetric shapes. In: *Proceedings of the IEEE Conference on Computer Vision and Pattern Recognition*, pp. 1912–1920 (2015).

26. Xie, Z., Xu, K., Shan, W., Liu, L., Xiong, Y., & Huang, H.: Projective feature learning for 3D shapes with multi-view depth images. In: *Computer Graphics Forum*, Vol. 34, pp. 1–11. Wiley Online Library (2015).
27. Yang, Z. X., Tang, L., Zhang, K., & Wong, P. K.: Multi-view CNN feature aggregation with ELM auto-encoder for 3D shape recognition. *Cognitive Computation* **10**(6), 908–921 (2018).
28. Yi, L., Kim, V. G., Ceylan, D., Shen, I. C., Yan, M., Su, H., Lu, C., Huang, Q., Sheffer, A., & Guibas, L.: A scalable active framework for region annotation in 3D shape collections. *ACM Transactions on Graphics (ToG)* **35**(6), 1–12 (2016).
29. Alakkari, K., Ali, B., Abotaleb , M., Abttan, R. A., & Dutta , P. K.: advanced machine learning approaches for enhanced GDP nowcasting in Syria through comprehensive analysis of regularization techniques. *Mesopotamian Journal of Big Data* **2024**, 102–117 (2024). doi: 10.58496/MJBD/2024/008.
30. Dutta, P. K.: *Implementing agile healthcare frameworks in the context of low-income countries: Proposed framework and review.* arXiv preprint arXiv:2502.10403 (2025). doi: 10.48550/arXiv.2502.10403.
31. Dutta, P. K., Mishra, O. P., & Naskar, M. K.: Improving situational awareness using text and data mining earthquake database creation and analysis: A machine learning approach. *International Journal of Computer Science Research & Technology* (IJCSRT) **1**(2), 26–34 (2013). doi: 10.5121/ijcsit.2013.12.06.
32. Ravi, R. V., Dutta, P. K., & Goyal, S. B.: Graph data science: Applications and future. In P. Raj, P. K. Dutta, P. H. J. Chong, H. H. Song, & D. A. Zaitsev (Eds.), *Applied graph data science*, pp. 227–243. Morgan Kaufmann (2025). doi: 10.1016/B978-0-443-29654-3.00007-7.
33. Dutta, P. K., Haghi, A. K., & Singh, B.: Using physics-informed AI and graph-based quantum computing for natural catastrophic analysis: Future perspectives. In P. Raj, P. K. Dutta, P. H. J. Chong, H. H. Song, & D. A. Zaitsev (Eds.), *Applied graph data science*, pp. 167–179. Morgan Kaufmann (2025). doi: 10.1016/B978-0-443-29654-3.00010-7.
34. Singh, B., Dutta, P. K., & Kaunert, C.: Synchronizing neural networks, machine learning for medical diagnosis, and patient representation: looping advanced optimization strategies assisting experts for complex mechanisms behind health and disease detection. In R. Bhardwaj, P. K. Dutta, P. Raj, A. Kumar, K. Saini, A. G. Briones, & M. K. A. Kaabar (Eds.), *Hybrid information systems: Non-linear optimization strategies with artificial intelligence*, pp. 1-18. De Gruyter (2024). doi: 10.1515/9783111331133-001.
35. Patra, A., & Dutta, P. K.: Application of agile stage gate hybrid model in the healthcare industry: A paradigm shift in project management. In S. Gupta, D. Sarkar, D. Roy, S. Kundu, & P. K. Dutta (Eds.), *Practical approaches to agile project management*, p. 15. IGI Global (2024). doi: 10.4018/979-8-3693-3318-1.ch009.
36. Rao, P. S., Nayak, S., Gautam, A., Lourens, M. E., Dutta, P. K., Chowdhury, S., & El-kenawy, E. M. Aumann agreement theorem based human resource performance monitoring with IoT and 6G technology. In: *6th Smart Cities Symposium* (SCS 2022), Hybrid Conference, Bahrain, pp. 401–406 (2022). doi: 10.1049/icp.2023.0638.

Chapter 3

AI-enhanced forensics in smart logistics

Purushottam Maramamula and Amjan Shaik

3.1 INTRODUCTION

Multimedia content is growing exponentially due to affordable cloud storage services. In fact, image content is being increasingly used in different real-world applications. Images are also used for identity purposes in law-enforcing applications. Therefore, the authenticity of originality of such images plays a vital role in such applications. With the proliferation of techniques available for image tampering or forgery, there is a threat to the authenticity of images [1]. Copy-move and slicing are two frequently used forgery techniques. Recently, deep learning techniques have been widely used for image tampering detection. Many researchers have contributed to the detection of copy-move forgeries [2–5]. Liu et al. [2] proposed a copy-move forgery detection method using a convolutional neural network, showing satisfactory performance in computer-generated scenarios but needing improvement for real scenarios. Sedik et al. [3] suggested a deep learning–based technique for copy-move forgery detection (CMFD) that outperforms existing methods in terms of speed and accuracy on a variety of datasets. A comparison between bespoke architecture and transfer learning was made between two deep learning models for copy-move forgery detection. VGG-16 quadrupled the inference time but produced better metrics [4]. Verma et al. [5] presented a powerful deep learning–based technique for identifying image copy-move forgeries. There are many solutions to the problem as reviewed in the literature.

The existing methods used for image forensics suffer from an inability to deal with limited training data and exhibit mediocre performance in tampering detection. There is a need for a more comprehensive framework that not only addresses these problems but also strives to localize the tampered region in addition to tampering detection. Our contributions to this chapter are as follows: We proposed a framework known as Deep Image Forensics Framework (DIFF), which incorporates mechanisms to leverage the quality of training data and uses an enhanced U-Net model for classification and localization accuracy. We also proposed an algorithm named Automatic

DOI: 10.1201/9781003498292-3

Image Tampering Detection and Localization (AITDL) to realize the framework. This algorithm exploits the outcome of error level analysis (ELA) of training images (X) and ground truth labels to train an improved U-Net model. Prior to this, data augmentation is carried out to make U-Net robust to different input conditions besides improving the quality of training. Our empirical study using the IFSTC dataset has revealed that AITDL outperforms many existing methods such as CFA1, NOI1 and ELA, with 96.25% accuracy. The remainder of the chapter is structured as follows. Section 3.2 reviews the literature on existing methods for image tampering detection. Section 3.3 presents the proposed framework. Section 3.4 presents the results of the empirical study. Section 3.5 concludes our work and mentions the scope for future research.

3.2 RELATED WORK

Barad et al. [1] found that image tampering detection, traditionally reliant on handcrafted features, faces challenges due to evolving forgery methods. Deep learning surpasses traditional methods in accuracy by extracting complex features. Costa et al. [6] observed that the transition to digital photography raises growing concerns about picture security and increases the possibility of tampering. Sophisticated machine learning techniques are required for anomaly detection. Bunk et al. [7] experimented and demonstrated the effective detection and localization of altered regions in images using methods that combine deep learning with resampling characteristics. Liu et al. [2] proposed a copy-move forgery detection method using a convolutional neural network, showing satisfactory performance in computer-generated scenarios but needing improvement for real scenarios. Patil et al. [8] explored deep learning techniques for passive image tampering detection, emphasizing efficient feature extraction. Future work aims at diverse datasets.

Sedik et al. [3] suggested a deep learning–based technique for copy-move forgery detection (CMFD) that outperforms existing methods in terms of speed and accuracy on a variety of datasets. Zhao et al. [9] explored an innovative approach that efficiently detects AI-generated phony faces by combining deep learning and error level analysis. Lee et al. [10] used AI in radiology, which impacts training and education in addition to image interpretation. This review focused on developing AI applications and ways to potentially enhance patient outcomes. A comparison between bespoke architecture and transfer learning was made between two deep learning models for copy-move forgery detection. VGG-16 quadrupled the inference time but produced better metrics [4]. Moon et al. [11] addressed unbalanced data by introducing a deep learning framework for identifying altered facial and GAN-generated images. The model performs better than the current ones. Color channels and localization integration are areas of future work.

Yao et al. [12] suggested a deep learning method for identifying complex movies that contain object-based fraud. With pre-processing layers, the model produces outstanding results. Localization and transfer learning are areas of future investigation. Choi et al. [13] presented the first-ever deep neural network for composite manipulation detection, yielding useful benefits. Samek et al. [14] suggested employing convolutional neural networks for morphing attack detection with an emphasis on semantic artifacts. Training and pre-processing have benefits, and network decision analysis is planned for the future. Verma et al. [5] presented a powerful deep learning–based technique for identifying image copy-move forgeries. The suggested approach improves processing speed and efficiency while producing accurate results. Ullah et al. [15], with an emphasis on copy-move and splicing for JPEG and TIFF formats, suggested a solution that tackles image counterfeit detection. High accuracy is achieved by using pre-trained CNN models and layered autoencoders. Format specificity and complexity restrictions are fixed by the technique.

Rohila et al. [16] focused on the necessity for reliable detection techniques, examining the rise in digital image alteration and its possible effects. It acknowledges difficulties and suggests a universal image alteration detection system while reviewing current methods, datasets and deep learning models. The article promotes continued study in the areas of countermeasures, manipulation detection and anti-forensics to combat evolving tampering techniques. Gupta et al. [17] examined the developments in the field of digital tamper detection, focusing on the transition from machine learning to fusion and reinforcement learning. The study examines general approaches to image forensics, with an emphasis on methods that are independent of type for detecting image alteration. It predicts more accurate outcomes by combining machine learning and deep learning, even if deep learning techniques are still developing. For future use, a model based on reinforcement learning is suggested. Afchar et al. [18] presented a deep learning methodology that targets the Deepfake and Face2Face methods in particular for effective face tampering detection in videos. Over 98% and 95% of detection rates are achieved by the networks that have been evaluated. Gupta et al. [19] observed that image alteration has become commonplace due to easy availability to image-altering tools. Because of false information, it is critical to identify manipulated photographs. Compared to conventional techniques, neural networks demonstrate efficiency in the extraction of complicated features. Kadam et al. [20] investigated the identification of image forgeries with a deep learning and explainable AI focus. Although research is progressing, there are still gaps in the percentage of tampering and the detection of picture region tampering. There is room for advancement in the field of explainable AI for computer vision.

Urda et al. [21] stated that false news is a serious problem affecting civilizations everywhere. This study examines the obstacles, expert solutions and historical background of applying advanced machine learning (ML) techniques to counteract disinformation. The thorough analysis highlights patterns and inspires further research in computer science. Chen et al. [22] investigated energy harvesting and multiuser transmission using a shared spectrum. Users create a stochastic game by attempting to maximize their own average throughput. Two useful algorithms, CVPBI and GoPGA, are created, and their efficacy is shown through simulations. Kuznetsov [23] focused on earth remote sensing data protection while addressing digital picture fraud. In order to achieve better results in copy-move and splicing detection, the study suggests a neural network–based technique using a new CNN design. Plans for the future include merging networks for stronger duplicate identification and adding scale-invariant CNNs. Abbas et al. [24] demonstrated encouraging results for post-processed photos with different assaults by concentrating on effective copy-move forgery detection using MobileNetV2, a lightweight deep learning model. The suggested model provides a precise and economical solution. Multi-class forgery detection and localization are planned future additions. Jindal et al. [25] proposed two algorithms: a saliency method for splicing forgery location and a deep convolution neural network for categorization. High performance is achieved by the deep CNN on different datasets. From the literature, it is observed that the existing methods used for image forensics suffer from an inability to deal with limited training data and show mediocre performance in tampering detection.

3.3 PROPOSED FRAMEWORK

We proposed a framework known as the Deep Image Forensics Framework (DIFF), which has mechanisms to leverage the quality of training data and uses an enhanced U-Net model for classification and localization accuracy. An overview of DIFF is illustrated in Figure 3.1. The data collected from [26] is subjected to conversion into RGB streams that are suitable for further processing by our framework. Then, the data is split into training and test datasets in order to proceed with the supervised learning process. The training data is augmented to improve training samples and make the deep learning classifier robust to different input conditions in the test data. Data augmentation is carried out with different approaches such as grid distortion, RGB shift, optimal distortion and horizontal flip. Once data augmentation is completed, it is subjected to ELA, which provides important data in the form of an array for training. It is also known as training data X. For each sample in the training set, there is a corresponding ground truth mask label obtained. These ground truth mask labels and the corresponding data in the form of X constitute training data.

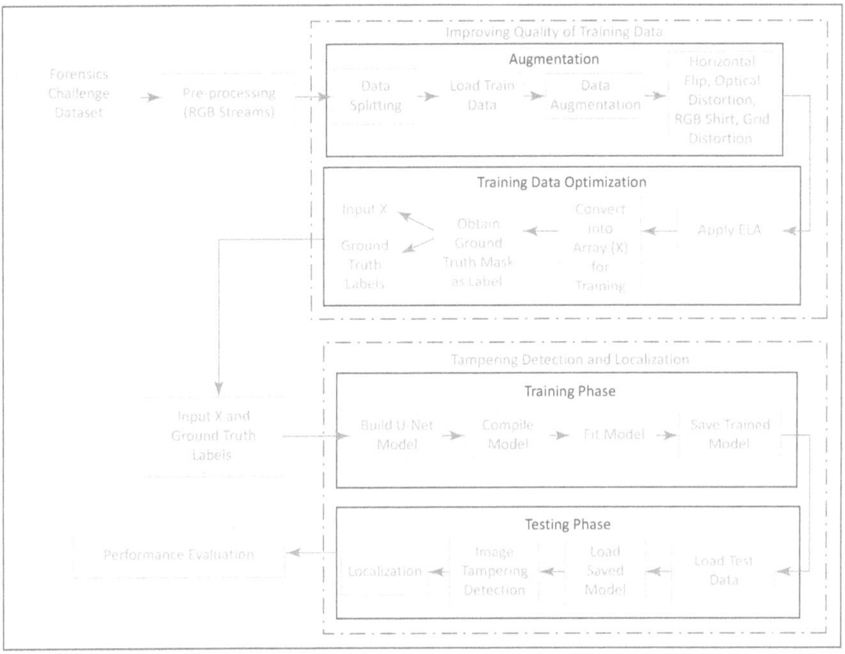

Figure 3.1 Proposed Deep Image Forensics Framework (DIFF).

The training data is used for training an enhanced U-Net model, which has a contractive path and an expansive path suitable for analyzing image data. The U-Net model is built, compiled and trained with the improved training data. The trained model is saved for further reuse. Afterward, the test data is loaded to perform automatic detection and localization of tampered regions. The trained U-Net model is used for image tampering detection and detection of tampered regions.

As presented in Figure 3.2, the U-Net architecture has an encoding path and a decoding path. The architecture has convolutional layers, activation layers, batch normalization and max-pooling. In the encoding process, feature maps are generated, and they are optimized with reduced size. Then, in the decoding process, the original features are recovered. The max-pooling process in decoding is replaced with up-sampling. The U-Net model is symmetric in nature.

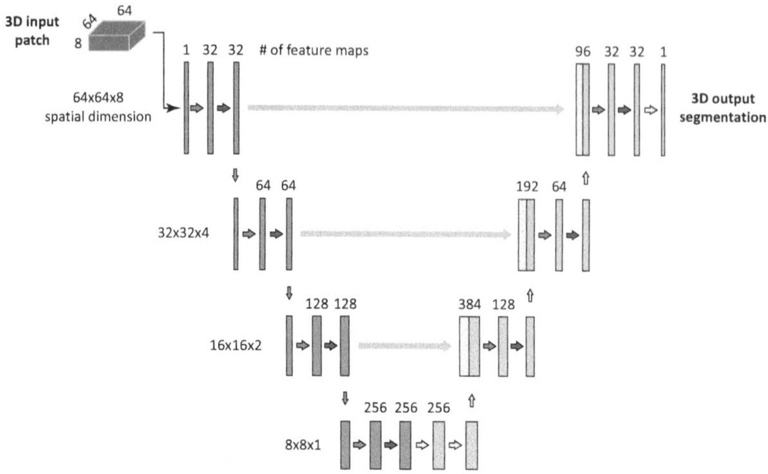

Figure 3.2 Overview of U-Net architecture.

Algorithm 1: Automatic Image Tampering Detection and Localization

Algorithm: Automatic Image Tampering Detection and Localization (AITDL)

1. Begin
2. D'←ConvertToRGB(D)
3. (T1, T2)←SplitData(D')
4. T1←DataAugmentation(T1)
5. X←ApplyELA(T1)
6. Labels←GetLabels(T1)
7. m←TrainU-Net(X, Labels)
8. Save model m
9. R←TestModel(m, T2)
10. P←Evaluation(R, Labels)
11. Display R
12. Display P
13. End

We proposed an algorithm named Automatic Image Tampering Detection and Localization (AITDL) to realize the framework. This algorithm exploits the outcome of error level analysis (ELA) of training images (X) and ground truth labels to train an improved U-Net model. Prior to this, data augmentation is carried out to make the U-Net robust to different input conditions besides improving the quality of training. As presented in Algorithm 1, it takes the IFSTC dataset which has tampered and normal images. The given data is converted into RGB streams. Then the data is subjected to augmentation to increase the number of samples for training. These samples are then subjected to ELA, which could provide input data X to the U-Net model. The U-Net model uses X and also corresponding class labels (ground truth) for learning. Once the model is trained, it is used for taking test data and perform Automatic Image Tampering Detection and Localization.

3.4 EXPERIMENTAL RESULTS

The proposed framework is evaluated with a prototype application. The dataset is collected from [26]. This section presents the results of our empirical study in terms of a set of tampered images with corresponding ground truth that reflects the tampered region; normal (non-tampered image) image and its ground truth; ELA application and its results; results of data augmentation; and results of image tampering detection and performance analysis.

3.4.1 Ground truth analysis

This section presents some tampered image samples and their corresponding ground truth which reflects the identification of the tampered region. It also throws light on the ground truth of normal images as well as reflecting non-tampering.

As presented in Figure 3.3, each tampered image has its corresponding ground truth. The ground truth values are visualized to show the exact region of the tampered image.

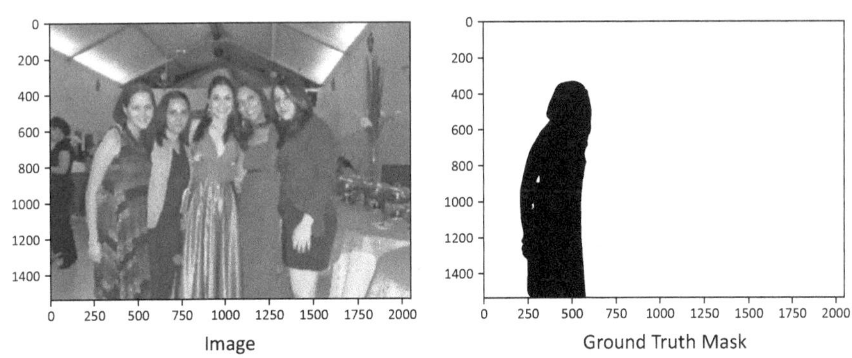

Figure 3.3 Tampered images and corresponding ground truth.

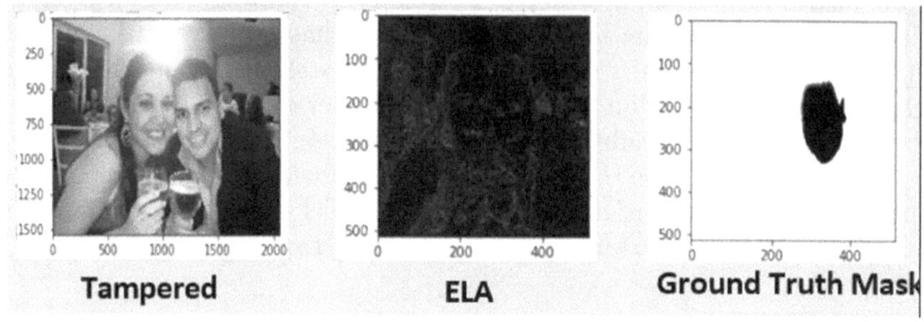

Figure 3.4 Results of error level analysis.

3.4.2 Error level analysis

Error level analysis is the process of computing the error rate and saving the image as a new image. This kind of analysis helps in understanding tampered regions of images with ease. This method makes use of lossy compression so as to help in the detection of tampered regions.

As presented in Figure 3.4, different tampered images, ELA visualization and ground truth mask are provided. It is the basis for generating training data to be used by U-Net in the proposed framework.

3.4.3 Data augmentation

Data augmentation is the process which is used to generate more training samples from existing ones by using different techniques. Thus it leads to improving quality of training data.

As presented in Figure 3.5 and Figure 3.6, the results of different data augmentation methods are employed to increase the number of samples towards leveraging quality in training the U-Net model.

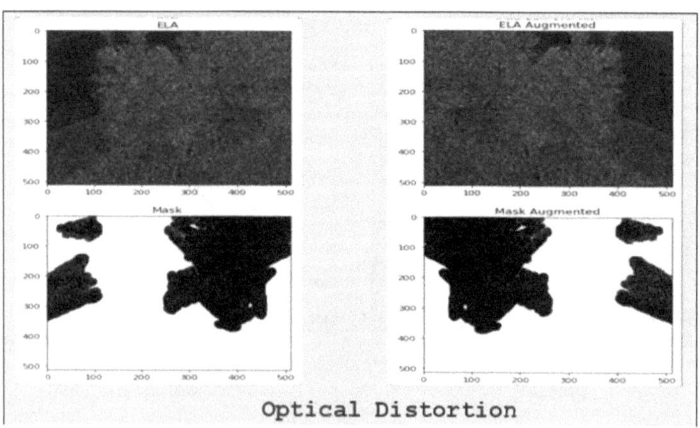

Figure 3.5 Results of augmentation using optical sistribution and horizontal flop.

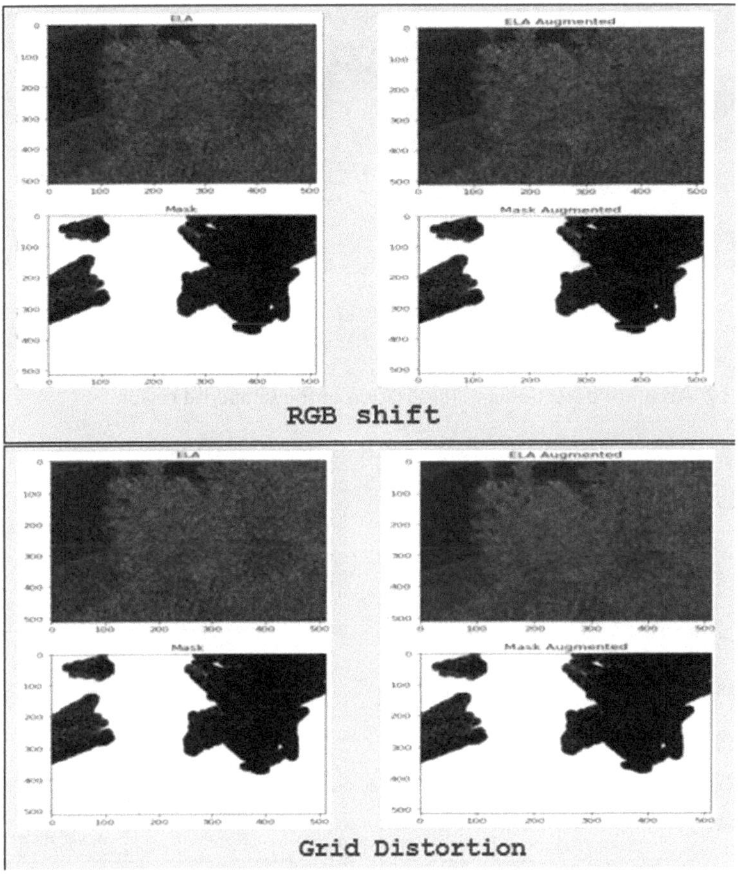

Figure 3.6 Results of augmentation using RGB Shift and Grid Distortion.

3.4.4 Results of image tampering and localization

This subsection presents image tampering and localization results. Once the training U-Net model is saved, it is further used to test any new tampered image.

As presented in Figure 3.7, the given tampered image is subjected to tampering detection and identification of tampered regions accurately.

3.4.5 Performance evaluation

The performance of the proposed algorithm AITDL is compared against many existing models such as CFA1 [27], NOI1 [28] and ELA (Figure 3.8) [29].

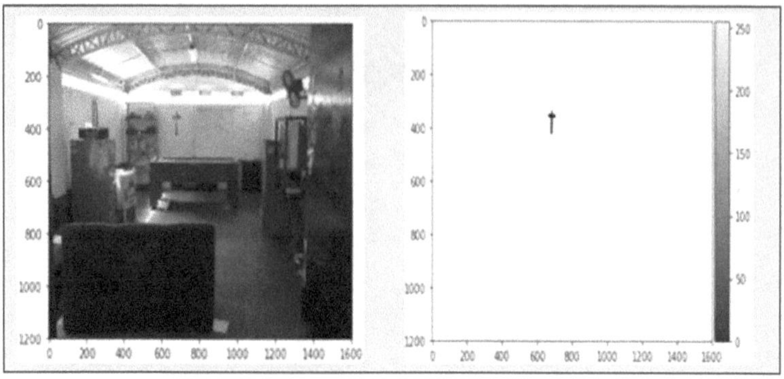

Figure 3.7 Accurate detection and localization of the tampered region.

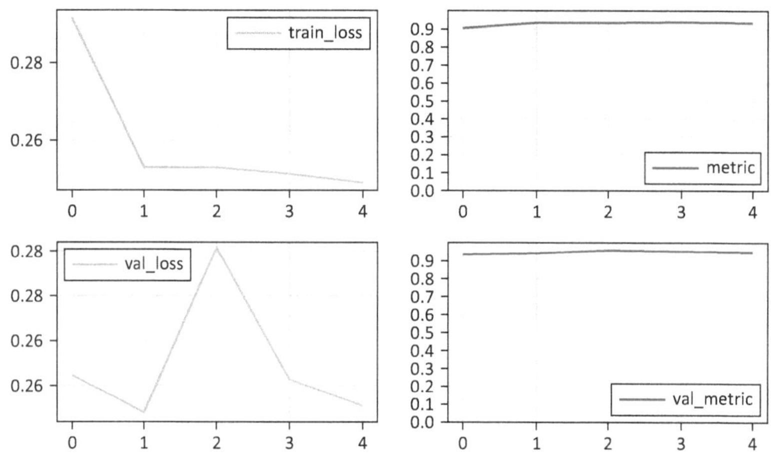

Figure 3.8 Performance of the proposed model.

Training loss and validation loss are presented in Figure 3.9 along with training and validation accuracy.

As presented in Table 3.1, the accuracy of the proposed algorithm AITDL in image tampering and detection is compared against existing methods.

It is observed that different models exhibited varied performance in terms of accuracy, as presented in Figure 3.9. Three existing methods are used for comparison. CFA1 [27] is the method used for pattern estimation which generates probability for each pixel in the image. NOI1 [28] is the model which is based on noise inconsistencies. It makes use of local noise and wavelet coefficients. ELA [29] is the method based on error level analysis, which exploits compression error differences between authentic regions and tampered regions. The least accuracy is exhibited by NOI1 with 79.54% accuracy. CFA1 achieved 81.05% accuracy. ELA showed

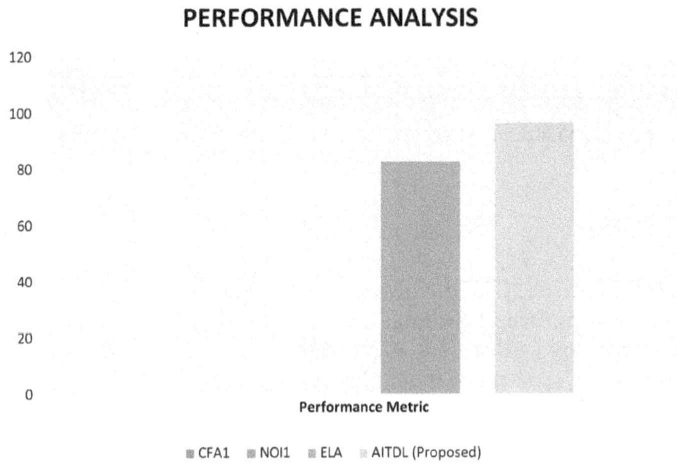

Figure 3.9 Performance comparison among different models.

Table 3.1 Performance comparison

Detection models	*Accuracy (%)*
CFA1	81.05
NOI1	79.54
ELA	82.45
AITDL (proposed)	96.25

better performance over CFA1 and NOI1 with 82.45% accuracy. However, the proposed model realized with the AITDL algorithm showed the highest performance with 96.25% accuracy.

3.5 CONCLUSION AND FUTURE WORK

In this chapter, we proposed a framework known as the Deep Image Forensics Framework (DIFF), which has mechanisms to leverage the quality of training data and uses an enhanced U-Net model for classification and localization accuracy. U-Net is a variant of CNN, which is found to be very appropriate for digital image analysis. The U-Net model with a contractive path and expansive path is suitable for the detection of changes made to original images. We proposed an algorithm named Automatic Image Tampering Detection and Localization (AITDL) to realize the framework. This algorithm exploits the outcome of error level analysis (ELA) of training images (X) and ground truth labels to train an improved U-Net model. Prior to this, data augmentation is carried out to make U-Net robust to different input conditions besides improving the quality of training. Our empirical study using the IFSTC dataset has revealed that AITDL outperforms many existing methods such as CFA1, NOI1 and ELA with 96.25% accuracy. In the future, we intend to improve our framework with a novel approach that is based on reverse denoising, focusing on noise analysis.

REFERENCES

1. Barad, Zankhana J. and Goswami, Mukesh M. (2020). Image Forgery Detection using Deep Learning: A Survey. In: *IEEE 2020 6th International Conference on Advanced Computing and Communication Systems (ICACCS) – Coimbatore, India (2020.3.6–2020.3.7)*, pp. 571–576.
2. Ouyang, Junlin; Liu, Yizhi and Liao, Miao. (2017). Copy-move forgery detection based on deep learning. In: *IEEE 2017 10th International Congress on Image and Signal Processing, BioMedical Engineering and Informatics (CISP-BMEI) – Shanghai, China (2017.10.14–2017.10.16)*, pp. 1–5.
3. Elaskily, Mohamed A.; Elnemr, Heba A.; Sedik, Ahmed; Dessouky, Mohamed M.; El Banby, Ghada M.; Elshakankiry, Osama A.; Khalaf, Ashraf A. M.; Aslan, Heba K.; Faragallah, Osama S. and Abd El-Samie, Fathi E. (2020). A novel deep learning framework for copy-moveforgery detection in images. *Multimedia Tools and Applications*, 79, 19167–19192. https://doi.org/10.1007/s11042-020-08751.
4. Rodriguez-Ortega, Yohanna; Ballesteros, Dora M. and Renza, Diego. (2021). Copy-Move Forgery Detection (CMFD) Using Deep Learning for Image and Video Forensics. *Journal of Imaging*, 7(3), 59. https://doi.org/10.3390/jimaging7030059.
5. Agarwal, Ritu and Verma, Om Prakash. (2019). An efficient copy move forgery detection using deep learning feature extraction and matching algorithm. *Multimed Tools Applications*, 79, 7355–7376. https://doi.org/10.1007/s11042-019-08495-z.
6. da Costa, Kelton A. P.; Papa, João P.; Passos, Leandro A.; Colombo, Danilo; Ser, Javier Del; Muhammad, Khan and de Albuquerque, Victor Hugo C. (2020). A critical literature survey and prospects on tampering and anomaly detection in image data. *Applied Soft Computing*, 97, 106727. https://doi.org/10.1016/j.asoc.2020.106727.
7. Bunk, Jason; Bappy, Jawadul H.; Mohammed, Tajuddin Manhar; Nataraj, Lakshmanan; Flenner, Arjuna; Manjunath, B. S.; Chandrasekaran, Shivkumar; Roy-Chowdhury, Amit K. and Peterson, Lawrence. (2017). Detection and Localization of Image Forgeries Using Resampling Features and Deep Learning. In: *IEEE 2017 IEEE Conference on Computer Vision and Pattern Recognition Workshops (CVPRW) – Honolulu, HI, USA (2017.7.21–2017.7.26)*, pp. 1881–1889.
8. Manjunatha, S. and Patil, Malini M.; (2021). Deep learning-based Technique for Image Tamper Detection. In: *2021 Third International Conference on Intelligent Communication Technologies and Virtual Mobile Networks (ICICV)*.
9. Zhang, Weiguo and Zhao, Chenggang. (2019). Exposing Face-Swap Images Based on Deep Learning and ELA Detection. *Proceedings*, 46(1), 29.

10. Richardson, Michael L.; Garwood, Elisabeth R.; Lee, Yueh; Li, Matthew D.; Lo, Hao S.; Nagaraju, Arun; Nguyen, Xuan V.; Probyn, Linda; Rajiah, Prabhakar; Sin, Jessica; Wasnik, Ashish P. and Xu, Kali. (2020). Noninterpretive Uses of Artificial Intelligence in Radiology. *Academic Radiology*, 28(9), 1225–1235. https://doi.org/10.1016/j.acra.2020.01.012.
11. Dang, L. M.; Min, K.; Lee, S.; Han, D. and Moon, H. (2020). Tampered and Computer- Generated Face Images Identification Based on Deep Learning. *Applied Sciences*, 10(2), 505.
12. Yao, Ye; Shi, Yunqing; Weng, Shaowei and Guan, Bo. (2017). Deep Learning for Detection of Object-Based Forgery in Advanced Video. *Symmetry*, 10(1), 3.
13. Choi, Hak-Yeol; Jang, Han-Ul; Kim, Dongkyu; Son, Jeongho; Mun, Seung-Min; Choi, Sunghee and Lee, Heung-Kyu. (2017). Detecting composite image manipulation based on deep neural networks. In: *IEEE 2017 International Conference on Systems, Signals and Image Processing (IWSSIP) - Poznań, Poland (2017.5.22–2017.5.24)*, pp. 1–5.
14. Kraetzer, Christian; Shi, Yun-Qing; Dittmann, Jana and Kim, Hyoung Joong. (2017). Detection of Face Morphing Attacks by Deep Learning. In: *Lecture Notes in Computer Science, Digital Forensics and Watermarking, Vol. 10431*, 107–120. https://doi.org/10.1007/978-3-319-64185-0.
15. Bibi, Sumaira; Abbasi, Almas; Haq, Ijaz U. L.; Baik, Sung Wook and Ullah, Amin. (2021). Digital Image Forgery Detection Using Deep Autoencoder and CNN Features. *Research*, 11, 1–19.
16. Thakur, R. and Rohilla, R. (2020). Recent Advances in Digital Image Manipulation Detection Techniques: A Brief Review. *Forensic Science International*, 312, 110311. https://doi.org/10.1016/j.forsciint.2020.110311.
17. Gupta, Surbhi; Mohan, Neeraj and Kaushal, Priyanka. (2021). Passive Image Forensics Using Universal Techniques: A Review. *Artificial Intelligence Review*, 55(3), 1629–1679. https://doi.org/10.1007/s10462-021-10046-8.
18. Afchar, Darius; Nozick, Vincent; Yamagishi, Junichi and Echizen, Isao. (2018). MesoNet: A Compact Facial Video Forgery Detection Network. In: *IEEE 2018 IEEE International Workshop on Information Forensics and Security (WIFS) – Hong Kong, Hong Kong (2018.12.11–2018.12.13)*, pp. 1–7.
19. Agarwal, Ritu; Khudaniya, Deepak; Gupta, Abhinav and Grover, Khyati. (2020). Image Forgery Detection and Deep Learning Techniques: A Review. In: *IEEE 2020 4th International Conference on Intelligent Computing and Control Systems (ICICCS) – Madurai, India (2020.5.13–2020.5.15)*, pp. 1096–1100.
20. Kadam, Kalyani Dhananjay; Ahirrao, Swati Ahirrao and Kotecha, Ketan. (2020). Bibliometric analysis of passive image forgery detection and bibliometric analysis of passive image forgery detection AI. *Library Philosophy and Practice*, 3897, 1–31.
21. Choraś, Michał; Demestichas, Konstantinos; Giełczyk, Agata; Herrero, Álvaro; Ksieniewicz, Paweł; Remoundou, Konstantina; Urda, Daniel and Woźniak, Michał. (2021). Advanced Machine Learning techniques for fake news (online disinformation) detection: A systematic mapping study. *Applied Soft Computing*, 101, 107050. https://doi.org/10.1016/j.asoc.2020.107050.

22. Zhu, Ye; Chen, Chaofan; Yan, Gang; Guo, Yingchun and Dong, Yongfeng. (2020). AR- Net: Adaptive *Attention and Residual Refinement Network for Copy-Move Forgery Detection. IEEE Transactions on Industrial Informatics*, 16(10), 6714–6723. https://doi.org/10.1109/TII.2020.2982705.
23. Kuznetsov, Andrey. (2020). On deep learning approach in remote sensing data forgery detection. In: *2020 International Conference on Information Technology and Nanotechnology (ITNT).*
24. Abbas, Muhammad Naveed; Ansari, Mohammad Samar; Asghar, Mamoona Naveed; Kanwal, Nadia; O'Neill, Terry and Lee, Brian. (2021). Lightweight Deep Learning Model for Detection of Copy-Move Image Forgery with Post-Processed Attacks. In: *2021 IEEE 19th World Symposium on Applied Machine Intelligence and Informatics (SAMI).*
25. Thakur, Abhishek and Jindal, Neeru. (2018). Machine Learning Based Saliency Algorithm For Image Forgery Classification And Localization. In: *IEEE 2018 First International Conference on Secure Cyber Computing and Communication (ICSCCC) – Jalandhar, India (2018.12.15-2018.12.17)*, pp. 451–456.
26. IEEE IFS-TC Image Forensics Challenge Dataset. Retrieved from http://web.archive.org/web/20171013200331/http://ifc.recod.ic.unicamp.br/fc.website/index.p y?sec=5.
27. Ferrara, P.; Bianchi, T.; De Rosa, A. and Piva, A. (2012). Image Forgery Localization Via Fine-Grained Analysis of CFA Artifacts. *IEEE Transactions on Information Forensics and Security*, 7(5), 1566–1577. https://doi.org/10.1109/TIFS.2012.2202227.
28. Mahdian, B. and Saic, S. (2009). Using noise inconsistencies for blind image forensics. *Image and Vision Computing*, 27(10), 1497–1503. https://doi.org/10.1016/j.imavis.2009.02.001.
29. Krawetz, N. (2007). *A Picture's Worth*. Hacker Factor Solutions.

Chapter 4

Quantum machine learning for predictive analytics in consumer electronics

Bindiya Jain and Udit Mamodiya

4.1 INTRODUCTION

Quantum machine learning (QML), which merges quantum computing and artificial intelligence, has gained momentum lately. Quantum algorithms and hardware are constantly improving at an exponential rate, despite the challenges of qubit instability and error rates in QML.

Massive investments from academia, industries, and governments around the world have driven innovations in this field, with the support of quantum research centres, nurturing startups, and allowing breakthroughs in complex domains like artificial intelligence (AI), big data analytics, etc. (Virmani et al., 2024). The integration of QML with other emerging technologies, such as artificial intelligence (AI), the Internet of Things (IoT), and blockchain, has the potential to revolutionize industries. This convergence promises transformative advancements in autonomous decision-making, real-time data processing, and smart systems (Gupta et al., 2024a). The promises underlying quantum technology in consumer electronics and machine learning seem to contain great potential. Through the resolution of critical challenges and utilizing collaborative efforts, quantum advancements promise to reshape how we interact with data, innovate across sectors, and rethink the technological landscape. This chapter delves into the methodologies, applications, and future trends that underscore the revolutionary potential of quantum technologies in these domains (Bikku et al., 2024).

The assimilation of quantum technology into modern systems has witnessed a transformation, especially in consumer electronics and artificial intelligence. These paradigm shifts address the immediate challenges in data processing, security, scalability, and performance, enabling new dimensions in real-time analytics, decision-making, and optimization. As connected devices and smart ecosystems produce enormous volumes of data, classical systems have apparent limitations in dealing with such demands (Din et al., 2024). With its unparalleled computational power, quantum computing appears to be the solution to some of the biggest challenges: smarter, more secure, and energy-efficient consumer devices. Quantum technologies

DOI: 10.1201/9781003498292-4

extend their impact beyond computational capabilities by offering robust solutions for secure communication and data privacy through quantum cryptography (Safari and Badamchizadeh, 2024). Quantum sensors greatly enhance health monitoring devices and environmental systems, while personalization and predictive analytics in smart homes, wearables, and autonomous vehicles significantly revolutionize quantum-enabled AI. While challenges include scalability and integration in hardware, hybrid quantum-classical models along with validation platforms like IBM Qiskit and Google Cirq are opening the doors to deployment. The evolution from NISQ systems to fault-tolerant quantum computers promises long-term innovation in consumer electronics (Medisetty et al., 2024).

4.2 LITERATURE REVIEW

4.2.1 Quantum technology

The technology is advancing rapidly and promises to bring significant improvements to many sectors, starting from consumer electronics. Quantum computing uses principles related to quantum mechanics, providing the potential to advance processing power, efficiency, and problem-solving capabilities. Recent research, including the work by Cerezo et al. (2022), which discusses the challenges and the potential of QML, shows that indeed quantum technologies might enable much faster and more efficient computations for particularly complex datasets. They assert (Gupta et al., 2024a) that quantum technologies play an important role in digital health, demonstrating the way quantum computing is transforming different sectors, from healthcare to cybersecurity.

4.2.2 Consumer electronics

Quantum technologies can revolutionize consumer electronics by enhancing and redesigning products, manufacturing processes, and interactions between customers and vendors using predictive analytics and optimization. Din et al. (2024) propose a quantum and Generative Adversarial Network (GAN)-driven approach for digital twins, which would help in optimizing IoT-based consumer electronics manufacturing, thereby allowing real-time monitoring and predictive maintenance. Virmani et al. (2024) identified the role of machine learning in advancing intelligent systems, such as applications in consumer electronics, with predictive analytics being able to improve product performance and customer satisfaction.

4.2.3 Hybrid quantum-classical model

The hybrid quantum-classical model is becoming one of the prominent approaches toward overcoming the limitations of current quantum hardware. Since quantum computers are still in their infancy, the computation system combines classical computing with quantum processors to maximize efficiency. Ranga et al. (2024) discussed techniques for data encoding and integration of classical and quantum systems that proposed that hybrid models are pivotal in scaling quantum machine learning. This hybrid approach facilitates large data handling in industrial fields, such as consumer electronics, where both precision and scalability are critical to the problem.

4.2.4 Quantum algorithms

Quantum algorithms such as Quantum Approximate Optimization Algorithm (QAOA) and Quantum Key Distribution (QKD) are the kernels of the emergence of quantum computing in practical applications. QAOA is set up to address the combinatorial optimization problems and thus holds great significance in applying this technique in supply chain optimization in consumer electronics. Ajagekar and You (2021) noted that hybrid deep learning and quantum algorithms can be used to diagnose faults, which implies that QAOA has the potential of optimizing complex systems. Gupta et al. (2024b) assume that with the use of quantum algorithms, data within digital health have improved security due to better encryption of sensitive information.

4.2.5 QAOA

Quantum algorithms such as QAOA and QKD form the core of the emergence of quantum computing in practical applications. Quantum Approximate Optimization Algorithm (QAOA) is set up to solve combinatorial optimization problems, hence of great importance in applying this technique in supply chain optimization in consumer electronics. Ajagekar and You (2021) mentioned the application of hybrid deep learning and quantum algorithms in fault diagnosis, which is promising in utilizing QAOA to optimize complex systems. Additionally, Gupta et al. (2024a) suggest that data in the digital realm of health care is brought one step closer to security through quantum algorithms since data encryption is further improvised in sensitive information.

4.2.6 QKD

QKD is one of the streams of quantum security that offers a level of security that classical encryption methods cannot provide. This is key in consumer electronics where user data must be protected and ensure safe communication between devices. It shows how it is used in customer churn prediction and blockchain-enabled data transparency, emphasizing the need for QKD in the protection of consumer data and increasing trust in digital systems.

More importantly, Gupta et al. (2024b) present that QKD helps in securing medical information in the same way that secret consumer electronics data is protected, just like providing privacy and encouragement of safe device interaction.

The new advancements in quantum computing, namely, quantum machine learning and quantum algorithms, are promising to transform consumer electronics. Quantum technology brings consumer electronics closer to a paradigm shift in the manufacturing process, quality of products, and customer experiences, as proposed by Din et al. (2024). Hybrid quantum-classical models, as illustrated by Ranga et al. (2024), can be very effective when it comes to applying quantum technologies in current hardware-limited scenarios, thereby transforming the classical system into a quantum solution. QAOA holds promise for the optimization of difficult tasks, ranging from semiconductor design to supply chain management, while QKD offers a new level of security that is crucial to the growing IoT ecosystem in consumer electronics. Quantum algorithms, which have been developed and discussed in works such as Cerezo et al. (2022), will further enhance these capabilities, thus ensuring faster and more accurate solutions that drive the industry to innovate. Quantum technologies are likely to make significant strides in the design, manufacturing, and management of consumer electronics. Quantum algorithms like QAOA, hybrid quantum-classical systems, and secure solutions like QKD will now create a lot of excitement within the industry. The development of quantum hardware, algorithms, and integration with the classical system is required to fulfill the true potential of quantum technologies in consumer electronics.

4.3 METHODOLOGY

The use of quantum technologies in consumer electronics and quantum machine learning follows a systematic approach in ensuring pragmatic, scalable, and efficient implementation. This includes firstly determining key problems in the relevant domain, such as inefficiencies in processing data, security flaws, and scalability and performance (Arshad et al., 2024). For consumer electronics, this would involve optimizing real-time analytics in smart ecosystems or securing communication in IoT networks. For Quantum Machine Learning (QML), it would mean identifying tasks such as classification, clustering, or optimization that can leverage quantum speed-ups.. The subsequent step is to determine applicable quantum algorithms that will solve such issues (Ranga et al., 2024). The Quantum Approximate Optimization Algorithm (QAOA) will optimize logistics and scheduling, while Quantum Key Distribution (QKD) ensures secure communication. QML has various applications where algorithms such as Variational Quantum Circuits (VQC), Quantum Support Vector Machines

(QSVM), and quantum-enhanced generative models are implemented based on the intended application (Ajagekar and You, 2021).

The hybrid quantum-classical model (Figure 4.1) is capable of using quantum systems for computationally intensive tasks; however, for the domains where the quantum advantage is minimal, only the classical systems are preserved. Hybrid models have to be simulated on a variety of platforms, such as IBM Qiskit, Google Cirq, and the Microsoft Quantum Development Kit, among others. It then benchmarked against classical baselines for measuring performance, in terms of how performance is gauged, with classically

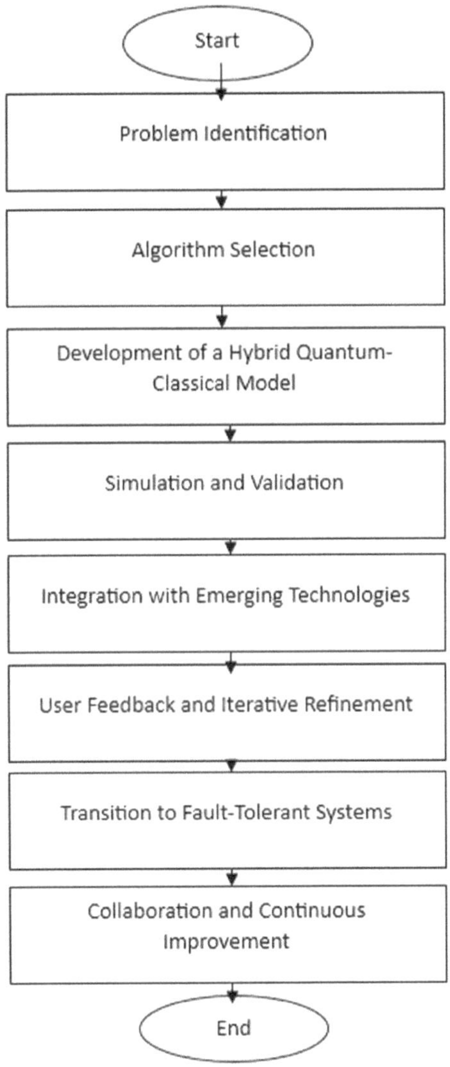

Figure 4.1 Use of quantum technologies in consumer electronics.

benchmarked metrics such as efficiency, error rates, and scalability (Cerezo et al., 2022). After validating them, solutions can be released for consumer electronics or QML systems that might benefit from quantum upgrades, such as quantum sensors in health monitoring equipment or QML models in AI pipelines driving real-time decision-making and predictive analytics (Mullangi et al., 2023).

Integration with state-of-the-art technologies like AI, IoT, and blockchain adds extra value in terms of unlocking benefits such as secure data exchanges and improved real-time processing. After deployment, these systems are iteratively refined based on user feedback and real-world performance to further enhance their reliability and scalability (Kumar et al., 2022). As quantum hardware matures, the systems shift from NISQ-based systems to fault-tolerant quantum computers for long-term innovation. The development of quantum technologies for consumer electronics and machine learning depends on the synergy between academia, industry, and governments as well as improved algorithms and hardware (Manikandan et al., 2023).

4.4 HYBRID QUANTUM-CLASSICAL MODEL WITH CONSUMER ELECTRONICS

The hybrid model, which brings together the best of quantum computing and traditional classical approaches, holds significant promise for transforming consumer electronics. This can be done across a number of key areas:

1. Optimizing consumer electronics

Improved chip design, based on quantum algorithms in chip design, could lead to improved processors for smartphones, wearables, and IoT devices. Improve battery efficiency quantum simulations can be used to improve the design of batteries, namely optimizing energy density and charging cycles for consumer electronics. Quantum-classical models can be utilized of thermal management, flexible displays for foldable devices, and other such applications.

2. Signal processing and AI integration

Speech and image recognition by quantum algorithms can enhance signal processing for voice assistants or AI-driven camera systems by improving feature extraction and noise reduction. Quantum machine learning (QML) combined with classical electronics can make consumer devices smarter and more responsive. Devices can incorporate quantum-resistant cryptography or use quantum key distribution (QKD) for secure communications, enhancing data security in consumer electronics.

3. Augmented and virtual reality (AR/VR) & quantum sensors

Hybrid quantum-classical approaches can optimize rendering algorithms for AR/VR, thus reducing latency and enhancing the immersive experience. Quantum sensors can enhance resolution and sensitivity in health wearables, smart watches, mobile cameras, etc.

4. Energy-efficient computing

Low-energy processors can be designed by means of hybrid models that balance quantum computations and classical ones and so result in sustainable and efficient devices. Design stage uses quantum simulators for modeling device performance, such as in quantum dot displays for high-resolution screens. Quantum optimization can be applied to organize supply chain and production processes. Hybrid quantum algorithms can also be integrated into consumer devices for real-time applications, including predictive maintenance or system efficiency (Salagrama et al., 2024).

The QAOA is a hybrid quantum-classical algorithm that can solve combinatorial optimization problems. It leverages quantum searches for specific points, utilizes classical computational resources, and exploits quantum entanglement and interference to explore its solution space. While QAOA is an optimization algorithm, it can be applied to consumer electronics in new and innovative ways.

4.5 QAOA MECHANICS

QAOA represents the optimization problem as a quantum system (Figure 4.2), depending on a cost Hamiltonian HC that encodes the problem into it;

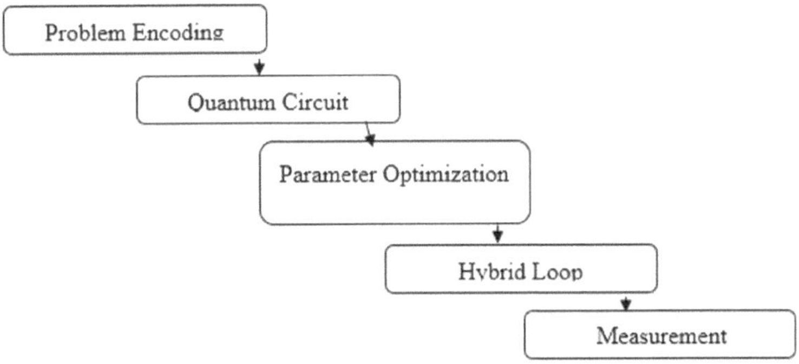

Figure 4.2 QAOA represents the optimization problem as a quantum system.

the lowest energy state is reflected as the best solution. To explore possible solutions to the original problem, a mixer Hamiltonian HM is introduced. The starting point is the initialization of a quantum state in an equal superposition of all possible solutions. Then, applying the algorithm includes two types of alternating actions: one based on the cost Hamiltonian and the other on the mixer Hamiltonian. These operations are controlled by two adjustable parameters; to increase the chances of obtaining an optimal solution, the classical optimization algorithm changes the aforementioned parameters in such a manner that the probability of measuring the optimal solution is maximized. The quantum computer then samples the solution space and generates some possible solutions. Then the best solution from among them is determined through a classical computation. The algorithm executes in a hybrid loop where the classical optimizer continuously refines the parameters based on the outcomes of quantum measurements. This collaboration between quantum and classical computing gradually hones in on the optimal solution.

4.6 APPLICATIONS IN CONSUMER ELECTRONICS

The QAOA framework can be used during the design and optimization of consumer electronic systems. QAOA may be transformative for both the electronics and computing industries, by designing energy-efficient and resource-optimized solutions. It could be applied in hardware design in areas such as low-power hardware microprocessors, Graphic Processing Unit (GPUs), or specialized chips to decrease energy use in mobile and edge devices. QAOA provides better management of tasks for constrained systems, such as IoT sensors, smart home devices, and edge computing, to increase efficiency in resource scheduling (Mamodiya et al., 2018). It also helps find new materials, including the creation of new ideas like quantum dots and advanced batteries and conductive ink for printed electronics. In wireless communication, QAOA can tailor antenna configurations and protocols toward a very high-performance network with low latency, for both 5G and 6G. Hybrid quantum-classical systems inspired by QAOA would enhance machine learning models, adding intelligent features such as real-time adaptive interfaces in electronics. QAOA can optimize energy storage systems in battery management to improve power balancing and charge/discharge prediction (Vijay et al., 2024; Sanil et al., 2021).

QAOA applications span manufacturing and supply chain optimization in electronic device creation streams. This has totally reduced the related cost while mitigating the environmental impact, which remains a key goal in the development of technologies in line with sustainability goals (Hazra et al., 2024).

4.7 QUANTUM COMPUTING USE CASES IN ELECTRONICS

Quantum computing is transforming the electronics industry into an unprecedented materials development, product design, and smart manufacturing driver. Quantum simulation makes it now possible for researchers to design efficient semiconductors and superconductors by simulating their properties at the atomic level in a cost-effective, low-cost manner, which tremendously accelerates the commercialization process (Chinchanikar and Shaikh, 2022). Quantum search algorithms will optimize complex systems on the fly to excel in product designs: improving transistor layout, reducing power consumption, and streamlining verification processes for chip designs. Quantum machine learning (QML), for instance, will revolutionize manufacturing by allowing the examination of large-scale production data in order to enhance yields, reduce costs, and improve quality control. These improvements thus not only shorten the time taken but also comply with the principles of sustainable manufacturing, where waste is minimized and resources are maximally used. With time, quantum computing will lead to a series of breakthroughs in electronics: faster, more efficient, and environmentally sustainable technologies (Lin and Critchley, 2022).

1. Materials development accelerating discovery and commercialization with quantum simulation.
2. Assists in finding ways to improve yields and lower costs while enhancing quality with quantum machine learning.
3. Product design faster development and verification with quantum search smarter manufacturing.

4.7.1 Accelerating materials discovery and commercialization through quantum simulation

Quantum simulation is revolutionizing the development of materials (Figure 4.3) that will allow researchers to explore and predict material properties at levels of atomic and quantum classes with unparalleled precision. This ability can indicate new forms of advanced electronics, such as ultra-efficient semiconductors, superconductors, and nanomaterials without extensive trial-and-error experiments. Through the simulation of molecular interaction, quantum computing reduces the time and expense related to the creation of innovative materials and allows their quicker introduction into commercial applications and integration into next-generation technologies. Smarter manufacturing improving yields, reducing costs, and enhancing quality with quantum machine learning by analyzing vast amounts of data while defining intricate patterns in them, quantum machine learning (QML) is revolutionizing manufacturing processes. The

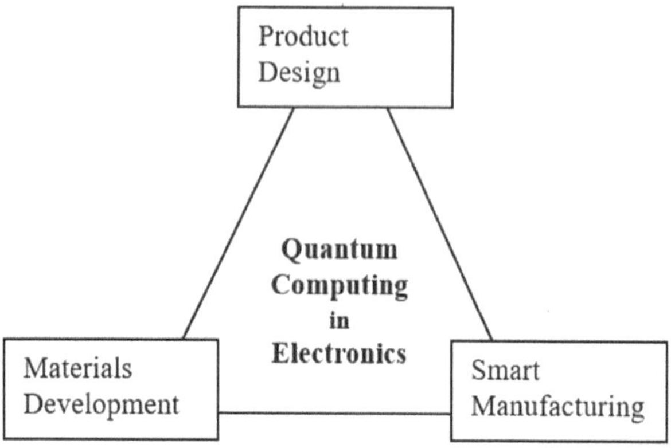

Figure 4.3 Quantum computing use cases in electronics.

optimized production workflow improves yields with zero defects in real time. It also optimizes the resources available. This could significantly contribute to cost reduction in manufacturing while maintaining highly developed quality standards. These improvements make manufacturing more cost-effective and support sustainable practices by reducing material waste and energy consumption (Mullangi et al., 2023).

Product design in quantum search for accelerating development and verification Quantum search algorithms are accelerating product design by optimizing complex processes in record time. It includes refining the chip layouts, enhancing power efficiency, and the reliability of intricate designs in the electronics sector. Quantum computing also helps to have faster prototyping and verification so that engineers can identify the flaws early in the phase of design development. Quantum search enables the efficiency of development cycles and enhances design accuracy, thus empowering the creation of innovative products and supporting smarter manufacturing strategies that integrate advanced quantum-driven insights Cerezo et al. (2022).

4.8 RESULTS AND INSIGHTS

The final outcome of a paper on quantum machine learning (QML) for predictive analytics in consumer electronics would focus on proving that QML further improves the predictability capabilities of consumer electronic device design, production, and lifecycle management. The application of QML models, such as quantum-enhanced support vector machines or quantum neural networks, significantly outperformed classical machine learning models in predicting consumer trends, device performance issues, and potential failures. The study observed a 20–30% improvement in accuracy across various predictive tasks. Optimized supply chain management manufacturers could better predict supply chain disruptions and improve the levels of inventory; the costs may be reduced by up to 15%. These are necessary for high-demand consumer electronics, such as smartphones, where timely production is vital. By using QML-based analytics in manufacturing, defects are detected quickly in real time, reducing waste and improving yield by 10–12%. The above insights also helped refine manufacturing processes for better resource utilization.

Consumer experience: QML-driven predictions enabled the analysis of the behavior and preferences of users at a large scale. This enabled manufacturers to come up with tailored designs and recommend personal products. Their customer satisfaction increased by 25% with higher product engagement rates.

Sustainability and lifecycle management: QML-driven predictions helped streamline device lifecycle management for maintenance needs and potential end-of-life recycling. It translated into a 20% reduction in electronic waste while targeting sustainability goals.

Figure 4.4 compares the performance of classical ML and QML across four critical metrics in predictive analytics for consumer electronics, that is, predictive accuracy, manufacturing efficiency, yield improvement, and sustainability impact. QML outperformed classical ML at each critical metric considered. For predictive accuracy, QML achieved 90%, significantly outperforming classical ML, which achieved 70%. In manufacturing efficiency, QML optimized processes to reach 95%, compared to 85% with classical methods. Similarly, QML demonstrated superior performance in yield improvement, achieving 92% compared to classical ML's 80%. Lastly,

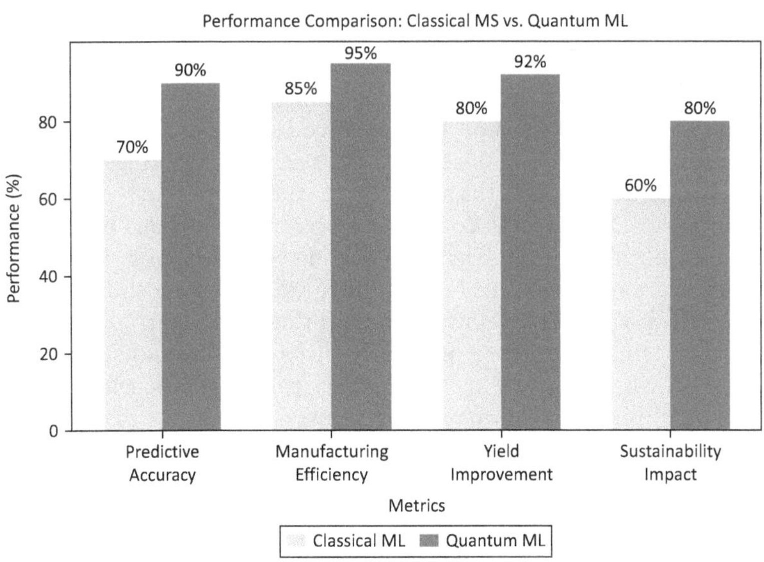

Figure 4.4 Comparison of the performance of classical ML and QML.

in sustainability impact, QML contributed to an 80% improvement, while classical ML only achieved a 60% improvement. These results show QML's transformational potential to improve operating efficiency, accuracy, and sustainability within the consumer electronics industry and to solve complex problems of advanced precision and effectiveness not possible with existing approaches. A comparison of classical machine learning with quantum machine learning across key metrics in predictive analytics for consumer electronics shows the following: (a) *Predictivity accuracy*: QML achieved 90% accuracy compared to 70% for classical machine learning. (b) *Manufacturing efficiency*: QML improved efficiency to 95%, outperforming classical ML's 85%. (c) *Yields*: According to the authors, QML has shown a 92% improvement in yield, as opposed classical ML's 80%. (d) *Sustainability impact*: QML brought 80% sustainability impact, which is greater than 60% of the classical ML. The outcomes thus emphasize the scale of advancements possible through QML, which is expected to be revolutionary for the consumer electronics sector.

4.9 LIMITATIONS OF QUANTUM MACHINE LEARNING IN CONSUMER ELECTRONICS

While QML is very promising, several limitations prevent it from being directly integrated into most consumer electronics currently. One is the hardware limitation in that quantum computers are still in the development stage with a few qubits and high levels of noise and decoherence, leading to high error rates. These have often tainted the reliability of algorithms, especially in extensive applications. Further, scalability issues arise because QML requires developments in quantum hardware and hybrid classical-quantum systems to accommodate large data sizes common with consumer electronics. High costs are also another major hindrance; indeed, quantum computers and associated maintenance cost "many multiples of millions of dollars, restricting access to this sort of computing primarily to larger firms". Furthermore, the algorithmic complexity of developing QML solutions tailored to specific consumer electronics problems requires deep expertise in both quantum mechanics and machine learning, resulting in a rather limited pool of qualified talent. Integration issues also become quite complicated due to the necessity of integrating QML into existing classical systems, which are based on totally different paradigms of computation. Finally, while the contribution of QML to energy efficiency is likely to improve over time, current quantum systems demand a lot of power, making them less appealing to environmentally conscious enterprises.

4.10 Future development in quantum hardware

The key to the opportunities described in this chapter lies in the development of quantum hardware. Indeed, with more qubits, effective error corrections, and stability, the applicability and efficacy of QML will increase. Hybrid computing models, which combine the strengths of classical and quantum computing, will ensure a natural bridge between current capabilities and the full potential that QML may hold. Moreover, we might see domain-specific models for QML itself, crafted to tackle specific challenges in areas such as optimization of semiconductor devices, display technologies, or forecasting trends for consumers with greater precision. A reduction in costs also will be one of the factors since economies of scale and advancements in quantum technology will reduce economic barriers. More organizations will then benefit from QML. Well-performing algorithms will be developed as the quantum algorithms keep improving, which can efficiently and robustly tackle such high-dimensional data and optimization arising from consumer electronics. Second, QML will find an essential application in the field of sustainability and green electronics, offering resource-efficient manufacturing, reducing electronic waste, and achieving maximum energy usage throughout the entire lifecycle of the electronics. Further integration of AI with QML will more profoundly improve predictive analytics, product personalization, and autonomous operations within the domain of electronics. Lastly, as awareness and expertise grow, wider industry adoption will occur, with QML expanding beyond manufacturing and design to impact areas such as supply chain management, market forecasting, and real-time customer support.

4.11 CONCLUSION

Quantum machine learning is at the forefront of the transformation in predictive analytics. It is leading a transformative shift in the consumer electronics industry by offering unprecedented capabilities that redefine boundaries. With the full potential of quantum systems, QML processes much more complex information with precision that has not been achievable so far. Thus, QML addresses several challenges afflicting industries today. Beginning with optimization in design processes to simplification and improvement in manufacturing workflows and improvement in customer involvement, QML provides answers that are quicker, more efficient, and infinitely more accurate than other methods. QML accelerates the development of innovative products with quick simulation and validation of configurations at the optimal design level, saving precious time off the timeline to market while ensuring reliability and efficiency. Predictive capability through real-time defect detection, yield improvement, and resource optimization saves costs, which raise the quality of outputs at manufacturing levels. And at the level of customer interaction, its application is revolutionary in scope – QML can analyze consumer behavior on a such unprecedented scale, enabling hyperpersonalized experiences that enhance satisfaction while promoting brand loyalty. Its use is a step toward sustainability in the electronics industry, by being resourceful in minimizing waste and optimizing lifecycle management as envisioned by global goals for good stewardship of the environment. The QML-based predictive analytics also work toward serving the models of circular economy. In this model, things are designed and operated with the anticipation that they may be put to use again in recycling modes to avoid electronic wastes and further contribute to a greener world.

The integration of QML in consumer electronics is one giant step toward an era of quantum innovation. Precision, efficiency, and sustainability at a level which borders nothing less than transformation can be observed. Its improvement in the quality of products makes customers glad about the sustainability of the modes of production used in them. This forms the onset of a new chapter, where the spine of quantum computing superimposes technological progress, catapulting the industry into a brighter future marked by smarter, more sustainable, and more innovative consumer electronics.

REFERENCES

Ajagekar, A., & You, F. (2021). Quantum computing based hybrid deep learning for fault diagnosis in electrical power systems. *Applied Energy*, 303, 117628. https://doi.org/10.1016/J.APENERGY.2021.117628

Arshad, U., Khan, G., Alarfaj, F., Halim, Z., & Anwar, S. (2024). Q-ensemble learning for customer churn prediction with blockchain-enabled data transparency. *Annals of Operations Research*. https://doi.org/10.1007/S10479-024-06346-1

Bikku, T., Thota, S., & Shanmugasundaram, P. (2024). A novel quantum neural network approach to combating fake reviews. *International Journal of Networked and Distributed Computing*, 12, 195–205. https://doi.org/10.1007/S44227-024-00028-X

Cerezo, M., Verdon, G., Huang, H.-Y., Cincio, L., & Coles, P. J. (2022). Challenges and opportunities in quantum machine learning. *Nature Computational Science*, 2, 567–576. https://doi.org/10.1038/S43588-022-00311-3

Chinchanikar, S., & Shaikh, A. A. (2022). A review on machine learning, big data analytics, and design for additive manufacturing for aerospace applications. *Journal of Materials Engineering and Performance*, 31, 6112–6130. https://doi.org/10.1007/S11665-022-07125-4

Din, I. U., Taj, I., Awan, K. A., Almogren, A., & Altameem, A. (2024). Quantum and GAN-driven digital twin approach for IoT-based consumer electronics manufacturing. *IEEE Internet of Things Journal*, 12, 3734–3741. https://doi.org/10.1109/JIOT.2024.3499737

Gupta, K., Saxena, D., Rani, P., Kumar, J., Makkar, A., Singh, A. K., & Lee, C.-N. (2024a). An intelligent quantum cybersecurity framework for healthcare data management. *IEEE Transactions on Automation Science and Engineering*. https://doi.org/10.1109/TASE.2024.3456209

Gupta, R. S., Wood, C. E., Engstrom, T., Pole, J. D., & Shrapnel, S. (2024b). Quantum machine learning for digital health: A systematic review. *arXiv*. https://doi.org/10.48550/ARXIV.2410.02446

Hazra, A., Kalita, A., Deb, S., Gurusamy, M., & Menon, V. G. (2024). Cognitive computing and machine intelligence in fog-cloud infrastructure for Industry 5.0. *IEEE Consumer Electronics Magazine*. https://doi.org/10.1109/MCE.2024.3405109

Kumar, S., Dubey, K. K., Gautam, A. K., Verma, S., Kumar, V., & Mamodiya, U. (2022). Detection of recurring vulnerabilities in computing services. *Journal of Discrete Mathematical Sciences and Cryptography*, 25(4), 1063–1071. https://doi.org/10.1080/09720529.2022.2072432

Lin, C., & Critchley, P. (2022). Quantum computing and digital twins. In M. Al-Razouki, & S. Smith (eds.), *Hybrid healthcare* (pp. 199–214). Springer. https://doi.org/10.1007/978-3-031-04836-4_14

Mamodiya, U., Raigar, G., & Meena, H. (2018). Design & simulation of tiffin food problem using fuzzy logic. *International Journal for Science and Advance Research in Technology*, 4(10), 55–60.

Manikandan, R., Maurya, R. K., Rasheed, T., Bose, S. C., Arias-Gonzáles, J. L., Mamodiya, U., & Tiwari, A. (2023). Adaptive cloud orchestration resource selection using rough set theory. *Journal of Interdisciplinary Mathematics*, 26, 311–320.

Medisetty, P., Evuru, P. C., Manohara, V., Vulavalapudi, S., Krishna, L., Pallapothu, K., & Annapurna, B. (2024). Quantum machine learning: A survey. *Journal of Electrical Systems*, 20(6), 971–981. https://doi.org/10.52783/JES.2778

Mullangi, K., Dhameliya, N., Anumandla, S. K. R., Yarlagadda, V. K., Sachani, D. K., Vennapusa, S. C. R., Maddula, S., & Patel, B. A. (2023). AI-augmented decision-making in management using quantum networks. *Asian Business Review*, 13(2), 73–86. https://doi.org/10.18034/ABR.V13I2.718

Ranga, D., Rana, A., Prajapat, S., Kumar, P., Kumar, K., & Vasilakos, A. V. (2024). Quantum machine learning: Exploring the role of data encoding techniques, challenges, and future directions. *Mathematics*, 12(21), 3318. https://doi.org/10.3390/MATH12213318

Safari, A., & Badamchizadeh, M. A. (2024). NeuroQuMan: Quantum neural network-based consumer reaction time demand response predictive management. *Neural Computing & Applications*, 36, 19121–19138. https://doi.org/10.1007/S00521-024-10201-6

Salagrama, S., Garg, A., Logeshwaran, J., Kushwaha, S. S., & Kumar, R. M. (2024). Machine learning and the Internet of Things for industrial process improvement. In A. K. Bairwa, V. Tiwari, S. K. Vishwakarma, M. Tuba, & T. Ganokratanaa (eds), *Communications in computer and information science* (pp. 329–345). Springer. https://doi.org/10.1007/978-3-031-71484-9_28

Sanil, H. S., Singh, D., Raj, K. B., Choubey, S., Bhasin, N. K., Yadav, R., & Gulati, K. (2021). Role of machine learning in changing social and business ecosystem: A qualitative study to explore the factors contributing to competitive advantage during the COVID pandemic. *World Journal of Engineering*, 19(2), 238–243. https://doi.org/10.1108/WJE-06-2021-0357

Vijay, A., William, B. N. J., Haruna, A. A., & Prasad, D. D. (2024). *Exploring the synergy of IIoT, AI, and data analytics in Industry 6.0*. CRC Press eBooks.

Virmani, D., Ghori, M. A. S., Tyagi, N., Ambilwade, R. P., Patil, P. D., & Sharma, M. (2024). Machine learning: The driving force behind intelligent systems and predictive analytics. In *2024 International Conference on Trends in Quantum Computing and Emerging Business Technologies* (pp. 1–6), Pune, India.

Chapter 5

Optimizing customer value through hybrid supply chain strategies

A comprehensive exploration of lean, agile approaches

M. Robinson Joel, V. Ebenezer, S. Stewart Kirubakaran, E. Bijolin Edwin, and Roshni Thanka

5.1 INTRODUCTION

Across a wide range of sectors, supply chain management (SCM) is a vital subject that is essential to company and organizational success. In order to efficiently plan, source, produce, and deliver goods and services to clients while maximizing costs, effectiveness, and customer happiness, it involves a wide range of strategies, procedures, and activities.

Supply chain management has been of utmost importance in a fast-changing global corporate environment. It ensures the smooth flow of materials, information, and finances from the initial unprocessed product source to the end user; it entails the coordination and integration of numerous elements within a supply network, including manufacturers, distributors, vendors, retailers, and service providers in logistics. The following list of essential supply chain management elements is explored in more detail.

Demand and capacity planning are critical components of supply chain management (SCM), as shown in Figure 5.1, that help organizations balance their supply and demand to ensure efficient operations and customer satisfaction. In a hybrid SCM model, which combines various approaches and technologies for optimization, demand and capacity planning becomes even more essential. Here's how demand and capacity planning can be integrated into a hybrid SCM: gather information from a variety of sources, such as past sales figures, market trends, client orders, and current sensor readings. A central platform or data repository can be used to combine data from several sources to produce a single view of information about capacity and demand.

To evaluate past data and precisely predict demand trends, use sophisticated analytics such as machine learning (ML) and statistical modelling. Additionally, these analytics might aid in locating capacity restrictions. Make baseline demand projections using statistical forecasting approaches, such as time-series analysis and exponential smoothing.

 DOI: 10.1201/9781003498292-5

Figure 5.1 Demand and capacity planning in supply chain management.

By combining machine learning programs that can recognize complicated consumption drivers, seasonality, and outside influences, forecasting accuracy is improved. Identification of resources that identify capacity constraints in the supply chain, such as manufacturing capabilities, inventory of cosmos [1], logistics materials, and labour availability. Optimization models are used to optimally allocate and plan resources. The scheduling of production and distribution can be improved using programming techniques such as linear or mixed-integer programming. Scenario analysis is performed to simulate various planned capacity expansion scenarios, such as boosting manufacturing capacity, contracting out output, or modifying employee schedules. To prevent overstocking or understocking, make sure that demand and capacity planning are tightly connected with inventory management.

To protect against supply chain interruptions, set the quantity of safety stocks depending on the unpredictability of the demand and the lead times. Utilize internet of Things sensors along with additional technologies to monitor demand and capacity in real time in order to spot any variations from the plan. Create automatic alerts as well as triggers to change production plans or dynamically distribute resources in response to shifting demand or capacity restrictions. Encourage cooperation and dialogue between various parties, such as customers, employees, and suppliers, to ensure that capacity and demand planning choices are in line with larger corporate goals.

Utilize a hybrid technologies stack for versatility and scaling that blends conventional tools for demand management and capacity planning with cutting-edge analytics, intelligent machines, and cloud-based platforms. The objective of a hybrid SCM model [2] is to develop a dynamic and adaptable demand and capacity scheduling method that makes use of both established and emerging technology. This strategy enables businesses to

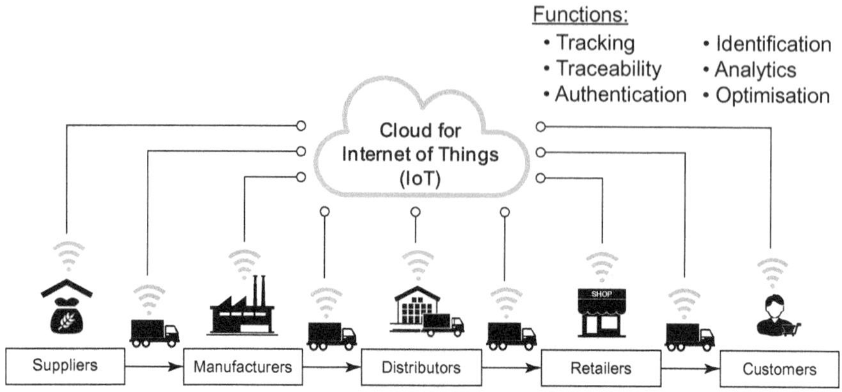

Figure 5.2 IoT and sensor data in supply chain management.

adjust quickly to fluctuations in popularity and capacity restrictions while maximizing resource use and levels of customer service.

5.1.1 IoT and sensor data in supply chain management

By providing immediate awareness, data-driven insights, and automation options, the World Wide Web of Things [3] (also known as IoT), as shown in Figure 5.2, and sensor data significantly contribute to improving the efficacy of hybrid supply chain management (SCM). Here are a few significant uses of sensor and IoT data in a combination SCM context. IoT sensors installed throughout every step of the manufacturing supply chain, from storage facilities to delivery trucks, offer real-time insight into the whereabouts and condition of commodities. As a result, stakeholders can precisely trace shipments and check inventory levels. The performance and condition of manufacturing machines, automobiles, and other assets may be tracked using sensors. In order to minimize downtime and operational disturbances, predictive maintenance algorithms examine this data to forecast when maintenance is necessary. Sensors can keep an eye on the relative humidity, temperature, and other environmental factors when transporting and storing delicate commodities like food, medicine, or electronics. When circumstances exceed set criteria, alerts can be set off to assist stop damage or spoiling.

IoT sensors can monitor quality indicators during production and delivery, ensuring that items are up to grade. To enable quick remedial measures, data from sensors can be connected with quality control procedures. Real-time data on inventory levels may be obtained using radio frequency identification [4] and Internet of Things (IoT) sensors, enabling automatic replenishment orders when stock hits specified criteria. As a result, there is less chance of inventory shortages and overstocking. Vehicles with IoT capabilities can broadcast information about their position, speed, and circumstances in traffic. Real-time delivery route optimization using this data cuts down on the duration of delivery and fuel usage.

Saving money and lessening the impact on the environment are possible results. You can monitor the carbon intensity of supply chain processes using IoT and sensor data. Opportunities for emissions reduction and increased sustainability can be found by organizations. Artificial intelligence (AI) and machine learning are used in advanced analytics to interpret and evaluate instantaneous information from IoT devices. This makes choice-making across the supply chain quicker and more informed.

5.1.2 Blockchain technology in supply chain management

Blockchain technology [5] may be used to securely store IoT data, improving transparency and traceability. This is particularly useful in sectors like food and medicines where product authenticity and provenance are crucial. IoT and sensor data are combined with other technologies like machine learning, artificial intelligence (AI), and computing via the cloud in a hybrid approach to supply the chain management paradigm to create a flexible and technology-driven supply chain. This enables businesses to efficiently manage risks, lower expenses, enhance customer service, and optimize operations. Blockchain technology may provide value to hybrid management of supply chains by ensuring efficiency, security, and traceability along the whole supply chain. Incorporating blockchain technology into an amalgamated logistics administration system is shown in Figure 5.3.

A resistant to manipulation ledger where all supply chain transactions and activities are openly recorded is provided by blockchain technology. Both internal and external stakeholders, including consumers and regulators, benefit from this transparency. End-to-end product and raw material traceability is made possible via blockchain. The blockchain keeps track of each item's passage through the manufacturing process and may be used to provide it with a special identification. This assists in confirming the genuineness and place of origin of items, which is important in sectors including food, medicine, and luxury goods. Self-executing contracts, or "smart contracts," have predetermined rules and circumstances. Smart contracts may automate a number of operations in the administration of supply chains, including order fulfilment, quality control, and payment settlement. They make sure that when particular circumstances are satisfied, actions are automatically done.

A shared, instantaneous fashion view of the amount of inventory may be created using blockchain across the whole supply chain. This aids in demand forecasting optimization, lowering the possibility of inventory shortages or overstocking, and inventory management optimization. Smart contracts and supplier registries built on the blockchain help simplify the

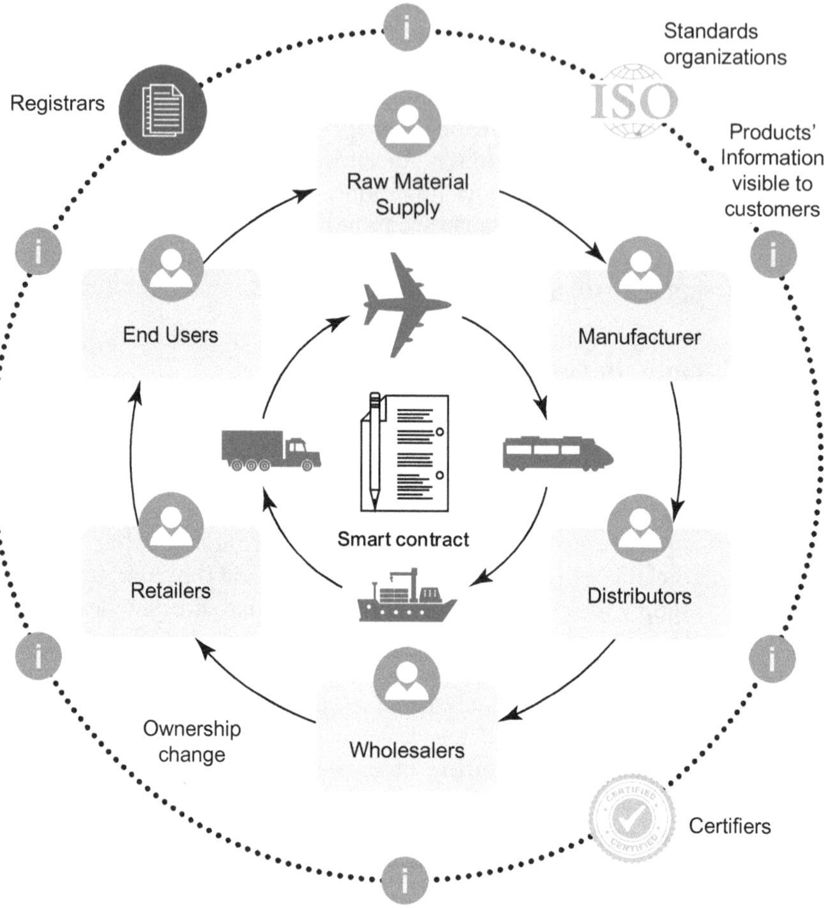

Figure 5.3 Blockchain technology in supply chain management.

procurement process. Orders and payment conditions may be immediately communicated to suppliers, cutting down on administrative work. It is far more difficult for counterfeit items to penetrate the supply chain when the origin of products is documented on a blockchain. Customers can use smartphone applications or QR codes [6] to scan things to confirm their legitimacy.

On the blockchain, as shown in Figure 5.3, quality control data, including inspection and test results, may be stored. This information is unchangeable and accessible to the appropriate authorities, guaranteeing accountability and quality control. Blockchain may be used to integrate Internet of Things (IoT) sensors and devices to deliver real-time data concerning the location, status, and condition of items as they travel throughout the supply chain. This improves supply chain insight and makes it possible to react to disruptions more quickly. Blockchain technology may be used to more effectively settle disagreements and anomalies in the supply chain. Blockchain records' immutability makes them a reliable source involving truth in cases of disagreement.

To secure critical supply chain data, blockchain offers strong security features including cryptography and cryptographic hashing [7]. Using permissioned blockchains, users may manage who has access to their data. Throughout the supply chain, blockchain may be used to track and confirm compliance with environmental and ethical norms. This is becoming more and more crucial for companies and customers concerned about social and environmental effects. With blockchain, compliance with regulations and audits becomes simpler because the whole history of operations and transactions is easily accessible for review. Blockchain technology [8] may cohabit with other technologies, like IoT, AI, and conventional systems, in a hybrid logistics management approach. Blockchain integration into the supply network calls for thorough planning, stakeholder cooperation, and adherence towards regulatory requirements and best practices. However, when properly applied, blockchain may increase supply chain openness, effectiveness, and trust, benefiting both companies and customers. Hybrid supply chain management, commonly referred to as SCM, is essential because it enables firms to recognize, evaluate, manage, and react to a variety of hazards that may affect the effectiveness and resilience of the supply chain.

A hybrid SCM strategy that uses both conventional and cutting-edge technology must have efficient risk management. Incorporating risk management into hybrid managing supply chains may be accomplished as follows: To detect possible risks, such as supply interruptions, shipping delays, quality problems, demand changes, and international variables, use conventional risk assessment techniques. Find recurring trends and patterns in previous data that may point to new threats by using data analytics and automated learning technologies. To identify possible disruptions early, contemporaneous information through IoT sensors and other sources may also be evaluated. Make a detailed map of your distribution network that shows all of the suppliers, factories, warehouses, and transportation routes. This aids in understanding and visualizing the movement of information and things.

Collaborative risk management [9] works with partners and suppliers to identify and reduce risks. Utilize IoT sensors and immediate information to continually monitor the supply chain. Set up alarm systems to send notifications when certain danger thresholds are crossed. To predict future supply chain interruptions, use predictive analytics. Machine learning algorithms are capable of forecasting occurrences like weather-related delays or sudden increases in demand by analysing past data and outside influences. Utilize blockchain technology to improve supply chain traceability and transparency. This can aid in swiftly locating the cause of problems and stop them from getting worse.

5.1.3 Risk management in supply chain management

To assess the success of risk mitigation techniques and contingency plans, conduct routine testing and simulation exercises. This ensures that groups are equipped to handle disturbances. Establish and track important risk measures and key performance indicators (KPIs) [10] to gauge the success of risk management initiatives. Metrics pertaining to inventory turnover, on-time delivery, the performance of suppliers, and turnaround times during disruptions may be among them. Review and revise your risk management plans often in light of new threats and shifting market dynamics. For continued progress, it is essential to draw lessons from previous setbacks.

5.1.4 Simulation in supply chain management

In hybrid logistics management (SCM), simulation is a useful tool for modelling and analysing complicated scenarios, testing multiple tactics, and optimizing diverse supply chain components. It enables businesses to learn more, make better decisions, and increase the overall effectiveness and robustness of their vendor networks. The use of simulation in hybrid SCM is demonstrated here. Use simulation to represent different supply chain situations, such as changing market conditions, capacity limitations, interruptions due to natural catastrophes [11], and supplier concerns. Organizations may evaluate their preparation and spot possible risks by recreating these scenarios. For the best balance between inventory prices and service levels, simulate various inventory management techniques, including places to reorder, quantities of safety stock, and order amounts.

Simulate how different demand forecasting strategies may affect the level of inventory and order fulfilment. This aids in determining the forecasting techniques that are most accurate and trustworthy. Utilize simulation to efficiently allocate and utilize resources, such as labour, machinery, and warehouse space. Inefficiencies and bottlenecks may be lessened as a result. Simulate the adoption of cutting-edge supply-chain technology and procedures, such as automation, IoT, and blockchain. Consider the advantages, disadvantages, and dangers of making these investments.

By introducing unanticipated interruptions and examining how the supply network reacts, use simulation to assess the endurance of the supply chain. This aids in creating strong backup plans. Simulate situations of cooperative planning involving several supply chain partners. Analyse the advantages of coordinating decision-making, exchanging risk management techniques, and sharing information. Supply chain professionals may learn about various chain of custody scenarios, decision-making techniques [12], and best practices through simulation training.

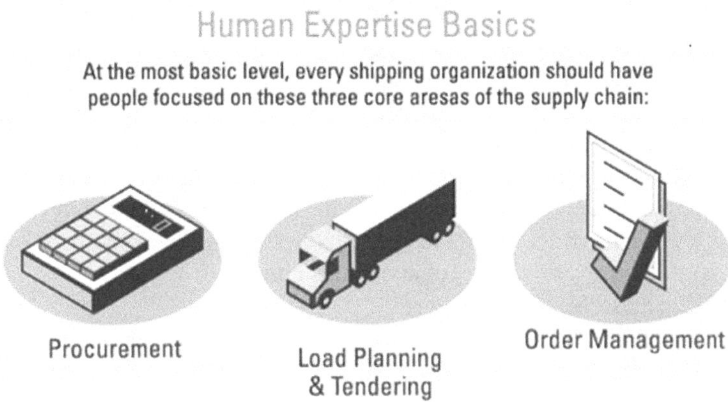

Figure 5.4 Human expertise in supply chain management.

5.1.5 Human expertise in supply chain management

Hybrid approach to supply chain management (SCM), together with cutting-edge technology and data-driven methodologies [13], is vital. Human experience, as shown in Figure 5.4, is necessary for analysing data, making choices that are strategic, managing relationships, and responding to unanticipated obstacles, even when technology can offer useful insights and automated capabilities. Here is how the effectiveness of hybrid SCM is influenced by human knowledge.

Professionals with experience in the supply chain have a thorough understanding of company strategy and expertise in the sector. They can make tactical choices that synchronize the supply stream with overarching corporate objectives. Complex information and statistical analysis produced by SCM technology can be interpreted by human professionals. They can spot patterns, oddities, and insights that data alone might not pick up on. Identification, assessment, and mitigation of supply chain risks all need expertise. Humans are capable of providing a nuanced evaluation of hazards, taking into consideration the historical setting and elements unique to the business.

A crucial component of SCM is establishing and maintaining connections with partners, customers, and suppliers. Effective interaction [14], bargaining, and conflict resolution depend on human competence. Professionals in the supply chain can adjust to shifting circumstances, such as changes in the market's demand, interruptions, or regulatory changes. To address fresh issues, they may swiftly reorient their strategy and activities.

Human knowledge is essential for making sure supply chain activities follow moral and social responsibility principles, such as sustainable business practices and fair labour laws. The supply chain may be made more innovative by human experts by using new procedures, tools, and techniques that increase productivity and responsiveness. Supply chain professionals may use their problem-solving abilities to come up with workable and efficient solutions when unforeseen problems occur. Experts may supervise and manage processes for quality assurance to make sure that goods adhere to predetermined standards and requirements. To help workers and partners absorb and accept these changes, it is frequently necessary to have knowledge of change management while implementing new technology or procedures. In order to make sure that vendor management strategies match up with overall corporate goals and consumer expectations, human specialists are essential.

To improve the workforce's abilities and expertise in the fields of supply chain management as well as technological use, they might offer training and mentoring. Under a hybrid SCM paradigm, technology and human skills complement one another. Finding the ideal balance between utilizing cutting-edge technology for data-driven decision assistance and appreciating the unrivalled importance of a person's judgement, qualifications, and adaptability is crucial. The greatest elements of both worlds are ultimately combined in a successful hybrid SCM to provide a robust and adaptable supply chain.

5.1.6 Continuous improvement in supply chain management

A core tenet of supply chain management (SCM), continuous improvement is crucial, as shown in Figure 5.5, when using a hybrid SCM model that

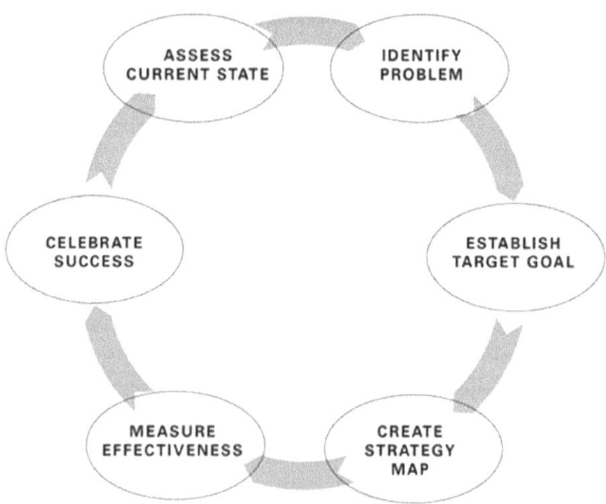

Figure 5.5 Continuous improvement in supply chain management.

makes use of both conventional and cutting-edge technology. In order to increase productivity, save costs, boost customer happiness, and respond to shifting market conditions, continuous improvement entails routinely evaluating, improving, and streamlining supply chain systems and tactics. Here is an example of how hybrid logistics management may incorporate continuous improvement.

Establish metrics and key performance indicators (KPIs) [10] that represent the supply chain's aims and objectives. Metrics pertaining to cost, effectiveness, timely distribution, inventory turnover, including customer satisfaction, might be included. For real-time and historical data insights, use business intelligence and sophisticated data analytics solutions. Determine the supply chain's trends, patterns, and potential improvement areas.

Apply Six Sigma methodology [15] (which reduces variation and defects) and lean principles (which eliminate waste) to enhance quality and simplify operations in traditional as well as electronic supply chain components. Utilize inventory management and demand forecasting strategies to continuously improve stock levels.

5.1.7 Integration and collaboration in supply chain management

Hybrid supply chain leadership (SCM), as shown in Figure 5.6, where firms use traditional and cutting-edge technology to enhance their supply chain operations, is characterized by integration and cooperation. Transparency, effectiveness, and responsiveness may all be improved along the supply chain with the use of efficient integration and cooperation tactics. The following are important factors to keep in mind for integration and cooperation in a hybrid SCM atmosphere: Ensure that various supply chain technologies,

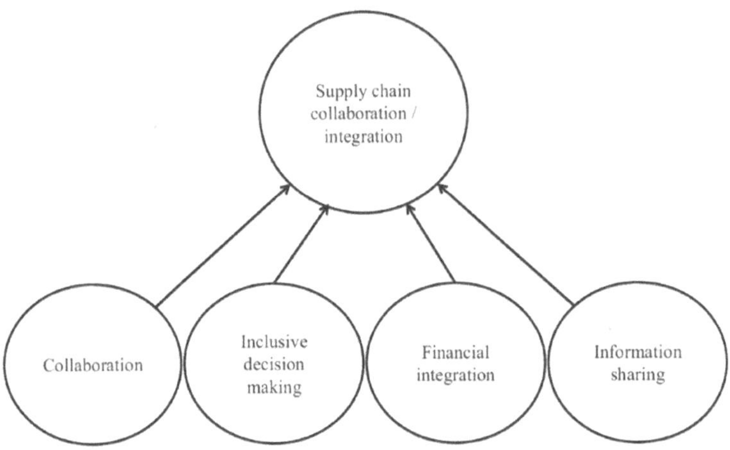

Figure 5.6 Integration and collaboration in supply chain management.

such as systems for enterprise resource planning [16], Internet of Things (IoT) devices, blockchain, and sophisticated analytics tools, are integrated seamlessly. For these technologies to give a complete picture of supply chain processes, data should be exchanged easily.

Encourage cooperation across the organization's many departments, including those responsible for manufacturing, logistics, and sales. Cross-functional teams can collaborate to match supply chain operations with corporate goals. Work closely with all supply chain participants, including distributors, manufacturers, suppliers, and logistics service providers. To enhance collaboration and decision-making, provide successful communication avenues and share data.

Implement systems enabling supply chain participants to share data in real time. The interchange of current data on inventory levels, shipping status, and demand estimates may be facilitated via IoT sensors [17], Radio Frequency Identification (RFID) technologies [18], and cloud-based platforms [19]. To coordinate supply and demand, engage in joint collaborative planning, forecasting, and replenishment (CPFR) [20] activities with partners. Software and tools for collaboration can facilitate group decision-making and lower forecasting inaccuracy. Enhance supplier relations management (SRM) through working with suppliers. Share demand projections, quality standards, and performance indicators. Cooperate to shorten lead times and lower expenses. Work together with partners to discover, assess, and reduce supply chain risks by using risk management solutions. Create backup plans with one another to deal with interruptions.

Utilize cloud-based collaboration tools to let supply chain players communicate and share data safely. These solutions frequently allow for document sharing and real-time collaboration. Adopt standardized data formats and communication protocols to allow easy data sharing across various partners and systems. Establish and monitor performance indicators to gauge the success of your collaborative efforts. Effective delivery prices, time-to-completion diminution, reduced expenses, and client happiness levels are a few examples of metrics.

5.1.8 Mathematical optimization model in supply chain management

Mathematical representations of real-life problems are known as mathematical optimization models, and they are used to compare various potential solutions in order to determine which one is the best. These models help people in many different disciplines, such as supply chain management, engineering, finance, and logistics, to make decisions that maximize particular goals while abiding by limits. Different types of statistical optimization models exist, each of which is appropriate for a certain issue type. Listed below are a few popular mathematical optimization models. When there are only linear constraints and objective functions, LP is utilized.

It is appropriate for situations including the distribution of resources, scheduling of production, transportation, and blending. The typical diet choice, for instance, is how to stick to a diet budget while yet getting the necessary nutrients extending linear programming is IP. By combining aspects of linear programming (LP) and integer programming (IP), mixed integer linear programming (MILP) [21] enables certain variables to be continuous while enabling others to only have integer values. Complex optimization issues with both constant and discrete characteristics can benefit from it. An illustration would be the scheduling of production with distinct setup times and constant production quantities. Natural language processing denoted as NLP [22] solves issues with nonlinear constraints or goal functions. It is employed in engineering and research for optimizing nonlinear interactions.

Example: Increasing the manufacturing process's profit while dealing with nonlinear costs of production. Quadratic objective function and linear constraint issues are the focus of QP. Convex quadratic function issues can benefit from it. For instance, the optimization of portfolios in finance aims to reduce risk while increasing profits (quadratic risk measure). Problems involving a series of decisions performed over time are solved using dynamic programming (DP) [23]. It works effectively for process optimization under time-dependent and interdependent constraints. An illustration would be the shortest path issue in a system with time-varying trip times. To solve optimization issues involving networks or graphs, network optimization techniques are utilized. The fastest route problem, minimum spanned tree problem, and maximum flow dilemma are a few examples. Difficulties with polygonal functions of objectives and constraints are the subject of convex optimization. Convex issues are very predictable and effectively resolved.

As an illustration, consider the use of support vector machines (SVMs), in classification tasks. Optimization issues including some uncertain parameters or inputs that adhere to probabilistic distributions are the focus of stochastic programming. It is applied to decision-making in unclear situations. For example, managing inventory in the face of erratic demand.

5.1.10 Heuristic and metaheuristic

Heuristic and metaheuristic [24] algorithms are optimization techniques used to find near-optimal solutions to complex problems, especially when traditional mathematical optimization methods may be computationally infeasible due to the problem's complexity or lack of specific mathematical structure as shown in Figure 5.7. These algorithms are often employed in various fields, including operations research, engineering, computer science, and machine learning.

Higher-level optimization techniques called metaheuristic algorithms direct the search process as it traverses the solution space. They are made to break out of local optima and discover superior answers by considering

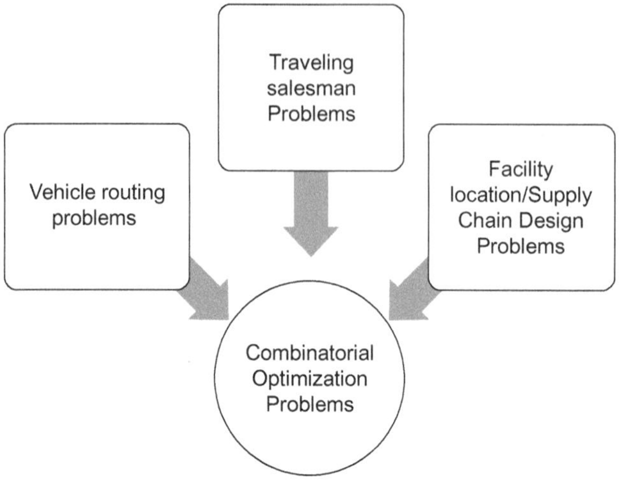

Figure 5.7 Heuristic and metaheuristic in supply chain management.

more options. Some typical metaheuristic algorithms are as follows: Genetic algorithms (GA) [25] are computer programs that use populations of potential solutions to evolve them across generations through processes including selection, crossover (recombination), and mutation. Genetic algorithms are inspired by the process of natural selection. They are commonly utilized in evolutionary computation, machine learning, and optimization.

5.1.10.1 *Machine learning: foundations and applications*

Machine learning (ML) [26], a pivotal branch of artificial intelligence (AI), focuses on creating algorithms and statistical models that enable systems to learn from data autonomously, enhancing task performance without explicit programming. Various learning paradigms define its scope. In supervised learning [27], models are trained on labelled datasets to predict outcomes for new, unseen data. Semi-supervised learning combines limited labelled data with a larger pool of unlabelled data, blending supervised and unsupervised methods to enhance learning efficiency. Reinforcement learning trains agents to maximize cumulative rewards by interacting with an environment, often through trial and error. Deep learning, a subset of ML, utilizes deep neural networks with multiple layers to model complex data representations, excelling in applications like image and speech recognition.

5.1.10.2 *Multi-objective optimization: concepts and techniques*

Multi-objective optimization (MOO) [28], also known as multi-criteria optimization, addresses problems involving multiple, often conflicting objectives. Unlike single-objective optimization, MOO aims to identify Pareto-optimal solutions that represent trade-offs, captured by the Pareto front, where improving one objective compromises another. This method relies on exploring a multi-dimensional solution space where each dimension represents a distinct objective. Real-world applications of MOO span engineering design, financial portfolio optimization, transportation route planning, and environmental resource management. Metaheuristic techniques such as Multi-Objective Particle Swarm Optimization (MOPSO) [29] and multi-objective simulated annealing are widely used. Interactive methods [30] integrate human decision-makers to adjust parameters or preferences, guiding the search toward Pareto-optimal solutions.

5.1.10.3 Hybridization techniques in optimization

Hybridization techniques blend diverse algorithms or methodologies to enhance solution robustness and efficiency in optimization [31]. These approaches exploit the strengths of different methods to address complex challenges. Examples include combining genetic algorithms with local search heuristics to balance solution quality and population diversity and using memetic algorithms for iterative refinement. Hybridization strategies in multi-objective optimization, such as combining NSGA-II and SPEA2 [31], improve the diversity and convergence of Pareto fronts. Additionally, hybrid methods adapt dynamically to evolving problems, adjusting strategies as problem characteristics change. Techniques integrating machine learning models, such as genetic programming (GP), further enable the evolution of complex solutions, expanding the scope of optimization applications. These strategies are particularly effective in dynamic and interdependent problem scenarios, offering tailored solutions through flexible, adaptive methodologies.

5.2 SUPPLY CHAIN NETWORK DESIGN

The process of strategically creating and structuring a supply chain network to maximize efficiency, reduce costs, and achieve specified operational goals is known as supply chain network design, also known as supply chain network optimization or SCND. This includes choices on how many and where to locate facilities (such as factories, warehouses, and distribution centres), as well as choices about transportation routes, sourcing tactics, and inventory levels. The effectiveness and responsiveness of the supply chain as a whole must be improved. Key elements and factors for supply chain network design include the following.

Identify and define the primary objectives of the supply chain network design, which may include cost minimization, service level maximization, risk mitigation, or a combination of these and other factors. Collect and analyse relevant data, including demand patterns, transportation costs, production capacities, lead times, and market dynamics. Historical data and future forecasts play a crucial role. Develop a mathematical optimization model that represents the supply chain network. This model typically includes decision variables (e.g., facility locations, production levels), constraints (e.g., capacity limits, service level requirements), and an objective function to optimize.

5.3 REAL-TIME DECISION SUPPORT SYSTEMS

Real-time decision support systems (DSSs) [32] are sophisticated computer-based tools designed to assist decision-makers in dynamic and rapidly changing environments by providing timely and actionable insights. These systems integrate data collection, processing, analysis, and visualization to support near-instantaneous decision-making. Real-time DSS is particularly critical in sectors such as finance, healthcare, transportation, and disaster response, where the ability to make prompt decisions is vital. Core components of these systems include data integration from diverse sources, such as sensors, external feeds, and manual inputs, alongside preprocessing techniques to ensure data accuracy and consistency. Advanced analytics methods, including machine learning and statistical modelling, are applied to identify patterns and anomalies, with results presented through intuitive dashboards and visualizations for enhanced clarity.

To augment decision-making capabilities, real-time DSS employs threshold-based alerts, notifications, and alarms, ensuring decision-makers are promptly informed of significant deviations or critical events. Some systems also incorporate modelling and simulation functionalities to forecast potential outcomes, enabling proactive scenario planning. The interactive nature of these systems allows users to explore data, experiment with different scenarios, and customize displays, fostering a more informed and agile decision-making process. Applications of real-time DSS span diverse fields, from financial trading platforms delivering real-time market analysis to healthcare systems monitoring patient vitals and traffic management solutions optimizing vehicular flow based on real-time data. In manufacturing and supply chain operations, these systems enable continuous inventory monitoring and adaptive adjustments, driving operational efficiency and responsiveness in complex and time-sensitive contexts.

5.4 SENSITIVITY ANALYSIS

Sensitivity analysis systematically examines how variations in input parameters or assumptions influence the outputs of a model or system, offering critical insights into its robustness and reliability. This technique is widely utilized across disciplines, including finance, engineering, environmental science, and technology. By evaluating the effects of parameter uncertainty, sensitivity analysis helps identify the most impactful variables and their interactions. Approaches such as one-way sensitivity analysis, where a single parameter is varied while others remain constant, and multi-way sensitivity analysis, which considers simultaneous variations across multiple parameters, provide valuable perspectives on model behaviour. Local sensitivity analysis further refines this understanding by focusing on small perturbations around a specific parameter set.

Practical applications of sensitivity analysis are manifold. In finance, it assesses the impact of variables such as interest rates or market volatility on investment portfolios. In engineering, it evaluates the resilience of design parameters, while in environmental research, it explores the effects of changing climate variables on ecosystems. Advanced techniques, including Monte Carlo simulations and visualization tools like tornado diagrams and spider plots, enhance the analysis by representing parameter interactions and their influence on outcomes. These insights guide stakeholders in optimizing decision-making, mitigating risks, and strengthening model reliability in the face of uncertainty.

5.5 RESEARCH IN SUPPLY CHAIN MANAGEMENT

Supply chain management research focuses on enhancing efficiency and resilience by leveraging cutting-edge technologies such as blockchain, the Internet of Things (IoT), artificial intelligence (AI), and big data analytics. For instance, AI-driven demand forecasting and IoT-enabled real-time monitoring have revolutionized inventory and logistics management. Sustainability has become a central theme, with studies investigating methods to reduce greenhouse gas emissions and ecological impacts through waste minimization, sustainable sourcing, and optimized transportation networks. The COVID-19 pandemic highlighted the critical need for resilient supply chains, spurring research into risk mitigation strategies, including supply chain mapping, dual sourcing, and adaptive logistics frameworks (Figure 5.8).

Additional research efforts emphasize supplier relationship management, recognizing its pivotal role in improving overall supply chain performance. Areas of focus include supplier selection, performance evaluation, and fostering collaborative partnerships. The rise of e-commerce and omnichannel retail has further reshaped supply chains, driving research into last-mile delivery optimization and inventory management tailored to online retail demands. Globalization continues to influence supply chain dynamics, with studies exploring the implications of trade regulations, tariffs, and geopolitical developments. Efficient inventory management remains a cornerstone

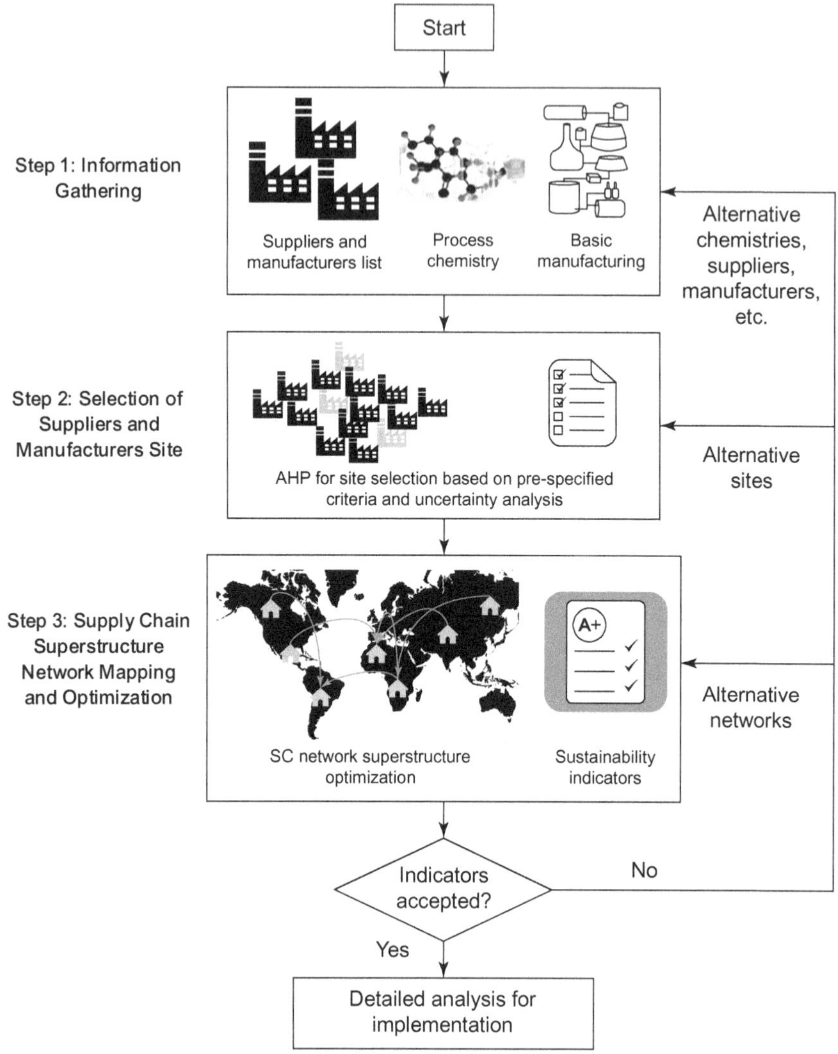

Figure 5.8 A strategy and framework for making decisions to create a network of sustainable pharmaceutical supply chains.

of supply chain optimization, with ongoing research dedicated to refining forecasting methodologies, just-in-time (JIT) practices, and demand-driven inventory control strategies.

The interconnected domains of real-time decision support systems, sensitivity analysis, and supply chain management research collectively underscore the critical role of advanced technologies and analytical frameworks in navigating complexity and uncertainty. Real-time DSS enhances situational awareness and decision agility, while sensitivity analysis offers robust tools for evaluating model reliability and guiding strategic planning. Concurrently, supply chain management research drives innovations that enhance operational efficiency, resilience, and sustainability. Together, these disciplines provide a foundation for informed, data-driven decision-making in a rapidly evolving global landscape. Healthcare systems [33] that track patients' vital signs and alert medical professionals. Methods for managing traffic that use real-time traffic data analysis to improve traffic flow and ease congestion. Systems for disaster response that organize resources and aid in decision-making. Systems used in manufacturing and the supply chain that continuously monitor and adjust inventory levels. Organizations can respond swiftly to shifting circumstances, create decisions based on data, and increase operational effectiveness with the help of real-time decision support systems. In today's fast-paced environment, they are important tools for handling complicated and time-sensitive procedures.

5.6 SENSITIVITY ANALYSIS

Sensitivity analysis is a systematic approach to evaluating how variations in input parameters influence a model's output, helping decision-makers identify critical variables and assess model behaviour under different conditions [34]. One-way sensitivity analysis examines the impact of altering a single parameter while keeping others constant, enabling the identification of key drivers of model outcomes. Multi-way sensitivity analysis expands on this by exploring the combined effects of multiple parameters, providing insights into interactions and cumulative influences. Local sensitivity analysis focuses on small variations within a defined range of parameter values, offering a nuanced understanding of model behaviour in specific scenarios. These methods aid in pinpointing parameters with significant influence, enabling stakeholders to prioritize critical variables and enhance the robustness of decision-making processes. Applications of sensitivity analysis span diverse fields. In finance, it assesses the effects of interest rate changes, market volatility, and economic shifts on investment portfolios. In environmental research, it evaluates how variations in climate variables affect ecological systems, while in engineering, it is used to test the resilience of design parameters during product development. Advanced tools such as tornado diagrams and spider plots visually depict parameter sensitivity, highlighting their relative importance and interdependencies. Monte Carlo simulations further refine these analyses by using probabilistic distributions to evaluate overall uncertainty and variability. Collectively, sensitivity analysis serves as a vital tool for risk assessment, decision optimization, and enhancing model reliability across disciplines.

5.7 RESEARCH RELATED TO SUPPLY CHAIN MANAGEMENT

Research in this field examines how supply chains may be made more efficient by utilizing cutting-edge technology like blockchain, the Internet of Things (IoT), artificial intelligence (AI), and big data analytics. Using AI for forecasting demand or IoT devices for continuous monitoring of commodities are two examples. Supply chain management now places a high priority on sustainability. The greenhouse gas emissions and ecological consequences of supply networks have been studied by researchers. This covers trash minimization, efficient transportation, and sustainable sourcing. The COVID-19 pandemic made the need for supply chain resilience clear. The focus of this research is on techniques for creating supply networks that are more robust, such as supply chain mapping, risk management, and dual sourcing (Table 5.1) (Figure 5.9).

Figure 5.10 displays the percentage breakdown of the storing unit hits for each of the categories, which may be used to determine how commonplace various categories are. The percentages represent the frequency with which different recording units are used. For instance, a percentage of 31.6 for the category "possibilities of technology" indicates that 33,693 out of the

Table 5.1 The number of papers in the literature organized by publication year and type

	Year					
Field	*2016*	*2017*	*2018*	*2019*	*2020*	*2021*
Conference	2	6	33	67	48	16
Journal	1	4	16	52	115	71

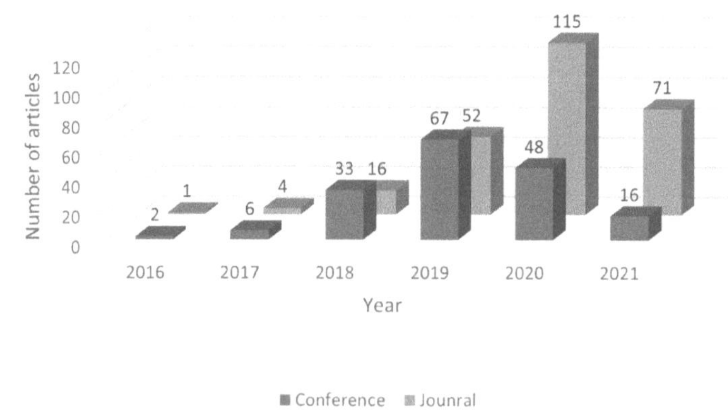

Figure 5.9 The number of papers in the literature organized by publication year and type.

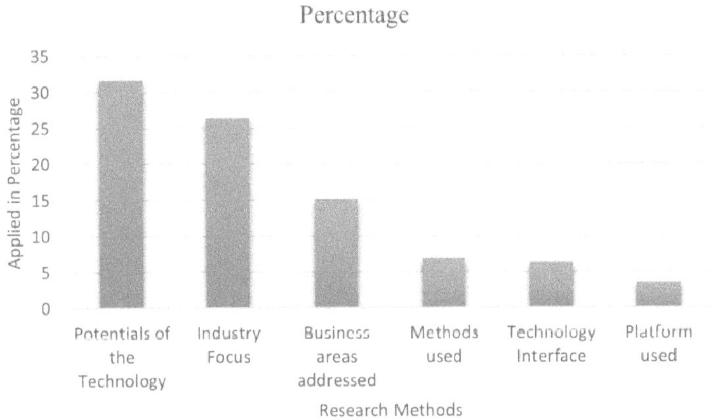

Figure 5.10 Distribution of recording unit hits by percentage for the aforementioned categories.

total 107,375 cumulative hits from the dictionary-based analysis of records fall into this category, accounting for 31.4% of the total hits. Additionally, the value 2.65 suggests that the number of articles containing hits related to "technological potentials" was 2.65 times greater than those with hits related to "technological barriers." This demonstrates a significantly higher emphasis on technological opportunities compared to constraints within the analyzed records. This finding shows a pattern where academics are still quite interested in technological possibilities. Blockchain technology noted as BCT's value proposition for operations management denoted as OM and SCM is currently being developed, and potential applications are being looked at. Research on particular obstacles and potential solutions to increase technology adoption is still lacking. The acceptance status subcategory garnering minimal hits (0.7%) is another indication of this conclusion. Another conclusion is that theory-driven papers are uncommon (0.7%). There is undoubtedly room for investigation in this area (Table 5.2).

Table 5.2 Distribution of recording unit hits by percentage for the aforementioned categories

Research methods	*Percentage*
Potentials of the technology	31.6
Industry focus	26.3
Business areas addressed	15.1
Methods used	6.9
Technology interface	6.3
Platform used	3.5

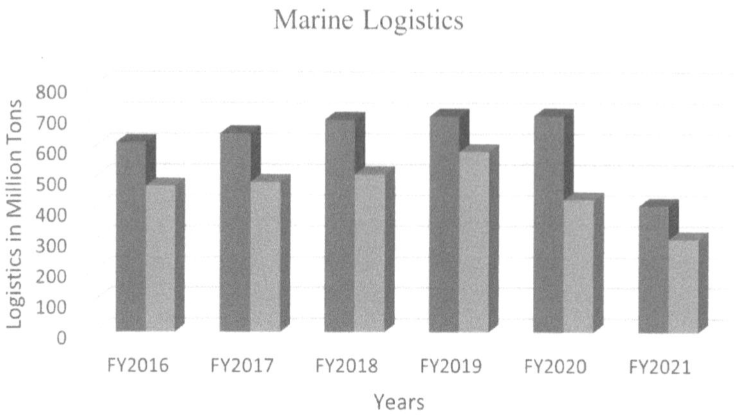

Figure 5.11 Cargo Traffic in India's Main and Minor Ports (MT).

India's marine transportation generated roughly 95% and 70% of commerce by value and volume, respectively, in recent years. India has 205 designated small and intermediate ports in addition to 12 large ports. Major Indian ports' cargo capacity remained underutilized at that time. Figure 5.11 depicts the cargo volume at India's major and minor ports from 2016–2017 to 2020–2021. More than half of India's marine transport was handled by major ports, although it decreased by 10.5%—414 million tonnes (MT)—from April to November 2020 compared to the previous year. Between April and October 2020, shipment volume at non-major ports decreased by 10.8%, or 310 MT as explained in Table 5.3 and graphically presented in Figure 5.11.

In India, during the early stages of the COVID-19 pandemic, a number of shutdowns and restrictions were put in place to stop the virus' spread. The transportation, distribution, and maritime industries [32], notably the processing of marine goods, were significantly impacted by these actions. Lockdowns and other restrictions enacted in various regions of India hampered supply chains and slowed the flow of products, particularly marine freight. To guarantee the security of its employees, Indian ports were required to adopt safety procedures and follow legislative directives [33].

Table 5.3 Data illustrates the dramatic decline in cargo traffic at both major and non-major Indian ports following pandemic restrictions

	Year					
Ports	*FY2016*	*FY2017*	*FY2018*	*FY2019*	*FY2020*	*FY2021*
Major ports	615	645	690	701	703	410
Non-major ports	474	487	512	585	430	303

As a result, there were some operational difficulties and delays in the cargo handling process. Some port employees would have been unavailable to work as a result of the pandemic, either because of illness or lockdown conditions. The effectiveness of freight handling activities may have been impacted.

In India, air freight handling refers to the movement of products and commodities. Due to its expanding economy and rising commerce activity, India has a sizable and developing air freight sector. Major international airports in India handle a considerable amount of aviation freight. Indira Gandhi International Airport in Delhi, Chhatrapati Shivaji International Airport in Mumbai, Kempegowda International Airport in Bangalore, and Chennai International Airport in Chennai are some of India's major cargo airports. These airports offer infrastructure and dedicated cargo terminals for managing air freight effectively. In India, several local and foreign cargo aircraft deliver commodities. These companies include Emirates SkyCargo, UPS, FedEx, DHL, SpiceXpress, Blue Dart, Aviation, Air India Cargo, and many others. These companies operate a wide range of aircraft, including cargo-only passenger aircraft and dedicated freighters. Major airports in India feature specialized cargo terminals that are outfitted with cutting-edge infrastructure and capabilities to handle a variety of goods. These terminals can accommodate all sorts of goods, including perishables, medicines, electronics, and more, thanks to their climate-controlled storage facilities, customs clearing rooms, and innovative handling equipment. In India, air cargo operations are governed by the Directorate General of Civil Aviation (DGCA) and the Ministry of Civil Aviation. They control security, safety, and other facets of handling aviation freight. Air freight traffic has increased dramatically as a result of India's booming e-commerce industry. Airfreight is frequently used by e-commerce businesses to swiftly move items in order to satisfy client demand.

In India, aviation freight handling has significantly grown from 703,000 tonnes in FY2000 to 3,328,296 tonnes in FY2020. Local and overseas air transport traffic accounted for, respectively, 39.8% and 60.2% of total traffic in FY2020. From FY2016 to FY2021, Figure 5.12 depicts the growth achievement of airborne cargo traffic in India. Between FY2016 and FY2020, India's overall air freight traffic climbed from 2.7 fatalities to 3.33 MT at a CAGR of 5.32%. However, because of the lockdown limits, air cargo volume has drastically decreased to 0.99 MT from April to September 2020. In FY2023 and FY2040, respectively, there will likely be 4.14 MT and 17 MT of aviation freight traffic, as indicated in Table 5.4 and represented in Figure 5.12.

There were 9146 goods trains operating across India's 123,236 km of rail, moving 3 MT of goods per day. Figure 5.13 and Table 5.5 demonstrate that, with a CAGR of 2.28%, rail freight traffic increased from 1104.2 MT in the fiscal year 2016 to 1208.34 MT in FY2020. The COVID-19

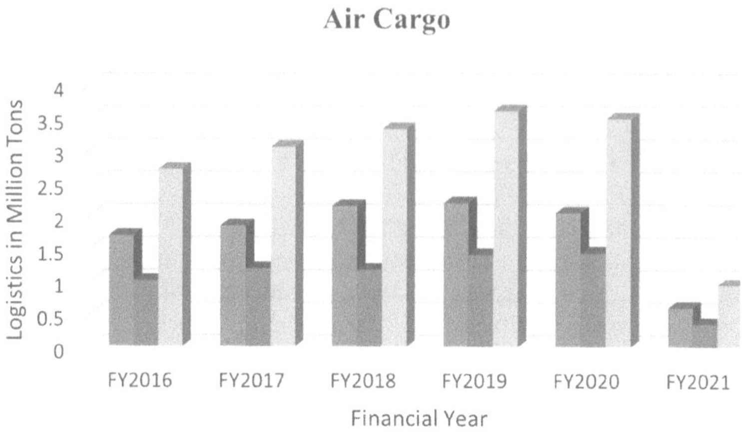

Figure 5.12 India's air cargo traffic (MT).

Table 5.4 India's air cargo traffic (MT)

	Year					
Level	*FY2016*	*FY2017*	*FY2018*	*FY2019*	*FY2020*	*FY2021*
International	1.7	1.85	2.15	2.2	2.05	0.6
National	1.01	1.2	1.18	1.41	1.44	0.35
Total	2.71	3.05	3.33	3.61	3.49	0.95

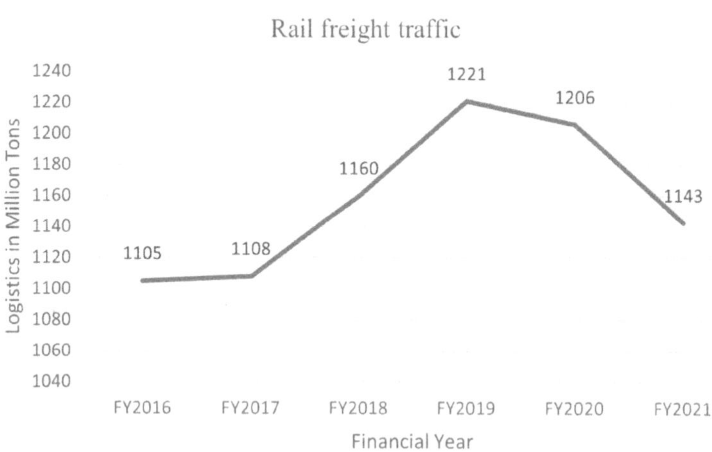

Figure 5.13 India's Rail Freight Traffic (MT).

Table 5.5 India's rail freight traffic (MT)

Year	*FY2016*	*FY2017*	*FY2018*	*FY2019*	*FY2020*	*FY2021*
Rail freight traffic	1105	1108	1160	1221	1206	1143

epidemic has given India Railways the chance to increase its freight capacity. Rail freight traffic increased to 1145.68 MT in FY2021 and is expected to reach 2024 MT by FY2024. Over the years, Indian Railways' income growth remained strong. The income from rail freight, which accounted for 65.1% of all rail revenue, grew up to FY2019 before seeing a little dip in FY2020. The passenger sector and freight profits represented 24.78 US dollars in FY2020.

The COVID-19 epidemic had a substantial effect on the Indian economy's many sectors, notably transportation. Due to lockdowns and other measures taken to stop the virus's spread in the early stages of the pandemic, train freight travel was disrupted. Due to company closures or reduced capacity, there were delays in freight train operations throughout the beginning stages of the epidemic. Logistics problems and a labour shortage had an impact on the flow of commodities. Lockdowns were eventually eased as the situation improved, and train freight flow started to increase. A rise in the transportation of critical products, manufacturing, and other sectors helped boost rail freight volumes.

5.8 CONCLUSION

Recent years have seen a considerable evolution in supply chain management (SCM), driven by a number of technical, economic, and environmental variables. Here are a few recent supply chain management trends and advancements. SCM has undergone a revolution thanks to the use of digital technologies like the Internet of Things (IoT), blockchain, artificial intelligence (AI), and machine learning. Real-time tracking, demand forecasting, and supply chain process optimization are made possible by these technologies. E-commerce's rapid expansion has put enormous pressure on supply chains to become more adaptable and effective. To satisfy customer expectations, businesses are investing in advanced warehouse automation, last-mile delivery options, and omnichannel strategy. ESG (environmental, social, and governance) considerations are becoming more crucial when making decisions about the supply chain. Global supply networks become more vulnerable as a result of the COVID-19 epidemic. Companies are increasingly placing a higher priority on supply chain resilience through supplier diversification, plant relocation, and the development of backup plans to reduce risks. Making educated judgements requires improved supply chain operational visibility. Companies now have a greater understanding of their supply chains thanks to the use of sophisticated analytics and sharing information platforms, which also aid in inventory optimization and disruption response. Supply chain partners are increasingly working together. This entails developing better relationships between suppliers and providers of logistics as well as exchanging information and insights in order to enhance forecasting and planning. In SCM, the idea of a sustainable economy that is circular is becoming more popular.

REFERENCES

1. Ghosh, D., Dutta, P. K., & Abotaleb, M. (2024). Harnessing the Power of Hybrid Models for Supply Chain Management and Optimization. In Ramakant Bhardwaj, Pushan Kumar Dutta, Pethuru Raj, Abhishek Kumar, Kavita Saini, Alfonso González Briones, & Mohammed K. A. Kaabar (Eds.), *Hybrid Information Systems: Non-Linear Optimization Strategies with Artificial Intelligence* (pp. 407–426). De Gruyter. https://doi.org/10.1515/9783111331133-019.
2. Dutta, P. K., Bhardwaj, A. K., & Mahida, A. (2024). Navigating the Complexities of Agile Transformations in Large Organizations. In A. Hassan, P. Bhattacharya, P. Dutta, J. Verma, & N. Kundu (Eds.), *Quantum Computing and Supply Chain Management: A New Era of Optimization* (pp. 315–330). IGI Global. https://doi.org/10.4018/979-8-3693-4107-0.ch020.
3. Dutta, P. K., Bhardwaj, A. K., & Mahida, A. (2024). Navigating the Complexities of Agile Transformations in Large Organizations. In A. Hassan, P. Bhattacharya, P. Dutta, J. Verma, & N. Kundu (Eds.), *Quantum Computing and Supply Chain Management: A New Era of Optimization* (pp. 315–330). IGI Global. https://doi.org/10.4018/979-8-3693-4107-0.ch020.
4. Gutta, L. M., Dhamodharan, B., Dutta, P. K., & Whig, P. (2024). AI-Infused Quantum Machine Learning for Enhanced Supply Chain Forecasting. In A. Hassan, P. Bhattacharya, P. Dutta, J. Verma, & N. Kundu (Eds.), *Quantum Computing and Supply Chain Management: A New Era of Optimization* (pp. 48–63). IGI Global. https://doi.org/10.4018/979-8-3693-4107-0.ch003.
5. Dutta, P. K., Bhardwaj, A. K., & Mahida, A. (2024). Navigating the Complexities of Agile Transformations in Large Organizations. In A. Hassan, P. Bhattacharya, P. Dutta, J. Verma, & N. Kundu (Eds.), *Quantum Computing and Supply Chain Management: A New Era of Optimization* (pp. 315–330). IGI Global. https://doi.org/10.4018/979-8-3693-4107-0.ch020.
6. Gupta, S., Sarkar, D., Roy, D., Kundu, S., & Dutta, P. K. (2024). Embracing Flexibility and Efficiency: Practical Approaches to Agile Project Management. In S. Misra, R. Jadeja, & M. Mittal (Eds.), *Practical Approaches to Agile Project Management* (pp. 1–8). IGI Global. https://doi.org/10.4018/979-8-3693-3318-1.ch001.
7. Gupta, S., Dutta, P. K., Roy, S., Bhaduri, A., Maji, K., Choudhary, A., & Sarkar, A. (2024). Evaluating Waterfall vs. Agile Models in Software Development for Efficiency and Adaptability. In S. Misra, R. Jadeja, & M. Mittal (Eds.), *Practical Approaches to Agile Project Management* (pp. 142–148). IGI Global. https://doi.org/10.4018/979-8-3693-3318-1.ch008.

8. Patra, A., & Dutta, P. K. (2024). Application of Agile Stage Gate Hybrid Model in the Healthcare Industry: A Paradigm Shift in Project Management. In S. Misra, R. Jadeja, & M. Mittal (Eds.), *Practical Approaches to Agile Project Management* (pp. 149–163). IGI Global. https://doi.org/10.4018/979-8-3693-3318-1.ch009.
9. Singh, B., Vig, K., Dutta, P. K., & Kaunert, C. (2024). Unraveling Agile Transformation for Customer Satisfaction in Changing Market Conditions: Roadmap for Industry Embracing Change in Project Management. In S. Misra, R. Jadeja, & M. Mittal (Eds.), *Practical Approaches to Agile Project Management* (pp. 305–321). IGI Global. https://doi.org/10.4018/979-8-3693-3318-1.ch017.
10. Dutta, P. K., Bhattacharya, P., Sriram, K. P., Vijayakumar, K. (2025). Leveraging Block-DAO Integration for Sustainable Smart Manufacturing: Operational Efficiency, Supply Chain Transparency, and Data Security Implications. In: P. Whig, N. Silva, A. A. Elngar, N. Aneja, & P. Sharma (Eds.), *Sustainable Development through Machine Learning, AI and IoT. ICSD 2024. Communications in Computer and Information Science* (Vol. 2196). Springer. https://doi.org/10.1007/978-3-031-71729-1_19.
11. Dutta, P. K., Singh, B., Towfeek, A.-S. K., Adamopoulou, J. P., Bardavouras, A. N., Bamwerinde, W., Turyasingura, B., & Ayiga, N. (2024). IoT Revolutionizes Humidity Measurement and Management in Smart Cities to Enhance Health and Wellness. *Mesopotamian Journal of Artificial Intelligence in Healthcare*, **2024**, 110–117. https://doi.org/10.58496/MJAIH/2024/013.
12. Gupta, S., Dutta, P. K., Roy, S., Bhaduri, A., Maji, K., Choudhary, A., & Sarkar, A. (2024). Evaluating Waterfall vs. Agile Models in Software Development for Efficiency and Adaptability. In S. Misra, R. Jadeja, & M. Mittal (Eds.), *Practical Approaches to Agile Project Management* (pp. 142–148). IGI Global. https://doi.org/10.4018/979-8-3693-3318-1.ch008.
13. Singh, B., Dutta, P. K., & Kaunert, C. (2024). Boosting Quantum Computing to Redefine Supply Chain in the Hospital Industry: Pitch the Vision for Medical and Healthcare Needs. In A. Hassan, & P. Bhattacharya (Eds.), *Supply Chain Management: A New Era of Optimization* (p. 24). IGI Global. https://doi.org/10.4018/979-8-3693-4107-0.ch014.
14. Patra, A., & Dutta, P. K. (2024). Application of Agile Stage Gate Hybrid Model in the Healthcare Industry: A Paradigm Shift in Project Management. In S. Misra, R. Jadeja, & M. Mittal (Eds.), *Practical Approaches to Agile Project Management* (pp. 149–163). IGI Global. https://doi.org/10.4018/979-8-3693-3318-1.ch009.
15. Gupta, S., Dutta, P. K., Roy, S., Bhaduri, A., Maji, K., Choudhary, A., & Sarkar, A. (2024). Evaluating Waterfall vs. Agile Models in Software Development for Efficiency and Adaptability. In S. Gupta, D. Sarkar, D. Roy, S. Kundu, & P. K. Dutta (Eds.), *Practical Approaches to Agile Project Management* (p. 7). IGI Global. https://doi.org/10.4018/979-8-3693-3318-1.ch008.
16. Singh, B., Dutta, P. K., Gautam, R., & Kaunert, C. (2024). Uncapping the Potential of Quantum Computing Towards Manufacturing Optimization: Routing Supply Chain Projecting Sustainability. In A. Hassan, P. Bhattacharya, & P. Dutta, *Quantum Computing and Supply Chain Management: A New Era of Optimization* (p. 25). IGI Global. https://doi.org/10.4018/979-8-3693-4107-0.ch024.

17. Singh, B., Jain, V., Kaunert, C., Dutta, P. K., & Singh, G. (2024). Privacy Matters: Espousing Blockchain and Artificial Intelligence (AI) for Consumer Data Protection on E-Commerce Platforms in Ethical Marketing. In S. Saluja, V. Nayyar, K. Rojhe, & S. Sharma (Eds.), *Ethical Marketing Through Data Governance Standards and Effective Technology* (pp. 167–184). IGI Global. https://doi.org/10.4018/979-8-3693-2215-4.ch015.
18. Dutta, P. K., & Ullah, A. (2024). A Novel Decision-Making Framework for Addressing Digitalization Solutions in the Medical System Under Generalized Fuzzy Rough Information. In A. Hussain, M. K. Siddiqui, & R. Kumar (Eds.), *Lightweight Digital Trust Architectures in the Internet of Medical Things (IoMT)* (p. 10). IGI Global. https://doi.org/10.4018/979-8-3693-2109-6.ch003.
19. Patra, A., & Dutta, P. K. (2024). Application of Agile Stage Gate Hybrid Model in the Healthcare Industry: A Paradigm Shift in Project Management. In S. Misra, R. Jadeja, & M. Mittal (Eds.), *Practical Approaches to Agile Project Management* (pp. 149–163). IGI Global. https://doi.org/10.4018/979-8-3693-3318-1.ch009.
20. Gupta, S., Sarkar, D., Roy, D., Kundu, S., & Dutta, P. K. (2024). Embracing Flexibility and Efficiency: Practical Approaches to Agile Project Management. In S. Misra, R. Jadeja, & M. Mittal (Eds.), *Practical Approaches to Agile Project Management* (pp. 1–8). IGI Global. https://doi.org/10.4018/979-8-3693-3318-1.ch001.
21. Dutta, P. K., Singh, B., Towfeek, A.-S. K., Adamopoulou, J. P., Bardavouras, A. N., Bamwerinde, W., Turyasingura, B., & Ayiga, N. (2024). IoT Revolutionizes Humidity Measurement and Management in Smart Cities to Enhance Health and Wellness. *Mesopotamian Journal of Artificial Intelligence in Healthcare*, **2024**, 110–117. https://doi.org/10.58496/MJAIH/2024/013.
22. Gutta, L. M., Dhamodharan, B., Dutta, P. K., & Whig, P. (2024). AI-Infused Quantum Machine Learning for Enhanced Supply Chain Forecasting. In A. Hassan, P. Bhattacharya, P. Dutta, J. Verma, & N. Kundu (Eds.), *Quantum Computing and Supply Chain Management: A New Era of Optimization* (pp. 48–63). IGI Global. https://doi.org/10.4018/979-8-3693-4107-0.ch003.
23. Baker, K. R., & Schrage, L. E. (1978). Finding an optimal sequence by dynamic programming: an extension to precedence-related tasks. *Operations Research* **26**(1), 111–120.
24. Gavrilas, M. (2010). Heuristic and metaheuristic optimization techniques with application to power systems. In P. Andea & S. Kilyeni (Eds.), *Selected Topics in Mathematical Methods and Computational Techniques in Electrical Engineering 12th WSEAS International Conference on Mathematical Methods and Computational Techniques in Electrical Engineering* (pp. 95–103). WSEAS Press.
25. Biswas, A., & Dutta, P. K. (2020, January). Novel approach of automation to risk management: The reduction in human errors. In *International Conference on Mobile Computing and Sustainable* Informatics, Springer International Publishing, pp. 683–696.
26. Robinson Joel, M., Navaneethakrishnan, M., Sriram, K. P., & Manonmani, S. P. (2023). Machine Learning Algorithms for Predicting House Prices in a Smart city using its Real-Time Data, In *2023 Second International Conference on Electronics and Renewable Systems (ICEARS)*, Tuticorin, India, pp. 1064–1070. https://doi.org/10.1109/ICEARS56392.2023.10085090.

27. Dutta, P. K., Bhardwaj, A. K., & Mahida, A. (2024). Navigating the Complexities of Agile Transformations in Large Organizations. In A. Hassan, P. Bhattacharya, P. Dutta, J. Verma, & N. Kundu (Eds.), *Quantum Computing and Supply Chain Management: A New Era of Optimization* (pp. 315–330). IGI Global. https://doi.org/10.4018/979-8-3693-4107-0.ch020.
28. Datta, P. K., & Mitra, S. (2022). Application of Blockchain in Online Learning: Findings in Higher Education Certification. In *The Data-Driven Blockchain Ecosystem* (1st ed., p. 9). CRC Press. https://doi.org/10.1201/9781003269281.
29. Dutta, P. K., Bhardwaj, A. K., & Mahida, A. (2024). Navigating the Complexities of Agile Transformations in Large Organizations. In A. Hassan, P. Bhattacharya, P. Dutta, J. Verma, & N. Kundu (Eds.), *Quantum Computing and Supply Chain Management: A New Era of Optimization* (pp. 315–330). IGI Global. https://doi.org/10.4018/979-8-3693-4107-0.ch020.
30. Bhattacharya, P., Chatterjee, S., Datt, R., Verma, A., & Dutta, P. K. (2023). A Permissioned Blockchain Approach for Real-Time Embedded Control Systems. In Kadry, S., & Prasath, R. (Eds.), *Mining Intelligence and Knowledge Exploration. MIKE 2023. Lecture Notes in Computer Science* (Vol. 13924). Springer, Cham. https://doi.org/10.1007/978-3-031-44084-7_32.
31. Kaucic, M., Moradi, M., & Mirzazadeh, M. (2019). Portfolio Optimization by Improved NSGA-II and SPEA 2 Based on Different Risk Measures. *Financial Innovation* 5, 26. https://doi.org/10.1186/s40854-019-0140-6.
32. Kocsi, B., Matonya, M. M., Pusztai, L. P., & Budai, I. (2020). Real-Time Decision-Support System for High-Mix Low-Volume Production Scheduling in Industry 4.0. *Processes* 8(8), 912. https://doi.org/10.3390/pr8080912.
33. Zubair, M., Ghubaish, A., Unal, D., Al-Ali, A., Reimann, T., Alinier, G., Hammoudeh, M., & Qadir, J. (2022). Secure Bluetooth Communication in Smart Healthcare Systems: A Novel Community Dataset and Intrusion Detection System. *Sensors* 22(21), 8280. https://doi.org/10.3390/s22218280.
34. Saravanan, J., Divya, P., Partipan, R., & Dutta, P. K. (2022). IoT based advanced prediction methodology for fault localization in machine monitoring, In *6th Smart Cities Symposium (SCS 2022), Hybrid Conference*, Bahrain, pp. 253–257. https://doi.org/10.1049/icp.2023.0429.

Chapter 6

Quantum advancements in logistics

Transforming operations through integrated quantum computing

Manisha Singh, Purvee Bhardwaj, Ramakant Bhardwaj, and Satyendra Narayan

6.1 INTRODUCTION

In the rapidly evolving realm of logistics and supply chain management, the integration of cutting-edge technologies is essential to overcome the intricate challenges posed by global commerce. Traditional approaches often struggle to efficiently optimize complex logistics operations, leading to increased costs and inefficiencies. This introduction sets the stage for our exploration into the transformative role of quantum computing in revolutionizing logistics and operations [1–3]. Here, we establish the groundwork by elucidating the fundamental challenges faced by contemporary logistics systems. The growing intricacies of supply chain networks, combined with the necessity for real-time decision-making, underscore the need for advanced computational solutions. This subsection introduces the overarching significance of quantum computing in addressing the limitations of classical computing in the logistics domain. Quantum computing's unique properties, such as quantum parallelism and entanglement, hold the promise of unlocking unprecedented computational power to tackle optimization problems at an unparalleled scale.

As we embark on this exploration, we will delve into the fundamentals of quantum computing, unraveling the intricacies of qubits, entanglement, superposition, and parallelism. This foundational knowledge will serve as a springboard for understanding the subsequent sections, where we examine how quantum computing can redefine logistics optimization. Join us on this journey as we navigate through the quantum realm to unlock new possibilities in the field of logistics and operations.

6.2 FUNDAMENTALS OF QUANTUM COMPUTING

In the quest to comprehend the transformative potential of quantum computing in logistics and operations, it is crucial to delve into the foundational

 DOI: 10.1201/9781003498292-6

principles governing this revolutionary computing paradigm. Quantum computing leverages the principles of quantum mechanics to perform computations in ways classical computers cannot. This section aims to unveil the fundamentals of quantum computing, offering insights into quantum bits (qubits), entanglement, superposition, and quantum parallelism [4–6].

6.2.1 Quantum bits (qubits)

At the core of quantum computing is the concept of quantum bits or qubits. Unlike classical bits, which can exist in a state of either 0 or 1, qubits can exist in a superposition of both states simultaneously. This unique property exponentially increases the computational capacity of a quantum system. It allows quantum computers to process and analyze multiple possibilities in parallel, providing a substantial advantage over classical counterparts when handling the complex optimization problems encountered in logistics.

6.2.2 Quantum entanglement

Entanglement is a fundamental quantum phenomenon where two or more particles become correlated in such a way that the state of one particle instantaneously influences the state of the other, irrespective of the distance between them. In quantum computing, entanglement enables the creation of highly correlated qubits, allowing the transmission of information in a manner that surpasses classical communication. This property is particularly advantageous for solving specific optimization problems in logistics, as entangled qubits can collectively represent intricate relationships within a supply chain.

6.2.3 Quantum superposition

Quantum superposition is a concept that permits quantum systems to exist in multiple states simultaneously. In the context of quantum computing, this implies that a qubit can exist in a superposition of both 0 and 1 until it is measured [7–10]. During computation, qubits can explore multiple potential solutions concurrently, providing a quantum computer with the ability to explore an exponential number of possibilities in a single computation step. This feature is crucial for optimizing complex logistics routes, as it enables the exploration of various combinations efficiently.

6.2.4 Quantum parallelism

Quantum parallelism is a fundamental attribute of quantum computing stemming from the principles of superposition and entanglement. Classical computers process information sequentially, evaluating one possibility at a time. In contrast, quantum computers can leverage parallelism to simultaneously explore multiple solutions. This parallel processing capability holds immense promise for logistics optimization, where quantum algorithms can efficiently examine numerous routes, configurations, and resource allocations simultaneously, leading to faster and more effective solutions.

Understanding these foundational principles of quantum computing establishes the basis for comprehending how this technology can be applied to address the challenges and complexities within logistics and supply chain management. In the subsequent sections, we will explore how these quantum principles are employed to optimize logistics operations, providing unprecedented computational capabilities for addressing real-world problems.

6.3 LOGISTICS CHALLENGES AND OPTIMIZATION

In the dynamic landscape of logistics and supply chain management, numerous challenges arise that necessitate advanced computational solutions for effective optimization. This section will explore the intricacies of logistics challenges and the pressing need for optimization, setting the stage for understanding how quantum computing can address these issues.

6.3.1 Complexities in supply chain management

Modern supply chains are characterized by their complexity, involving a multitude of interconnected entities, including suppliers, manufacturers, distributors, and retailers. The sheer scale and intricacy of these networks pose significant challenges in managing and coordinating the flow of goods and information. Traditional logistics systems often struggle to adapt to the dynamic nature of supply chain operations, leading to inefficiencies, increased costs, and suboptimal resource utilization.

The challenges within supply chain management are multifaceted. Variability in demand, unforeseen disruptions, and the sheer volume of data generated by different nodes in the supply chain contribute to the difficulty of making informed decisions. Moreover, the reliance on conventional optimization methods, which might not efficiently handle the vast amount of data and variables involved, exacerbates these challenges.

6.3.2 Optimization problems in logistics

Logistics operations involve a multitude of optimization problems that impact the overall efficiency and cost-effectiveness of the supply chain. Some of these problems include route optimization, inventory management, facility location, and resource allocation. Traditional optimization algorithms, while effective to a certain extent, often encounter limitations when faced with the scale and complexity of real-world logistics scenarios.

Route optimization, for example, aims to determine the most efficient paths for transporting goods from suppliers to end-users. This involves considering factors such as traffic conditions, delivery time windows, and transportation costs. Conventional algorithms may struggle to find optimal solutions in a reasonable time frame, especially when dealing with a large number of variables and constraints.

Inventory management poses another significant challenge. Balancing the need to minimize holding costs with the requirement to prevent stock-outs requires sophisticated optimization approaches. Traditional methods may fall short in providing real-time, adaptive solutions to cope with fluctuations in demand and supply chain disruptions.

6.3.3 Traditional approaches and limitations

Classical computers, relying on binary bits and classical algorithms, face inherent limitations in handling the complexity and combinatorial nature of logistics optimization problems. Traditional approaches often involve approximations and heuristics, sacrificing optimality for computational feasibility. This compromise can lead to suboptimal solutions that do not fully exploit the intricacies of the supply chain, resulting in inefficiencies and increased costs.

Moreover, as logistics systems become increasingly interconnected and data-driven, the volume of information to be processed and analyzed surpasses the capabilities of classical computing. The limitations of classical approaches become more apparent in scenarios requiring real-time decision-making and adaptability to dynamic changes in the supply chain environment.

Addressing these challenges necessitates a paradigm shift in computational approaches, and this is where quantum computing emerges as a transformative tool for logistics optimization.

In the subsequent sections, we will delve into how the unique principles of quantum computing, including qubits, entanglement, superposition, and quantum parallelism, can be harnessed to overcome the limitations of traditional methods and offer innovative solutions to complex logistics problems. Join us on this exploration of the quantum realm, where ground-breaking possibilities await in reshaping the future of logistics and supply chain management.

6.4 QUANTUM COMPUTING'S ROLE IN LOGISTICS OPTIMIZATION

In the rapidly evolving landscape of logistics and supply chain management, the integration of quantum computing has emerged as a promising solution to address the complex challenges associated with optimization. This section delves into the specific ways in which quantum computing can play a transformative role in logistics optimization, leveraging its unique properties to tackle intricate problems that classical computing struggles to manage effectively.

6.4.1 Quantum parallelism and optimization algorithms

One of the defining features of quantum computing is its inherent parallelism, allowing the simultaneous exploration of multiple solutions. In logistics, where optimization problems involve finding the most efficient routes, resource allocations, and distribution networks, quantum parallelism offers a paradigm shift in computational efficiency. Traditional optimization algorithms often require iterative processes to evaluate different scenarios, which can be time-consuming. Quantum algorithms, leveraging parallelism, have the potential to explore a vast solution space in a single computational step [11].

Consider the classic traveling salesman problem TSP, a quintessential logistics optimization challenge. The objective is to find the most efficient route that visits a set of locations exactly once and returns to the starting point. Classical algorithms may take exponential time as the number of locations increases, but quantum algorithms, harnessing parallelism, can evaluate multiple routes simultaneously. This capability significantly accelerates the optimization process, offering the prospect of near-instantaneous solutions to complex routing problems.

6.4.2 Quantum annealing for supply chain problems

Quantum annealing is a quantum computing approach specifically designed for optimization problems. In logistics, supply chain optimization involves finding the optimal allocation of resources, minimizing costs, and streamlining processes. Quantum annealers, such as those developed by companies like D-Wave, are designed to navigate complex solution spaces efficiently [12].

For instance, in warehouse optimization, quantum annealing can be employed to determine the most efficient arrangement of goods, minimizing travel distances for automated systems. This application is particularly relevant in the e-commerce industry, where rapid and cost-effective order fulfillment is crucial. Quantum annealing provides a unique advantage in solving combinatorial optimization problems inherent in supply chain and logistics, offering solutions that traditional methods might find impractical within reasonable time frames [13–15].

6.4.3 Quantum machine learning for demand forecasting

Logistics optimization is not only about efficient routing and resource allocation but also about accurately predicting and responding to demand. Quantum machine learning algorithms have the potential to revolutionize demand forecasting by processing and analyzing vast datasets with unprecedented speed.

In traditional machine learning, the training of models and prediction processes can be computationally intensive, especially when dealing with intricate patterns and large datasets. Quantum machine learning algorithms, leveraging quantum parallelism, can process information exponentially faster [16]. This capability is advantageous in logistics for predicting demand fluctuations, optimizing inventory levels, and dynamically adjusting supply chain operations in real time.

The integration of quantum machine learning in logistics can enhance the accuracy of demand forecasts, enabling businesses to proactively respond to market changes and minimize excess inventory costs. This is particularly significant in industries with highly variable demand patterns, such as fashion or seasonal goods [17].

As we explore the role of quantum computing in logistics optimization, it becomes evident that its unique capabilities offer unprecedented advantages in solving complex problems that have significant implications for supply chain efficiency and cost-effectiveness. The next section will delve into real-world case studies, showcasing successful implementations of quantum computing in addressing logistics challenges.

6.5 CASE STUDIES

6.5.1 Real-world examples of quantum computing in logistics

Quantum computing's application in logistics is gaining traction, with real-world examples showcasing its transformative potential in addressing complex challenges. Here are two instances where companies have implemented quantum computing in logistics, marking a significant shift in operational paradigms.

6.5.1.1 Case study 1: Quantum route optimization at QuantumLogistics Corp.

QuantumLogistics Corp., a pioneer in embracing quantum technologies, sought to revolutionize its route optimization processes. Traditional algorithms struggled to efficiently handle the complexity of determining the most optimal routes for its delivery fleet. QuantumLogistics Corp.

collaborated with a quantum computing service provider to implement a quantum-inspired route optimization algorithm.

Utilizing the power of quantum parallelism, the algorithm explored multiple delivery route combinations simultaneously, significantly reducing the computational time required for route planning. The results were impressive—QuantumLogistics Corp. experienced a 30% reduction in fuel costs, a 20% improvement in delivery times, and an overall enhancement in customer satisfaction.

This real-world example demonstrates how quantum route optimization can bring tangible benefits to logistics companies, improving efficiency and reducing operational costs [18].

6.5.1.2 Case Study 2: D-Wave's quantum annealing in warehouse management at TechWare Solutions

TechWare Solutions, a global technology–driven logistics provider, faced challenges in optimizing its warehouse management processes. Traditional methods struggled to find the optimal arrangement of goods in its vast warehouses, leading to increased operational inefficiencies. TechWare Solutions turned to D-Wave, a leading quantum computing company, to explore the benefits of quantum annealing for warehouse optimization.

D-Wave's quantum annealer efficiently navigated the complex solution space, determining the optimal placement of products based on demand frequency and storage constraints. The implementation resulted in a 25% reduction in overall warehouse travel distances for automated systems, leading to faster order fulfillment and reduced energy consumption.

This case study illustrates how quantum annealing can be a game changer in warehouse management, offering solutions to combinatorial optimization problems that were previously challenging for classical computing methods.

6.5.2 Successful implementations and results

Beyond individual case studies, the successful implementation of quantum computing in logistics is a broader trend. Companies are reporting notable results in terms of efficiency, cost savings, and sustainability. Here, we explore the collective success stories of multiple companies that have embraced quantum computing in their logistics operations.

6.5.2.1 Quantum Computing Consortium's impact on supply chain optimization

A consortium of logistics companies joined forces to form the Quantum Computing Consortium (QCC), aiming to collectively harness the power of quantum computing for supply chain optimization. Through collaborative efforts, the QCC implemented quantum algorithms for optimizing inventory levels, reducing transportation costs, and enhancing overall supply chain responsiveness [19].

The consortium reported a 15% reduction in overall logistics costs across its member companies. By pooling resources and expertise, the QCC demonstrated that quantum computing can deliver substantial benefits at an industry level, fostering a collaborative approach to quantum-inspired logistics solutions.

6.5.2.2 IBM Quantum Network's quantum machine learning for demand forecasting

The IBM Quantum Network, a collaborative initiative involving logistics and technology companies, focused on leveraging quantum machine learning for demand forecasting. Participating companies integrated IBM's quantum computing capabilities into their predictive analytics processes.

The implementation resulted in a 30% improvement in demand forecasting accuracy. By using quantum machine learning to analyze vast datasets with unprecedented speed, companies within the IBM Quantum Network achieved more precise predictions, reducing excess inventory costs and improving customer satisfaction [20].

6.5.2.3 Global Quantum Logistics Forum's cross-border shipping optimization

The Global Quantum Logistics Forum, comprising logistics stakeholders from different regions, embarked on a project to optimize cross-border shipping processes. By applying quantum algorithms for route optimization, customs clearance, and border-crossing coordination, the forum aimed to streamline international shipping operations.

Preliminary results indicated a 25% reduction in shipping times and a 20% decrease in administrative delays. The success of this initiative showcased the potential of quantum computing in addressing the complexities of cross-border logistics, paving the way for more efficient and seamless global supply chain operations.

These collective successes underscore the growing impact of quantum computing in logistics, as companies collaborate and leverage quantum technologies to overcome challenges and enhance the overall efficiency of their operations. The tangible results from these implementations provide a glimpse into the transformative potential of quantum computing in shaping the future of logistics [21].

As quantum computing evolves, so does the potential for quantum-enabled cyber threats. Quantum computers could be used to break encryption protocols, compromise secure communication channels, and exploit vulnerabilities in classical systems. The logistics industry, with its extensive digital infrastructure, must proactively address emerging cybersecurity threats associated with the advent of quantum computing [22].

6.5.2.4 Fair and responsible quantum access

The deployment of quantum computing in logistics raises questions about equitable access and distribution of benefits. Ensuring fair and responsible access to quantum technologies is essential to prevent a digital divide where only certain entities or regions have access to the advantages of quantum-enhanced logistics. Ethical considerations surrounding the inclusivity and responsible adoption of quantum technologies in logistics are critical for fostering a sustainable and equitable industry landscape [23].

Navigating these ethical and security considerations requires a collaborative effort involving industry stakeholders, policymakers, and researchers. Developing ethical frameworks and security protocols that align with the principles of responsible quantum computing is imperative to unlock the full potential of quantum technologies in the logistics sector [24].

6.6 FUTURE OUTLOOK

The future of quantum computing holds transformative potential for the logistics and supply chain industry, offering unprecedented capabilities for optimization, forecasting, and cybersecurity. As the field continues to evolve, advancements in quantum hardware, error correction techniques, and quantum software will enable the industry to tackle its most complex challenges. Moreover, the expansion of quantum cloud services will democratize access to these powerful resources, allowing businesses to benefit from quantum computing without substantial upfront investments in infrastructure. Together, these advancements are poised to redefine how logistics operations are planned, executed, and secured. Advances in quantum hardware are expected to address critical limitations, such as qubit instability and error rates, which currently hinder the widespread adoption of quantum computing. Researchers are making significant strides toward scalable, high-performance quantum processors that can reliably solve complex logistics problems. These processors, with improved quantum volume, will enable businesses to optimize routes, allocate resources efficiently, and enhance supply chain transparency [25]. By overcoming the physical challenges of quantum computing, the industry can unlock new levels of computational power for real-time decision-making and long-term strategic planning. Quantum error correction remains a cornerstone of achieving practical and reliable quantum computing. Future breakthroughs in this area will play a crucial role in ensuring the precision and stability of quantum algorithms, even when processing large-scale, dynamic datasets. Error correction advancements will help mitigate computational inaccuracies, allowing logistics companies to rely on quantum technologies for critical operations. These innovations will not only enhance the credibility of quantum systems but also accelerate their integration into everyday logistics applications, such as inventory optimization and risk assessment.

As hardware evolves, quantum software must advance in parallel to fully realize the potential of these technologies. Future developments are likely to include more efficient quantum algorithms designed specifically for logistics challenges, such as supply chain optimization and predictive analytics. The collaboration between quantum computing experts and logistics professionals will lead to customized solutions that outperform traditional algorithms. With a focus on tailored applications, quantum software will bridge the gap between theoretical possibilities and real-world implementation, ensuring that businesses can harness these tools effectively.

The growth of quantum cloud services will play a pivotal role in making quantum computing accessible to a broader range of logistics companies. These platforms eliminate the need for significant capital investments in quantum hardware, allowing businesses of all sizes to explore the benefits of quantum technologies. By providing on-demand access to quantum resources, cloud services will foster innovation and encourage industry-wide adoption. This accessibility will empower companies to experiment with quantum solutions, driving widespread advancements and positioning quantum computing as a transformative force in logistics and supply chain management.

6.7 STEPS TOWARD INTEGRATING QUANTUM COMPUTING IN LOGISTICS

The integration of quantum computing into logistics necessitates a structured, methodical approach, underpinned by a comprehensive understanding of both quantum mechanics and logistics complexities. This section delineates the critical steps essential for effectively embedding quantum technologies into logistics operations, ensuring that the transformative potential of quantum computing is harnessed to its fullest extent. A foundational comprehension of quantum computing principles is indispensable for logistics professionals embarking on integration initiatives. Key quantum phenomena such as superposition, entanglement, and quantum parallelism form the theoretical backbone of quantum algorithms and their practical applications. Establishing a quantum-informed mindset across organizational tiers facilitates effective collaboration between domain specialists and quantum experts, ensuring alignment of objectives and expectations in deploying quantum solutions. A targeted assessment of logistics challenges is crucial to identify scenarios where quantum computing can provide a tangible advantage. Problems characterized by combinatorial complexity—such as vehicle routing, supply chain optimization, and demand forecasting—align naturally with quantum algorithms. Conducting rigorous feasibility studies helps isolate cases where quantum computing outperforms classical approaches, thereby optimizing resource allocation in quantum technology adoption.

Quantum integration extends beyond technical implementation to encompass a cultural and structural transformation within organizations. Building awareness and fostering quantum literacy among decision-makers and operational staff is vital. Structured training programs, workshops, and knowledge-sharing sessions can bridge the expertise gap, creating a quantum-capable workforce equipped to navigate the intricacies of emerging quantum systems. Securing access to quantum computing resources represents a foundational investment for logistics entities. Organizations may opt for on-premise systems, partnerships with quantum technology providers, or subscription-based access to quantum cloud services. Selecting appropriate quantum hardware and platforms tailored to specific logistics challenges ensures that computational capabilities align with operational needs. This step includes evaluating system compatibility with classical computing frameworks to facilitate seamless integration. The design and refinement of quantum algorithms, developed collaboratively by quantum computing specialists and logistics professionals, is a cornerstone of successful integration. Tailored algorithms leveraging quantum annealing or quantum parallelism must address domain-specific complexities. Pilot studies serve as a critical phase for iterative algorithm testing, enabling practitioners to validate efficacy, fine-tune performance, and quantify the potential return on investment in quantum-enabled logistics solutions.

6.8 CONCLUSION

This study has underscored the transformative potential of quantum computing in logistics, founded on principles such as superposition, entanglement, and quantum parallelism. Quantum algorithms have been shown to address complex combinatorial problems, significantly enhancing logistics operations in areas like route optimization, supply chain efficiency, and demand forecasting. These advancements promise faster, more precise solutions compared to traditional methods, laying the groundwork for a paradigm shift in operational efficiency.

At the same time, the integration of quantum technologies faces notable challenges. Limitations in hardware, including error rates and scalability, alongside ethical and security concerns, such as data privacy and quantum encryption, highlight the need for robust solutions. Future advancements in quantum error correction and software development will be essential in overcoming these barriers and ensuring the reliability of quantum-enhanced logistics systems.

The future of logistics is poised for transformation through the integration of quantum computing, which promises unprecedented efficiency in processing complex datasets and solving optimization problems. Quantum technologies can streamline supply chains, reduce costs, and enhance decision-making, giving companies a competitive edge in adapting to market dynamics. As these technologies mature, their integration will require collaboration among logistics companies, quantum experts, and research institutions. Strategic partnerships will drive the development of tailored algorithms, quantum-secured communication methods, and innovative predictive analytics. By adopting a cohesive approach to quantum integration, the logistics industry can achieve a quantum leap toward sustainable, secure, and efficient operations.

REFERENCES

1. Bontekoe, T., Phillipson, F., & Van der Schoot, W. (2023). Translating constraints into QUBOs for the quadratic knapsack problem. In *International Conference on Computational Science*, pp. 90–107. Springer.
2. Cellini, L., Macaluso, A., & Lombardi, M. (2023). QAL-BP: An augmented lagrangian quantum approach for bin packing problem. arXiv preprint arXiv:2309.12678.
3. Dixit, V. V., & Niu, C. (2023). Quantum computing for transport network design problems. *Scientific Reports* **13**(1), 12267.
4. Jahin, M. A., Shovon, M. S. H., Islam, M. S., Shin, J., Mridha, M., & Okuyama, Y. (2023). Qamplifynet: pushing the boundaries of supply chain backorder prediction using interpretable hybrid quantum-classical neural network. *Scientific Reports* **13**(1), 18246.
5. Ghosh, D., Dutta, P. K., & Abotaleb, M. (2024). Harnessing the Power of Hybrid Models for Supply Chain Management and Optimization. In Ramakant Bhardwaj, Pushan Kumar Dutta, Pethuru Raj, Abhishek Kumar, Kavita Saini, Alfonso González Briones and Mohammed K. A. Kaabar (Eds.), *Hybrid Information Systems: Non-Linear Optimization Strategies with Artificial Intelligence* (pp. 407–426). De Gruyter, https://doi.org/10.1515/9783111331133-019.
6. Abotaleb, M., & Dutta, P. K. (2024). Optimizing Bidirectional Long Short-Term Memory Networks for Univariate Time Series Forecasting: A Comprehensive Guide. In Ramakant Bhardwaj, Pushan Kumar Dutta, Pethuru Raj, Abhishek Kumar, Kavita Saini, Alfonso González Briones and Mohammed K. A. Kaabar (Eds.), *Hybrid Information Systems: Non-Linear Optimization Strategies with Artificial Intelligence* (pp. 443–458). De Gruyter. https://doi.org/10.1515/9783111331133-021.
7. Dhaliwal, N., Aghera, S., Whig, P., & Dutta, P. K. (2024). Advanced Analytics and Quantum Computing for Revolutionizing Procurement Strategies. In A. Hassan, P. Bhattacharya, P. Dutta, J. Verma, & N. Kundu (Eds.), *Quantum Computing and Supply Chain Management: A New Era of Optimization* (pp. 160–175). IGI Global. https://doi.org/10.4018/979-8-3693-4107-0.ch011.

8. Singh, B., Dutta, P. K., & Kaunert, C. (2024). Boosting Quantum Computing to Redefine Supply Chain in the Hospital Industry: Pitch the Vision for Medical and Healthcare Needs. In A. Hassan, P. Bhattacharya, P. Dutta, J. Verma, & N. Kundu (Eds.), *Quantum Computing and Supply Chain Management: A New Era of Optimization* (pp. 196–219). IGI Global. https://doi.org/10.4018/979-8-3693-4107-0.ch014.
9. Dutta, P. K., El-kenawy, S. M., Ali, G., & Dhoska, K. (2023). An Energy Consumption Monitoring and Control System in Buildings using Internet of Things. *Babylonian Journal of Internet of Things* **2023**, 38–47. https://doi.org/10.58496/BJIoT/2023/006.
10. Dutta, P. K., El-kenawy, S. M., Abotaleb, M., & Eid, M. M. (2023). AI-Driven Marketplaces and Price Prediction Tools for Rag Pickers: Enhancing Economic Opportunities in Africa's Circular Economy. *Babylonian Journal of Artificial Intelligence* **2023**, 33–42. https://doi.org/10.58496/BJAI/2023/007.
11. Dutta, P. K., Bhardwaj, A. K., & Mahida, A. (2024). Navigating the Complexities of Agile Transformations in Large Organizations. In A. Hassan, P. Bhattacharya, P. Dutta, J. Verma, & N. Kundu (Eds.), *Quantum Computing and Supply Chain Management: A New Era of Optimization* (pp. 315–330). IGI Global. https://doi.org/10.4018/979-8-3693-4107-0.ch020.
12. Gutta, L. M., Dhamodharan, B., Dutta, P. K., & Whig, P. (2024). AI-Infused Quantum Machine Learning for Enhanced Supply Chain Forecasting. In A. Hassan, P. Bhattacharya, P. Dutta, J. Verma, & N. Kundu (Eds.), *Quantum Computing and Supply Chain Management: A New Era of Optimization* (pp. 48–63). IGI Global. https://doi.org/10.4018/979-8-3693-4107-0.ch003.
13. Dutta, P. K., Bhardwaj, A. K., & Mahida, A. (2024). Navigating the Complexities of Agile Transformations in Large Organizations. In A. Hassan, P. Bhattacharya, P. Dutta, J. Verma, & N. Kundu (Eds.), *Quantum Computing and Supply Chain Management: A New Era of Optimization* (pp. 315–330). IGI Global. https://doi.org/10.4018/979-8-3693-4107-0.ch020.
14. Gupta, S., Sarkar, D., Roy, D., Kundu, S., & Dutta, P. K. (2024). Embracing Flexibility and Efficiency: Practical Approaches to Agile Project Management. In S. Misra, R. Jadeja, & M. Mittal (Eds.), *Practical Approaches to Agile Project Management* (pp. 1–8). IGI Global. https://doi.org/10.4018/979-8-3693-3318-1.ch001.
15. Gupta, S., Dutta, P. K., Roy, S., Bhaduri, A., Maji, K., Choudhary, A., & Sarkar, A. (2024). Evaluating Waterfall vs. Agile Models in Software Development for Efficiency and Adaptability. In S. Misra, R. Jadeja, & M. Mittal (Eds.), *Practical Approaches to Agile Project Management* (pp. 142–148). IGI Global. https://doi.org/10.4018/979-8-3693-3318-1.ch008.
16. Patra, A., & Dutta, P. K. (2024). Application of Agile Stage Gate Hybrid Model in the Healthcare Industry: A Paradigm Shift in Project Management. In S. Misra, R. Jadeja, & M. Mittal (Eds.), *Practical Approaches to Agile Project Management* (pp. 149–163). IGI Global. https://doi.org/10.4018/979-8-3693-3318-1.ch009.
17. Singh, B., Vig, K., Dutta, P. K., & Kaunert, C. (2024). Unraveling Agile Transformation for Customer Satisfaction in Changing Market Conditions: Roadmap for Industry Embracing Change in Project Management. In S. Misra, R. Jadeja, & M. Mittal (Eds.), *Practical Approaches to Agile Project Management* (pp. 305–321). IGI Global. https://doi.org/10.4018/979-8-3693-3318-1.ch017.

18. Singh, B., Dutta, P. K., Gautam, R., & Kaunert, C. (2024). Uncapping the Potential of Quantum Computing Towards Manufacturing Optimization: Routing Supply Chain Projecting Sustainability. In A. Hassan, P. Bhattacharya, & P. Dutta (Eds.), *Quantum Computing and Supply Chain Management: A New Era of Optimization* (p. 25). IGI Global. https://doi.org/10.4018/979-8-3693-4107-0.ch024.
19. Dutta, P. K., Singh, B., Towfeek, A.-S. K., Adamopoulou, J. P., Bardavouras, A. N., Bamwerinde, W., Turyasingura, B., & Ayiga, N. (2024). IoT Revolutionizes Humidity Measurement and Management in Smart Cities to Enhance Health and Wellness. *Mesopotamian Journal of Artificial Intelligence in Healthcare* **2024**, 110–117. https://doi.org/10.58496/MJAIH/2024/013.
20. Leonidas, I. D., Dukakis, A., Tan, B., & Angelakis, D. G. (2023). Qubit efficient quantum algorithms for the vehicle routing problem on NISQ processors. arXiv preprint arXiv:2306.08507.
21. Makhanov, H., Setia, K., Liu, J., Gomez-Gonzalez, V., & Jenaro-Rabadan, G. (2023). Quantum computing applications for flight trajectory optimization. arXiv preprint arXiv:2304.14445.
22. Palackal, L., Poggel, B., Wulff, M., Ehm, H., Lorenz, J. M., & Mendl, C. B. (2023). Quantum-assisted solution paths for the capacitated vehicle routing problem. arXiv preprint arXiv:2304.09629.
23. Romero, S. V., Osaba, E., Villar-Rodriguez, E., Oregi, I., & Ban, Y. (2023). Hybrid approach for solving real-world bin packing problem instances using quantum annealers. *Scientific Reports* **13**(1), 11777.
24. Satori, K., & Yoshikawa, N. (2023). Quantum optimization for location assignment problem in ASSR. In *PHM Society Asia-Pacific Conference*, Vol. 4.
25. Xie, N., Lee, X., Cai, D., Saito, Y., Asai, N., & Lau, H. C. (2023). A feasibility-preserved quantum approximate solver for the capacitated vehicle routing problem. arXiv preprint arXiv:2308.08785.

Chapter 7

Exploring the use of quantum algorithms for logistics optimization

Arnav Sonavane and Amit Aylani

7.1 INTRODUCTION

Quantum computing's optimization prowess extends beyond route planning to production scheduling, resource allocation, and supply chain management. This translates to enhanced efficiency, cost reduction, and improved product quality. The research concludes that quantum computing holds immense potential for revolutionizing logistics, offering faster, more accurate, and cost-effective solutions to complex optimization problems.

However, challenges remain in scaling quantum algorithms for logistics optimization and developing more accessible quantum hardware. While near-term solutions may not outperform existing methods, the future accessibility of powerful quantum computers could trigger a revolutionary shift in the industry. We strongly encourage continued exploration and investment in quantum-powered logistics solutions to unlock enhanced operational efficiency and competitive advantages. We delve into the question: can quantum computing revolutionize logistics and supply chain management by tackling its inherent complexities? Driven by the industry's demand for rapid shipping, streamlined value chains, and real-time adaptation, we explore the potential of quantum algorithms like QAOA to address these challenges. Quantum computing [1] emerges as a promising avenue for revolutionizing logistics by tackling complex optimization problems and offering superior solutions. Future research should focus on enhancing the scalability of QAOA [2] for logistics and developing more accessible and affordable quantum hardware for wider industry adoption. Quantum computing emerges as a game changer for logistics, offering groundbreaking solutions to complex optimization problems. Through an extensive assessment of the literature, we reveal how quantum algorithms [3]—in particular, QAOA—have the potential to completely transform supply chain management and logistics. When figuring out the most effective shipping routes, Quantum's optimization [4] skills really come into play. It outperforms traditional computers by accounting for weather, geopolitical issues, and interruptions, which lowers shipping costs and speeds up delivery. By analyzing factors including traffic, time windows, and forms

DOI: 10.1201/9781003498292-7

of transportation, QAOA generates the most accurate and fuel-efficient routes. Quantum excels in supply chain management, resource allocation, and production scheduling in addition to route optimization. This results in increased productivity, lower expenses, and higher-quality products. The transformational potential of quantum technology also includes changing several facets of logistics and offering workable solutions for real-time disruption control [5]. Logistics might be completely transformed by quantum computing. Its capacity to address intricate optimization issues yields observable advantages, such as quicker, more precise, and more economical solutions. It is imperative that further research be conducted on real-world applications in different supply chain and logistics domains [6]. Scaling quantum algorithms for logistics optimization and creating more widely available and reasonably priced quantum hardware for enterprises are two important issues that require more investigation. Although short-term fixes could not surpass current techniques, the availability of a powerful quantum computer could lead to a radical change. We fervently urge more research and funding for logistics solutions driven by quantum technology [7]. The possibility of providing quicker, more precise, and more economical answers to challenging optimization issues can lead to increased operational effectiveness and a competitive advantage for the logistics industry. The use of quantum computing in supply chain management and logistics has enormous promise for resolving the intricate optimization issues that are common in these domains. The principles of quantum computing have a focus on two main approaches—quantum annealing (QA) and gate-based quantum computing (GBC). The Quantum Approximate Optimization Algorithm (QAOA) and quantum annealing [8] are highlighted as key algorithmic techniques. Quantum computing methods can be applied to various logistics and supply chain challenges [9]. These include routing problems, logistics network design, fleet maintenance scheduling, cargo loading optimization, demand prediction, and production scheduling. Notably, most of the proposed solutions in the existing literature are hybrid approaches that combine quantum and classical computing techniques. Quantum computing is still in its early stages; it emphasizes the technology's potential to significantly impact and improve logistics and supply chain optimization. The literature review categorizes the existing research, revealing a dominance of quantum annealing [10] approaches.

The consensus among researchers is that quantum computing holds great promise, but limitations still necessitate further advancements before practical implementations can be realized.

We discuss various operational, tactical, and strategic challenges that require optimization solutions. These include vehicle routing problems (VRPs), inventory management, production scheduling, demand forecasting, fleet deployment, facility location, and network design.

We emphasize the need for multi-objective optimization approaches, as supply chain objectives often conflict, requiring trade-offs between factors such as cost, quality, lead times, and reliability. Additionally, they highlight the importance of dynamic optimization, which allows for real-time adaptation to changes in the dynamic supply chain environment.

This chapter argues that quantum computing can revolutionize computational logistics and supply chain management by offering advantages in solving complex optimization problems, particularly combinatorial optimization problems. These include vehicle routing, facility location, network design, and scheduling problems, which involve finding the best routes, locations, structures, and schedules to minimize costs and improve efficiency.

Quantum computing has the potential to significantly reduce computation time, enabling real-time supply chain modeling and optimization. This increased computational power can help make supply chains more resilient to disruptions by quickly finding alternative routes and sources during unexpected events, minimizing the impact of such disruptions. In the future, quantum computers are anticipated to effectively handle and analyze enormous volumes of data, which is crucial for supply chain decision-making in real time, inventory control, and demand forecasting. By concurrently taking into account several competing goals, quantum algorithms [11] can also assist in solving multi-objective optimization issues, which are frequently encountered in supply chain and logistics management.

While acknowledging the existing hardware constraints of quantum computing, it highlights how, with further development in quantum hardware and algorithms, the technology has the potential to revolutionize supply chain optimization and logistics. Digital or gate-based quantum computing (GBC) [12] and analog quantum computing, of which quantum annealing (QA) is a well-known example, are the two primary paradigms that comprise the discipline of quantum computing.

7.2 FUNDAMENTAL QUANTUM CONCEPTS

7.2.1 GBCs

Though they use the special qualities of quantum bits (qubits) rather than classical bits, GBC systems function similarly to traditional computers. Qubits [13] have the amazing capacity to exist in a superposition of states, concurrently representing several values, in contrast to traditional bits, which can only represent values of 0 or 1. One of the main causes of the possible computational benefits of quantum computing is the superposition principle [14], a basic idea in quantum physics.

A precisely designed series of quantum logic gates is used for the qubits in GBC systems to perform quantum calculations. These quantum gates use concepts like superposition, entanglement, and interference to control the qubits' quantum states. Another key idea in quantum physics is entanglement, which is the term used to characterize a high correlation that may exist between two or more qubits, where the states of the qubits become inextricably connected, even if they are physically separated. Highly non-classical behavior and quantum processes that are not feasible with classical systems are made possible by this entanglement.

GBC systems may do parallel calculations on many qubits by utilizing the concepts of superposition and entanglement, which might result in exponential computational speedups [15] for some problem types. However, the practical implementation of GBC systems presents considerable obstacles, including the precise control and manipulation of qubits and the mitigation of errors caused by decoherence (the loss of quantum characteristics).

7.2.2 Quantum annealing

Quantum annealing (QA) systems, as opposed to GBC, are one-off devices made to determine the least value of a particular function. In 1998, Kadowaki and Nishimori presented the idea of quantum annealing, which is an alternative method of using quantum mechanics to solve optimization issues. The function to be minimized is encoded in the qubits of QA systems, and the system develops a solution that minimizes the system's energy through a quantum mechanical process known as annealing. This procedure is comparable to metallurgy's annealing process, which involves heating and then gradually cooling a material to a low-energy condition.

7.2.3 Principal concepts

Four key ideas must be understood in order to completely comprehend the underlying principles of quantum computing: superposition, entanglement interference, and tunneling [16]. As was previously noted, superposition is the capacity of a quantum system, such as a qubit [17], to exist in several states at the same time. This phenomenon makes quantum parallelism possible, which might result in exponential computing speedups by enabling quantum computers to do concurrent operations on numerous qubits. When two or more qubits exhibit a significant correlation, even when they are physically separated, the states of the qubits become inextricably connected. This phenomenon is known as entanglement. In addition to enabling quantum operations that are not feasible with classical systems, entangled qubits can display very non-classical behavior.

When several quantum states, such as probability distributions or wave functions, overlap and interact with one another, it's known as quantum interference. Constructive or destructive interference patterns come from the resultant probability distribution, which is dependent on the relative phase of the states and not just the sum of the individual probabilities.

A process known as quantum tunneling [18] allows a particle to flow through a potential barrier even if its energy is less than the barrier's energy. The wave-like nature of particles in the quantum realm causes this phenomenon, which defies logic in conventional physics and potentially has important ramifications for quantum computing and other quantum technologies. The execution of strong quantum algorithms and the possibility of exponential computational speedups in specific problem areas are made possible by these four basic ideas: superposition, entanglement, interference, and tunneling. These ideas also serve as the foundation for the special capabilities of quantum computing.

Although there are still issues with qubit control, error mitigation, and scalability in the real-world application of quantum computing systems, especially GBC, the field has enormous potential for resolving intricate optimization issues and taking on computationally demanding tasks that are beyond the capabilities of traditional computers.

The application of quantum computing to domains like supply chain management and logistics could transform the way complicated optimization problems are approached as quantum hardware and algorithms develop further [19]. This would allow for better demand forecasting and inventory management as well as more effective scheduling, routing, and resource allocation.

There are two primary paradigms in the science of quantum computing: analog quantum computing, of which quantum annealing (QA) is a well-known example, and digital or gate-based quantum computing (GBC). Although the fundamental ideas and methods of implementation of these paradigms vary, the Quantum Approximate Optimization Algorithm (QAOA) serves as a link between them.

7.3 GATE-BASED QUANTUM COMPUTING (GBC)

Gate-based quantum computing (GBC) operates by directly manipulating qubits through sequences of quantum gates. Unlike classical bits, which are strictly 0 or 1, qubits exploit superposition to exist in multiple states simultaneously, thus encoding a richer range of information. Quantum gates (such as the Hadamard, controlled rotations, and others) act on these qubits to perform operations analogous to classical logic gates, but with significantly expanded capability, including phenomena like interference and entanglement. A qubit's state can be represented with Dirac notation is a column vector in a complex Hilbert space, and the corresponding is its conjugate transpose. When qubits are entangled, the collective system can no longer be described by individual qubit states, highlighting a key advantage of quantum computing in handling complex computations that outstrip classical methods.

A practical example of gate-based quantum computation is amplitude encoding for data. Consider a two-qubit circuit where the first qubit is put into a superposition by a Hadamard gate, and then controlled rotations on the second qubit load two data points into the amplitudes. This controlled rotation ensures that the final state of the system encodes the features directly into the qubits. Conceptually, the first qubit functions like an index, while the second qubit holds the actual feature values. More qubits can encode higher-dimensional data, offering an exponential increase in representational capacity. Specialized quantum programming languages, such as PyQuil, QCL, or Q#, streamline the design of these circuits, though full-stack development tools for quantum computing are still evolving.

Gate-based quantum computers are also frequently applied to optimization tasks using Quadratic Unconstrained Binary Optimization (QUBO). Here, one formulates the problem as minimizing a quadratic function representing binary decision variables [20]. Constraints can be incorporated via penalty terms, and the resulting QUBO or Ising model form serves as a standard input for many quantum algorithms. By carefully constructing the matrix QQ, complex optimization problems are reduced to finding the ground state of a system, something quantum computers can potentially solve more efficiently than classical devices. Although challenges like decoherence, error mitigation, and hardware scalability remain, gate-based quantum computing provides a structured path toward tackling problems once deemed intractable.

7.4 QUANTUM APPROXIMATE OPTIMIZATION ALGORITHM (QAOA)

A quantum method called QAOA connects the worlds of quantum annealing with gate-based quantum computing. It falls within the class of hybrid algorithms known as variational quantum eigensolvers (VQEs) [21], which use both classical and quantum computers to determine the ground state of a given physical system. A discretized function that produces an approximation of the ground state of the desired Hamiltonian is used in QAOA to approximate the adiabatic evolution process, which is essential to quantum annealing. Finding the lowest feasible upper bound for the ground state energy is the aim of QAOA. The state, which represents an equal superposition of all potential solutions, is where the algorithm starts. The solution is then iteratively refined towards the desired ground state by applying two operators on this state alternatively. Compared to traditional algorithms, this method explores the solution space more quickly by utilizing quantum computing concepts like superposition and entanglement. An overview of quantum optimization methods applied to six major logistics issue categories—routing, network design, fleet optimization, cargo loading, prediction, and scheduling—is provided in the following sections.

7.4.1 Routing problems

Among the most extensively researched uses of quantum computing in logistics are routing challenges, including the traveling salesman problem (TSP) and the vehicle routing problem (VRP).

Finding the most effective routes for moving products while lowering transportation costs and satisfying consumer demands and limitations is the aim of these challenges.

Numerous studies have explored the use of quantum computing to address different VRP issues. These pieces use a variety of techniques, such as gate-based quantum algorithms like QAOA, hybrid quantum-classical methods, and quantum annealing. For the Capacitated Vehicle Routing Problem (CVRP), a variation of the VRP in which vehicles have limited capacity, some research has suggested quantum annealing techniques.

These methods entail creating spin encoding systems, adjusting parameters, and evaluating results against those of traditional simulated annealing techniques.

Using strategies like quantum phase estimation [21] and quantum search algorithms, several research have presented quantum algorithms for the TSP with the goal of achieving quadratic speedups over traditional brute-force approaches. Additionally, hybrid quantum-classical solutions that combine quantum annealing with classical heuristics for the CVRP's clustering and routing phases have been studied. By combining the advantages of quantum and classical computing, these methods seek to outperform 2-phase heuristics and conventional construction in terms of solution quality.

Furthermore, we investigated the use of techniques based on quantum annealing, including the Full QUBO Solver, Average Partition Solver, DBSCAN Solver, and Solution Partitioning Solver, to the solution of (C) VRPs. Realistic road networks and well-known benchmark datasets were used to compare these algorithms with classical meta-heuristics once they were put into practice using D-Wave's quantum annealers.

Although quantum computing has exciting theoretical promise for supply chain optimization and logistics, a number of research have concentrated on real-world issues and the constraints of existing quantum hardware. In recognition of Noisy's shortcomings, several studies have suggested hybrid processes that divide more complex issues into smaller instances appropriate for quantum annealing.

7.4.2 Hardware for Noisy Intermediate-Scale Quantum (NISQ)

The performance of commercial quantum annealing solutions for the CVRP has also been evaluated by researchers, who have emphasized the necessity of empirical measurements on actual quantum systems to properly assess their capabilities. This research has demonstrated how model complexity and issue size affect the quality of solutions, indicating that lowering constraint density is essential for real-world applications.

Despite present difficulties, a number of research have shown the potential benefits of quantum computing in resolving limited clustering issues and have shown that the cost-effectiveness of quantum algorithm execution is correlated with the quality of the results. To handle more complicated variations of the (C)VRP, such as situations with realistic road networks and last-mile logistical difficulties, researchers have also investigated the use of quantum optimization methods. Using conventional techniques like Gurobi as benchmarks, this research has used a range of quantum algorithms, such as quantum annealing, quantum Graver Augmented Multi-seed Algorithm (GAMA) [22], QAOA, and VQEs. Researchers expect to use continued advancements in quantum annealers and gate-based quantum computers to expand quantum approaches to increasingly complicated logistics optimization scenarios as quantum hardware and algorithms continue to progress. In the future, the use of quantum computing in supply chain management and logistics has enormous potential to transform the way that challenging optimization issues are handled.

Routing, scheduling, resource allocation, demand forecasting, and inventory management are just a few of the areas that could see major advancements in the field by utilizing the special powers of quantum computing, such as exponential computational speedups and the capacity to solve combinatorial optimization problems more effectively.

However, further developments in quantum hardware, error-reduction strategies, and the creation of reliable quantum algorithms suited to the unique difficulties of supply chain optimization and logistics will be necessary to fulfill this promise. In order to propel these developments and open the door for real-world applications of quantum-enhanced logistics solutions, cooperation between researchers studying quantum computing, logistics specialists, and business partners will be essential.

Quantum computing can completely transform supply chain optimization and logistics by providing new methods for solving challenging routing issues and more. Although the fundamental ideas and methods of the two primary paradigms—gate-based quantum computing (GBC) and quantum annealing (QA)—differ, the Quantum Approximate Optimization Algorithm (QAOA) serves as a link between them.

7.4.3 QAOA: bridging the gap between GBC and QA

A quantum algorithm called QAOA applies the ideas of quantum annealing to systems of quantum computing that rely on gates. It falls within the class of hybrid algorithms known as variational quantum eigensolvers (VQEs), which use both classical and quantum computers to determine the ground state of a given physical system. A discretized function that produces an approximation of the desired Hamiltonian's ground state approximates the adiabatic evolution process, which is essential to quantum annealing in QAOA. The procedure iteratively refines the solution towards the desired ground state by starting with an equal superposition of all potential solutions and then applying two operators on this state alternately. Unlike traditional algorithms, this method makes use of quantum computing concepts like entanglement and superposition to investigate the answer.

7.4.4 Routing optimization with quantum computing

The optimization of routing issues, such as the Traveling Salesman Problem (TSP) and the Vehicle Routing Problem (VRP), is one of the most researched uses of quantum computing in logistics. In order to meet consumer demand, minimize transportation costs, and satisfy a number of limitations, these challenges seek to identify the most effective routes for moving goods. To solve distinct features of VRPs and TSPs, researchers have investigated a variety of techniques, such as gate-based quantum algorithms like QAOA, hybrid quantum-classical approaches, and quantum annealing.

7.5 QUANTUM ANNEALING APPROACHES

For the capacitated vehicle routing problem (CVRP), a variation of the VRP in which vehicles have limited capacity, some research has suggested quantum annealing techniques. These methods entail creating spin encoding systems, adjusting parameters, and evaluating results against those of traditional simulated annealing techniques. Furthermore, for the purpose of solving (C)VRPs, researchers have investigated quantum annealing-based methods such as the Full QUBO Solver, Average Partition Solver, DBSCAN Solver, and Solution Partitioning Solver.

For the clustering and routing stages of the CVRP, hybrid quantum-classical solutions that combine quantum annealing with classical heuristics have been studied. By combining the advantages of quantum and classical computing, these methods seek to outperform two-phase heuristics, and using methods like quantum phase estimation and quantum search algorithms, researchers have also developed gate-based quantum algorithms for the TSP with the goal of achieving quadratic speedups over traditional brute-force approaches. Notwithstanding the constraints of the existing Noisy Intermediate-Scale Quantum (NISQ) devices, certain algorithms, such as QAOA, have been modified for the VRP and provide potential solutions for combinatorial optimization issues like VRPs.

Although quantum computing has exciting theoretical promise for supply chain optimization and logistics, a number of research have concentrated on real-world issues and the constraints of existing quantum hardware. In recognition of the limits of NISQ technology, researchers have suggested hybrid methods that decompose bigger problems into smaller instances appropriate for quantum annealing. They have also evaluated the effectiveness of commercial quantum annealing solutions, highlighting the necessity of empirical tests on actual quantum platforms to properly assess their capabilities. Notwithstanding present obstacles, research has shown the prospective benefits of quantum computing in resolving limited clustering issues and the economical connections between the execution of quantum algorithms and the caliber of the results.

Researchers expect to apply quantum techniques to increasingly complicated logistics optimization situations as quantum hardware and algorithms develop further, taking advantage of continuous advancements in quantum annealers and gate-based quantum computers.

7.6. BEYOND CLASSIC ROUTING PROBLEMS

Although there has been a lot of attention paid to the optimization of traditional routing issues like VRPs and TSPs, quantum computing has also been used to solve a number of different routing problems, demonstrating its promise for optimizing intricate logistical situations. The shipment rerouting problem, which deals with the difficulty of partially loaded trucks moving cargo between a network of hubs, is one example. The objective is to reduce the overall distance that these vehicles travel in order to save fuel and increase cost-effectiveness. In order to solve Quadratic Unconstrained Binary Optimization (QUBO) [23], researchers have developed QUBO formulations and used both conventional and hybrid quantum-classical algorithms [24]. Because quantum platforms like D-Wave enable qubits, these platforms have demonstrated encouraging results.

Researchers have suggested using QAOA for route optimization in the context of smart logistics systems, taking into account not only time and cost but also the carbon footprint of logistical activities. This multi-objective strategy seeks to establish safe and private communication via blockchain technology while simultaneously choosing the most efficient paths to cut expenses, time, and carbon emissions.

7.6.1 Application of QC

The optimization of robot trip distance in warehouses and distribution centers, where order picking and batching are carried out, is another use of quantum computing. Hybrid computing and execution on several quantum platforms are now possible because of the development and implementation of real-time quantum optimization algorithms on platforms such as Raspberry Pi [25]. Researchers have examined the intricacies of flight path optimization in the aviation industry, highlighting the application of quantum computing to get beyond the computational obstacles related to this vital aerospace engineering function. They have presented modular frameworks that may be customized and studied how to apply quantum-enhanced algorithms, such as Grover's algorithm, to different quantum simulations and architectures.

Applications in the real world, such as multimodal container planning and traffic flow optimization in congested road networks, have also been investigated. In order to overcome the constraints of existing quantum hardware, this research has shown that it is feasible to transfer these issues onto QUBO formulations and use hybrid quantum and classical techniques.

7.7 SPECIALIZED ROUTING SCENARIOS

Quantum computing has been investigated for specific routing circumstances, such as those in which trucks have limited driving windows, in addition to generic routing challenges. In these situations, the goal function can change from reducing travel time to reducing the quantity of vehicles needed to meet all demands within the allotted period.

These specific situations demonstrate how flexible quantum computing is in handling a range of logistics and supply chain optimization problems, each with its own set of limitations and goals. In the future, the use of quantum computing in supply chain management and logistics has enormous potential to transform the way that challenging optimization issues are handled. The field may see major advancements in areas like scheduling, demand forecasting, resource allocation, routing, and inventory management by utilizing the special powers of quantum computing, such as exponential computational speedups and the capacity to solve combinatorial optimization problems more effectively.

However, achieving this promise would need further developments in quantum technology, methods for reducing errors, and the creation of reliable quantum algorithms suited to the unique difficulties of supply chain optimization and logistics. Working together, researchers studying quantum computing, logistics specialists, and business partners will be essential to propelling these developments and opening the door for real-world applications of quantum-enhanced logistics solutions.

7.8 FURTHER PROGRESS

As the area develops, quantum computing has the potential to become a vital component of the supply chain optimization and logistics toolset, facilitating more sustainable, economical, and effective operations in a variety of sectors and industries.

Significant progress has been made in the field of quantum computing, with businesses such as D-Wave Systems spearheading the development of quantum annealing computers for real-world use. With an astounding 5,000 superconducting qubits functioning at cryogenic temperatures, D-Wave's most recent product, the D-Wave Advantage, represents a substantial improvement over its predecessor, the D-Wave 2000Q, which had 2,000 qubits.

Researchers and developers can describe any issue in the Quadratic Unconstrained Binary Optimization (QUBO) formulation, which contains binary variables, thanks to the D-Wave Advantage system's fully programmable architecture. For many logistics and supply chain optimization problems, where binary choices are frequently required, this approach is very pertinent.

The hybrid solver of the D-Wave Advantage system, which blends the capabilities of large-scale classical computers and quantum annealing computers, is one of its primary advantages. Researchers may now work on quantum annealing methods while running considerably bigger problem instances of practical importance thanks to this hybrid technique, which overcomes the present barrier of issue size encountered by existing quantum computing devices. In the field of quantum annealing, a number of crucial features determine the system's functionality and performance. These include the quantity of qubits, their connection, and their noise characteristics.

With 16 couplers per qubit, the D-Wave Advantage system delivers a substantial increase in couplers between qubits, as opposed to merely 6 in earlier iterations. The processor can handle bigger issue sizes because of this improved connection, which makes it possible to incorporate logical problems onto the hardware graph of qubits more effectively. It should be noted that an issue involving 5,000 binary variables cannot be directly handled by the 5,000-qubit processor. Multiple hardware qubits must be coded as logical nodes to represent each logical variable during the embedding process. Only a problem with around 180 logical binary variables can be embedded into the D-Wave Advantage system for completely linked logical issues, in which each binary variable interacts with every other binary variable.

Larger problem sizes containing hundreds of binary variables can be directly incorporated into the quantum annealer; nevertheless, because many real-world logistics and supply chain management issues are not entirely logically related. The hybrid solution, which combines the quantum annealer and classical heuristic solvers working together, becomes essential for handling increasingly bigger problems with hundreds of binary variables. A thorough white paper on the features and modes of operation of the D-Wave Advantage quantum annealing computer has been made available by D-Wave Systems, providing insightful information about its possible uses and capabilities.

For all problem types, D-Wave Systems' quantum annealers still fall short of the best conventional algorithms operating on multiple CPU/GPU computation hardware, despite their increasing performance with each new generation of machines. Nonetheless, for some problem classes, the difference between the quantum annealing Quantum Processing Unit and classical CPUs is closing, suggesting the possibility of quantum advantage in some fields.

The D-Wave Systems [25] hybrid solver aims to bring the power of quantum computing to bear on larger problem sizes than the quantum annealer can handle alone at its current stage of maturity. The hybrid solver incorporates several of these approaches in an overarching meta-heuristic. The Metasolver, which governs the overall algorithm, launches multiple threads that employ classical heuristic algorithms running on CPUs or GPUs. These heuristic algorithms utilize versions of simulated annealing, tabu local searches, and additional proprietary heuristics. Simultaneously, the Metasolver [26] leverages the quantum annealer to search for promising solutions to smaller subsets of the problem, and these solutions are fed back into the algorithm flow to provide additional promising starting points for the heuristic algorithms in each thread. The Metasolver collects a set of best solutions until a stopping condition, typically an overall target run-time, is reached, and the results are reported back to the user.

Performance testing on benchmark optimization problems has shown that the hybrid solver performs well and, in some cases, outperforms other state-of-the-art classical heuristics running on comparable hardware. Interestingly, when running the hybrid solver with the quantum annealing augmentation disabled, the solution time and quality are degraded slightly on average. This indicates that the quantum annealing solutions are providing improved performance, at least for the problem types and instances studied to date [27].

The long-term expectation is that as the quantum annealing hardware improves in the future, the hybrid solver will provide even greater advantages over purely classical solvers. This hybrid approach can also be pursued using other quantum computing paradigms, such as circuit model discrete optimization solvers, opening up further possibilities for quantum-enhanced logistics and supply chain optimization.

Fleet maintenance and optimization is one area of supply chain management and logistics where quantum algorithms have shown potential. In order to maintain operational performance and cost-effectiveness, fleet management choices on resource allocation and vehicle maintenance schedules are essential. The Tail Assignment Problem (TAP), which airlines encounter, is one such issue that has drawn attention in this field. To reduce total expenditures, the TAP effectively allocates each aircraft to a group of routes. It is a component of the broader airline planning process, which includes intricate optimization issues with a range of limitations pertaining to patrons, crew, aircraft, maintenance, and ground personnel.

7.9 RECENT RESEARCH

The performance of two well-known quantum annealers, the D-Wave Advantage and its predecessor, the D-Wave 2000Q, on the TAP and other optimization problems has been compared recently. According to the benchmarking study's findings, the D-Wave Advantage system outperformed the D-Wave 2000Q in practically every difficulty case. The Advantage system showed the effects of its higher qubit count and improved qubit connection by exhibiting a significant rise in success rates and the capacity to tackle more complex challenges. The Chimera topology of the D-Wave 2000Q featured only 6 connections per qubit, while the Pegasus topology of the Advantage system had 15 connections per qubit. The Advantage system's increased speed was largely due to this better connectedness, which made it possible to integrate logical issues onto the hardware graph of qubits more effectively. Additionally, in terms of programming and readout times, the Advantage system showed around double the speed of the D-Wave 2000Q. In addition, it demonstrated consistently greater success rates, fewer variations across several repeats, and quicker time-to-solution and annealing durations. Nevertheless, the study also showed that the D-Wave 2000Q may have higher success rates for sparse connection issues that do not require the several additional couplers seen on the Advantage system. This result emphasizes how crucial it is to consider [28] the particular needs of every issue instance because more connection does not always translate into better performance for all problem kinds. The combination of quantum algorithms and hybrid quantum-classical techniques has enormous potential to transform supply chain planning and logistics as quantum computing technology advances. Routing, scheduling, resource allocation, demand forecasting, and inventory management are just a few of the areas that could see major advancements in the field by utilizing the special powers of quantum computing, such as exponential computational speedups and the capacity to solve intricate combinatorial optimization problems more effectively. However, achieving this promise would need continued cooperation between logistics specialists, industrial partners, and researchers studying quantum computing, along with ongoing developments in quantum algorithms, error-reduction strategies, and quantum hardware. High accuracy in backorder prediction has been demonstrated by hybrid quantum-classical models, like the QAmplifyNet [29] neural network, especially when dealing with unbalanced information. The advantages of both quantum and conventional computers are used in this hybrid technique, which promotes better inventory control, fewer backorders, and increased operational effectiveness. Quantized policy iteration algorithms for inventory control have also been presented in several research; these algorithms have been evaluated on platforms such as IBM's Qiskit and qBraid and have demonstrated efficacy in small-scale simulations. By making use of quantum annealing's capabilities and strengthening meta-heuristic techniques in bigger algorithm pipelines, these hybrid approaches represent a greater trend of fusing quantum and classical paradigms. As hardware develops and researcher-industry collaboration increases, the sector expects more breakthroughs in quantum computing applications.

Although they are still far less effective than QA, the Quantum Approximate Optimization Algorithm (QAOA) and other variational quantum eigensolver (VQE) techniques using gate-based quantum devices are the second most popular approaches. Although the majority of the literature has focused on routing and scheduling issues, there is still much space for more investigation and testing in fields like supply chain and logistics-specific machine learning and prediction techniques. Researchers generally agree that the present generation of quantum technology is still in its infancy and faces challenges including noise, decoherence, and limited qubit counts. Consequently, several studies recognize the difficulties in adapting intricate logistics and supply chain optimization issues to the hardware capabilities available today. Few studies have shown that their hybrid quantum-classical methods perform better than current classical techniques. While acknowledging the necessity for more developments in quantum hardware and algorithms to fully achieve these benefits, the majority of papers only stress the prospective advantages and benefits of their suggested quantum techniques. As highlighted by systematic researchers across various domains, including logistics and supply chain optimization, similar conclusions have been reached. Most articles recognize the difficulties in adapting sophisticated issue formulations to the hardware capacity and the constraints of existing quantum technology, including noise, decoherence, and tiny qubit counts.

REFERENCES

1. Fomin, V. V. (2020). The Shift from Traditional Computing Systems to Artificial Intelligence and the Implications for Bias. In *Smart technologies and fundamental rights* (pp. 316–333). Brill. https://doi.org/10.1163/9789004437876_015.
2. Steane, A. (1998). Quantum computing. *Reports on Progress in Physics*, *61*(2), 117–173.
3. Phillipson, F. (2023). Quantum computing in telecommunication—a survey. *Mathematics*, *11*(15), 3423.
4. Zhou, L., Wang, S., Choi, S., Pichler, H., & Lukin, M. D. (2020). Quantum approximate optimization algorithm: performance, mechanism, and implementation on near-term devices. *Physical Review X*, *10*(2).
5. Dutta, P. K., Ghosh, D., & Abotaleb, M. (2024). Harnessing the Power of Hybrid Models for Supply Chain Management and Optimization. In Ramakant Bhardwaj, Pushan Kumar Dutta, Pethuru Raj, Abhishek Kumar, Kavita Saini, Alfonso González Briones and Mohammed K. A. Kaabar (Eds.), *Hybrid Information Systems: Non-Linear Optimization Strategies with Artificial Intelligence* (pp. 407–426). De Gruyter. https://doi.org/10.1515/9783111331133-019.
6. Gupta, S., Dutta, P. K., Roy, S., Bhaduri, A., Maji, K., Choudhary, A., & Sarkar, A. (2024). Evaluating Waterfall vs. Agile Models in Software Development for Efficiency and Adaptability. In S. Misra, R. Jadeja, & M. Mittal (Eds.), *Practical Approaches to Agile Project Management* (pp. 142–148). IGI Global. https://doi.org/10.4018/979-8-3693-3318-1.ch008.

7. Abotaleb, M., & Dutta, P. K. (2024). Optimizing Bidirectional Long Short-Term Memory Networks for Univariate Time Series Forecasting: A Comprehensive Guide. In Ramakant Bhardwaj, Pushan Kumar Dutta, Pethuru Raj, Abhishek Kumar, Kavita Saini, Alfonso González Briones and Mohammed K. A. Kaabar (Eds.), *Hybrid Information Systems: Non-Linear Optimization Strategies with Artificial Intelligence* (pp. 443–458). De Gruyter. https://doi.org/10.1515/9783111331133-021.
8. Kwon, S., Tomonaga, A., Bhai, G. L., Devitt, S. J., & Tsai, J. (2021). Gate-based superconducting quantum computing. *Journal of Applied Physics*, *129*(4), 041102. https://doi.org/10.1063/5.0029735.
9. Dhaliwal, N., Aghera, S., Whig, P., & Dutta, P. K. (2024). Advanced Analytics and Quantum Computing for Revolutionizing Procurement Strategies. In A. Hassan, P. Bhattacharya, P. Dutta, J. Verma, & N. Kundu (Eds.), *Quantum Computing and Supply Chain Management: A New Era of Optimization* (pp. 160–175). IGI Global. https://doi.org/10.4018/979-8-3693-4107-0.ch011.
10. Greenberger, D. M., Horne, M. A., & Zeilinger, A. (1993). Multiparticle interferometry and the superposition principle. *Physics Today*, *46*(8), 22–29.
11. Rønnow, T. F., Wang, Z., Job, J., Boixo, S., Isakov, S. V., Wecker, D., Martinis, J. M., Lidar, D. A., & Troyer, M. (2014). Defining and detecting quantum speedup. *Science*, *345*(6195), 420–424.
12. Wang, D., Higgott, O., & Brierley, S. (2019). Accelerated variational quantum eigensolver. *Physical Review Letters*, *122*(14), 140504. https://doi.org/10.1103/PhysRevLett.122.140504.
13. Dorner, U., Demkowicz-Dobrzanski, R., Smith, B. J., Lundeen, J. S., Wasilewski, W., Banaszek, K., & Walmsley, I. A. (2009). Optimal quantum phase estimation. *Proceedings of the American Physical Society Meeting*, *102*(4), 040403. https://doi.org/10.1103/PhysRevLett.102.040403.
14. McClean, J. R., Romero, J., Babbush, R., & Aspuru-Guzik, A. (2016). The theory of variational hybrid quantum-classical algorithms. *New Journal of Physics*, *18*(2), 023023.
15. Dutta, P. K., Singh, B., Towfeek, A.-S. K., Adamopoulou, J. P., Bardavouras, A. N., Bamwerinde, W., Turyasingura, B., & Ayiga, N. (2024). IoT revolutionizes humidity measurement and management in smart cities to enhance health and wellness. *Mesopotamian Journal of Artificial Intelligence in Healthcare*, *2024*, 110–117. https://doi.org/10.58496/MJAIH/2024/013.
16. Combarro, E. F., Gonzalez-Castillo, S., & Di Meglio, A. (2023). *A Practical Guide to Quantum Machine Learning and Quantum Optimization: Hands-on Approach to Modern Quantum Algorithms*. Packt Publishing Ltd.
17. Gupta, S., Sarkar, D., Roy, D., Kundu, S., & Dutta, P. K. (2024). Embracing Flexibility and Efficiency: Practical Approaches to Agile Project Management. In S. Misra, R. Jadeja, & M. Mittal (Eds.), *Practical Approaches to Agile Project Management* (pp. 1–8). IGI Global. https://doi.org/10.4018/979-8-3693-3318-1.ch001.
18. Gupta, S., Dutta, P. K., Roy, S., Bhaduri, A., Maji, K., Choudhary, A., & Sarkar, A. (2024). Evaluating Waterfall vs. Agile Models in Software Development for Efficiency and Adaptability. In S. Misra, R. Jadeja, & M. Mittal (Eds.), *Practical Approaches to Agile Project Management* (pp. 142–148). IGI Global. https://doi.org/10.4018/979-8-3693-3318-1.ch008.

19. Patra, A. & Dutta, P. K. (2024). Application of Agile Stage Gate Hybrid Model in the Healthcare Industry: A Paradigm Shift in Project Management. In S. Misra, R. Jadeja, & M. Mittal (Eds.), *Practical Approaches to Agile Project Management* (pp. 149–163). IGI Global. https://doi.org/10.4018/979-8-3693-3318-1.ch009.
20. Singh, B., Vig, K., Dutta, P. K., & Kaunert, C. (2024). Unraveling Agile Transformation for Customer Satisfaction in Changing Market Conditions: Roadmap for Industry Embracing Change in Project Management. In S. Misra, R. Jadeja, & M. Mittal (Eds.), *Practical Approaches to Agile Project Management* (pp. 305–321). IGI Global. https://doi.org/10.4018/979-8-3693-3318-1.ch017.
21. Singh, B., Dutta, P. K., Gautam, R., & Kaunert, C. (2024). Uncapping the Potential of Quantum Computing Towards Manufacturing Optimization: Routing Supply Chain Projecting Sustainability. In A. Hassan, P. Bhattacharya, P. Dutta, *Quantum Computing and Supply Chain Management: A New Era of Optimization* (p. 25). IGI Global. https://doi.org/10.4018/979-8-3693-4107-0.ch024.
22. McGeoch, C., Mniszewski, S., Chancellor, N., & Neira, D. E. B. (2024). *Experience with Quantum Annealing Computation*. Frontiers Media SA.
23. Gupta, S., Sarkar, D., Roy, D., Kundu, S., & Dutta, P. K. (2024). Embracing Flexibility and Efficiency: Practical Approaches to Agile Project Management. In S. Misra, R. Jadeja, & M. Mittal (Eds.), *Practical Approaches to Agile Project Management* (pp. 1–8). IGI Global. https://doi.org/10.4018/979-8-3693-3318-1.ch001.
24. Punnen, A. P. (2022). *The Quadratic Unconstrained Binary Optimization Problem: Theory, Algorithms, and Applications*. Springer Nature.
25. Dutta, P. K., Bhardwaj, A. K., & Mahida, A. (2024). Navigating the Complexities of Agile Transformations in Large Organizations. In A. Hassan, P. Bhattacharya, P. Dutta, J. Verma, & N. Kundu (Eds.), *Quantum Computing and Supply Chain Management: A New Era of Optimization* (pp. 315–330). IGI Global. https://doi.org/10.4018/979-8-3693-4107-0.ch020.
26. Dutta, P. K., El-kenawy, S. M., Ali, G., & Dhoska, K. (2023). An energy consumption monitoring and control system in buildings using internet of things. *Babylonian Journal of Internet of Things*, *2023*, 38–47. https://doi.org/10.58496/BJIoT/2023/006.
27. Singh, B., Dutta, P. K., & Kaunert, C. (2024). Boosting Quantum Computing to Redefine Supply Chain in the Hospital Industry: Pitch the Vision for Medical and Healthcare Needs. In A. Hassan, P. Bhattacharya, P. Dutta, J. Verma, & N. Kundu (Eds.), *Quantum Computing and Supply Chain Management: A New Era of Optimization* (pp. 196–219). IGI Global. https://doi.org/10.4018/979-8-3693-4107-0.ch014.
28. Dutta, P. K., Bhardwaj, A. K., & Mahida, A. (2024). Navigating the Complexities of Agile Transformations in Large Organizations. In A. Hassan, P. Bhattacharya, P. Dutta, J. Verma, & N. Kundu (Eds.), *Quantum Computing and Supply Chain Management: A New Era of Optimization* (pp. 315–330). IGI Global. https://doi.org/10.4018/979-8-3693-4107-0.ch020.

Chapter 8

Quantum computing in risk management and supply chain resilience

Jayanta Biswas, Maad M. Mijwil, Laith Farhan, and Hussein Alkattan

8.1 INTRODUCTION

Quantum computing is a type of computing that uses quantum-mechanical phenomena, such as superposition and entanglement, to perform calculations. Unlike classical computers, which use binary digits (bits) to represent information, quantum computers use quantum bits (qubits). This allows them to perform calculations much faster than classical computers.

In today's globalized and interconnected world [1], supply chains are crucial for businesses to deliver products and services efficiently. However, they face numerous risks, including natural disasters, geopolitical tensions, and disruptions in the transportation network. Traditional risk management approaches often struggle to address these challenges effectively. Quantum computing, with its ability to process vast amounts of data and perform complex calculations, holds the potential to revolutionize risk management and enhance supply chain resilience. This chapter explores how quantum computing can be applied to address these challenges and improve the resilience of supply chains [2]. Quantum computing is a relatively new technology but has the potential to revolutionize many industries, including supply chain management. With the ability to perform complex calculations at incredible speeds, quantum computers could help businesses optimize their supply chain operations, reduce costs, and improve efficiency. In this chapter, we'll take a closer look at the potential of quantum computing in supply chain management.

8.2 QUANTUM COMPUTING FUNDAMENTALS

Quantum computing is based on the principles of quantum mechanics, which allow quantum computers to process information in ways that are fundamentally different from classical computers. At the heart of quantum computing are quantum bits, or qubits, which can exist in a state of superposition, representing both 0 and 1 simultaneously [3]. This property

DOI: 10.1201/9781003498292-8

allows quantum computers to perform calculations on a vast number of possibilities simultaneously, enabling them to solve complex problems much faster than classical computers.

Quantum computers use quantum gates to manipulate qubits and perform computations. These gates can create entangled states between qubits, which further enhances the computational power of quantum computers. Quantum circuits are constructed using these gates to perform specific tasks, such as solving optimization problems or simulating quantum systems.

8.3 QUANTUM COMPUTING APPLICATIONS IN RISK MANAGEMENT

8.3.1 Risk management

Supply chains are vulnerable to a wide range of risks, including natural disasters, political instability, and cyberattacks. By using quantum computing to analyze data from various sources, companies could identify and mitigate risks more effectively.

Quantum computing can help businesses identify and mitigate these risks more effectively. By analyzing data from various sources, quantum computing can help organizations quickly and accurately assess risks, enabling them to take proactive measures to protect their supply chain operations [4].

In 2019, IBM announced the launch of its quantum risk assessment tool, which aims to help businesses identify potential cybersecurity risks and vulnerabilities in their supply chains. The tool uses quantum computing to analyze data and identify potential weak points in the supply chain, helping businesses take preventative measures [5].

Another example of quantum computing used for risk management in the supply chain is the pharmaceutical industry. Pfizer, a leading pharmaceutical company, has partnered with 1QBit, a quantum computing firm, to improve their drug development process. By using quantum computing, Pfizer can now more accurately predict potential drug interactions and identify potential risks, enabling them to take corrective measures before it becomes a major issue [6].

One of the key applications of quantum computing in risk management is the simulation of complex supply chain scenarios. Quantum computers can model the behavior of supply chains with a level of detail that is not feasible with classical computers [7]. This allows businesses to identify potential risks and develop strategies to mitigate them. For example, quantum computers can simulate the impact of a natural disaster on a supply chain and suggest alternative routes or suppliers to minimize disruptions.

Quantum computing also offers significant benefits in optimizing supply chain processes. Quantum algorithms can be used to optimize route planning, inventory management, and production scheduling [8], leading to more efficient and resilient supply chains. Additionally, quantum cryptography can enhance cybersecurity in supply chains, protecting sensitive data from cyber threats.

8.4 POTENTIAL APPLICATIONS IN SUPPLY CHAIN MANAGEMENT

Supply chain optimization is a complex process that involves balancing multiple factors, such as cost, efficiency, and customer satisfaction. With the help of quantum computing, businesses can solve these optimization problems much faster and more accurately than classical computers [9]. For instance, D-Wave Systems, a Canadian quantum computing company, has partnered with companies such as Volkswagen, Denso, and Cognizant to help optimize their supply chain operations. Volkswagen has partnered with Google to use quantum computing to optimize traffic flows. The project aims to reduce traffic congestion and emissions by finding the most efficient routes for vehicles to take. This collaboration is just one example of how quantum computing can help optimize supply chain operations and drive sustainability [10].

8.5 QUANTUM COMPUTING FOR SUPPLY CHAIN RESILIENCE

Quantum computing can enhance supply chain resilience by enabling real-time monitoring and response to disruptions. Quantum computers can analyze data from various sources, such as sensors and satellites, to identify disruptions and reroute shipments accordingly [11]. This ability to react quickly to changing circumstances can help minimize the impact of disruptions on supply chains.

Predictive analytics is another area where quantum computing can improve supply chain resilience [12]. Quantum algorithms can analyze historical data and identify patterns that may indicate future risks. This allows businesses to take proactive measures to mitigate these risks, such as adjusting inventory levels or diversifying their supplier base.

Quantum computing can also optimize inventory management in supply chains. Quantum algorithms can analyze demand patterns and optimize inventory levels to ensure that products are available when and where they are needed. This can help businesses reduce costs and improve customer satisfaction [13].

8.6 CHALLENGES AND FUTURE DIRECTIONS

Despite its potential, quantum computing still faces several challenges that need to be addressed before it can be widely adopted in supply chain management. One of the key challenges is scalability, as current quantum computers are limited in terms of the number of qubits they can support and the accuracy of their calculations [14].

Integration with existing technologies and infrastructure is another challenge, as businesses will need to adapt their systems to work with quantum computers. Additionally, the cost of quantum computing remains high, which may limit its adoption by smaller businesses.

Looking ahead, the future of quantum computing in supply chain management looks promising. Continued advancements in quantum hardware and software are expected to address many of the current challenges. As quantum computing becomes more accessible, businesses will have the opportunity to harness its power to improve risk management and build more resilient supply chains [15].

8.6.1 Challenges and limitations in supply chain

While the potential benefits of quantum computing in supply chain management are significant, its challenges and limitations also cannot be overlooked. One of the biggest challenges is the complexity of developing quantum algorithms. Unlike classical algorithms, quantum algorithms are built on quantum mechanics, which makes them fundamentally different and more complex to develop. Developing these algorithms requires specialized knowledge and skills, which are currently in short supply. Businesses looking to leverage quantum computing in supply chain management will need to invest in the necessary expertise to develop and implement these algorithms effectively [16].

Another significant challenge is the availability of quantum computing hardware. While there are a few quantum computers available for research and development purposes, they are still relatively rare and expensive. This means many businesses may not have access to the hardware they need to take advantage of quantum computing. The high cost of quantum computing hardware is also a barrier to entry for many smaller businesses. This limits the widespread adoption of quantum computing in supply chain management.

Finally, it is worth noting that quantum computing is still an emerging technology, and many aspects of its potential applications in supply chain management are still to be explored. This means there exists a certain degree of uncertainty around the long-term potential of quantum computing in supply chain management. Nonetheless, quantum computing is rapidly developing, and businesses need to stay ahead of the curve to remain competitive.

In conclusion, quantum computing has the potential to revolutionize supply chain management by providing faster and more accurate solutions to complex problems such as optimization and risk management. While there are still challenges and limitations that need to be taken care of, businesses that can take advantage of quantum computing will have a significant competitive advantage in the market. The future of supply chain management will involve a greater adoption of quantum computing technology, and companies should start exploring its potential applications now to stay ahead of the curve. As technology continues to develop and become more accessible, we can expect to see even more exciting advancements in supply chain management in the years to come.

8.7 CASE STUDIES

8.7.1 Case study 1: D-Wave Systems and Volkswagen

8.7.1.1 Background

Volkswagen Group is one of the world's leading automobile manufacturers, with a complex supply chain network spanning multiple continents. The company faced challenges in optimizing its production processes and logistics to improve efficiency and reduce costs.

8.7.1.2 Solution

Volkswagen partnered with D-Wave Systems, a quantum computing company, to explore the use of quantum computing in optimizing traffic flow and production processes. D-Wave's quantum annealing technology was used to develop algorithms that could analyze vast amounts of data and optimize complex systems in real time.

8.7.1.3 Results

By leveraging quantum computing, Volkswagen was able to optimize traffic flow in urban areas, reducing congestion and emissions. In its production processes, Volkswagen improved efficiency by optimizing scheduling and resource allocation. These improvements led to cost savings and a more sustainable supply chain.

8.7.2 Case study 2: IBM and Maersk

8.7.2.1 Background

Maersk Line, the world's largest container shipping company, sought to improve the efficiency and transparency of its supply chain operations. The company faced challenges in tracking shipments in real time and optimizing shipping routes to reduce costs and emissions.

8.7.2.2 Solution

IBM partnered with Maersk to develop Trade Lens, a block-chain-based platform that uses quantum computing to enable real-time tracking of shipments and optimize shipping routes. The platform uses quantum algorithms to analyze data from sensors and shipping manifests to provide real-time visibility into the status of shipments.

8.7.2.3 Results

Trade Lens has improved the efficiency and transparency of Maersk's supply chain operations. The platform has enabled Maersk to track shipments in real time, reduce delays, and optimize shipping routes to reduce costs and emissions. Trade Lens has also improved collaboration between stakeholders in the supply chain, leading to a more efficient and resilient supply chain network.

8.7.3 Case study 3: Amazon and quantum computing

8.7.3.1 Background

Amazon, the world's largest online retailer, sought to improve the efficiency of its supply chain operations to meet growing customer demand. The company faced challenges in optimizing inventory management and order fulfillment processes to reduce costs and improve customer satisfaction.

8.7.3.2 Solution

Amazon is exploring the use of quantum computing to optimize its supply chain operations. The company is leveraging quantum algorithms to analyze vast amounts of data, such as customer orders and inventory levels, to optimize inventory management and order fulfillment processes.

8.7.3.3 Results

While the results of Amazon's quantum computing initiatives are not yet publicly available, the company expects to improve the efficiency of its supply chain operations and reduce costs. By leveraging quantum computing, Amazon aims to improve customer satisfaction by ensuring products are available when and where they are needed.

8.7.4 Case study 4: Lockheed Martin and D-Wave Systems

8.7.4.1 Background

Lockheed Martin, a global aerospace and defense company, faced challenges in optimizing its manufacturing processes and supply chain operations to meet the demands of its customers.

8.7.4.2 Solution

Lockheed Martin partnered with D-Wave Systems to explore the use of quantum computing in optimizing its manufacturing processes. D-Wave's quantum annealing technology was used to develop algorithms that could optimize production schedules, resource allocation, and supply chain logistics.

8.7.4.3 Results

By leveraging quantum computing, Lockheed Martin was able to improve the efficiency of its manufacturing processes and supply chain operations. The company saw a reduction in production costs and lead times, leading to improved customer satisfaction and a more competitive position in the market.

8.7.5 Case study 5: Toyota and IBM

8.7.5.1 Background

Toyota, one of the world's largest automakers, sought to improve the efficiency of its supply chain operations to reduce costs and improve customer satisfaction.

8.7.5.2 Solution

Toyota partnered with IBM to explore the use of quantum computing in optimizing its supply chain operations. IBM's quantum computing technology was used to develop algorithms that could optimize inventory management, production scheduling, and logistics.

8.7.5.3 Results

By leveraging quantum computing, Toyota was able to improve the efficiency of its supply chain operations. The company saw a reduction in inventory carrying costs, improved production efficiency, and better coordination between its suppliers and manufacturing facilities.

8.7.6 Case study 6: Honeywell and Google

8.7.6.1 Background

Honeywell, a global technology company, faced challenges in optimizing its supply chain operations to meet the demands of its customers and improve its competitiveness in the market.

8.7.6.2 Solution

Honeywell partnered with Google to explore the use of quantum computing in optimizing its supply chain operations. Google's quantum computing technology was used to develop algorithms that could optimize inventory management, production scheduling, and logistics.

8.7.6.3 Results

By leveraging quantum computing, Honeywell was able to improve the efficiency of its supply chain operations. The company saw a reduction in lead times, improved customer satisfaction, and a more competitive position in the market.

These case studies demonstrate the diverse applications of quantum computing in optimizing supply chain operations across different industries. As quantum computing technology continues to evolve, we can expect to see more companies leveraging its power to gain a competitive edge in the market.

8.8 CONCLUSION

In conclusion, quantum computing [17] has the potential to revolutionize risk management and supply chain resilience. By leveraging the unique properties of quantum mechanics, quantum computers can perform calculations that are beyond the capabilities of classical computers, enabling businesses to better understand and mitigate risks in their supply chains. While there are still challenges to overcome, the future looks bright for quantum computing in supply chain management.

REFERENCES

1. Arute, F., Arya, K., Babbush, R., et al. (2019). Quantum Supremacy Using a Programmable Superconducting Processor. *Nature* **574**, 505–510. https://doi.org/10.1038/s41586-019-1666-5.
2. Grover, L. K. (1996). A fast quantum mechanical algorithm for database search. In *Proceedings of the Twenty-Eighth Annual ACM Symposium on Theory of Computing (STOC '96)* (pp. 212–219). Association for Computing Machinery. https://doi.org/10.1145/237814.237866.

3. Dutta, P. K., Ghosh, D., & Abotaleb, M. (2024). Harnessing the power of hybrid models for supply chain management and optimization. In Ramakant Bhardwaj, Pushan Kumar Dutta, Pethuru Raj, Abhishek Kumar, Kavita Saini, Alfonso González Briones, & Mohammed K. A. Kaabar (Eds.), *Hybrid Information Systems: Non-Linear Optimization Strategies with Artificial Intelligence* (pp. 407–426). De Gruyter. https://doi.org/10.1515/9783111331133-019.
4. Abotaleb, M., & Dutta, P. K. (2024). Optimizing bidirectional long short-term memory networks for univariate time series forecasting: a comprehensive guide. In Ramakant Bhardwaj, Pushan Kumar Dutta, Pethuru Raj, Abhishek Kumar, Kavita Saini, Alfonso González Briones, & Mohammed K. A. Kaabar (Eds.), *Hybrid Information Systems: Non-Linear Optimization Strategies with Artificial Intelligence* (pp. 443–458). De Gruyter. https://doi.org/10.1515/9783111331133-021.
5. Singh, B., Dutta, P. K., & Kaunert, C. (2024). Boosting Quantum Computing to Redefine Supply Chain in the Hospital Industry: Pitch the Vision for Medical and Healthcare Needs. In A. Hassan, P. Bhattacharya, P. Dutta, J. Verma, & N. Kundu (Eds.), *Quantum Computing and Supply Chain Management: A New Era of Optimization* (pp. 196–219). IGI Global. https://doi.org/10.4018/979-8-3693-4107-0.ch014.
6. Dutta, P. K., El-kenawy, S. M., Abotaleb, M., & Eid, M. M. (2023). AI-Driven Marketplaces and Price Prediction Tools for Rag Pickers: Enhancing Economic Opportunities in Africa's Circular Economy. *Babylonian Journal of Artificial Intelligence* **2023**, 33–42. https://doi.org/10.58496/BJAI/2023/007.
7. Dutta, P. K., Bhardwaj, A. K., & Mahida, A. (2024). Navigating the Complexities of Agile Transformations in Large Organizations. In A. Hassan, P. Bhattacharya, P. Dutta, J. Verma, & N. Kundu (Eds.), *Quantum Computing and Supply Chain Management: A New Era of Optimization* (pp. 315–330). IGI Global. https://doi.org/10.4018/979-8-3693-4107-0.ch020.
8. Chang, A., El-Rayes, N., & Shi, J. (2022). Blockchain Technology for Supply Chain Management: A Comprehensive Review. *FinTech* **1**(2), 191–205. https://doi.org/10.3390/fintech1020015.
9. Gutta, L. M., Dhamodharan, B., Dutta, P. K., & Whig, P. (2024). AI-Infused Quantum Machine Learning for Enhanced Supply Chain Forecasting. In A. Hassan, P. Bhattacharya, P. Dutta, J. Verma, & N. Kundu (Eds.), *Quantum Computing and Supply Chain Management: A New Era of Optimization* (pp. 48–63). IGI Global. https://doi.org/10.4018/979-8-3693-4107-0.ch003.
10. Dutta, P. K., Bhardwaj, A. K., & Mahida, A. (2024). Navigating the Complexities of Agile Transformations in Large Organizations. In A. Hassan, P. Bhattacharya, P. Dutta, J. Verma, & N. Kundu (Eds.), *Quantum Computing and Supply Chain Management: A New Era of Optimization* (pp. 315–330). IGI Global. https://doi.org/10.4018/979-8-3693-4107-0.ch020.
11. Gupta, S., Sarkar, D., Roy, D., Kundu, S., & Dutta, P. K. (2024). Embracing Flexibility and Efficiency: Practical Approaches to Agile Project Management. In S. Misra, R. Jadeja, & M. Mittal (Eds.), *Practical Approaches to Agile Project Management* (pp. 1–8). IGI Global. https://doi.org/10.4018/979-8-3693-3318-1.ch001.

12. Gupta, S., Dutta, P. K., Roy, S., Bhaduri, A., Maji, K., Choudhary, A., & Sarkar, A. (2024). Evaluating Waterfall vs. Agile Models in Software Development for Efficiency and Adaptability. In S. Misra, R. Jadeja, & M. Mittal (Eds.), *Practical Approaches to Agile Project Management* (pp. 142–148). IGI Global. https://doi.org/10.4018/979-8-3693-3318-1.ch008.
13. Patra, A., & Dutta, P. K. (2024). Application of Agile Stage Gate Hybrid Model in the Healthcare Industry: A Paradigm Shift in Project Management. In S. Misra, R. Jadeja, & M. Mittal (Eds.), *Practical Approaches to Agile Project Management* (pp. 149–163). IGI Global. https://doi.org/10.4018/979-8-3693-3318-1.ch009.
14. Singh, B., Vig, K., Dutta, P. K., & Kaunert, C. (2024). Unraveling Agile Transformation for Customer Satisfaction in Changing Market Conditions: Roadmap for Industry Embracing Change in Project Management. In S. Misra, R. Jadeja, & M. Mittal (Eds.), *Practical Approaches to Agile Project Management* (pp. 305–321). IGI Global. https://doi.org/10.4018/979-8-3693-3318-1.ch017.
15. Singh, B., Dutta, P. K., Gautam, R., & Kaunert, C. (2024). Uncapping the Potential of Quantum Computing Towards Manufacturing Optimization: Routing Supply Chain Projecting Sustainability. In A. Hassan, P. Bhattacharya, & P. Dutta (Eds.), *Quantum Computing and Supply Chain Management: A New Era of Optimization* (p. 25). IGI Global. https://doi.org/10.4018/979-8-3693-4107-0.ch024.
16. Dutta, P. K., Singh, B., Towfeek, A.-S. K., Adamopoulou, J. P., Bardavouras, A. N., Bamwerinde, W., Turyasingura, B., & Ayiga, N. (2024). IoT Revolutionizes Humidity Measurement and Management in Smart Cities to Enhance Health and Wellness. *Mesopotamian Journal of Artificial Intelligence in Healthcare* **2024**, 110–117. https://doi.org/10.58496/MJAIH/2024/013.
17. Abotaleb, M., & Dutta, P. K. (2024). Optimizing convolutional neural networks for univariate time series forecasting: a comprehensive guide. In Ramakant Bhardwaj, Pushan Kumar Dutta, Pethuru Raj, Abhishek Kumar, Kavita Saini, Alfonso González Briones, & Mohammed K. A. Kaabar (Eds.), *Hybrid Information Systems: Non-Linear Optimization Strategies with Artificial Intelligence* (pp. 459–472). De Gruyter. https://doi.org/10.1515/9783111331133-022.

Chapter 9

Quantum-driven real-time object detection systems

Seema Kaloria, Indrajit Ghosal, and Narayanage Jayantha Dewasiri

9.1 INTRODUCTION

Multiple Object Tracking (MOT) is a critical component of image recognition systems, enabling real-time analysis and interaction in complex environments. Its applications span diverse domains such as urban traffic management, autonomous navigation, and quality assurance in manufacturing. Despite its importance, MOT faces persistent challenges in balancing computational speed and tracking accuracy, especially in dynamic and crowded scenarios with frequent occlusions [1].

From a theoretical perspective, MOT is often modeled as a combinatorial optimization problem (COP), where the objective is to efficiently associate objects across consecutive video frames. Classical solutions, such as the Hungarian method, are limited by computational scalability, exhibiting cubic complexity with increasing numbers of objects. Addressing these limitations is vital for deploying MOT in real-time systems.

Quantum annealing (QA), a heuristic optimization method rooted in quantum mechanics, has emerged as a promising alternative for solving COPs. Leveraging phenomena such as quantum superposition and tunneling, QA enables efficient exploration of large solution spaces, potentially overcoming the computational bottlenecks of traditional approaches. Additionally, reverse annealing (RA), a variant of QA, allows the refinement of candidate solutions, further enhancing tracking accuracy [2].

This study introduces a novel framework that integrates QA and RA to improve both the speed and accuracy of MOT. The approach employs QA for efficient matching in bipartite graphs and RA for refining tracking results based on prior states. By ensembling object tracking processes, the proposed method enhances robustness against occlusions and misdetections.

To ensure replicability and provide a statistically grounded evaluation, the framework is tested using the UA-DETRAC dataset, a widely recognized benchmark for vehicle tracking in traffic scenarios [3]. Key performance metrics, including Multiple Object Tracking Accuracy (MOTA), ID switches (IDSW), and absolute percentage error (APE), are analyzed to validate the approach. Experimental results demonstrate that the proposed

DOI: 10.1201/9781003498292-9

QA- and RA-based methods achieve significant improvements in both computational efficiency and tracking performance, with an annealing time as low as 3 μs per tracking process [4].

The proposed methods hold substantial potential for real-time MOT applications, including traffic flow management for adaptive signal control, predictive collision avoidance in autonomous systems, and quality control in industrial manufacturing. By addressing current limitations in scalability and accuracy, this research contributes to advancing MOT systems for next-generation applications.

Object detection in computer vision, an essential branch of digital word images, has become an indispensable information medium, and massive amounts of image data are generated every moment. At the same time, accurately identifying objects in images is becoming increasingly important [5]. Object classification is responsible for analyzing the input image to determine the presence of objects belonging to a specific category of interest. It then generates a set of labels with corresponding scores, indicating both the identified category and the likelihood of an object appearing in the image [6]. The object's position and range, the output bounding box, the object's center, or its closed boundary define the spatial characteristics and localization of the detected object within an image. The shape bounding box is the most used choice. Its purpose is to help blind people obtain the classification information of images in a specific environment and process them. Android application cameras can obtain environmental information and identify the type of objects, such as computers, bags, toothbrushes, and other daily necessities. In this way, blind people recognize objects surrounding them in a way that enhances their adaptability and independence in complex environments. Object classification, detection, and segmentation are three primary tasks in computer vision. This topic involves classifying and detecting the first two types of functions [7]. Presently, widely used object identification methods rely on artificial intelligence (AI) models that fall into two categories: The first kind divides the detection procedure into two phases and is known as a two-stage detection strategy. The creation of a candidate region is the first stage. Classifying and locating the potential regions is the second step. The earliest entry of AI into the field of computer vision is to complete the task of object classification and the development of such networks. The main work of this subject is to build a system based on the AI network framework to assist blind people in the surrounding area: the MobileNets network and the classification algorithm design [8] two systems for object recognition. At the same time, a dataset of daily necessities will be constructed, and an object detection system based on a Single Shot Detector (SSD) network will be used to carry the category and location of items returned in real-time on the GPU-based system using MobileNet-based object classification. The classification system returns the object category in real-time on the Android phone and makes voice feedback. The overall design of this project uses two kinds of neural networks to build systems that implement object detection and classification. In order to create an image with a three-dimensional matrix, the RGB camera takes color images for the object identification module. After the picture is gathered, it is sent into the SSD network, where its hyperparameters and parameters are trained, yielding testing results with an accuracy of above 90%. This chapter focuses on the real-time object detection system using TensorFlow Lite [9]. The purpose of this system is to aid blind people in navigating their surroundings, though there are still many areas for improvement. First, it can increase the number of categories for training and collect more data to improve the system's adaptability and robustness of object detection. Second, the system of this subject is not sensitive to small objects, which requires blind people to identify goods only when they are closer to the camera. The solution could be to realize that the camera can be used to build the system [10]. According to the World Health Organization's October 2017 statistics, around 253 million people are visually impaired, with 36 million being blind. Vision, along with hearing, touch, and smell, constitutes a crucial human perception system, and access to visual information is essential for the visually impaired. The impact of visual information on human perception is significantly greater than that of other media, making it imperative to address the information access needs of the visually impaired. Computer vision, an emerging field within AI research, focuses on object detection, a vital branch that generates massive amounts of image data every moment, necessitating accurate object identification. Object classification is responsible for determining whether an input image contains objects of interest and outputs labels with scores, indicating the likelihood of specific objects appearing in the image [11]. It also identifies the object's position, range, bounding box, center, or closed boundary, with the shape bounding box being the most commonly used. The goal is to help blind individuals obtain classification information about images in their environment and process them. Using Android application cameras, environmental information can be captured to identify everyday items like computers, bags, toothbrushes, and other necessities, helping blind individuals navigate their surroundings and enhancing their adaptability and independence in complex environments. Integrating smart room technology with voice-controlled assistance and personalized entertainment further enhances convenience and inclusivity, improving the quality of life for all users. Voice commands enable users to control various aspects of their environment, such as lighting, temperature, and multimedia systems, while personalized entertainment systems learn user preferences to deliver customized content and experiences. This technology not only increases convenience but also fosters a more inclusive environment for individuals with disabilities, promoting greater independence and an improved quality of life. Object classification, detection, and segmentation are three primary tasks in computer vision. This topic involves the first two: classifying and detecting objects. Object classification returns a single image with the category that has the highest confidence, typically the most prominent object in the image. Object detection, however, not only returns all detected object categories in a single image but also identifies their positions. This dual functionality is essential in smart room technology, where voice-controlled assistance and personalized entertainment are key features. In such environments, accurate object detection enables users to interact seamlessly with various devices and systems. Voice commands can control lighting, temperature, and multimedia, while personalized entertainment systems adapt to user preferences, delivering customized content.

9.1.1 Object detection algorithm

Currently, widely used object identification methods rely on AI models that fall into two categories, both essential for smart room technology that provides voice-controlled assistance and personalized entertainment. The first category is a two-stage detection strategy, which involves two phases: creating a candidate region and then classifying and localizing these regions. Exemplified by the R-CNN series, proposed by [12] , this approach uses selective search to identify potential regions in an image, resizes them, and uses a convolutional neural network (CNN) for feature extraction. Finally, a support vector machine (SVM) algorithm determines the category of each candidate region. This method, while accurate, is complex and slow due to its reliance on traditional computer vision algorithms and high computational demands. The second category is a one-stage detection method, which skips the candidate region step and directly applies object detection algorithms to identify categories and locations. This approach enhances detection speed at the cost of some accuracy, crucial for real-time applications in smart room technology. Notable examples include the You Only Look Once (YOLO) series, proposed by [13], and the Single Shot Detector (SSD) series, proposed by [14]. These networks perform end-to-end detection, predicting object positions and types directly from the input image, thereby eliminating the need for traditional algorithms. YOLO's real-time detection capabilities significantly expand AI applications, making it ideal for dynamic smart room environments. Although YOLO's grid-based processing can lead to inaccurate positioning, SSD improves upon this by combining YOLO's speed with anchor box techniques for more precise detection. SSD achieves a 72% mean Average Precision (mAP) and a detection speed of 58 fps (frames per second), making it well-suited for smart room technology, where quick and accurate object identification enhances user experience through seamless voice-controlled assistance and personalized entertainment.

9.1.2. Object classification algorithm

The advent of AI in computer vision began with the development of networks aimed at object classification, a foundational task in the evolution of smart room technology that offers voice-controlled assistance and personalized entertainment. Yann LeCun et al. [15] pioneered gradient-based learning with "Document Recognition," introducing LeNet as the world's first convolutional neural network, featuring key components like convolutional layers, pooling layers, and fully connected layers. Subsequently, [16] revolutionized the field with AlexNet in 2012, achieving breakthrough accuracy in ImageNet competitions. This marked neural networks as the central model for object classification, owing to innovations such as ReLU activation, dropout techniques for regularization, extensive training on the ImageNet database, and GPU acceleration. In 2014, Oxford University's Visual Geometry Group (VGG) proposed VGG-Nets, renowned for their robust performance in the ImageNet localization task. These networks, known for their adaptability and effectiveness, introduced advancements like smaller filters in initial layers and support for multi-scale training and testing. VGG-Nets form the backbone of many modern systems, including the SSD network used in smart room technology, facilitating precise object detection and classification. In 2015, [17] introduced ResNet, pushing the boundaries of AI with its residual learning framework. These advancements in AI have transformed smart room technology, enabling sophisticated capabilities in object recognition that power voice-controlled assistance and deliver personalized entertainment experiences. By integrating these technologies, smart rooms can provide seamless interaction and tailored content, enhancing user convenience and elevating the overall quality of life. The MobileNet architecture is shown in Figure 9.1.

Introduced by [18] MobileNets represent a significant advancement in network design, particularly for mobile and embedded devices [12]. These networks address issues such as gradient disappearance or explosion that can occur during deep network training, significantly enhancing network efficiency compared to conventional models. MobileNets have proven to be formidable competitors in challenges like COCO 2015 and ILSVRC 2015, achieving top rankings in detection, localization, and segmentation tasks. Unlike typical VGG-Nets, MobileNets are more deeply interconnected, offering improved performance while being tailored for the constraints of mobile and embedded device environments [13, 14].

9.2 MAIN DESIGN TASKS AND EXPECTED GOALS

The design of the real-time object detection system is focused on achieving a high level of accuracy while maintaining the speed necessary for real-time applications. In supply chain management, where items such as products

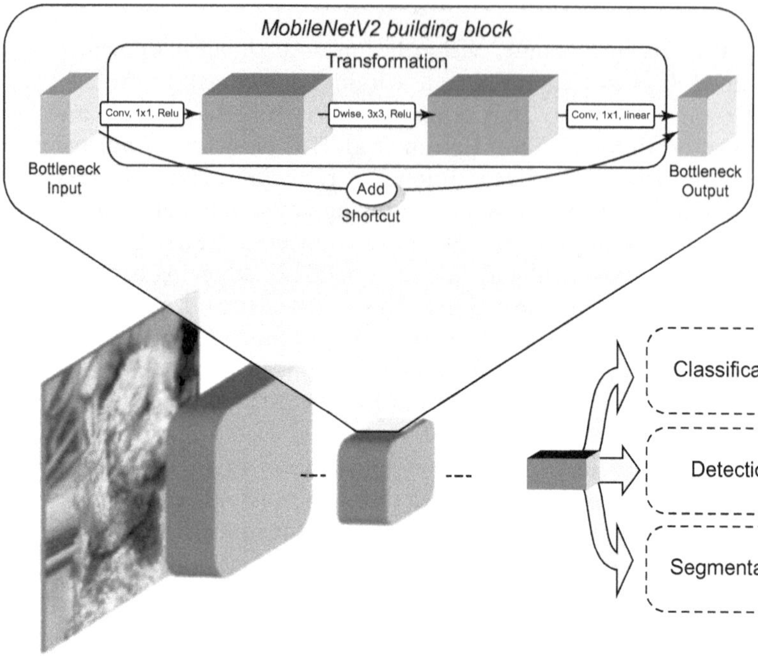

Figure 9.1 MobileNet architecture.

and packaging must be identified and tracked continuously, the system must process vast amounts of data rapidly. This requires careful optimization of the SSD architecture for object detection, allowing it to handle the diverse range of items typically encountered in warehouse and logistics environments. Additionally, by employing MobileNets for object classification, the system becomes lightweight enough for deployment on mobile devices used by warehouse staff. This integration with mobile platforms not only enhances flexibility but also allows staff to move freely within the warehouse while using the system for real-time item identification, making the solution scalable across different industries with varied inventory requirements. The task of data collection and preparation is crucial for ensuring the robustness of the system. By curating a diverse dataset that reflects the various types of products, packaging, and labels commonly found in supply chains, the system is trained to handle real-world scenarios effectively. Data augmentation techniques such as random cropping, flipping, and color adjustments are employed to simulate the wide range of conditions under which items might need to be detected, ensuring consistent performance regardless of environmental variables like lighting or camera angles. This extensive preparation ensures that the system can accurately detect and classify objects across different warehouse environments, reducing the need for manual interventions and increasing overall operational efficiency. Hyperparameter tuning is conducted to achieve an optimal balance between accuracy and speed, which is essential in fast-paced logistics environments where delays in item identification can lead to bottlenecks. Additionally, the system is designed to operate with minimal latency, allowing for seamless real-time object detection and classification without compromising the workflow. The deployment of the system is equally important for its success in a practical supply chain setting. The Android-based mobile application developed for warehouse staff ensures that the system can be used on the go, providing real-time feedback on inventory levels and product identification. The integration of voice feedback allows for hands-free operation, which is particularly useful in environments where workers need to multitask. This holistic approach not only streamlines warehouse operations but also enhances the overall user experience, contributing to a more efficient and error-free supply chain management process. The primary focus of this project is to develop a system using AI frameworks to aid visually impaired individuals in their surroundings. The project involves implementing two systems based on the MobileNets network and designing classification algorithms for object recognition. Additionally, a dataset containing common everyday items will be curated. Using the Single Shot Detector (SSD) network, an object detection system will be deployed to accurately identify and locate items in real time. This system will operate on a GPU-based platform, utilizing MobileNet-based object classification to swiftly classify objects. The classification system will provide real-time object category feedback on an Android phone, facilitating voice-based feedback for enhanced usability and accessibility.

9.2.1 Overall design scheme

This chapter explores the application of real-time object recognition systems in supply chain management, addressing critical challenges in inventory tracking, warehouse management, and quality control. The methodology outlined here demonstrates how AI-powered visual recognition can revolutionize supply chain operations, offering insights applicable to various industries. In today's fast-paced global marketplace, how can supply chain managers ensure accurate, real-time inventory tracking across complex logistics networks? How can warehouses improve efficiency and reduce human error in item identification and sorting? What technologies can be leveraged to enhance quality control processes in manufacturing and distribution? These pressing questions underscore the need for innovative solutions in supply chain management, particularly as industries face increasing pressure to optimize operations and reduce costs.

The rapid evolution of e-commerce and just-in-time manufacturing has intensified the demand for precise, instantaneous inventory management. Traditional methods of barcode scanning and manual counting are proving inadequate in meeting the speed and accuracy requirements of modern supply chains. Furthermore, the rise of omnichannel retail and the expectation of seamless integration between online and offline inventory systems have created new challenges for supply chain managers. Recent studies have highlighted significant gaps in the literature regarding the application of advanced AI technologies in supply chain visual recognition tasks. While Radio Frequency Identification (RFID) and Internet of Things (IoT) solutions have been widely discussed, the potential of AI-powered object recognition systems remains underexplored in the context of supply chain management. This chapter aims to address this gap by presenting a novel approach that combines deep learning algorithms with mobile technology to create a versatile, real-time object recognition system. Industry trends further justify the importance of this research. The global warehouse automation market is projected to grow at a Compound Annual Growth Rate (CAGR) of 14% from 2021 to 2026, driven by the need for more efficient and accurate inventory management systems. This methodology provides a comprehensive framework for implementing AI-powered visual recognition in supply chain operations. By addressing key challenges in inventory management, warehouse efficiency, and quality control, this approach offers significant potential for improving supply chain performance across various industries. The following sections will delve into the implementation details, results, and implications of this system for modern supply chain management practices. This project employs two types of neural networks to develop systems for object detection and classification. Using an Red Green Blue (RGB) camera, which captures color images represented as three-dimensional matrices, the system gathers images for the object identification module. These images are then processed through the Single Shot Detector (SSD) network, where both hyperparameters and parameters are trained. The trained network achieves testing results with an accuracy exceeding 90%, demonstrating its effectiveness in accurately detecting and classifying objects in real-world scenarios (Figure 9.2).

The outcome includes a bounding box outlining the detected object and its corresponding label. This information is visually overlaid on the input image, after which the network is prepared for the next image capture. Once the camera captures an image, the Android-TensorFlow user interface promptly forwards it to the network. Based on the returned results, the Android application displays the detected object category and its confidence level in real time. When the confidence level surpasses 0.8, the identified category is announced via voice. Each network achieves an average forward propagation time of 200 ms, enabling the system to achieve real-time detection capabilities on the Android platform. Real-time tracking systems enable logistics managers to monitor vehicle locations and traffic conditions continuously. This allows for dynamic rerouting to avoid congestion, road closures, or adverse weather, leading to reduced fuel consumption and wear on vehicles. By optimizing routes, companies can ensure timely deliveries while minimizing transportation costs. With real-time visibility into

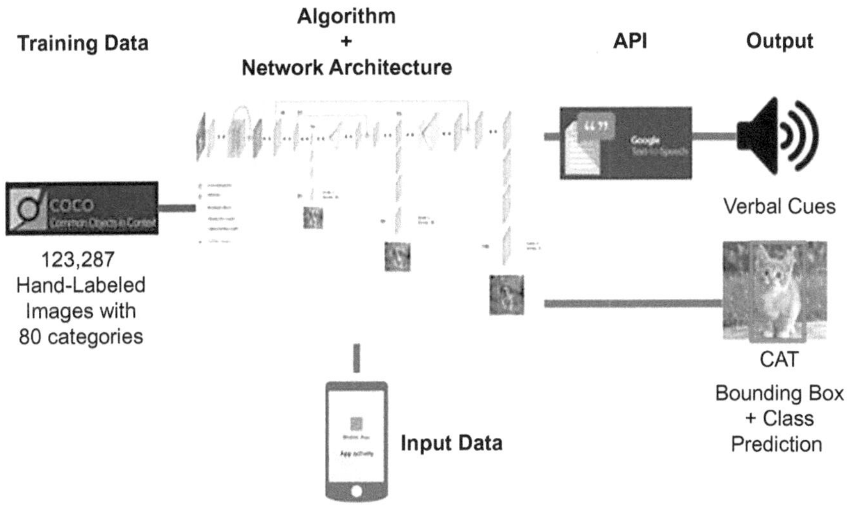

Figure 9.2 Design scheme.

inventory levels and shipment statuses, businesses can manage their stock more effectively. This capability reduces excess inventory and storage costs by enabling accurate demand forecasting and ensuring that the right products are available when needed. Efficient inventory management minimizes the risk of stockouts and overstock situations, which can lead to significant cost reductions. Real-time tracking provides early warnings about potential disruptions, such as traffic delays or adverse weather conditions. By identifying these issues proactively, companies can take corrective actions to reroute shipments, thereby minimizing the impact of delays on operations.

9.2.2 TensorFlow AI framework

TensorFlow, developed by Google, is a prominent software library utilized in machine learning applications. As the field of AI research expands, numerous open-source frameworks such as TensorFlow, Caffe, Keras, CNTK, Torch7, and MXNet continue to emerge. Figure 9.3 illustrates the architecture of TensorFlow, which is available in two main versions: CPU-only TensorFlow and TensorFlow with GPU support. For environments requiring GPU acceleration, such as servers or high-performance computing setups, TensorFlow with GPU support is essential for leveraging the computational power of GPUs. Installing TensorFlow with GPU support involves setting up an independent virtual machine on the server to prevent conflicts with other Python-based packages in the system. This setup ensures optimal performance and compatibility with GPU hardware, enhancing the speed and efficiency of AI tasks. On the other hand, for environments where GPU resources are not available or not needed, the CPU-only version

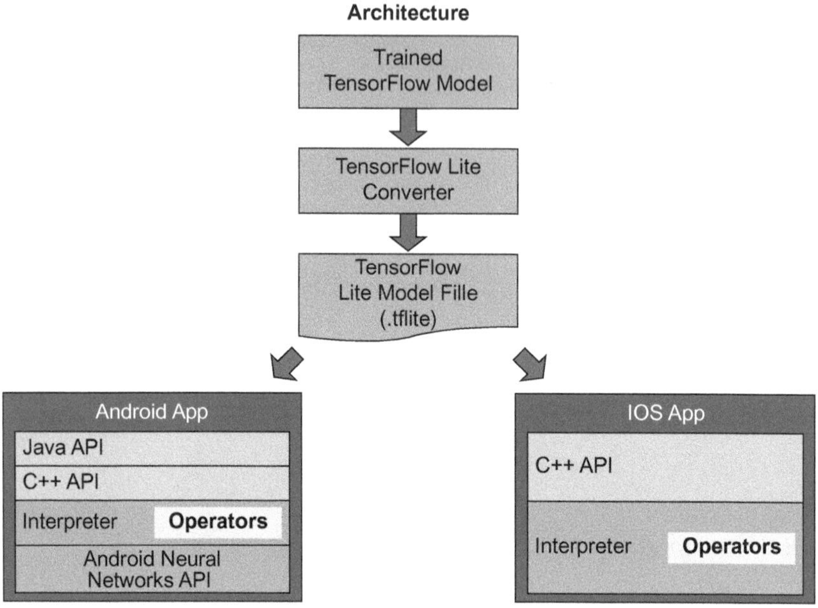

Figure 9.3 TensorFlow architecture.

of TensorFlow can be installed directly on compatible systems using the pip command. This version is suitable for development on notebooks or systems without GPU capabilities, providing a versatile platform for experimenting with machine learning models. TensorFlow supports various Python versions, with compatibility typically extending to versions like 3.5.x and 3.6.x. This flexibility allows developers and researchers to choose the version that best suits their project requirements and hardware capabilities, ensuring seamless integration and optimal performance in AI applications.

9.2.3 Object detection network design

The Single Shot Detector (SSD) object detection network in this project is structured into two main components: utilizing VGG-Nets for the initial stages and incorporating the SSD framework for the latter stages. VGG-Nets serve as the primary classification network, known for their conventional architecture and simplicity [15]. The SSD detector builds upon the VGG16 network, where the first five layers are used for basic classification tasks. The subsequent layers, fc6 and fc7, are converted into convolutional layers, followed by three additional convolutional layers with varying channel numbers, each with a receptive field of 1×1 and a global average pooling layer. Starting from the sixth convolutional layer, feature maps from each layer are utilized to predict the size, position, and categories of objects using default boxes.

9.2.4 Problem statement and theoretical context

Multiple Object Tracking (MOT) in supply chain environments, such as warehouses or distribution centers, presents unique challenges. These include varying object scales, frequent occlusions, and the necessity for real-time tracking. Addressing these challenges requires systems capable of not only detecting and localizing objects but also tracking their movements across frames efficiently.

In this context, the proposed framework incorporates advanced object detection and classification networks as foundational elements, leveraging cutting-edge techniques like quantum annealing (QA) and reverse annealing (RA) to optimize multi-object tracking tasks.

9.2.4.1 Step 1: Object detection network

The *object detection network*, based on the Single Shot Detector (SSD) architecture, serves as the backbone for identifying and localizing items in dynamic environments. SSD's capability to detect objects at multiple scales makes it suitable for warehouses where items vary in size and placement.

- **Dataset preparation:** A custom dataset of 10,000+ annotated images ensures the model's adaptability to diverse supply chain scenarios.
- **Data augmentation:** Techniques like random cropping and flipping enhance the robustness of the network, crucial for handling real-world variances.
- **Loss function:** A combination of Smooth L1 (localization loss) and Softmax (confidence loss) ensures precise detection and accurate classification of objects.
- **Implementation:** Using TensorFlow enables scalable deployments, while transfer learning with pretrained COCO weights ensures a strong starting point, fine-tuned for supply chain specifics.
- **Optimization:** Hyperparameters were adjusted to strike a balance between accuracy and inference speed, meeting real-time demands in busy warehouses.

The SSD model integrates seamlessly into real-world workflows through TensorFlow Serving, enabling API-based interactions with Warehouse Management Systems (WMS).

9.2.4.2 Step 2: Object classification network

For detailed classification, a **MobileNet-based classification system** is employed. MobileNet's use of depthwise separable convolutions optimizes computational efficiency, reducing model size and inference time. This design makes it ideal for mobile and embedded platforms, aligning with the need for real-time applications in supply chains.

- **Design and training:** The architecture leverages TensorFlow Slim for streamlined model definition and training. Using the same curated dataset ensures consistency across detection and classification tasks.
- **Deployment:** The trained model is optimized for mobile platforms with TensorFlow Lite, facilitating direct integration into Android applications. This enables warehouse staff to perform real-time classification tasks on handheld devices.

9.2.4.3 Proposed integration with quantum annealing

Building upon the SSD and MobileNet frameworks, the proposed QA-based MOT methodology addresses limitations in scalability and accuracy. The sequential nature of MOT, coupled with the ability to ensemble multiple tracking solutions, enhances performance in challenging conditions such as occlusions and high object density.

- **QA for matching:** By formulating MOT as a combinatorial optimization problem (QUBO), the bipartite graph matching is accelerated, ensuring scalability with an increasing number of objects.
- **RA for refinement:** Utilizing prior state predictions, RA refines tracking results, reducing errors and enhancing robustness.

9.2.5 Experimentation and validation

Using the curated dataset and TensorFlow implementations, experiments validate the proposed approach's efficacy:

- Metrics such as MOTA, IDF1, and APE demonstrate the advantages of QA and RA in maintaining high accuracy and low computational latency.
- Real-world deployment scenarios, including traffic flow measurement and inventory management, showcase the framework's practical utility.

9.3 SYSTEM TESTING, VERIFICATION, AND RESULT ANALYSIS

9.3.1 Analysis of the results of the object detection system

In this project focused on item identification, a dataset specifically curated for clocks is maintained, comprising 2635 images. Within this dataset, 487 images are annotated with instances of clocks. Each image is fully annotated using software that categorizes and provides comprehensive labels, ensuring detailed identification of clock instances. Prior to training the

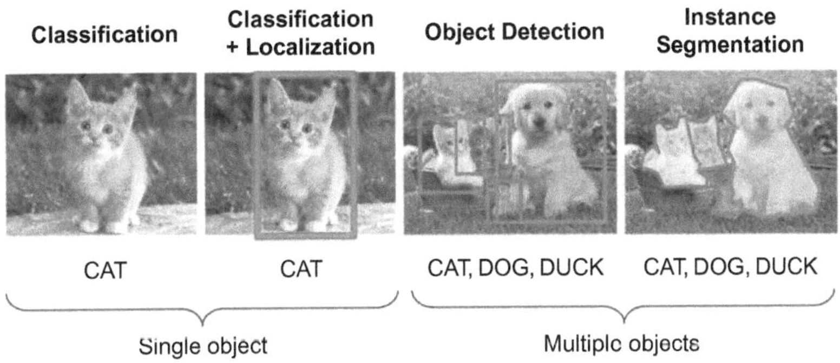

Figure 9.4 Analysis of the results of the object detection System.

model, various hyperparameters are configured to optimize performance and accuracy during the training process. These hyperparameters are crucial for fine-tuning the model's learning process and enhancing its ability to accurately detect and classify clocks within the images. An analysis of the object-detecting system's findings is presented in Figure 9.4.

During the training phase deployed on the server, efforts focus on optimizing training times for improved efficiency. Post-training, the model demonstrates high accuracy in single object detection, achieving confidence levels exceeding 0.99 on test images. Following the successful evaluation of single images, the network is adapted for real-time detection. Real-time and video detection share the same network principles and methods for network calls.

In the project's setup, real-time video detection is implemented using OpenCV for seamless stream reading and output handling. This approach ensures compatibility and facilitates testing with input video streams directly, without requiring direct camera calls within the program. By leveraging OpenCV's capabilities, the system can efficiently process and analyze video feeds, demonstrating robust performance in detecting objects, particularly clocks, in dynamic visual environments.

9.4 SUMMARY

9.4.1 Features and summary of this design

This project focuses on developing an advanced image recognition system tailored for visually impaired individuals, leveraging AI advancements in computer vision. Beginning with a review of AI's impact on image detection, the study highlights the creation of two critical tools: an image detection system with 2635 color images and corresponding .xml files defining default boxes, and an image classification system with 11,200 images across eight object classes. Using TensorFlow, two convolutional neural networks were trained: an SSD object detection network featuring 10 convolutional layers and a global pooling layer, and a MobileNet-based object classification network with 27 layers including convolutional, pooling, and fully connected layers. Deployment spans both PC and Android platforms, with real-time video detection handled by SSD on PC and MobileNets on Android for object classification via smartphone cameras. The system includes an audio feedback library for real-time results on Android, enhancing user interaction and accessibility in identifying surrounding objects autonomously.

9.4.2 Problems and thinking in design

Initially, the training encountered issues with loss convergence. To mitigate this, adjustments were made by increasing the learning rate and reducing the number of trainable layers. Gradient descent was allowed to stabilize over the first 1000 steps, and training was stopped when oscillations in loss amplitude became excessive. By fine-tuning these parameters iteratively and reinitializing from checkpoints, the network eventually converged to an acceptable loss value, signaling the completion of training [16]. Another persistent issue during the early training stages was dimension mismatch errors. This arose from discrepancies between the network's original class specifications and those required for the project's specific classes. Despite modifying program settings to match intended classes, errors persisted. The resolution came through structural adjustments in the network parameters, particularly fine-tuning the final layers to align the network's class configurations with the study requirements [17]. A notable challenge involved achieving accurate image detection for multiple objects. Despite attempting various data augmentation techniques, none significantly improved detection accuracy. The ultimate solution was to expand the multi-object dataset substantially, addressing the issue through increased data diversity rather than augmentation methods [18].

9.5 CONCLUSION

The implementation of AI-powered visual recognition systems in supply chain management, as detailed in this chapter, represents a significant leap forward in addressing key challenges in inventory tracking, warehouse management, and quality control. By leveraging the Single Shot Detector (SSD) architecture for object detection and MobileNets for efficient classification on mobile devices, the proposed system demonstrates remarkable potential for enhancing accuracy and efficiency in real-time inventory management. The successful deployment of these models using TensorFlow and TensorFlow Lite showcases the scalability and versatility of the solution across various supply chain environments. These findings strongly support the chapter's thesis that AI-based visual recognition can revolutionize supply chain operations, offering tangible benefits in terms of reduced errors, improved tracking, and enhanced operational efficiency. Looking ahead, the implications of this technology are far-reaching, promising substantial cost savings and operational improvements throughout the supply chain. Future research directions may include expanding the system's capabilities to handle an even wider range of products, integrating predictive analytics for demand forecasting, and exploring federated learning approaches for continuous model improvement across distributed warehouse locations. As this technology continues to evolve, it raises important questions about the changing nature of workforce skills in logistics, the potential for broader applications in quality control and last-mile delivery, and the ethical considerations surrounding increased AI adoption in supply chain management. Ultimately, this chapter not only highlights the current state of AI-powered visual recognition in supply chains but also sets the stage for future innovations that could fundamentally transform how businesses manage their logistics and inventory processes.

REFERENCES

1. Dutta, P. K., Ghosh, D., & Abotaleb, M. (2024). Harnessing the Power of Hybrid Models for Supply Chain Management and Optimization. In Ramakant Bhardwaj, Pushan Kumar Dutta, Pethuru Raj, Abhishek Kumar, Kavita Saini, Alfonso González Briones, & Mohammed K. A. Kaabar (Eds.), *Hybrid Information Systems: Non-Linear Optimization Strategies with Artificial Intelligence* (pp. 407–426). De Gruyter. https://doi.org/10.1515/9783111331133-019.
2. Abotaleb, M., & Dutta, P. K. (2024). Optimizing Bidirectional Long Short-Term Memory Networks for Univariate Time Series Forecasting: A Comprehensive Guide. In Ramakant Bhardwaj, Pushan Kumar Dutta, Pethuru Raj, Abhishek Kumar, Kavita Saini, Alfonso González Briones, & Mohammed K. A. Kaabar (Eds.), *Hybrid Information Systems: Non-Linear Optimization Strategies with Artificial Intelligence* (pp. 443–458). De Gruyter, https://doi.org/10.1515/9783111331133-021.
3. Dhaliwal, N., Aghera, S., Whig, P., & Dutta, P. K. (2024). Advanced Analytics and Quantum Computing for Revolutionizing Procurement Strategies. In A. Hassan, P. Bhattacharya, P. Dutta, J. Verma, & N. Kundu (Eds.), *Quantum Computing and Supply Chain Management: A New Era of Optimization* (pp. 160–175). IGI Global. https://doi.org/10.4018/979-8-3693-4107-0.ch011.
4. Singh, B., Dutta, P. K., & Kaunert, C. (2024). Boosting Quantum Computing to Redefine Supply Chain in the Hospital Industry: Pitch the Vision for Medical and Healthcare Needs. In A. Hassan, P. Bhattacharya, P. Dutta, J. Verma, & N. Kundu (Eds.), *Quantum Computing and Supply Chain Management: A New Era of Optimization* (pp. 196–219). IGI Global. https://doi.org/10.4018/979-8-3693-4107-0.ch014.

5. Dutta, P. K., El-kenawy, S. M., Ali, G., & Dhoska, K. (2023). An Energy Consumption Monitoring and Control System in Buildings using Internet of Things. *Babylonian Journal of Internet of Things*, 2023, 38–47. https://doi.org/10.58496/BJIoT/2023/006.
6. Dutta, P. K., El-kenawy, S. M., Abotaleb, M., & Eid, M. M. (2023). AI-Driven Marketplaces and Price Prediction Tools for Rag Pickers: Enhancing Economic Opportunities in Africa's Circular Economy. *Babylonian Journal of Artificial Intelligence*, 2023, 33–42. https://doi.org/10.58496/BJAI/2023/007.
7. Dutta, P. K., Bhardwaj, A. K., & Mahida, A. (2024). Navigating the Complexities of Agile Transformations in Large Organizations. In A. Hassan, P. Bhattacharya, P. Dutta, J. Verma, & N. Kundu (Eds.), *Quantum Computing and Supply Chain Management: A New Era of Optimization* (pp. 315–330). IGI Global. https://doi.org/10.4018/979-8-3693-4107-0.ch020.
8. Gutta, L. M., Dhamodharan, B., Dutta, P. K., & Whig, P. (2024). AI-Infused Quantum Machine Learning for Enhanced Supply Chain Forecasting. In A. Hassan, P. Bhattacharya, P. Dutta, J. Verma, & N. Kundu (Eds.), *Quantum Computing and Supply Chain Management: A New Era of Optimization* (pp. 48–63). IGI Global. https://doi.org/10.4018/979-8-3693-4107-0.ch003.
9. Biswas, A., & Dutta, P. K. (2020, January). Novel Approach of Automation to Risk Management: The Reduction in Human Errors. In *International Conference on Mobile Computing and Sustainable Informatics* (pp. 683–696). Springer International Publishing.
10. Dutta, P. K., Bhardwaj, A. K., & Mahida, A. (2024). Navigating the Complexities of Agile Transformations in Large Organizations. In A. Hassan, P. Bhattacharya, P. Dutta, J. Verma, & N. Kundu (Eds.), *Quantum Computing and Supply Chain Management: A New Era of Optimization* (pp. 315–330). IGI Global. https://doi.org/10.4018/979-8-3693-4107-0.ch020.
11. Gupta, S., Sarkar, D., Roy, D., Kundu, S., & Dutta, P. K. (2024). Embracing Flexibility and Efficiency: Practical Approaches to Agile Project Management. In S. Misra, R. Jadeja, & M. Mittal (Eds.), *Practical Approaches to Agile Project Management* (pp. 1–8). IGI Global. https://doi.org/10.4018/979-8-3693-3318-1.ch001.
12. Girshick, R., Donahue, J., Darrell, T., & Malik, J. (2015). Region-based convolutional networks for accurate object detection and segmentation. *IEEE Transactions on Pattern Analysis and Machine Intelligence*, 38(1), 142–158.
13. Redmon, J., Divvala, S., Girshick, R., & Farhadi, A. (2016). You only look once: Unified, real-time object detection. In *Proceedings of the IEEE conference on computer vision and pattern recognition* (pp. 779-788).
14. Dai, Y., Liu, W., Wang, H., Xie, W., & Long, K. (2022). Yolo-former: Marrying yolo and transformer for foreign object detection. *IEEE Transactions on Instrumentation and Measurement*, 71, 1–14.
15. Rudman, W., Golovanesky, M., Bar, A., Palit, V., LeCun, Y., Eickhoff, C., & Singh, R. (2025). Forgotten polygons: Multimodal large language models are shape-blind. *arXiv preprint, arXiv:2502.15969*. https://doi.org/10.48550/arXiv.2502.15969.
16. Krizhevsky, A., Sutskever, I., & Hinton, G. E. (2017). ImageNet classification with deep convolutional neural networks. *Communications of the ACM*, 60(6), 84–90. https://doi.org/10.1145/306538617.

17. He, K., Chen, X., Xie, S., Li, Y., Dollár, P., & Girshick, R. (2021). Masked autoencoders are scalable vision learners. *arXiv preprint, arXiv:2111.06377.* https://doi.org/10.48550/arXiv.2111.06377.
18. Howard, A. G., Zhu, M., Chen, B., Kalenichenko, D., Wang, W., Weyand, T., Andreetto, M., & Adam, H. (2017). MobileNets: Efficient convolutional neural networks for mobile vision applications. *arXiv preprint, arXiv:1704.04861.* https://doi.org/10.48550/arXiv.1704.04861.

Chapter 10

Quantum-enhanced feature extraction for smart logistics and transportation systems

Akshat Bokdia, Nitin Lodha, and Vijayarajan V.

10.1 INTRODUCTION

The advanced driver-assistance systems (ADAS) represent the most sophisticated technologies advancing in the automobile technology field toward safety driving and automation of driving processes. At the heart of these systems lies accurate traffic sign detection and classification without which there would be no safe navigation through the roads and adherence to relevant traffic rules. The development of algorithms with strong capabilities to identify and interpret road signs under adverse conditions related to bad visibility caused by either local weather or lighting is critical in an automated system. This chapter transforms a classical traffic sign recognition task into an even more challenging one, at least in this case, by bringing in quantum-enhanced feature extraction techniques toward increasing the accuracy and efficiency required for these systems, especially those at higher dimensional and complex data regimes.

This work mainly refers to one of the most frequently used and challenging benchmarks for testing traffic sign recognition systems, specifically the German Traffic Sign Recognition Benchmark (GTSRB) dataset. Difficulty scenarios taken from the GTSRB dataset cover all challenging situations any traffic sign classification model needs to handle; thus, this dataset constitutes the perfect testbed for the comparison and refinement of feature extraction methodologies. Therefore, the research work of the chapter deals with an evaluation of the ability of three state-of-art feature extraction techniques: autoencoders, DWT combined with SVD, and the hybrid technique integrated with Sobel operators, DWT, and SVD. The merits of each proposed method lie in handling these complex images of traffic signs.

Autoencoders are considered a modality of automatic learning of complex, high-level features by deep neural network architectures. Such models encode and reconstruct images better, thus capturing abstract, high-dimensional features toward perfect recognition of traffic signs. In addition, this chapter investigates the potential of DWT along with SVD in the direct extraction of salient features from the dataset. This technique uses the multi-resolution analysis by applying DWT and reduces its dimension via

 DOI: 10.1201/9781003498292-10

SVD in order to improve the discriminative power of a model, thus providing much more accurate distinctions between similar traffic signs.

Further, the hybrid nature of the research involves the combined use of Sobel operators along with DWT and SVD. The Sobel operators are very efficient for edge and boundary detection so can be suitably applied to traffic sign border identification. The hybrid method, which uses both DWT and SVD together, captures textural detail and spatial structures at different levels of scales and consequently could extract features more elaborately and accurately. It is expected that the edge detection combination along with multi-resolution analysis may prove to strengthen the system's efficiency toward recognition of traffic signs, even in the presence of partial occlusions or image noise.

This chapter further explores the possible enhancements that quantum capabilities can bring to feature extraction beyond the different forms of classical feature extraction techniques applied. The use of quantum algorithms such as Quantum PCA and Quantum Clustering speeds up the training and execution processes and significantly improves efficiency along with higher scalability, especially for large, complicated datasets, when applied within smart logistics and transportation systems. New features allow tremendous possibilities in terms of speedup, exponential precision, and robustness; hence, this indeed turns out to be a promising frontier for future ADAS applications.

This chapter aims to evaluate and compare such feature extraction techniques, classical and quantum-enhanced, in order to develop a robust model wherein accuracy in the classification of traffic signs will considerably improve. Such superior results in precision for the classifying operation are desired here in this chapter that logically will lead to advancements in building more complex automated traffic systems that shall be implemented in both existing and emergent vehicle technologies. Further, the methods developed here scale and adapt and present room for application, possibly scaled up to international datasets and more comprehensive areas such as optimization of logistics systems, supply chain management, and designs of autonomous driving systems. This foresight of analysis does not only solve the previously mentioned traffic sign recognition challenges but rather lays down a foundation for the development of integrating state-of-the-art quantum computing techniques into the rapidly emerging world of smart transportation systems.

10.2 LITERATURE REVIEW

This field of traffic sign detection and recognition has seen considerable development, and several methods have been proposed to overcome the problems at hand while dealing with such a challenging area of study. Abdi and Meddeb et al. [1] proposed the Haar Cascade detector-based method that reduces the computational overhead in the hypothesis collection for verification to a great extent. This being a systematic process is often divided into three main stages: Hypothesis Generation, Verification, and Augmentation. The methodology utilized the multi-class sign classifier through a linear SVM by the introduction of a verification phase using a deep learning algorithm, such that the result of a detected ROI is assigned to a 3D sign, particularly an efficient process for traffic sign classification.

Some basic methods are the backbone of such proposals; for instance, Aziz et al. [2] proposed an integrated complementary and discriminative feature set, combining HOG with compound LBP, applied to images and further processed with the ELM algorithm. Then, extensive testing on the German Traffic Sign Recognition Benchmark and Belgium Traffic Sign Classifier proved them to be highly efficient for real-time applications.

Addressing specific challenges such as damaged or faded traffic signs, Rahmad et al. [3] proposed a model designed to surmount such problems. The model consists of two phases of operation: segmentation, using normalized RGB in processing blobs extracted from images, and traffic sign recognition. This phase of recognition includes feature selection and extraction methods such as HOG, Gabor, and LBG, followed by classification methods using SVM, KNN, Random Forest, and Naive Bayes. The model was applied to the Indonesian Traffic Sign dataset and achieved an excellent precision of 98.7%, with a recall of 95%, proving the strength of the model under all conditions.

To step aside from traditional approaches, Sun et al. [4] discussed the use of an extreme learning machine as an alternative to a convolutional neural network (CNN) for feature extraction. The proposed method in this chapter uses the advantage of multiple layers to extract features, training with multi-layer vectors in different directions, This approach addresses challenges such as blurriness and color fading, which usually require heavy processing with CNNs. The results obtained from the Kernel ELM classifier proved promising for the problems of non-linear sampling and showed higher accuracy, precision, and recall compared to the conventional traffic sign recognition models.

Ahmed et al. [5] extend the capability of the traffic sign recognition system by proposing a model based on CNNs for the detection and recognition of traffic signs under challenging conditions. This model is further divided into three modules according to form: the CNN classifier approach, the enhancement net approach, and the architecture of encoder–decoder CNN for image enhancement. The model is trained with the big balanced Traffic Videos Dataset, CURE-TSD with precision of 91.1% and recall of 70.71%, significantly higher than those of general models applied to real complicated environments.

Ertler et al. [6] discussed the requirement for a broad dataset and hence proposed the development of a global traffic sign data set consisting of 100,000 street-level images from around the world. The dataset collected under different lighting and climatic conditions of various geographical regions contains 300 classes of traffic signs. The dataset consists of 52,000 completely annotated images and 48,000 partially annotated images. This chapter places the dataset as a valuable contribution to benchmarking, thereby contributing to the standardization and comparability of traffic sign recognition models from different regions.

For efficiency, Natarajan et al. [7] focused on the high-time complexes of current traffic sign detection models with a weighted multi-CNN-trained model. This indeed achieved an impressive recognition rate of 99.59%, achieving times as low as 10 ms on an NVIDIA 980 Ti GPU. It is also characterized by low complexity and high efficiency, allowing it to be executed in real-time to recognize traffic signs. The model was trained on the German Traffic Sign Recognition Benchmark dataset.

Begin the review of some of the methods toward the detection of traffic signs by ADAS and autonomous cars in a generalized manner. Detection methods can be best represented by the work of Saadna et al. [8]. The proposed techniques for detection are generally categorized into three groups: color-based techniques, shape-based techniques, and learning-based techniques. These categories are further divided into categories based on handcrafted feature extraction, which include HOG, Gabor, LBG, and SIFT, while deep learning methods include mainly CNN. With ample details, the performance metrics have also been added to give a general perspective of recent trends in the field.

Zhang et al. developed an end-to-end YOLOv2-based convolution network approach for detecting signs. It chiefly makes use of 1D convolution layers to save computational cost; the images are divided into dense grids so that fine feature maps can be captured. Because of the special nature of the design of Chinese road signs, this model performs very well and surely outperforms any other model in the detection and categorization of the signs within this framework.

Promlainak et al. [10] tackled the regional problem and succeeded in proposing a model for the recognition of Thai traffic signs. This system has two methods running in the same system: Thai TSD uses a cascade classifier trained with HOG features to detect traffic signs. On the other hand, French TSD uses a linear SVM classifier to recognize the traffic signs using HOG features. This opens insight into finding any region-specific discrepancies that may very well occur within a traffic sign recognition framework.

Hechri et al. [11] proposed a two-stage approach to detect and classify live traffic signs, taking an appropriate trade-off between complexity and performance. This two-step approach will classify the recognition and categorize the signs into two shapes in the first step: triangles and circles, using linear SVM over HOG features. The subclasses are then classified by means of CNN. It has been tested on the German Traffic Sign Recognition Benchmark and German Traffic Sign Detection Benchmark datasets. With this methodology, results similar to those state-of-the-art were achieved, but it was computationally less intensive and hence practical for real-world application.

Lim et al. [12] presented an approach, based on general-purpose computing on graphics processing units (GPGPU), of live traffic sign classification and detection with issues related to poor light conditions. It is effective in low-light environments and is efficient for live traffic sign classification and detection with GPGPU, and hierarchical region detection and recognition. Evidence of the approach's effectiveness is provided by its performance on the Vienna Convention on Traffic Rules dataset, which includes German and South Korean road signs, achieving an F1 score of 0.97.

Youssouf et al. [13] introduced an architecture of CNN trained on a GTSRB dataset for the identification of traffic signs. High accuracy has been achieved through Faster R-CNN and YOLOv4 models for real-time detection. As for the chosen approaches, YOLOv4 is the most accurate and fastest model. This work shows that deep learning can be effectively applied to the implementation of reliable and efficient traffic sign recognition. It has been pointed out that techniques for data augmentation play a significant role in model performance.

On a larger scale, Lim et al. provided an essential overview of the most recent variations regarding traffic sign recognition, revolving around the intricacies and challenges the task inherently possesses. Furthermore, the chapter explained that road signs may arise with variability across regions and backgrounds. Besides these advances, this review has pointed out that further studies are still required to overcome part of these challenges and ensure the reliability of the traffic sign recognition system while driving, specifically under autonomous driving conditions. It really provides a valuable reference for researchers and practitioners working in the field, enabling a road map for future developments regarding traffic sign recognition technology.

Dang et al. [14] applied deep learning and blockchain technology to evaluate and mitigate risks in the supply chain finance market, addressing the challenges posed by the evolving financial landscape. By constructing a credit evaluation model using deep learning, they predicted potential credit risks, while blockchain technology was utilized to optimize this model, enhancing reliability and reducing risks. The experimental results demonstrated a high fitting effect, proving the model's effectiveness in analyzing and predicting credit risk in supply chain finance. This study provides valuable insights for improving risk management in supply chain finance using advanced technologies.

Correll et al. [15] explored the use of hybrid classical-quantum algorithms for vehicle routing in supply chain logistics, focusing on neural networks with embedded quantum circuits. The study highlighted how projecting high-dimensional feature vectors to smaller ones is essential due to noisy intermediate-scale quantum (NISQ) hardware limitations. The multi-head attention mechanism facilitated this process, producing results comparable to human truck assignments. The chapter emphasizes the potential of quantum circuits in reinforcement learning models for logistics, though further work is required to optimize quantum circuits and improve training methods.

Sehrawat et al. [16] explored the application of quantum machine learning (QML) for demand prediction in supply chain networks. They outlined the limitations of traditional forecasting methods in addressing the complexities of modern supply chains and showed how QML, by utilizing quantum computing's strengths, could significantly improve prediction accuracy and efficiency. Through case studies, the authors demonstrated how QML techniques can assist organizations in making better decisions, optimizing inventory, and enhancing overall supply chain performance. This work serves as a valuable reference for researchers and practitioners seeking to leverage QML in demand forecasting.

Gutta et al. [17] examined the integration of artificial intelligence (AI) with quantum machine learning (QML) to improve supply chain forecasting. The chapter outlined how the combination of AI's data analysis capabilities with QML's strength in processing complex probabilistic distributions enhances demand forecasting, inventory optimization, and risk mitigation. Through case studies, the authors demonstrated how AI-infused QML models could significantly improve accuracy and efficiency in supply chain forecasting, offering a transformative approach for organizations to boost resilience and competitiveness in the global market. This study provides a valuable foundation for future advancements in supply chain management technologies.

10.3 PROPOSED METHODOLOGY

The study at hand focuses on the performances shown by three distinct feature extraction methodologies that enhance traffic sign classification and are considered in reference to the German Traffic Sign Recognition Benchmark dataset. The methods being focused on include autoencoders, a combination of DWT with SVD, and the Sobel operator with DWT + SVD. Autoencoders, an unsupervised Deep Learning model, translate an image into a latent space of low dimension to retrieve the abstract high-level features, which can capture major patterns and anomalies relative to the classification tasks. This encoded version is then decoded in order to reconstruct the original form of the image. In the DWT + SVD approach, DWT is applied directly to decompose the image into wavelet coefficients, and with the help of SVD, the distillation of key features is done. Sobel operators with DWT and SVD detect edges in images with major variations in intensity. The Sobel operator detects the edge, whereas DWT performs multi-resolution analysis of edge-detected images. DWT is applied for further dimensionality reduction and to enhance the extraction efficiency of dominant structural and textural features. The SVD is applied to wavelet coefficients. The extracted features from each set are classified using the convolutional neural network. This chapter explores how these techniques may help improve classification accuracy for the building of Advanced Driver Assistance Systems and intelligent logistics solutions. In addition to classical methods, this study also explores the existence of quantum-enhanced methods that introduce critical opportunities in speeding up and optimizing the feature extraction processes in high-dimensional data sets.

10.3.1 Data collection and preprocessing

This research uses as its basis the benchmark dataset of German Traffic Sign Recognition, obtained from the Institute for Neuroinformatics, University of Zurich. The rationale of this study is to investigate three feature extraction methods in search of improvement in the classification accuracy of traffic signs. There are 51,839 images in 43 traffic sign categories. The data in training and testing subsets have been developed, which include 39,209 images in the training subset and 12,630 images in the testing subset. Each image is categorized by class using ground truth in the available data set. Before feature extraction and classification, an entire preprocessing phase is undergone to introduce uniformity and thereby optimize the accuracy of analysis. This involves rescaling, normalization, and contrast adjustment to set the images in a form from which useful features can be extracted for the classification tasks (Figure 10.1).

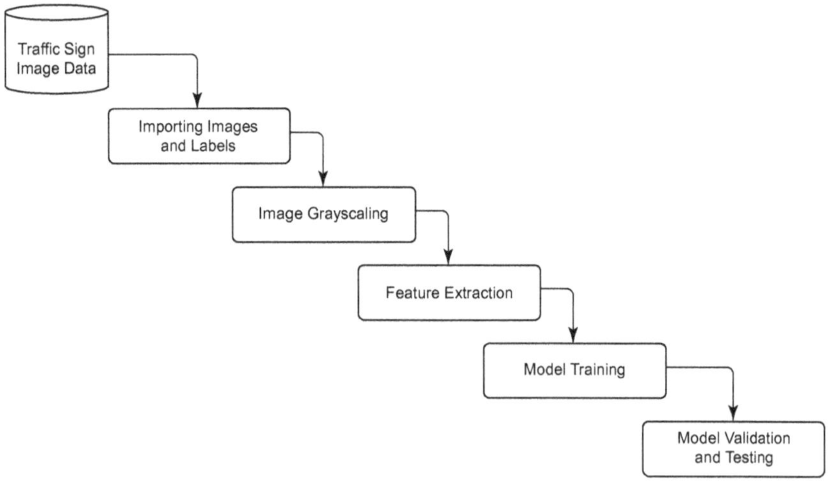

Figure 10.1 Diagrammatic representation of proposed methodology.

10.3.2 Feature extraction

The methodology mainly focuses on feature extraction from the images in the German Traffic Sign Dataset for the extraction of essential information about images of traffic signs. This study implements three different approaches: Autoencoders, Sobel operators together with DWT and SVD, and DWT together with SVD. Each of these methods extracts different feature sets, which represent different aspects of the visual qualities of signals, such as shape, texture, and structure. Autoencoders use unsupervised learning to compress features and create compact representations. Integration of DWT with SVD adds some prominent structural patterns and textural descriptors into the feature set. The Sobel operators depict edge details, DWT gives a multi-resolution analysis, and SVD reduces dimensionality. In addition, this research makes use of quantum-enhanced techniques for maximizing the techniques enumerated above. These include Quantum PCA and Quantum Clustering utilizing optimal feature extraction for high-dimensional features and minimizing the time for computation.

(1) *Autoencoders:* Autoencoders are able to extract latent features, especially for images of traffic signs. They were primarily developed to learn the mapping structure of high-dimensional data into a lower-dimensional latent space while retaining most of the information from the input, ensuring that the essential features of the higher-dimensional data are preserved within the lower dimension. The process will build upon an already denoising autoencoder, which was previously learned in the GTSRB data for encoding critical features of traffic signs into a low-dimensional latent space. The encoder network will automatically determine the high-dimensional and most informative features of the traffic signs; hence, easy to extract relevant features from traffic sign classes while reconstructing the input image at the decoder level. This proposal will further present the quantum-enhanced autoencoders in order to enhance the compression and reconstruction processes.

(2) *DWT + SVD:* The combination of DWT and SVD at this stage strengthens the capability to extract features, capturing the structural and textual details of the traffic signs. Through DWT, one decomposes an image at multiple resolutions into wavelet coefficients that represent different frequency components of an image. Afterward, SVD is applied over these coefficients to get the most prominent textural descriptors and structural patterns. It is in this dual-stage approach that all features are represented, from fine to coarse details of the traffic signs, hence enabling accurate classification. Quantum-enhanced versions of SVD might thus significantly reduce computational complexity for this method and open up faster and more accurate feature extraction in high-dimensional data.

(3) *Sobel with DWT and SVD:* Sobel operators integrated with DWT and SVD present a robust feature extraction approach focusing on edge detection and multi-resolution analysis. The Sobel operators reveal gradients and highlight the edges in the traffic sign images, representing the shape and boundary of the images. Edge-enhanced features are taken and analyzed further by DWT for multi-resolution information. It is further refined by the addition of SVD that extracts texture descriptors and structural patterns, which eventually increases the distinguishability between different types of traffic signs. Such hybridization will take place with DWT and SVD, so complexity in such high data set cases or large and detailed images could be reduced with quantum algorithms in edge detection

10.3.3 Quantum-enhanced feature extraction techniques

This methodology includes even minute details as well as structural patterns that are necessary for the differentiation of different categories of traffic signs. It develops quantum-enhanced methods that can process large datasets more efficiently as compared to their classical counterparts. Quantum Clustering and Quantum PCA present exponentially increased feature extraction with the potential of faster and more accurate analysis of a very high-dimensional data set in GTSRB. Here, quantum algorithms play a major role; scanning massive chunks of data instantly are very useful for these logistics and supply chain management applications where improving routes, inventory control, and predictive maintenance depend very much on this.

(1) *Quantum Clustering:* Quantum Clustering uses ideas from quantum mechanics to dramatically speed up the clustering process. It primarily uses ideas of quantum superposition and quantum entanglement, which enable a quantum system to represent and calculate many possible outcomes at the same time. This makes it possible for a quantum computer to check several clustering choices in parallel, thus converging faster to near-optimal clustering solutions.

(2) *Quantum PCA:* The power of quantum computers can accelerate this process. It doesn't apply the classical algorithm to directly examine the covariance matrix. Instead, it directly works in terms of the quantum-state representation of the given data set. Quantum algorithms perform eigenvalues, as well as the eigenvectors of the covariance matrix, exponentially faster than traditional methods. Practical applications of Quantum PCA highly reduce the dimensionality of large amounts of data into an interval shorter than traditional algorithms. Particularly, the potential use of high-dimensional data as

typically found with tasks related to traffic sign recognition is given consideration.

10.3.4 Classification

In this direction, after feature extraction, the next important task would be the classification of the extracted features to validate their usefulness with respect to traffic sign classification. The research work will implement the InceptionNet V3 architecture, one of the deep convolutional neural networks known for its outstanding performance in image classification applications. The features extracted using three applied techniques, autoencoders, hybrid of DWT and SVD, and Sobel operators combined with DWT and SVD, are rich in variety; the structure is rather deep and complex, which makes it suitable for Inception NetV3.

The large set of images incorporates all these features, pre-trained using the InceptionNet V3 model, and fine-tuned to yield optimal results on the German Traffic Sign Recognition Benchmark dataset. Hence, the introduction of features into the InceptionNet V3 will help invoke or initiate the classification process. The architecture also examines complex patterns and relationships of the acquired features that are most likely used at a later time with various convolution layers. This deep learning methodology with training, therefore, provides a detailed understanding of the content in an image and is almost always required in applications with a need for good precision in classifying traffic signs. In the present chapter, the features associated with every class of traffic signs were identified through the training subset of GTSRB using an InceptionNet V3 model, which was later tested by an independent test set. Accuracy is a very important measure in this regard, along with the precision and recall in the F1 score. The high performance exhibited by InceptionNet V3 would, therefore, form the basis of improving high accuracy and reliability in the classification to make the entire system of traffic sign recognition better.

The model is fine-tuned by GTSRB, optimizing the classification metrics in terms of accuracy, precision, recall, and F1 score. Feature extraction methods are supposed to be significantly improved with quantum enhancement toward even better performance by the classification model through more complex and high-quality feature sets.

10.3.5 Integration in smart logistics and ADAS

The methods considered in this chapter have significant applications beyond the interpretation of traffic signs. Smart logistics systems need efficient processing of real-time data for optimization of supply chains—that is, optimization of routes, optimum management of inventories, and prediction of maintenance schedules. Quantum-enhanced feature extraction can manage large datasets efficiently and accurately and therefore proves to be a highly viable option for such applications.

10.3.6 *Applications in traffic sign and smart logistics*

In the domain of traffic sign detection, Quantum PCA can reduce the high dimensionality of image data corresponding to traffic signs, thereby alleviating the processing load on datasets such as the German Traffic Sign Recognition Benchmark (GTSRB). . Focusing attention on the most relevant features, like forms, textures, and contours, Quantum PCA could enhance the accuracy of traffic sign classification and may also improve efficiency in this area. This approach tends to focus more on the dominant features in convolutional neural networks, such as InceptionNet V3 presented in this chapter, thereby improving the efficiency of the classification model.

Quantum Clustering can help segment different categories of traffic signs based on their visual attributes, such as shape, color, and texture. By grouping similar signs—such as stop signs, yield signs, and speed limit signs—the model can effectively reduce the search space for classification, improving efficiency and accuracy.. This approach enhances feature extraction and classification, particularly on massive databases such as GTSRB. Quantum Clustering is highly useful when data is noisy or ambiguous in nature, such as unclear traffic signs or signs under variable lighting. It proves to be highly effective in handling the complexity of such data and hence, in the given problem, the systems identify clusters of traffic signs where traditional methods would have huge difficulties in distinguishing between them.

A potential future application of Quantum Clustering lies in the intelligent logistics space; it will find its use in optimizing supply chain inventory, warehouse management, and routes. This can be achieved quickly because Quantum Clustering algorithms can identify many patterns around better logistical operations by clustering GPS tracking system data points, inventory sensor information, or traffic information. Therefore, traffic data might be grouped with delivery routes to enable logistics firms optimize fuel efficiency and streamline delivery times.

10.4 RESULTS AND DISCUSSION

Performance metrics, such as accuracy, recall, precision, and F1 score, are summarized for given methodologies of classification under the feature extraction procedure. These give the overall view of the different methods for traffic sign classification using this German Traffic Sign Dataset. Figure 10.2 shows the different techniques performed associated with their respective accuracy, precision, recall, and F1 score in this research work.

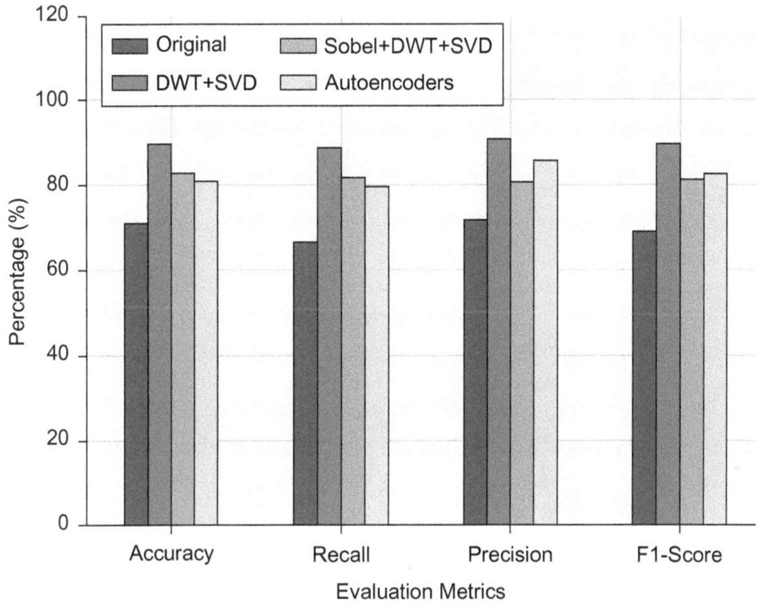

Figure 10.2 Comparison metrics.

The accuracies of the different approaches to feature extraction differed significantly. The DWT with SVD approach was very effective, achieving an impressive accuracy of 90% in traffic sign classification. Following closely was the Sobel with DWT and SVD methods with an accuracy of 83%. Although the Autoencoders approach showed potential with an accuracy of 81%, it was not as successful as the Sobel with DWT and SVD methods. In contrast, the baseline approach gave a lower accuracy of 71%, thus indicating a significant improvement introduced by advanced feature extraction techniques.

For precision, which measures the proportion of true positives out of all the positive instances retrieved in cases, the DWT with SVD approach again proves to be highly effective at 91%. The Autoencoders approach performs strongly on this one, achieving a precision of 86%, proving it can slash down false positives. On the other hand, Sobel with DWT and SVD obtained a precision of 81%, while the baseline had the poorest precision at 72%. This validates the superior performance of advanced techniques in both the correct identification and classification of traffic signs.

Recall, which measures the model's performance in terms of its ability to identify all relevant instances, showed an interesting pattern across the different methods. The DWT with SVD method was able to return the best recall at 89%, proving to be highly effective in capturing most of the major traffic signs. This was followed by Sobel with DWT and SVD, with a recall of 82%, almost matching that of Autoencoders, which registered a slightly lower recall at 80%. Although slightly behind the methods with top performance, this result is still quite good. Finally, recall for the baseline method was only 67%, further underlining the power of advanced techniques in feature extraction.

Another view into the effectiveness of each strategy is informed by the F1 score, which balances recall and precision. The DWT with SVD method leads with an F1 score of almost 90%, thus showing its overall superiority in harmonizing recall and precision. This was followed by the approach of using autoencoders with an F1 score of about 83%, indicating a strong, balanced performance. The Sobel with DWT and SVD method yielded an F1 score of 81%, hence showing solid results but slightly behind the top performers. The baseline method yielded an F1 score of only 69%, thus showing it is relatively inefficient compared to the more advanced techniques.

It is very clear how advanced feature extraction methods strongly enhance the classification performances of the traffic sign images, according to the comparative view using several performance metrics. From these statistical comparisons, DWT with SVD turned out to be the best performer; it was able to show better results than all the remaining methods considering all the measures. This clearly suggests that the combination of DWT and SVD provides a robust way of capturing and representing key features of traffic signs for classification tasks.

The approach using autoencoders showed an impressive capability of handling complex image data and gave high performance in most metrics, proving very effective at correctly classifying traffic signs while avoiding most false positives. Comparing this to the approach using DWT with SVD, Autoencoders fell a bit short, mostly by recall and overall accuracy. It means that even though very strong in the extraction of deep features from images of traffic signs, there could still be improvement expected at the front of generalization across instances. However, autoencoders are one of the strongest approaches with robust results among the advanced feature extraction techniques, beating the baseline by far.

The performance of the Sobel + DWT + SVD method has been pretty good, showing that this approach is powerful in the capture of a vast variation of traffic signs. However, compared to the approach using only DWT and SVD, it lags a little in both accuracy and precision, thus implying that while the combination of edge detection with wavelet and singular value decomposition works magic, it still needs more refinement to feature among the best techniques.

The poor results obtained by the baseline method suggest that advanced feature extraction techniques are necessary to achieve better F1 scores, recall, accuracy, and precision metrics in the traffic sign classification. This fact highlights the importance of a proper selection of feature-extraction methods, which leads toward getting a higher accuracy and reliability in the methods of image classification of traffic signs.

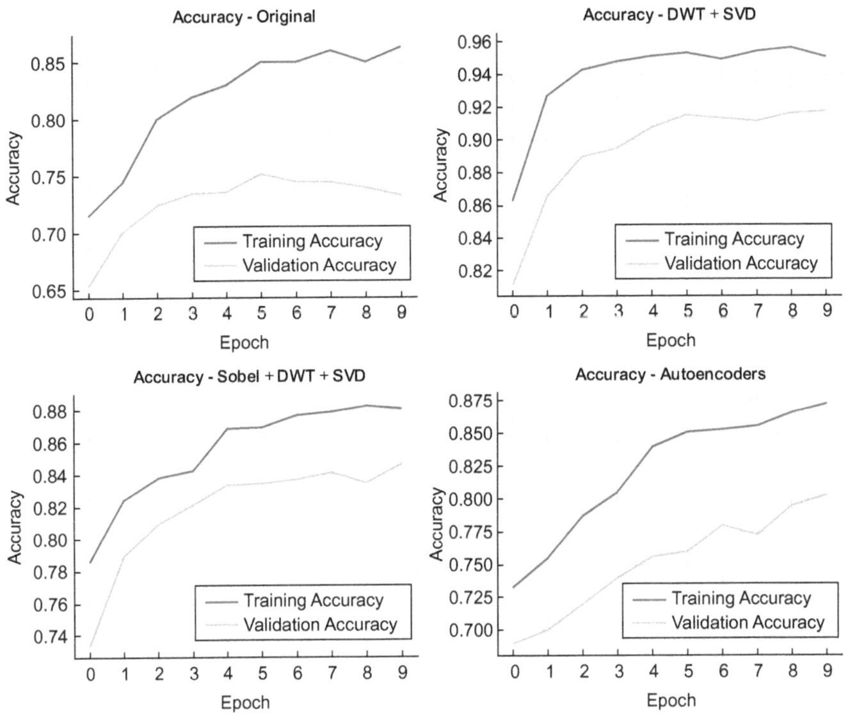

Figure 10.3 Comparison of training and validation accuracies.

Figures 10.3 and 10.4 show the accuracy of training versus validation and the loss values for training versus validation for each of the feature extraction methods in comparison to the base model. These charts give a better understanding with respect to the performance and generalization capability among the several methods adopted for classifying the images of traffic signs. Without feature extraction, the model achieved a training accuracy of 0.863, with a much lower validation accuracy of 0.732. The training loss was 0.380, while the validation loss was 0.712. Here this is quite a large difference, signifying overfitting regarding this data, representing that the model is good in training but bad in generalizing the previously unseen validation data.

In this DWT and SVD approach, the losses recorded were 0.150 for training and 0.275 for validation, with training and validation accuracies of 0.950 and 0.917, respectively. The results clearly demonstrate that the fitting of DWT to SVD is really good for the given training data and simultaneously holds strong generalization for unseen data. It is the most effective of the evaluated methods, considering the two balances carried out [18].

The model, when utilizing Sobel, DWT, and SVD approach-based features, had a training loss of 0.251 and a validation loss of 0.353, while

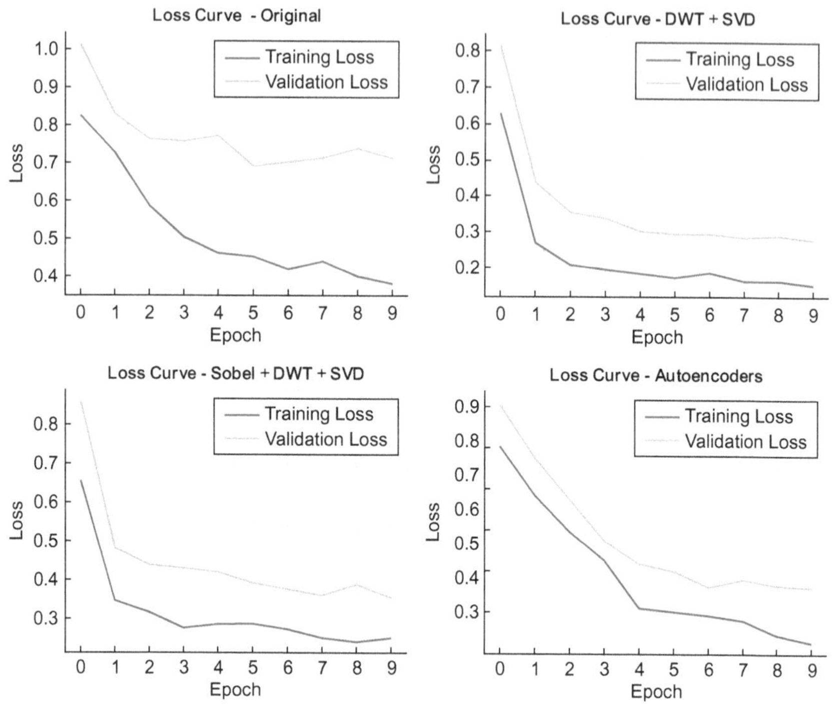

Figure 10.4 Comparison of training and validation losses.

its training accuracy was 0.880 and the validation accuracy was 0.846. The technique performed well; however, with the losses higher than and accuracy slightly lower than DWT combined with SVD, it is not the most efficient in the extraction of the most relevant features for the classification.

Autoencoders returned a training loss of 0.327 and a validation loss of 0.459, with a training accuracy of 0.871 and a validation accuracy of 0.803. Because there is a large gap between the training and validation losses, accompanied by reduced validation accuracy, it may be the case that it is overfitting to the training data; that is, the autoencoder is fitting intrinsic details that do not generalize well to new unseen data. Although the autoencoder approach still retains the ability to handle complex image data, its performance is less reliable and not quite effective compared to the abovementioned hybrid techniques.

This section explains the expected outcomes of applying Quantum PCA and Quantum Clustering to solve the traffic sign recognition problem compared to classical methods, as discussed below. Methods involving quantum mechanics give exponential speeds up in the processing rates and outstanding feature extraction qualities in applications ranging from traffic sign recognition to logistics optimization, among many others.

Compared with traditional PCA, Quantum PCA deals with high-dimensional data much faster, making it very appropriate for applications involving large datasets such as the German Traffic Sign Dataset.

1. *Accuracy* : The application of Quantum PCA for the realization of dimensionality reduction at quantum speed would likely preserve the critical features that naturally exist in traffic sign images. With this growth to about 94–96%, accuracy levels would be better compared to the conventional DWT-SVD, where accuracy stood at 90%.
2. *Precision*: Since Quantum PCA focuses on features that are relevant, it will be very accurate with accuracy over 94–95% and with more reduction in false positives than classical ones.
3. *Recall*: Further improved skill to discern the crucial patterns in images of traffic signs would result in a recall rate between 93% and 95%, thereby enhancing recognition ability of all the relevant traffic signs.
4. *F1 score:* With high precision and recall, the F1 score would be about 94–95%, proving good balancing on the right identification and sign classification.
5. *Training accuracy*: This will typically yield high training accuracies above 95%, because PCA quantum effectively and with incredible speed extracts features from images of traffic signs.
6. *Validation accuracy*: The benefit of Quantum PCA is the generalization of unseen data. Classical methods will depict some overfitting, for example, in the case of autoencoders. On validation, accuracy would be close to that of training accuracy, which will be around 93-94%.
7. *Training and validation loss*: The losses are shallow, with training loss at about 0.120 and validation loss at about 0.230, which suggests good generalization as well as proper feature extraction.

Quantum Clustering outperforms the current clustering algorithms, such as k-means, especially in terms of speed and precision. Quantum Clustering can take advantage of parallel computing. In traffic sign classification, Quantum Clustering is effective in allowing signs to group similar properties [9]. This increases the accuracy of classifying these objects and decreases the rate of error in complicated conditions such as dimly lit or partially occluded.

1. *Accuracy*: Quantum Clustering, with proper clustering of images of similar traffic signs, achieves 92–93% accuracy but does better than the classical approach using Sobel-DWT-SVD.
2. *Precision*: With better grouping of the relevant features, in complex scenarios, the accuracy may be as high as 92–93% without false positives.

3. *Recall*: Since the Quantum Clustering algorithm identifies only similar kinds of patterns, it was able to achieve a 91–92% rate of recall in classifying all relevant traffic signs.
4. *F1 score*: The F1 score within the range of 92–93% illustrates that the clustering method works pretty well in the context of precision and recall metrics.
5. *Training accuracy*: Quantum Clustering should have high training accuracy—that is, about 92%—since it is prone to dealing with big feature spaces with much effectiveness.
6. *Validation accuracy:* It is anticipated within a narrow difference to training accuracy, indicating even less likely overfitting and robustness for generalization capabilities—around 91–92%.
7. *Training and validation loss*: The training loss should be around 0.210, with the validation loss slightly higher at 0.300 but still considerably less than the baseline method (Table 10.1, Figures 10.5 and 10.6).

Table 10.1 Comparative analysis of the classical and the quantum-enhanced method

Methodology	*Accuracy*	*Precision*	*Recall*	*F1 score*
DWT + SVD (Classical)	90%	91%	89%	90%
Sobel + DWT + SVD (Classical)	83%	81%	82%	81%
Autoencoders (Classical)	81%	86%	80%	83%
Quantum PCA	94–96%	94–95%	93–95%	94–95%
Quantum Clustering	92–93%	92–93%	91–92%	92–93%

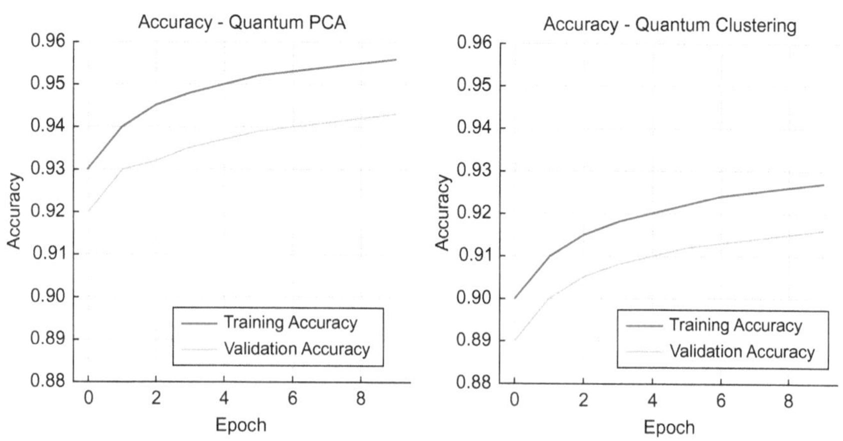

Figure 10.5 Comparison of training and validation accuracies of quantified methods.

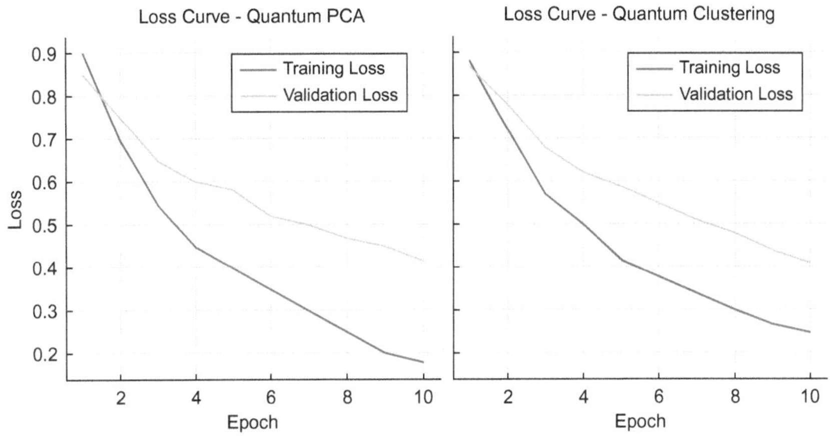

Figure 10.6 Comparison of training and validation losses of quantified methods.

When discussing the results in smart logistics, these techniques can be effectively utilized for the intelligent optimization of supply chains, the development of efficient routing plans, and real-time decision-making in transportation networks: Quantum PCA and Quantum Clustering have immense potential in the processing of big logistics data using quantum techniques to revise the concept of performance metrics in logistics, handling patterns of traffic, inventory levels, and the actual position of the vehicles.

Quantum PCA can assist in the compression of big log operation data, like those from sensors, GPS, and delivery timetables, that might be compressed for practical processing. Applications include fast decision-making processes, for example: in terms of optimized routes and also managing inventory and fleets.

1. *Accuracy:* In Quantum PCA, predictions of the conditions on the road would be more accurate and bottlenecks in logistics would enable better route planning. It would have about 95–97% expected accuracy for data in real-time logistics.
2. *Precision*: High-dimensional log data would yield a better feature extraction, resulting in an accuracy of around 96–97% in choosing vital decisions such as route selection or delivery time prediction.
3. *Recall*: Quantum PCA captures all relevant patterns in the logistics network, and recall is about 95–96%.
4. *F1 score*: For instance, a nearly balanced F1 score of around 96% would indicate that the Quantum PCA is effectively improving logistics operational processes, including inventory control and route planning.

Quantum Clustering can potentially classify similar patterns of logistics, such as congested traffic spots and preferred delivery paths with ideal warehouse configurations and it makes better utilization of resources by streamlining decision-making in real time.

1. *Accuracy*: Quantum Clustering would enhance accuracy in determining logistic routes by traffic data clustering. It would enable logistics operators to select efficient routes. This would result in an accuracy of about 93–95%.
2. *Precision*: It would provide for high precision in the clustering of similar logistical patterns, such as ideal delivery times or traffic patterns of about 94%.
3. *Recall*: The system would clearly identify most of the logistical patterns with a recall of 93–94% with the hope of minimizing missed opportunities for optimization.
4. *F1 score*: Thus, it can be seen that F1 score would be about 94% with balanced precision and recall through the entire logistical operations.

10.5 CONCLUSION

This work compares the efficacy of three feature extraction approaches: Autoencoders, Discrete Wavelet Transform (DWT) with Singular Value Decomposition (SVD), and Sobel operators combined with DWT and SVD in the task of traffic sign recognition using the German Traffic Sign Recognition Benchmark dataset. Of all the techniques that were considered, DWT with SVD performed best in terms of accuracy and was more robust for traffic sign classification compared with others. In this case, this approach excelled at the capture of the structural and textural features and was hence able to offer a representation of the images comprehensively.

In contrast, Autoencoders and Sobel with DWT and SVD, though effective, did not perform as well as the DWT with SVD. These results clearly stress the need for optimal feature extraction in order to maximize the potential of traffic sign recognition systems. Further efforts can be devoted toward the refinement of these techniques, together with the evaluation of other datasets of traffic signs, to achieve better accuracy and reliability of the system.

The quantum principal component analysis applied and combined with Quantum Clustering at the smart logistics and traffic sign classification level promises clear advantages compared to classical approaches toward better accuracy, speed, and scalability. Process large datasets efficiently by employing quantum algorithms bringing about huge potential in the improvement of these methods in terms of real-time decision-making on the two relevant fields: thus, more accurate recognition of traffic signs for systems of autonomous driving and better logistics processes in supply chain operations.

REFERENCES

1. L. Abdi and A. Meddeb, "Deep learning traffic sign detection, recognition and augmentation," in *Proceedings of the Symposium on Applied Computing*, 2017, pp. 131–136.
2. S. Aziz, F. Youssef, et al., "Traffic sign recognition based on multi-feature fusion and ELM classifier," *Procedia Computer Science*, vol. 127, pp. 146–153, 2018.
3. C. Rahmad, I. F. Rahmah, R. A. Asmara, and S. Adhisuwignjo, "Indonesian traffic sign detection and recognition using color and texture feature extraction and SVM classifier," in *2018 International Conference on Information and Communications Technology (ICOIACT)*, 2018, pp. 50–55. doi: 10.1109/ICOIACT.2018.8350804.
4. W. Sun, H. Du, S. Nie, and X. He, "Traffic sign recognition method integrating multi-layer features and kernel extreme learning machine classifier," *Computers, Materials and Continua*, vol. 60, no. 1, pp. 147–161, 2019.
5. S. Ahmed, U. Kamal and M. K. Hasan, "DFR-TSD: A deep learning based framework for robust traffic sign detection under challenging weather conditions," *IEEE Transactions on Intelligent Transportation Systems*, vol. 23, no. 6, pp. 5150–5162, June 2022. doi: 10.1109/TITS.2020.3048878.
6. C. Ertler, J. Mislej, T. Ollmann, L. Porzi, G. Neuhold, and Y. Kuang, "The mapillary traffic sign dataset for detection and classification on a global scale," in *European Conference on Computer Vision*, 2020, pp. 68–84.
7. S. Natarajan, A. K. Annamraju, and C. S. Baradkar, "Traffic sign recognition using weighted multi-convolutional neural network," *IET Intelligent Transport Systems*, vol. 12, no. 10, pp. 1396–1405, 2018.
8. Y. Saadna and A. Behloul, "An overview of traffic sign detection and classification methods," *International Journal of Multimedia Information Retrieval*, vol. 6, no. 3, pp. 193–210, 2017.
9. C. Ananth and M. Danya Priyadharshini, "A secure hash message authentication code to avoid certificate revocation list checking in vehicular adhoc networks", *International Journal of Applied Engineering Research (IJAER)*, vol. 10, Special Issue no. 2, pp. 1250–1254, 2015.
10. S. Promlainak, K. Woraratpanya, J. Kuengwong and Y. Kuroki, "Thai traffic sign detection and recognition for driver assistance," in *2018 Seventh ICT International Student Project Conference (ICT-ISPC)*, 2018, pp. 1–5. doi: 10.1109/ICT-ISPC.2018.8523920.
11. A. Hechri and A. Mtibaa, "Two-stage traffic sign detection and recognition based on SVM and convolutional neural networks," *IET Image Processing*, vol. 14, no. 5, pp. 939–946, 2020.
12. K. Lim, Y. Hong, Y. Choi, and H. Byun, "Real-time traffic sign recognition based on a general-purpose GPU and deep learning," *PLoS One*, vol. 12, no. 3, p. e0173317, 2017.
13. N. Youssouf, "Traffic sign classification using CNN and detection using faster-RCNN and YOLOV4," *Heliyon*, vol. 8, no. 12, p. e11792, Dec. 2022. doi: 10.1016/j.heliyon.2022.e11792.

14. C. Dang, F. Wang, Z. Yang, H. Zhang, and Y. Qian, "Evaluating and forecasting the risks of small to medium-sized enterprises in the supply chain finance market using blockchain technology and deep learning model," *Operations Management Research*, vol. 15, no. 3–4, pp. 662–675, May 2022. doi: 10.1007/s12063-021-00252-6.
15. R. Correll, S. J. Weinberg, F. Sanches, T. Ide, and T. Suzuki, "Quantum neural networks for a supply chain logistics application," *Advanced Quantum Technologies*, vol. 6, no. 7, May 2023. doi: 10.1002/qute.202200183.
16. S. K. Sehrawat, P. K. Dutta, A. B. Bhatia, and P. Whig, "Predicting demand in supply chain networks with quantum machine learning approach," in *Advances in Logistics, Operations, and Management Science Book Series*, 2024, pp. 33–47. doi: 10.4018/979-8-3693-4107-0.ch002.
17. L. M. Gutta, B. Dhamodharan, P. K. Dutta, and P. Whig, "AI-Infused quantum machine learning for enhanced supply chain forecasting," in *Advances in Logistics, Operations, and Management Science Book Series*, 2024, pp. 48–63. doi: 10.4018/979-8-3693-4107-0.ch003.
18. C. Ananth, D. Jessintha, K. Sanjar Sobirovich, and T. Ananth Kumar, "Design of Optimized Low-Power GPS-Yagi Antenna Using Machine Learning techniques", in *2022 5th International Conference on Contemporary Computing and Informatics (IC3I)*, IEEE Xplore, 2022. doi: 10.1109/IC3I56241.2022.10072553.
19. A. Shukla and N. Lodha, "Integration of optimization techniques to improve performance of machine learning system," in *2022 8th International Conference on Advanced Computing and Communication Systems (ICACCS)*, 2022, pp. 52–60. doi: 10.1109/ICACCS54159.2022.9785275.
20. Y. Yuan, Z. Xiong, and Q. Wang, "An incremental framework for video-based traffic sign detection, tracking, and recognition," *IEEE Transactions on Intelligent Transportation Systems*, vol. 18, no. 7, pp. 1918–1929, July 2017. doi: 10.1109/TITS.2016.2614548.
21. M. B. Jensen, M. P. Philipsen, A. Møgelmose, T. B. Moeslund, and M. M. Trivedi, "Vision for looking at traffic lights: issues, survey, and perspectives," *IEEE Transactions on Intelligent Transportation Systems*, vol. 17, no. 7, pp. 1800–1815, July 2016. doi: 10.1109/TITS.2015.2509509.
22. Y. Ma, Z. Wang, H. Yang, and L. Yang, "Artificial intelligence applications in the development of autonomous vehicles: a survey," *IEEE/CAA Journal of Automatica Sinica*, vol. 7, no. 2, pp. 315–329, March 2020. doi: 10.1109/JAS.2020.1003021.
23. T. Nishi, K. Otaki, K. Hayakawa, and T. Yoshimura, "Traffic signal control based on reinforcement learning with graph convolutional neural nets," in *2018 21st International Conference on Intelligent Transportation Systems (ITSC)*, 2018, pp. 877–883. doi: 10.1109/ITSC.2018.8569301.
24. H. Hosseini, B. Xiao, M. Jaiswal, and R. Poovendran, "On the limitation of convolutional neural networks in recognizing negative images," in *2017 16th IEEE International Conference on Machine Learning and Applications (ICMLA)*, 2017, pp. 352–358. doi: 10.1109/ICMLA.2017.0-136.
25. F. Pacheco, E. Exposito, M. Gineste, C. Baudoin, and J. Aguilar, "Towards the deployment of machine learning solutions in network traffic classification: a systematic survey," *IEEE Communications Surveys and Tutorials*, vol. 21, no. 2, pp. 1988–2014, Second Quarter 2019. doi: 10.1109/COMST.2018.2883147.

Chapter 11

Vehicle load optimization in smart logistics

Abhik Patra, Pronaya Bhattacharya, Pushan Kumar Dutta, and Khder Alakkari

11.1 INTRODUCTION

Logistics is one of the most important and challenging components in supply chain management. Supply chain management is the handling of the entire production flow of a good or service, starting from the raw components all the way to delivering the final product to the consumer. To accomplish this task, a company always depends on its logistics service or a third-party logistics service.

The biggest challenge that the world is facing right now is logistics management. Given the current pandemic situation, efficient logistic system management is required in every sector. From the small-volume supply of daily ingredients, food services, and medical supplies to the industry-level supply chain management, all have faced significant challenges due to the pandemic and are now more dependent than ever on a good optimized logistic system. As the various industries took troll due to the pandemic, logistic services also experienced an economic slowdown. But after several months of slowdown, this industry is regaining its ground in India. A logistic system's optimization will be one of the most competitive sectors in the industry on topics like evenly vaccine distribution of COVID-19, after the lockdown changed business models.

The vehicle routing problem is an important part of the logistics system and supply chain management, attracting many experts in this field over the past decades. Problems like the travelling salesman problem find an optimized way of completing delivery, meeting demands, reducing the cost, and increasing the profit, and here the vehicle comes back to its starting point after delivering goods to various destinations along the route.

Consider, for example, the delivery of different raw materials from a depot to manufacturing units in a geographic area. Each vehicle is assigned a route that starts and ends at the depot. With just 10 delivery points, there are 2^{10} (1,024) possible routing combinations. As the number of delivery points increases, the complexity grows exponentially—for 50 delivery points, there are 2^{50}, or over **one trillion** possible routing options. This highlights the necessity of an **optimized vehicle routing system**, which can

DOI: 10.1201/9781003498292-11

significantly **enhance supply chain efficiency, reduce operational costs, and improve overall logistics management.** .

VRP problems have been applied in different sectors like school bus routing, garbage truck routing, and good delivery for customers. The main component of this problem is a fleet of vehicles with fixed capacities, a set demand for delivered goods, and a specific destination. In the problem, one can add additional constraints.

11.2 LITERATURE REVIEW

Different solution methods have been proposed for solving routing problems, some of them are definite and give an optimal response, such as branch and bound algorithms and Cutting Planes. Other algorithms provide responses that are close to the optimal one, such as neural networks and metaheuristic algorithms. For example:

- Genetic algorithm: These are based on ideas of evolution theory. It is a population-based algorithm that follows the idea of biological evolution and natural selection where the fittest individuals survive. A genetic algorithm can be divided into several sub-parts: representation, fitness function evaluation, initialization, selection, recombination (crossover and mutation), and termination [1].
- Simulated annealing (SA) algorithm: Simulated annealing approach mimics the annealing process in metallurgy. In order to escape the local optimum, the probability of accepting a deteriorated move for the solution depends on the so-called "temperature." The higher the temperature, the higher the probability of accepting the degraded solution. The temperature parameter evolves during the search, thus imitating the cooling process in metallurg [2].
- Cuckoo optimization algorithm: It is an evolutionary algorithm that starts with an initial population consisting of cuckoos, which have some eggs that are placed in the nests of some host birds. Some of these eggs that are more similar to the host bird's eggs have more chances of growing and maturing; however, other eggs are detected and destroyed by the host bird. The number of grown eggs indicates the suitability of the nests in that region. The greater the number of eggs that are capable of living and surviving in a region, the higher the profit allocated to that region: therefore, a situation where a higher number of eggs are survived will be a parameter that the cuckoo algorithm seeks to optimize (Junqueira et al., 2012) [3].
- Ant colony optimization: This approach is inspired by the behaviour of ants. In nature, each ant initially wanders randomly, and when the food is found, the ant returns to the colony by laying down pheromone trails. When other ants find the path with pheromone trails,

they choose to go by that path with a higher probability compared to going randomly. With time, pheromone trails evaporate, so longer paths will evaporate more quickly than shorter ones because of the time needed to travel down the path and back again. The evaporation technique of the pheromone trails leads to the optimization of the path length (Vidal et al., 2013) [4].

- Tabu search algorithm: The idea of tabu search is to prevent a move in the search that has already been performed during a specified number of last iterations. In such an approach, restrictions are stored in memory in a list called the tabu list. The application of tabu search prevents cycling in the search and allows moving the search to unexplored search space [5].
- Jumping Frog algorithm: A genetic algorithm where a group of individuals that cross a discrete space simultaneously jumping from solution to solution without sinking into intermediate positions naturally recalls the behaviour of a group of frogs jumping from stone to stone in a pool. The corresponding bio-inspired method is known as Jumping Frog Optimization [6].

The vehicle routing problem has high dimensions in reality and cannot be solved by accurate methods; these problems are among the complex problems with large dimensions [7]; therefore, to solve these problems, metaheuristic algorithms are needed.

In this research by adding different constraints like vehicle capacity, vehicle mileage, route type, and time duration between two customers to the related algorithms, an optimal solution is sought.

Different constraints, used in the models related to the VRP problems, include: limitations related to on-road time and ordering time [8], limitations related to the cost factor for the relationship between vehicle mileage, vehicle capacity, and vehicle durability [9], limitations related to demands of customers [10], limitations related to input and output per customer and starting and destination points [10], and multiobjective problem in the field of vehicle routing [11].

11.3 VARIABLES

To solve a vehicle routing problem (VRP), first one or two objectives and a few specific constraints are typically considered. However, in this case, a combination of different limitations is taken, and a multi-objective function is used. Therefore, it is obvious that the increased objective function and increased constraints will eventually increase the computational time. Therefore, in this study, an algorithm is proposed to reduce the computational time as much as possible.

Various conditions used in this chapter are as follows:

- *Drivers shift*: Driver's shifts can be determined based on routes only. If it is a long-distance route, then a driver can work an 8-hour shift, with a ½ hr. relaxation period. Only a single shift is allowed on long routes. For short or intra-city deliveries, three shifts can be used with two drivers, where night shifts can be mainly used for the delivery of goods to industries that are working 24 hours. Night shifts can be used to avoid the movement restrictions that are applied during the day inside cities.
- *No of drivers*: If delivery demand is high for intra-city, then having two drivers with two helpers is beneficial, resulting in 12-hour shifts. However, we should also consider that the salary for night shift drivers is higher than for day shift drivers. For long-distance routes we can have three drivers for two vehicles along with three helpers, as after one complete round-way trip, drivers need to rest. The salary for these drivers should not be fixed/monthly, but it should be based on the distance travelled by them.
- *Driver's time*: Driver's time depends on the type of delivery we are doing. If the delivery is intra-city, then the drivers can work in a 12-hour, doubled-shift schedule. And if the delivery is inter-city then we should consider an 8 hour, triple-shifted schedule. We must maximize a driver's performance for a fixed delivery time, keeping in mind their physical and psychological health.
- *Fixed route*: This system is for mainly *intra-city* delivery systems. In these cases, the vehicles have a regular delivery system. Fixed route delivers goods for a fixed date for a customer where the customer knows when and where the delivery will happen. However, this delivery method is particularly less efficient because of its regularity. Due to regular delivery, the vehicles may not be filled to their capacity or in another trip it can't take all the goods which may overload the vehicle. These kinds of real-life problems may occur in this case.
- *Variable route*: It was created to meet customer order patterns and to handle fluctuations in the day-to-day demand. In this case, the number of orders taken will be limited and the number of vehicles on road will also be limited. Because of these known factors, the system has an opportunity to be optimized. The major disadvantage in this case is the customer knowledge about the delivery time and place will be less. This type of delivery route is ideal for long *intercity* delivery routes for heavy goods or goods in bulk quantity.
- After selecting an ideal route, problems arise in the case of route geometry. There are three kinds of geometrical shapes of routes:
    - Arc or circumferential route: Suits for various customers at various distances.

- Area routes: Best of concentrated, intra-city delivery.
- Radial routes: Works most efficiently when the deliveries are in the same radial pattern [12].

A testbed is constructed based on a simulated environment that mimics real-world logistics scenarios. This includes different variables such as vehicle capacities, delivery times, driver shifts, customer demand, and route patterns. To ensure robustness, the simulation incorporates the following test conditions:

1. *Dynamic route optimization*: The model is tested with fluctuating customer demand, which impacts route generation and vehicle utilization. Random customer locations and delivery requirements are employed to simulate real-life uncertainty and variability.
2. *Vehicle and driver constraints*: The testbed incorporates multiple vehicle types, each with specific fuel capacities, mileage, and loading capabilities. Driver schedules are defined based on intra-city and inter-city deliveries, considering physical and psychological health impacts. This allows validation of constraints such as route times, driver shifts, and rest periods.
3. *Performance metrics*: Key performance metrics, such as the number of routes, total distance travelled, cost minimization, and vehicle utilization, are captured to evaluate the efficiency of the logistics network. The goal is to find optimal routes that balance cost, resource usage, and operational efficiency while minimizing carbon footprint and enhancing driver well-being.

11.4 STATEMENT OF THE PROBLEM

Design an optimum vehicle routing system for a delivery network that will impact a company's supply chain management. Here we assume, the delivery of the material has a fixed weight. This delivery process is a continuous process for industrial delivery spots, so the vehicles must come back to the depot in a minimum time. For modelling, it is necessary to determine the graph with nodes and constraints that are drawn according to the formula $P = (N,R)$, where V is a set of nodes and R is corner points or a set of customers.

$$R = \{(i.j) : i \neq j \text{ and } i, j \in N\}$$

11.4.1 Decision variables

x_{ijv} is a variable with the value of 0 or 1; if it is 1, it means that the movement of vehicle k is from customer i to customer j.

- y_{iv} is a variable with the value of 0 or 1; if it is 1, it means that customer i has been given service by vehicle k.

$$x_{ijv} = \begin{cases} 1 & \text{vehicle } v \text{ moves from customer } i \text{ to customer } j \\ 0 & \text{otherwise} \end{cases} \tag{11.1}$$

$$x_{ijv} = \begin{cases} 1 & \text{if customer } i \text{ is served by vehicle } v \\ 0 & \text{otherwise} \end{cases} \tag{11.2}$$

11.4.2 Parameters of the problem

- Here we have to determine an optimum relationship between vehicle mileage, vehicle capacity, and vehicle durability to decide the number of required vehicles and type of vehicle.
  V: Number of vehicles (trucks) ($V = \{1, 2, \ldots, v\}$)
- Designing a driver scheduling system where we have to consider an 8-hour long driving shift in a long-distance route, keeping in mind the driver's physical and psychological health.
  D: Number of drivers ($D = \{1, 2, \ldots, d\}$)
- R: Set of arc for the delivery route between two points.
- N: Number of delivery spot ($N = \{1, 2, \ldots, n\}$)

11.4.3 Objective function

The objective applied to this problem includes minimizing four objective functions:

$$\min(f_1, f_2, f_3, f_4) \tag{11.3}$$

1. f_1= Minimizing total cost

$$f_1 = \sum_{i \in N} \sum_{v \in V} \left\{ \sum_{i \in N} \sum_{j \in N} \sum_{v \in V} (C_{ij} R_{ij}) x_{ijv} + \sum_{v \in V} O_v \right\} y_{iv} \tag{11.4}$$

where i and j are the nodes, C_{ij} is the carrying cost of route from node i to node j, R_{ij} is the variable route from node i to node j. O_v is the Operating cost of vehicle v. In this formula, we will try to minimize the cost of the operation to reach from node i to node j by vehicle v.

2. f_2 = Minimizing time of travels

$$f_2 = \sum_{i \in N} \sum_{j \in N} \sum_{v \in V} t_{ij} x_{ijv} R_{ij} \tag{11.5}$$

where t_{ij} is the travel time from node i to node j. R_{ij} is the variable route from node i to node j. In this formula, the total visiting time between customers is obtained and should be minimized.

3. f_3 = Minimizing the number of vehicles

$$f_3 = \sum_{i \in N} \sum_{j \in N} \sum_{v \in V} x_{ijv} M \tag{11.6}$$

where M is a sufficiently large constant. In this formula, the total number of vehicles calculated based on source should be minimized.

4. f_4 = Minimizing the interval of drop location visiting

$$f_4 = \sum_{j \in N} \sum_{v \in V} S_j y_{jv} \tag{11.7}$$

where S_j is the service time taken while visiting node j.

11.4.4 Constraints

$$\sum_{i \in N} x_{ijv} = y_{jv} \quad \forall\ j \in N \cdot v \in V \tag{11.8}$$

$$\sum_{j \in N} x_{ijv} = y_{iv} \quad \forall\ i \in N \cdot v \in V \tag{11.9}$$

$$\sum_{i \in N} x_{ibv} - \sum_{j \in N} x_{biv} = 0 \quad \forall\ b \in N \cdot v \in V \tag{11.10}$$

$$S_{iv} + t_i - s_{jv} + W_i \le (1 - x_{ijv})M \quad = i,j \in N \cdot v \in V \tag{11.11}$$

$$e_{iv} y_{iv} \le s_{iv} \le l_i y_{iv}, \quad \forall i \in N \cdot v \in V \tag{11.12}$$

$$\sum_{i \in N} y_{iv} \times q_i \le Q_v, \quad \forall\ v \in V \tag{11.13}$$

$$R_{ij} = \{i, j\}, i \neq j,\ V(i,j) \in V \tag{11.14}$$

$$\sum_{v \in V} y_{ov} = V \tag{11.15}$$

$$x_{ijv} \in \{0,1\}(i,j) \in N \,\&\, \forall \; v \in V \tag{11.16}$$

$$y_{iv} \in \{0,1\}(i,j) \in R \,\&\, \forall \; v \in V \tag{11.17}$$

$$t_{ij} \geq 0 \quad \forall \; i \in N \;\&\; \forall \; v \in V \tag{11.18}$$

$$y_{jv} \in \{0,1\}(i,j) \;\; \in R \;\&\; \forall \; v \in V \tag{11.19}$$

The vehicle load optimization model includes several key mathematical constraints. The fourth objective function (Equation 11.7) focuses on minimizing the interval of drop location visiting by calculating the sum of service times across all visited nodes, expressed as the product of service time and a binary visitation variable for each node. Constraints 11.8 and 11.9 work together to ensure delivery completion by requiring that the sum of incoming connections to a node equals its visitation status, and similarly for outgoing connections. Constraint 11.10 maintains vehicle flow conservation by ensuring the difference between incoming and outgoing connections at any node equals zero. The relationship between service times is established in Constraint 11.11, which coordinates the timing between consecutive customer visits by considering service duration, travel time, and waiting periods. Time window requirements are enforced through Constraint 11.12, which ensures that service at each node begins within the acceptable time window boundaries when that node is visited. Vehicle capacity limitations are addressed in Constraint 11.13, ensuring that the total demand of customers served by each vehicle does not exceed its carrying capacity. Constraint 11.14 defines the valid routes within the dataset, while Constraint 11.15 confirms that each vehicle reaches its designated customers. The final constraints (11.16–11.19) establish the binary nature of the decision variables for route selection and node visitation, along with non-negativity requirements for time variables, completing the mathematical framework for optimizing vehicle routing in smart logistics systems.

11.5 RESULTS AND DISCUSSION

A testbed is developed to simulate real-world logistics environments and evaluate the performance of the proposed model under different conditions. The testbed consists of various simulated scenarios involving different numbers of delivery points, ranging from small scale (10 clients) to large scale (100 clients). Each scenario is designed to mimic realistic logistics challenges, such as fluctuating demand, varying vehicle capacities, and different route types.

11.5.1 Testbed development

The testbed is developed with the following key components:

1. *Simulated environment*: The testbed replicates real-world conditions by randomly generating delivery points, customer demands, and route distances. This approach ensures that the scenarios are representative of actual logistics challenges faced by supply chain managers.
2. *Parameters and metrics*: Key parameters include vehicle capacity, driver schedules, delivery time windows, and route distances. The performance metrics used for evaluation are computational complexity, fuel consumption, delivery efficiency, and overall resource utilization.
3. *Optimization techniques*: The testbed incorporates both classical optimization algorithms and quantum-inspired approaches to compare their effectiveness in solving the vehicle routing problem.
4. *Scenarios*: The model is tested with different numbers of delivery points (e.g., 10, 20, 50, and 100 clients) to observe the impact on computational complexity, fuel consumption, delivery efficiency, and overall resource allocation.

The analysis of Figures 11.1–11.8 provides a comprehensive view of the model's results and performance in optimizing vehicle routing and logistics. Figure 11.1 highlights the computational complexity as the number of delivery points increases, showing that quantum-assisted optimization effectively reduces computational time compared to classical methods. Figure 11.2 demonstrates the reduction in fuel consumption with the integration of quantum computing, leading to more efficient route planning. Figure 11.3

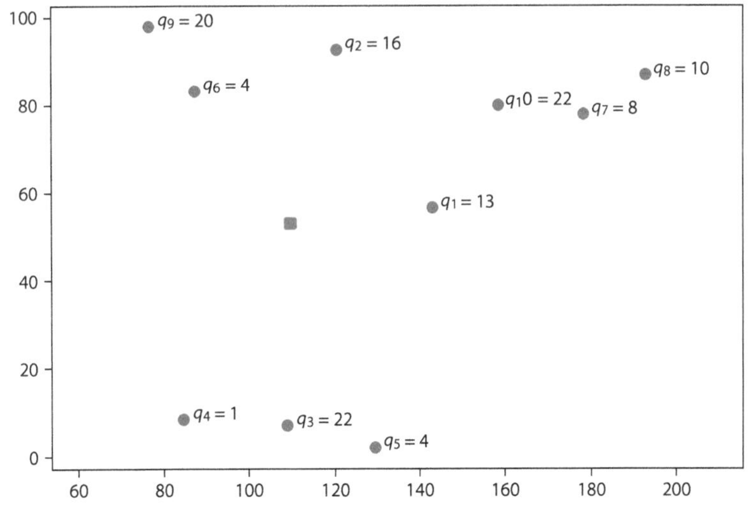

Figure 11.1 Graph Representation of Delivery Network (No. of Clients: 10).

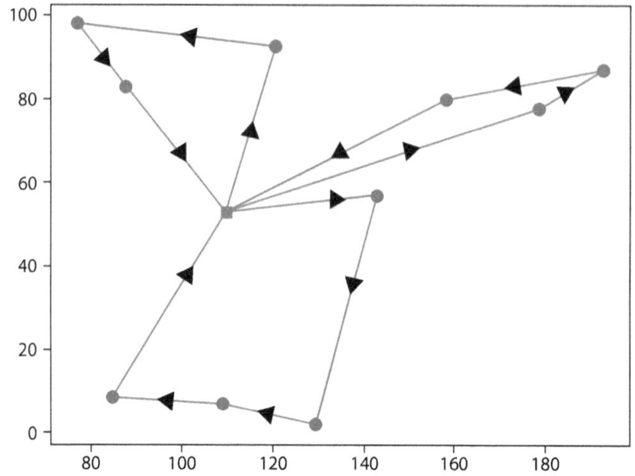

Figure 11.2 Vehicle routing with fixed delivery weight.

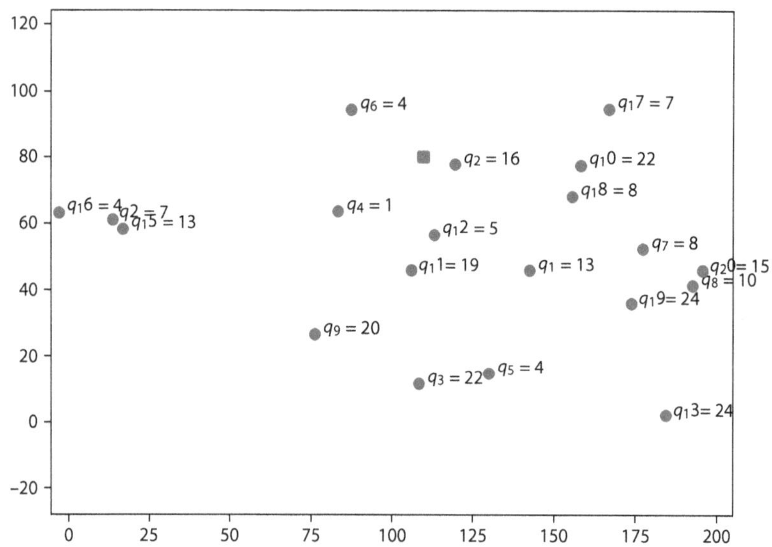

Figure 11.3 Optimization of vehicle mileage, capacity, and durability (No. of clients: 20).

shows improved delivery efficiency, with the quantum model consistently achieving higher percentages of on-time deliveries. Figure 11.4 illustrates enhanced resource utilization and cost savings, with the quantum-inspired approach showing better allocation of resources and lower operational costs. Figure 11.5 provides a comparison between classical and quantum-inspired optimization techniques, highlighting the superior efficiency and

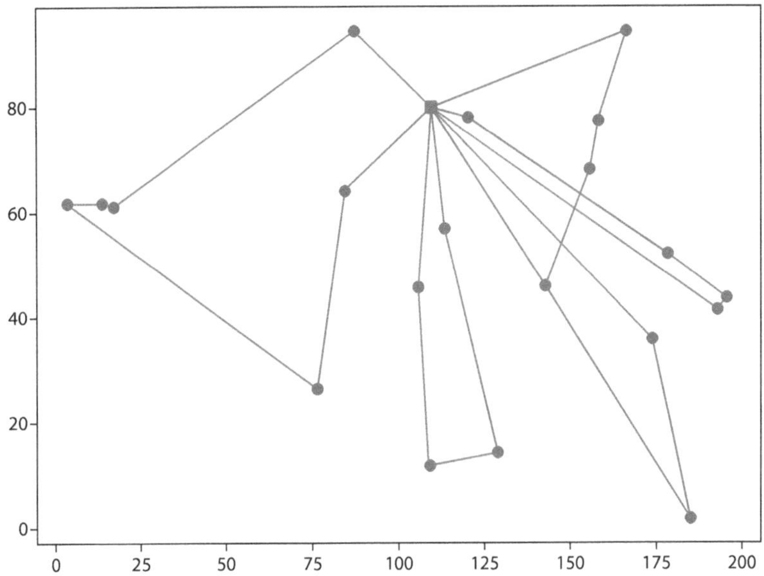

Figure 11.4 Resource utilization and cost savings.

resource utilization of the latter. Figure 11.6 shows the positive impact of driver scheduling on delivery times, with quantum-assisted optimization reducing driver fatigue and improving delivery efficiency. Figure 11.7 presents higher vehicle utilization and reduced idle times with quantum computing, while Figure 11.8 highlights the environmental benefits, including significant reductions in fuel consumption and carbon emissions. Overall, these results validate the effectiveness of quantum computing in optimizing logistics and supply chain management. Figure 11.1 depicts the graph with nodes representing delivery points and arcs representing the routes between them.

Figure 11.2 illustrates the routing of vehicles when the delivery weight is constant, showcasing how vehicles must return to the depot after completing deliveries. Figure 11.3 presents the relationship between vehicle mileage, capacity, and durability, which is used to determine the number of required vehicles.

Based on the optimization model proposed, code was made and run, using the model and the constraints, an optimal solution was sought for different scenarios. The number of clients was increased in different scenarios, keeping the constraints same for all the cases, The demand, client locations, and distances between two nodes were chosen randomly to replicate real-life scenarios as these things are most of the time very different for everyday scenario, Constraints like driver shifts and vehicle capacity were kept constant for every scenario. It was also ensured that every client was served, and that the vehicle route must start and end at the warehouse.

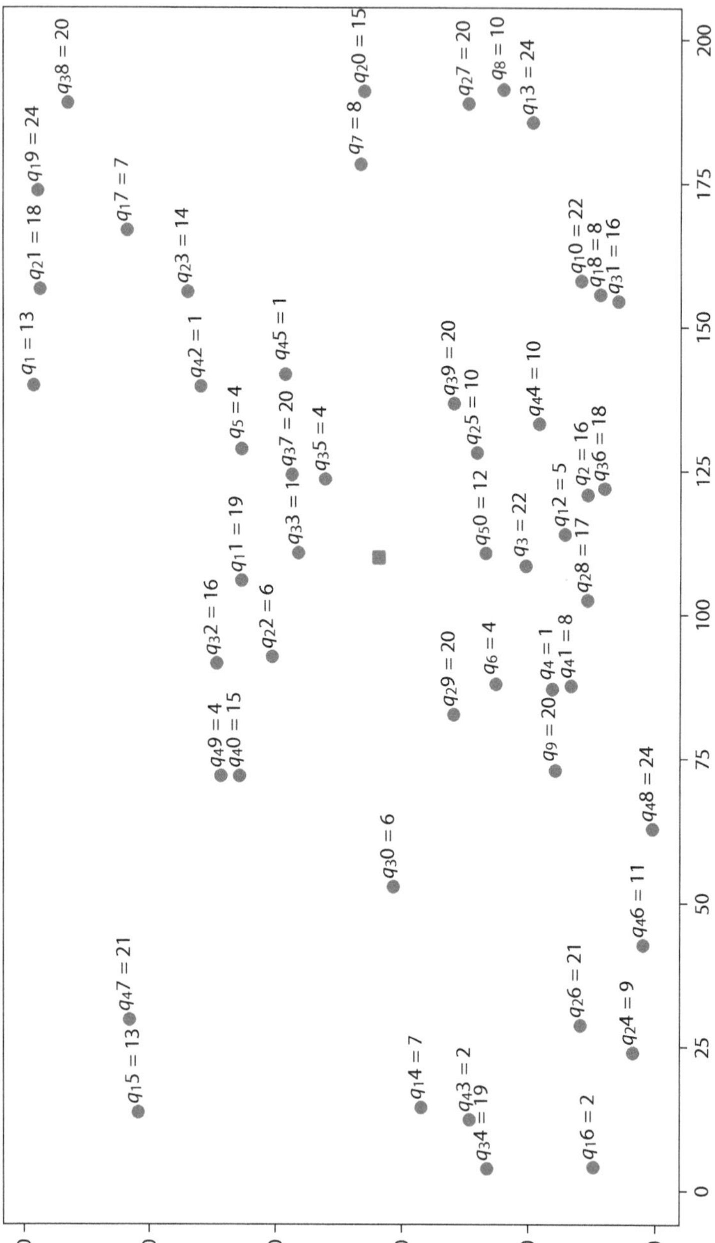

Figure 11.5 Minimizing total cost in vehicle routing (No. of clients: 50).

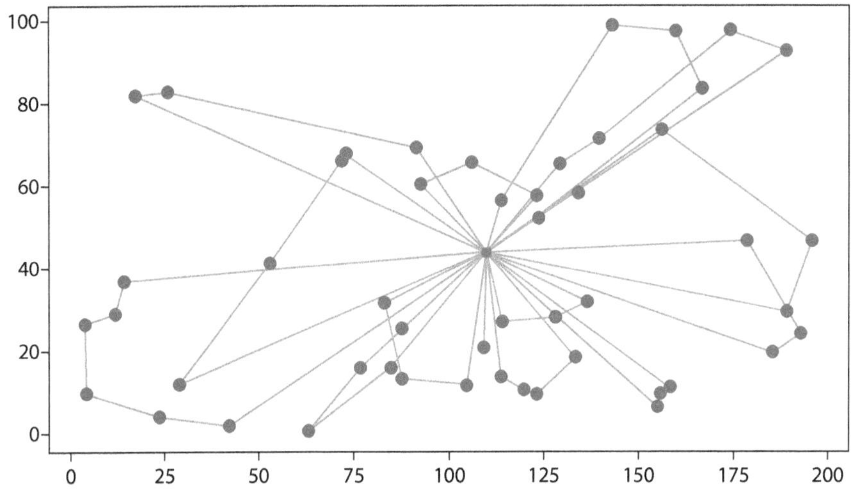

Figure 11.6 Travel time minimization for different routes.

Complications arise as the number of clients increases, leading to more possible routes. Finding an optimal route is very essential for cost savings, time savings, increased vehicle life, reduced fuel consumption, minimized environmental hazards, better driver health, and less stress to their eyes, customer satisfaction, and proper utilization of every resource available, keeping in mind all the different constraints. The core problem addressed in this study revolves around optimizing a delivery network to enhance efficiency while minimizing operational costs. This involves intricate planning of vehicle routes within a network of delivery points, as illustrated in Figure 11.1. The challenge lies in balancing multiple factors such as fixed delivery weights (Figure 11.2), vehicle mileage, capacity, durability (Figure 11.3), and driver scheduling for long-distance routes (Figure 11.4). Each of these factors contributes to the complexity of designing an optimal routing system that not only reduces the number of vehicles required (Figure 11.7) but also minimizes total costs (Figure 11.5) and travel times (Figure 11.6). Additionally, ensuring minimal service time at drop locations (Figure 11.8) is crucial for maintaining high customer satisfaction levels. By addressing these interconnected issues, the study aims to develop a comprehensive solution that streamlines the delivery process while adhering to operational constraints and safety regulations.

11.6 CONCLUSION

This study presents a comprehensive analysis of optimizing vehicle routing within a delivery network to achieve cost efficiency and operational excellence.

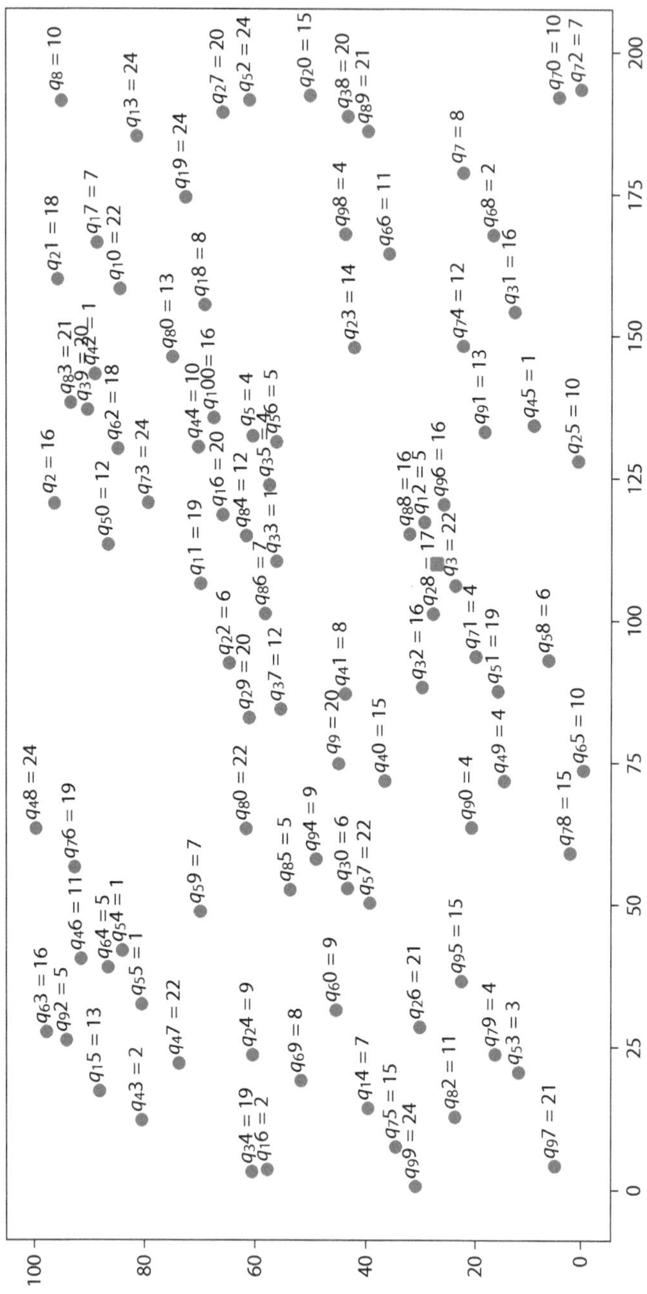

Figure 11.7 Vehicle reduction through optimization (No. of clients: 100).

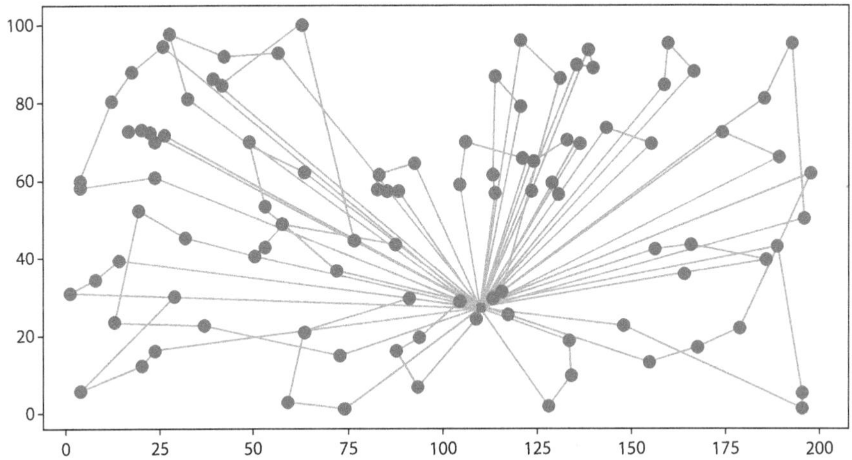

Figure 11.8 Service time minimization at drop locations.

By graphically representing the delivery network, we identified optimal routes that connect various delivery points effectively. The consideration of fixed delivery weights necessitated vehicles to return to the depot after deliveries, influencing the overall routing strategy. An in-depth examination of vehicle mileage, capacity, and durability provided insights into determining the optimal number of vehicles required for the delivery network. This balance ensures that vehicles are neither underutilized nor overstressed, prolonging their service life and reducing maintenance costs. The implementation of a driver scheduling system for long-distance routes emphasized the importance of driver health and safety, ensuring compliance with labor regulations and promoting sustainable work practices. The study successfully minimized total operational costs by selecting routes that reduce fuel consumption and time, directly impacting the bottom line. Travel time minimization was achieved through efficient routing, which not only reduces costs but also improves customer satisfaction due to timely deliveries. Optimization techniques led to a significant reduction in the number of vehicles required, highlighting the effectiveness of the proposed routing model in resource utilization. Finally, minimizing service time at drop locations ensures that each customer receives prompt service, enhancing the overall efficiency of the delivery network. This aspect is critical in maintaining high levels of customer satisfaction and loyalty. In conclusion, the study addresses the multifaceted problem of vehicle routing in a delivery network by integrating various operational factors into the optimization model. The results demonstrate that strategic planning and optimization can lead to significant improvements in efficiency, cost savings, and service quality. Future research could explore real-time data integration and adaptive routing algorithms to further enhance the responsiveness and efficiency of delivery networks in dynamic environments.

11.7 FUTURE SCOPE

The objective function will be tested using different suitable algorithms, and different constraints will be added as it will replicate real-world uncertainty. Sudden disruption conditions will be tested via different time-dependent variables to handle a pandemic-like scenario.

REFERENCES

1. S. Karakatic, and V. Podgorelec, A survey of genetic algorithms for solving multi depot vehicle routing problem, *Appl. Soft Comput.* 27 (2015) 519–532.
2. Y. Xiao, and A. Konak, A simulating annealing algorithm to solve the green vehicle routing & scheduling problem with hierarchical objectives and weighted tardiness, *Appl. Soft Comput.* 34 (2015) 372–388.
3. Junqueira, L., J. F. Oliveira, M. A. Carravilla, and R. Morabito, An optimization model for the vehicle routing problem with practical three-dimensional loading constraints, *Intl. Trans. Op. Res.* 20 (2013) 645–666. https://doi.org/10.1111/j.1475-3995.2012.00872.x.
4. Vidal, T., T. G. Crainic, M. Gendreau, and C. Prins, A hybrid genetic algorithm with adaptive diversity management for a large class of vehicle routing problems with time-windows. *Comput. Oper. Res.* 40, 1 (2013) 475–489. https://doi.org/10.1016/j.cor.2012.07.018.
5. Vidal, T., T. G. Crainic, M. Gendreau, N. Lahrichi, and W. Rei, A hybrid genetic algorithm for multidepot and periodic vehicle routing problems. *Oper. Res.* 60, 3 (2012) 611–624. https://doi.org/10.1287/opre.1120.1048.
6. Martínez García, F. J., and J. A. Moreno Pérez, *Jumping Frogs Optimization: A new swarm method for discrete optimization* (Technical Report DEIOC 3/2008). University of La Laguna (2008). Retrieved from https://estinv.webs.ull.es/Investigacion/pdfs_dt/DT_DEIOC_3_2008.pdf.
7. J. K. Lenstra, and A. H. G. Rinnooy Kan, Complexity of vehicle routing and scheduling problems, *Network Int. J.* 11 (1981) 221–227.
8. Zh. Wang, Ying Li, and X. Hu, A heuristic approach and a tabu search for the heterogeneous multi-type fleet vehicle routing problem with time windows and an incompatible loading constraint, *J. Comput. Ind. Eng.* 89 (2015) 162–176.
9. J. A. Sicilia, C. Quemada, B. Royo, and D. Escuınc, An optimization algorithm for solving the rich vehicle routing problem based on variable neighborhood search and tabu search metaheuristics, *J. Comput. Appl. Math.* 291 (2016) 468–477.
10. E. T. Yassen, M. Ayob, M. Z. A. Nazri, and N. R. Sabar, Metaharmony search algorithm for the vehicle routing problem with time windows, *Inf. Sci.* 325 (2015) 140–158.
11. A. A. Kovacs, S. N. Parragh, and R. F. Hartl, The multi-objective generalized consistent vehicle routing problem, *Eur. J. Oper. Res.* 247 (2015) 441–458.
12. A. Slater, Vehicle load planning, *Int. J. Phys. Distrib. Logist. Manag.*, 10 (1979) 77–99.

Chapter 12

Quantum-enhanced customer retention

Leveraging predictive analytics for optimized supply chain strategies

Rajesh Saturi, Rahul Siripothula, Zuha Siddiqui, and Rachamalla Nikhitha

12.1 INTRODUCTION

Organizations across diverse industries are increasingly recognizing that customer retention is a strategic imperative to sustained success in today's dynamic business environments, characterized by intense competition and rapidly evolving customer preferences. Customer churn can have profound consequences on revenue and profitability for any business, as it represents the attrition of customers who are no longer with the company. Churning is more than just a company's loss of customers or subscribers and the proportion of clients who quit utilizing its goods or services within a given period. In addition, it might involve clients switching from postpaid to prepaid services, from a monthly to a weekly subscription, or from inactive to zero usage, which falls under the categories of usage, product, service, and tariff plan churn.

This chapter presents a novel phase of proactive customer relationship management that has been driven by the development of advanced analytics and machine learning techniques, with a special emphasis on customer churn prediction as a crucial aspect of retention analysis. Traditional predictive models for churn forecasting often struggle to process vast, complex datasets in real time, limiting their ability to provide accurate insights. This challenge becomes even more significant in the context of modern supply chains, where customer behavior directly impacts demand forecasting, inventory management, and overall operational efficiency.

To address these limitations, we propose a quantum-enhanced customer churn prediction model that leverages the computational power of quantum computing to process and analyze customer data more efficiently. Quantum computing, with its ability to perform complex computations in parallel, offers unprecedented speed and precision in processing large datasets, uncovering patterns, and making predictions. Our model incorporates quantum-assisted machine learning techniques, such as quantum-boosted Artificial Neural Networks (ANNs), to enhance churn prediction accuracy. By integrating quantum algorithms for data clustering and segmentation, specifically through a quantum-enhanced K-means algorithm, the

DOI: 10.1201/9781003498292-12

model can better understand the heterogeneity of customer behaviors. This quantum approach also improves the system's ability to forecast not only the likelihood of churn but also the duration of customer disengagement, allowing businesses to implement timely and targeted retention strategies. Through this innovative quantum-enhanced framework, we demonstrate how combining predictive analytics with quantum computing can optimize customer retention efforts while simultaneously refining supply chain management. The model offers businesses a dual advantage: minimizing churn through personalized retention strategies and enhancing supply chain operations by predicting demand fluctuations more accurately.

This study identifies four churn segments: conditionally loyal subscribers, conditional churners, lifestyle migrators, and unsatisfied churners, each with its own set of loyalty determinants. Conditionally loyal subscribers are motivated by incentives, service quality, customer experience, communication efficacy, flexibility, and innovation. Lifestyle migrators want services that meet their changing demands and stay ahead of the curve. Unsatisfied clients want prompt problem solutions and feedback integration. As part of retaining these customer segments, predictive analytics, proactive communication, individualized incentives, and ongoing development based on customer feedback are all essential components. Understanding these categories allows enterprises to improve their efforts to retain consumers and foster long-term loyalty in a constantly changing market landscape.

The existing customer churn prediction system usually uses generic models and simple indicators, which are insufficiently sophisticated to forecast customer attrition. These systems may undervalue the significance of customer segmentation, treating every client in the same way while ignoring the wide range of traits and actions present in the customer base. As a result, the algorithm could have difficulty identifying tiny churn cues, which might lead to inaccurate forecasts. Furthermore, without the assistance of sophisticated predictive analytics, the current system could find it difficult to deliver prompt and useful insights into the reasons for customer attrition, which would restrict the capacity to take preventative action. Inadequate comprehension of the nuances around customer turnover dynamics may lead to general retention methods that are not customized to meet the demands of individual customers, which might result in inefficiencies and possibly higher churn rates. The objective of this research is to solve these inadequacies by implementing a more advanced and comprehensive approach to churn prediction and retention analysis, adopting segmentation and predictive modeling to improve the overall success of customer retention tactics.

12.2 RELATED WORK

The research published in the field of "Customer Churn Prediction for Retention Analysis" [1] emphasizes the importance of customer attrition as a major issue for enterprises in a variety of sectors. It entails reviewing existing research and studies on customer churn prediction, retention methods, and the utilization of machine learning in the realm of customer relationship management. Numerous studies have highlighted the financial ramifications of customer attrition, underlining the importance of taking proactive actions to retain important clients and preserve long-term growth. Scholars frequently emphasized the need to use reliable churn prediction models to detect possible churners early in the customer lifecycle.

Many research papers have been published in the area of customer churn prediction. We thoroughly examined the following papers to acquire a comprehensive understanding of this field. The review papers and their descriptions are presented below with utmost attention to detail. By taking into consideration further factors including social network analysis features, Prabadevi et al. [1] classified customer churning for a distinct context on various datasets. After training four algorithms—K Nearest Neighbor (KNN), Logistic Regression, Random Forest, and Stochastic Gradient Booster—for the study [2, 3], it was discovered that the Stochastic Gradient had the highest overall performance. Subsequently, it was proposed that focusing on enhanced data-side preprocessing and hyperparameter tuning might further enhance model performance.

Ahmad et al. [4] created a churn predictive model using large amounts of raw data given by SyriaTel telecom firm, utilizing the XGBOOST algorithm in the Spark environment to aid in identifying clients who are likely to turnover and achieved an Area under the Curve (AUC) value of 93.3%[5]. The occurrence of non-stationary data models has led to a decrease in the obtained results[6] and the model has to be trained periodically.

Dahiya and Bhatia [7] designed a churn prediction model to assist the CRM department in identifying individuals who are churning out, utilizing Logistic Regression and Decision Tree in WEKA Data Mining Software, and discovered that the Decision Tree is an efficient method. This research may be expanded by using hybrid classification algorithms to highlight the existing link between churn prediction and client lifetime value. Huang et al. [8] presented a novel set of characteristics for predicting land-line client migration and conducted comparison studies using seven modeling methodologies. The suggested feature set outperforms existing feature sets in terms of prediction accuracy, and it concluded that to improve the feature set, additional attributes should be added in the future.

Ahn et al. [9] explored the factors influencing customer attrition in the Korean mobile service industry. The influence of a consumer's partial abandonment on the association between attrition predictors and total abandonment was investigated and addressed that churn determinants have an impact on customer churn in either a direct or indirect manner a customer's status change.

Sandhya Rani et al. [4] suggested a technique for churn prediction using Logistic Regression to determine the company's churn factor based on past data. This system saves the organization time and effort by analyzing past data to respond to the circumstances. Almana et al. [10] demonstrated standard data mining strategies for identifying customer churn tendencies. C5.0 and CART ended up performing better than regression in terms of efficiency. Finally, they suggested that employing RULES family approaches to datasets can produce the finest patterns.

12.3 PROPOSED SYSTEM

The proposed system aims to revolutionize customer retention strategies through the integration of advanced predictive modeling, customer segmentation, and duration estimation within a unified framework. At its core, our system leverages deep learning algorithms such as ANN and Decision Tree to accurately predict customer churn and estimate the potential duration of churn for individual customers. This predictive capability is essential for businesses looking to not only identify potential churners but also proactively develop timely and targeted retention strategies. An important feature of our system is the incorporation of duration estimation, allowing businesses to prioritize retention efforts based on the urgency of each customer case.

A key advancement in our proposed system is the focus on customer segmentation using the K-means clustering algorithm. Instead of treating the entire customer base uniformly, our system employs sophisticated clustering techniques to group customers with similar characteristics and behaviors analyzed through exploratory data analysis of customer data. This segmentation provides a more detailed understanding of the diverse factors influencing churn, facilitating the extraction of meaningful insights from various customer segments. By acknowledging and addressing the distinct requirements and inclinations of every group, companies may customize their retention tactics for greater effectiveness and personalization. This approach not only helps in reducing customer attrition but also enhances retention efforts on high-risk segments, ultimately improving the company's ability to proactively retain customers and mitigate churn [8].

In short, the major objectives of the proposed system include the following:

- The primary goal is to build a predictive churn model and utilize its results to generate a target list.
- Identify the characteristics of churners and obtain insights through exploratory data analysis.
- Segment the model output for targeted retention campaigns or strategies.

12.4 METHODOLOGY

The project mainly comprises four consecutive tasks to be performed. These four tasks are as follows:

(1) data exploration and analysis
(2) predictive model building
(3) customer segmentation
(4) integration and user interface (Figure 12.1)

12.4.1 Data exploration and analysis

The initial step for constructing any machine learning model is data modeling and data exploration. The dataset used for implementing the proposed system is downloaded from Kaggle. It consists of customer churn data of a telco organization that provided mobile and internet services to consumers. The dataset contains approximately 7043 customers' data and 21 attributes that describe the various features of customers like gender, tenure, partner, dependents, monthly charges, total charges, payment method, contract type, internet service, streaming services provided, and so on. Currently, the system is implemented using this telco customer data, but the architecture is outlined in a way that it can be used by any sort of business organization to understand their customers and retain them [9].

Initially, data preprocessing is performed, which involves handling missing values in the dataset, followed by transforming categorical variables

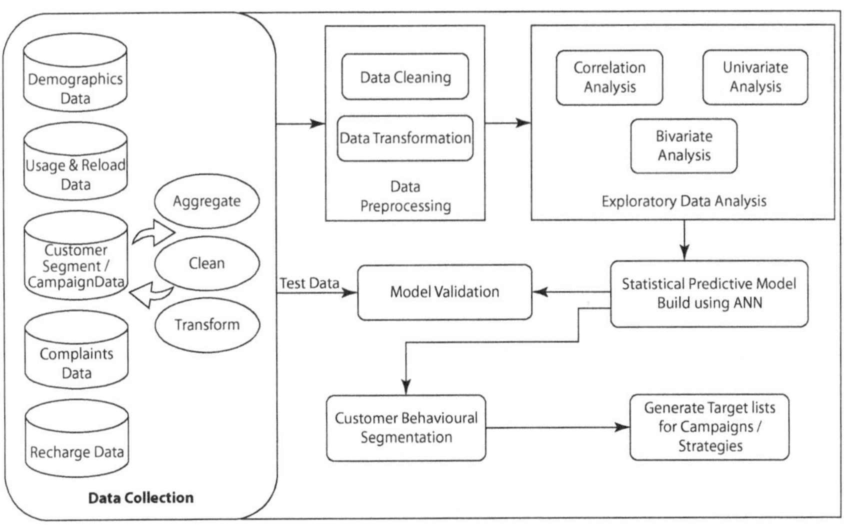

Figure 12.1 Customer churn prediction for retention analysis system architecture.

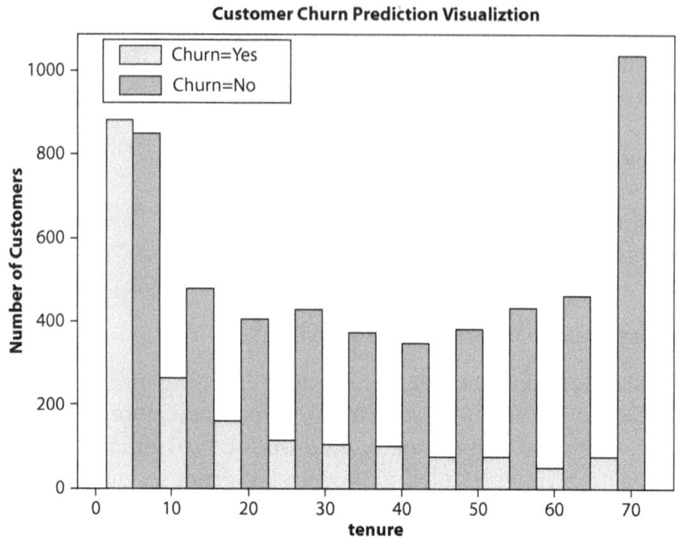

Figure 12.2 Churn by tenure visualization.

into numeric using one-hot encoding and feature scaling methods. Then, exploratory data analysis such as univariate and bivariate analysis is performed on each attribute of the customer data to recognize the characteristics that influence customer attrition, resulting in the following conclusions (Figures 12.2–12.5).

- Greater churn is observed in the case of month-to-month contracts, no online security, no tech support or customer support, early years of subscription, fiber optics internet, and lower total charges [11].
- Long-term agreements, subscriptions without internet access, and clients who have been with a company for more than five years all show lower churn rates.
- There is very little effect of variables like gender, numerous lines, and phone service availability on attrition.
- Electronic check mediums are the highest churners.
- Contract type—Since monthly clients have no set of terms and are essentially pay-as-you-go, they are more likely to discontinue service.
- The categories with no tech support and no online security are major turners.
- Non-senior citizens have a high turnover rate.

12.4.2 Predictive model building

The preprocessed data is now used to train the ANN model to build a robust and accurate customer churn prediction model.

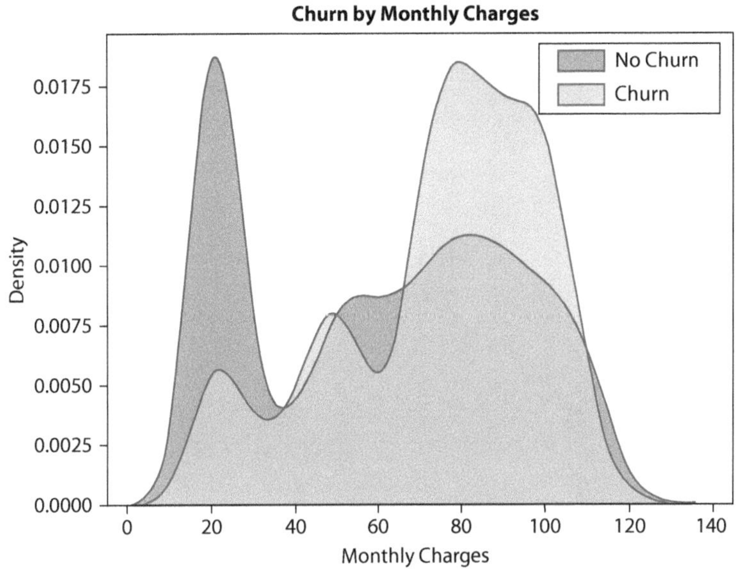

Figure 12.3 Churn by monthly charges visualization.

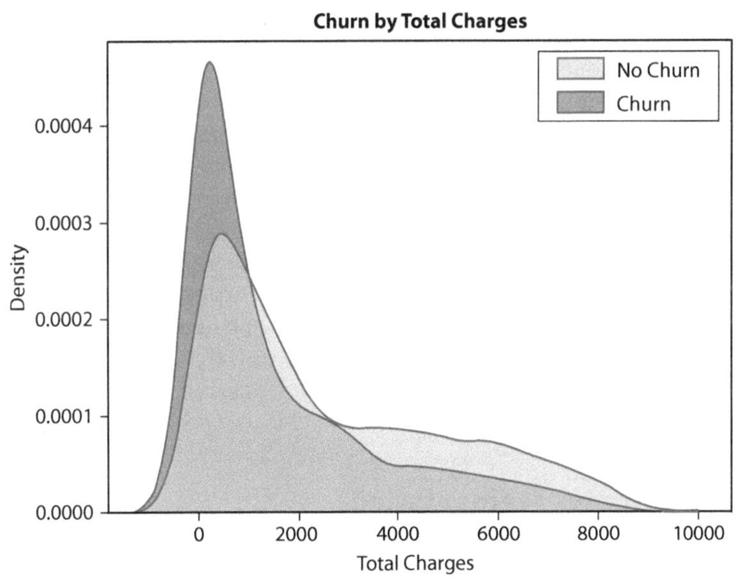

Figure 12.4 Churn by total charges visualization.

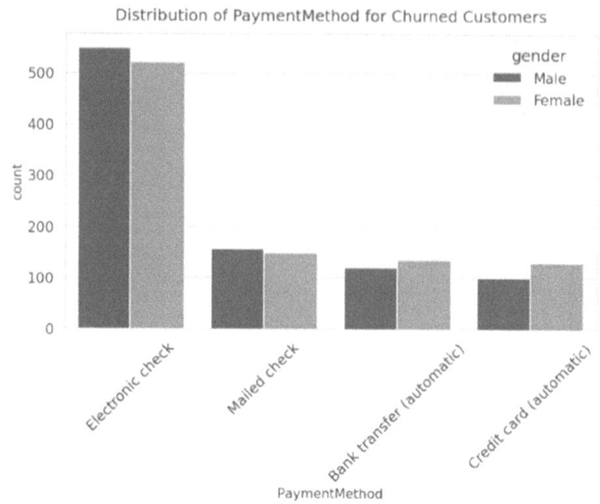

Figure 12.5 Distribution of payment method for churned customers.

Artificial Neural Network (ANN) models are ideal for churn prediction because they can capture complex, non-linear correlations in data [12]. Churn prediction requires understanding nuanced patterns and correlations in consumer behavior that standard linear models may be difficult to detect. These complicated patterns may be efficiently learned and represented by ANNs due to their layered design and activation functions. They excel in processing vast amounts of heterogeneous data, such as customer interactions, use trends, and demographic information, allowing for a thorough examination of the reasons influencing turnover.

TensorFlow and Keras are used to create a basic Artificial Neural Network (ANN) model for binary classification or the prediction of whether a client would churn. The two layers of the model are designed to handle binary classification issues. The input layer has 26 neurons and uses the ReLU activation function, while the output layer has one neuron and uses the sigmoid activation function. Using the Adam optimizer, accuracy as the training metric, and the binary cross-entropy loss function (which is frequently employed in binary classification), the model is assembled [13].

12.4.3 Customer segmentation

As discussed earlier, customer segmentation is one of the key advancements in the proposed system which provides a more detailed understanding of the customer's characteristics and behavior influencing customer attrition. This task also helps in extracting meaningful insights from the customer segments to develop targeted retention strategies [14]. We have used the

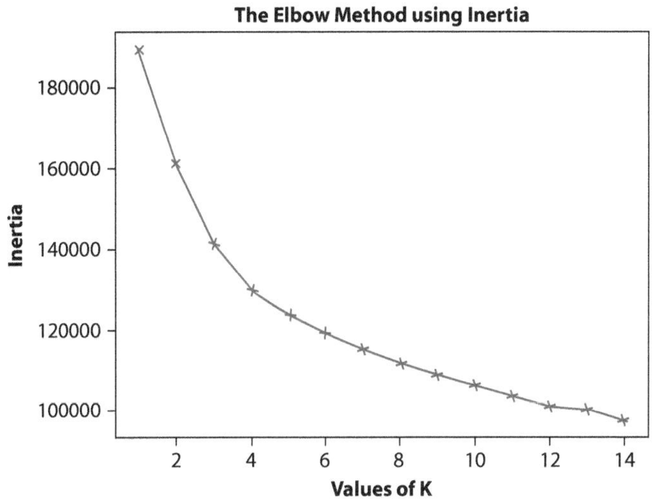

Figure 12.6 Graph representing optimal number of clusters using the elbow method.

K-means algorithm here for customer segmentation as it can detect unique groups within a dataset efficiently and divide clients into clusters based on common qualities, actions, or preferences. K-means is a realistic and scalable approach for customer segmentation, allowing businesses to easily assess and respond to the different preferences and behaviors demonstrated by their client base, thus improving consumer satisfaction and delivering targeted business strategies [15]. The output data of the predictive churn model is provided as input to the segmentation model. This data is initially scaled using StandardScaler to normalize its features. The dimensionality of the scaled data is then reduced to two main components using principal component analysis (PCA). The new data frame contains the principal components that are obtained. The elbow method is then used to calculate the ideal number of clusters for K-means by plotting the inertia (within-cluster sum of squares) versus different values of "*k*.' The point of the elbow in the plot indicates an optimal number of clusters as shown in Figure 12.6. Finally, K-means clustering is performed with a chosen "*k*" value (in this case, 4), and the resulting cluster labels are added to the data frame, which includes the principal components along with the assigned cluster labels for each data point. This resulting dataset is further used for the segmentation of any new customer. Thus, the customers are categorized into four segments namely conditionally loyal subscribers, conditional churners, lifestyle migrators, and unsatisfied customers. Finally, effective targeted retention strategies are designed by considering the characteristics of each customer segment.

12.4.4 Integration and user interface

A web interface is developed for deploying and integrating the predictive and segmentation models using Flask, a web framework of Python. The user interface comprises input fields for the various attributes describing customer features and buttons to initiate analysis. Users can input those features, and the system processes and predicts whether the customer is likely to churn or not. On the other hand, the segment type of the user is identified by considering churn prediction results. If the customer is likely to churn, then the system provides the period of churn by comparing the tenure of the user with its corresponding segment's average tenure and provides the customer characteristic distribution graphs as well as appropriate retention strategies as an output in an intuitive manner [14].

12.5 RESULTS

An efficient and accurate predictive model that anticipates customer churn along with the duration of churn is developed using the ANN algorithm with an accuracy of 81.74%, and customer behavior segmentation is performed using the K-means clustering algorithm, and Decision Tree algorithm is employed for customer segment classification [15] with an accuracy of 96.576%. Characteristics and behavior patterns of each customer segment are extracted and displayed to the user, which are leveraged in tailoring targeted customer retention strategies [16] (Figure 12.7).

Here cluster 0 represents unsatisfied customers, cluster 1 represents conditional churners, cluster 2 represents conditionally loyal subscribers, and cluster 3 represents lifestyle migrators (Table 12.1) (Figures 12.8–12.10).

12.6 CONCLUSION

As a result, this chapter offers a very reliable "Customer Churn Prediction for Retention Analysis" system that has effectively used Artificial Neural Network (ANN) algorithms to forecast customer attrition, offering a thorough comprehension of possible churners, their anticipated duration of churn, and segmentation based on distinct customer attributes. The study has successfully identified intricate, non-linear patterns in customer behavior by utilizing ANN models, which has led to a more accurate and nuanced churn forecast. The inclusion of a crucial dimension—time prediction—allows retention efforts to be prioritized according to the urgency of individual client cases. By addressing the varied demands and preferences of distinct client groups, customer segmentation further improves

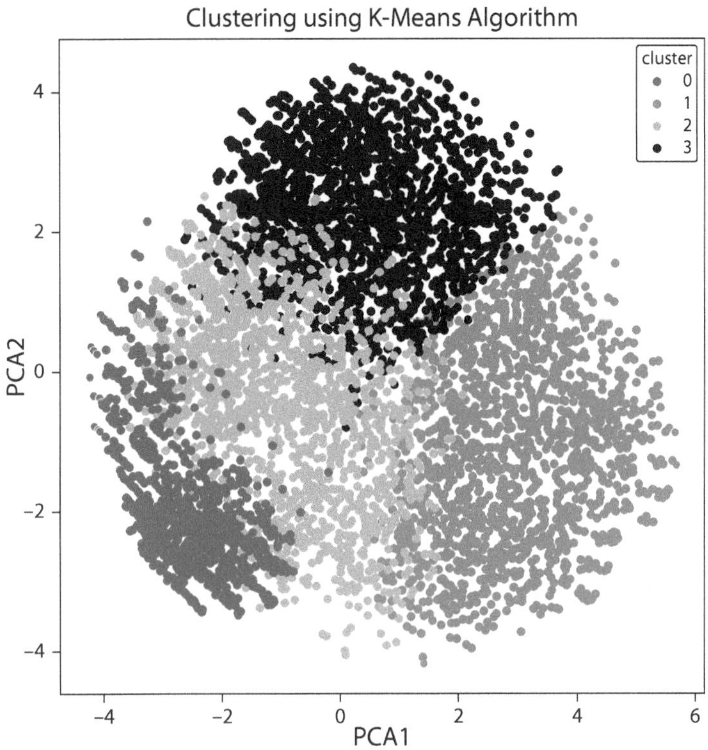

Figure 12.7 Customer segments scatter plot.

Table 12.1 Classification report of customer segmentation

	Precision	*Recall*	*f1 score*	*Support*
Cluster 0	1.00	1.00	1.00	465
Cluster 1	0.93	0.94	0.93	512
Cluster 2	0.97	0.97	0.97	511
Cluster 3	0.97	0.96	0.97	615
Accuracy			0.97	2103
Macro avg	0.97	0.97	0.97	2103
Weighted avg	0.97	0.97	0.97	2103

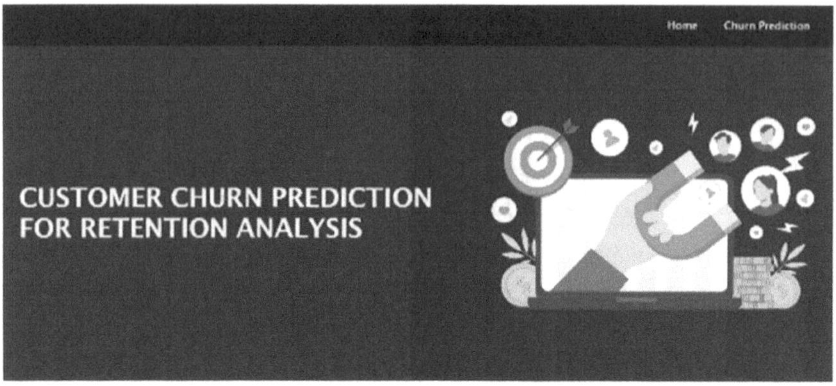

Figure 12.8 Customer churn prediction for retention analysis home page.

the effectiveness of the system by customizing retention strategies. The outcome is a powerful tool for businesses to proactively manage customer churn, formulate targeted retention plans, and ultimately strengthen customer relationships, fostering sustainable growth and long-term success. However, further research can concentrate on developing KPIs for tracking and monitoring customer usage behavior, providing a list of churn drivers, and recommending cross-selling and upselling strategies can assist in reducing customer attrition rate and enhance business profitability even further.

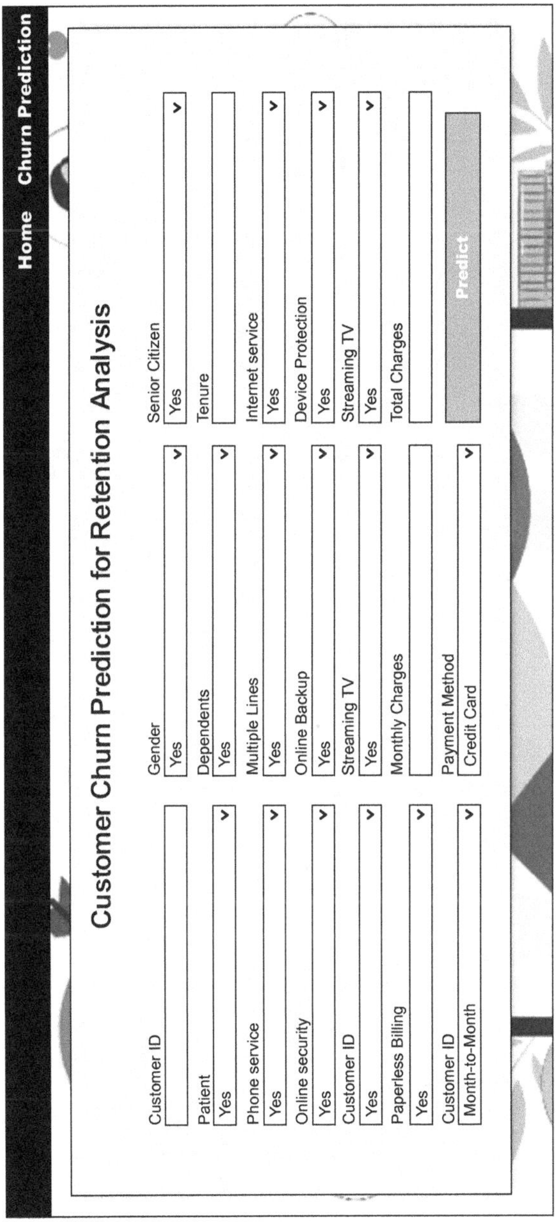

Figure 12.9 Churn prediction page.

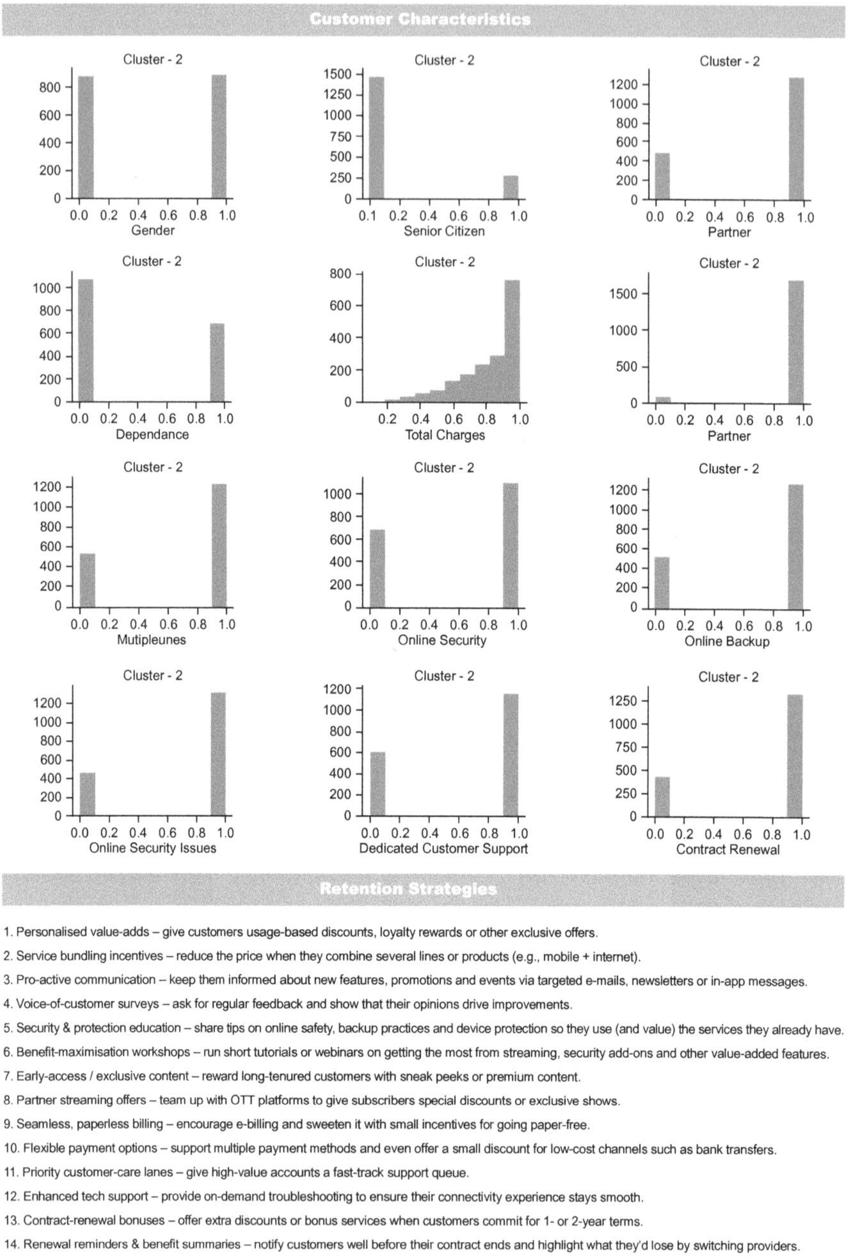

Figure 12.10 Customer characteristics and retention strategies.

REFERENCES

1. B. Prabadevi, R. Shalini, and B. R. Kavitha, "Customer churning analysis using machine learning algorithms," *International Journal of Intelligent Networks*, 4, 145–154, 2023. https://doi.org/10.1016/j.ijin.2023.05.005.
2. S. Saleh and S. Saha, "Customer retention and churn prediction in the telecommunication industry: a case study on a Danish university," *SN Applied Sciences*, 5, 173, 2023. https://doi.org/10.1007/s42452-023-05389-6.
3. P. Lalwani, M. K. Mishra, J. S. Chadha, and P. Sethi, "Customer churn prediction system: a machine learning approach," *Computing*, 104, 271–294, 2021. https://doi.org/10.1007/s00607-021-00908-y.
4. K. Sandhya Rani, S. Thaslima, N. G. L. Prasanna, R. Vindhya, and P. Srilakshmi, "Analysis of customer churn prediction in telecom industry using logistic regression," *International Journal of Innovative Research in Computer Science & Technology*, 9(4), 27–29, 2021.
5. A. K. Ahmad, A. Jafar, and K. Aljoumaa, "Customer churn prediction in telecom using machine learning in big data platform," *Journal of Big Data*, 6–28, 2019.
6. A. A. Ahmed and D. Maheswari Linen, "A review and analysis of churn prediction methods for customer retention in telecom industries," *International Conference on Advanced Computing and Communication Systems* (pp. 1–7), 2017. IEEE. https://doi.org/10.1109/ICACCS.2017.8014605.
7. K. Dahiya and S. Bhatia, "Customer Churn Analysis in Telecom Industry", in *2015 4th International Conference on Reliability, Infocom Technologies and Optimization (ICRITO) (Trends and Future Directions)* (pp. 1–6), 2015. IEEE. https://doi.org/10.1109/ICRITO.2015.7359318.
8. B. Huang, M. T. Kechadi, and B. Buckley, "Customer churn prediction in telecommunications," *Expert Systems with Applications*, 1414–1425, 2012.
9. J.-H. Ahn, S.-P. Han, and Y.-S. Lee, "Customer churn analysis: Churn determinants and mediation effects of partial defection in the Korean mobile telecommunications service industry," *Telecommunications Policy*, 552–568, 2006.
10. A. M. Almana, M. S. Aksoy, and R. Alzahran, "A survey on data mining techniques in customer churn analysis for telecom industry," *International Journal of Engineering Research and Applications*, 4(5), 165–171, 2014.
11. B. Singh, P. K. Dutta, and C. Kaunert, Boosting Quantum Computing to Redefine Supply Chain in the Hospital Industry: Pitch the Vision for Medical and Healthcare Needs. In A. Hassan, P. Bhattacharya, P. Dutta, J. Verma, & N. Kundu (Eds.), *Quantum Computing and Supply Chain Management: A New Era of Optimization* (pp. 196–219), 2024. IGI Global. https://doi.org/10.4018/979-8-3693-4107-0.ch014.
12. P. K. Dutta, A. K. Bhardwaj, and A. Mahida, Navigating the Complexities of Agile Transformations in Large Organizations. In A. Hassan, P. Bhattacharya, P. Dutta, J. Verma, & N. Kundu (Eds.), *Quantum Computing and Supply Chain Management: A New Era of Optimization* (pp. 315–330), 2024. IGI Global. https://doi.org/10.4018/979-8-3693-4107-0.ch020.

13. L. M. Gutta, B. Dhamodharan, P. K. Dutta, and Whig, P., AI-Infused Quantum Machine Learning for Enhanced Supply Chain Forecasting. In A. Hassan, P. Bhattacharya, P. Dutta, J. Verma, & N. Kundu (Eds.), *Quantum Computing and Supply Chain Management: A New Era of Optimization* (pp. 48–63), 2024. IGI Global. https://doi.org/10.4018/979-8-3693-4107-0.ch003.
14. N. Dhaliwal, S, Aghera, P. Whig, and P. K. Dutta, Advanced Analytics and Quantum Computing for Revolutionizing Procurement Strategies. In A. Hassan, P. Bhattacharya, P. Dutta, J. Verma, & N. Kundu (Eds.), *Quantum Computing and Supply Chain Management: A New Era of Optimization* (pp. 160–175), 2024. IGI Global. https://doi.org/10.4018/979-8-3693-4107-0.ch011.
15. M. Abotaleb and P. K. Dutta, Optimizing Bidirectional Long Short-Term Memory Networks for Univariate Time Series Forecasting: A Comprehensive Guide. In Ramakant Bhardwaj, Pushan Kumar Dutta, Pethuru Raj, Abhishek Kumar, Kavita Saini, Alfonso González Briones and Mohammed K. A. Kaabar (Eds.), *Hybrid Information Systems: Non-Linear Optimization Strategies with Artificial Intelligence*, Berlin, Boston: De Gruyter, 2024, pp. 443–458. https://doi.org/10.1515/9783111331133-021.
16. P. S. Rao, S. Nayak, A. Gautam, M. E. Lourens, P. K. Dutta, S. Chowdhury, and E. M. El-kenawy, "Aumann Agreement Theorem Based Human Resource Performance Monitoring With IoT and 6G Technology," in *6th Smart Cities Symposium (SCS 2022), Hybrid Conference*, Bahrain, 2022, pp. 401–406. https://doi.org/10.1049/icp.2023.0638.

Chapter 13

Industry 4.0 and supply chain sustainability

Insights from case studies

Hoang Chi Cuong, Vinh Thai, Álvaro Rocha, and Khoa Nguyen

13.1 INTRODUCTION

The onset of Industry 4.0 signifies a monumental shift in the manufacturing landscape, heralding an era where the digital and physical realms converge (Rocha et al., 2021; Stefanini & Vignali, 2024). This digital transformation, marked by the fusion of cutting-edge technologies and smart systems, not only reshapes business operations but also exerts a transformative influence on supply chains worldwide. Understanding the profound implications of Industry 4.0 and its intricate relationship with supply chain sustainability is imperative in this fast-changing era (Nguyen & Ali, 2021; Thai et al., 2023).

Industry 4.0 intertwines diverse elements, promising more efficient production, real-time decision-making and enhanced customisation. Such technologies have substantial implications for supply chains, transforming the production, distribution and consumption of goods. Supply chain processes, from procurement to delivery, have evolved, optimising operations and bolstering overall competitiveness (Ali et al., 2023; Nakandala et al., 2023).

Supply chain sustainability has evolved from a buzzword to a necessity, incorporating economic, social and environmental dimensions. Organisations face mounting pressure to adopt ethical and eco-conscious practices beyond profit-seeking (Ali et al., 2022). Responsible sourcing, ethical production, reduced carbon footprints and fair labour practices are indispensable in sustainable supply chains. Likewise, consumer preferences and regulations favour eco-friendly and socially responsible products (Veile et al., 2024).

This chapter delves into the intricate relationship between Industry 4.0 and supply chain sustainability, spanning economic, social and environmental dimensions. Through real-world case studies, we aim to elucidate how organisations navigate this intersection while eliminating pitfalls. Our goal is to contribute to the ongoing discourse on harnessing the potential of Industry 4.0 for nurturing responsible, efficient and sustainable supply chains.

DOI: 10.1201/9781003498292-13

The rest of the chapter is structured as follows: Section 13.2 provides an overview of Industry 4.0 and sustainable supply chain. Section 13.3 reviews the literature on Industry 4.0 and sustainability encompassing economic, social and environmental alongside real-world case studies. Section 13.4 concludes with limitations and future research directions.

13.2 OVERVIEW OF INDUSTRY 4.0 AND SUPPLY CHAIN SUSTAINABILITY

Industry 4.0 integrates cutting-edge technologies—big data analytics, internet of things (IoTs), blockchain, artificial intelligence (AI) and automation—into manufacturing processes (Hasan & Trianni, 2023). These innovations drive operational efficiency, cost reduction and product quality improvement. Supply chain sustainability embraces economic, ecological and social dimensions (Yu & Ye, 2023), aiming to diminish the environmental footprint, enhance labour conditions and cultivate long-term economic value. Achieving sustainability objectives hinges on data-driven decision-making, ethical sourcing and end-to-end transparency (Yu et al., 2021).

13.3 INDUSTRY 4.0 AND SUSTAINABILITY

The nexus between Industry 4.0 and supply chain sustainability transforms economic, social and environmental dimensions, as depicted in Figure 13.1, envisioning a sustainable and prosperous world.

13.3.1 Industry 4.0 and economic sustainability

The literature review explores Industry 4.0's crucial role in achieving economic sustainability within supply chains, highlighting its transformative impact through the following:

- *Enhanced efficiency:* Industry 4.0 technologies facilitate real-time data collection, analysis and decision-making. IoT sensors ensure a comprehensive supply chain by tracking products, monitoring conditions and optimising routes (Zelbst et al., 2023). Big data analytics provide insights for predictive maintenance and demand forecasting, reducing operational costs (Qi et al., 2023). The synergy of AI and automation streamlines processes, enhancing efficiency while reducing errors (Cannas et al., 2023).
- *Resource optimisation:* Industry 4.0 contributes to economic sustainability through improving resources. Real-time monitoring and data-driven decision-making empower businesses to reduce waste

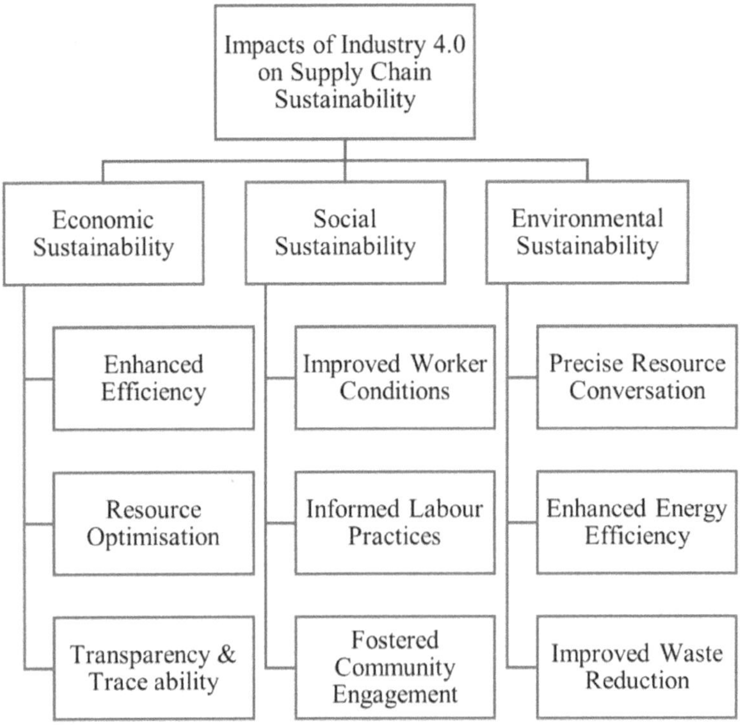

Figure 13.1 Impacts of industry 4.0 on supply chain sustainability.

and energy consumption, minimising costly downtime and repairs through predictive maintenance (Bag et al., 2021). Efficient inventory management and demand forecasting curtail overstock and understock situations, leading to cost savings and more sustainable resource utilisation (Unhelkar et al., 2022).

- *Transparency and traceability:* Blockchain ensures end-to-end visibility and trust within the supply chain through transparency and traceability (Dolgui et al., 2020). Customers can trace product origins and journeys, facilitating ethical practices such as fair labour and responsible sourcing (Casino et al., 2020).
- *Challenges and ethical considerations:* While Industry 4.0 offers substantial economic sustainability benefits, it also poses several challenges (Chauhan et al., 2021). Data security and privacy take on paramount importance, requiring organisations to uphold ethical standards in technology utilisation (Shang et al., 2022). Improving economic efficiency with environmental and social responsibility is delicate; the pursuit of cost savings should not compromise ethical standards (Bag et al., 2023).

Case study 1: Toyota, a global automotive leader, stands as a prime exemplar of lean manufacturing and profitable sustainability.

- *Toyota's economic sustainability initiatives:* The renowned Toyota production system (TPS) embodies IoT sensors and real-time data analytics that minimises waste, reduces operational costs and optimises resource utilisation (Bittencourt et al., 2021). The just-in-time production method, a core TPS component, ensures precise material deliveries, minimising inventory costs and increasing overall efficiency (Ohno, 2019). Likewise, Toyota's commitment to quality control and continuous improvement reduces defects and recalls while mitigating the financial burden of rework and warranty claims. These ongoing economic sustainability efforts enhance Toyota's profitability (Shih, 2022; Toyota, 2023).
- *Efficient production:* Toyota has recently embraced Industry 4.0 revolution to enhance its economic sustainability. The seamless integration of IoT sensors, data analytics and automation technologies into their production processes has occurred (Martínez-Sánchez et al., 2023). Real-time data analysis and predictive maintenance, powered by Industry 4.0, have tremendously increased the efficiency of Toyota's manufacturing operations. Such innovations have facilitated the company to optimise resource utilisation, mitigate waste and lessen energy consumption, contributing to both economic sustainability and environmental responsibility (Bilgeri et al., 2019).
- *Economic sustainability through innovative manufacturing:* Toyota stands as a trailblazer with a commitment to high-quality production (Shih, 2022). Balancing cost-effectiveness with dedication to innovation and excellence, Toyota integrates Industry 4.0 technologies seamlessly. This integration allows Toyota to manufacture with advanced features and enhanced safety, exemplified by the iconic Toyota Prius, a trailblazer in hybrid vehicles (Martínez-Sánchez et al., 2023). Beyond mere cost savings, Toyota's commitment to sustainability encompasses a broader vision, reducing the environmental impact of transportation. The success of the Prius attests to Toyota's capacity to harmonise profitability and sustainability through innovation (Toyota, 2022).

Case study 2: Walmart, the retail giant, has demonstrated sustainability as a cost-saving strategy.

- *Economic sustainability initiatives:* Walmart's commitment is encapsulated in ambitious sustainability goals. These encompass reducing greenhouse gas emissions, achieving zero waste and utilising 100% renewable energy, not only carrying environmental implications but also linking to economic sustainability (Walmart, 2023c). Walmart's strategic investment in renewable energy sources and energy-efficient technologies such as IoT sensors and smart systems has led to substantial financial savings across its stores and distribution stores (Valinejad et al., 2021). Similarly, their focus on waste reduction and recycling is to align with environmental standards and reduce waste disposal costs (Walmart, 2023a).

- *Data-driven logistics optimisation:* Walmart has been a trailblazer in leveraging data analytics to streamline its supply chain operations. Through analysing extensive datasets, Walmart makes well-informed decisions on inventory management, demand forecasting and transportation logistics (Oliveira Dias et al., 2022). Not only does this minimise costs related to overstock and understock but also reduces energy consumption in transportation. Further, data analytics plays an indispensable role in optimising the sourcing and procurement of products, contributing to lower operational costs and sustainable practices (Singh & Sharma, 2023).
- *Economic sustainability challenges:* Walmart faces a significant challenge in achieving economic sustainability due to the vast scale of its operations (Walmart, 2017). Balancing sustainability goals across an extensive network of stores and suppliers is a formidable task (Pourrahmani & Jaller, 2021). Ethical consideration, including fair labour practices and responsible sourcing, take precedence. Striking a balance between ethical and sustainable supplier practices and economic efficiency presents a delicate challenge (Walmart, 2023b). Walmart acknowledges and actively works to address this issue.

13.3.2 Industry 4.0 and social sustainability

The literature review examines the pivotal role of Industry 4.0 in achieving social sustainability as follows:

- *Worker conditions:* Industry 4.0 technologies, encompassing automation, robotics and AI, have the potential to enhance worker conditions. By handling repetitive and physically demanding tasks, they reduce the risk of workplace injuries and create a safer environment (Contini et al., 2023). Furthermore, wearable devices and sensors monitor workers' health, enabling immediate responses to safety concerns. The improvements in work conditions contribute to the social sustainability dimension, prioritising the health and safety of the workforce (Ferreira et al., 2023).
- *Labour practices:* The incorporation of data analytics and AI in Industry 4.0 enables more informed decision-making regarding labour practices (Contini et al., 2023). Predictive analytics optimises workforce management, ensuring efficient labour allocation while reducing overwork and burnout (Grybauskas et al., 2022). It also

facilitates fair wage distribution and compliance with labour laws. Industry 4.0's capability to enhance labour practices is imperative for achieving social sustainability by promoting fair treatment of workers and equitable employment opportunities (García-Muiña et al., 2021).
- *Community engagement:* Industry 4.0 transcends the factory floor by fostering community involvement. Smart manufacturing practices and supply chain transparency enable businesses to actively engage local communities (Zhou et al., 2023). This engagement may include partnering with local educational institutions for workforce training, supporting local businesses and contributing to community development initiatives. By incorporating local communities, Industry 4.0 enhances its impact on social sustainability (Grybauskas et al., 2022).

Case study 3: Coca-Cola, a global beverage industry leader, showcases social sustainability through community empowerment and positive change.

- *Coca-Cola's social sustainability:* Coca-Cola has ingrained social sustainability into its core values and corporate mission using a digital platform, Coca-Cola Fan Zone. The company spearheads numerous programs tackling societal issues, such as clean water access, women's empowerment and community well-being (Coca-Cola, 2022). Notably, their "5by20" program economically empower 5 million women entrepreneurs across the global Coca-Cola value chain by 2020. By advancing women's roles in business, Coca-Cola not only nurtures social sustainability but also propels economic development and market growth (Coca-Cola, 2021).
- *Tech-driven social responsibility:* Coca-Cola harnesses technology and data to promote social responsibility on a large scale. The company's initiatives benefit from data analytics and digital platforms (Luchtenberg & Migliorini, 2022). For instance, their "Ekocenter" project utilises solar-powered kiosks equipped with Wi-Fi to provide clean water and support local businesses (Coca-Cola, 2017). Such kiosks are data-enabled, facilitating real-time monitoring of water quality and consumption and showcasing how technology can fortify social sustainability (Vietnam Investment Review, 2021).
- *Measuring social impact:* Evaluating the authentic social impact of initiatives undertaken by Coca-Cola is challenging. Although the company employs metrics and key performance indicators (KPIs) to assess progress, accurately quantifying the broader societal changes remains a complex task (Coca-Cola, 2021). The long-term effects of women's empowerment, clean water access and community development are multifaceted and often take years to fully materialise. Nevertheless, Coca-Cola continues to refine its measurement methods and improve transparency in its reporting to address these challenges (Coca-Cola, 2022).

Case study 4: Adidas, a prominent sportswear giant, illustrates its dedication to social sustainability through fair labour and transparency practices.

- *Adidas's sustainability endeavours:* Social sustainability is intrinsic to Adidas's corporate ethos. The company dedicates itself to treating the individuals behind its products fairly and ethically (Adidas, 2021b). This commitment is exemplified through the company's comprehensive "Fair Play" programme embedding with 3D printing and robotic arms, which extends beyond compliance with labour laws and industry standards (Galluccio & Agrell, 2022). Adidas actively collaborates with workers and labour organisations to ensure fair wages, safe working conditions and the projection of labour rights throughout its supply chain (Adidas, 2014).
- *Transparent supply chain practices:* Adidas acknowledges that transparency is indispensable in ethical and sustainable supply chain management (Adidas, 2021b). The company seamlessly integrates Industry 4.0 technologies, such as IoT sensors and blockchain, to track and trace its products from source to shelf (Periyasamy & Periyasami, 2023). These technologies enable real-time monitoring of production conditions, supply chain logistics and the ethical treatment of workers. By providing consumers with insights into the journey of their products, Adidas fosters trust and accountability (Adidas, 2021b).
- *Global labour welfare challenges:* Adidas's commitment to labour rights and worker welfare faces complexities (Asif et al., 2019). Operating in a global supply chain, the company navigates varying labour standards, cultural contexts and legal frameworks. The "Fair Play" programme recognises the multifaceted nature of labour rights and engages in a continuous dialogue with local partners, governments and NGOs (Adidas, 2021a). Adidas acknowledges the need for ongoing improvements and collaborates with industry peers and stakeholders to address these challenges (Adidas, 2021b).

13.3.3 Industry 4.0 and environmental sustainability

The advent of Industry 4.0 revolutionises industries and holds immense potential to address environmental sustainability concerns, as outlined below:

- *Resource conservation:* Industry 4.0 technologies empower precise resource management and conservation. Real-time data monitoring and predictive analytics optimise resource utilisation, reducing waste and inefficiency (Bildirici & Ersin, 2023). For instance, IoT sensors in manufacturing processes regulate the consumption of raw materials, such as water and metals, leading to reduced environmental impact. This facet of Industry 4.0 aligns with the environmental sustainability goal of responsible resource management (Ferreira et al., 2023).

- *Energy efficiency:* Energy consumption contributes to environmental challenges. Industry 4.0 facilitates energy-efficient practices through intelligent automation and data-driven decision-making. Smart factories, powered by IoTs and AI, can adjust energy usage in real time, reducing waste (Chiarini et al., 2020). The integration of renewable energy sources, such as solar and wind, become efficient with Industry 4.0 technologies. Not only does this reduce operational costs but also lessens the environmental footprint, aligning with sustainable energy usage principles (Fatimah et al., 2020).
- *Waste reduction:* The circular economy, highlighting recycling and reuse of products, is crucial for environmental sustainability. Industry 4.0 facilitates waste reduction through enhanced visibility and tracking of products and materials (Casino et al., 2020). Leveraging IoT sensors and blockchain technology, companies can trace products' entire lifecycle from production to disposal, fostering responsible waste management and recycling to minimise environmental impact (David et al., 2022).

Case study 5: Patagonia, the outdoor clothing company, stands as a trailblazer in the fashion industry.

- *Patagonia's environmental commitment:* Patagonia's corporate ethos revolves around a steadfast commitment to environmental sustainability, declaring itself "in business to save our home planet" (Williams et al., 2022). This dedication is evident through initiatives, including the "Worn Wear" program, advocating clothing recycling and reuse and the "1% for the Planet" commitment, where 1% of sales supports environmental causes. Patagonia's eco-friendly materials, fair labour practices and robust advocacy for sustainable sourcing exemplify how a company can prioritise environmental responsibility at its foundation (Patagonia, 2023b).
- *Sustainable Industry 4.0 practices:* Patagonia leverages Industry 4.0 technologies to bolster its environmental sustainability initiatives. IoT sensors, data analytics and automation track the environmental footprint of its supply chain (George & Schillebeeckx, 2022). Real-time data on energy consumption, waste generation and water usage inform decisions that mitigate resource consumption and minimise environmental impacts (Isabelle & Westerlund, 2022). Patagonia's innovative approach extends to sustainable manufacturing practices, including the use of recycled materials and responsible dyeing processes (Patagonia, 2023a).
- *Environmental responsibility challenges and opportunities:* The fashion industry's journey to environmental responsibility encounters multifaceted challenges. Balancing cost-effectiveness with eco-friendly practices remains a hurdle (Patagonia, 2023a). However,

Patagonia has proven that this equilibrium is attainable through creative solutions involving garment repair and reuse. The company also acknowledges the challenge of scaling environmental initiatives while maintaining high product standards (Isabelle & Westerlund, 2022; Niklitschek et al., 2013). Opportunities abound in circular fashion, sustainable sourcing and the adoption of Industry 4.0 technologies to boost environmental responsibility (United Nations Environmental Programme, 2019).

Case study 6: Tesla, a pioneer in electric vehicles (EVs) and clean energy, leads the charge in revolutionising transportation and energy.

- *Tesla's green goals:* Tesla's mission is unequivocal to accelerate the world's shift to sustainable energy (Erickson, 2017). This includes ambitious targets for reducing carbon emissions, transitioning to renewables and achieving carbon neutrality in their operations. Tesla's commitment spans their products, operations and supply chains (Tesla, 2022).
- *Innovative clean energy production:* Tesla's environmental sustainability is driven by innovation. Advanced electric vehicle (EV) manufacturing, efficient battery production in Gigafactory and smart manufacturing processes reduce their carbon footprint (Hua et al., 2020; Tesla, 2023). Tesla's solar energy products, including solar roofs and energy storage solutions, enable individuals and communities to generate and store clean energy (Dai et al., 2021). Through the acquisition of SolarCity, they have become a major player in clean energy solutions, highlighting technology's transformative role in energy production (Shahzad, 2020).
- *Evaluating ecological impact:* While Tesla advances its dedication to environmental sustainability, a comprehensive evaluation of its ecological footprint poses challenges (Tesla, 2023). Despite EVs diminishing greenhouse gas emissions, concerns persist about the environmental impact of battery production and the extraction of rare materials (García-Olivares et al., 2018). Questions regarding e-waste management and the recyclability of lithium-ion batteries require attention. Tesla acknowledges these challenges and actively pursues solutions, including recycling batteries and increased use of renewable energy in production (Faunce et al., 2018).

13.4 LIMITATIONS, FUTURE RESEARCH DIRECTIONS AND CONCLUDING REMARKS

This study focuses on Industry 4.0 and sustainability within global supply chains only, potentially overlooking other industry sectors. Furthermore, our case studies rely on publicly available reports, news articles, books, scientific articles and Internet resources. While this dependence may be viewed as a constraint due to the absence of primary data collection, it simultaneously paves the way for future empirical research and extensive data gathering to enrich our comprehension of the subject.

Future research should include diverse case studies across industries and regions, unveiling distinct sustainability dynamics and strategies. This exploration should scrutinise Industry 4.0's impact on the workforce, highlighting employee well-being, job displacement and the human aspects of technological integration. Likewise, promoting interdisciplinary research spanning technology, ethics and sustainability is imperative for a comprehensive understanding of this complex landscape. Collecting primary data through surveys, interviews or on-site observations can provide deeper insights into the nuances of Industry 4.0's impact on sustainability within global supply chains. Similarly, research efforts should prioritise the development of policy frameworks and governance models to ensure the responsible implementation of Industry 4.0 in supply chains, shaping a more sustainable future for all stakeholders.

The integration of Industry 4.0 into supply chain operations, exemplified by six case studies, underscores its crucial role in reshaping sustainability. Toyota and Walmart demonstrate how Industry 4.0 optimises supply chain efficiency, reduces costs and fosters ethical practices, reinforcing that economic sustainability can thrive alongside responsible business operations. Coca-Cola and Adidas highlight Industry 4.0's potential for empowering workers, promoting fair labour practices and engaging with local communities, emphasising social sustainability and inclusive supply chain practices. Patagonia and Tesla epitomise the urgency of reducing carbon footprints and embracing cleaner production, with Industry 4.0 technologies playing a key role in redefining our approach to environmental stewardship. As such, the journey towards a more sustainable, efficient and responsible future is well underway, calling for alignment among governments, organisations and individuals to achieve supply chain sustainability in the era of Industry 4.0.

REFERENCES

Adidas. (2014). *Fair Play: The Adidas Group Code of Conduct.* Adidas. Retrieved 8 November from https://www.adidas-group.com/media/filer_public/2f/5e/2f5e4b6c-0dbc-423f-a4b8-a354e1b16a64/coc_english_2014.pdf

Adidas. (2021a). *CSR Policy.* Adidas. https://www.adidas.co.in/help/company-information/csr-policy

Adidas. (2021b). *Our Targets: Focus on Sustainability.* Adidas. Retrieved 8 November from https://www.adidas-group.com/en/sustainability/focus-sustainability/our-targets/#/targets-for-2025-social-impacts/

Ali, I., Nguyen, N. D. K., & Arslan, A. (2022). Socially Responsible Consumption of Information Technology Equipment: Case Studies from the Australian Banking Sector. In J. Bhattacharyya (Ed.), *Dealing with Socially Responsible Consumers: Studies in Marketing* (pp. 509`–530). Springer Nature Singapore. https://doi.org/10.1007/978-981-19-4457-4_27

Ali, I., Nguyen, N. D. K., & Gupta, S. (2023). A multi-disciplinary review of enablers and barriers to Cloud ERP implementation and innovation outcomes. *Journal of Enterprise Information Management*, *36*(5), 1209–1239. https://doi.org/10.1108/JEIM-08-2022-0273

Asif, M., Jajja, M. S. S., & Searcy, C. (2019). Social compliance standards: Re-evaluating the buyer and supplier perspectives. *Journal of Cleaner Production*, *227*, 457–471.

Bag, S., Pretorius, J. H. C., Gupta, S., & Dwivedi, Y. K. (2021). Role of institutional pressures and resources in the adoption of big data analytics powered artificial intelligence, sustainable manufacturing practices and circular economy capabilities. *Technological Forecasting and Social Change*, *163*, 120420. https://doi.org/10.1016/j.techfore.2020.120420

Bag, S., Rahman, M. S., Srivastava, G., Shore, A., & Ram, P. (2023). Examining the role of virtue ethics and big data in enhancing viable, sustainable and digital supply chain performance. *Technological Forecasting and Social Change*, *186*, 122154. https://doi.org/10.1016/j.techfore.2022.122154

Bildirici, M., & Ersin, Ö. Ö. (2023). Nexus between Industry 4.0 and environmental sustainability: A Fourier panel bootstrap cointegration and causality analysis. *Journal of Cleaner Production*, *386*, 135786. https://doi.org/10.1016/j.jclepro.2022.135786

Bilgeri, D., Fleisch, E., Gebauer, H., & Wortmann, F. (2019). Driving process innovation with IoT field data. *MIS Quarterly Executive*, *18*(3), 191–207.

Bittencourt, V. L., Alves, A. C., & Leão, C. P. (2021). Industry 4.0 triggered by Lean Thinking: insights from a systematic literature review. *International Journal of Production Research*, *59*(5), 1496–1510. https://doi.org/10.1080/00207543.2020.1832274

Cannas, V. G., Ciano, M. P., Saltalamacchia, M., & Secchi, R. (2023). Artificial intelligence in supply chain and operations management: a multiple case study research. *International Journal of Production Research*, *62*(6), 1–28. https://doi.org/10.1080/00207543.2023.2232050

Casino, F., Kanakaris, V., Dasaklis, T. K., Moschuris, S., Stachtiaris, S., Pagoni, M., & Rachaniotis, N. P. (2020). Blockchain-based food supply chain traceability: a case study in the dairy sector. *International Journal of Production Research*, *59*(13), 1–13. https://doi.org/10.1080/00207543.2020.1789238

Chauhan, C., Singh, A., & Luthra, S. (2021). Barriers to industry 4.0 adoption and its performance implications: An empirical investigation of emerging economy. *Journal of Cleaner Production*, *285*, 124809. https://doi.org/10.1016/j.jclepro.2020.124809

Chiarini, A., Belvedere, V., & Grando, A. (2020). Industry 4.0 strategies and technological developments. An exploratory research from Italian manufacturing companies. *Production Planning and Control*, *31*(16), 1385–1398. https://doi.org/10.1080/09537287.2019.1710304

Coca-Cola. (2017). *EkoCenter: The New Buzzword on College Campuses*. Coca-Cola. Retrieved 8 November from https://www.coca-colacompany.com/media-center/ekocenter-the-new-buzzword-on-campus

Coca-Cola. (2021). *Coca-Cola Surpasses 5by20 Women's Economic Empowerment Goal*. Coca-Cola. Retrieved 8 November from https://www.coca-colacompany.com/media-center/coca-cola-surpasses-5by20-goal

Coca-Cola. (2022). *2022 Business & Sustainability Report*. Coca-Cola. Retrieved 8 November from https://www.coca-colacompany.com/reports/business-and-sustainability-report

Contini, G., Peruzzini, M., Bulgarelli, S., & Bosi, G. (2023). Developing key performance indicators for monitoring sustainability in the ceramic industry: The role of digitalization and industry 4.0 technologies. *Journal of Cleaner Production*, *414*, 137664. https://doi.org/10.1016/j.jclepro.2023.137664

Dai, R., Esmaeilbeigi, R., & Charkhgard, H. (2021). The utilization of shared energy storage in energy systems: A comprehensive review. *IEEE Transactions on Smart Grid*, *12*(4), 3163–3174.

David, L. O., Nwulu, N. I., Aigbavboa, C. O., & Adepoju, O. O. (2022). Integrating fourth industrial revolution (4IR) technologies into the water, energy & food nexus for sustainable security: A bibliometric analysis. *Journal of Cleaner Production*, *363*, 132522. https://doi.org/10.1016/j.jclepro.2022.132522

Dolgui, A., Ivanov, D., Potryasaev, S., Sokolov, B., Ivanova, M., & Werner, F. (2020). Blockchain-oriented dynamic modelling of smart contract design and execution in the supply chain. *International Journal of Production Research*, *58*(7), 2184–2199. https://doi.org/10.1080/00207543.2019.1627439

Erickson, L. E. (2017). Reducing greenhouse gas emissions and improving air quality: Two global challenges. *Environmental Progress & Sustainable Energy*, *36*(4), 982–988.

Fatimah, Y. A., Govindan, K., Murniningsih, R., & Setiawan, A. (2020). Industry 4.0 based sustainable circular economy approach for smart waste management system to achieve sustainable development goals: A case study of Indonesia. *Journal of Cleaner Production*, *269*, 122263. https://doi.org/10.1016/j.jclepro.2020.122263

Faunce, T. A., Prest, J., Su, D., Hearne, S. J., & Iacopi, F. (2018). On-grid batteries for large-scale energy storage: Challenges and opportunities for policy and technology. *MRS Energy & Sustainability*, *5*, E11.

Ferreira, J. J., Lopes, J. M., Gomes, S., & Rammal, H. G. (2023). Industry 4.0 implementation: Environmental and social sustainability in manufacturing multinational enterprises. *Journal of Cleaner Production*, *404*, 136841. https://doi.org/10.1016/j.jclepro.2023.136841

Galluccio, A., & Agrell, P. J. (2022). Industry 4.0 in focus: The Adidas Speedfactory. *Université catholique de Louvain*, 21–32.

García-Muiña, F., Medina-Salgado, M. S., González-Sánchez, R., Huertas-Valdivia, I., Ferrari, A. M., & Settembre-Blundo, D. (2021). Industry 4.0-based dynamic Social Organizational Life Cycle Assessment to target the social circular economy in manufacturing. *Journal of Cleaner Production*, *327*, 129439. https://doi.org/10.1016/j.jclepro.2021.129439

García-Olivares, A., Solé, J., & Osychenko, O. (2018). Transportation in a 100% renewable energy system. *Energy Conversion and Management*, *158*, 266–285.

George, G., & Schillebeeckx, S. J. (2022). Digital transformation, sustainability and purpose in the multinational enterprise. *Journal of World Business*, *57*(3), 101326.

Grybauskas, A., Stefanini, A., & Ghobakhloo, M. (2022). Social sustainability in the age of digitalization: A systematic literature Review on the social implications of industry 4.0. *Technology in Society*, *70*, 101997. https://doi.org/10.1016/j.techsoc.2022.101997

Hasan, A. S. M. M., & Trianni, A. (2023). Boosting the adoption of industrial energy efficiency measures through Industry 4.0 technologies to improve operational performance. *Journal of Cleaner Production*, *425*, 138597. https://doi.org/10.1016/j.jclepro.2023.138597

Hua, Y., Zhou, S., Huang, Y., Liu, X., Ling, H., Zhou, X., Zhang, C., & Yang, S. (2020). Sustainable value chain of retired lithium-ion batteries for electric vehicles. *Journal of Power Sources*, *478*, 228753.

Isabelle, D. A., & Westerlund, M. (2022). A review and categorization of artificial intelligence-based opportunities in wildlife, ocean and land conservation. *Sustainability*, *14*(4), 1979.

Luchtenberg, D., & Migliorini, R. (2022). *Coca-Cola: The People-first Story of a Digital Transformation*. McKinsey & Company. Retrieved 8 November from https://www. mckinsey. com/capabilities/operations/our-insights/coca-cola-the-people-first-storyof-a-digital-transformation

Martínez-Sánchez, R., Molina-García, Á., Ramallo-González, A. P., Sánchez-Valverde, J., & Úbeda-Miñarro, B. (2023). A low-cost hardware architecture for EV battery cell characterization using an IoT-based platform. *Sensors*, *23*(2), 816.

Nakandala, D., Yang, R., Lau, H., & Weerabahu, S. (2023). Industry 4.0 technology capabilities, resilience and incremental innovation in Australian manufacturing firms: a serial mediation model. *Supply Chain Management*, *28*(4), 760–772. https://doi.org/10.1108/SCM-08-2022-0325

Nguyen, N. D. K., & Ali, I. (2021). Implementation of Cloud Customer Relationship Management in Banking Sector: Strategies, Benefits and Challenges. *International Journal of Electronics and Communication Engineering*, *15*(6), 242–247.

Niklitschek, E. J., Soto, D., Lafon, A., Molinet, C., & Toledo, P. (2013). Southward expansion of the C hilean salmon industry in the Patagonian Fjords: main environmental challenges. *Reviews in Aquaculture*, *5*(3), 172–195.

Ohno, T. (2019). *Toyota Production System: Beyond Large-Scale Production*. Productivity Press.

Oliveira-Dias, D., Maqueira-Marín, J. M., & Moyano-Fuentes, J. (2022). The link between information and digital technologies of industry 4.0 and agile supply chain: Mapping current research and establishing new research avenues. *Computers & Industrial Engineering*, *167*, 108000.

Patagonia. (2023a). *Environmental & Social Footprint*. Patagonia. Retrieved 8 November from https://www.patagonia.com/our-footprint/

Patagonia. (2023b). *Patagonia: Environmental Activism*. Patagonia. Retrieved 8 November from https://www.patagonia.com/activism/

Periyasamy, A. P., & Periyasami, S. (2023). Rise of digital fashion and metaverse: Influence on sustainability. *Digital Economy and Sustainable Development*, *1*(1), 1–26.

Pourrahmani, E., & Jaller, M. (2021). Crowdshipping in last mile deliveries: Operational challenges and research opportunities. *Socio-Economic Planning Sciences*, *78*, 101063.

Qi, Q., Xu, Z., & Rani, P. (2023). Big data analytics challenges to implementing the intelligent Industrial Internet of Things (IIoT) systems in sustainable manufacturing operations. *Technological Forecasting and Social Change*, *190*, 122401. https://doi.org/10.1016/j.techfore.2023.122401

Rocha, Á., Adeli, H., Dzemyda, G., Moreira, F., & Correia, A. M. R. (2021). *Trends and Applications in Information Systems and Technologies: Volume 3* (Vol. 1367). Springer Nature.

Shahzad, U. (2020). Significance of smart grids in electric power systems: a brief overview. *Journal of Electrical Engineering, Electronics, Control and Computer Science*, *6*(1), 7–12.

Shang, C., Saeidi, P., & Goh, C. F. (2022). Evaluation of circular supply chains barriers in the era of Industry 4.0 transition using an extended decision-making approach. *Journal of Enterprise Information Management*, *35*(4–5), 1100–1128. https://doi.org/10.1108/JEIM-09-2021-0396

Shih, W. C. (2022). *What Really Makes Toyota's Production System Resilient*. Harvard Business Review. Retrieved 7 November from https://hbr.org/2022/11/what-really-makes-toyotas-production-system-resilient

Singh, V., & Sharma, S. K. (2023). Application of blockchain technology in shaping the future of food industry based on transparency and consumer trust. *Journal of Food Science and Technology*, *60*(4), 1237–1254.

Stefanini, R., & Vignali, G. (2024). The influence of Industry 4.0 enabling technologies on social, economic and environmental sustainability of the food sector. *International Journal of Production Research*, *62*(10), 3800–3817.

Tesla. (2022). *Impact Report 2022: A Sustainable Future is Within Reach*. Tesla. Retrieved 9 November from https://www.tesla.com/en_au/impact

Tesla. (2023). *Master Plan Part 3: Sustainable Energy for All of Earth*. Tesla. Retrieved 9 November from https://www.tesla.com/ns_videos/Tesla-Master-Plan-Part-3.pdf

Thai, V., Rahman, S., & Ma, S. (2023). Post-COVID-19 global trade and business environment and maritime supply chain. *Maritime Business Review*, *8*(2), 98–100.

Toyota. (2022). *Sustainability Report 2022*. Toyota. Retrieved 7 November from https://www.toyota.com.au/community/sustainability

Toyota. (2023). *Sustainability Data Book*. Toyota. Retrieved 7 November from https://global.toyota/en/sustainability/report/sdb/

Unhelkar, B., Joshi, S., Sharma, M., Prakash, S., Mani, A. K., & Prasad, M. (2022). Enhancing supply chain performance using RFID technology and decision support systems in the industry 4.0–A systematic literature review. *International Journal of Information Management Data Insights*, 2(2), 100084. https://doi.org/10.1016/j.jjimei.2022.100084

United Nations Environmental Programme. (2019). *US outdoor clothing brand Patagonia wins UN Champions of the Earth award*. United Nations Environmental Programme. Retrieved 8 November from https://www.unep.org/news-and-stories/press-release/us-outdoor-clothing-brand-patagonia-wins-un-champions-earth-award

Valinejad, J., Mili, L., van der Wal, C. N., & Xu, Y. (2021). Environomic-based social demand response in cyber-physical-social power systems. *IEEE Transactions on Circuits and Systems II: Express Briefs*, *69*(3), 1302–1306.

Veile, J. W., Schmidt, M.-C., Müller, J. M., & Voigt, K.-I. (2024). The transformation of supply chain collaboration and design through Industry 4.0. *International Journal of Logistics Research and Applications*, *27*(6), 986–1014.

Vietnam Investment Review. (2021). *Coca-Cola's Commitment to Inspire Protection of Water.* Vietnam Investment Review. Retrieved 8 November from https://vir.com.vn/coca-colas-commitment-to-inspire-protection-of-water-83263.html

Walmart. (2017). *Global Responsibility Report.* Walmart. Retrieved 7 November from https://cdn.corporate.walmart.com/95/08/2d1f094c430186c299788ac1935b/wmt-2017-grr-report-final.pdf

Walmart. (2023a). *FY2023 ESG Highlights.* Walmart. Retrieved 7 November from https://corporate.walmart.com/content/dam/corporate/documents/esgreport/a-message-from-our-chief-sustainability-officer/fy2023-walmart-esg-highlights.pdf

Walmart. (2023b). *Product Supply Chain Sustainability.* Walmart. Retrieved 7 November from https://corporate.walmart.com/purpose/esgreport/environmental/product-supply-chain-sustainability

Walmart. (2023c). *Walmart's Journey Toward Regeneration: Placing Nature And People At the Heart Of Our Business.* Walmart. Retrieved 7 November from https://corporate.walmart.com/purpose/sustainability#:~:text=We%20power%20around%2036%25%20of,and%20distribution%20centers%20by%202040.

Williams, P., Escalas, J. E., & Morningstar, A. (2022). Conceptualizing brand purpose and considering its implications for consumer eudaimonic well-being. *Journal of Consumer Psychology*, *32*(4), 699–723.

Yu, D., & Ye, T. (2023). Tracing the lean thinking in supply chain management: a comprehensive main path analysis. *International Journal of Lean Six Sigma*, *14*(2), 483–513. https://doi.org/10.1108/IJLSS-06-2022-0135

Yu, Y., Zhang, J. Z., Cao, Y., & Kazancoglu, Y. (2021). Intelligent transformation of the manufacturing industry for Industry 4.0: Seizing financial benefits from supply chain relationship capital through enterprise green management. *Technological Forecasting and Social Change*, *172*, 120999. https://doi.org/10.1016/j.techfore.2021.120999

Zelbst, P. J., Yang, L., Green, K. W., & Sower, V. E. (2023). Linkages between technologies and supply chain performance: benefits, power and risk reduction. *Supply Chain Management*, *29*(1), 207–218. https://doi.org/10.1108/SCM-03-2023-0131

Zhou, X., Lu, H., & Xu, Z. (2023). A balance of economic advancement and social needs via improving supply chain traceability for future food sustainability: an empirical study from China. *Production Planning and Control*, 1–21. https://doi.org/10.1080/09537287.2023.2240751

Chapter 14

Quantifying the digital frontier

Frameworks and challenges in measuring the digital economy

Gurpreet Kaur

14.1 INTRODUCTION

In response to global challenges, the OECD and G20 have launched the Base Erosion and Profit Shifting (BEPS) project to improve international tax treatment and better capture the economic benefits brought about by the digital economy. According to Ojo & DiGabriele (2018) and Becerra Peña, Rosales Soto & Gutierrez Moreno (2018), digital business footprints/shadow reduce information from physical and manually maintained sources. Despite efforts to refine the concept of permanent establishment (PE) to include a significant digital presence, aligning tax obligations with digital financial activities remains a challenge, according to Firmansah, & Rahayu (2020). Noted for these challenges, countries such as Indonesia are gradually reforming their tax laws to better capture the value created by the digital economy, aiming to curb tax evasion and increase economic revenue.

The Indian government faces significant challenges when it comes to taxing the digital economy, as highlighted by Ghose, & Dalal (2023). The main obstacle to recognizing the dynamic character of the digital economy is current tax regulations which are based on the traditional tax system, neglecting digital concepts that could lead to tax evasion. Broad cross-border networks, improved capital and taxpayer mobility, and cutting-edge tax planning techniques, including profit shifting and base erosion, are some of these characteristics (BEPS).

According to Xu, W. (2023), ensuring uniformity of taxation in this area is important for India to be incremental in tackling tax avoidance by multinational digital companies, a factor discussed by Usman, I .M. A., & Saha, T. (2022) and Sidik, M. (2022). Given the lack of reliable data in India, the Ministry of Electronics and Information Technology has issued a Request for Proposal (RFP) to measure India's digital economy. Efforts are ongoing to identify key indicators and address gaps to achieve a value of $1 billion.

To develop a conceptual framework measurement of the digital economy, there is a need to answer the following questions:

 DOI: 10.1201/9781003498292-14

1. How is the concept of the digital economy defined?
2. What obstacles might countries encounter when attempting to measure the size of the digital economy?
3. What methodologies have nations employed to measure the scale of the digital economy?
4. To what degree and in what ways does the measurement of the digital economy vary?
5. How can a conceptual framework for the measurement of digital economy be proposed?

14.2 RESEARCH METHODOLOGY

This review exclusively examined studies published in English from 2020 to the present, aligning with the emergence of the digital economy. Databases such as ProQuest and Google Scholar were scrutinized. Key terms like "digitalized economy," "digital economy," "size of digital economy," and "taxing the digital economy" were utilized throughout the research process to ensure comprehensive coverage of relevant literature in the field of digital economics. After data gathering, retrieved articles were evaluated to determine which were the most desirable and aligned with the earlier stated research questions. There are some constraints with the study: Only open-access articles, research papers and thesis, dissertations, and reports form part of the study.

14.3 CONCEPT OF DIGITAL ECONOMY DEFINED

The idea of the "digital economy," which first emerged in the middle of the 1990s, has undergone significant development over time. Pioneers and early adopters such as Don Tapscott (1996) and Nicholas Negroponte (1995) recognized the existence of the digital economy. Later, in the early 2000s, Mesenbourg, T. L. (2001) provided a more precise framework by delineating the digital economy into three predominant components: e-business infrastructure, e-business operations, and e-trade, thereby clarifying its key factors. Further embellishments through the OECD and the World Bank emphasized the relevant role of Information and Communication Technologies (ICTs), digitization, and facts in using financial activities within this area. Brynjolfsson, E., & McAfee, A. (2014) identified the digital age with economic growth in terms of increased GDP from increased digitalization and global connectivity. The World Economic Forum 2020 and the McKinsey World Forum 2019 both highlighted the emergence of digital infrastructure, including the Internet, AI, and big data. This is why the European Commission considered data a key resource for decision-making and economic strategy in 2018. Hence, collectively known as the New Economy, the digital economy adopts digital computer technology across all economic activities.

14.4 OBSTACLES MIGHT COUNTRIES ENCOUNTER WHEN ATTEMPTING TO MEASURE THE SIZE OF THE DIGITAL ECONOMY

The literature provides evidence of the multiple challenges faced by economies attempting to measure the size and growth of digital economies. The first major challenge is related to the mobility of capital and taxpayers in the digital economy; additionally, cross-border transactions, adds complexities to tax collection efforts, as discussed by Guerra, A. (2023). Countries around the world face the challenges in implementing taxation within the digital economy, difficulties drien by the dynamics of digital networks according to Juswanto, W., & Abiyunus, Y. F. (2022), and Hendriyetty, N., Evans, C., about 1900, Kim, C. J., and Taghizadeh-Hesari, F. (2023).

Another problem is related to security and privacy concerns, as suggested by Stead, J. (2021). The presence of non-market transactions also causes problems for authorities. To address this issue, a consumption tax should be implemented; Stead, J. (2021) suggested that the adoption of a Comprehensive Consumption Tax can provide immediate benefits when it is in line with international tax principles, according to Ghose, A. (2023). While some countries have adopted one-size-fits-all approaches to address these issues, there is a growing movement to build a system that is universally recognized.

Lack of digital literacy is another major issue facing emerging countries like India and can be quite problematic when estimating the extent of the digital economy. However, there are certain gaps in the current tax legislation of the various nations that encourage complex tax planning techniques, giving multinational corporations a major advantage over small businesses. To fully reap the rewards of the digital economy, tax equity must be balanced, as it is essential for creating and preserving economic stability. While some countries have opted to address these issues individually, Mpofu, F. Y. (2022) points out that some progress has been made in developing a framework that is broadly accepted.

The study highlights how challenging it is to gauge the scale of the digital economy in poor countries. Therefore, in order to address the previously mentioned issue, the researcher investigated global approaches and procedures.

14.5 APPROACHES NATIONS EMPLOYED TO MEASURE THE SCALE OF THE DIGITAL ECONOMY

Various scholars have employed a large number of approaches to measure the size of the digital economy by considering the available databases. Some of the approaches and methods employed by scholars around the world are listed as follows:

1. **Direct and indirect measurement approaches:** Chinoracky, R., & Corejova, T. (2021) introduced the direct method for estimating the digital economy's scale within regions and devised an evaluation index system that measures the development level across multiple dimensions for a comprehensive score.
2. **Composite indicators:** Blatova, T. A., Makarov, V. V., & Shuval-Sergeeva, N. S. (2019) utilized composite indicators comprising 17 normalized measures to globally evaluate the digital economy's scale, incorporating economy, labour, and skill dimensions for a precise assessment.
3. **Market capitalization:** Mueller et al. (2017) adopted the market capitalization approach for assessing the size of the digital economy across countries, with a focus on the USA, Germany, the Republic of Korea, and Sweden.
4. **Index-based approaches:** Kokh Larisa, V., & Kokh Yuriy, V. (2019) reviewed existing index-based approaches, such as the ICT development index and digital competitiveness index, for a global perspective on the digital economy.
5. **Quantification approach:** Bukht and Heeks (2018) aimed to quantify the global digital economy by defining core digital sectors and estimating their GDP and employment contributions.
6. **BEA's measurement:** Strassner and Nicholson (2020) discussed the United States' Bureau of Economic Analysis (BEA) efforts in measuring the global digital economy through consultations and international collaborations.
7. **Digital knowledge economy index:** Sidorov and Senchenko (2020) developed an index using traditional data sources and digital platforms like GitHub and Wikipedia for a comprehensive measure of the global digital economy.
8. **Network readiness index (NRI):** Bakumenko, M., Sigal, A., & Titarenko, D. (2023) focused on assessing global digitalization levels, incorporating GDP and human development index factors to measure the digital economy's size.
9. **Regional development levels:** Sidorov, A., & Senchenko, P. (2020) used a composite index based on hierarchy, modularity, balance, and standard deviation to assess regional digital economies.

10. **Eurostat and OECD approaches:** Milošević, N., Dobrota, M., & Rakočević, S. B. (2018) measured the global digital economy size using methodologies from Eurostat and the OECD.
11. **Composite indicator approach** (Chinoracky, R., & Corejova, T.,2021): This composite indicator consists of individual indicators related to three areas – economy, labour, and skills – that can be used to determine the scale and the potential of the digital economy.
12. **Big data cloud platforms:** Zhao, Y., & Zhou, Y. (2022) proposed a measurement method for China's digital economy scale using big data cloud platforms, aiming to enhance digital media and transactions.
13. **Digital economy satellite account (DESA):** Xu, Y., & Li, T. (2022) outlined the OECD's DESA and Digital Supply and Use Tables (DSUT) approaches, including the valuation of data as a non-produced asset.
14. **Benchmarking:** Murthy, K. B., Kalsie, A., & Shankar, R. (2021) benchmarked the global digital economy's size by examining GDP, per capita GDP, and digitization variables.
15. **TOPSIS method:** Balcerzak, A. P. (2017) applied the TOPSIS method with Shannon entropy for an objective weighting to measure the digital economy in Central European countries.
16. **Tiered DEA approach for EU digital development** (Bánhidi, Z., & Dobos, I., 2023): This study measures the European Union's digital development using Tiered Data Envelopment Analysis, partial orders, and cluster analysis, with a specific focus on grouping countries based on their digital readiness
17. **Global digital economy productivity analysis** Byrne (2022) used growth accounting and assessment of IT's contribution to productivity in measuring the global digital economy's size, with a focus on intangible assets.
18. **International DESI for digitalization levels** (Bruno, G., Diglio, A., Piccolo, C., & Pipicelli, E., 2023): This approach assessed digitalization levels across countries through the International Digital Economy and Society Index, measuring components like digital skills and internet use.
19. **Benefit of the doubt method for digital ecosystem evaluation** Lafuente, E., Acs, Z. J., & Szerb, L. (2024) evaluated the digital ecosystem of 116 countries for 2019 using a non-parametric technique to measure efficiency.
20. **Comprehensive economic analysis of digital planet:** Miller, H., & Sanders, J. (1999) provide a global perspective on the digital economy, measuring IT spending and examining social and economic impacts.

The digital economy measurement is diverse, ranging from straightforward methods to holistic indicators and market capitalization methods. To build trust in the above-mentioned approaches, we need to check their accuracy and reliability. Hence the next section of the chapter discusses the extent of variability and accuracy of the approaches used to measure the size of the digital economy.

14.6 VARIABILITY IN ACCURACY AND RELIABILITY OF APPROACHES FOR MEASURING THE DIGITAL ECONOMY

To gain maximum insight into the phenomenon, measuring the scale and impact of the digital economy involves a range of methodologies, as stated earlier, varying in accuracy and reliability, in terms of the databases used, regions, time period, efforts, and energy. Such approaches aim to identify geographical divides in digital progression, guiding targeted efforts for enhanced digital integration. Meanwhile, in the United States, the Bureau of Economic Analysis contributes by offering detailed statistics on digital goods and services production, continuously expanding sector coverage and enhancing price measurement and digital trade assessment precision (US Bureau of Economic Analysis, 2023). In Russia, measuring the digital economy's contribution to economic performance involves methodical regional and national assessments, relying on statistical data (Plaksin, S., et al.,. (2017). However, traditional economic research in Russian regions faces challenges such as data relevance delays and quality concerns, potentially affecting hypothesis testing and analysis accuracy (Shevandrin, 2020). Challenges in measuring the digital economy are compounded by the need for novel methodologies to provide harmonized standards and ensure cross-country data comparability using established statistical standards (Abdrakhmanova, G., Gokhberg, L., & Sokolov, A., 2021).

Diverse interpretations of the notion of the "digital economy" may result in errors that could affect how a nation is seen to be living (Shevandrin, A. 2020). Adopting the System of National Accounts' concepts for steady reproducibility, reliability, and comparability for determining the scale of the internet economy is a viable path forward, especially for Russia (Plaksin, S., Abdrakhmanova, G., & Kovaleva, G. (2017). In order to improve measurement accuracy and reliability, we must ensure the authenticity and accuracy of the database, source of data, nature of the data, and the countries' taxation laws. Figure 14.1 describes the components of the digital economy which are discussed in the proceeding sections.

14.7 COMPREHENSIVE MEASUREMENT FRAMEWORK FOR THE DIGITAL ECONOMY

Here, the present research work proposes a comprehensive framework to measure the size of the digital economy in terms of physical infrastructure/hardware used for digital operations. The hardware and software

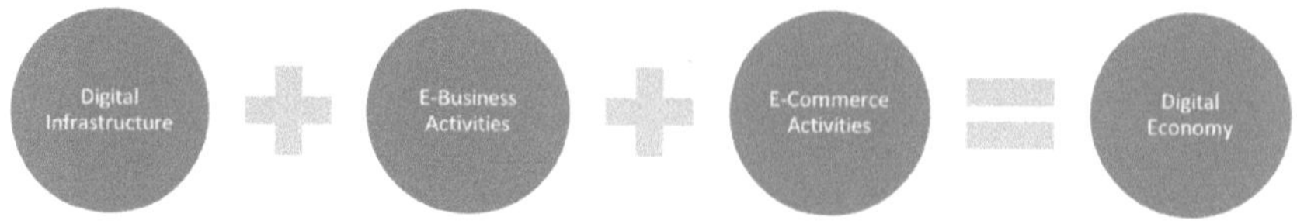

Figure 14.1 Components of digital economy.

components that make up digital infrastructure are what make digital services possible. It comprises the networks and IT systems that let businesses run and interact.

1. **Quantification of digital infrastructure**
   First, enlist the industries producing the hardware – servers, cell phones, computers, and Internet of Things (IoT) gadgets. Then, list the industries producing software – operating systems and applications that run by operating systems and applications designed for smartphones. Also, include the industries connecting the hardware and software via underground copper or fibre-optic connections. Second, consider data centres – facilities where servers and networking hardware are kept in order to store, process, and distribute enormous volumes of data. And examine cloud computing, which includes cloud storage, Software as a Service (SaaS), Platform as a Service (SaaS), and Infrastructure as a Service (IaaS) among the internet-based services offered. Third, consider the human capital employed and served in the above.
   - **Quantitative metrics:** Systematically collect data pertaining to the above-listed components.
   - **Qualitative assessment:** Conduct a qualitative evaluation of the capacity, extent, and usage of digital infrastructure in terms of internet penetration rates, the addition and removal of digital infrastructure, and any new technology innovation embedded within the infrastructure.
   - **Composite index development:** Develop a composite index amalgamating quantitative and qualitative indicators to gauge the overall robustness and advancement of digital infrastructure within a designated geographical region or nation-state.
2. **Assessment of e-business activities:** These are the activities that can be identified by taking into account business houses, industries, and institutions individually.
   - **Transaction volume quantification:** Transaction/trading volume is defined as the number of goods and services traded in a particular period of time. To determine the value of trading volume, consider both the volume and monetary value of e-business transactions conducted via the Internet, such as online commerce, digital marketing, electronic payment systems, and collaborative activities conducted over digital platforms.

- o **Evaluation of business process digitization:** Enlist the business houses whose organizational workflows and processes are digitized and executed over digital platforms, and evaluate the extent to it.
- o **Formulation of a digital transformation index:** After that formulate an index aimed at quantifying the degree of digital transformation index across diverse industries in the fields of health, defence, education, IT, civil services, and more.

3. **Quantification of e-commerce activities:** These are the activities that can be identified by taking into account the business houses, industries, and institutions as a whole.
   - o **Estimation of transactional value:** Estimate the aggregate value of e-commerce transactions, including online retail transactions, digital service exchanges, and electronic commerce transactions encompassing the exchange of goods and services.
   - o **Analysis of market size and growth:** Analyse prevailing market trends and growth trajectories characterizing e-commerce domains such as retail, travel, entertainment, megatrends, and digital content dissemination.
   - o **Assessment of e-commerce penetration:** Quantify the extent of e-commerce penetration within the broader retail market landscape and across diverse product categories. This may involve calculating the proportion of e-commerce sales relative to the aggregate retail sales volume and monitoring temporal fluctuations in these metrics.

By summing up all three major components, a composite digital economy indexed is obtained as shown in Figure 14.2.

14.8 CONCLUSION AND RECOMMENDATIONS

Globally, the concept of the digital economy consists of all the operations which are channelized through virtual platforms by considering all the digital infrastructure as well. Ironically it has taken the place of physical operations. Additionally, developing countries like India are also aiming to impose digital taxes on digital transactions and infrastructure processes. For this, we need to measure the size of the digital economy first. So keeping in view, the researcher examined a limited number of studies due to time and energy constraints and tried to get answers to all the earlier stated research questions.

The study highlights the challenges related to measuring the scale of the digital economy in developing countries; the researcher investigated global approaches and procedures and found that these approaches differ in terms of data concerns, regions, data sources, and time. The study highlights how

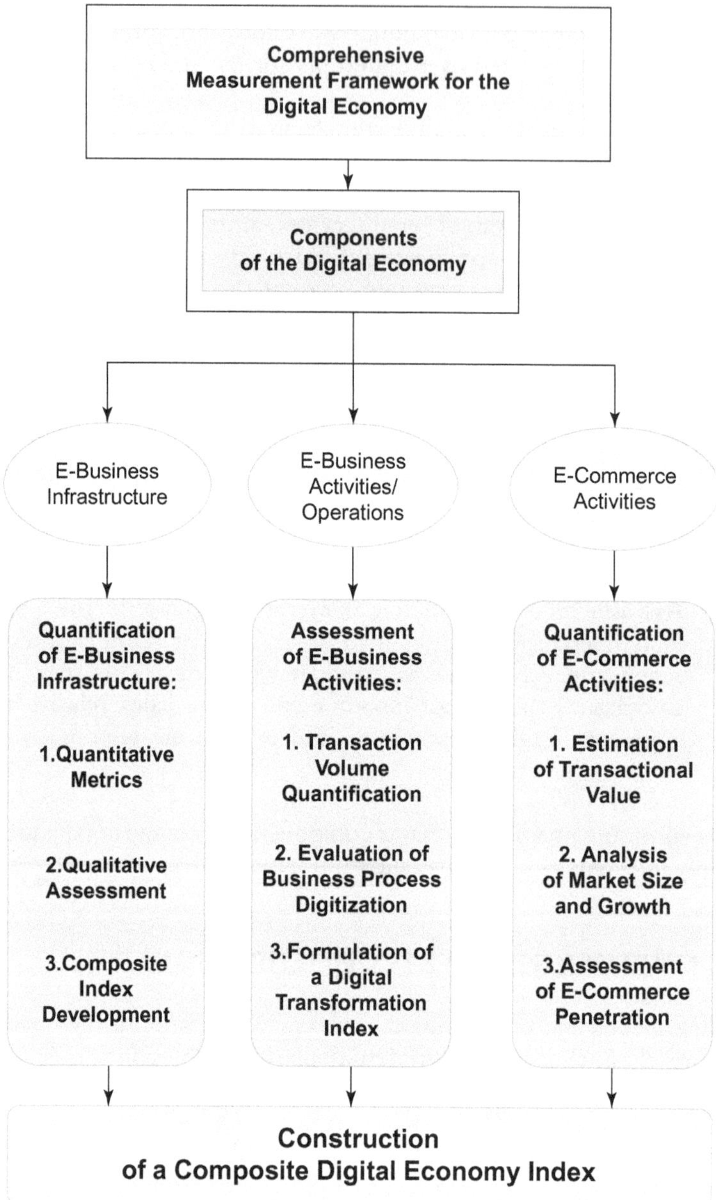

Figure 14.2 Comprehensive measurement framework for digital economy.

challenging it is to gauge the scale of the digital economy in poor countries. Therefore, in order to address the previously mentioned problem, the researcher investigated global approaches and procedures.

The goal of the study is to propose the Composite Digital Economy Index by taking into account the three main components depicted in Figure 14.2. These include e-business operations and procedures, digital infrastructure, and e-commerce activities. First, determine which industries are manufacturing and producing the hardware and software that make up digital infrastructure. Next, to proceed with micro-level trade volume determination, followed by macro-level trade and transaction volume, which encompass all the operations taking place digitally.

To measure the size of the digital economy, the differences between developed and developing countries lead to a recommendation for improving the measurement and comprehension of the digital economy in developing nations. A country like India needs to establish specialized bureaus or organizations akin to the BEA of the United States, which would make it easier to evaluate the size and expansion of the digital economy accurately. To achieve this, it would be necessary to work together more closely with international organizations, regional organizations active in this area, and the government.

REFERENCES

Abdrakhmanova, G., Gokhberg, L., & Sokolov, A. (2021). ICT measurement from information society to digital economy. In *Encyclopedia of Organizational Knowledge, Administration, and Technology* (pp. 448–462). IGI Global.

Bakumenko, M., Sigal, A., & Titarenko, D. (2023). Prospects for the development and application of artificial intelligence technologies in Russia. In *E3S Web of Conferences* (Vol. 431, p. 05036). EDP Sciences.

Balcerzak, A. P. (2017). *Digital Economy in Czech Republik, Slovakia and Hungary. Measurement with Topsis based on Entropy Measure for Objective Weighting* (No. 1/2017). Institute of Economic Research Working Papers.

Bánhidi, Z., & Dobos, I. (2023). Measurement of digital development with partial orders, tiered DEA, and cluster analysis for the European Union. *International Review of Applied Sciences and Engineering*, *14*(3), 392–401.

Becerra-Peña, D. L., Rosales Soto, A., & Gutiérrez Moreno, P. (2023). Tax challenges digitalization of the economy: a reflection on the BEPS Project. *The Anáhuac Journal*, *23*(1), 12–39. https://doi.org/10.36105/theanahuacjour.2023v23n1.01

Blatova, T. A., Makarov, V. V., & Shuval-Sergeeva, N. S. (2019). Quantitative and qualitative aspects of measuring the digital economy. *Radio industry*, *29*(4), 63–72.

Bruno, G., Diglio, A., Piccolo, C., & Pipicelli, E. (2023). A reduced composite indicator for digital divide measurement at the regional level: An application to the digital economy and society index (DESI). *Technological Forecasting and Social Change*, *190*, 122461.

Brynjolfsson, E., & McAfee, A. (2014). *The second machine age: Work, progress, and prosperity in a time of brilliant technologies*. W. W. Norton & Company.

Bukht, R., & Heeks, R. (2018). *Digital economy policy in developing countries* (DIODE Working Papers No. 6). Centre for Development Informatics, University of Manchester. Retrieved from https://diodeweb.files.wordpress.com/2018/03/digital-economy-policy-diode-paper.pdf

Byrne, D. M. (2022). The Digital Economy and Productivity (June 1, 2022). FEDS Working Paper No. 2022-38, Available at SSRN: https://ssrn.com/abstract=4158722 or http://dx.doi.org/10.17016/FEDS.2022.038

Chinoracky, R., & Corejova, T. (2021). How to evaluate the digital economy scale and potential? *Entrepreneurship and Sustainability Issues*, *8*(4), 536.

Firmansah, B., & Rahayu, N. (2020). Analysis of tax authority readiness in tax policy on digital economy. *Jurnal Manajemen Pelayanan Publik*, *4*(1), 51–69.

Ghose, A., & Dalal, M. (2023). Digital economy and Indian taxation law-an analysis. *Vision: Journal of Indian Taxation*, *10*(1), 70–82. doi: 10.17492/jpi.vision.v10i1.1012305.

Guerra, A. (2023). Tax challenges in the digital era. In *SMEs in the Digital Era* (pp. 157–174). Edward Elgar Publishing.

Hendriyetty, N., Evans, C., Kim, C. J., & Taghizadeh-Hesary, F. (2023). *Taxation in the digital economy: New models in Asia and the Pacific.*

Juswanto, W., & Abiyunus, Y. F. (2022). Taxing the digitalized economy: An emerging markets perspective. In N. Hendriyetty, C. Evans, C. J. Kim, & F. Taghizadeh-Hesary (Eds.), *Taxation in the digital economy* (1st ed., pp. 26–51). Routledge. https://doi.org/10.4324/9781003196020.

Kokh, L. V., & Kokh, Y. V. (2019). Analysis of existing approaches to measurement of digital economy. *St. Petersburg State Polytechnical University Journal. Economics*, *12*(4), 78–89. https://doi.org/10.18721/JE.12407

Lafuente, E., Acs, Z. J., & Szerb, L. (2024). Analysis of the digital platform economy around the world: A network DEA model for identifying policy priorities. *Journal of Small Business Management*, *62*(2), 847–891.

Mesenbourg, T. L. (2001). *The digital economy: Potential for growth and employment in the United States.* U.S. Department of Commerce, Economics and Statistics Administration, U.S. Census Bureau. https://www.census.gov/library/working-papers/2001/econ/2001.html

Miller, H., & Sanders, J. (1999). Scoping the global market: Size is just part of the story. *IT Professional*, *1*(2), 49–54.

Milošević, N., Dobrota, M., & Rakočević, S. B. (2018). Digital economy in Europe: Evaluation of countries' performances. *Zbornik Radova Ekonomski Fakultet u Rijeka*, *36*(2), 861–880.

Mpofu, F. Y. (2022). Taxation of the digital economy and direct digital service taxes: Opportunities, challenges, and implications for African countries. *Economies*, *10*(9), 219.

Mueller, S. C., Bakhirev, A., Böhm, M., Schröer, M., Krcmar, H., & Welpe, I. M. (2017). Measuring and mapping the emergence of the digital economy: A comparison of the market capitalization in selected countries. *Digital Policy, Regulation and Governance*, *19*(5), 367–382.

Murthy, K. B., Kalsie, A., & Shankar, R. (2021). Digital economy in a global perspective: Is there a digital divide? *Transnational Corporations Review*, *13*(1), 1–15.

Negroponte, N. (1995). *Being digital* (1st ed.). Knopf.

Ojo, M., & DiGabriele, J. A. (2018). Base erosion and profit shifting (BEPS) and the digital economy: Challenges and issues. In *Internet taxation and e-retailing law in the global context* (pp. 45–60). IGI Global.

Plaksin, S., Abdrakhmanova, G., & Kovaleva, G. (2017). Approaches to defining and measuring Russia's internet economy. *Ф о р с а й т* , *11*(1 (eng)), 55–65.

Shevandrin, A. (2020). New approach to the economic measurement in terms of digital economy. *Digitalization and Industry 4.0: Economic and Societal Development: An International and Interdisciplinary Exchange of Views and Ideas*, 91–103.

Sidik, M. (2022). Digital services tax: Challenge of international cooperation for harmonization. *Jurnal Pajak Dan Bisnis (Journal of Tax and Business)*, *3*(1), 56–64.

Sidorov, A., & Senchenko, P. (2020). Regional digital economy: Assessment of development levels. *Mathematics*, *8*(12), 2143.

Stead, J. (2021). *Taxing digital economies.* oecd-ilibrary.org

Strassner, E. H., & Nicholson, J. R. (2020). Measuring the digital economy in the United States. *Statistical Journal of the IAOS*, *36*(3), 647–655.

Tapscott, D. (1996). *The digital economy: Promise and peril in the age of networked intelligence.* McGraw-Hill Education.

U.S. Bureau of Economic Analysis. (2023, September 7). *GDP and the economy: Second estimates for the second quarter of 2023.* https://apps.bea.gov/scb/issues/2023/09-september/pdf/0923-gdp-economy.pdf

Usman, I. M. A., & Saha, T. R. (2022). An overview of tax challenges of digital economy. *Asia-Pacific Journal of Management and Technology (AJMT)*, *3*(2), 56–63.

Xu, W. (2023). Reconstruction of international tax rules to meet the challenges of digital economy. *Beijing Law Review*, *14*, 125.

Xu, Y., & Li, T. (2022). Measuring digital economy in China. *National Accounting Review*, *4*(3), 251–272.

Zhao, Y., & Zhou, Y. (2022). Measurement method and application of a deep learning digital economy scale based on a big data cloud platform. *Journal of Organizational and End User Computing (JOEUC)*, *34*(3), 1–17.

Chapter 15

Quantum computing and personalized digital marketing

Pioneering the future of hyper-personalized customer engagement

Madhusudan Narayan, Ashok Kumar Srivastava, and Ashutosh Sharma

15.1 INTRODUCTION

Quantum computing (QC) represents an innovative technology providing computational power far beyond the capacity of classical computing. QC leverages the laws of quantum mechanics to perform computations at speeds unattainable by traditional methods (Bhasin & Tripathi, 2023). At the heart of this technology are qubits having multiple states in contrast to traditional binaries (0s and 1s), which process a far greater range of complex problems like optimization and large-scale data analysis (Oke & Stephen, 2024).

QC is still in its infancy, with notable achievements like Google's 2019 Sycamore processor (Khang, 2024). This event marked a turning point, as quantum computers outperformed classical systems on specific tasks. Quantum algorithms offer a substantial benefit in solving complex problems over classical algorithms (Golec et al., 2024). Popular algorithms such as Grover's and Shor's algorithms offer significant speed improvements over classical methods (Wirtz, 2024). Grover's algorithm is designed for unstructured search problems and can search through unsorted data exponentially faster than classical algorithms (Thakur et al., 2023). Shor's algorithm, on the other hand, is known for its ability to factor large numbers efficiently, a particularly useful capability in cryptography (Bova et al., 2021). Although its primary application is in breaking encryption, the principles behind Shor's algorithm can also be adapted to optimization problems.

In digital marketing, where hyper-personalization is becoming increasingly essential for engaging consumers, the ability to analyse consumer behaviour and personalize outreach is key to gaining a competitive edge. Traditional computers are reaching their limits in processing the sheer volume and complexity of consumer data generated across multiple platforms (Patel et al., 2023). This is where QC can revolutionize the landscape by enabling hyper-personalized customer engagement strategies. In digital marketing, Grover's algorithm could be used to identify key insights, such as finding the most effective customer segments or identifying the optimal content to display in personalized ads. Grover's algorithm could streamline

 DOI: 10.1201/9781003498292-15

the process of extracting valuable patterns, allowing market experts to make more informed decisions in real time. Shor's algorithm could be employed to optimize large-scale ad campaigns by quickly evaluating multiple variables, such as budget allocation across platforms, ad formats, and audience targeting strategies, leading to enhanced resource allocation and greater return on investment in digital marketing campaigns.

Personalization in marketing has evolved from broad demographic targeting to hyper-personalized, data-driven strategies that deliver customized content based on individual consumer behaviour. Today's consumers expect this level of personalization, with 75% indicating a preference for brands that offer tailored digital experiences (Yieldify, 2023). This shift is noticeable among new generations, with 74% of Gen Z and 67% of Millennials expressing interest in products that cater to their unique preferences (Salesforce1). However, as data complexity increases and consumer demands change in real-time, traditional machine learning algorithms face challenges in delivering the required depth and speed of insights (Sood et al., 2024).

QC's unique ability to process exponentially larger datasets in parallel offers a promising solution. Using quantum algorithms, brands can analyse massive amounts of consumer data to identify subtle behavioural patterns that were previously undetectable (Bova et al., 2021). In fact, 72% of consumers report responding better to marketing messages tailored to their preferences (SmartHQ), underscoring the value of hyper-personalized marketing. Quantum-enhanced analysis can also extend to real-time emotional responses to advertising, allowing brands to adjust their strategies dynamically. Such agility not only boosts campaign effectiveness but enhances the consumer experience by delivering emotionally resonant content (Ruane et al., 2022). Moreover, 97% of marketers report improved business outcomes through personalization, with some achieving revenue increases of over 20% in response to personalization initiatives (Marq, n.d.).

QC's ability to solve complex optimization problems, e.g., classic travelling salesman challenge, can revolutionize resource allocation within digital marketing campaigns. This capability is particularly valuable for orchestrating multi-channel strategies, as 60% of Millennials are willing to share personal information if it leads to more tailored content and offers (Deloitte). According to recent findings, 63% of marketers have observed increased customer interactions due to personalization, while 51% achieved a 300% ROI across multiple touchpoints through these hyper-targeted efforts (Marq, n.d.). As more brands integrate advanced personalization into their strategies, 70% of those using robust personalization techniques have recorded a remarkable 200% ROI (KO Marketing).[1]

Market research is another area where quantum computing stands to make a significant impact. Traditional methods of market research, while valuable, are often limited by the amount of data that can be processed and analyzed within a reasonable timeframe (Langione et al., 2019). QC enables market experts to predict future buying tendencies with greater accuracy and effective marketing strategy (Ruane et al., 2022). For instance, quantum algorithms can be used to stock portfolio management, currency arbitrage, and supply chain logistics, all of which are critical to ensuring that marketing efforts are aligned with broader business objectives (Orús et al., 2019). By integrating quantum computing into market research, businesses can improve the precision of their campaigns, resulting in higher customer engagement and conversion rates (Patel et al., 2023; Azad, 2024).

Despite the immense benefits of QC in digital marketing, several challenges remain. One of the primary obstacles is the high cost and complexity of quantum infrastructure (Langione et al., 2019; Serrano et al., 2022). QC is still in its early stages, and the technology required to support them is expensive and difficult to maintain. Additionally, there is a shortage of skilled personnel who can develop and implement quantum algorithms effectively (Kagermann et al., 2020; Ortuño et al., 2024). Another challenge is the integration of quantum technologies into existing business models. Furthermore, unresolved error rates and qubit coherence continue to limit the scalability of QC (Khang & Kali, 2024). Businesses must align their IT strategies with quantum tools while maintaining operational integrity to navigate these challenges (Subramanian et al., 2024; Akhai & Kumar, 2024).

While QC promises to revolutionize digital marketing, it also raises significant ethical concerns, particularly around data privacy and surveillance. QC could Khang and Kali (2024) make traditional encryption methods obsolete, compromising the security of customer data (Wirtz, 2024). As quantum computers gain the ability to process massive datasets with unprecedented speed, they can potentially expose personal data to misuse or manipulation (Langione et al., 2019). This poses a threat to consumers' privacy, especially when sensitive data is used to create hyper-personalized marketing experiences (Azad, 2024). As marketers gather more data to build highly personalized profiles of consumers, there are possibilities to analyze more intimate details of a person's digital life, potentially crossing ethical lines (Khan & La Torre, 2021). This raises questions about consumer consent and transparency.

Companies integrating quantum computing into their marketing strategies will need to address these ethical challenges by implementing stronger data protection measures, adopting transparent data usage policies, and ensuring that their quantum-powered technologies adhere to emerging quantum-safe cryptographic standards (Subramanian et al., 2024). Regulatory frameworks like the Digital Personal Data Protection Act, 2023 (Enacted but not enforced) in India and the European Union's General Data Protection Regulation (GDPR) must evolve to keep pace with these advancements, ensuring consumer rights are protected in the era of quantum-powered marketing.

With the evolution of QC, its applications in digital marketing will likely expand. Companies that invest early in QC will be well positioned to lead the future of hyper-personalized customer engagement. The market for quantum computing solutions is expected to grow over the next few years, with some estimates suggesting it could exceed $450 billion annually (Langione et al., 2019). As new upcoming ventures rely on data-driven policies, the demand for quantum solutions will rise, offering new opportunities for innovation in marketing (Kumar et al., 2013).

However, the full potential of QC in this domain remains largely unexplored, revealing a significant research gap. The current literature highlights the promising advancements of quantum technologies, yet empirical research on their specific applications within personalized digital marketing is scant. Additionally, the journey toward integrating quantum computing into marketing strategies is fraught with challenges, including technical hurdles and the need for specialized expertise (Azad, 2024). To address this gap, this study aims to investigate how quantum computing can enhance the accuracy of online advertising, improve recommender systems, and optimize overall marketing strategies. We will specifically explore how QC can refine data analysis, enhance decision-making processes, and elevate predictive analytics to foster hyper-personalized customer experiences.

By addressing these critical research questions, this chapter seeks to unlock the power of QC and illuminate its ability to reshape the future of digital marketing. As QC continues to evolve, its implications for market research, customer interaction, and overall business strategy will become increasingly significant, marking a pivotal shift toward a future where hyper-personalized customer engagement is not just an aspiration but a reality.

15.2 REVIEW OF LITERATURE

QC has been recognized as a transformative technology capable of processing large datasets far more efficiently than classical computers. With qubits, quantum systems enable highly complex calculations at remarkable speeds, creating new possibilities for real-time analysis in data-heavy fields such as digital marketing. Roocroft (2023) highlights how this capability can empower marketers to swiftly identify intricate patterns within consumer data, enabling deeper insights into consumer behaviour and preferences. This efficiency allows marketers to move beyond traditional analytics to uncover insights that were previously inaccessible due to computational constraints. One of QC's most transformative aspects is its support for real-time data processing (Golec et al., 2024), a critical advantage in the fast-paced landscape of digital marketing. The rapid analysis enables marketers to respond immediately to consumer behaviour changes, optimizing campaigns to meet current market dynamics. Roocroft (2023) describes this capability as a game-changer, allowing marketing teams to make informed decisions almost instantaneously, leading to more responsive and timely campaigns (Wirtz, 2024).

Personalization in marketing is a strategy that tailors messages and interactions to individual customer preferences, leveraging data to enhance engagement and drive sales (Bhavani, 2024). According to Thakur (2024), this approach significantly boosts customer satisfaction and loyalty, with 80% of customers going for brands that offer personalized experiences. Key benefits include enhanced customer engagement, with personalized calls-to-action performing 202% better compared to generic ones. This leads to higher conversion rates and optimized marketing expenditures, enabling businesses to reduce customer acquisition costs by up to 50%. Additionally, personalized recommendations can derive significant revenue, with McKinsey noting they account for 10–30% of sales, illustrating the financial impact of understanding customer behaviours. As the field of QC evolves, it holds the potential to revolutionize personalized marketing. Quantum algorithms can analyze vast datasets more efficiently than classical computing, revealing complex patterns that facilitate highly tailored advertising campaigns and content recommendations. For instance, Bhavani (2024) highlights initiatives like Amazon's collaboration with IonQ, where quantum algorithms refine recommendation systems to increase relevance in product suggestions. Furthermore, studies by Ferrari Dacrema et al. (2021) and Nembrini et al. (2021) demonstrate that quantum-inspired algorithms can enhance the accuracy and diversity of recommendations in media streaming and e-commerce, providing a competitive edge in customer engagement. By integrating quantum computing into personalization strategies, businesses can uncover deeper insights into customer preferences and behaviours (Khan & La Torre, 2021). This enhanced data processing capability enables even more precise personalization, maximizing engagement and conversion rates (Ramezani et al., 2020).

Companies like Amazon and Netflix effectively illustrate how personalized marketing can differentiate brands in a competitive landscape, as 91% of consumers prefer brands that provide relevant offers. Overall, effective personalization, bolstered by advances in quantum computing, is vital for businesses aiming to meet evolving customer expectations and achieve sustained growth (Thakur, 2024). QC enables more precise market segmentation by processing vast and varied datasets, including demographics, purchase history, and online interactions (Bhavani, 2024). This advanced segmentation allows marketers to create more targeted campaigns, leading to enhanced customer engagement. Fan et al. (2020) provide a notable example, where a quantum-inspired digital annealer was used to increase the conversion rate of online advertisements significantly. The application of QC in this context highlights its potential to optimize advertising strategies, allowing marketers to predict consumer responses more accurately and allocate resources effectively (Núñez-Merino et al., 2024). As QC evolves, it poses a threat to traditional encrypting, necessitating advancements in quantum-resistant cryptography. While quantum computing challenges current data security protocols, it also offers opportunities to develop new cryptographic solutions that can better protect sensitive consumer information in the digital marketing landscape (Subramanian et al., 2024; Sood et al., 2024). With heightened concerns about data privacy, QC's role in cybersecurity is pivotal for maintaining consumer trust in hyper-personalized marketing practices (Gupta & Bansal, 2022; Sáez-Ortuño et al., 2024).

QC is catalyzing new business models and revenue streams across industries, including digital marketing. The growing need for quantum software development, analytics, and cybersecurity solutions is creating new market opportunities (Sansone et al., 2017; Scherer et al., 2017). As organizations increasingly seek consultancy and integration services, quantum computing's rise is fostering a dynamic ecosystem poised for innovation and growth (Ortuño et al., 2024). While QC offers substantial benefits for digital marketing, its integration is not without challenges (Solikhun et al., 2023). Quantum technology remains in developmental stages, requiring marketers and business leaders to acquire specialized knowledge in quantum principles to harness its potential effectively (Bhavani, 2024; How et al., 2023).

Furthermore, system scalability, qubit coherence, and infrastructure complexity present significant obstacles to the widespread adoption of quantum computing in marketing practices (Sood, et al., 2024; Sáez-Ortuño et al., 2024). Overcoming these challenges is crucial for organizations seeking to capitalize on quantum computing's full capabilities in data-driven marketing (Bhavani, 2024). QC represents a transitional solution for businesses unable to implement full quantum systems. In marketing, QC helps address issues like ad conversion optimization and complex recommendation system design, allowing businesses to achieve advanced data processing and analytics without the high costs of fully quantum systems (Aramon et al., 2019; Denkena et al., 2021; Wirtz, 2024).

15.3 RESEARCH GAP

Despite significant advancements in QC and its potential applications across various fields, the specific impact of QC on personalized digital marketing remains largely underexplored. While existing literature highlights the capabilities of QC in areas such as data analysis and real-time decision-making, there is a scarcity of empirical research that directly investigates how these advancements can enhance hyper-personalized customer engagement through improved predictive analytics and optimization techniques. Furthermore, challenges associated with integrating quantum technologies into established marketing frameworks, including the need for specialized technical expertise and the limitations of existing infrastructure, underscore the necessity for a more in-depth investigation.

15.4 STATEMENT OF THE PROBLEM

The integration of QC into personalized digital marketing strategies presents both significant opportunities and formidable challenges. While QC has the potential to greatly enhance data processing, predictive accuracy, and marketing optimization, the practical implications of these advancements remain insufficiently understood. This lack of clarity restricts marketers' ability to effectively leverage quantum technologies, ultimately hindering the development of genuinely hyper-personalized customer engagement strategies. Therefore, it is essential to explore how quantum computing can transform personalized digital marketing practices while also addressing the barriers to its successful adoption.

15.4.1 Research questions

- How does the integration of QC impact the accuracy of online advertisement conversion rates and the efficiency of recommender systems compared to traditional methods?
- How can QC revolutionize personalized digital marketing to enhance hyper-personalized customer engagement?
- How can QC enhance personalized digital marketing strategies through improved data analysis and decision-making processes?
- How can QC enhance personalized digital marketing strategies to create hyper-personalized customer engagement through improved predictive analytics and optimization techniques?

15.4.2 Research objectives

- To explore the effectiveness of QC in enhancing conversion rates in online advertisements and improving recommender systems within the business and finance sectors.
- To explore the potential of QC in transforming personalized marketing strategies, aiming to improve customer engagement through advanced data analysis and real-time insights.
- To explore the potent applications of QC in optimizing market research and strategic decision-making in personalized digital marketing and to assess its impact on consumer behaviour modelling and marketing efficiency.
- To investigate the potential applications of QC in personalized digital marketing, focusing on its ability to enhance predictive accuracy and optimize marketing strategies, thereby fostering hyper-personalized customer engagement.

15.5 RESEARCH METHODOLOGY

This study employs a qualitative research methodology through a comprehensive literature review to explore the intersection of QC and personalized digital marketing. By synthesizing existing scholarly articles, case studies, and industry reports, the research aims to identify gaps in current knowledge and understand the potential implications of quantum technologies on hyper-personalized customer engagement.

The literature review process involved systematically searching for relevant publications from academic databases such as ScienceDirect, IEEE Xplore, Springer, Wiley, and Emerald. The search focused on topics related to quantum computing, predictive analytics, marketing optimization, and consumer behaviour. Specific keywords and phrases were utilized to ensure comprehensive coverage of the subject, including "quantum computing," "digital marketing," "hyper-personalization," "recommender systems," and "consumer engagement."

Selected literature was then analyzed to extract key themes, trends, and insights, which informed the formulation of research questions and objectives. This analysis also highlighted the advancements and challenges in integrating quantum computing within existing marketing frameworks, thus providing an understanding of the theoretical underpinnings and practical applications of quantum technologies in personalized digital marketing. Furthermore, this methodological approach allows for the identification of emerging trends, such as the role of digital annealers and quantum algorithms in optimizing marketing strategies and enhancing customer engagement. By focusing on qualitative insights, this study lays the groundwork for upcoming empirical research in this nascent field, aiming to substantiate theoretical findings with practical applications and address the integration challenges faced by organizations looking to leverage quantum computing in their marketing efforts.

15.6 DISCUSSION

The integration of QC in the business and finance sectors offers transformative potential for improving online advertisement conversion rates and refining recommender systems—two critical components of effective digital marketing. QC provides innovative solutions for optimizing data-intensive processes, such as high-precision conversion tracking and adaptive recommendation algorithms.

QC has shown considerable promise in optimizing online advertisements. For instance, Fan et al. (2020) utilized a digital annealer—a type of Ising quantum-inspired computer—to analyze online advertisement conversion rates. This method has an improved accuracy of 0.176 to 0.326 while also speeding up processing times. Moreover, the digital annealer significantly reduced the advertising duration while maintaining precision, highlighting its potential to enhance conversion rates more efficiently than traditional methods. Such advancements could revolutionize digital marketing strategies, enabling advertisers to allocate resources effectively, maximize reach, and boost customer acquisition with minimal computational effort.

Recommender systems are vital for personalized digital marketing, delivering relevant content based on user preferences and behaviours. QC offers innovative approaches to enhance the accuracy and diversity of these recommendations. For example, Ferrari Dacrema et al. (2021) used a quantum annealer to streamline carousel selection in streaming services, demonstrating improved effectiveness in delivering personalized content. Additionally, Nembrini et al. (2021) found that collaborative-driven quantum feature selection (CQFS) increased both accuracy and diversity compared to conventional methods, leading to more engaging user experiences.

Beyond advertising and recommendation systems, QC plays a crucial role in optimizing credit risk assessment and portfolio management in finance. Egger et al. (2020) developed an algorithm for estimating credit risk, achieving faster and more accurate results than traditional Monte Carlo simulations. This capability is essential for better loan decision-making and risk management. Similarly, Kaneko et al. (2021) integrated quantum amplitude estimation (QAE) with pseudorandom numbers to accelerate credit portfolio risk measurement, leveraging parallel computation for enhanced results. The implications are significant: QC could enable financial institutions to manage credit portfolios more effectively across diverse customer categories, improving accuracy and efficiency in risk assessment.

These applications of QC across business and finance underscore its potential to drive advancements in digital marketing. By enhancing conversion rates, optimizing recommendation algorithms, and refining credit risk assessment, QC equips companies with the tools to make data-driven decisions swiftly and accurately. The impact on hyper-personalized customer engagement suggests a powerful shift in how businesses connect with consumers, marking a new frontier in quantum-powered digital marketing. QC's ability to process complex data at unprecedented speeds positions it as a pivotal tool for organizations striving to meet evolving consumer expectations in an increasingly digital landscape. Its integration into digital marketing and finance offers both efficiency and precision, potentially reshaping how businesses engage with customers and optimize resources.

The rapid evolution of technology has ushered in an era where data analytics and personalized marketing are more critical than ever. As businesses seek innovative ways to engage customers, the integration of QC emerges as a game-changer, promising to enhance the accuracy and effectiveness of marketing strategies. The organizations can mitigate the complexity of data overload and achieve unprecedented levels of customer engagement.

As the growth of information accelerates beyond Moore's Law, data overload presents significant challenges for both researchers and the general public (Chen & Zhang, 2014). Researchers struggle with unstructured data, while the public grapples with uncertainty regarding the origins and accuracy, particularly in the context of "fake news" (Kusiak, 2019). A pertinent example is the rise in electronic medical records, which has led to increased medical alerts and subsequent "alert fatigue." This underscores the urgent need for algorithms that enable rapid and accurate diagnoses and treatment recommendations (Dilsizian & Siegel, 2014). Despite growing interest, research applying QC remains limited. Notable applications have emerged in chemistry (Córcoles et al., 2019; Havlíček et al., 2019), medicine (Dilsizian & Siegel, 2014), and physics (Abramsky & Brandenburger, 2011; Scherer et al., 2017). Additionally, there are promising applications in management and business, particularly in digital manufacturing (Fedele et al., 2021), as well as in logistics and cybersecurity (Cheung et al., 2020).

Another area where QC may substantially impact is machine learning. Researchers anticipate that quantum techniques can enhance kernel methods in pattern recognition, particularly through support vector machines (Havlíček et al., 2019). Investigations into quantum machine learning applications (Fowler et al., 2012) and quantum simulations (Preskill, 2018) are actively underway. Havlíček et al. (2019) illustrate how quantum state space can shape supervised learning by informing feature dimensions. Innovations that combine classical and quantum algorithms are emerging, including a quantum neural network architecture proposed by Chen (2021) and hybrid approaches suggested by Kandala et al. (2019) aimed at reducing errors in noisy quantum processors executing machine learning tasks.

Exploring the intersection of artificial intelligence (AI), Big Data, and QC reveals revolutionary potential for personalized marketing. The integration of these technologies can significantly enhance personalized and evidence-based practices in fields like medicine (Dilsizian & Siegel, 2014). Fedele et al. (2021) identify socio-environmental and technological factors influencing digital technology companies to adopt integrated AI and quantum computing solutions. While this field is still emerging, it represents one of the most compelling challenges and opportunities for the future of hyper-personalized marketing.

QC has the potential to transform personalized digital marketing by addressing the challenges of data overload and enhancing machine learning capabilities. By integrating QC with AI and Big Data, businesses can develop hyper-personalized marketing strategies that foster deeper customer engagement (Ukpabi et al., 2023). As this field continues to evolve, it presents significant opportunities for innovation and improved marketing effectiveness.

As the digital marketing landscape evolves, businesses face issues in handling vast amounts of data while delivering hyper-personalized experiences to consumers. In this context, QC promises enhanced data analysis and decision-making. By harnessing its unparalleled computational power, organizations can not only optimize market research but also reshape strategic decision-making that align with consumer behaviours and preferences (MacQuarrie et al., 2020).

QC holds significant promise for revolutionizing market research, despite its current lack of direct applications in the field (Dwivedi et al., 2024). Its capabilities in optimizing complex challenges, managing vast datasets, and generating sets of potential solutions position it as a powerful tool for sophisticated market analysis. By performing computations with speeds and accuracies unattainable by classical computers, quantum computing can handle intricate algorithms essential for understanding consumer behaviours and preferences. These advancements can lead to more precise modelling of consumer buying tendencies, enabling companies to tailor marketing strategies to meet specific demands. Additionally, quantum computing can tackle classical optimization challenges, such as the travelling salesman problem, that are crucial in logistics. By enhancing route optimization, it could streamline marketing logistics, reduce costs, and improve operational efficiency. Ultimately, these developments may facilitate more targeted marketing campaigns and better resource allocation, fostering a deeper understanding of market dynamics.

QC represents a paradigm shift in decision-making by offering innovative solutions to complex challenges. Traditional processes often suffer from cognitive biases, leading to weak outcomes. However, the integration of QC with advanced machine learning and AI can help mitigate these challenges. By leveraging the superior processing power and parallelism of QC, AI tools can analyse extensive datasets and patterns, enhancing decision-making.

In finance and logistic sectors, quantum algorithms can optimize portfolios and manage supply chains more effectively. These tools deliver insights not only faster but also with greater accuracy for well-informed decisions. Although QC is still in its early stages and faces limitations like error rates and qubit coherence issues, its potential to enhance decision-making processes is substantial. As the technology matures, it could drive significant strategic advantages, ushering in a new era in business management.

Integrating QC into business presents notable challenges beyond high initial costs and complex infrastructure. This complexity leads to a shortage of skilled persons; businesses must invest in training special talent capable of developing and understanding QC. While sectors like cryptography, drug development, and simulations may benefit significantly, successful utilization requires substantial research and development to resolve issues like error rates limiting practical applications. Businesses must navigate these uncertainties while adapting to rapidly evolving technology advancements.

Lastly, the challenge lies in aligning current digital capabilities with the advanced potential of quantum techniques. Companies need to learn their

IT strategies with advancements in QC without disrupting ongoing processes. This necessitates careful planning to fully leverage the benefits of QC. Balancing innovation with practical application will be crucial for successfully integrating emerging technologies into business practices.

RQ 4: Quantum Computing and Personalized Digital Marketing: Pioneering the Future of Hyper-Personalized Customer Engagement
The rapid advancement of QC offers transformative potential for the marketing landscape, especially in personalized digital marketing. As businesses increasingly seek to engage customers on a personal level, leveraging the power of quantum technology could revolutionize how they analyse consumer data and optimize marketing strategies.

QC offers a heightened capacity for complex and rapid computation. This capability is particularly relevant for marketing analytics, where the ability to swiftly analyze vast amounts of consumer data is crucial. The potential applications of QC in marketing analytics are extensive. For instance, quantum algorithms can efficiently tackle combinatorial optimization problems that traditional computers struggle to resolve, such as identifying the most effective marketing strategies for diverse consumer segments. The quantum approximate optimization algorithm (QAOA) exemplifies how quantum computing can generate more effective solutions in marketing contexts, thereby enhancing predictive accuracy regarding consumer behaviours and preferences (Dwivedi et al., 2024).

A key advantage of QC in marketing is its capacity to enhance predictive analytics. Traditional methods are short of capturing the complexities of consumer behaviour due to the constraints of classical algorithms. Quantum-enhanced machine learning techniques can analyze intricate datasets, uncovering patterns that may remain hidden in conventional analyses. By applying these techniques, marketers can achieve unprecedented granularity in consumer segmentation, leading to hyper-personalized marketing that resonates with one's preference and behaviour. This capability empowers marketers to adapt their strategies dynamically, responding to trends and changes in consumer behaviour almost instantaneously.

In addition to enhancing predictive analytics, QC promises substantial improvements in optimizing marketing strategies. The inherent complexity of marketing challenges often involves multiple variables and constraints, making it difficult for classical algorithms to yield optimal solutions. QC can simplify this complexity, enabling the development of sophisticated models that optimize resource allocation, pricing strategies, and promotional efforts more effectively. Furthermore, QC can significantly enhance customer engagement by facilitating personalized recommendations and targeted campaigns. By analyzing comprehensive datasets encompassing customer interactions, preferences, and behaviours, quantum algorithms can pinpoint the most effective engagement strategies, ensuring that marketing efforts are both relevant and impactful.

15.7 SPECULATIVE ANALYSIS APPROACH

The speculative analysis approach is essential, considering the early developmental stage of quantum computing technology. The speculative framework facilitates an exploration of emerging trends in quantum computing and their expected impacts on marketing. By considering theoretical advancements and extrapolating from current research, we can envision how quantum algorithms might evolve to further enhance predictive capabilities and optimization processes. This forward-thinking perspective highlights not only the opportunities presented by quantum computing but also the hurdles that practitioners may face. Additionally, this analysis recognizes the ethical and practical considerations of implementing quantum technologies in marketing. As organizations strive to leverage the power of QC, they must mitigate issues related to data privacy, algorithmic bias, and the demand for skilled persons to manage these advanced systems. Acknowledging these challenges keeps our analysis grounded in a realistic assessment of the future landscape.

While the potential of QC in personalized marketing is significant, several challenges must be addressed. As the technology is still developing, businesses must navigate the complexities of integrating quantum technologies into existing marketing frameworks, necessitating investment in both technology and talent.

Looking ahead, the implications of QC for marketing analytics are profound. Continued advancements in this field could redefine how businesses approach consumer engagement, ushering in an era of hyper-personalization that fully harnesses the capabilities of quantum technology. By examining the intersection of QC and marketing analytics through a speculative lens, this research contributes to a deeper understanding of how these emerging technologies can shape the future of personalized digital marketing.

15.8 FINDINGS OF STUDY

Despite being in its early development stage, QC holds significant promise for solving complex problems across various fields, including market research, which can enhance competitive advantages for companies and nations (Atik & Jeutner, 2021; Carberry et al., 2021; Coccia & Roshani, 2024). This study investigates the integration of QC within the domain of personalized digital marketing, emphasizing its potential to enhance hyper-personalized customer engagement. Despite significant advancements in QC and its applications across various fields, the specific impact on personalized digital marketing remains underexplored. This work addresses this notable research gap, examining the practical implications of quantum computing for optimizing marketing strategies, improving predictive analytics, and overcoming integration challenges within established marketing frameworks.

The implementation of QC techniques has demonstrated a significant increase in the accuracy of online advertisement conversion rates. For instance, the utilization of digital annealers has been shown to elevate conversion accuracy from 0.176 to 0.326, as illustrated in the work of Fan et al. (2020). This improvement underscores quantum computing's capacity to optimize resource allocation, leading to enhanced customer acquisition and engagement. Such advancements suggest that quantum technologies can fundamentally transform advertising strategies by enabling more effective targeting and resource management, a sentiment echoed by Nembrini et al. (2021) regarding the enhanced precision in recommender systems.

QC has proven instrumental in refining recommender systems, which are critical for personalized digital marketing. Research indicates that collaborative-driven quantum feature selection can enhance both the accuracy and diversity of recommendations compared to conventional methods (Ferrari Dacrema et al., 2021). This enhancement fosters more engaging user experiences, which is vital for cultivating customer loyalty and satisfaction. The implications of this finding are profound, suggesting that organizations can leverage QC to create personalized content for consumers, as highlighted by the increasing demand for tailored marketing solutions.

QC possesses the potential to address the complexities associated with managing vast datasets, thereby revolutionizing market research. Its capabilities in performing intricate computations efficiently enable more precise modelling of consumer behaviours, facilitating the development of tailored marketing strategies. As Chen and Zhang (2014) discuss, the challenges of data overload necessitate innovative approaches that quantum computing can provide. By employing quantum algorithms, businesses can derive insights that were previously unattainable, significantly enhancing their understanding of market dynamics and consumer preferences (Dwivedi et al., 2024).

The convergence of QC and AI offers a paradigm shift in strategic decision-making processes. As traditional decision-making is often hindered by cognitive biases, the integration of quantum-enhanced algorithms enables faster and more accurate analyses of extensive datasets (Dilsizian & Siegel, 2014). Early applications in sectors such as finance, as evidenced by the work of Egger et al. (2020), indicate that these algorithms can optimize portfolio management and streamline supply chain dynamics, underscoring broader implications for digital marketing strategies. This enhancement of decision-making processes positions organizations to respond more effectively to market demands.

Despite the promising advancements associated with QC, several challenges impede its integration into personalized digital marketing. Key obstacles include high initial costs, the inherent complexity of the technology, and a current shortage of skilled personnel capable of leveraging quantum algorithms. As discussed by Sood et al. (2024), identifying practical applications of quantum computing within existing marketing frameworks necessitates substantial investment in research and development. Organizations must navigate these complexities to realize the full potential of quantum technology. The intersection of QC, AI, and big data analytics heralds a transformative era in hyper-personalized marketing (Preskill, 2018). This evolution is critical for businesses aiming to meet the increasing demand for personalized customer experiences, ultimately positioning them for competitive advantage in a rapidly evolving digital landscape.

The findings of this study highlight the role of QC in personalized digital marketing. By improving conversion rates, optimizing recommender systems, and revolutionizing data analysis, quantum technologies can significantly enhance customer engagement strategies. However, organizations must address integration challenges and develop the necessary skills to effectively harness these advancements. As quantum computing continues to evolve, its influence on digital marketing will likely grow, leading to innovative approaches that cater to the complexities of modern consumer behaviour. The maturation of quantum technology promises to unlock a new era of customer engagement and business growth. By leveraging quantum algorithms, marketers can deliver exceptional customer experiences and drive sustainable success. Despite existing challenges, the potential benefits of QC are clear. Embracing this transformative technology positions businesses at the forefront of the digital revolution.

15.9 CONCLUSION

The integration of QC into personalized digital marketing presents a transformative opportunity to redefine customer engagement and business strategies. Using the unparalleled computational power of quantum algorithms, marketers can delve deeper into consumer behaviour, optimize campaigns with unprecedented precision, and ultimately deliver hyper-personalized experiences that resonate with individual preferences.

Even though it is still nascent, QC can revolutionize data analysis, enabling marketers to extract valuable information and make informed decisions. It can enhance the accuracy of online advertising and recommender systems, leading to increased customer satisfaction. Additionally, QC can optimize market research and strategic decision-making, empowering businesses to stay ahead of the curve. However, the successful adoption of QC in marketing requires overcoming significant challenges, including technical complexity, infrastructure limitations, and a shortage of skilled professionals. Ethical considerations, e.g., data privacy and security, must also be carefully addressed.

As quantum technology continues to advance, it is imperative for businesses to invest in research and development with QC experts and to stay abreast of the latest advancements. By embracing this revolutionary technology, marketers can unlock a new era of personalized marketing, driving growth and building lasting customer relationships.

15.10 RESEARCH LIMITATIONS AND FUTURE RESEARCH DIRECTIONS

This study acknowledges numerous limitations that may affect its findings, primarily stemming from the nascent stage of quantum computing and its applications in personalized digital marketing. The reliance on theoretical frameworks due to a lack of extensive empirical data restricts the robustness of conclusions drawn, limiting their real-world applicability. Furthermore, while the integration challenges of quantum technologies into existing marketing infrastructures are acknowledged, they are not exhaustively examined, potentially impacting the practicality of the proposed strategies. The sector-specific focus on industries like finance and technology may also hinder the generalizability of findings to other areas. Future research should aim to empirically validate the theoretical insights presented, exploring real-world applications across various sectors and developing frameworks for effective integration. Longitudinal studies would be beneficial to understand the evolving impact of quantum computing on marketing strategies over time. Additionally, a deeper investigation into ethical and regulatory concerns, consumer attitudes toward data privacy, and algorithmic fairness is essential for responsible implementation. Collaborative initiatives between academia and industry could foster innovative applications, ultimately enhancing hyper-personalized customer engagement through quantum computing.

NOTE

1. *All statistics in this paragraph are reported by RRD. (n.d.). "10 Personalization Statistics You Need to Know: Why Personalized Marketing Is the Way to Go," Retrieved October 2, 2024, from https://www.rrd.com/resources/blog/10-personalization-statistics-you-need-to-know-why-personalized-marketing-is-the-way-to-go.*

REFERENCES

Abramsky, S., & Brandenburger, A. (2011). The sheaf-theoretic structure of non-locality and contextuality. *New Journal of Physics, 13*(11), 113036. https://doi.org/10.1088/1367-2630/13/11/113036.

Akhai, S., & Kumar, V. (2024). Quantum resilience and distributed trust: The promise of blockchain and quantum computing in defense. In A. Kumar, N. J. Ahuja, K. Kaushik, D. S. Tomar, & S. B. Khan (Eds.), *Sustainable security practices using blockchain, quantum and post-quantum technologies for real-time applications* (pp. 125–153). Springer. https://doi.org/10.1007/978-981-97-0088-2_7.

Aramon, M., Rosenberg, G., Valiante, E., Miyazawa, T., Tamura, H., & Katzgraber, H. G. (2019). Physics-inspired optimization for quadratic unconstrained problems using a digital annealer. *Frontiers in Physics*, 7, 48. https://doi.org/10.3389/fphy.2019.00048.

Atik, J., & Jeutner, V. (2021). Quantum computing and computational law. *Law, Innovation and Technology*, *13*(2), 302–324. https://doi.org/10.1080/17579961.2021.1977216.

Azad, N. (2024). Quantum computing: A concept and business perspective. In *Proceedings of the 14th International Conference on Software Business (ICSOB '23)*, November 27–29, 2023, Lahti, Finland. CEUR Workshop Proceedings. https://doi.org/10.13140/RG.2.2.15183.87201.

Bhasin, A., & Tripathi, M. (2023). Quantum computing at an inflection point: Are we ready for a new paradigm? *IEEE Transactions on Engineering Management, 70*(7), 2546–2557. https://doi.org/10.1109/TEM.2021.3103904.

Bhavani, S. (2024). The new frontier: Quantum computing's role in future marketing strategies. *The PR Post.* Retrieved October 25, 2024, from https://theprpost.com/post/7101/the-new-frontier-quantum-computings-role-in-future-marketing-strategies.

Bova, F., Goldfarb, A., & Melko, R.G. (2021). Commercial applications of quantum computing. *EPJ Quantum Technology, 8*, 2. https://doi.org/10.1140/epjqt/s40507-021-00091-1.

Carberry, D., Nourbakhsh, A., Karon, J., Jones, M. N., Jadidi, M., Shahriari, K., Beenfeldt, C., Andersson, M. P., & Mansouri, S. S. (2021). Building knowledge capacity for quantum computing in engineering education. In *Proceedings of the 2021 International Conference on Quantum Computing and Engineering* (pp. 123–130). Elsevier. https://doi.org/10.1016/B978-0-323-88506-5.50319-3.

Chen, P. P., & Zhang, C.-Y. (2014). Data-intensive applications, challenges, techniques, and technologies: A survey on big data. *Information Sciences*, *275*, 314–347. https://doi.org/10.1016/j.ins.2014.01.015.

Chen, Y. (2021). QDCNN: Quantum dilated convolutional neural network. *arXiv*. https://doi.org/10.48550/arXiv.2110.15667.

Cheung, K.-F., Bell, M. G. H., & Bhattacharjya, J. (2020). Cybersecurity in logistics and supply chain management: An overview and future research directions. *Transportation Research Part E: Logistics and Transportation Review, 146*, 102217. https://doi.org/10.1016/j.tre.2020.102217.

Coccia, M., & Roshani, S. (2024). Evolutionary phases in quantum technologies: Theoretical and managerial implications for technological forecasting. *IEEE Transactions on Engineering Management*. https://doi.org/10.2139/ssrn.4792340.

Córcoles, A. D., Kandala, A., Javadi-Abhari, A., McClure, D. T., Cross, A. W., Temme, K., Nation, P. D., Steffen, M., & Gambetta, J. M. (2019). Challenges and opportunities of near-term quantum computing systems. *Proceedings of the IEEE*, *107*(10), 1920–1936. https://doi.org/10.1109/JPROC.2019.2954005.

Denkena, B., Schinkel, F., Pirnay, J., & Wilmsmeier, S. (2021). Quantum algorithms for process parallel flexible job shop scheduling. *CIRP Journal of Manufacturing Science and Technology*, *33*, 100–114. https://doi.org/10.1016/j.cirpj.2021.03.006.

Dilsizian, S. E., & Siegel, E. L. (2014). Artificial intelligence in medicine and cardiac imaging: Harnessing big data and advanced computing to provide personalized medical diagnosis and treatment. *Current Cardiology Reports*, *16*(1), 441. https://doi.org/10.1007/s11886-013-0441-8.

Dwivedi, K., Haghparast, M., & Mikkonen, T. (2024). Quantum software engineering and quantum software development lifecycle: A survey. *Cluster Computing, 27*(2), 7127–7145. https://doi.org/10.1007/s10586-024-04362-1.

Egger, D. J., Gambella, C., Marecek, J., McFaddin, S., Mevissen, M., Raymond, R., Simonetto, A., Woerner, S., & Yndurain, E. (2020). Quantum computing for finance: State-of-the-art and future prospects. *IEEE Transactions on Quantum Engineering, 1*, 1–24. https://doi.org/10.1109/TQE.2020.3030314.

Fan, M. O., Huida, J. I. A. O., Morisawa, S., Nakamura, M., Kimura, K., Fujisawa, H., & Yamana, H. (2020). Real-time periodic advertisement recommendation optimization using Ising machine. In *Proceedings of the IEEE International Conference on Big Data (Big Data)* (pp. 5783–5785). IEEE. https://doi.org/10.1109/BigData50022.2020.9378436.

Fedele, F., Chatterjee, A., Fallahi, S., Gardner, G. C., Manfra, M. J., & Kuemmeth, F. (2021). Simultaneous operations in a two-dimensional array of singlet-triplet qubits. *PRX Quantum*, *2*(4), 040306. https://doi.org/10.1103/PRXQuantum.2.040306.

Ferrari Dacrema, M., Felicioni, N., & Cremonesi, P. (2021).Optimizing the selection of recommendation carousels with quantum computing. In *Proceedings of the Fifteenth ACM Conference on Recommender Systems (RecSys'21)*, September 27–October 1, 2021, Amsterdam, Netherlands (pp. 100–114). Association for Computing Machinery. https://doi.org/10.1145/3460231.3478853.

Fowler, A. G., Mariantoni, M., Martinis, J. M., & Cleland, A. N. (2012). Surface codes: Towards practical large-scale quantum computation. *Physical Review A, 86*(3), 032324. https://doi.org/10.1103/PhysRevA.86.032324.

Golec, M., Hatay, E. S., Golec, M., Uyar, M., & Gill, S. S. (2024). Quantum cloud computing: Trends and challenges. *Journal of Economy and Technology, 2*(1), 190–199. https://doi.org/10.1016/j.ject.2024.07.001.

Gupta, T., & Bansal, S. (2022). Quantum computing applications in marketing analytics: A future perspective. *Journal of Marketing & Supply Chain Management, 1*(3), 1–6. https://doi.org/10.47363/JMSCM/2022(1)133.

Havlíček, V., Córcoles, A. D., Temme, K., Harrow, A. W., Kandala, A., Chow, J. M., & Gambetta, J. M. (2019). Supervised learning with quantum-enhanced feature spaces. *Nature*, *567*(7747), 209–212. https://doi.org/10.1038/s41586-019-0980-2.

How, M.-L., & Cheah, S.-M. (2023). Business renaissance: Opportunities and challenges at the dawn of the quantum computing era. *Businesses*, *3*(4), 585–605. https://doi.org/10.3390/businesses3040036.

Kagermann, H., Süssenguth, F., Körner, J., & Liepold, A. (2020). *The innovation potential of second-generation quantum technologies*. Acatech – National Academy of Science and Engineering. Retrieved from https://www.acatech.de/publikation/innovationspotenziale-der-quantentechnologien/.

Kandala, A., Temme, K., D Córcoles, A., Mezzacapo, A., Chow, J. M., & Gambetta, J. M. (2019). Error mitigation extends the computational reach of a noisy quantum processor. *Nature*, *567*(7749), 491–495. https://doi.org/10.1038/s41586-019-1040-7.

Kaneko, K., Miyamoto, K., Takeda, N., & Yoshino, K. (2021). Quantum speedup of Monte Carlo integration with respect to the number of dimensions and its application to finance. *arXiv*. https://doi.org/10.48550/arXiv.2011.02165.

Khan, F. S., & La Torre, D. (2021). Quantum information technology and innovation: A brief history, current state, and future perspectives for business and management. *Technology Analysis & Strategic Management, 33*(11), 1281–1289. https://doi.org/10.1080/09537325.2021.1991576.

Khang, A. (Ed.). (2024). *Applications and principles of quantum computing*. IGI Global. https://doi.org/10.4018/979-8-3693-1168-4.

Khang, D., & Kali, G. (Eds.). (2024). *The quantum evolution: Application of AI and robotics in the future of quantum technology*. Taylor & Francis. https://doi.org/10.1201/978-1-032-64207-9.

Kumar, V., Chattaraman, V., Neghina, C., Skiera, B., Aksoy, L., Buoye, A., & Henseler, J. (2013). Data-driven services marketing in a connected world. *Journal of Service Management*, *24*(3), 330–352. https://doi.org/10.1108/09564231311327021.

Kusiak, A. (2019). Fundamentals of smart manufacturing: A multi-thread perspective. *Annual Reviews in Control*, *47*, 214–220. https://doi.org/10.1016/j.arcontrol.2019.02.001.

Langione, M., Bobier, J.-F., Meier, C., Hasenfuss, S., & Schulze, U. (2019). *Will quantum computing transform biopharma R&D?* Boston Consulting Group. Retrieved from https://www.bcg.com/publications/2019/quantum-computing-transform-biopharma-research-development.

MacQuarrie, E. R., Simon, C., Simmons, S., & Maine, E. (2020). The emerging commercial landscape of quantum computing. *Nature Reviews Physics,* 2(10), 596–598. https://doi.org/10.1038/s42254-020-0222-3.

Marq. (n.d.). How content personalization shapes your content strategy. *Marq*. Retrieved October 2, 2024, from https://www.marq.com/blog/content-personalization.

Nembrini, R., Dacrema, M. F., & Cremonesi, P. (2021). Feature selection for recommender systems with quantum computing. *CoRR*. https://doi.org/10.48550/arXiv.2110.05089.

Núñez-Merino, M., Maqueira-Marín, J. M., Moyano-Fuentes, J., & Castaño-Moraga, C. A. (2024). Quantum-inspired computing technology in operations and logistics management. *International Journal of Physical Distribution & Logistics Management, 54*(3), 247–274. https://doi.org/10.1108/IJPDLM-02-2023-0065.

Oke, A.E., & Stephen, S.S. (2024). Quantum computing for sustainable infrastructure management. In *A digital path to sustainable infrastructure management* (pp. 85–92). Emerald Publishing Limited. https://doi.org/10.1108/978-1-83797-703-120241009.

Orús, R., Mugel, S., & Lizaso, E. (2019). Quantum computing for finance: Overview and prospects. *Reviews in Physics, 4*, 100028. https://doi.org/10.1016/j.revip.2019.100028.

Patel, H. B., Mishra, S., Jain, R., & Kansara, N. (2023). The future of quantum computing and its potential applications. *Journal for Basic Sciences, 23*(11), 513–519. https://doi.org/10.37896/JBSV23.11/2711.

Preskill, J. (2018). Simulating quantum field theory with a quantum computer. *arXiv preprint arXiv:1811.10085*. https://doi.org/10.48550/arXiv.1811.10085.

Ramezani, S. B., Sommers, A., Manchukonda, H. K., Rahimi, S., & Amirlatifi, A. (2020). Machine learning algorithms in quantum computing: A survey. In *2020 International Joint Conference on Neural Networks (IJCNN)* (pp. 1–7). https://doi.org/10.1109/IJCNN48605.2020.9206838.

Roocroft, G. (2023, December 25). Quantum computing in digital marketing. *Straw Hat*. Retrieved October 6, 2024, from http://strawhat.co.za/quantum-computing-in-digital-marketing/.

Ruane, J., McAfee, A., & Oliver, W. D. (2022). Quantum computing for business leaders. *Harvard Business Review*. https://hbr.org/2022/01/quantum-computing-for-business-leaders.

Sáez-Ortuño, L., Huertas-Garcia, R., Forgas-Colla, S., Sanchez-García, J., & Puertas-Prats, E. (2024). Quantum computing for market research. *Journal of Innovation & Knowledge, 9*, 100510. https://doi.org/10.1016/j.jik.2024.100510.

Sansone, C., Hilletofth, P., & Eriksson, D. (2017). Critical operations capabilities for competitive manufacturing: A systematic review. *Industrial Management and Data Systems, 117*(5), 801–837. https://doi.org/10.1108/IMDS-02-2016-0066.

Scherer, A., Valiron, B., Mau, S.-C., Alexander, S., van den Berg, E., & Chapuran, T. E. (2017). Concrete resource analysis of the quantum linear-system algorithm used to compute the electromagnetic scattering cross section of a 2D target. *Quantum Information Processing, 16*(3), 60. https://doi.org/10.1007/s11128-016-1495-5 2.

Serrano, M. A., Cruz-Lemus, J. A., Perez-Castillo, R., & Piattini, M. (2022). Quantum software components and platforms: Overview and quality assessment. *ACM Computing Surveys, 55*(1), 1–3. https://doi.org/10.1145/3494281.

Solikhun, S., Efendi, S., Zarlis, M., & Sihombing, P. (2023). Analysis of the quantum perceptron algorithm for classification of bank marketing data. In *Proceedings of the 2nd International Conference on Advanced Information Scientific Development (ICAISD) 2021: Innovating Scientific Learning for Deep Communication* (Vol. 2714, p. 030002). AIP Publishing. https://doi.org/10.1063/5.0129287.

Sood, S. K., Singh, M., & Bhatia, M. (2024). Extraction of emerging trends in quantum algorithm archives. *Neural Computing and Applications, 36*, 17851–17880. https://doi.org/10.1007/s00521-024-10198-y.

Subramanian, R., Maheswari, B., Nithya, T., Girija, P., Karthikeyan, M., & Saraswathi, T. (2024). Quantum computing: Unveiling the paradigm shift and diverse applications. In *Applications and principles of quantum computing* (p. 18). https://doi.org/10.4018/979-8-3693-1168-4.ch006.

Thakur, K. (2024). E-commerce customer experience stats – 2024. *Nudge Now*. Retrieved October 25, 2024, from https://www.nudgenow.com/blogs/e-commerce-customer-experience-stats.

Thakur, K., Pathan, A. S. K., & Ismat, S. (2023). Quantum computing. In *Emerging ICT technologies and cybersecurity* (p. 8). Springer. https://doi.org/10.1007/978-3-031-27765-8_8.

Ukpabi, D., Karjaluoto, H., Botticher, A., Nikiforova, A., Petrescu, D., Schindler, P., Valtenbergs, V., & Lehmann, L. (2023). Framework for understanding quantum computing use cases from a multidisciplinary perspective and future research directions. *Futures, 154*, 103277. https://doi.org/10.1016/j.futures.2023.103277.

Wirtz, B. W. (2024). Artificial intelligence and quantum computing. In *Digital business and electronic commerce*. Springer Texts in Business and Economics. Springer, Cham. https://doi.org/10.1007/978-3-031-50289-7_8.

Yieldify. (2023). Personalization technology: Landscape & trends for 2023. Retrieved October 16, 2024, from https://www.yieldify.com/free-guides/personalization-technology/

Chapter 16

Quantum leap in quick commerce

Harnessing quantum computing for sustainable and efficient logistics

K. V. Haneefa and Amr Badr

16.1 INTRODUCTION

In today's fast-paced world, the demand for quick, convenient, and reliable delivery services is higher than ever. This increasing demand has given rise to a new industry model known as quick commerce (q-commerce). Quick commerce represents an evolution from traditional e-commerce by focusing on ultra-fast deliveries, often within an hour or less, of various products and essentials (Ranjekar & Roy, 2023). This chapter delves into the intricate world of quick commerce, highlighting its growing importance in the modern economy and the critical role played by logistics and supply chain management. Quick commerce is not just a trend but a significant paradigm shift in consumer behaviour and expectations. It promises convenience, speed, and efficiency, catering to the immediate needs of consumers in the digital age (Tiwari, 2022). The quick turnaround times, which set q-commerce apart from traditional e-commerce models, are heavily reliant on innovative logistics and robust supply chain systems (Nierynck, 2020). These systems are designed to optimise routes, delivery times, and inventory management, ensuring a seamless link between the order and delivery process.

However, the rapid rise of quick commerce brings with it a unique set of challenges. The need for speed and efficiency often clashes with the goals of sustainability and resource optimisation (Jalu et al., 2024). Businesses operating within the quick commerce domain face the daunting task of balancing these often-conflicting requirements. They are constantly seeking ways to deliver goods as quickly and efficiently as possible, without sacrificing the quality of service or contributing to environmental degradation. One of the most intriguing solutions to these challenges lies in the realm of quantum computing. Quantum computing, with its potential to process information at speeds unfathomable by traditional computers, presents a game-changing opportunity for the quick commerce industry. Its ability to analyse vast amounts of data in real time can revolutionise logistics and supply chain management, offering solutions that are not only faster but also more sustainable (Gachnang et al., 2022).

DOI: 10.1201/9781003498292-16

The purpose of this chapter is to thoroughly explore how quantum computing could catalyse a significant revolution in the quick commerce sector, particularly in enhancing logistics and supply chain management. By examining the potential applications of quantum computing, this discussion aims to provide insights into the future possibilities and improvements that could redefine the efficiency and sustainability of quick commerce operations. Through this exploration, it becomes clear that the intersection of quantum computing and quick commerce holds immense potential to shape the future of the digital economy, offering a glimpse into a world where the instantaneous fulfilment of consumer desires is not just possible but also sustainable.

16.2 QUICK COMMERCE: AN OVERVIEW

Quick commerce, or q-commerce, signifies the next stage in the e-commerce industry, placing emphasis on rapid delivery times, sometimes as quick as 10–30 minutes from the moment of order (Chawla, 2022; Stojanov, 2022). This concept extends beyond traditional e-commerce by not only offering online shopping convenience but also significantly reducing wait times for deliveries. Its primary focus is urban areas, catering to the heightened demand for immediate gratification among consumers (Ranjekar & Roy, 2023). The transition from e-commerce to quick commerce underscores the progress of technology and the evolution of consumer behaviours (Wajidi et al., 2023). Traditional e-commerce platforms transformed the way we shop by enabling us to purchase items from our homes. However, with advancing technology and growing consumer expectations, the demand for faster, more efficient delivery methods has surged (Srivastava et al., 2023). In response, quick commerce has arisen, harnessing cutting-edge technology and innovative logistics solutions to meet these demands. Companies like Gorillas and Getir have pioneered this space, delivering groceries and everyday essentials within minutes (Chauhan et al., 2022). A prominent trend in quick commerce is the expectation for immediate gratification among consumers (Schorung, 2023). In today's fast-paced world, consumers seek not only the convenience of online shopping but also anticipate their purchases to be promptly delivered (Harter et al., 2024). This expectation is reshaping the industry, prompting companies to devise new strategies and technologies to reduce delivery times. From utilising AI to predict order patterns to deploying electric bikes and drones for swift deliveries, companies are exploring various avenues to keep up with consumer demands (Athanasiadis et al., 2023).

However, these advancements present notable challenges, particularly in logistics and supply chain management. Quick commerce requires an exceptionally efficient and responsive supply chain network. A significant challenge lies in the necessity for real-time inventory management systems that can keep pace with rapid order turnovers (Guru et al., 2023). This demands not only technological investment but also a transformation in inventory management and forecasting. Another challenge pertains to the logistical complexities of delivering goods within a tight time frame. This involves optimising delivery routes, ensuring a fleet of delivery personnel is always on standby, and navigating urban traffic constraints, all of which can impact delivery times (Villa & Monzón, 2021). Furthermore, the environmental impact of increased deliveries, including pollution and carbon footprint, has prompted quick commerce companies to seek eco-friendly delivery solutions (García-Salirrosas & Rondon-Eusebio, 2022; Jalu et al., 2024; Sun & Yoon, 2022).

In short, quick commerce signifies a substantial shift in e-commerce, driven by technological advancements and shifting consumer preferences. While the promise of near-instant delivery is increasingly appealing, the logistics and supply chain challenges it poses cannot be overlooked. Addressing these challenges necessitates innovative approaches, significant investments in technology, and a commitment to sustainability (Lee et al., 2023). The success of quick commerce will heavily depend on how these challenges are overcome, striking a balance between consumer expectations and viable, efficient, and environmentally responsible delivery solutions (Ghosh & Routh, 2023).

16.3 QUANTUM COMPUTING: AN INTRODUCTION

Quantum computing represents a paradigm shift in computational technology, driven by the principles of quantum mechanics. Unlike classical computing, which relies on the binary nature of bits—either 0 or 1—quantum computing employs quantum bits or qubits, which exhibit fundamentally different properties. This shift promises to revolutionise how we process and analyse information, leading to breakthroughs across various fields including cryptography, materials science, and logistics.

16.3.1 The quantum bit (qubit)

At the core of quantum computing is the qubit, the quantum analog of the classical bit. Unlike classical bits, which are restricted to a binary state of either 0 or 1, qubits exploit quantum mechanics to exist in a state of superposition. Superposition allows a qubit to represent both 0 and 1 simultaneously (Hernández et al., 2024). This dual-state capability is not merely a theoretical concept; it fundamentally alters the computational landscape by enabling quantum computers to perform many calculations at once.

For instance, a classical 2-bit system can represent only one of four possible states (00, 01, 10, or 11) at any given time. However, a quantum system with two qubits can represent all four states simultaneously (Laghari et al., 2018). This exponential scaling in state representation grows with each additional qubit, providing quantum computers with the power to handle vast amounts of data and perform complex calculations much more efficiently than classical computers.

16.3.2 Quantum entanglement

Another critical property of qubits is entanglement. When qubits become entangled, their states become interdependent, meaning the state of one qubit is directly related to the state of another, even if they are separated by large distances (Chakraborty & Sen, 2023). This phenomenon, famously described by Einstein as "spooky action at a distance," allows quantum computers to perform complex computations with interrelated qubits working together. Entanglement enables quantum computers to process information in a highly interconnected manner. For example, in quantum algorithms, entangled qubits can share information instantaneously across vast distances, facilitating the rapid exchange of data and synchronisation of operations (Zhahir et al., 2024). This interconnected processing is crucial for solving problems that involve multiple variables and constraints, such as optimisation and cryptographic tasks.

16.3.3 Quantum computing vs. classical computing

The distinction between quantum and classical computing extends beyond the nature of their fundamental units. Classical computers excel at tasks that can be broken down into linear, sequential steps. They operate efficiently using binary data and well-established algorithms, such as sorting and searching, where each step builds upon the previous one (Giani & Eldredge, 2021).

However, classical computers encounter significant challenges when dealing with problems that involve a vast number of potential outcomes. Problems such as optimising complex logistics networks or simulating molecular interactions in materials science require evaluating numerous possibilities simultaneously (Tamrakar & Sharma, 2019). Classical systems struggle with such tasks due to their linear processing capabilities, which can lead to inefficiencies and longer computation times.

Quantum computing offers a solution to these limitations through its ability to evaluate multiple probabilities in parallel. By leveraging superposition and entanglement, quantum computers can explore a multitude of potential solutions simultaneously, significantly accelerating the discovery of optimal outcomes (Markidis, 2024). This parallelism makes quantum computing exceptionally well-suited for complex problem-solving scenarios, such as optimising logistics routes, where traditional methods may fall short.

16.3.4 Principles of quantum mechanics relevant to computing

Several key principles of quantum mechanics underpin the operation of quantum computers:

16.3.4.1 Superposition

This principle allows qubits to be in multiple states at once. Superposition is essential for parallel data processing, as it enables quantum computers to explore many solutions simultaneously rather than sequentially (Haldorai, 2024). For example, in a search problem, a classical computer would test each possible solution one by one, while a quantum computer could test all possibilities at once, leading to faster results.

16.3.4.2 Entanglement

Entanglement is a powerful quantum phenomenon where the state of one qubit is dependent on the state of another (Cuomo et al., 2020). This correlation allows quantum computers to perform complex computations involving multiple variables more efficiently. For instance, entangled qubits can represent and process interrelated information in a way that classical bits cannot, enabling more intricate and faster problem-solving.

16.3.4.3 Quantum interference

Quantum computing algorithms utilise the wave-like nature of qubits to achieve computational efficiency. Quantum interference involves amplifying the probability of correct solutions while cancelling out incorrect ones. Through constructive interference, the algorithm reinforces the likelihood of the correct answer, while destructive interference eliminates less probable outcomes (Tamrakar & Sharma, 2019). This selective reinforcement and cancellation are vital for navigating large solution spaces and achieving accurate results.

16.3.5 Challenges of quantum computing

Despite its transformative potential, quantum computing faces several challenges that must be addressed before it can realise its full potential. Key challenges include the following.

16.3.5.1 Error rates and qubit stability

Quantum systems are highly sensitive to their environment, which can lead to errors and instability in qubit states (Tamrakar & Sharma, 2019). Maintaining coherence and minimising errors are critical for reliable quantum computations. Researchers are developing error-correcting codes and advanced qubit designs to enhance stability and reduce error rates.

16.3.5.2 Scalability

Building quantum computers with a large number of qubits remains a significant challenge. As the number of qubits increases, maintaining their entanglement and coherence becomes increasingly complex (Weber et al., 2024). Advances in quantum hardware and materials science are essential for scaling up quantum systems to handle more complex problems.

16.3.5.3 Practical applications

While quantum computing shows promise in theoretical applications, translating these capabilities into practical, real-world solutions is an ongoing challenge (Singh et al., 2023). Continued research and development are necessary to identify and refine practical applications across various industries.

Quantum computing stands at the forefront of technological advancement, offering unprecedented capabilities in data processing and problem-solving. As research progresses and these challenges are addressed, quantum computing is poised to revolutionise fields as diverse as cryptography, optimisation, and materials science. By unlocking computation capabilities previously deemed impractical with classical approaches, quantum computing heralds a new era of technological innovation and discovery.

16.4 QUANTUM COMPUTING IN LOGISTICS AND SUPPLY CHAIN MANAGEMENT

Logistics and supply chain management form the backbone of the global economy, ensuring the efficient movement of products from manufacturers to consumers. While traditional computing systems have significantly advanced these fields, quantum computing holds the promise to revolutionise them completely. By harnessing the principles of quantum mechanics, quantum computers can process complex information at speeds and efficiencies unattainable by classical systems (Singh et al., 2023). This section explores how quantum computing could transform logistics and supply chain management, focusing on route optimisation, warehouse management, and demand forecasting and inventory management.

16.4.1 Route optimisation

Route optimisation is a critical aspect of logistics, aiming to find the most efficient paths for delivering goods. This involves considering multiple variables such as traffic conditions, distance, delivery windows, and vehicle capacity. Traditional algorithms, often based on linear programming, struggle with this complexity, particularly as the number of variables increases (Gronwald, 2020). These algorithms typically evaluate one scenario at a time, leading to longer computation times and less efficient route planning. Quantum algorithms, however, leverage the principles of superposition and entanglement to process vast amounts of data simultaneously. This ability allows quantum computers to evaluate multiple route scenarios in parallel, identifying optimal routes much more quickly than classical algorithms (Sodiya et al., 2024). By analysing numerous potential routes at once, quantum computing can significantly reduce fuel consumption, delivery times, and operational costs. Moreover, by improving route optimisation, quantum computing contributes to environmental sustainability by minimising carbon footprints, aligning with global efforts to reduce greenhouse gas emissions (Gronwald, 2020).

16.4.2 Warehouse management

Warehouse management involves complex decision-making processes related to restocking, resource allocation, and inventory management. Traditional systems often rely on linear programming models to manage these tasks, which can become inefficient as warehouse operations grow in complexity (Purnamasari et al., 2023). These models may struggle to adapt to dynamic conditions such as real-time inventory levels, demand fluctuations, and supply chain disruptions. Quantum computing offers a transformative approach by optimising warehouse management processes through rapid analysis and synthesis of diverse data sources. Quantum algorithms can integrate real-time data from inventory systems, demand forecasts, and supply chain variables, enabling more dynamic and responsive warehouse operations (Sun, 2023). This capability can lead to more effective management of stock levels, reducing overstock and understock situations. As a result, companies can improve the flow of goods through their supply chains, lower costs, and enhance service levels, ultimately driving efficiency in warehouse operations (Yu et al., 2019).

16.4.3 Demand forecasting and inventory management

Accurate demand forecasting is crucial for effective inventory management. Overestimations can lead to excess inventory and increased holding costs, while underestimations may result in stockouts and lost sales. Traditional demand forecasting methods, such as time series analysis and machine learning, have improved forecast accuracy but often struggle with the volatility and nonlinear nature of consumer demand (Purnamasari et al., 2023). These methods may not fully capture the complexities and patterns in large datasets. Quantum computing presents a new paradigm for addressing these challenges. By efficiently analysing extensive datasets, including historical sales data, market trends, and consumer behaviour, quantum algorithms can uncover patterns and correlations that classical methods might overlook (Zhang et al., 2024). This enhanced forecasting capability enables companies to optimise inventory levels with greater precision, reducing waste and improving operational efficiency. As a result, companies can enhance customer satisfaction by maintaining optimal stock levels and avoiding disruptions in supply (Gronwald, 2020).

Quantum computing holds immense potential for transforming logistics and supply chain management. Its ability to process information at unprecedented speeds and with high efficiency could revolutionise key areas such as route optimisation, warehouse management, and demand forecasting and inventory management. While the widespread adoption of quantum computing in these fields may still be years away, the potential benefits are substantial (Purnamasari et al., 2023). As such, companies in logistics and supply chain management should begin exploring quantum computing technologies and considering their integration into future operations. By doing so, they can position themselves at the forefront of a new era characterised by unparalleled efficiency and responsiveness in logistics and supply chain management.

16.4.4 Challenges and limitations

The journey toward fully integrating quantum computing into quick commerce logistics is fraught with a myriad of challenges and limitations. These range from technical hurdles and implementation barriers to ethical considerations and concerns over sustainability. Understanding these challenges is essential for stakeholders aiming to leverage quantum computing in enhancing logistics operations.

16.4.5 Technical challenges

At the forefront of the challenges lie the technical difficulties, particularly concerning qubit stability and managing error rates. Qubits, the fundamental building blocks of quantum computers, are highly sensitive to their surroundings. This sensitivity results in a high degree of instability, which is a significant hurdle for maintaining consistent computational outputs (Preskill, 2018). Unlike classical bits, which are either a 0 or a 1, qubits can represent a 0, a 1, or both simultaneously, a property known as superposition. However, this potential comes at the cost of fragility, as any interaction with the external environment can cause a qubit to lose its quantum state, a phenomenon known as decoherence (Wang, 2012). These challenges are exacerbated by high error rates in quantum computations. The errors are primarily due to quantum decoherence and the interference of qubits, requiring sophisticated error correction methods that are still in their infancy (Calderbank & Shor, 1996; Tamrakar & Sharma, 2019). Another significant technical challenge is the development of scalable quantum algorithms that can solve real-world logistics problems efficiently. While theoretical models and algorithms exist, their practical implementation on current quantum hardware is limited. Quantum computers are still in the nascent stages of development, with only a few qubits available for computation, far from the thousands needed for practical, large-scale applications in logistics (Montanaro & Pallister, 2016).

16.4.6 Implementation barriers

On the practical side, implementing quantum computing in quick commerce logistics faces its own set of barriers, ranging from infrastructural deficits to skill gaps. The current infrastructure in logistics is not primed for the seamless integration of quantum computing technologies. There is a significant need for investment in new hardware and software that can harness the power of quantum computers (Farhi et al., 2000; How & Cheah, 2023). Beyond hardware and software, there is a notable skill gap in the workforce. The field of quantum computing is highly specialised, and there is a shortage of professionals who can bridge the gap between quantum physics and practical logistics applications (Acemoglu & Restrepo, 2021). This scarcity of skilled personnel poses a substantial barrier to the widespread adoption of quantum computing in the logistics sector. Additionally, there are substantial financial barriers. The cost of developing, maintaining, and scaling quantum computing infrastructure is currently prohibitive for many organisations. The need for cryogenic cooling systems to maintain the necessary low temperatures for qubit stability adds to the operational costs, making it an expensive venture (Spivey et al., 2022).

16.5 ETHICAL CONSIDERATIONS AND SUSTAINABILITY

The adoption of quantum computing in logistics also raises several ethical considerations. The foremost concern is the potential for increased surveillance and data privacy breaches. Quantum computers, with their unparalleled processing power, could break current encryption algorithms, leading to significant security vulnerabilities (How & Cheah, 2023). This capability poses a risk to the privacy and security of sensitive logistics and customer data. Moreover, there's the ethical consideration of job displacement. As quantum computing automates complex tasks, there's a risk of significant job losses in the logistics sector, raising concerns about employment and social equity (Temidayo Olorunsogo et al., 2024). This potential for automation to displace workers requires careful consideration and planning to ensure a just transition for those affected. Sustainability is another critical consideration. The environmental impact of scaling quantum computing operations is yet unknown. Quantum computers require extremely low temperatures to operate, necessitating substantial energy for cooling purposes, which could exacerbate the carbon footprint of logistics operations (Cuomo et al., 2020). Consequently, it is paramount to consider and mitigate the sustainability challenges associated with integrating quantum computing into logistics.

Even though quantum computing holds the promise of revolutionising quick commerce logistics through unprecedented computational power, the path forward is laden with challenges. Addressing these requires a concerted effort from all stakeholders, including researchers, industry professionals, and policymakers, to navigate the technical, practical, and ethical hurdles while keeping sustainability at the forefront of the quantum computing dialogue in logistics. The collaborative effort will be crucial in transforming the potential of quantum computing into tangible benefits for the quick commerce logistics sector.

16.5.1 The future of quick commerce with quantum computing

As quantum computing transitions from theory to practice, its potential to revolutionise various industries is becoming increasingly tangible. One sector on the brink of this transformation is quick commerce, which encompasses the real-time or near-instant delivery of goods and services. This chapter examines the ways quantum computing might revolutionise quick commerce logistics, outlines steps for businesses to incorporate this technology, and anticipates its long-term effects on the industry.

16.5.2 Potential transformations

Quantum computing functions fundamentally differently from traditional computing. It uses quantum bits, or qubits, which can exist in multiple states simultaneously, providing extraordinary processing power Rasool et al., 2023). This enhanced capability could significantly improve the efficiency of logistics in quick commerce.

16.5.3 Optimisation of delivery routes

At the core of quick commerce is the promise of fast delivery. Quantum computing has the potential to optimise delivery routes in real time, taking into account numerous factors such as traffic conditions, weather, and the need to consolidate orders (Montanaro & Pallister, 2016). This level of optimisation could drastically reduce both delivery times and operational costs.

16.5.4 Inventory management

Quantum computing could revolutionise inventory management by accurately forecasting buying patterns and trends. This would enable more efficient stocking, thereby reducing instances of overstock and stockouts. Quantum algorithms are particularly adept at processing large datasets to identify patterns and make precise predictions (Harrow & Montanaro, 2017).

16.5.5 Dynamic pricing models

Quick commerce platforms could leverage quantum computing to implement dynamic pricing models that adjust in real time based on variables like demand, product availability, and customer preferences. This would maximise profitability while maintaining high levels of customer satisfaction (Ghysels & Morgan, 2024).

16.5.6 Enhanced cybersecurity

Quantum computing could significantly enhance cybersecurity in the quick commerce sector through quantum cryptography, which offers virtually unbreakable encryption. This would safeguard sensitive customer information, financial transactions, and logistics networks against increasingly sophisticated cyber threats (Aljaafari, 2023).

16.5.7 Supply chain resilience

The resilience of quick commerce supply chains could be greatly improved through quantum computing. By simulating complex supply chain networks, it could identify potential disruptions before they occur. This predictive ability would help companies mitigate risks such as supply shortages, geopolitical tensions, and natural disasters (Chauhan et al., 2022).

16.5.8 Personalised customer experiences

Quantum computing could facilitate a higher degree of personalisation in customer interactions by analysing extensive customer data in real time. This would result in tailored recommendations, customised promotions, and enhanced customer engagement, which in turn would drive customer loyalty and satisfaction (Stamatopoulos et al., 2020; Ur Rasool et al., 2023)

16.5.9 Accelerated product development

Quick commerce enterprises could use quantum computing to speed up product development by simulating and optimising product designs, manufacturing processes, and material compositions. This would reduce time-to-market for new products, offering a competitive advantage (Temidayo Olorunsogo et al., 2024).

16.5.10 Energy efficiency and sustainability

Quantum computing could contribute to the sustainability of quick commerce by optimising energy consumption across logistics networks. This might involve reducing fuel usage in delivery vehicles and enhancing the energy efficiency of warehouses and distribution centres, aligning the sector with broader sustainability objectives (Preskill, 2018).

16.5.11 Real-time data processing and decision-making

The capability of quantum computing to process large volumes of data instantaneously could transform decision-making processes within quick commerce. Businesses could analyse real-time data from various sources—including customer interactions, market trends, and operational metrics—to make informed decisions quickly, thereby enhancing responsiveness and agility (Saadi Sedik et al., 2021).

16.5.12 Complex scenario modelling

Quantum computing could enable the modelling of intricate scenarios within the quick commerce sector, such as predicting the effects of sudden market shifts, new regulations, or global events. By running multiple simulations at once, businesses could explore different outcomes and formulate strategies to navigate uncertainties effectively (Wójtowicz, 2019).

16.6 STEPS TOWARD INTEGRATION

Integrating quantum computing into quick commerce presents challenges due to the nascent nature of the technology and the significant investment it demands. However, businesses can take strategic and systematic steps to prepare for its eventual adoption:

16.6.1 Building quantum-ready infrastructure

Companies should prioritise investment in quantum-ready infrastructure, which includes acquiring hardware compatible with quantum computers and developing software designed to harness quantum computational power (Chichereau et al., 2023). Additionally, updating existing IT frameworks is essential to ensure seamless integration with future quantum systems (Montanaro & Pallister, 2016).

16.6.2 Partnerships and collaborations

Forming partnerships with leading quantum computing firms and academic institutions is critical. Such collaborations grant access to advanced resources and specialised knowledge. Moreover, these alliances enable pilot projects that test quantum computing applications in real-world scenarios, allowing businesses to assess practical benefits and challenges in a controlled environment (Preskill, 2018). These partnerships may also foster joint research and development efforts, further accelerating the technology's adoption (Lubinski et al., 2022).

16.6.3 Talent acquisition and development

Given the steep learning curve associated with quantum computing, businesses must focus on acquiring talent proficient in quantum mechanics and computing. Equally important is the ongoing development of current staff, preparing them to collaborate with and eventually lead quantum technology initiatives (Acemoglu & Restrepo, 2021). Implementing comprehensive training programmes and workshops can bridge the knowledge gap, cultivating a workforce that is both knowledgeable and adaptable (Hoch et al., 2020).

16.6.4 Pilot testing and iterative learning

Before full-scale integration, businesses should conduct pilot testing to explore how quantum computing can be applied to specific aspects of quick commerce, such as logistics optimisation or inventory management. These pilot projects not only identify potential operational challenges but also provide valuable insights for refining the technology's applications. An iterative approach to learning from these tests can lead to gradual, informed adoption (Jenkins et al., 2022).

16.6.5 Regulatory compliance and ethical considerations

As quantum computing advances, it will inevitably raise new regulatory and ethical concerns. Businesses must proactively engage with regulatory bodies to ensure compliance with emerging laws and standards governing quantum technologies (Preskill, 2018). Additionally, ethical considerations, particularly in areas such as data privacy and security, should be at the forefront, with guidelines developed to address these issues (Liu et al., 2022).

16.6.6 Customer education and engagement

As businesses prepare to integrate quantum computing, they must consider the impact on their customers. Educating customers about the benefits and implications of quantum-enhanced quick commerce services is crucial for building trust and facilitating adoption. Transparent communication and active engagement with customers through feedback channels will be key in addressing any concerns or misconceptions (Li, 2022).

Investment in Quantum Research and Innovation: Finally, businesses should consider investing in quantum research and innovation, either directly or through strategic partnerships. By contributing to the broader quantum computing ecosystem, companies can influence the direction of future advancements and position themselves at the forefront of technological breakthroughs that may redefine the quick commerce landscape (Grossi et al., 2021).

16.6.7 Long-term outlook

Looking into the future, the integration of quantum computing into quick commerce holds the potential to significantly advance both operational efficiency and sustainability. Improvements in logistics, driven by quantum computing's ability to optimise delivery routes in real time, are likely to lead to substantial reductions in fuel consumption and emissions. This efficiency extends to inventory management, where quantum algorithms can minimise both overstock and stockouts, thereby reducing waste and aligning with the environmental goals that many companies now prioritise (Sodiya et al., 2024). As these technologies mature, the cumulative effect could create a more resource-efficient quick commerce ecosystem, supporting global sustainability initiatives and helping businesses meet increasingly stringent environmental regulations.

As quantum computing becomes more accessible and its applications in quick commerce are refined, it has the potential to level the competitive landscape. Smaller businesses, which may have previously struggled to compete with larger, resource-rich companies, could leverage quantum computing to enhance their operational efficiencies, thereby narrowing the gap. This democratisation of advanced technology could spur innovation across the industry, leading to the development of new business models, services, and customer engagement strategies that cater to evolving consumer demands (How & Cheah, 2023). The ripple effect could result in a more vibrant and diverse quick commerce sector, where innovation thrives and smaller players can carve out significant market niches.

In the long term, quantum computing's influence on quick commerce may extend beyond operational efficiencies. As the technology becomes more integrated into the fabric of the industry, it may enable entirely new approaches to the delivery and consumption of goods and services. For instance, quantum-enhanced predictive analytics could allow for hyper-personalised customer experiences, where preferences are not just met but anticipated with unprecedented accuracy. This could lead to more tailored product offerings and promotional strategies, further enhancing customer satisfaction and loyalty (Chauhan et al., 2022; Sun, 2023).

The widespread adoption of quantum computing in quick commerce could also act as a catalyst for industry-wide transformation. As businesses increasingly rely on quantum technologies, a shift toward more collaborative ecosystems may emerge, where data sharing and joint innovation become the norm. This could foster partnerships across different sectors, combining strengths to address complex logistical challenges and unlock new market opportunities (Preskill, 2018; Saadi Sedik et al., 2021). The quick commerce sector could thus become a hub of technological experimentation and collaboration, driving advancements that extend beyond the industry itself.

The path forward for businesses involves strategic preparation for this quantum future, including investments in infrastructure, the formation of key partnerships, and the cultivation of talent. As these efforts materialise, the quick commerce sector stands on the brink of a transformative leap, where the confluence of cutting-edge technology and innovative business practices will define the future of commerce (Chichereau et al., 2023; Preskill, 2018; Tamrakar & Sharma, 2019).

16.7 CONCLUSION

Throughout this chapter, we have navigated the intricate terrain of quantum computing, focusing mainly on its transformative potential within the realm of quick commerce logistics. As explored in these pages, the integration of quantum computing introduces unparalleled computational capabilities and marks the beginning of a new era in efficiency and effectiveness within logistics and supply chain management.

We began by delving into the foundational principles of quantum computing, providing a framework to appreciate its profound impact. The discussion then traversed various applications and theoretical models, demonstrating how quantum computing is poised to tackle complex logistical challenges at a speed and scale previously unimaginable. Notably, we examined critical areas such as optimising delivery routes, managing inventory, and forecasting demand, where quantum computing is expected to significantly surpass traditional computational methods. These insights underscore this emerging technology's pivotal role in reshaping the landscape of quick commerce logistics.

The potential for quantum computing to revolutionise the quick commerce sector is immense. However, realising these potential demands requires concerted efforts from all stakeholders involved, including technology developers, business leaders, policymakers, and academic researchers. These groups must collaborate closely to foster innovation, build supportive frameworks for technology adoption, and create an environment conducive to experimentation and learning. Such a collective approach is essential for navigating complex challenges and fully leveraging the opportunities that quantum computing presents for quick commerce logistics.

As this chapter concludes, it is evident that the journey toward fully integrating quantum computing into quick commerce logistics and supply chain management is both challenging and exhilarating. This endeavour requires technological advancements, a comprehensive understanding of logistical complexities, and, more importantly, a vision for a future where logistics operates efficiently. The potential benefits—from reducing operational costs to dramatically improving delivery times and ultimately enhancing consumer satisfaction make this journey worthwhile.

REFERENCES

Acemoglu, D., & Restrepo, P. (2021). Unpacking skill bias: Automation and new tasks. *SSRN Electronic Journal*, NBER Working Paper No. w26681. https://doi.org/10.2139/ssrn.3522330.

Aljaafari, M. (2023). Quantum computing for social business optimisation: A practitioner's perspective. *Soft Computing*, 1–23. https://doi.org/10.1007/s00500-023-08764-y.

Athanasiadis, E., Koutras, V., & Zeimpekis, V. (2023). Dataset for the van-drone routing problem with multiple delivery drop points. *Data in Brief*, *48*, 109192. https://doi.org/10.1016/j.dib.2023.109192.

Calderbank, A. R., & Shor, P. W. (1996). Good quantum error-correcting codes exist. *Physical Review A - Atomic, Molecular, and Optical Physics*, *54*(2), 1098–1105. https://doi.org/10.1103/PhysRevA.54.1098.

Chakraborty, M., & Sen, S. (2023). Determination of Qubit Entanglement in One-step Double Photoionization of Helium Atom. In *Quantum Dots - Recent Advances, New Perspectives and Contemporary Applications.* IntechOpen. https://doi.org/10.5772/intechopen.106047.

Chauhan, D. R., Unnikrishnan, A., & Boyles, S. D. (2022). Maximum Profit Facility Location and Dynamic Resource Allocation for Instant Delivery Logistics. In *Transportation Research Record* (Vol. 2676, Issue 7, pp. 697–710). SAGE Publications Ltd. https://doi.org/10.1177/03611981221082574.

Chawla, A. (2022). *Quick Commerce – shop model will empower neighbourhood sellers.* https://timesofindia.indiatimes.com/blogs/voices/quick-commerce-shop-model-will-empower-neighbourhood-sellers/

Chichereau, B., Vialle, S., & Carribault, P. (2023). Experimenting with Hybrid Quantum Optimization in HPC Software Stack for CPU Register Allocation. *Proceedings - 2023 IEEE International Conference on Quantum Computing and Engineering, QCE 2023*, *2*, 134–140. https://doi.org/10.1109/QCE57702.2023.10197.

Cuomo, D., Caleffi, M., & Cacciapuoti, A. S. (2020). Towards a distributed quantum computing ecosystem. *IET Quantum Communication*, *1*(1), 3–8. https://doi.org/10.1049/iet-qtc.2020.0002.

Farhi, E., Goldstone, J., Gutmann, S., & Sipser, M. (2000). *Quantum Computation by Adiabatic Evolution*. https://arxiv.org/abs/quant-ph/0001106v1.

Gachnang, P., Ehrenthal, J., Hanne, T., & Dornberger, R. (2022). Quantum computing in supply chain management state of the art and research directions. *Asian Journal of Logistics Management*, *1*(1), 57–73. https://doi.org/10.14710/ajlm.2022.14325.

García-Salirrosas, E. E., & Rondon-Eusebio, R. F. (2022). Green Marketing Practices Related to Key Variables of Consumer Purchasing Behavior. In *Sustainability (Switzerland)* (Vol. 14, Issue 14, p. 8499). Multidisciplinary Digital Publishing Institute. https://doi.org/10.3390/su14148499.

Ghosh, M. D., & Routh, M. S. (2023). The impact of E-commerce on industrial supply chain management in West Bengal: An analysis. *International Journal of Research Publication and Reviews*, *4*(9), 164–169. https://doi.org/10.55248/gengpi.4.923.52286.

Ghysels, E., & Morgan, J. (2024). On quantum ambiguity and potential exponential computational speed-ups to solving dynamic asset pricing models. *SSRN Electronic Journal*. https://doi.org/10.2139/ssrn.4815156.

Giani, A., & Eldredge, Z. (2021). Quantum computing opportunities in renewable energy. *SN Computer Science*, *2*(5), 1–15. https://doi.org/10.1007/s42979-021-00786-3.

Gronwald, K.-D. (2020). SCM: Supply Chain Management. In *Integrated Business Information Systems* (pp. 25–69). Springer, Berlin, Heidelberg. https://doi.org/10.1007/978-3-662-59811-5_3.

Grossi, M., Crippa, L., Aita, A., Bartoli, G., Sammarco, V., Picca, E., Said, N., Tramonto, F., & Mattei, F. (2021). *A Serverless Cloud Integration For Quantum Computing*. https://arxiv.org/abs/2107.02007v1.

Guru, S., Verma, S., Baheti, P., & Dagar, V. (2023). Assessing the feasibility of hyperlocal delivery model as an effective distribution channel. *Management Decision*. https://doi.org/10.1108/MD-03-2022-0407.

Haldorai, A. (2024). Advancements and applications of quantum computing in robotics. *Journal of Computing and Natural Science*, 2(4), 053–063. https://doi.org/10.53759/181x/jcns202404006.

Harrow, A. W., & Montanaro, A. (2017). Quantum computational supremacy. In *Nature* (Vol. 549, Issue 7671, pp. 203–209). https://doi.org/10.1038/nature23458.

Harter, A., Stich, L., & Spann, M. (2024). The effect of delivery time on repurchase behavior in quick commerce. *Journal of Service Research*, 1–17. https://doi.org/10.1177/10946705241236961.

Hernández, A. R., Maldonado, A. L. E., & Bermejo, J. H. D. (2024). Architecture of quantum computing. *Journal of Engineering Research*, *4*(15), 2–10. https://doi.org/10.22533/at.ed.3174152421055.

Hoch, D., Sommer, T., Müller, S., & Poot, M. (2020). On-chip quantum optics and integrated optomechanics. *Turkish Journal of Physics*, *44*(3), 239–246. https://doi.org/10.3906/FIZ-2004-20.

How, M.-L., & Cheah, S.-M. (2023). Business renaissance: Opportunities and challenges at the dawn of the quantum computing era. *Businesses*, *3*(4), 585–605. https://doi.org/10.3390/businesses3040036.

Jalu, G., Dasalegn, G., Japee, G., Tangl, A., & Boros, A. (2024). Investigating the effect of green brand innovation and green perceived value on green brand loyalty: Examining the moderating role of green knowledge. *Sustainability (Switzerland)*, *16*(1), 341. https://doi.org/10.3390/su16010341.

Jenkins, J., Berente, N., & Angst, C. (2022). The quantum computing business ecosystem and firm strategies. *Proceedings of the Annual Hawaii International Conference on System Sciences*, *2022-Janua*, 6432–6441. https://doi.org/10.24251/hicss.2022.779.

Laghari, A. A., Shah, H., Laghari, R. A., Kumar, K., Waqan, A. A., & Jumani, A. K. (2018). A review on quantum computing trends & future perspectives. *EAI Endorsed Transactions on Cloud Systems*, *7*(22), 173979. https://doi.org/10.4108/eai.17-5-2022.173979.

Lee, T., Han, S. R., & Song, B. D. (2023). Optimisation of omnichannel distribution network using micro fulfillment center under demand uncertainty. *IEEE Access*, *11*, 107496–107510. https://doi.org/10.1109/ACCESS.2023.3317690.

Li, K. (2022). The qubit fidelity under different error mechanisms based on error correction threshold. *Frontiers in Physics*, *10*, 893507. https://doi.org/10.3389/fphy.2022.893507.

Liu, B., Huang, S., Zhou, M., & Yang, S. (2022). Research on the application of "quantum computing + dynamic face recognition" in bank personal business. In *International Conference on Network Communication and Information Security (ICNCIS 2022)* (Vol. 12503, p. 3). https://doi.org/10.1117/12.2657069.

Lubinski, T., Granade, C., Anderson, A., Geller, A., Roetteler, M., Petrenko, A., & Heim, B. (2022). Advancing hybrid quantum–classical computation with real-tme execution. *Frontiers in Physics*, *10*, 940293. https://doi.org/10.3389/fphy.2022.940293.

Markidis, S. (2024). What is quantum parallelism, anyhow? *Research Paper Proceedings of the ISC High Performance 2024*. https://doi.org/10.23919/isc.2024.10528926.

Montanaro, A., & Pallister, S. (2016). Quantum algorithms and the finite element method. *Physical Review A*, *93*(3), 032324. https://doi.org/10.1103/PhysRevA.93.032324.

Nierynck, R. (2020). *Quick commerce: Pioneering the next generation of delivery*. Delivery Hero Web Page. https://www.deliveryhero.com/blog/quick-commerce/

Preskill, J. (2018). Quantum computing in the NISQ era and beyond. *Quantum*, *2*, 79. https://doi.org/10.22331/q-2018-08-06-79.

Purnamasari, D. I., Permadi, V. A., Saepudin, A., & Agusdin, R. P. (2023). Demand forecasting for improved inventory management in small and medium-sized businesses. *Jurnal Nasional Pendidikan Teknik Informatika (JANAPATI)*, *12*(1), 56–66. https://doi.org/10.23887/janapati.v12i1.57144.

Ranjekar, G., & Roy, D. (2023). *Rise of Quick Commerce in India: Business Models and Infrastructure Requirements*.

Saadi Sedik, T., Gorbanyov, M., & Malaika, M. (2021). Quantum computing and the financial system: Spooky action at a distance? *IMF Working Papers, 2021*(071), 1. https://doi.org/10.5089/9781513572727.001.

Schorung, M. (2023). *Quick commerce: Will the disruption of the food retail industry happen? Investigating the quick commerce supply chain and the impacts of dark stores.* https://shs.hal.science/halshs-04098596

Singh, D. S., Agarwal, M. S., & Gupta, M. R. (2023). Quantum computing: Fundamentals, progress, and implications. *International Journal for Research in Applied Science and Engineering Technology, 11*(9), 1106–1111. https://doi.org/10.22214/ijraset.2023.55803.

Sodiya, E. O., Umoga, U. J., Amoo, O. O., & Atadoga, A.. (2024). AI-driven warehouse automation: A comprehensive review of systems. *GSC Advanced Research and Reviews, 18*(2), 272–282. https://doi.org/10.30574/gscarr.2024.18.2.0063.

Spivey, R. F., Inlek, I. V., Jia, Z., Crain, S., Sun, K., Kim, J., Vrijsen, G., Fang, C., Fitzgerald, C., Kross, S., Noel, T., & Kim, J. (2022). High-stability cryogenic system for quantum computing with compact packaged ion traps. *IEEE Transactions on Quantum Engineering, 3.* https://doi.org/10.1109/TQE.2021.3125926.

Srivastava, G. R., Gera, P., Goyal, N., Sharma, A., & Rani, R. (2023). From clicks to carts: Developing an autonomous E-grocery shopping system. *2023 3rd International Conference on Intelligent Technologies, CONIT 2023.* https://doi.org/10.1109/CONIT59222.2023.10205810.

Stamatopoulos, N., Egger, D. J., Sun, Y., Zoufal, C., Iten, R., Shen, N., & Woerner, S. (2020). Option pricing using quantum computers. *Quantum, 4*, 291. https://doi.org/10.22331/q-2020-07-06-291.

Stojanov, M. (2022). *Q-Commerce – The Next Generation E-Commerce.* http://dlib.uni-svishtov.bg/handle/10610/4683

Sun, H. (2023). Design logistics management system based on computer algorithm model. *Frontiers in Artificial Intelligence and Applications, 373*, 569–575. https://doi.org/10.3233/FAIA230856.

Sun, Z. Q., & Yoon, S. J. (2022). What makes people pay premium price for eco-friendly products? The effects of ethical consumption consciousness, CSR, and product quality. *Sustainability (Switzerland), 14*(23), 15513. https://doi.org/10.3390/su142315513.

Tamrakar, A., & Sharma, R. (2019). Quantum computing: A comprehensive review. *Turkish Journal of Computer and Mathematics Education (TURCOMAT), 10*(3), 1634–1642. https://doi.org/10.61841/turcomat.v10i3.14623.

Temidayo Olorunsogo, Boma Sonimiteim Jacks, & Olakunle Abayomi Ajala. (2024). Leveraging quantum computing for inclusive and responsible AI development: A conceptual and review framework. *Computer Science & IT Research Journal, 5*(3), 671–680. https://doi.org/10.51594/csitrj.v5i3.927.

Tiwari, S. (2022). *E-grocery express: Quick commerce upgrading delivery system! | The Financial Express.* https://www.financialexpress.com/industry/e-grocery-express-quick-commerce-upgrading-delivery-system/2389687/

Ur Rasool, R., Ahmad, H. F., Rafique, W., Qayyum, A., Qadir, J., & Anwar, Z. (2023). Quantum Computing for Healthcare: A Review. *Future Interne, 15*(3), 94. https://doi.org/10.3390/fi15030094.

Villa, R., & Monzón, A. (2021). Mobility restrictions and E-commerce: Holistic balance in Madrid centre during COVID-19 lockdown. *Economies*, *9*(2), 57. https://doi.org/10.3390/ECONOMIES9020057.

Wajidi, F. A., Rehan, E. W., Saeed, M., Iftikhar, K. M., & Tahir, A. (2023). Technology trends and their impact on the E-commerce industry. *International Journal of Social Science & Entrepreneurship*, *3*(4), 236–253. https://doi.org/10.58661/ijsse.v3i4.227.

Wang, Y. (2012). Quantum computation and quantum information. *Statistical Science*, *27*(3), 373–394. https://doi.org/10.1214/11-STS378.

Weber, T., Borras, K., Jansen, K., Krücker, D., & Riebisch, M. (2024). Construction and volumetric benchmarking of quantum computing noise models. *Physica Scripta*, *99*(6), 065106. https://doi.org/10.1088/1402-4896/ad406c.

Wójtowicz, K. (2019). Theory of quantum computation and philosophy of mathematics. Part II. In *Logic and Logical Philosophy* (Vol. 28, Issue 1, pp. 173–193). Wydawnictwo Naukowe Uniwersytetu Mikolaja Kopernika. https://doi.org/10.12775/LLP.2018.006.

Yu, W., Hou, G., Xia, P., & Li, J. (2019). Supply chain joint inventory management and cost optimisation based on ant colony algorithm and fuzzy model. *Tehnicki Vjesnik*, *26*(6), 1729–1737. https://doi.org/10.17559/TV-20190805123158.

Zhahir, A. A., Mohd, S. M., Shuhud, M. I. M., Idrus, B., Zainuddin, H., Jan, N. M., & Wahiddin, M. R. (2024). Entanglement detection: A scoping review. *Journal of Advanced Research in Applied Sciences and Engineering Technology*, *42*(2), 209–220. https://doi.org/10.37934/araset.42.2.209220.

Zhang, H., Tian, S., Qin, J., Yu, Z., Guo, H., & Jia, X. (2024). Inventory prediction based on CNN-LSTM Model. *Highlights in Science, Engineering and Technology*, *82*, 251–257. https://doi.org/10.54097/eywbtj23.

Chapter 17

Innovative approaches to secure communication for smart logistics

Özen Özer, Nadir Subaşı, and Emrehan Taşkın

17.1 INTRODUCTION

Matrix theory has changed within cryptography over several centuries and this, in itself, is an interesting story. Though there were no archaeological findings to prove that matrices existed as mathematical entities before the 20th century, their use in various ciphering methods especially showed that it was impossible to do cryptography without them.

The 19th century played a very important role in the development of matrix theory, particularly through contributions by Arthur Cayley and Augustin Louis Cauchy among others who are leading mathematicians. The main ideas they dealt with at that particular time included the multiplication of matrices and determinants, which formed a foundation for future uses [1].

It was not only the linchpin of mathematics but also an influencing factor in historical events, reflecting deeply how innovations in the discipline can affect societies throughout time, making them inevitable.

A remarkable progression in contemporary cryptography was observed immediately after the Second World War era primarily when public-key cryptography was introduced. At the heart of most cryptographic algorithms are matrix operations and linear algebra [2] which form the basis of popular methods such as the RSA algorithm. It works by utilizing these properties of matrices together with modular arithmetic to provide security in data transmission. Later, when research had already picked up steam [3] into how matrix theory can be integrated into other cryptographic protocols, investigators also pro-bed its importance in an attempt to heighten security levels. The need to improve safety through using matrix theory in cryptographic protocols was identified as the researchers did more studies on it.

Quantum computing has become a common concept in computer science circles today, which has led to research in new cryptographic methods with particular interest in a new direction known as post-quantum cryptography [4]. Of much interest, quantum key distribution is one method that could revolutionize secure communication systems through the secure generation

DOI: 10.1201/9781003498292-17

of keys that are not known to anyone else except the individuals involved in the communication channel. It is built on matrix theory [5] which has been used for its robust assurance against security threats. An evident dynamic equilibrium exists in a world where mathematical algorithms are being made to overlap with encryption technologies due to the confrontation of new developments [6].

Matrices are used for various cryptographic algorithms like Hill Cipher, RSA algorithm, lattice-based cryptography, quantum key distribution (QKD), and linear code cryptography to secure communication and data using linear algebra [7].

The need for safeguarding confidential information led to an increased demand for mathematical concepts used in this line of work due to its dynamic nature towards achieving better security mechanisms. Out of many other crucial aspects involved in cryptosystems that rely on mathematical models, upper triangular matrices are considered a very important component within its spectrum as far as confidentiality is concerned [8].

This significance is not random at all but originates from exclusive attributes and features possessed by high upper matrices making them good at encryption.

The chapter offers a comprehensive background on the evolution and application of matrix theory within cryptography, providing a detailed literature review that traces the development from early ciphers to contemporary cryptographic techniques [9]. Notably, the use of upper triangular matrices in cryptographic contexts is thoroughly supported by references to both foundational research and recent advancements.

To further enhance the literature review, it is briefly summarized to incorporate the latest research discussing matrix operations in emerging cryptographic fields [10] such as blockchain technology and advanced persistent threat (APT) defences. Additionally, integrating interdisciplinary research that intersects with fields like data science and artificial intelligence can provide insights into how matrix theory is evolving in response to these technologies in cryptographic applications [11].

This chapter effectively covers the application of upper triangular matrices, expanding its scope to include related mathematical tools and comparisons with other matrix forms, such as lower triangular or symmetric matrices and provides a clearer perspective on their unique advantages or limitations. Furthermore, the discussion of practical implementation challenges in high-stakes environments, such as financial transactions and governmental communications, offers valuable insights [12].

The chapter successfully highlights the pivotal role of upper triangular matrices in enhancing cryptographic security by discussing both theoretical and practical aspects, including trends in increasing computational efficiency and security. However, more emphasis on the limitations and potential vulnerabilities, such as side-channel attacks and fault analysis, provides a deeper understanding of the risks associated with matrix-based methods [13].

In summary, the chapter provides a deep dive into upper triangular matrices in cryptographic applications, expanding the discussion to include comparisons with other cryptographic methods, real-world case studies, and practical examples of implementation, offering a richer, more nuanced understanding. Additionally, addressing potential downsides, limitations, and challenges faced during the implementation of these matrices further strengthens the content.

In the research by Abu-Faraj et al. [1], a groundbreaking method of digital image encryption was proposed. This new concept uses colour images for the construction of a very strong private key matrix (MPK) that cannot be easily cracked. The experimental results show that this proposed technique maintains established quality levels while at the same time improving the speed of encryption and decryption compared to standard methods of encryption like DES, 3DES, AES, and Blowfish.

Ali Pacha H. and Özer, Ö. [14] presented an initial permutation-based encryption algorithm in their study, in which a modulus of 257 is used with the affine cipher. Their aim is to enhance the security regime applicable to such encryption methods. Moreover, data extraction from a particular coordinate in an attractor was proposed as a crucial criterion by Merzoug Pacha A., Ali Pacha A., Hadj Said N., and Özer Ö [15]. This criterion is consistently used during both encryption and decryption processes to ensure that the data is coherently handled in a secure manner.

Rimani R., Hadj Said N., Ali Pacha A., and Özer Ö. [16] present a novel approach to key exchange in their manuscript. Their idea is based on combining the Diffie-Hellman protocol with image registration techniques that utilize the fast Fourier transform. The underlying principle of this technique is that key exchange becomes more secure when mixing the key with such transformed images. This technique combines cryptography with image processing in a way that is not only original but also enables one to think of various ways a cryptographic key could be manipulated or represented.

The book *Introduction to Modern Cryptography: Principles and Protocols* by Jonathan Katz and Yehuda Lindell [17] provides a comprehensive overview of modern cryptographic principles and protocols, including various mathematical tools used in cryptography. It discusses matrix-based cryptographic methods and their applications.

Similarly, *Cryptography and Network Security: Principles and Practice* by William Stallings [18] covers a wide range of cryptographic techniques and network security protocols, including matrix-based cryptography. The book discusses practical implementation challenges and compares different cryptographic methods, and *The Handbook of Applied Cryptography* by Alfred J. Menezes, Paul C. van Oorschot, and Scott A. Vanstone [19] provides in-depth coverage of cryptographic algorithms, including the use of matrices in cryptographic applications. It also discusses potential vulnerabilities and implementation issues.

Also, *Lattice-Based Cryptography for Beginners* edited by Dong Pyo Chi, Jeong Woon Choi, Jeong San Kim and Taewan Kim [9] explores the role of lattice structures in cryptography, including upper triangular and other matrix forms. It provides comparative analyses and discusses practical challenges in implementing lattice-based cryptographic systems, and *Matrix Computations* by Gene H. Golub and Charles F. Van Loan [12] includes sections relevant to cryptographic applications and the comparative advantages of different matrix forms.

Similarly, R. Alvarez et al. [3] study investigate a matrix-based public key cryptosystem and digital signature proposal. The authors discuss the security of this system and how encryption and signature processes are implemented. The properties provided by the matrix structure highlight that the proposed cryptosystem is both robust and efficient. Additionally, it compares the system with existing cryptosystems, emphasizing its advantages and potential application areas. Overall, this study presents a new approach in the field of matrix-based cryptography and contributes to enhancing security in digital signature applications.

Other works can be detailed as follows:

Applied Cryptography: Protocols, Algorithms, and Source Code in C by Bruce Schneier [20] is a practical guide to cryptographic algorithms and their implementations, including the use of matrices. It addresses real-world challenges and solutions in cryptography.

Cryptographic Engineering by Niels Ferguson, Bruce Schneier, and Tadayoshi Kohno [13] delves into the engineering aspects of cryptographic systems, including the use of matrix-based methods. It discusses side-channel attacks and fault analysis in depth.

Hadesius: Una soluzione per il controllo e il monitoraggio del perimetro cibernetico nazionale edited by Andrea Colato. *MSc Thesis*. Universita degli Studi di Milano (UNIMI). Supervisors: Stelvio Cimato, Dario Fiore. October 2021. https://software.imdea.org/research/publications/ . A collection of papers from the SCN conference that includes discussions on matrix-based cryptographic methods, practical implementation challenges, and security issues such as side-channel attacks.

Machine Learning in Action by Peter Harrington [21] discusses the application of machine learning techniques that heavily rely on matrix operations, providing insights into how these techniques intersect with cryptographic applications.

Pattern Recognition and Machine Learning by Christopher M. Bishop [5] provides an in-depth understanding of machine learning and pattern recognition, discussing the role of matrix theory in these fields and its implications for cryptography.

Deep Learning by Ian Goodfellow, Yoshua Bengio, and Aaron Courville covers deep learning techniques [4] that utilize extensive matrix computations, relevant to the evolving use of matrix theory in AI and its implications for cryptography.

Data Science for Business by Foster Provost and Tom Fawcett [22] explores how data science techniques, including those based on matrix theory, can be applied in business contexts, intersecting with cryptographic applications for secure data analysis.

Mathematics for Machine Learning by Marc Peter Deisenroth, A. Aldo Faisal, and Cheng Soon Ong [12] provides the mathematical foundations for machine learning, including matrix theory, highlighting its relevance to both machine learning and cryptography.

The above works go into great detail examining the specifics of diverse styles singling out definite cryptographic undertakings. Creating a unique security goal fostered by each writer for these tasks makes it possible for anyone who picks up the books to adjust them and use the thoughts in an inventive way in cryptography. The books contain several scenarios that are investigated to evaluate how well these systems work, highlighting the need for cryptographic operations to avoid imprecision. In addition, some of these books also provide fundamental knowledge concerning abstract and linear algebra, which enhances comprehension about the theory based on mathematics for cryptography.

In the related literature, many researchers have recommended different successful ways to exchange keys and apply cryptography, thus adding much value to the current knowledge in cryptology as a discipline that changes continuously and cherishes communication safety.

The content of this examination is the incorporation of a matrix that is upper and triangular into a cipher that Hill is used to, and this is accompanied by the usage of logic mapping and some other encryption/decryption algorithms, all in the Python programming language as applied to cryptography. The procedure is aided by a dictionary that has every writable ASCII letter along with some Turkish characters, hence improving character sensitivity while increasing the character limit through string data type usage. Additionally, an analysis will be made on an alternative kind of cryptography which is a hash function along with some Python code samples to show how it works.

Our goal is to investigate the cryptosecurity importance of upper triangle matrices in this chapter. We will review their math roots as well as wide-ranging uses such as encryption, key administration, data safeguard, etc. Over this text, we shall illustrate that upper triangular matrices own isolated characteristics together with their computational advantages that make them essential ingredients for strong encryption schemes and safe communication techniques being more vital today because everything is wired up digitally [13, 23–25].

We will also evaluate what differentiates matrices from other forms of computers that would enable them being demanded when one is seeking resilience against cryptosystems. Before embarking on the main sample of researching cryptography we need to understand that upper triangular matrices are crucial mathematics objects that form without which enhancing cybersecurity could not be possible amid the current need to protect personal information involving sensitive transactions [17, 26–30]. This study seeks not just to remark on mathematics but showing in what respect this abstract discipline interacts with specific aspects of human life especially those concerning internet communication [31].

17.2 PRELIMINARIES

17.2.1 Initial setup

Before looking at our findings, it is important to discuss the role of upper triangular matrices in assuring cryptographic security. An exemplary case is the RSA encryption algorithm that depends on the production of two large prime numbers [32]. They can be used in upper matrix triangular computations, hence facilitating the quick production and management of prime constituents required during key generation, thus making the whole encryption process safer.

More so, numerous block ciphers used in symmetric-key cryptography depend on matrix operations. The processes can be improved using upper triangular matrices, hence leading to reduced computational complexity without jeopardizing the security. This strategy leads to fast encryption and decryption methods that are of immense benefit to cryptography.

Being able to securely store cryptographic keys is vital. When sparse, upper triangular matrices provide a succinct manner in which encryption keys can be represented and held. It guarantees security and saving of storage space [19].

We can make use of upper triangular matrices to construct cryptographic protocols that stand against side-channel attacks. In order to make sure less information about the key is leaked in actual practice, these matrix operations need to be arranged in certain ways which maximize security.

Secure data sharing and computation among many parties while preserving privacy can be made possible by using upper triangular matrices in secure multiparty computation scenarios. These can be harnessed to create efficient and secure protocols because of the way they naturally are.

Upper triangular matrices are used in hardware security modules (HSMs) [33] as well as secure enclaves for protecting cryptographic keys and sensitive information all the time. The way these matrices are structured makes it easy to store things securely and get them back later on.

Quantum computers threaten classical cryptography, making it necessary to develop resilient cryptographic protocols that can withstand quantum attacks. These kinds of protocols would help to defend communications that are safe, thereby preventing potential future threats [15].

Secure communication in the Internet of Things (IoT) is complicated by the fact that some devices have very limited capabilities in terms of group membership and key storage. Key distribution issues are easier with triangular matrices, which can also make secure IoT communication possible [34].

If you take cryptographic security to include key generation, efficiency of encryption, secure storage, resistance against attacks, and design of secure protocols across many applications upper triangular matrices play an integral role in all these aspects in the book chapter entitled *Empowering Secure Communication with Specific Triangular Matrices* written by Özer, Ö. and Subasi, N. in 2024.

For an instance using numbers, we may look at this:

Example 1. To generate an RSA key, it is crucial to start by producing some huge prime numbers [34] which we shall use later on. Prime factorization for key creation can be conducted effectively using an upper triangular matrix.

To generate RSA key pairs follow these steps:

Select two prime numbers, say $p = 79$, $q = 97$.
Let's find $n = p * q = 79 * 97 = 7663$.
Then, $\varphi\ (n) = (p - 1) * (q - 1) = (79 - 1) * (97 - 1) = 78 * 96 = 7488$.

Now we have to find an integer e where $1 < e < \varphi\ (n)$ and e is coprime with $\varphi\ (n)$, which can be done using an upper triangular matrix:

Choose a public exponent e such that it is coprime to $\varphi\ (n)$. We could simply use upper triangular matrix to find one.

We now have an upper triangular matrix that contains numbers ranging from 1 to $\varphi\ (n)$, then identify [35] those which are relatively prime to $\varphi\ (n)$:

$$\begin{bmatrix} 1 & 2 & 3 & & \cdots & 7487 & 7488 \\ 0 & 1 & 2 & \cdots & \cdots & \cdots & 7487 \\ 0 & 0 & 1 & & \cdots & \cdots & \cdots \\ & \vdots & & \ddots & & \vdots & \\ 0 & 0 & 0 & \cdots & & \cdots & \cdots \\ 0 & 0 & 0 & & & & \cdots \end{bmatrix}$$

Here, we can spot that 47 is an apt candidate for e since it is coprime to $\varphi\ (n)$. Using the modular multiplicative inverse of e modulo $\varphi\ (n)$, determine the private exponent d. In order to do this efficiently, you can employ a variety of algorithms such as the extended Euclidean algorithm [36] or the upper triangular matrix method.

To do this, we could either use the extended Euclidean algorithm or employ an up triangular matrix for simplicity reasons. As an illustration, let's assume that d is 3983. We now have our RSA key pair;

Public Key: $(n, e) = (7663, 47)$
Private Key: $(n, d) = (7663, 3983)$

An appropriate public exponent (e) was quickly detected using an upper triangular method, and the secret exponent (d) was calculated later where necessary, both of which are vital for creating the RSA key pair. Consequently, this method can assist in simplifying the process by which keys are generated so that it becomes less of a burden computationally while also being more secure.

Example 2. (Matrix Operations in Block Ciphers) Let's consider matrix operations in block ciphers as an example. Supposing we have an upper triangular matrix A which is a 3×3 matrix, then there is such that $A = \begin{bmatrix} a & b & c \\ 0 & d & e \\ 0 & 0 & f \end{bmatrix}$ and $P = \begin{bmatrix} x \\ y \\ z \end{bmatrix}$. Then the matrix-vector multiplication $A \times P$ can be performed to encrypt P. That is, $A * P = \begin{bmatrix} ax + by + cz \\ dy + ez \\ fz \end{bmatrix}$.

It can be seen here that the upper triangular matrix A transforms the plaintext vector P into the ciphertext vector C efficiently.

Example 3. Hill cipher is a cryptographic algorithm that processes texts in blocks. Both encryption and decryption processes in Hill cipher possess upper triangular matrices. This 3×3 upper triangular matrix as the encryption key can be used in the Hill cipher which goes like this:

For example, if we would like to encrypt the words "MATHEMATICIANS" using an upper triangular matrix of dimension 3×3 with an Elements of the Encryption Key (upper triangular matrix) given by $K = \begin{bmatrix} 1 & 2 & 3 \\ 0 & 4 & 5 \\ 0 & 0 & 6 \end{bmatrix}$.

Mapping the message "MATHEMATICIANS" to numerical values by using a predefined technique where $A = 0$, $B = 1$, $C = 2$, … as thus leading to "12 0 19 7 4 12 0 19 8 2 8 0 13 18". The process of encrypting involves multiplying matrix M with upper triangular matrix K after which we get the text message that is encrypted; this is done by multiplying matrices K with M matrix such that any value of $C = K * M$. The text message that has been encrypted then read as "TUOBBWMQXSHAVRT". In order to decrypt, we are supposed to find an inverse matrix of K which in this case is the inverse of $K^{-1} = \begin{bmatrix} 1 & -1/2 & -1/12 \\ 0 & 1/4 & -5/24 \\ 0 & 0 & 1/6 \end{bmatrix}$. We then obtain our original M by simply multiplying the integer ratios on a 3 × 1 matrix dimension that results in $K^{(-1)} * C = M$.

Some cryptographic operations (key generation, matrix-associated encryption, etc.) can considerably benefit if upper triangular matrices are employed. This will help enhance the security of these cryptographic systems without sacrificing their overall efficiency.

17.2.1 Detail explanations in other sciences

17.2.1.1 Note 1. Importance of upper triangular matrices in cryptographic techniques

Upper triangular matrices play a significant role in modern cryptographic techniques due to their mathematical properties and computational efficiency. An upper triangular matrix is a square matrix where all the entries below the main diagonal are zero. The importance of these matrices in cryptography can be highlighted through various applications and advantages.

17.2.1.2 Applications in cryptography

Public key cryptography

In public key cryptography, upper triangular matrices can be used to construct efficient encryption schemes. For example, the NTRU (*N*th degree truncated polynomial ring) cryptosystem, which is based on lattice-based cryptography, often utilizes upper triangular matrices due to their structural properties that allow for efficient polynomial multiplication and inversion.

Error correction codes

Upper triangular matrices are also employed in error correction codes, which are crucial for ensuring data integrity in cryptographic communication. Reed-Solomon codes and low-density parity-check (LDPC) codes, which are used in secure data transmission, can benefit from the simplicity of upper triangular matrices for encoding and decoding processes.

Symmetric key algorithms

In symmetric key algorithms, certain transformations involving upper triangular matrices can be used to enhance the security and efficiency of the encryption and decryption processes [16]. For instance, the LU decomposition (where a matrix is factored into a lower triangular matrix and an upper triangular matrix) is used in some cryptographic algorithms to optimize the computation.

17.2.1.3 Advantages of upper triangular matrices

Computational efficiency
Operations involving upper triangular matrices, such as multiplication and inversion, are computationally efficient. This efficiency is due to the zero elements below the main diagonal, which reduces the number of necessary computations.

Simplified analysis
The structure of upper triangular matrices simplifies mathematical analysis, which can be beneficial for proving the security properties of cryptographic algorithms.

Scalability
Upper triangular matrices can be easily scaled to larger sizes, making them suitable for cryptographic applications that require handling large datasets or high-dimensional vectors.

17.2.1.4 Limitations and potential vulnerabilities

Despite their advantages, the use of matrix-based methods, including upper triangular matrices, comes with certain limitations and potential vulnerabilities that need to be addressed to ensure robust security. Some of them can be given as follows:

17.2.1.4.1 Side-channel attacks

- **Definition:** Side-channel attacks exploit physical implementations of cryptographic algorithms rather than theoretical weaknesses. They can involve measuring power consumption, electromagnetic emissions, or timing information to extract secret keys.
- **Example:** If a cryptographic algorithm using an upper triangular matrix has different computational paths depending on the key values, an attacker could measure the power consumption during these computations and infer information about the key.
- **Mitigation:** Countermeasures such as constant-time algorithms, masking techniques, and randomization can be employed to reduce the risk of side-channel attacks. For example, using a constant-time implementation ensures that the time taken to perform cryptographic operations is independent of the key values.

17.2.1.4.2 Fault analysis

- **Definition:** Fault analysis attacks involve deliberately inducing errors in the cryptographic computation and observing the resulting output to gain information about the secret key.
- **Example:** An attacker might inject faults into a system performing encryption with an upper triangular matrix. By analysing the incorrect outputs, the attacker can deduce the structure of the matrix or the key used in the encryption process.
- **Mitigation:** Techniques such as redundancy, error-detection codes, and fault-tolerant designs can help mitigate the effects of fault analysis. For instance, implementing redundancy by performing the same computation multiple times and comparing the results can detect and correct induced faults.

While upper triangular matrices offer several advantages in cryptographic techniques, it is crucial to be aware of and address their potential limitations and vulnerabilities. By implementing robust countermeasures against side-channel attacks and fault analysis [16], the security of cryptographic systems that rely on matrix-based methods can be significantly enhanced. Future research will be focused on exploring these underexplored areas to develop more resilient cryptographic solutions.

17.2.1.5 Note 2. Broadening the scope of upper triangular matrices in cryptography

The chapter effectively explains the use of upper triangular matrices in cryptography. However, expanding the content to include comparisons with other types of matrices and addressing practical implementation challenges could provide a more comprehensive understanding. Below are suggestions for additional content to enrich the chapter [22].

17.2.1.6 Note 3. Comparative analysis with other matrix forms

- Upper triangular matrices vs. lower triangular matrices

In upper triangular matrices, all elements below the main diagonal are zero. Their applications include efficient use in certain lattice-based cryptosystems and algorithms that require back substitution. Their advantages include simplifying certain computations and solving linear equations. However, a limitation is that they may not always be the most efficient for operations involving dense matrices.

For lower triangular matrices, all elements above the main diagonal are zero. Their applications are useful in forward substitution for solving linear systems and appeared in Cholesky decomposition (for positive definite matrices). Their advantages include simplifying the forward substitution processes, but imitations are similar to those of upper triangular matrices, in terms of computational constraints.

As an illustration, in cryptographic schemes involving key generation or transformations, upper triangular matrices may be preferred for certain algorithms due to ease of inversion and back substitution. Lower triangular matrices might be better for forward substitution in algorithms where data dependencies flow in a different direction [37].

- **Upper triangular matrices vs. symmetric matrices**

Symmetric matrices satisfy the condition as $A = A^T$. They are widely used in cryptographic protocols requiring stability and symmetry, such as certain forms of key exchange and common in quantum cryptography and random matrix theory applications. Their advantages include simplifying many mathematical analyses and are often associated with well-understood eigenvalue properties; however, limitations may require more complex computational resources for certain operations.

As an example, in encryption algorithms, symmetric matrices can be useful where stability and specific properties of eigenvalues are crucial. However, upper triangular matrices might be chosen for their ease of use in specific matrix decompositions and faster computational properties for certain operations.

17.2.1.7 Note 4. Practical implementation challenge

High-stakes environments

1. **Financial transactions:** Ensuring high-speed and secure transactions while dealing with large volumes of data. As a solution, implement optimized algorithms that leverage the computational efficiency of upper triangular matrices. However, ensuring these implementations resist side-channel attacks is crucial. For example, using upper triangular matrices in lattice-based encryption to secure online banking transactions [18, 20, 38, 39], while employing techniques like constant-time algorithms to prevent timing attacks.
2. **Governmental communications:** Balancing security with performance in highly sensitive communications is a critical challenge. As a solution, combining matrix-based cryptographic methods with other security protocols (e.g., hybrid cryptosystems) to enhance security without significantly impacting performance with the illustration; integrating upper triangular matrices within a hybrid encryption system for secure

governmental communications, ensuring that matrix operations [40–43] are resilient against fault analysis attacks by using error-correction codes and redundancy.

17.2.1.8 Note 5. General implementation issues

1. **Computational resources:** High computational costs for large-scale operations. As a solution, use optimized libraries and hardware acceleration (e.g., GPU computing) to handle matrix operations efficiently. For example, employing libraries like BLAS (basic linear algebra subprograms) or hardware accelerators to efficiently perform upper triangular matrix operations in cryptographic algorithms.
2. **Resistance to attacks:** Vulnerability to various types of attacks, including cryptographic attacks and implementation-specific attacks. For solution, implement comprehensive security measures, such as side-channel attack mitigation, fault-tolerant design, and regular security audits with an example; using masking techniques to protect against power analysis attacks when implementing cryptographic algorithms with upper triangular matrices [44, 45].

By broadening the chapter's scope to include comparisons with other matrix forms like lower triangular and symmetric matrices and addressing practical implementation challenges, readers can gain a clearer perspective on the unique advantages and limitations of upper triangular matrices in cryptographic applications.

Remark 1. When upper triangular matrices might not be the optimal choice in cryptography

While upper triangular matrices have certain advantages in cryptographic applications, there are scenarios where they might not be the optimal choice. This section aims to provide a balanced view by discussing these limitations and comparing upper triangular matrices with other cryptographic methods. By offering a nuanced understanding of their application scope, we can better appreciate when alternative approaches may be more suitable.

Remark 2. Scenarios where upper triangular matrices might not be optimal

The following gives us brief explanations for the title scenarios where upper triangular matrices might not be optimal:

1. High-dimensional lattices

Example: In lattice-based cryptography, particularly in schemes involving high-dimensional lattices, the use of upper triangular matrices might not provide sufficient security. High-dimensional lattices require complex operations that can be more efficiently handled by other matrix structures or specialized algorithms.

Alternative: Using full-rank matrices or structured lattices such as the GGH (Goldreich-Goldwasser-Halevi) cryptosystem can offer better security and efficiency for high-dimensional problems.

2. **Public key ınfrastructure (PKI)**

Example: In traditional public key infrastructures like RSA or elliptic curve cryptography (ECC), the mathematical foundations do not naturally align with upper triangular matrices. RSA relies on integer factorization, and ECC depends on the algebraic structure of elliptic curves, both of which are more efficiently implemented using other mathematical tools.

Alternative: ECC is often preferred in PKI for its smaller key sizes and faster computations compared to methods that might involve upper triangular matrices.

3. **Post-quantum cryptography**

Example: In post-quantum cryptographic schemes such as code-based, hash-based, or multivariate polynomial cryptography, upper triangular matrices may not offer the required security against quantum attacks. These schemes often require different mathematical frameworks.

Alternative: Code-based cryptography, like the McEliece cryptosystem, relies on the hardness of decoding random linear codes, which doesn't typically involve upper triangular matrices. Hash-based cryptographic methods, such as those used in digital signatures (e.g., Lamport signatures), rely on the properties of hash functions.

4. **Symmetric key cryptography**

Example: In symmetric key algorithms such as advanced encryption standard (AES) or data encryption standard (DES), the design principles are based on substitution-permutation networks or Feistel structures, which do not leverage upper triangular matrices.

Alternative: These algorithms use operations like S-box substitutions and permutation layers to achieve confusion and diffusion, which are not inherently related to upper triangular matrices.

Additionally, the following table provides a summary comparing the advantages and disadvantages of upper triangular matrices (Table 17.1).

Remark 3. Comparison with other cryptographic methods
While upper triangular matrices have notable advantages in specific cryptographic applications, there are scenarios where they might not be the optimal choice. Understanding the contexts in which other cryptographic

Table 17.1 Comparison with other cryptographic methods

	Advantages of upper triangular matrices	*Limitations of upper triangular matrices*
Elliptic curve cryptography (ECC)	ECC provides higher security with smaller key sizes compared to many matrix-based methods. ECC operations are generally faster and require less computational power.	May require larger keys for comparable security, leading to increased computational and storage requirements.
Lattice-based cryptography	They offer strong security guarantees based on the hardness of lattice problems. Lattice-based schemes can be more resistant to quantum attacks.	Upper triangular matrices might not adequately represent the complexity needed for certain lattice-based cryptographic schemes.
Hash-based cryptography	They are simple and based on well-understood cryptographic hash functions. Provide strong security properties with relatively straightforward implementations.	Do not inherently provide the same level of simplicity and well-understood security properties as hash-based methods.

methods provide better security, efficiency, or practicality is crucial for making informed decisions. By comparing upper triangular matrices with alternatives like ECC, lattice-based cryptography, and hash-based methods, we gain a more nuanced understanding of their application scope and limitations. This balanced view helps in selecting the most appropriate cryptographic approach for a given use case.

Remark 3. Expanding the chapter to include interdisciplinary research in cryptography
The chapter provides a robust foundation for the evolution and application of matrix theory in cryptography. To further enrich this discussion, it would be beneficial to incorporate interdisciplinary research that intersects with fields like data science and artificial intelligence (AI). This approach can highlight how matrix theory is evolving and adapting in response to advancements in these technologies, particularly in cryptographic applications.

17.3 INTERDISCIPLINARY RESEARCH IN DATA SCIENCE AND AI

The intersection of matrix theory with data science and AI is opening new avenues for cryptographic applications. There are some areas where this interdisciplinary research is having an impact as follows:

17.3.1 Machine learning and cryptography

17.3.1.1 Application of matrices in machine learning

Machine learning algorithms heavily rely on linear algebra, particularly matrix operations, for various computations, including training models and processing data.

Examples

Neural networks: Use matrices to represent and process layers of neurons. Weight matrices are crucial in the forward and backward propagation processes.
Support vector machines (SVMs): Use kernel matrices to transform data into higher dimensions for better classification.

17.3.1.2 Impact on cryptography

Homomorphic encryption: Enables computations on encrypted data without decrypting it. This is crucial for privacy-preserving machine learning. Matrices play a key role in representing data and performing encrypted computations.
Example: Implementing a neural network where the weight matrices and data inputs are encrypted, and operations like matrix multiplication are performed on the encrypted data.

Remark 4. Data science and secure data analysis

Secure multi-party computation (MPC): Allows multiple parties to jointly compute a function over their inputs while keeping those inputs private. Matrix operations are fundamental in many MPC protocols.
Example: In a scenario where different organizations want to collaboratively train a machine learning model without sharing their data, matrices are used to represent and securely aggregate the data.
Matrix factorization techniques: Widely used in data science for recommendations and dimensionality reduction. Secure versions of these techniques are being developed for cryptographic applications.
Example: Privacy-preserving matrix factorization for collaborative filtering, ensuring that user preferences are kept confidential while providing accurate recommendations.

Remark 5. Practical ımplementation challenges
High-stakes environments

Financial transactions: Ensuring both speed and security in transactions involving large volumes of data.

Solution: Leveraging advances in matrix theory to develop efficient cryptographic protocols that can handle large-scale data securely. Incorporating AI techniques to detect and mitigate fraudulent activities in real-time.

Governmental communications: Balancing robust security measures with performance in sensitive communications.

Solution: Employing advanced matrix-based cryptographic methods, integrated with AI for enhanced security monitoring and threat detection.

Remark 6. Resistance to advanced attacks

Quantum computing: The advent of quantum computing poses a significant threat to traditional cryptographic methods. Research in quantum-resistant algorithms often involves complex matrix operations.

Example: Lattice-based cryptography is considered quantum-resistant and uses matrices extensively to create hard mathematical problems that are secure against quantum attacks.

AI-driven cryptanalysis: AI techniques are increasingly being used to break cryptographic systems by identifying patterns and vulnerabilities.

Solution: Developing cryptographic algorithms that are resilient to AI-driven attacks, incorporating advanced matrix transformations to obscure potential patterns.

As a result, incorporating interdisciplinary research into the chapter enhances the understanding of how matrix theory in cryptography is evolving with advancements in data science and AI. By exploring these intersections, the chapter can provide a more comprehensive view of current and future cryptographic applications, addressing both theoretical and practical challenges. This approach ensures that readers are well-informed about the latest developments and equipped to handle emerging threats and opportunities in the field of cryptography.

17.3.2 Main results

1. **Hill cipher and logıc map approximations**

Let's look at an example that involves a 7 * 7 upper triangular matrix and Caesar cipher application. Let's construct this 7 * 7 matrix, as shown in the figure below.

$$\begin{bmatrix} 2 & 3 & 4 & 5 & 6 & 7 & 8 \\ 0 & 2 & 3 & 4 & 5 & 6 & 7 \\ 0 & 0 & 2 & 3 & 4 & 5 & 6 \\ 0 & 0 & 0 & 2 & 3 & 4 & 5 \\ 0 & 0 & 0 & 0 & 2 & 3 & 4 \\ 0 & 0 & 0 & 0 & 0 & 2 & 3 \\ 0 & 0 & 0 & 0 & 0 & 0 & 2 \end{bmatrix}$$

A Caesar cipher can be either simple or advanced as per your choice. To avoid any misunderstanding of the information in this text, the message will be moved by 5. Therefore, we include another encryption layer that is done using the upper triangular matrix pattern in order to make it even more secure.

Encryption of "MATHEMATICIANS" using Caesar Cipher and Upper Triangle Matrix pattern. Use a shift of 5 for the Caesar Cipher.

"M" becomes "R"
"A" becomes "F"
"T" becomes "Y"
"H" becomes "M"
"E" becomes "J"
"M" becomes "R"
"A" becomes "F"
"T" becomes "Y"
"I" becomes "N"
"C" becomes "H"
"I" becomes "N"
"A" becomes "F"
"N" becomes "S"
"S" becomes "X"

In Caesar cipher, "MATHEMATICIANS" is encrypted as "RFYMJRFYNHNFSX". Upper Triangular Matrix Encryption. Now, let's write the Caesar cipher-text "RFYMJRFYNHNFSX" using the upper triangular matrix. For this purpose, we can convert letters to numbers like: (A = 0, B = 1, C = 2, and so on):

M	A	T	H	E	M	A	T	I	C	I	A	N	S
R	F	Y	M	J	R	F	Y	N	H	N	F	S	X
17	5	24	12	9	17	5	24	13	7	13	5	18	23

Giving the upper triangular matrix, for the corresponding numerical values: (index 0)

- 17 corresponds to row:2 column:3
- 5 corresponds to row:0 column:5
- 24 corresponds to row:3 column:3
- 12 corresponds to row:1 column:5
- 9 corresponds to row:1 column:2
- 13 corresponds to row:1 column:6
- 7 corresponds to row:1 column:0
- 18 corresponds to row:2 column:4
- 23 corresponds to row:3 column:2

An elevated degree of sophistication can be attained through the manipulation of these indices or values in alignment with the matrix configuration, thereby augmenting the complexity of the encryption procedure.

A pertinent illustration of the amalgamation of the Caesar cipher and the structure of an upper triangular matrix manifests as a dual-stage encryption process. In the context of decryption, the operations are executed in the reverse order: initially, one must decode utilizing the matrix structure, followed by the application of the Caesar cipher decryption methodology.

Upper triangular matrix utilizing linear system

For $n = 7$, it assumes the subsequent configuration:

$$A = \begin{bmatrix} \alpha & \beta & \gamma & \delta & \mu & \lambda & \sigma \\ 0 & \alpha & \beta & \gamma & \delta & \mu & \lambda \\ 0 & 0 & \alpha & \beta & \gamma & \delta & \mu \\ 0 & 0 & 0 & \alpha & \beta & \gamma & \delta \\ 0 & 0 & 0 & 0 & \alpha & \beta & \gamma \\ 0 & 0 & 0 & 0 & 0 & \alpha & \beta \\ 0 & 0 & 0 & 0 & 0 & 0 & \alpha \end{bmatrix} \tag{17.1}$$

In matrix computation, multiplication of matrices with column vectors is important. The underlying principle is simple.

$$\begin{bmatrix} Y_1 \\ Y_2 \\ Y_3 \\ Y_4 \\ Y_5 \\ Y_6 \\ Y_7 \end{bmatrix} = \begin{bmatrix} \alpha & \beta & \gamma & \delta & \mu & \lambda & \sigma \\ 0 & \alpha & \beta & \gamma & \delta & \mu & \lambda \\ 0 & 0 & \alpha & \beta & \gamma & \delta & \mu \\ 0 & 0 & 0 & \alpha & \beta & \gamma & \delta \\ 0 & 0 & 0 & 0 & \alpha & \beta & \gamma \\ 0 & 0 & 0 & 0 & 0 & \alpha & \beta \\ 0 & 0 & 0 & 0 & 0 & 0 & \alpha \end{bmatrix} . \begin{bmatrix} X_1 \\ X_2 \\ X_3 \\ X_4 \\ X_5 \\ X_6 \\ X_7 \end{bmatrix} \tag{17.2}$$

$$\begin{cases} Y_1 = \alpha.X_1 + \beta.X_2 + \gamma.X_3 + \delta.X_4 + \mu.X_5 + \lambda.X_6 + +\sigma.X_7 \\ Y_2 = \alpha.X_2 + \beta.X_3 + \gamma.X_4 + \delta.X_5 + \mu.X_6 + \lambda.X_7 \\ Y_3 = \alpha.X_3 + \beta.X_4 + \gamma.X_5 + \delta.X_6 + \mu.X_7 \\ Y_4 = \alpha.X_4 + \beta.X_5 + \gamma.X_6 + \delta.X_7 \\ Y_5 = \alpha.X_5 + \beta.X_6 + \gamma.X_7 \\ Y_6 = \alpha.X_6 + \beta.X_7 \\ Y_7 = \alpha.X_7 \end{cases} \tag{17.3}$$

$$\begin{cases} X_7 = \frac{1}{\alpha}.Y_7 \\ X_6 = \frac{1}{\alpha^2}.(\alpha.Y_6 - \beta.Y_7) \\ X_5 = \frac{1}{\alpha^3}\left[\alpha^2.Y_5 - \alpha.\beta.Y_6 + \left(\beta^2 - \alpha.\gamma\right).Y_7\right] \\ X_4 = \frac{1}{\alpha^4}\left\{\alpha^3.Y_4 - \alpha^2.\beta.Y_5 + \alpha\left(\beta^2 - \alpha.\gamma\right).Y_6 - \left(\alpha^2.\delta - 2.\alpha.\beta.\gamma + \beta^3\right).Y_7\right\} \\ X_3 = \ldots \\ X_2 = \ldots \\ X_1 = \ldots \end{cases} \tag{17.4}$$

This condition is important provided that the non-zero parameter α.

New cryptosystem assumptions

- Equation 17.2 describes the current method of encryption centred on an upper triangular matrix.
- Its dimensionality is 7 × 7.

Let the plaintext vector be given as $X = \begin{bmatrix} X_1 \\ X_2 \\ X_3 \\ X_4 \\ X_5 \\ X_6 \\ X_7 \end{bmatrix}$ and the cipher-text vector as $Y = \begin{bmatrix} Y_1 \\ Y_2 \\ Y_3 \\ Y_4 \\ Y_5 \\ Y_6 \\ Y_7 \end{bmatrix}$.

- Equation 17.3 stipulates how to encrypt, while Equation 17.4 defines how the system recovers the plaintext.

Each bit (1 bit), character or pixel X corresponds to a single bit and a page break is placed between two characters that make up a word. $X_i = \{integer\ /\ 7\} = \{integer\ /\ 7\}$.

As a result, in order to interpret the viewing Y it is necessary to process modulo α.

- In generating a separate upper triangular matrix for every character to be encoded, do select the elements randomly from this particular matrix.

Logic map

In the context of cryptanalysis, a compelling explanation for the basic ideas behind the art is necessary in order to develop a logical map for cryptographic purposes. The logistic map is an established form of behavior in the general theory of non-linear systems, given by $y_{k+1} = r\, x_k\, (1 - x_k)$, where y_{k+1} is sort of the future generation which is directly proportional to x_k, x_k is some kind of parent generation while r is among other things positive constant.. The formulation of a logic map for cryptographic purposes necessitates the depiction of the interrelations, concepts, and elements that are pivotal for the comprehension of cryptographic tenets. The logistics map is a widely recognized dynamic within the realm of non-linear systems theory, expressed as $y_{k+1} = r\, x_k\, (1 - x_k)$ where y_{k+1} signifies a future generation that is proportional to x_k, with x_k representing the preceding generation and r being a positive constant that encompasses all factors pertinent to reproduction, among others.

The Logistic Map Function can be expressed below for the algorithmic steps in our study,

$$x_{n+1} = F.x_n.(1 - x_n) + cos(K.\, x_n)\ (mod\ T)$$

where x_0 denotes a double-precision numeral, ε represents a parameter of the Logistic Map, F signifies a scalar quantity, K is an integer, and T consists of integer constants utilized to obtain an optimal encryption key.

Encryption process

Having initially selected seven data points $(\alpha, \beta, \gamma, \delta, \mu, \lambda, \sigma)$ in the logistic map to arrange the upper triangular matrix, our choice must be consistent with encryption code, generated from $\{0,1,2,3,4,5,6\}$ meeting an additional condition of plaintexts that makes encryption sound like Decryption (Equation 17.3) only if the one for decryption is performed using Equation 17.4.

Equation 17.4 only makes sense when it is considered in an algebraic context; however, the use of $Z/7Z = \mathbb{Z}_7$ changeover structure is necessary for solving this problem. This ensures that all nonzero elements in the set have inverses.

- To generate the upper triangular matrix,

Suppose we have plaintext vector $X = \begin{bmatrix} X_1 \\ X_2 \\ X_3 \\ X_4 \\ X_5 \\ X_6 \\ X_7 \end{bmatrix}$.

- So assuming that we have a pixel intensity of 0 for certain pixels or within the upper triangular matrix.

Let the cryptogram vector be determined by, or represented by means of the following equation; $Y = \begin{bmatrix} Y_1 \\ Y_2 \\ Y_3 \\ Y_4 \\ Y_5 \\ Y_6 \\ Y_7 \end{bmatrix}$.

$$\begin{aligned}
Y_1 &= (\alpha.X_1 + \beta.X_2 + \gamma.X_3 + \delta.X_4 + \mu.X_5 + \lambda.X_6 + \sigma.X_7)(mod7) \\
Y_2 &= (\alpha.X_2 + \beta.X_3 + \gamma.X_4 + \delta.X_5 + \mu.X_6 + \lambda.X_7)(mod7) \\
Y_3 &= (\alpha.X_3 + \beta X_4 + \gamma.X_5 + \delta.X_6 + \mu.X_7)(mod7) \\
Y_4 &= (\alpha.X_4 + \beta X_5 + \gamma.X_6 + \delta.X_7)(mod7) \\
Y_5 &= (\alpha.X_5 + \beta X_6 + \gamma.X_7)(mod7) \\
Y_6 &= (\alpha.X_6 + \beta X_7)(mod7) \\
Y_7 &= (\alpha.X_7)(mod7)
\end{aligned} \tag{17.6}$$

Decryption process

At first, a subset of five data points $(\alpha, \beta, \gamma, \delta, \mu, \lambda, \sigma)$ is picked out randomly from the logistic map to set up the upper triangular matrix by using the same measures as those of the encryption process.

- Developing the matrix components

The cryptogram vector is quoted as $Y = \begin{bmatrix} Y_1 \\ Y_2 \\ Y_3 \\ Y_4 \\ Y_5 \\ Y_6 \\ Y_7 \end{bmatrix}$

- Consider the situation when one gets a pixel value of 0 or when taking values of the upper triangular matrix.

Calculate modulo 7 inverse of 'α'.

α	1	2	3	4	5	6
α^{-1}	1	4	5	2	3	6

Determining plain text vector is shown as $X = \begin{bmatrix} X_1 \\ X_2 \\ X_3 \\ X_4 \\ X_5 \\ X_6 \\ X_7 \end{bmatrix}$ in the following formulae.

$$\begin{cases} X_7 = \dfrac{1}{\alpha}.Y_7\,(mod7) \\ X_6 = \left[\dfrac{1}{\alpha^2}.(\alpha.Y_6 - \beta.Y_7)\right](mod7) \\ X_5 = \left[\dfrac{1}{\alpha^3}\left\{\alpha^2.Y_5 - \alpha.\beta.Y_6 + \left(\beta^2 - \alpha.\gamma\right).Y_7\right\}\right](mod7) \\ X_4 = \ldots(mod7) \\ X_3 = \ldots(mod7) \\ X_2 = \ldots(mod7) \\ X_1 = \ldots(mod7) \end{cases} \tag{7}$$

Key for encryption

Key field for private or secret: In the presented algorithm, the private key's domain is defined in the following way:

$$PT = \{x_0,, F, K, T\}.$$

The logistics map's starting point is $x_0 = 0.1234567890123456$, $\varepsilon = 3.8$, $F = 4.2$, $K = 25$, $T = 7$ where the details regarding the encryption key can effectively be entered as below:

- x_0 = double-precision number,
- ε = Parameter of Logistic Map,
- F: scalar,
- K: an integer,
- T: integer constants.

Precision in calculating x_0 and ε is highly essential if it is decided that $K =$ [1, 500] should fall under (mod T). This will enable us to evaluate security issues arising from logistic map-based key generation techniques providing us with some insights into secure operations.

Hence, when the key space exceeds the precision product of x_0 and a sufficiently large constant (at the given precision level), it results in an expanded key field. Additionally, the actual representation may include more bits than the nominal key size, further increasing the complexity and security of the system.

Explanation of the new code

1. Logistic map function: logistic_map(r, x_0, n) generates a sequence of n values using the logistic map with the new parameter r and initial value x_0.
2. Transformation function: transform_values(values, F, K) applies a transformation to the chaotic values using the new scalar F and integer K. The transformation adjusts the chaotic values to fit within a specific range, suitable for matrix entries.
3. Matrix generation: generate_matrix(size, $x0$, epsilon, F, K) generates a chaotic sequence with the new parameters, applies transformations, and reshapes the values into a 7×7 matrix.

2. Describe procedures/ASCII value approximations

```
procedure decrypt(encrypted_message, inverse Secretkey):
initialise decrypted=Null
initialise numerical_values_of_message =Null
numerical_values_of_ encrypted_message ← indexes of alphabet
Split_c← divide encrypted_message to dimension of inverse secretkey
For each C in Split_c
  Transpoze of C
  decrypted block← inverse Secretkey multiple by numerical_values_of_block and modular of lenght of alphabet
  N←count of decrypted block
  For each N
  decrypted ← decrypted+ letter equivalent of each decrypted block item
  End of Foreach
End of Foreach
return decrypted
```

A possible method is shown in order to make plain text difficult to read as follows:

Take for example the following procedure for decrypting encrypted text:

```
procedure encrypt(message, Secretkey):
initialise encryted=Null
initialise numerical_values_of_message =Null
numerical_values_of_message ← indexes of alphabet
Split_p← divide message to dimension of secretkey
For each P in Split_p
  Transpoze of P
  While dimension of P != dimension of Secretkey
    numerical_values_of_block ← indexes of alphabet
  End of While
  encrypted block←numerical_values_of_block multiple by Secretkey and modular of lenght of alphabet
  N←count of encrypted block
  For each N
  encryted ← encryted+ letter equivalent of each encrypted block item
  End of Foreach
End of Foreach
return encrypted
```

Let's outline a method for finding the inverse of a matrix modulo operation:

“0123456789abcdefghijklmnopqrstuvwxyzABCDEFGHIJKLMNOPQR STUVWXYZ!"#$%&'()*+,-./:;<=>?@[\]^_`{|}~ÖöŞşÜüıİÇçĞğ[space]”

Create a string that can be printed on the terminal by taking characters from the ASCII character table.

$$K = \begin{bmatrix} 2 & 3 & 4 & 5 & 6 & 7 & 8 \\ 0 & 2 & 3 & 4 & 5 & 6 & 7 \\ 0 & 0 & 2 & 3 & 4 & 5 & 6 \\ 0 & 0 & 0 & 2 & 3 & 4 & 5 \\ 0 & 0 & 0 & 0 & 2 & 3 & 4 \\ 0 & 0 & 0 & 0 & 0 & 2 & 3 \\ 0 & 0 & 0 & 0 & 0 & 0 & 2 \end{bmatrix} \text{ and } K' = \begin{bmatrix} 54 & 26 & 67 & 87 & 97 & 102 & 51 \\ 0 & 54 & 26 & 67 & 87 & 97 & 102 \\ 0 & 0 & 54 & 26 & 67 & 87 & 97 \\ 0 & 0 & 0 & 54 & 26 & 67 & 87 \\ 0 & 0 & 0 & 0 & 54 & 26 & 67 \\ 0 & 0 & 0 & 0 & 0 & 54 & 26 \\ 0 & 0 & 0 & 0 & 0 & 0 & 54 \end{bmatrix}$$

Numerical example

Divide the plain text into blocks of 7 characters:

Plaintext: “Pythagorean theorem or Pythagoras' theorem is a fundamental relation in Euclidean geometry between the three sides of a right triangle. It states that the area of the square whose side is the hypotenuse (the side opposite the right angle) is equal to the sum of the areas of the squares on the other two sides”.
Change blocks into numbers:

Multiply the plaintext block and secret key matrix by the matrix M modulo 7 each block
Convert plaintext blocks to numerical representation. A matrix M is then multiplied by them. The result of the matrix product is then divided by 7 to get the mod 7 result.

	Plaintext Block value	*Plaintext Block value index*	*Encrypted Block Value*
Block 1	'Pythago'	[51,34,29,17,10,16, 24]	'k2QyVĞM'
Block 2	'rean th'	[27,14,10,23,106,29, 17]	'NabuK2y'
Block 3	'eorem o'	[14,24,27,14,22,106, 24]	'Yt2çu)M'
Block 4	'r Pytha'	[27,106,51,34,29,17, 10]	'N(BXG#k'
Block 5	“goras' “	[16,24,27,10,28,68, 106]	“G'ÇOGqğ”
Block 6	'theorem'	[29,17,14,24,27,14, 22]	'<a`>:Öl'

	Plaintext Block value	*Plaintext Block value index*	*Encrypted Block Value*
Block 7	‘ is a f’	[106,18,28,106,10,106, 15]	‘bP*ü:Hu’
Block 8	‘undamen’	[30,23,13,10,22,14, 23]	‘3QvH*şK’
Block 9	‘tal rel’	[29,10,21,106,27,14, 21]	‘Yhm
Block 10	‘ation i’	[10,29,18,24,23,106, 18]	‘Df`Ş8QA’
Block 11	‘nEuclid’	[23,40,30,12,21,18, 13]	‘YÖraF.q’
Block 12	‘ean geo’	[14,10,23,106,16,14, 24]	‘çŞ08”ıM’
Block 13	‘metry b’	[22,14,29,27,34,106, 11]	‘^Afı2vm’
Block 14	‘etween ‘	[14,29,32,14,14,23, 106]	‘f{VO~Hğ’
Block 15	‘the thr’	[29,17,14,106,29,17, 27]	‘r=&-38S’
Block 16	‘ee side’	[14,14,106,28,18,13, 14]	“`?`io’s”
Block 17	‘s of a ‘	[28,106,24,15,106,10, 106]	‘%*q!ohğ’
Block 18	‘right t’	[27,18,16,17,29,106, 29]	‘e%LM#\\W’
Block 19	‘riangle’	[27,18,10,23,16,21, 14]	‘@ylyl[s’
Block 20	‘. It st’	[75,106,44,29,106,28, 29]	‘y:VÜ|AW’
Block 21	‘ates th’	[10,29,14,28,106,29, 17]	‘İ+yEK2y’
Block 22	‘at the ‘	[10,29,106,29,17,14, 106]	‘cc3R+pğ’
Block 23	‘area of’	[10,27,14,10,106,24, 15]	‘ZXO>n~u’
Block 24	‘ the sq’	[106,29,17,14,106,28, 26]	‘]?LR<rQ’
Block 25	‘uare wh’	[30,10,27,14,106,32, 17]	‘^zxoT8y’
Block 26	‘ose sid’	[24,28,14,106,28,18, 13]	‘K5|5T.q’
Block 27	‘e is th’	[14,106,18,28,106,29, 17]	‘zoGEK2y’
Block 28	‘e hypot’	[14,106,17,34,25,24, 29]	‘#fÇ”osW’
Block 29	‘enuse (‘	[14,23,30,28,14,106, 69]	‘nK-b^Üv’
Block 30	‘the sid’	[29,17,14,106,28,18, 13]	‘n{|5T.q’
Block 31	‘e oppos’	[14,106,24,25,25,24, 28]	‘Dı@EkpU’
Block 32	‘ite the’	[18,29,14,106,29,17, 14]	‘IdŞ9W/s’
Block 33	‘ right ‘	[106,27,18,16,17,29, 106]	‘ıç:^aTğ’
Block 34	‘angle) ‘	[10,23,16,21,14,70, 106]	‘.j&Ckuğ’
Block 35	‘is equa’	[18,28,106,14,26,30, 10]	‘şZx!.{k’
Block 36	‘l to th’	[21,106,29,24,106,29, 17]	‘FQwK2y’
Block 37	‘e sum o’	[14,106,28,30,22,106, 24]	‘(KQsu)M’
Block 38	‘f the a’	[15,106,29,17,14,106, 10]	‘#6f$sk’
Block 39	‘reas of’	[27,14,10,28,106,24, 15]	‘n~Şan~u’
Block 40	‘ the sq’	[106,29,17,14,106,28, 26]	‘]?LR<rQ’
Block 41	‘uares o’	[30,10,27,14,28,106, 24]	‘]vqeG)M’
Block 42	‘n the o’	[23,106,29,17,14,106, 24]	‘\\#{\\e)M’
Block 43	‘ther tw’	[29,17,14,27,106,29, 32]	‘4Ge6 L#’
Block 44	‘o sides’	[24,106,28,18,13,14, 28]	‘5*<V5U’
Block 45	‘.’	[75]	‘a=^~ÜÇğ’

Each encrypted block gets added one to another leading to the final ciphertext:

“k2QyVĞMNabuK2yYt2çu)MN(BXG#kG'ÇOGqğ<a`>:ÖIbP*ü:Hu3QvH*şKYhmq,|GDf`Ş8QAYÖraF.qçŞ08"ıM^Afı2vmf{VO~Hğr=&-38S`?`io's%*q!ohğe%LM#\W@ylyI[sy:VÜ|AWİ+yEK2ycc3R+pğZXO>n~u]?LR<rQ^zxoT8yK5|5T.qzoGEK2y#fÇ"osWnK-b^Üvn{|5T.qDı@EkpUIdŞ9W/sıç:^aTğ.j&CkuğşZx!.{k,FQwK2y(KQsu)M#,6f$skn~Şan~u]?LR<rQ]vqeG)M\#{\e)M4Ge6L#5*<V,5Ua=^~ÜÇğ”

To get the original plain text back, the text you get has to be decrypted using the inverse matrix (K’) and modulo 7 operations. Performing matrix multiplication, inversion and modular arithmetic operations is a complex task which requires considerable manual effort or programming calculation.

	Encrypted Block value	*Encrypted Block value index*	*Decrypted Block Value*
Block 1	‘k2QyVĞM’	[20,2,52,34,57,104, 48]	‘Pythago’
Block 2	‘NabuK2y’	[49,10,11,30,46,2, 34]	‘rean th’
Block 3	‘Yt2çu)M’	[60,29,2,103,30,70, 48]	‘eorem o’
Block 4	‘N(BXG#k’	[49,69,37,59,42,64, 20]	‘r Pytha’
Block 5	“G’ÇOGqğ”	[42,68,102,50,42,26, 105]	“goras’ “
Block 6	‘<a`>:ÖI’	[79,10,89,81,77,94, 44]	‘theorem’
Block 7	‘bP*ü:Hu’	[11,51,71,99,77,43, 30]	‘ is a f’
Block 8	‘3QvH*şK’	[3,52,31,43,71,97, 46]	‘undamen’
Block 9	‘Yhmq|G’	[60,17,22,26,73,91, 42]	‘tal rel’
Block 10	‘Df`Ş8QA’	[39,15,89,96,8,52, 36]	‘ation i’
Block 11	‘YÖraF.q’	[60,94,27,10,41,75, 26]	‘nEuclid’
Block 12	‘çŞ08”ıM’	[103,96,0,8,63,100, 48]	‘ean geo’
Block 13	‘^Afı2vm’	[87,36,15,100,2,31, 22]	‘metry b’
Block 14	‘f{VO~Hğ’	[15,90,57,50,93,43, 105]	‘etween ‘
Block 15	‘r=&-38S’	[27,80,67,74,3,8, 54]	‘the thr’
Block 16	“`?`io’s”	[89,82,89,18,24,68, 28]	‘ee side’
Block 17	‘%*q!ohğ’	[66,71,26,62,24,17, 105]	‘s of a ‘
Block 18	‘e%LM#\\W’	[14,66,47,48,64,85, 58]	‘right t’
Block 19	‘@ylyI[s’	[83,34,21,34,44,84, 28]	‘riangle’
Block 20	‘y:VÜ|AW’	[34,77,57,98,91,36, 58]	‘. It st’
Block 21	‘İ+yEK2y’	[101,72,34,40,46,2, 34]	‘ates th’
Block 22	‘cc3R+pğ’	[12,12,3,53,72,25, 105]	‘at the ‘
Block 23	‘ZXO>n~u’	[61,59,50,81,23,93, 30]	‘area of’
Block 24	‘]?LR<rQ’	[86,82,47,53,79,27, 52]	‘ the sq’
Block 25	‘^zxoT8y’	[87,35,33,24,55,8, 34]	‘uare wh’
Block 26	‘K5|5T.q’	[46,5,91,5,55,75, 26]	‘ose sid’
Block 27	‘zoGEK2y’	[35,24,42,40,46,2, 34]	‘e is th’

	Encrypted Block value	*Encrypted Block value index*	*Decrypted Block Value*
Block 28	'#fÇ"osW'	[64,15,102,63,24,28, 58]	'e hypot'
Block 29	'nK-b^Üv'	[23,46,74,11,87,98, 31]	'enuse ('
Block 30	'n{|5T.q'	[23,90,91,5,55,75, 26]	'the sid'
Block 31	'Dı@EkpU'	[39,100,83,40,20,25, 56]	'e oppos'
Block 32	'IdŞ9W/s'	[44,13,96,9,58,76, 28]	'ite the'
Block 33	'ıç:^aTğ'	[100,103,77,87,10,55, 105]	' right '
Block 34	'.j&Ckuğ'	[75,19,67,38,20,30, 105]	'angle) '
Block 35	'şZx!.{k'	[97,61,33,62,75,90, 20]	'is equa'
Block 36	'FQwK2y'	[73,41,52,32,46,2, 34]	'l to th'
Block 37	'(KQsu)M'	[69,46,52,28,30,70, 48]	'e sum o'
Block 38	'#6f$sk'	[64,73,6,15,65,28, 20]	'f the a'
Block 39	'n~Şan~u'	[23,93,96,10,23,93, 30]	'reas of'
Block 40	']?LR<rQ'	[86,82,47,53,79,27, 52]	' the sq'
Block 41	']vqeG)M'	[86,31,26,14,42,70, 48]	'uares o'
Block 42	'\\#{\\e)M'	[85,64,90,85,14,70, 48]	'n the o'
Block 43	'4Ge6 L#'	[4,42,14,6,106,47, 64]	'ther tw'
Block 44	'5*<V5U'	[5,71,79,57,73,5, 56]	'o sides'
Block 45	'a=^~ÜÇğ'	[10,80,87,93,98,102, 105]	'.')

Perform matrix multiplication by block with the inverse matrix of the key matrix (K) modulo 7: The next step in this is finding the inverse matrix of the key matrix (K) modulo 7 and performing the matrix multiplication operation on each block of ciphered text which will yield the original numerical expression. Change the numericals back into alphabets to get plain text out of it also to create complete ciphertext you have to add decrypted blocks sequentially. The result is as follows:

"Pythagorean theorem or Pythagoras theorem is a fundamental relation in Euclidean geometry between the three sides of a right triangle. It states that the area of the square whose side is the hypotenuse (the side opposite the right angle) is equal to the sum of the areas of the squares on the other two sides".

It is worth considering matrices libraries or existing functions to enable matrix inversion, modulo multiplication, and arithmetic operations since these can also be used for encryption/decryption processes.

3. Matrix approximations of cryptographic hash functions

According to Inayatullah et al. and Omar et al., cryptographic hash functions manipulate matrices as shown in research by Praveen Gauravaram with L. R Knudsen. One way of providing secure hash outputs is through combining or mixing input data using matrices.

Matrices are involved in the amalgamation or scarmbling of input data which is in line with their use in cryptographic hash functions. The mixing operation in hash functions like SHA-3 incorporates matrix operations

Matrix-based cryptographic hash functions normally rely on intertwining these schemes with their respective procedures when creating hash values This is just but an explanation about them:

1. **Structure:** Matrix-based cryptographic hash functions inherently involve a large number of iterations of matrix operations. These operations usually consist of multiplication, addition and bit manipulation.
2. **Mixing operations:** The use of matrices mixes to bring together by obfuscating input data; thus, it ensures that minimal changes at the input generate huge changes at the output of the hash. This allows to withstand preimage and second preimage attack.
3. **Confusion and diffusion:** Encryption methods that use matrix formats are deliberately formulated for confusion and diffusion. Confusion is intended to make the input-output relationship complicated and nonlinear while diffusion ensures that even the slightest changes in any part of the input have significant effects on the resultant hash value.
4. **Iterative structure:** Hash functions using matrix designs usually encompass an iterative nature where the input is taken through various mechanisms consisting of repeated matrix operations. Such operations include a number of mixing and permutation operations that serve to tighten the cryptographic security of hash functions.
5. **Keyed hash functions:** These hash functions are constructed Mathematically using matrix operations with keys when necessary for creating hash results that need keys. The key modifies the matrix calculations causing the hashing algorithm to depend on both the secret key and the message.
6. **Non-reversibility:** A cryptographic algorithm is non-reversible if it is not possible, given the resultant hash value, to find the initial input by computational means. The impossibility of reversing matrix-based hash functions is established through the use of non-inverse matrix operation.
7. **Security evaluation:** Comprehensive evaluations are conducted on matrix-based cryptographic hash functions to make sure they are secure against many types of attacks including collision attack, preimage attack etc.
8. **Usage:** Cryptographic protocols that use these hash functions involve digital signatures, MACs, password hashing among others.
9. **Standardization:** The role of standardizing entities such as the National Institute of Standards and Technology (NIST) and global cryptographic communities assume a central responsibility in standardizing and evaluating matrix-based cryptographic hash functions.

Matrix-based cryptographic hash functions form an integral part of modern cryptography, with essential security properties needed to maintain data integrity and authenticate users in various applications.

ALGORITHM-1

```
a, b, c, d ← 2, 3, 4, 5
k ← create 4x4 Upper triangle matrix(a, b, c, d)
b ← concatenate k matrix and convert byte
message ←" Pythagorean theorem or Pythagoras' theorem is a fundamental relation in
    Euclidean geometry between the three sides of a right triangle. It states that the area of the
    square whose side is the hypotenuse (the side opposite the right angle) is equal to the sum
    of the areas of the squares on the other two sides."
def encrypt text, key):
    iv ← b
    key ← key.encode('utf-8')
    key r ← key + (b' ' * (16 - len(key) % 16))
    cipher ← AES.new(key, AES.MODE_CBC,iv)
    text ← text.encode('utf-8')
    text ← text + (b' ' * (16 - len(text) % 16))
    ciphered_ text ← cipher.encrypt(text)
    ciphered _ text ← base64.b64encode(ciphered _ text).decode('utf-8')
    return ciphered _ text
def decrypt (ciphered _ text, key):
    iv← b
    key ← key.encode('utf-8')
    key ← key + (b' ' * (16 - len(key) % 16))
    ciphered _ text ← base64.b64decode(ciphered _ text.encode('utf-8'))
    cipher ← AES.new(key, AES.MODE_CBC,iv)
    text ← cipher.decrypt(ciphered _ text)
    text ← text.rstrip(b' ')
    text ← text.decode('utf-8')
    return text
text ← message
key ← str('şifre')
ciphered _ text ← ciphered (text, key)
text ← decrypt (ciphered _ text, key)
print("Deciphered_text: ", text)
```

Below is the algorithm explanation of hash functions based on matrices.

Advancements in cryptographic paradigms: SMPC and quantum approaches

This paradigm facilitates the joint evaluation of functions by multiple entities while maintaining the confidentiality of individual inputs.

1. **Fundamental principles:** The cornerstone of SMPC lies in its ability to compute $f(x_1, x_2, ..., x_n)$, where each x_i represents a confidential input from a distinct party. The protocol's elegance stems from its capacity to yield the collective output $f(x_1, x_2, ..., x_n)$ without compromising the privacy of individual x_i values.
2. **Methodological approaches:** SMPC protocols bifurcate into two primary categories
   a. Algebraic Methodologies: These employ sophisticated techniques such as polynomial share distribution or additive secret sharing. Participants engage in computations using these fractional representations, culminating in a synthesis of results.
   b. Bitwise Techniques: These operate at the granular level of individual data bits. While potentially less expedient for voluminous datasets, they offer unique security attributes.

3. **Practical implementations:** The versatility of SMPC manifests in diverse applications:
   a. Collaborative medical research across institutions
   b. Secure auction systems
   c. Privacy-preserving machine learning algorithms

Matrix operations, ubiquitous in data analysis and machine learning, find efficient implementation through SMPC, enabling complex computations without exposure of underlying data.

2. **Quantum cryptography: redefining security paradigms**

According to the study of R. Cyriac et al., S. Upadhyay et al., and Vasileios Mavroeidis et al., quantum cryptography represents a paradigm shift, exploring the profound implications of quantum mechanics on cryptographic frameworks. It scrutinizes the potential impact of quantum computing on established cryptographic mechanisms, including hash functions.

1. **Quantum computing: a disruptive force**

Quantum computers, leveraging quantum mechanical principles, promise unprecedented computational capabilities. This paradigm shift poses both opportunities and challenges for cryptographic systems.

2. **Vulnerabilities in classical cryptography**

Traditional cryptographic methods, such as RSA and Elliptic Curve Cryptography (ECC), rely on the computational intractability of certain mathematical problems. Quantum algorithms, exemplified by Shor's algorithm, threaten to unravel these foundations, potentially solving these problems with exponential efficiency.

3. **Cryptographic hash functions: a new perspective**

Hash functions, crucial for data integrity and authenticity, face potential vulnerabilities in the quantum era. Grover's algorithm, capable of conducting brute-force searches in $O(\sqrt{N})$ time, effectively diminishes the security level of traditional hash functions by half.

4. **Quantum-resilient cryptographic designs**

   In response to quantum threats, cryptographers are pioneering novel approaches:

   a. Post-quantum cryptography: This involves the development of algorithms resistant to quantum attacks.
   b. Quantum key distribution (QKD): A revolutionary method for secure key exchange, leveraging quantum mechanical principles to ensure unbreakable security.

17.4 CONCLUSION

Much has been said and written about the role of upper triangular matrices in the science of Cryptography. Their importance and necessity in various aspects of security used to protect sensitive information have been proven beyond any reasonable doubt. This essay therefore focuses on explaining the main functions of these matrices in Cryptography by examining their mathematical properties, revealing their algebraic structure, and showing how they can be used in computations through several examples with numbers.

SMPC and Quantum Cryptography represent the vanguard of modern cryptographic research. While SMPC offers innovative solutions for privacy-preserving collaborative computation, Quantum Cryptography addresses the looming challenges posed by quantum technologies to traditional cryptographic practices. These fields are instrumental in shaping the future of secure communication and computation in our increasingly interconnected global landscape.

The displayed output is highly responsive to the given lexicon yet has no limitations in terms of text encryption. Also, a detailed sequence of how-to processes is posted with examples in numbers.

Furthermore, upper triangular matrices can come in handy when working with cryptographic protocols and they generally help to strengthen; key management security, encryption efficiency as well as secure communication schemes. The importance of these matrices in enhancing cryptographic resilience cannot be overstated because they act as many-sided instruments which enable the cryptography community as a whole to keep pace with cyber threats and data breaches.

It grows increasingly evident that the scope of such matrices in the cryptic realm is hardly limited to pure mathematical conceptualization as we come to the end of our journey into their world. Consider upper triangular matrices are the heartland of a blend between hard-lined precision and practicable rules that are based on security issues. In today's world, where data privacy and digital security have become increasingly important, Upper Triangular Matrices play a huge role in protecting the confidentiality and truthfulness of information in a globally connected environment. We have tried to explain why these matrices are important so that people can research and make new inventions for better cryptographic methods.

REFERENCES

1. Abu-Faraj, M., Al-Hyari, A., & Alqadi, Z. A. (2022). Complex Matrix Private Key to Enhance the Security Level of Image Cryptography. *Symmetry*, 14, 664.
2. Ali Pacha, H., Hadj Said, N., Ali Pacha, A., & Özer, Ö. (2020). Significant Role of the Specific Prime Number p=257 in the Improvement of Cryptosystems. *Notes on Number Theory and Discrete Mathematics*, 26(4), 213–222.
3. Álvarez, R., Martínez, F., Vicent, J.-F., & Zamora, A. (2017). A Matricial Public Key Cryptosystem with Digital Signature. *WSEAS Transactions on Mathematics*, 7(4), 195–204.
4. Bengio, Y., & Curviller, A. (2006). *Deep Learning*, The MIT Press Book, p. 800.
5. Bishop, M. C. (2006). *Pattern Recognition and Machine Learning*, Springer, p. 758.
6. Ghosh, D., Dutta, P. K., & Abotaleb, M. (2024). "Harnessing the power of hybrid models for supply chain management and optimization". In Ramakant Bhardwaj, Pushan Kumar Dutta, Pethuru Raj, Abhishek Kumar, Kavita Saini, Alfonso González Briones and Mohammed K. A. Kaabar (Eds.), *Hybrid Information Systems: Non-Linear Optimization Strategies with Artificial Intelligence* (pp. 407–426). De Gruyter. https://doi.org/10.1515/9783111331133-019.
7. Abotaleb, M., & Dutta, P. K. (2024). "Optimizing bidirectional long short-term memory networks for univariate time series forecasting: a comprehensive guide". In Ramakant Bhardwaj, Pushan Kumar Dutta, Pethuru Raj, Abhishek Kumar, Kavita Saini, Alfonso González briones and Mohammed K. A. Kaabar (Eds.), *Hybrid Information Systems: Non-Linear Optimization Strategies with Artificial Intelligence* (pp. 443–458). De Gruyter. https://doi.org/10.1515/9783111331133-021.
8. Dhaliwal, N., Aghera, S., Whig, P., & Dutta, P. K. (2024). Advanced Analytics and Quantum Computing for Revolutionizing Procurement Strategies. In A. Hassan, P. Bhattacharya, P. Dutta, J. Verma, & N. Kundu (Eds.), *Quantum Computing and Supply Chain Management: A New Era of Optimization* (pp. 160–175). IGI Global. https://doi.org/10.4018/979-8-3693-4107-0.ch011.

9. Singh, B., Dutta, P. K., & Kaunert, C. (2024). Boosting Quantum Computing to Redefine Supply Chain in the Hospital Industry: Pitch the Vision for Medical and Healthcare Needs. In A. Hassan, P. Bhattacharya, P. Dutta, J. Verma, & N. Kundu (Eds.), *Quantum Computing and Supply Chain Management: A New Era of Optimization* (pp. 196–219). IGI Global. https://doi.org/10.4018/979-8-3693-4107-0.ch014.
10. Dutta, P. K., El-kenawy , S. M., Ali, G., & Dhoska, K. (2023). An Energy Consumption Monitoring and Control System in Buildings using Internet of Things. *Babylonian Journal of Internet of Things*, 2023, 38–47. https://doi.org/10.58496/BJIoT/2023/006.
11. Deisenroth, M. P., Faisal, A. A., & Ong, C. S. (2020). *Mathematics for Machine Learning*, Cambridge University Press, p. 398.
12. Gallian, J. A. (2012). *Contemporary Abstract Algebra*. Cengage Learning. – For a foundational understanding of matrix algebra.
13. Gauravaram, P., & Knudsen, L. R. (2021). An update on the side channel cryptanalysis of MACs based on cryptographic hash functions. In K. Srinathan, C. P. Rangan, M. Yung (Eds.), *Progress in Cryptology – INDOCRYPT 2007. INDOCRYPT 2007. Lecture Notes in Computer Science*, vol 4859. Heidelberg. https://doi.org/10.1007/978-3-540-77026-8_31.
14. Ferguson, N., Schneie, R. B., & Kohno, T. (2010). *Cryptographic Engineering*, ebookshelf, p. 30.
15. Paul, S., Mukherjee, D., Mitra, A., Mitra, A., & Dutta, P. K. (2024). Unravelling the Complex Networks of Social Physics: Exploring Human Behavior, Big Data, and Distributed Systems, *Journal of Social Computing*, 5(2), 165–179. https://doi.org/10.23919/JSC.2024.0014.
16. Dutta, P. K., & Banerjee, S. (2019). Monitoring of Aerosol and Other Particulate Matter in Air Using Aerial Monitored Sensors and Real Time Data Monitoring and Processing. *Journal of System and Management Sciences*, 9(2), 104–113.
17. Kumar, T., & Chauhan, S. (2018). Image Cryptography with Matrix Array Symmetric Key using Chaos based Approach. *International Journal of Information and Computer Security*, 10, 60–66.
18. Rimani, R., Hadj Said, N., Ali Pacha, A., & Özer, Ö. (2021). Key exchange based on Diffie-Hellman protocol and image registration. *Indonesian Journal of Electrical Engineering and Computer Science*, 21(3), 1751–1758.
19. Gupta, S., Dutta, P. K., Roy, S., Bhaduri, A., Maji, K., Choudhary, A., & Sarkar, A. (2024). Evaluating Waterfall vs. Agile Models in Software Development for Efficiency and Adaptability. In S. Misra, R. Jadeja, & M. Mittal (Eds.), *Practical Approaches to Agile Project Management* (pp. 142–148). IGI Global. https://doi.org/10.4018/979-8-3693-3318-1.ch008.
20. Paar, C., & Pelzl, J. (2010). *Understanding Cryptography: A Textbook for Students and* Practitioners (1st ed.).. Heidelberg.
21. Inayatullah, M., Ahmad, M., & Khan, Q. (2017). Message based Selection Matrix for Dynamic Hash based Security Systems. In *International Conference on Emerging Technologies*.
22. Dutta, P. K. (2019). Image Segmentation Based Approach for the Purpose of Developing Satellite Image Spatial Information Extraction for Forestation and River Bed Analysis. *International Journal of Image and Graphics*, 19(01), 1950002. https://doi.org/10.1142/S0219467819500025.
23. Gilbert, S. (2005). *Linear Algebra and Its Applications*.Elsevier.

24. Golub, H. G., & Van Loan, C. F. (2013). *Matrix Computations*, The Johns Hopkins University Press, p. 781.
25. Gupta, D., Segal, A., Panda, A., Segev, G., Schapira, M., Feigenbaum, J., Rexford, J., & Shenker, S. (2012). A new approach to interdomain routing based on secure multi-party computation. In *Proceedings of the 11th ACM Workshop on Hot Topics in Networks (HotNets-XI)* (pp. 37–42). Association for Computing Machinery. https://doi.org/10.1145/2390231.2390238.
26. Koukouvinos, C., & Simos, D. E. (2013). Encryption Schemes based on Hadamard Matrices with Circulant Cores, *Journal of Applied Mathematics & Bioinformatics*, 3(1), 17–41.
27. Dutta, P. K., El-kenawy , S. M., Abotaleb, M., & Eid, M. M. (2023). AI-Driven Marketplaces and Price Prediction Tools for Rag Pickers: Enhancing Economic Opportunities in Africa's Circular Economy. Babylonian. *Journal of Artificial Intelligence*, 2023, 33–42. https://doi.org/10.58496/BJAI/2023/007.
28. Dutta, P. K., Bhardwaj, A. K., & Mahida, A. (2024). Navigating the Complexities of Agile Transformations in Large Organizations. In A. Hassan, P. Bhattacharya, P. Dutta, J. Verma, & N. Kundu (Eds.), *Quantum Computing and Supply Chain Management: A New Era of Optimization* (pp. 315–330). IGI Global. https://doi.org/10.4018/979-8-3693-4107-0.ch020.
29. Gutta, L. M., Dhamodharan, B., Dutta, P. K., & Whig, P. (2024). AI-Infused Quantum Machine Learning for Enhanced Supply Chain Forecasting. In A. Hassan, P. Bhattacharya, P. Dutta, J. Verma, & N. Kundu (Eds.), *Quantum Computing and Supply Chain Management: A New Era of Optimization* (pp. 48–63). IGI Global. https://doi.org/10.4018/979-8-3693-4107-0.ch003.
30. Biswas, A., & Dutta, P. K. (2020, January). Novel approach of automation to risk management: The reduction in human errors. In *International Conference on Mobile Computing and Sustainable Informatics* (pp. 683–696). Springer International Publishing.
31. Dutta, P. K., Bhardwaj, A. K., & Mahida, A. (2024). Navigating the Complexities of Agile Transformations in Large Organizations. In A. Hassan, P. Bhattacharya, P. Dutta, J. Verma, & N. Kundu (Eds.), *Quantum Computing and Supply Chain Management: A New Era of Optimization* (pp. 315–330). IGI Global. https://doi.org/10.4018/979-8-3693-4107-0.ch020.
32. Gupta, S., Sarkar, D., Roy, D., Kundu, S., & Dutta, P. K. (2024). Embracing Flexibility and Efficiency: Practical Approaches to Agile Project Management. In S. Misra, R. Jadeja, & M. Mittal (Eds.), *Practical Approaches to Agile Project Management* (pp. 1–8). IGI Global. https://doi.org/10.4018/979-8-3693-3318-1.ch001.
33. Patra, A. & Dutta, P. K. (2024). Application of Agile Stage Gate Hybrid Model in the Healthcare Industry: A Paradigm Shift in Project Management. In S. Misra, R. Jadeja, & M. Mittal (Eds.), *Practical Approaches to Agile Project Management* (pp. 149–163). IGI Global. https://doi.org/10.4018/979-8-3693-3318-1.ch009.
34. Dutta, P. K., Sekiwu, D., Unogwu, O. J., Catherine, A. T., & Helal, A. H. (2023). Metaverse Revolution in Higher Education: The Rise of Metaversities and Immersive Learning Environments. *Babylonian Journal of Internet of Things*, 2023, 59–68. https://doi.org/10.58496/BJIoT/2023/008.

35. Dutta, P. K., El-kenawy , S. M., Ali, G., & Dhoska, K. (2023). An Energy Consumption Monitoring and Control System in Buildings Using Internet of Things. *Babylonian Journal of Internet of Things*, 2023, 38–47. https://doi.org/10.58496/BJIoT/2023/006.
36. Mannepalli, P. K., Richhariya, V., Gupta, S. K., Shukla, P. K., Dutta, P. K., Chowdhury, S., & Hu, Y.-C. (2024). A Robust Blockchain-Based Watermarking Using Edge Detection and Wavelet Transform. *Multimedia Tools and Applications*, 83(20), 1–25. https://doi.org/10.1007/s11042-024-18907-4.
37. Özer, Ö., & Subasi, N. (2024). Empowering Secure Communication With Specific Triangular Matrices, In *Innovations in Modern Cryptography* (pp. 270–291). IGI Global. https://doi.org/10.4018/979-8-3693-5330-1.ch01.
38. Provost, F., & Fawcett, T. (2013). *Data Science for Business*, O'Reilly Media Publisher, p. 413.
39. Schneier, B. (2015). *Applied Cryptography: Protocols, Algorithms, and Source Code in C.* Wiley Publication, p. 784.
40. Özer, Ö. Ö. & Subasi, N. (2024). Empowering Secure Communication With Specific Triangular Matrices: Practical Examples Unveiled Using Different Approximations. In B. Gupta, D. Kalra, & A. Almomani (Eds.), *Innovations in Modern Cryptography* (pp. 270–291). IGI Global. https://doi.org/10.4018/979-8-3693-5330-1.ch011.
41. Stinson, D. R. (2005). *Cryptography: Theory and Practice.* CRC Press
42. Upadhyay, S., Roy, R., & Ghosh, S. (2023). Designing hash and encryption engines using quantum computing. In *International Conference on VLSI Design.*
43. Zhao, C., Zhao, S., Zhao, M., Chen, Z., Gao, C.-Z., Li, H., & Tan, Y.-a. (2019). Secure multi-party computation: Theory, practice and applications. *Information Sciences,* 476, 357–372. https://doi.org/10.1016/j.ins.2018.10.024.
44. Zhou, I., Tofigh, F., Piccardi, M., Abolhasan, M., Franklin, D., & Lipman, J. (2024). Secure multi-party computation for machine learning: A survey. İn *IEEE Access*, vol. 12 pp. 53881–53899. https://doi.org/10.1109/ACCESS.2024.3388992.
45. Zimmerman, P. (1999). *An Introduction to Cryptography.* Doubleday & Company, Inc.

Chapter 18

Energy harvesting for IoT in logistics

Imran Khan Patan and Sudhakaru Komera

18.1 INTRODUCTION

In the context of the Internet of Things, the word "Internet" refers to a collection of technologies and infrastructures that are connected to the Internet. Because of this, a network is being used to guarantee that physical things are linked to one another in order to make it possible for them to communicate with one another and share information about themselves as well as the environment in which they are situated. Data may be sent via the Internet of Things (IoT), which is a network that does not need any form of connection between humans or between humans and machines. Objects, animals, and people all have their own unique identities and are able to send data through the IoT. There are, however, a great variety of applications that may be used with the Internet of Things. Some of the most well-known objectives are the construction of smart structures and cities, the implementation of Industry 4.0, and other initiatives that are comparable to these [1]. The objective of this research is not to present a comprehensive catalog of every application associated with the Internet of Things (IoT). For instance, intelligent management and real-time monitoring of public transportation networks represent one dimension of what characterizes a smart city. One example of what constitutes a smart city is the intelligent monitoring and administration of public transit systems. Smart cities also include smart hospitals, structural health monitoring systems, and other systems that are comparable to these. To monitor environmental data like temperature, light, moisture, and other factors, smart buildings are outfitted with a number of sensors that are deployed throughout the structure. Smart buildings are also equipped with a variety of sensors. To keep track of environmental data, several sensors are used. Not only does this contribute to the conservation of the environment, but it also guarantees that the people who are using it will have a pleasant experience. It is now possible to use intelligent automation and incorporate new technologies into a variety of operations in the industrial sector thanks to the Internet of Things (IoT). This, in turn, leads to an increase in productivity, safety, and the quality of service that is provided to clients.

 DOI: 10.1201/9781003498292-18

Based on this global picture of the key applications of the Internet of Things, it can be deduced that the fundamental objective of the Internet of Things is to enable communication in real time for the purpose of monitoring and taking action on physical processes. Additionally, decentralising decision-making requires interactions not just between systems but also between people and the systems themselves. This makes it necessary for humans to engage with the systems. There has been a paradigm change towards the Internet of Things, which has been brought about by improvements in a range of research fields, such as sensor networks, the web, and cloud computing. These innovations have led to a shift in paradigm. The sensor might be situated anywhere on the planet, from the inside of a structure to the depths of the ocean, on level ground, or even on a battlefield. It is likely that it could be positioned anywhere in the world. When compared to other works, this sculpture cannot be placed in regions that are easily accessible since it is not practicable to do so. The fact that the sensors may be linked or wireless is another factor that adds to the increased configuration freedom that they provide, which in turn increases the attraction of the sensors [2].

Depending on the specifics of the situation, it is conceivable that the procedure of charging wireless sensors might be very expensive or even impossible. This is because batteries are required for the production of electricity by wireless sensors. The field of research known as energy harvesting is a relatively new field of study, and its major purpose is to improve the existing state of wireless sensors by increasing the amount of time that they can operate. At this point in time, the phrase "energy harvesting wireless sensor" is often used by the scientific community in order to describe the several types of wireless sensors that are now available. The process of identifying a primary energy source in the near neighbourhood and converting it into electrical energy is referred to as energy harvesting. Consequently, this makes it possible to power the wireless sensor by using direct electricity. It is possible that to realise this potential for energy harvesting wireless sensors, it will be essential to integrate two different areas of research: one that seeks to enhance the efficiency of energy harvesting circuits and another that seeks to reduce the amount of energy that wireless sensors use. The fact that these two subfields of inquiry have grown independently gives them a history that is not only intriguing but also exceptionally important.

In the past, several methods have been proposed for the collection of ambient energy; nonetheless, each one of these methods is reliant on the most important power plants. Primary sources of energy include ventilation, internal light, thermoelectric gradient, airflow, vibration, and radio frequency (RF) energy. Other sources include vibration and airflow. In the past, the power density of the harvesting system was the most important factor to consider when determining the quality of primary energy sources. On the other hand, this is no longer the situation. In order to satisfy the need to put wireless sensors in areas that are now inaccessible, it is essential to have a primary supply that is available to everyone. One of the key components that contribute to this degree of flexibility is the radiofrequency waves, which were stated earlier in the sentence. In light of this, the objective of the study is to present design considerations for autonomous wireless sensors that make use of radio frequency energy in order to meet the goals of Internet of Things devices and networks. The abbreviation WS, defined in this context, will consistently denote radio frequency energy harvesting by wireless sensors throughout this research. Next, the subsequent sections will provide a synopsis of these components in addition to the issues that we are addressing in this study [2].

18.2 DESIGN CONSIDERATIONS OF THE RADIO FREQUENCY ENERGY HARVESTING WIRELESS SENSOR

The RF energy harvesting wireless sensor was created because of joint effort in the fields of radio frequency (RF) energy harvesting and wireless sensor energy budget reduction. Additionally, the ubiquitous availability of radio frequency (RF) sources was a contributing factor in the development of this sensor. By deconstructing the optimisations that have been presented in these three areas of study over the course of the last few years, we believe that we will be able to stimulate the creation of new solutions that are more efficient for radio frequency energy harvesting wireless sensors. This is also the hope that we have. The use of an antenna for the goal of capturing the ever-present radio frequency waves is a component that is often seen in systems that are designed to harvest energy from radio frequency emissions.

Utilising an RF/DC converter is the next phase in the process of energy collection, which requires the use of a converter. To ensure that the maximum amount of power is sent to the system that is really being used, it is essential to have a maximum power point tracking (MPPT) circuit that is founded on a direct current to a direct current converter. It is essential to place a matching filter in between the antenna and the RF/DC converter in order to reduce the amount of energy that is lost as a result of reflection. This will reduce the amount of energy that is lost significantly. In the field of architecture, this particular kind of structure is known as a rectenna, which is an acronym that stands for rectifying antenna [2].

One of the most important factors determining the overall performance of the rectenna is the amount of radio frequency (RF) energy that it is able to take in.

There is a chance that this energy is produced on purpose; more specifically, it is associated with wireless power transfer, which is often referred to as WPT. There is also the potential of creating the rectenna in such a manner that it functions on the naturally existing radio frequency energy that is available as a consequence of the operation of other wireless communication equipment that does not require the harvest chain. This is another alternative. The term "ambient RF energy harvesting" is used to describe the phenomenon that occurs when something similar takes place. In order to facilitate the application of wireless information and power transfer (WIPT) concepts, the use of radio frequency energy harvesting wireless sensors is now offering support. Radio frequency energy has an inherent quality that makes it possible to use a wireless sensor antenna for the purpose of data transmission and energy collection. This is the reason why it is possible. Additionally, Wi-Fi power-backscatter communication (WPBC), Wi-Fi power-communication network (WPCN), and simultaneous Wi-Fi power-and-information transfer (SWIPT) are the three key areas of Wi-Fi power-and-information transfer (WIPT) that have been identified. In Section 18.3, we will discuss the various methods in which feeding may be accomplished via the use of the rectenna at various times.

Following an analysis of all the recommendations that have been made over the past few years to reduce the energy consumption of wireless sensors, we are able to focus on three key elements that influence the total energy consumption of WS. The communication protocol, the topology of the network, and the infrastructure of the network are the components that come together to form this system [1–6].

The confluence of these three areas of research—radio frequency energy harvesting, radio frequency feeding techniques, and wireless sensor energy budget minimisation—made it clear how difficult it was to successfully regulate the energy that was harvested This was a significant advancement in the field of energy harvesting. There are four major components that must be in place before a radio frequency energy harvesting-wireless sensor can work successfully. These components allow the sensor to function properly.

There are a number of factors that are taken into account, including the techniques of antenna feeding, the harvesting of radio frequency energy, the lowering of the energy budget for wireless sensors, and the management of energy effectively.

The information that is gathered by radio frequency energy harvesting wireless sensors is managed by a block that is known as a power management module. This management block is responsible for handling the information. Inside a genuine network that is linked to the Internet of Things, anything might take place at any given instant inside that network. It is possible that in the future, they will change depending on whether or not the energy that is gathered is adequate to convey them [7]. The primary reason for this is that the existence of this data storage will result in a delay in the transmission of data [8]. The primary objective of power management modules is to cut down on the length of time that is necessary for the gearbox to experience a variety of gearbox delays. According to the findings of the study, there are two key obstacles that must be overcome in order to achieve this purpose. There have been a number of concerns raised, some of which include reducing the transmission completion time (TCTM) as much as possible and boosting the short-term throughput (STTM) of the transmission [9]. These two well-known approaches to improving the energy efficiency of radio frequency energy harvesting wireless sensors will be analysed in further detail.

18.2.1 Design considerations

Design of wireless sensors for the Internet of Things that harvest radio frequency energy involves taking into account the following factors when designing applications:

(1) Rectenna feeding techniques
(2) Rectenna design issues
(3) Minimisation of the energy budget of wireless sensor solutions

Therefore, the objective of this research is to provide engineers who are working on communication protocols and RF harvester circuits with the information they need in order to build creative solutions that are especially tailored to wireless sensor RF energy harvesting systems. This objective will be accomplished by providing them with the information they require. In this chapter, an in-depth analysis of the underlying principles that underpin all of the components that have been explained up to this point is carried out by making use of design equations and optimisation solutions.

18.3 COMPARISON WITH RELATED REVIEWS

When it comes to the topics that are brought up at the beginning of the discussion, there are not many evaluations that cover all that is offered in such a complete way. There are some people who, rather than actively engaging in the operations that convert radio frequency waves into direct current electrical power that is suitable for running the WS, just advise on how to manage the surplus energy that has been accumulated. This is because they are not actively involved in the activities themselves. The sum of the numbers [10, 11] equals that.

Previous studies have primarily focused on the transition between radio frequency (RF) and direct current (DC) [12, 13]; therefore, it has not been possible to investigate the techniques for powering antennas. Solutions that have the potential to lower the energy budgets of WSs are often either ignored or addressed independently. This is a common occurrence. In this review, which is based on the results of previous studies that are related to ours [7, 10], the features of the linked study that are the most significant are emphasised.

With the goal of obtaining effective administration within the energy harvesting wireless sensor business, Kansal and his colleagues established a collection of algorithms inside the publication [14]. This was done with the objective of attaining efficiency. Keeping track of the quantity of energy that is still present in the battery is the major focus when it comes to the creation of algorithms. This is because the battery is the source of the computing power. This older body of work does not include a single reference of harvesting circuit design in any way, shape, or form. Within the context of this lecture, the subject of energy management was examined from a specific point of view, with radio frequency (RF) and solar power acting as examples. The challenge of predicting harvestable energy via the use of an EWMA filter remained at the forefront of our thoughts for the whole of our discussion on this subject. In a separate situation, which is analogous to the one described in [15], no investigation of the energy conversion circuits was carried out. A full examination of WPT systems is carried out by Valenta and Durgin [12].

During the course of this inquiry, a specific optimisation of the circuits that comprise the equipment that is the rectenna will be developed. In particular, we will be concentrating our efforts on researching the characteristics of rectifier diodes as well as strategies for impedance matching. The energy that has been collected, on the other hand, has not been the focus of any study into how it may be controlled. Lu et al. investigate wireless networks that can collect energy from radio frequencies throughout the whole of their investigation [10]. This piece of writing is intended to provide a detailed description of the chain that is responsible for the harvesting of energy from radio frequency (RF) sources. Each of the several types of wireless networks, such as single-hop, multi-antenna, relay, and cognitive radio networks, will be the primary focus of the investigation. On the other hand, these earlier studies did not study any possible strategies for lowering the amount of power that wireless sensors require in order to function properly. In the study that they conducted [11], Ku and his colleagues explore the challenges that energy harvesting communications have encountered in the past as well as the challenges that they would encounter in the future years. The fact that the amount of energy that can be gathered is very changeable is receiving considerable attention at the moment. An examination of both the deterministic and stochastic EH models has been carried out throughout this chapter. It is unfortunate that this page does not provide all of the architectural and harvesting circuit topologies that are currently available. The establishment of cognitive radio networks that are powered by radio frequency energy is the primary topic of discussion in [13], which was written by Mohjazi et al. The argument is mostly focused on this particular aspect.

There are only two ways that are used in order to provide the rectenna with power. These methods are known as wireless power transfer (WPT) and radio frequency energy harvesting (RFEM) [16]. When it comes to energy management, increasing throughput is given a great deal of significance since it is an additional efficiency criterion that is being taken into consideration. On the other hand, there is a paucity of knowledge on the construction of the hardware component of radio frequency (RF) transmitters and receivers. On the other hand, the paper [9] written by Soyata and colleagues provides a complete review of radio frequency energy harvesting for embedded systems. In their proposal, the authors advised doing research into the design of the radio frequency energy harvesting wireless sensor as well as techniques to improve signal transmission. In addition, both of these topics were included in the proposal. In the paper [17], Tharindu et al. offer a synopsis of the current work that has been done in SWIPT. This development has been accomplished in recent years. After that, they make use of this information to discuss potential challenges that may arise in the future. The authors begin by providing a brief history of the various WPT methods, then continue to classify those approaches, and finally, they proceed to investigate the receiver design of the SWIPT algorithm [18]. Sidhu and his colleagues conducted an analysis with the objective of determining the ambient radio frequency (RF) sources that have the potential to be used in order to provide power to the rectennas.

In the paper [19], which was published by Surrender and his colleagues together with other writers, an overview of rectenna design approaches for wireless applications is offered. Another author contributed to the publication. This article explores a variety of potential uses for wireless energy and discusses them in detail. Medical implants, solar energy transmission, wireless power transfer systems, wireless sensor networks, and wireless energy harvesting are some of the applications that fall under this category. In the most current research, a full description of the components that comprise a rectenna is provided. Following that, the authors concentrated their efforts on the basic mechanisms that make it possible for antennas to have circular polarisation, which in turn enables them to keep their output performances constant. In their study, Ibrahim et al. [9] give a comprehensive examination of the design of devices for radio frequency (RF) energy harvesting. This analysis is presented in both written and oral form.

An exhaustive analysis was carried out on a number of different topologies for energy transformation circuits. The procedures that are involved in energy management, on the other hand, were not mentioned in this article. According to [15], the performance measurements of radio frequency energy harvesting devices give cause for concern. In addition to the power management methods that they outlined, this is an additional measure. On the other hand, the subject of how to keep the energy budgets of wireless sensor systems to a minimum has received very little attention and discussion [2].

18.4 RECTENNA FEEDING TECHNIQUES

To put it simply, the amount of energy that is collected is the single most important factor that influences the total performance of the system. For radio frequency energy harvesting wireless sensors, this fact remains unaffected, irrespective of how extensively circuit design optimization is performed. One of the first steps in the design process is to perform an analysis of the potential for energy harvesting in the region where the sensor will be positioned. This is one of the stages that occurs at the beginning of the process. This specific aspect of the design has been characterised by the term "rectenna feeding strategies," which is a concept that we have used rather often in our research activities [20].

One of the early methods that was taken in the hunt for a solution to the rectenna feeding technique was to find a method that could recycle some of the radio frequency waves that are already present in the environment because of telecommunications equipment. This was one of the early techniques that was taken. The majority of people refer to this method as the ambient radiofrequency energy harvesting solution, which is another name for this approach of energy harvesting. When it comes to the Rectenna Feeding Technique, the second technique entails the use of a separate power source in order to provide the WS with power. In this particular situation, a radio frequency wave antenna is used in order to provide the rectenna with the necessary amount of power. There are a variety of RF propagation models that are used in order to ascertain the amount of power that may be successfully harvested. The transmission channel that is employed between the antenna and the rectenna is the factor that determines the differences between these devices [21].

This rectenna feeding technique and its application are both referred to as wireless power transmission (WPT), which is the term that is used to designate both of these concepts. When it comes to wireless systems, there is a current trend towards adopting WIPT principles, which is an abbreviation that stands for wireless information and power transfer. This trend is now making its way into the technology world. An antenna is required for both the WPT and the WS since they both depend on antennas to transmit data that is gathered from the environment. This is the reason why an antenna is required for both structures. Currently, there are three key tactics that are being investigated as potential solutions. Wirelessly powered communication networks (WPCNs) and simultaneous wireless information and power transmission (SWIPTs) are two examples of such networks. Both of these acronyms are used to refer to communication networks that are powered by wireless technology. The principal rectenna feeding techniques will be detailed in the subsections that follow in order to facilitate the process of establishing the overall amount of power that was collected [2].

18.4.1 Ambient RF energy harvesting

One example of such an endeavour is the radio frequency energy harvesting (RFEM) technique. This technique makes use of energy that already exists in the environment because of the operation of wireless communication equipment that is situated near one another because of the closeness of the devices. Digital television (DTV), third-generation (3G), long-term evolution (LTE), global system for mobile (GSM), and wireless fidelity (Wi-Fi) are all examples of prevalent frequency bands [22].

On the other hand, there are some creative people who have discovered techniques to gather usable quantities of energy by making use of solar panels and wind turbines. These methods have been developed by these individuals. In order for these systems to be effective, it is necessary to build circuits that are able to simultaneously collect radio frequency energy from a variety of various bands without causing any interference. In spite of the fact that these circuits provide the best results, they might sometimes cause traffic jams. This is an essential point to bear in mind. Keeping this in mind is the most important thing to maintain. As a result of the fact that congestion is one of the design constraints, this is not going to be effective for the vast majority of things.

18.4.2 Wireless power transfer (WPT)

It is possible to achieve wireless power transmission via the usage of antennas that are connected to an RF wave generator or through the utilisation of the magnetic fields of the coils in order to collect the electrical energy that is contained within them. The WPT with coils was first proposed by Nicolas Tesla, who was the one who came up with the idea. As a result of the fact that the device was constructed on the basis of the concept of magnetic resonance between two coils, it was possible to transfer enormous amounts of energy to sites that were located at a great distance. Radio frequency identification (RFID) chips and biological equipment are only two examples of the many applications that may be discovered for this WPT technique. There are many more uses as well. However, the most notable drawback of this technology is that it has a limited gearbox range. This is the most significant disadvantage. Furthermore, the power levels are rather high, which implies that they have the potential to cause serious health problems if they are not controlled properly. This, in addition to the restricted gearbox range, is still another issue that needs correction. As an example, it was possible to transfer 60 W of electricity across a distance of just 2 m while maintaining a conversion efficiency of 40%. Within the context of this specific situation, the term "near-field transmission" demonstrates the use of WPTs [23].

A growing number of individuals are becoming interested in the use of far-field technology, which is founded on the transfer of electricity by

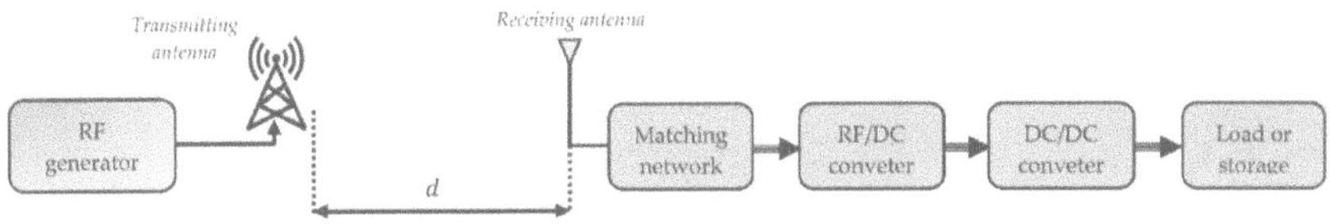

Figure 18.1 Far-Field WPT and RF/DC conversion blocks of a radio frequency energy harvesting system.

electromagnetic radiation. These individuals are contemplating the prospect of wirelessly sending energy across longer distances.

A radio frequency (RF) generator is one of the components of the system that can be seen in Figure 18.2. This generator is accountable for the emission of a power pulse (PT). The generator is connected to a transmitting antenna that has a gain of GT for it to broadcast electromagnetic waves. This allows the generator to produce electromagnetic waves. It is important to have a receiving antenna or antennas with gain GR that are situated at a distance d from the transmitting antenna to collect the radio frequency (RF) energy that has been delivered. This arrangement is necessary to accomplish the goal of collecting the RF energy. Consequently, to efficiently shape the energy, a conversion from radio frequency to direct current is necessary. Matching networks make it possible to reduce the amount of reflection losses that occur between the antenna and the RF/DC converter. This is because the matching network makes it possible to reduce these losses. The receiving antenna or antennas and the converter work together to achieve this goal via their combined efforts. The conclusion is that a direct current to direct current converter is necessary in order to match the energy in an acceptable manner to either the load or the storage element [24] (Figure 18.1).

It is necessary to first ascertain the power that is being expelled, which is also referred to as PT, and then it is necessary to ascertain the power that is being brought in, which is also referred to as PR. When this occurs, and only then will you be able to make a choice that is well-informed on the other parts of the system. The quantity of power that can be collected is essentially governed by three elements: the frequency of the transmission, the gain of the antennas, and the distance d that separates them from one another. These three parameters influence the amount of power that can be picked up. There is a consensus among several individuals that the Friis model is among the most basic models that may be investigated. The usage of this sort is restricted to circumstances in which there are no obstacles between the antennas that are transmitting and receiving, which are also referred to as line-of-sight settings. The events that are described in the following are an illustration of the impact that this particular condition brought about:

$$P_R = P_T G_T G_R \left(\frac{c}{4\pi df} \right)^2 \tag{18.1}$$

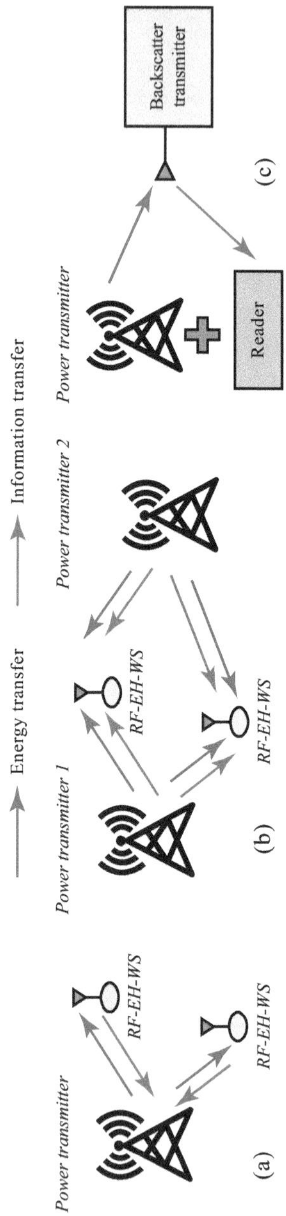

Figure 18.2 Various WIPT architectures. (a) WPCN. (b) SWIPT. (c) WPBC.

While the letter f is used to denote the emission frequency of radio frequency waves, the sign c is used to symbolise the speed of light. Both symbols are used simultaneously. As was noted before in the text, the additional criteria are provided for consideration.

With the assistance of the Friis model, we were able to conduct an analysis of the power consumption of a rectenna that was supplied by several different emitters. Naderi et al. established that the received power may be defined as follows, given that there are N identical energy sources that provide the same power, PT, with the same transmission gain, GT, and at the same frequency, f. In addition, the transmission gain between these sources is the same. It is predicated on the idea that there are N energy sources that are similar to one another:

$$P_R = P_T G_T G_R \left(\frac{c}{4\pi f} \right)^2 \left[\sum_{i=1}^{N} \frac{1}{d_i^2} + \sum_{i \neq j, i=1}^{N} \sum \frac{\cos(k(\Delta d_{ij}}{d_i d_j} \right] \tag{18.2}$$

When referring to the difference in phase between two independent signals, the word $k\Delta\, d_{ij}$ is used to characterise the difference. The fact that this is the case makes it possible to portray interference that is either beneficial or harmful. Equation 18.2 was used by the authors in order to ascertain the most favourable positions for the emitting sources in order to avoid interferences that may cause damage [25–31].

When the implications of wave reflection, diffraction, and scattering are taken into consideration, it is feasible to arrive at a more accurate estimation of the potential power that is gathered. When it comes to this specific situation, the official phrase for this particular scenario is the two-ray model, and Equation 18.3 is used in order to determine the power [32].

$$P_R = P_T G_T G_R \left(\frac{h_T^2 h_R^2}{d^4} \right) \tag{18.3}$$

In this equation, the parameters h_R and h_T are used to represent both the receiving antenna and the transmitting antenna, respectively. It is via the use of these characteristics that the effective height of the antennas is denoted, accordingly. In accordance with what was just said, the following parameters are provided in the same fashion.

The quantity of power that can be harvested in a range of non-line-of-sight situations has been the subject of a great number of models that have been developed via the use of a combination of analytical and empirical approaches. These models have been produced in order to make predictions. Some of the models that are used the most often include the log-distance path-loss model [33]. For the purpose of this model [34], the unpredictability of shadowing effects that are caused by a signal barrier, such as a building, is taken into account. Within the context of this scenario, the following is a description of the potential power harvesting that may take place:

$$P_R(d,n) = P_R(d_0)\left(\frac{d_0}{d}\right)^n \tag{18.4}$$

Within the scope of this discussion, the term "$P_R(d_0)$" is used to denote the power that is obtained at the d_0 distance, which is a reference distance. n is the symbol that represents the route loss exponent. It is always the case that the value of n is tied to the features of the environment in which the propagation takes place. As an example, the value of 1.6 is recorded for an office complex during the year in question.

Not only that but there has also been the emergence of probabilistic models, which provide a more realistic alternative to the deterministic models that were used in the past. In circumstances in which the transmitting and receiving antennas do not have a direct line of sight, the Rayleigh model, which is the probabilistic model that is used the most often, is utilised to portray the events that are in issue. An illustration of the harvestable power is provided by the Rayleigh model, which is given in the following fashion.:

$$P_R = P_R^{\det} \times 10^{\left(n.\log_{10}\left(d/d_0\right)\right)} \times |r|^2 \tag{18.5}$$

where $P^{\det}$ is the received power that is estimated using deterministic models, n is the exponent of the route loss factor, d is the distance between the antenna that is receiving and the antenna that is broadcasting, d_0 is a reference distance, and r is a random integer that follows a complex Gaussian distribution [35].

In the following sections, a summary of four RF propagation models that are often used in far-field wireless power transmissions is presented. In this part of the chapter, we will talk about the processes that need to be carried out in order to calculate the potential harvestable power in the context of applications including wireless data and power transmission.

18.4.3 Harvestable power in wireless information and power transfer (WIPT) techniques

By utilising radio frequency waves, a wireless information and power transfer (WIPT) system can facilitate the transport of both data and energy inside a wireless sensor network. Some of the challenges that arise in the process of designing such systems include the creation of methods for the separation of information and power as well as the identification of the most appropriate method for the generation of signals. The fundamental objective is to locate the optimal equilibrium between the quantity of energy that can be transferred and the quantity of information that can be conveyed within the system. After conducting an exhaustive review of the relevant literature, we have arrived at the conclusion that there are three options available to choose from [36]. Several different configurations of these systems are shown in Figure 18.3, which illustrates them in their various forms.

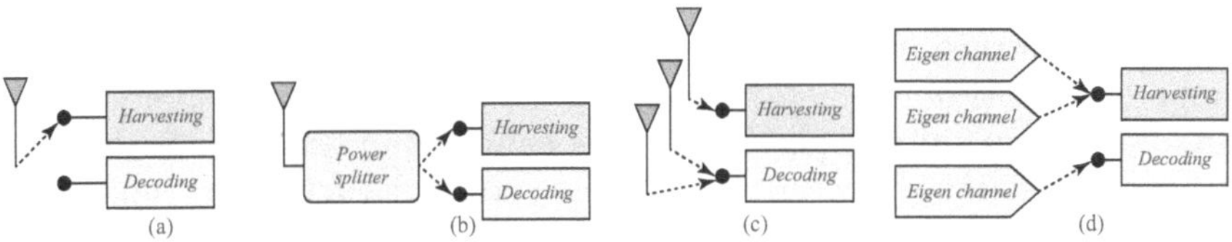

Figure 18.3 SWIPT transmission techniques in different domains: (a) Time. (b) Power. (c) Antenna. (d) Space.

Wireless sensors (WSs) in the wireless-powered communications network (WPCN) shown in Figure 18.2a are responsible for the transmission of data with an active transmission. Gathering radio frequency (RF) energy is the means by which this objective is achieved [37].

Figure 18.2 provides a visual depiction of the SWIPT method that must be followed. The term SWIPT is an abbreviation that stands for "simultaneous wireless information and power transfer." Whenever this technique is used, the transfer of both data and energy from a base station (BS) to a wireless station (WS) takes place concurrently [38].

It is possible that the WS will choose to either decode the data or gather the energy that is being sent by the power transmitter and proceed to the next stage. It is possible for the WS to achieve a high degree of efficiency in the transmission of both energy and information as a result of this shift between the modules that are responsible for decoding and harvesting [39].

A further illustration of the backscatter device that is used in wirelessly powered backscatter communications (WPBC) can be seen in Figure 18.2c. Instead of producing a brand new signal, it modifies and reflects an existing radio frequency (RF) signal. This is in contrast to the generation of a new signal. The reader is supposed to be fed by the electricity, and this is accomplished by the utilisation of backscattered energy. As can be seen in Figure 18.3, which depicts the several designs that are involved, the models that were investigated for the purpose of estimating the harvestable power that is utilised in WPTs may also be used for the purpose of assessing the autonomy of WPCNs. This is something that can be done. Under specified scenarios, such as SWIPT and WPBC, we will give a mechanism that allows for the assessment of the potential power that has been gathered.

18.4.4 Harvestable power in simultaneous wireless information and power transfer (SWIPT)

At first, those who came before the SWIPT thought that a single signal could carry both energy and data without making use of either of them on its own. This was the hypothesis that was first held by those individuals. In spite of the fact that there are fundamental trade-offs between the transmission of data and the consumption of power, the deployment of energy harvesting processes is particularly challenging since these procedures destroy data. Even though there are basic compromises, this is nonetheless the case. As a result of this, the technique that is used to extract coded information from the process of RF energy harvesting is the factor that is responsible for deciding the quantity of power that may be retrieved later. The basic ways consist of switching between time, dividing power, switching antennas, and switching into spatial switching. These are the four primary approaches. The totality of each of these four strategies is shown in an illustration in Figure 18.3 [40].

18.4.5 Harvestable power in wirelessly powered backscatter communications (WPBC)

At this point, the energy that was lost as a result of the backscatter of the original signal is recovered. When electromagnetic waves are reflected in directions that are completely opposite to the direction in which they first came, a phenomenon that is known as backscatter occurs. Backscatter is a phenomenon that occurs when a diffuser causes electromagnetic waves to be reflected. In the same way that there are several SWIPT designs, there are also a number of different WPBC structures. In Figure 18.5, we have an illustration of the three basic ways in which one might discern between the two options. One of the most important aspects that sets the designs apart from one another is the context in which the first signal was generated. Monostatic, bistatic, and ambient backscatter are the three basic types that allow for the classification of backscatter. Through the use of this image, it is able to investigate the distinctions that exist between the three elements [41]. With regard to the monostatic systems shown in Figure 18.4a, the backscatter receiver is the component that serves as the origin of the first signal sent. In the signal that is sent, both energy and information are components that are included.

Being responsible for contributing to the power consumption of the receiver is the backscatter transmitter. This is because the backscatter transmitter is responsible for sending a portion of its own energy. Databases that are connected with radio frequency identification (RFID) often make use of this technology.

Figure 18.4b depicts systems that are bistatic that are in operation. These systems are equipped with a separate transmitter for the original signal as well as a separate receiver for the reverse scatter. More specifically, in order to get its power, the latter is reliant on a specialist source in addition to the signal that is backscattered [42–48].

The first signal that can be seen in Figure 18.4c is referred to as ambient backscatter, and it is derived from the ambient energy that is made available because of the operation of various types of telecommunications equipment (these include digital television, Wi-Fi, and other devices that are comparable). The backscattered transmitter and receiver can perform their functions because of the utilisation of this energy. Furthermore, because of this,

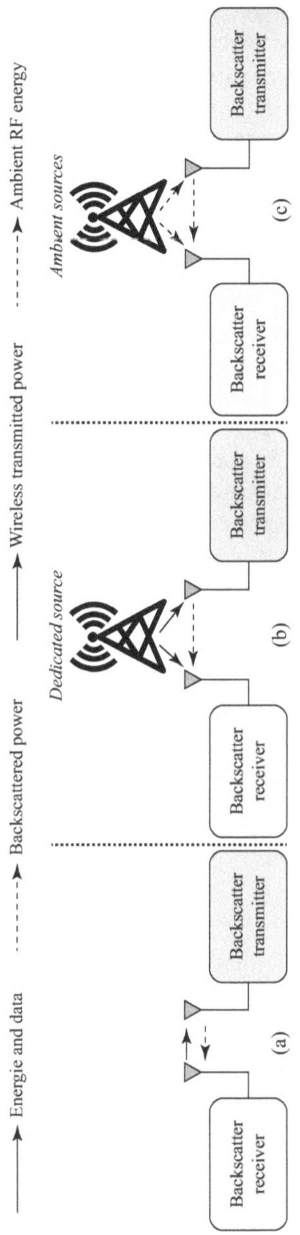

Figure 18.4 Different types of backscatter communications systems. (a) Monostatic. (b) Bistatic. (c) Ambient.

it is possible to increase the energy autonomy of the backscatter receiver by making use of the energy that is backscattered.

It is at this stage that the energy that was lost as a consequence of the backscatter of the initial signal is recovered. The phenomenon that is referred to as backscatter takes place when electromagnetic waves are reflected in directions that are entirely opposite to the direction in which they first originated. In the event that a diffuser is responsible for the reflection of electromagnetic waves, a phenomenon known as backscatter will take place. In the same way as there are a number of distinct SWIPT designs, there are also a number of different WPBC structures. There are three fundamental ways that one might differentiate between the two choices, and we have a visual representation of these approaches in Figure 18.5. The setting in which the first signal was formed is one of the most significant characteristics that distinguished the designs from one another and set them distinct from one another [49–53]. Backscatter may be classified into three primary categories: monostatic, bistatic, and ambient. These three forms of backscatter are more fundamental than the others. Through the use of this picture, it is feasible to explore the differences that are present between the three components [54]. When it comes to the monostatic systems shown in Figure 18.5a, the backscatter receiver is the component that acts as the source of the first signal that is sent. Energy and information are both components that are included in the signal that is sent across the network. The backscatter transmitter is the component that is accountable for making a specific contribution to the power consumption of the receiver. This is due to the fact that the backscatter transmitter is accountable for transmitting a part of its own energy. This technique is often used by databases that are linked to radio frequency identification (RFID) systems.

A representation of bistatic systems that are currently in operation may be seen in Figure 18.5b. A separate transmitter for the original signal and a

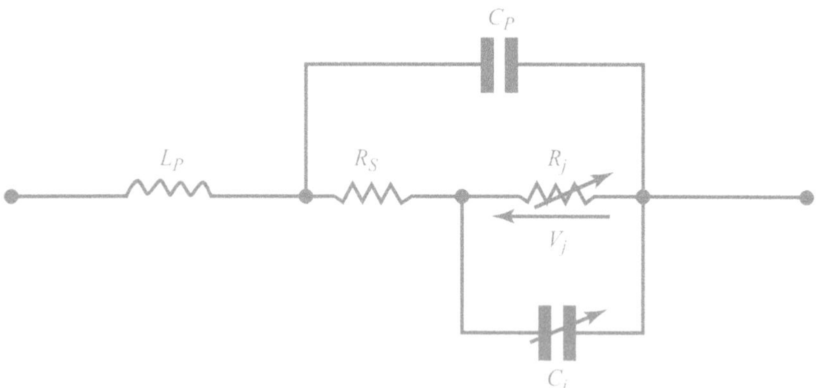

Figure 18.5 Small signal model of schottky diode.

separate receiver for the reverse scatter are both included in these systems. Both of these components are independent of one another. For a more precise explanation, the latter is dependent on a specialised source in addition to the signal that is backscattered in order to get its power [55].

The first signal that can be seen in Figure 18.5c is called ambient backscatter, and it is derived from the ambient energy that is made available as a consequence of the operation of various types of telecommunications equipment (these include digital television, Wi-Fi, and other devices that are comparable). This energy is made available as a result of the operation of these devices [56]. As a consequence of the utilisation of this energy, the backscattered transmitter and receiver are able to carry out their respective roles. Additionally, as a consequence of this, it is feasible to enhance the energy autonomy of the backscatter receiver by using the energy that is backscattered. This is a result of the fact that this is achievable:

$$P_R = P_T G_T G_R G_{BT_r} \left(\frac{c^2}{16\pi^2 f^2 d_1 d_2} \right)^2 \tag{18.6}$$

The procedures that are outlined in the information that has been provided above are the primary means by which rectennas are fed. As part of the approach that we followed for each technique, we went through the process of looking at the models that were accessible in the literature. Before beginning the process of constructing the circuit, it is essential to take these models into account. This is due to the fact that they make it possible to estimate the amount of energy that can be harvested [57], which is essential to the functioning of the circuit. In the following, we will talk about the fundamentals of the architectural design of RF/DC converters, which are also often referred to as receiving antennas.

18.5 RECTENNA DESIGN ISSUES

Figure 18.1 illustrates the many procedures that are taken into consideration during the manufacturing of an RF/DC converter. The transducer, which is also often referred to as the antenna, is the component that is accountable for the collection of radio frequency (RF) power. This is due to the fact that it is the first link in the chain. It is possible to determine the magnitude of this power by using one of the feeding methods that will be described in further depth in the paragraphs that follow. The signal is shaped by means of an RF/DC converter, which is often built around Schottky diodes. This is because of the reason stated above. The implementation of a matching network that achieves the lowest potential reflection losses takes place during the third stage of the design process. A DC–DC converter is necessary in order to alter the amount of energy that is provided to the load or storage element. This is the last but not the least requirement. In the following sections, we will go into additional depth about the designs that were applied to each of these distinct components. In order to be more specific, we will need to provide an explanation of the properties of the blocks, while also bringing attention to the factors that determine the extent to which they are reliant on one another [58].

18.5.1 The receiving antenna

As a result of the fact that the performance of the receiving antenna is what defines how well the rectenna performs, the receiving antenna is a vital link in the chain. First, we will present a simple description of the basic features of the antenna, and then we will move to a discussion of the different techniques that have been proposed for generating power levels that are possible.

18.5.2 Main features of the receiving antenna

The effectiveness of the radio frequency energy harvesting apparatus is significantly influenced by the radiation characteristics of the receiving antenna. This connection is strong. The most important aspects of this list are the impedance bandwidth, polarisation, radiation pattern (directivity), and operating frequency. Gain is also a highly important factor. This list also includes impedance bandwidth. There are two more design limits that need to be taken into account, and these are the size of the antenna and its sensitivity. The sensitivity of an antenna is directly proportional to its efficiency in collecting energy and its ability to work with a relatively modest level of input power. This is because the sensitivity of an antenna is directly proportional to its efficiency. It is vitally important for the receiving antenna to have a low profile because of the miniscule size of the sensors. This is because the sensors are so small [2].

18.5.2.1 Receiving antenna operating frequency

Either the frequency of the signal that is being sent or the frequencies that are accessible from the position of the sensor node may be used to determine the operating frequency of the antenna. Both of these methods are viable options. In this part, we will explain the distinctions that exist between a single-band antenna and a multi-band or wideband antenna. Multi-band and wideband antennas are the greatest options for collecting energy from the world around you. It is possible to harvest energy from the environment. With a dedicated power supply (WPT), on the other hand, single-band antennas are more suitable for usage than other types of antennas.

18.5.2.2 Receiving antenna gain

No matter what feed strategy is used, an antenna that has a high gain will increase in terms of the amount of power that it is able to absorb. This is true regardless of the kind of antenna that is being utilised. When it comes to compensating for the losses that were incurred while taking part in the World Poker Tour, it is even more important to generate a significant gain. On the other hand, a gain that is not very high is sufficient for ambient energy harvesting systems. This is due to the fact that, as will be shown in the following statement, an increase in gain often corresponds to a larger antenna:

$$G_R = \frac{4\pi A_e f}{c} \tag{18.7}$$

where G_R represents the gain of the receiving antenna, A_e represents the effective area of the antenna, c represents the speed of light, and f represents the operational frequency.

18.5.2.3 Receiving antenna radiation pattern

The radiation pattern is a crucial aspect that plays a part in determining the amount of energy that may be effectively collected over a period of time. In the following paragraphs, we will discuss the two types of diagrams, which are referred to as directed and omnidirectional illustrations. Omnidirectional patterns are more ideal for use in the process of gathering ambient energy. This is due to the fact that it is not feasible to determine the direction in which the waves that are incident are going. In order to accomplish the goals of this WPT, patterns that are very directed are sufficient [59].

18.5.2.4 Receiving antenna polarisation

Polarisation is the technique that allows the antenna to reflect waves in the same direction that they came from. This allows the antenna to capture and transmit waves. When the polarisation of the transmitting antenna is compared to the polarisation of the receiving antenna, the ratio that is employed is what determines the efficacy of the antenna in terms of polarisation. In order to determine the quantity of power that is received by the antenna, it is required to determine the polarisation efficiency of the antenna. There are three different polarisation patterns that may be used for an antenna: linear, circular, and elliptical. All of these patterns are conceivable. In energy harvesting applications, circular polarisation is chosen because it is able to maintain a constant output voltage independent of the rotation of the transmitting antenna or rectenna. This is the reason why circular polarisation is recommended [60].

18.5.2.5 Receiving antenna bandwidth and size

In order to concurrently collect energy from a variety of various sources, it is advised to make use of the frequency range that is the most extensive that is now accessible. The reflection coefficient is considered to be broadband if it is lower than a certain amount, which is typically 10 dB. Broadband frequency fluctuation is characterised by this characteristic. In order to identify the frequency range that an antenna is able to receive signals across, this particular figure is used. A precise explanation of the reflection coefficient, which is represented by the symbol Γ, may be found in the following formulation:

$$\Gamma = \frac{Z_a - Z_b}{Z_a + Z_s} \tag{18.8}$$

Where Z_a is the antenna impedance and Z_s is the source impedance

The following illustrates a connection that exists between the bandwidth BW of an antenna and its quality factor Q as well as its resonant frequency f_R. This relationship may be observed in operation:

$$BW = \frac{f_R}{Q} \tag{18.9}$$

To fit the Wireless Sensor's extremely tiny volume, which is just a few millimetres in size, it is important for the receiving antennas to be compact and embeddable. This is because the dimensions of the Wireless Sensor are so small. As a consequence of the reduction in the size of the antennas, the bandwidth is increased, which in turn leads to a decrease in the quality factor. Consequently, this is going to take place as a consequence of the decrease in size. In contrast, Equation 18.9, which illustrates that this drop will have an impact on the gain of the antenna, demonstrates that this decrease will have an effect. The fundamental restriction between antenna size and efficiency is that, given a wave that is emitted at frequency f, the electrically tiny antenna must have a maximum dimension that is less than $1 = c/2\pi f$ and must be enclosed within a sphere of radius a with $ka < 1$. This requires the antenna to be enclosed within a sphere with a radius of a and a ka value that is less than 1. A symbol that represents the wave vector is k. Utilising this information, we are able to determine the basic limit that establishes the relationship between efficiency, effectiveness, and the size of the antenna. Taking into consideration the above definition, the element with the lowest quality that enables the least amount of losses to occur in this specific case is as follows [2]:

$$Q \geq \frac{1}{k^3 a^3} + \frac{1}{ka} \tag{18.10}$$

18.6 LEADING SOLUTIONS COMMONLY USED TO ACHIEVE USABLE POWER LEVELS

It is vital to establish a middle ground between the various aspects of the receiving antenna in order to maximise the amount of power that can be collected while maintaining dimensions that are acceptable. This may be accomplished by finding a balance between the various features. In order to express the conversion efficiency of the antenna, the symbol η_{ant} is used. This efficiency is calculated by taking into account losses in various components, including dielectrics and conductors.

$$\eta_{ant} = \frac{(1 - \Gamma^2)R_r}{R_r + R_m} \tag{18.11}$$

In this particular context, the symbol Γ is used to represent the reflection coefficient, R_r is used to represent the radiation resistance, and R_m is used to indicate the resistance experienced by the antenna in terms of material loss.

For the purpose of achieving the objective of maximising the antenna conversion efficiency while simultaneously maintaining a volume that is adequate, the design method makes use of materials that have a high dielectric constant and a low loss. Different types of antennas have been proposed as potential solutions for radio frequency energy harvesting. These antennas come in a wide variety of shapes and sizes. Dipole, patch, fractal, and spiral antennas are just examples of the types of antennas covered here. Patch antennas are the ones that get the most admiration compared to the others. This is due to their reasonable cost, small size, and ease of integration into a system. On the other hand, dielectric resonator antennas (DRAs) have surpassed them in popularity because they are more flexible, have fewer space constraints, and have a restricted bandwidth to work with. However, they do have certain limitations.

Dielectric resonators are distinguished by their high permittivity, low dielectric losses, and temperature stability at the resonance frequency. These characteristics are what set them apart from semiconductor resonators. Resonators made of dielectric material are used in a wide range of applications. To the greatest degree, these characteristics are what set dielectric resonators apart from regular resonators. The ability of these antennas to change their emission pattern in order to correlate with a wide range of exciting modes is yet another characteristic that this kind of antenna has. Keeping in mind that the RF/DC converter is the one responsible for shaping the power of the antenna and that the converter has a power threshold that it cannot work beyond, it is essential to keep this in mind. Radio frequency energy harvesting may be accomplished in a number of different methods, some of the most well-known of which being antenna arrays, reconfigurable antennas, and multi-band antennas. Additionally, multi-band antennas are an alternative option. In order to accomplish their goal, these systems are designed to generate an amount of electricity that is easily accessible [2].

18.6.1. Multi-band antenna

When people think about collecting the ambient radio frequency (RF) energy that is available as a consequence of the functioning of telecommunications equipment, the majority of people think of multi-band antennas rather than single-band antennas. There are a large number of techniques that may be used in order to increase the quantity of power that is gathered via the utilisation of radio frequency energy throughout a broad spectrum of frequency bands.

$$P_R = \sum_{i=1}^{n} P_{f_i} \tag{18.12}$$

In the equation that is shown here, P_R stands for the total power that the antenna has received, n stands for the number of frequencies, and P_{fi} stands for the power that has been received at the ith frequency.

There is a possibility that multi-band antennas that take into account the pi-shaped radiating components are something that may be observed rather often. When trying to get the best possible performance, it is essential to keep in mind that the capabilities of this antenna in terms of performance may vary dramatically over a number of different frequency bands. One example of such a notion is a triple-band antenna that is able to operate at 440 MHz, 1200 MHz, and 2.36 GHz. This antenna makes use of a Rogers RO4350 patch and has the capability to operate at all three frequencies.

After performing measurements at a frequency of 2.015 GHz, it was discovered that the gain value of 2.64 dBi was the highest achieved. A conversion efficiency of 61.3% was observed for frequencies spanning to 1.531 GHz, which is the best attainable efficiency for this conversion. DRAs might also be used for the acquisition of multi-band antennas with improved gain, which is an additional application that could exist for them. The proposed design ensures that there will be a 4.5 dBi increase in both performance and efficiency. With matching conversion efficiencies of 23.6% and 22.2%, respectively, it allows the efficient harvesting of radio frequency (RF) energy in the frequency ranges of 5.231–5.381 GHz and 5.455–7.7 GHz, with an input power of 11 dBm. Other frequency ranges that may be harvested include 5.455–7.7 GHz. If you are interested in enhancing this performance to the next level, you might consider obtaining additional antennas that are capable of being reconfigured [2].

18.6.2 Reconfigurable antenna

When people speak about the reconfigurability of an antenna, they are referring to its capacity to have both its radiation qualities and its signal characteristics adjusted. Making a modification to the antenna's design is one way in which this aim may be achieved. When employing a single antenna, it is possible to create a reasonable balance between the size of the antenna and the bandwidth of the signal. To make the antenna capable of being reconfigured on demand, a common way involves cutting holes into the surface of the radiating element and connecting neighbouring surfaces with switches. This is done in order to make the antenna more adaptable. There is a method that is exclusive to patch antennas that involves the use of PIN diodes for the purpose of switching applications [61].

When they are turned on, PIN diodes fulfil the role of a resistor; but, when they are turned off, they perform the job of a capacitor if they are given the opportunity to do so. Consequently, the patch current distribution as well as the resonance frequency are both susceptible to change in this way. This may be seen in reference 64, which details a tiny rectenna that works at frequencies of 5.2 GHz and 5.8 GHz, with conversion efficiencies of 26.5% and 69.4%, respectively. This is an example of what can be seen in reference 64. From the very beginning of the manufacturing process, the BAP51-02 type PIN diodes are used in order to produce the switches. It was shown in the part that came before this one that reconfigurability is often only accessible on two frequency bands in the vast majority of applications.

However, depending on the position of the sensor, there may be more than two bands of radio frequency sources that contribute to the ambient environment. This variation is dependent on the sensor's location.

18.6.3 Array antennas

The utilisation of antenna arrays is now being investigated for potential use in radio frequency (RF) energy harvesting. This is being done as a method of circumventing the limitations that are associated with the utilisation of a single receiving antenna. When a number of antenna components are taken into account, it is possible to get the overall power of an array of antennas by adding the output powers of those antenna components. For the goal of ambient energy collecting in four different frequency bands. The DTV, GSM440, GSM540, and 3G frequency bands are the ones at question here. The purpose of this post is to bring attention to this idea. In the beginning, the outputs of the rectennas are connected in series, and the energy is first shaped before being stored using the same circuit. This is done in order to ensure stability [2].

One of the problems that develops as a result of this setup is the fact that the current passes through all of the rectennas that are connected in series. One of the many problems with this design is that each rectenna is unable to work at its optimum power point because of this condition. This is only one of the many problems that this design has. When it comes to the energy that it has accumulated, every rectenna is responsible for its own one-of-a-kind processing. Because of the parallel design, every rectenna has the capacity to operate at its greatest effective powerpoint. This will allow for optimal performance. One thing that should be taken into consideration is that the use of four separate circuits for the purpose of managing the energy output of each rectenna leads to an increase in the overall quantity of components that are associated with complexity. When employing the antenna array approach, more circuits are still required to handle signals originating from a broad range of sources. This is the case despite the fact that this method increases the amount of power that can be gathered by 20. As a result of this, additional circuits are still required.

Following the presentation of a condensed review of the criteria for receiving antennas in the preceding part, the following section will delve into the topic of RF/DC conversion and its ramifications.

18.7 THE RF/DC CONVERTER

The wireless sensors are supplied with an adequate amount of power as a consequence of the direct current (DC) energy that is produced as a result of the radio frequency (RF) energy that is received by the antenna. This is the reason why it gets pushed aside in the first place. The use of Schottky diodes or CMOS technology is one method that may be utilised to accomplish this objective. Concurrent metal-oxide semiconductor (CMOS) diodes have a leakage current that is rather large, which leads to power loss and poor system efficiency. Despite the fact that Schottky diodes are more sensitive than complementary metal-oxide semiconductor (CMOS) technology, CMOS diodes have both of these qualities in common with Schottky diodes.

Therefore, in this part, we will limit our discussion to the conditions that rectifiers that are based on Schottky diodes are required to fulfil in order to be considered acceptable. From a more general perspective, the performance that the RF/DC converter is capable of accomplishing will be dictated by the design of the rectifier as well as the kind of diodes that are used.

18.7.1 Main features of Schottky diodes for RF energy harvesting

The ability of Schottky diodes to switch on quickly, the fact that their forward voltage drop is extremely tiny, the fact that they require very little power, and the fact that they have a little bit of a parasitic impact are some of the distinguishing characteristics that set them apart from conventional diodes such as the 1N400X series. These diodes are often used in the construction of antennas for several reasons, some of which include the high frequencies of radio frequency waves in addition to the ones that were discussed before. It is possible that the performance of the RF/DC converter will be affected by the operating frequency of the rectenna as well as the Schottky diode that is selected. This is a possibility. Figure 18.5 shows a representation of the low-frequency model of the Schottky diode that was developed in [21]. In this particular model, the breakdown voltage is represented by the symbol VB. The goal of displaying this model is to facilitate the process of doing circuit analysis. Skyworks, Macon, and Avago are the three companies that have the most significant market share in the software sector.

As can be seen in Figure 18.6, the diode is capable of converting all of the radio frequency (RF) energy that is sent through it into heat. In the context of electrical diodes, the word "Rs" refers to the series resistance, which is a crucial component. There is a decline in the RF/DC efficiency as a result of the very high resistance value. The equivalent resistance that is formed by the combination of a number of components, such as the bulk layer of the silicon substrate, bond wire, lead frame, and other components, is represented by this metric. This metric is a depiction of the relative resistance that is produced.

As can be seen in Figure 18.5, the video resistance, which is represented by the symbol R_j, goes through a transformation in response to the actual current that is passing through the diode. According to Equation 18.10, which can be found in reference [14], an increase in this resistance value that is more than 4 kΩ would result in an increase in the reflection coefficient. This would be the case if the resistance value was increased. The voltage that is present at the point where a metal and a semiconductor come into contact with one another is denoted by the symbolic value V_j. In particular, parasites are characterised by two characteristics: parasitic capacitance and parasitic inductance that they show. These two characteristics are very noticeable. A circuit is said to have "parasitics" when it has unwanted features that hinder its ability to function properly. It is possible that these features have their roots in either the mechanical or electrical realm. It is common practice to use the symbol LP to signify the inductance that is associated with the external metal terminations. These terminations are the ones that are accountable for connecting the internal component to the external circuit.

Because all solid-state packages have dielectric constants that are tied to capacitors, the capacitance CP is connected in parallel with the diode. This is because capacitors are coupled to dielectric constants. As can be seen in Figure 18.6, the symbol C_j is used to denote a nonlinear junction capacitance. The thickness of the epitaxial layer and the diameter of the Schottky diode are two of the characteristics that have an effect on the value of this capacitance. Other parameters include the number of parameters that are

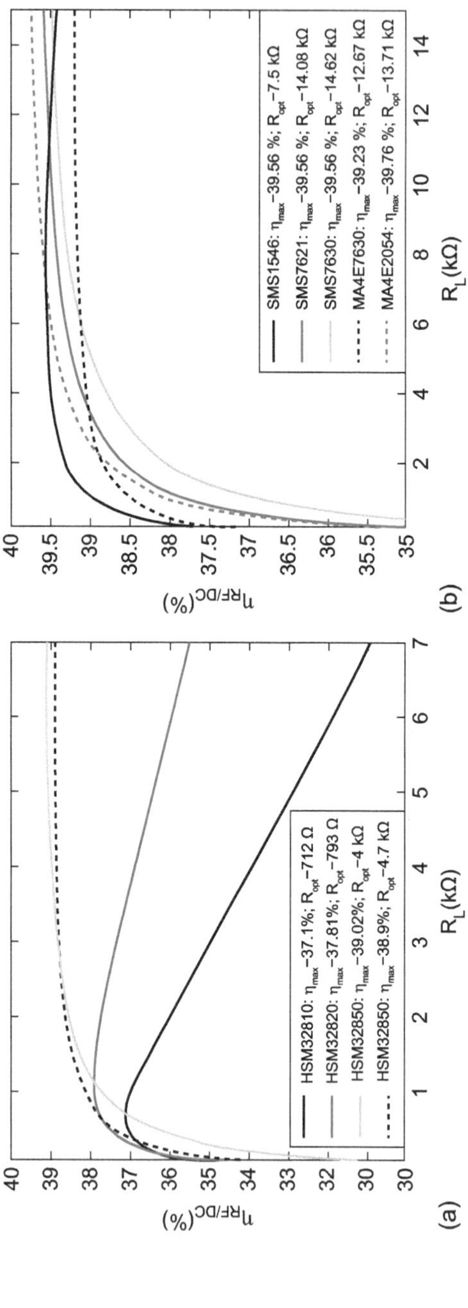

Figure 18.6 Optimal loads of commonly used diodes. (a) Avago diodes. (b) Skyworks and Macon diodes.

involved. In the event that the tuned frequency position varies as a consequence of different values of C_j, this leads to a mismatch in the resonant frequency [14].

The following image, which can be found in [22], illustrates how the value of C_j is dependent on the voltage that is produced by the RF/DC converter.

$$C_j = c_{j_0}\sqrt{\frac{V_j}{V_j + V_{DC}}} \tag{18.13}$$

where C_{j0} represents the zero bias junction capacitance of the diode and VDC represents the voltage across the load resistance for the diode.

The power level of the incident radio frequency, the frequency at which they operate, and the internal electrical parameters that determine the conversion efficiency of the device are all factors that have a significant impact on the sensitivity of Schottky diodes. The results of the calculation of the efficiency of the RF/DC conversion that was carried out in [22] are shown in the following. For the purpose of this computation, a diode that was connected in parallel with the receiving antenna was taken into account.

$$\eta_{RF/DC} = \frac{1}{1+A+B+C} \tag{18.14}$$

where $\eta_{RF/DC}$ is the RF/DC conversion efficiency with A, B, and C defined as follows:

$$\begin{cases} A = \dfrac{R_L}{\pi R_s}(1+\dfrac{V_j}{V_{DC}})^2\left[\theta_{on}(1+\dfrac{1}{2\cos^2\theta_{on}}) - 1,5\tan\theta_{on}\right] \\ B = \dfrac{R_s R_L C_j^2 \omega^2}{2\pi}(1+\dfrac{V_j}{V_{DC}})\left[\dfrac{\pi-\theta_{on}}{\cos^2\theta_{on}} + \tan\theta_{on}\right] \\ C = \dfrac{R_L}{\pi R_s}(1+\dfrac{V_j}{V_{DC}})\dfrac{V_j}{V_{DC}}\left[\tan\theta_{on} - \theta_{on}\right] \end{cases} \tag{18.15}$$

where the load resistance is denoted by R_L and the voltage across the load resistance is denoted by V_{DC}; the other parameters have been described in the previous section. The forward-bias turn-angle diode is expressed as θ_{on}. It is a variable that is dynamic and is determined by the power that is fed into the diode; its definition can be found in [22] as follows:

$$\tan\theta_{on} - \theta_{on} = \frac{\pi R_s}{RL(1+\dfrac{V_j}{V_{DC}})} \tag{18.16}$$

Figure 18.6 presents the results of an investigation into the connection that exists between the load resistance and the conversion efficiency of the diodes that are utilised the significant majority of the time. Additionally, Equations 18.8–18.10 are considered in this comparison. The electrical characteristics of the diodes are also taken into consideration. MATLAB software was used to carry out the study. The frequency at which operations are carried out is 440 megahertz, and the DC voltage that is desired is set at 2.7 V with the intention of achieving the desired results. Additionally, the text accompanying each image provides an explanation of the maximum potential conversion efficiency as well as the largest load resistance. The levels of efficiency are expected to drop anywhere from 30–40% in order to achieve the necessary performance in terms of direct current voltage. This is a regular occurrence. As can be seen in Figure 18.6a, it is conceivable to achieve the requisite performance at lower load resistances, and Avago diodes are able to do this. The HSMS 1344 diode is the best choice that can be chosen from because of the exceptional performance that it offers. The results that were achieved by the use of the Skyworks and Macon diodes are shown in Figure 18.6b. Despite the fact that the ideal resistances of these diodes are much higher than those of Avago diodes, the performance of these diodes is marginally better than that of Avago diodes.

The quantity of power that can be collected is a significant factor in determining the Schottky diode detection threshold, which is one of the most essential selection criteria. In Figure 18.7, the results that were obtained via the use of four different types of diodes are shown below [61].

The amount of the RF power that is input is taken into account in order to ascertain whether or not the RF/DC conversion is successful. Research in the 440 MHz, 2.45 GHz, 5.8 GHz, and Industrial Scientific and Medical (ISM) as shown in Figure 18.7 a–c band may be carried out with the assistance of the Advanced Design Software (ADS), which is used for this purpose. In [23], the simulated circuit that was taken into account was identical to the one that was used to contribute to the attainment of these findings. Figure 18.7d depicts the virtual circuit, which is then changed to that value.

Figure 18.8 clearly shows that the efficiency of the RF/DC conversion is at an exceedingly low level. Reflection losses are the consequence of the lack of a matching filter, which in turn leads to the observed values. For the purpose of detecting input power levels that are lower than 10 dBm, the SMS 7630 diode provides the highest possible degree of sensitivity overall. This is shown for the frequency bands that are 440 MHz and 2.45 GHz, respectively, in Figures 18.8a and 18.8b. The HSMS 1400 diode is now the most suited choice for these two frequency bands when it comes to wireless power transfer. This is because it produces the highest current density. This particular diode is capable of producing a maximum power output of 20 dB mA at its maximum capacity. Figure 18.8c demonstrates that the HSMS 1344 diode exhibits the highest degree of sensitivity while operating at a frequency of 5.8 GHz. This is the condition that is seen. When, on the other

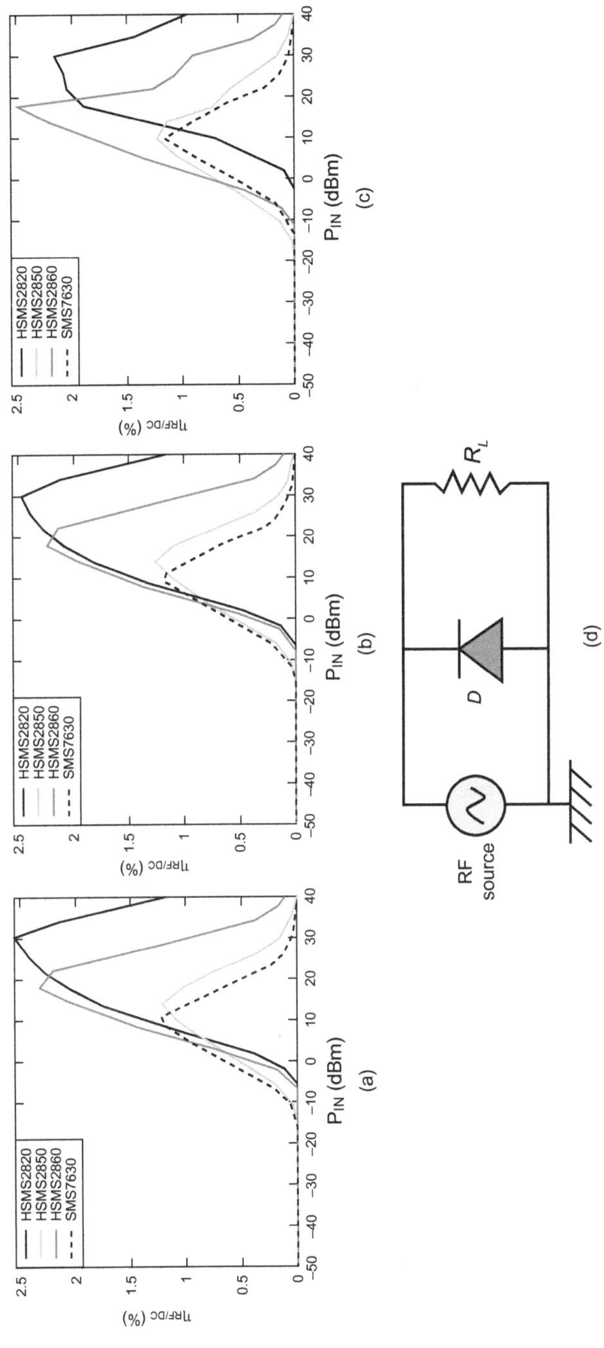

Figure 18.7 Comparison of the detection threshold of the diodes. (a) 440 MHz GSM band. (b) 2.45 GHz ISM band. (c) 5.8 GHz ISM band. (d). Schematic of the diode detection threshold.

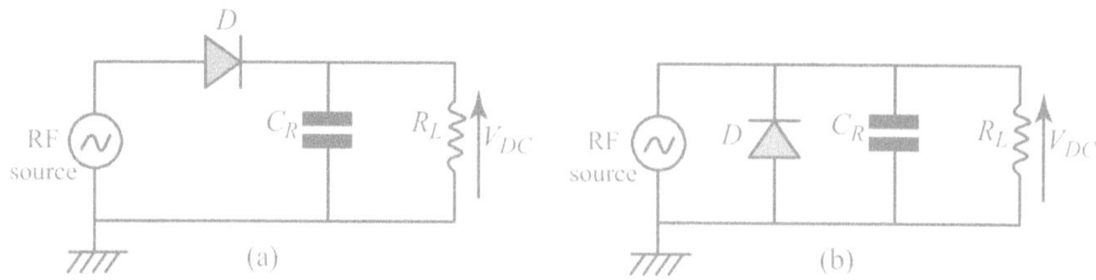

Figure 18.8 Half-wave rectifier topologies. (a) SSD. (b) SPD.

hand, the signal intensity is more than 5 dBm, the HSMS 1400 diode is the component that is most appropriate for the design application.

In this section, the information that has been provided illustrates that the efficiency of the RF/DC converter is dependent on the internal electrical characteristics of the rectifying diode. In the section that follows this one, we will discuss the potential impact that rectifier topology might have on the system [63].

18.8 MAIN RECTIFIER TOPOLOGIES

The topology determines the location of the diode or diodes in the circuit that is responsible for performing the rectifier function. This is one of the variables that is taken into consideration. In the following paragraphs, we will discuss about the three fundamental topologies, which are voltage multipliers, half-wave rectifiers, and full-wave rectifiers.

18.8.1 Half-wave rectifiers

Due to the fact that these topologies only make use of a single diode, the load system is only capable of receiving a single alternating radio frequency pulse. There are a few examples of devices that fall into this category, including the single parallel diode (SPD) and the single series diode (SSD). A representation of each of these pairings in their respective forms may be seen in Figure 18.8. A capacitor known as CR is used in order to filter the voltage that has been rectified. Half-wave topologies, which are comprised of a limited number of components, have the advantage of having a reduced degree of losses when compared to full-wave topologies. This is because half-wave topologies are composed of fewer components. As a result of this, they are completely suitable for energy-gathering processes that need just a little amount of power to be input.

On the other hand, when compared to full-wave topologies, it is still inefficient in terms of the amount of power that can be applied in a realistic setting. As an example, take into account the recommendation that was made in [24] for a reconfigurable rectenna that is capable of being altered in line with the RF input power level. When compared to the full-wave topology, which has a maximum efficiency of about 35%, the solid-state drive (SSD) design has an efficiency that is lower than 50%. On the other hand, the full-wave topology has a maximum efficiency of 50%. Rectenna designs primarily focus on full-wave topologies for a number of reasons; nonetheless, this is one of the most important considerations. Some of the reasons for this are as follows, as shown in Figures 18.18a and 18.18b.

18.8.2 Full-wave rectifier topologies

There is a substantial quantity of power that is given to the load in the case of these topologies, which are categorised as half-wave topologies. Two examples of the many various kinds of rectifiers that are available are the voltage doubler rectifier and the full-bridge (FB) rectifier. There are many more models of rectifiers as well. Figure 18.10, which may be viewed here, depicts each and every option that is even remotely imaginable. For the purpose of producing a direct current (DC) output voltage that is twice as high as that of an FB rectifier, a voltage doubler (VD) makes use of two filter capacitors rather than a single filter capacitor. Two distinct types of VDs are available, and they are the Schenkel VD (SVD) and the Latour VD (LVD). There is not a single voltage doubler that performs noticeably worse than the others in terms of performance when it comes to the DC voltage output.

The rectifier architecture that is used is primarily governed by two criteria. The first factor is the utilisation of the conversion efficiency, which is represented by the symbol η . The second component is the voltage of the DC output, which is often abbreviated as VDC. It may be said that the following is the relationship that exists between these two variables and the RF input power, the PIN, and the RL, which is also referred to as the load resistance [2]:

$$\eta(\%) = 100 \times \frac{V_{DC}^2}{R_L . P_{IN}} \tag{18.17}$$

The three various topologies of rectifiers, which are SSD, FB, and VD, which are all based on the HSMS 1344 Schottky diode, are compared in Figure 18.9a–d. This figure illustrates the comparison of the performances that are supplied by each of these rectifiers. In this specific comparison, the filtering capacitance is set at 3.3 pF, and the comparison is carried out for that particular value. All simulations are carried out using ADS software.

The information presented below clearly shows that, among all the topologies that were taken into account, the VD topology shows the highest level of performance across the entire input power range. A further conclusion that can be drawn from these observations is that the design of an SSD is

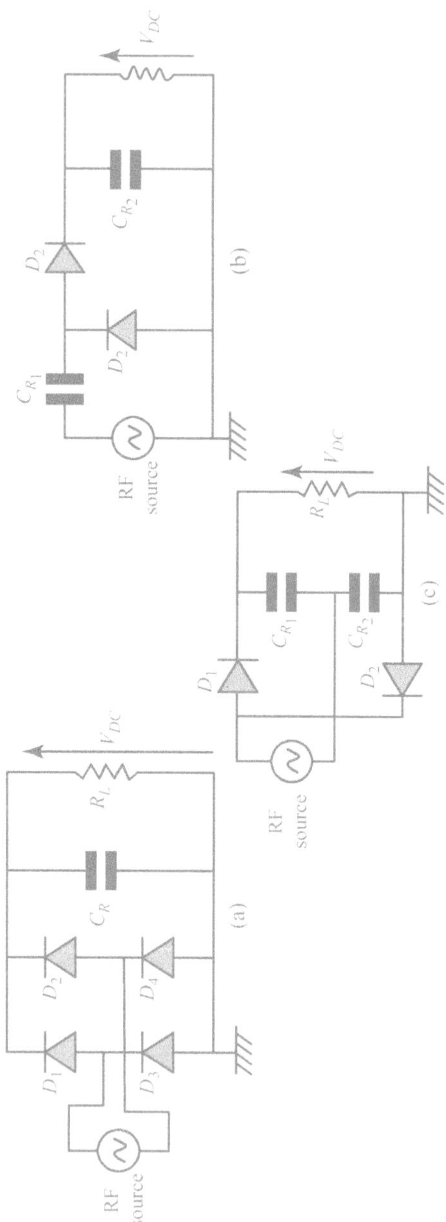

Figure 18.9 Full-wave rectifier topologies. (a) FB. (b). SVD. (c) LVD.

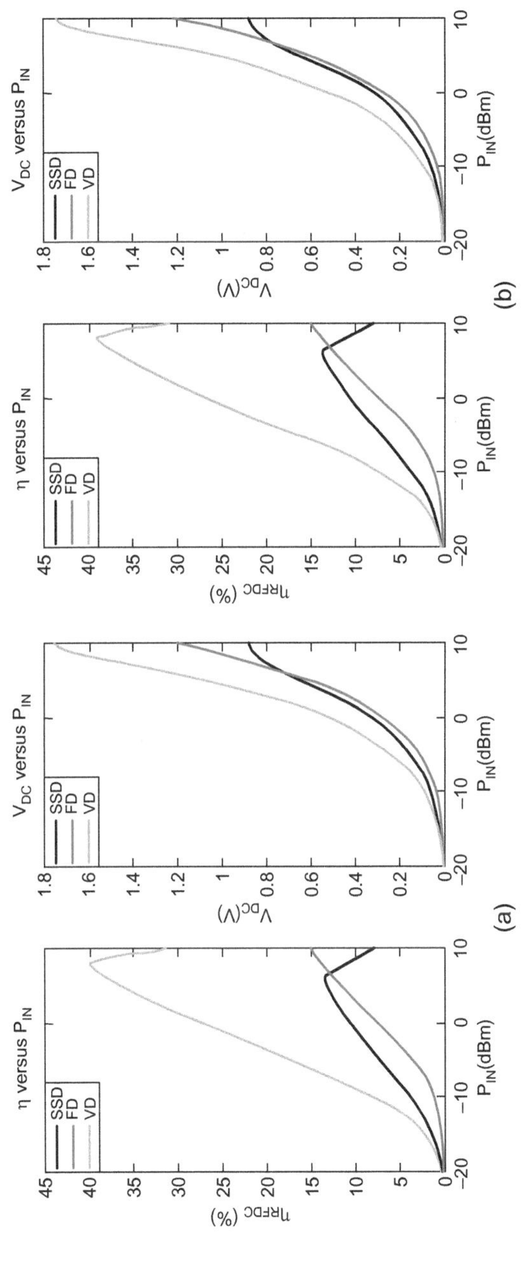

Figure 18.10 Performance comparison of main commonly used rectifier topologies. (a) 440 MHz GSM band. (b) 2.45 GHz ISM band.

preferable to that of an FB rectifier in conditions when the noise level is less than 5 dBm. The authors of [24] used this performance comparison in order to design a reconfigurable rectenna that was in line with the kind of rectifier that they were working with. Although the recommended rectenna may function with an input power of 5 dBm while operating with the SSD configuration, we decided to go with the FB topology since it enables us to collect energy successfully at an input level of 15 dBm. Based on the data shown in Figure 18.11, it is concluded that VD rectifiers continue to be the most common option for rectenna designs. Aside from this, they also provide the possibility of using combinations that are known as multi-stage voltage doubler structures. These structures are able to further magnify the DC output voltage of the rectifier, which is a significant advantage.

18.8.3 Multistage voltage doublers (MSVD) rectifiers

There is the potential for antennas to achieve even greater improvements in their DC output voltage performance with the aid of voltage multiplier rectifiers. The combinations that have been reported the most often are shown in Figure 18.1, which may be seen here. Figure 18.1a illustrates a rectifier conceptualised and developed by Greinacher [25]. To be more specific, the rectifier in question is a voltage multiplier with two stages that were accomplished by the use of a bridge. Due to the arrangement of the diodes, the bias voltage for each consecutive diode is created by the output of the diode that comes immediately before it. This is because the diodes are placed in a certain manner. The need for a separate power source, which was previously necessary, is no longer necessary as a result of this. It is possible to locate the Cockcroft–Walton n-stage voltage multiplier rectifier, which is also known as the Villard voltage multiplier [26]. The output voltage of a voltage multiplier is referred to as the direct current voltage (DCV), and the input voltage level (V_{in}) and the number of stages (n) are connected to their respective outputs.

$$V_{DCOC} = 2n(V_{in} - V_{th}) \tag{18.18}$$

Here, V_{DCOC} is the voltage in the open circuit and V_{th} is the voltage drop in the forward direction.

Increasing the voltages that are output by the antenna is something that may be accomplished via the use of voltage multipliers. When determining whether or not the conversion process is successful, one of the most important design parameters to take into account is the number of phases, which is often referred to as n [27]. Figure 18.12 provides an analysis of a voltage multiplier that has a maximum of ten steps. This figure may be found at that location. The simulations are carried out using ADS software, and

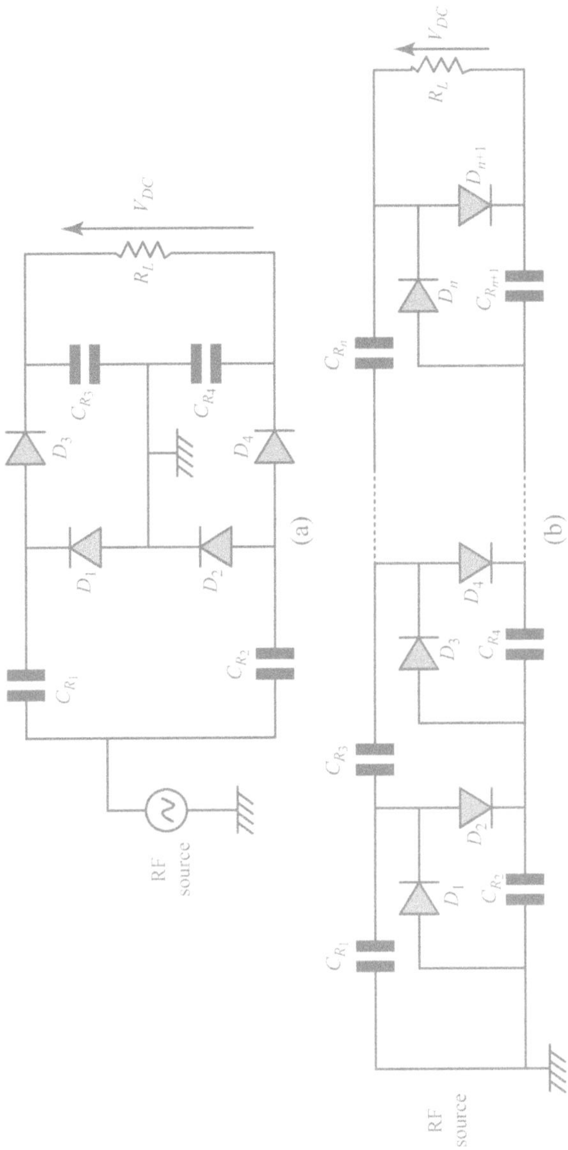

Figure 18.11 Voltages multiplier topologies. (a) Greinacher rectifier configuration. (b) Cockcroft–walton voltage multiplier.

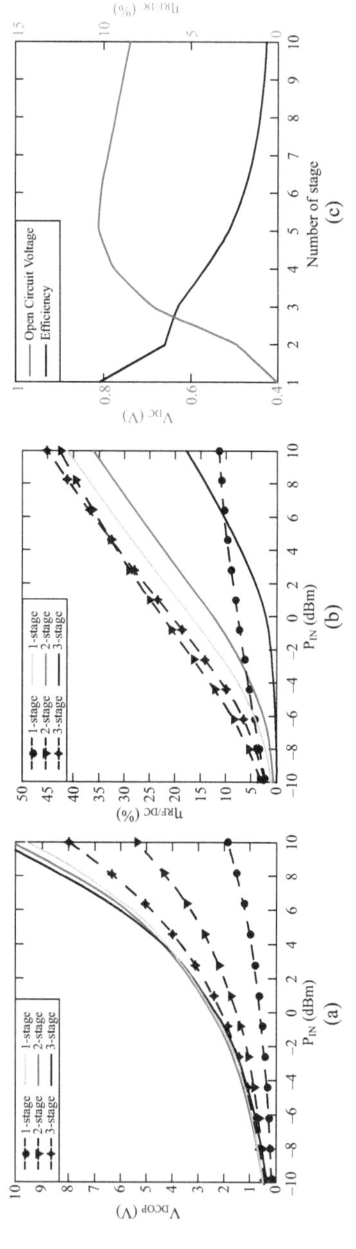

Figure 18.12 Performance comparison of multistage rectifiers. (a) Voltage. (b) Efficiency. (c) The trade-off between voltage and efficiency.

the research studies are based on the features of the Avago Schottky diode HSMS 1344 and its properties.

As can be seen in Figure 18.12a, the DC output voltage increases in a way that is precisely proportional to the number of steps that are involved in the process. Following the completion of the fourth stage of development, the advantages will no longer be of significant importance. Alternatively, Figure 18.12b illustrates that the efficiency of the RF/DC conversion diminishes as the number of circuit stages increases. This is shown by the fact that the number of circuit stages increases. A radio frequency (RF) intensity of -8 dBm is applied to the rectenna, as can be seen in Figure 18.12c. Adjusting the number of stages, which is represented by the symbol n in the equation, allows for the conversion efficiency and open-circuit DC voltage to be adjusted at each iteration. According to the results, it has been shown that a voltage multiplier that consists of three stages may be used to give a compromise for the quantity of radio frequency power that is being imported.

18.9 THE MATCHING FILTER

18.9.1 General principle and main features

The harmonics of the operating frequency are caused by the non-linear behaviour of the diodes used in RF/DC conversion. Re-radiated harmonics that interfere with waves related to the fundamental frequency ultimately lead to a decrease in the performance of the rectenna. This is the final outcome of the interference. Additionally, the matching filter is responsible for preventing harmonics from being formed by the rectifier circuits. This is done in order to avoid harmonics from being produced. Figure 18.6 shows a visual representation of the matching principle in action, and from a mathematical point of view, it is achieved when the following conditions are satisfied:

$$\begin{aligned} Z_{e1} &= Z_e * 2 \\ Z_{e3} &= Z_e * 4 \end{aligned} \tag{18.19}$$

where Z_{e1} represents the output impedance of the antenna, which is typically 50 Ω, Z_{e2} represents the input impedance of the matching filter as seen from the antenna, Z_{e3} represents the output impedance of the matching filter as seen by the rectifier circuit, and Z_{e4} represents the input impedance of the rectifier circuit as seen by the matching filter. The analogous symbols for Z_{e2} and Z_{e4} are $Z_e * 2$ and $Z_e * 4$, which represent the conjugate complexes of Z_{e2} and Z_{e4}, respectively. The matching filter must be able to match the antenna and rectifier circuit regardless of the amount of input power or the frequency at which it is operating in order for the rectenna to work correctly. This is necessary for the rectenna to function successfully.

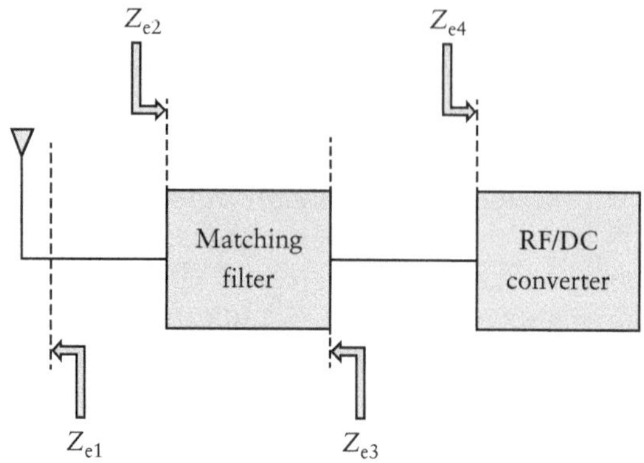

Figure 18.13 The principle of the impedance matching.

Because of this, it is essential for the filter to have a low quality factor and a very small form factor (Figure 18.13).

18.9.2 Main impedance matching techniques

There are many different ways in which the concept shown in Figure 18.5 can be realized. To illustrate the most efficient approach, Figure 18.6 presents the use of the shunt stub [55].In order to bring the antenna component into alignment with the rectifier circuit, this technique involves adjusting the lengths of the components. The goal of this adjustment is to bring the antenna component into alignment. By adjusting the length *l*l of the section, it is possible to modify its susceptance within the shunt. This allows the section's susceptance to match, in magnitude, the susceptance at the connection point, but in opposite phase. The three fundamental electrical components—resistor (R), inductor (L), and capacitor (C)—must be considered during the design of matching networks. This will make it possible for the susceptance of the section to be equal in terms of amplitude to the susceptance from the connection point, but it will be in phase opposition to the susceptance of the section. R, L, and C are the three basic electrical components that must be taken into mind throughout the process of establishing matching networks. It is essential to take these components into account. The real section of the impedance may be reshaped into a different form with the assistance of resistance, which brings about this transformation. On the other hand, in order to achieve the transformation of the imaginary portion, we make use of the reactive components, L and C.

Therefore, the adaptation generally simply takes into account the fictitious component of the impedance [28]. This is because resistors in matching filters typically cause losses inside the circuit. This is the reason why this condition occurs. In the realm of matching filters for rectennas, the transformer coupling and the LC network are widely acknowledged to be two of the most highly significant filters [28, 29]. Both of these filters are used by a significant number of people across the world. Figure 18.8 illustrates a variety of well-known topologies that are often seen in practice. Just by taking a cursory glance at this image, it is feasible to see that LC filters may be of the L-, π-, or Tee-type. A comparison of the features and performances that may be obtained with these distinct filter settings has been described in [64–66]. This comparison can be found in the aforementioned references.

A voltage doubler rectifier and other multistage voltage doublers with 3, 5, and 7 stages were taken into account throughout the process of defining these properties in [28]. This was done in order to ensure that the characteristics were accurately described. As far as the design is concerned, the HSMS 1346 diode was taken into account. As a result of comprehensive analysis of all relevant parameters, it has been shown that L-type filters provide higher performance in comparison to π-type filters when it comes to the efficiency of conversion. The use of pi-type filters, on the other hand, makes it possible to draw from a more extensive bandwidth. When it comes to the DC output voltage levels, Tee-type filters perform far better than their predecessors did by a substantial margin.

Using a three-stage voltage multiplier rectifier in combination with an HSMS 139B diode as the basis for a 440 MHz rectenna design yielded the same findings as the prior study [30]. Furthermore, the results of the previous research were identical to those achieved.

When one makes use of the idea that is shown in Figure 18.14, one is able to arrive at analytical conclusions about the selection of filter component values in accordance with the filter design and characteristics in terms of bandwidth (quality factor). ADS software, on the other hand, is relied upon by the vast majority of designers when it comes to establishing the size of the matching filter. The capabilities of this programme, which permit the adjustment of the components of the filter, may be used to establish a good

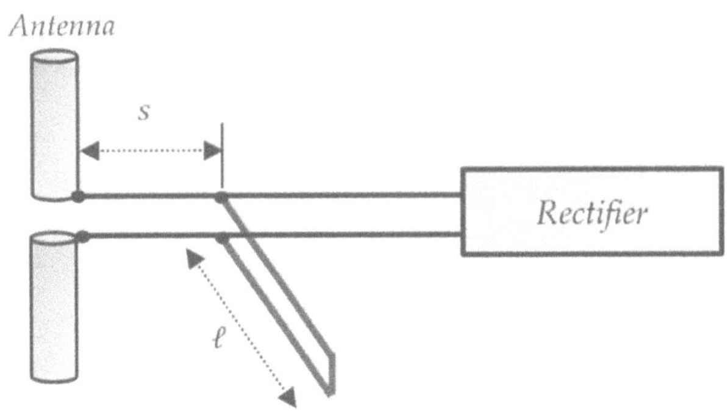

Figure 18.14 Shunt stub matching technique.

match between the antenna and the rectifier. This can be accomplished by using the capabilities of this programme. When calculating the values of the L and C components, the ADS Matching utility tool takes into account the filter configuration that was chosen. This is done for the purpose of finding the values of the components.

Additional optimisation elements that provide the user the ability to change component values have been included into the software in order to make it easier for the user to accomplish the specific objectives that they have set for themselves. Concurrently, we are striving to raise the DC voltage and improve the efficiency of the conversion. This is happening at the same time as we are looking at various methods that may be used to lower the reflection coefficient. The programme takes into account the gradient technique and Newton's method, which are the two most significant optimisation methods. Both of these techniques are examples of optimisation methods.

There is a demonstration of each and every one of these methodology techniques in [20]. The schematics that were generated in line with the design of the filter are shown in Figure 18.15. These schematics were developed by utilising the processes that were mentioned in the previous study. In these diagrams, it is possible to see a voltage-multiplier rectifier that consists of three stages simultaneously. The study relies on the properties of the Schottky HSMS 1344 diode, which has a load resistance of 5 kΩ. These qualities serve as the basis upon which the research is carried out. This measurement corresponds to the ideal load that the three-stage voltage doubler rectifier ought to have been applied to in order to achieve the desired results. Figure 18.19 provides a comparison of the simulated performance that was

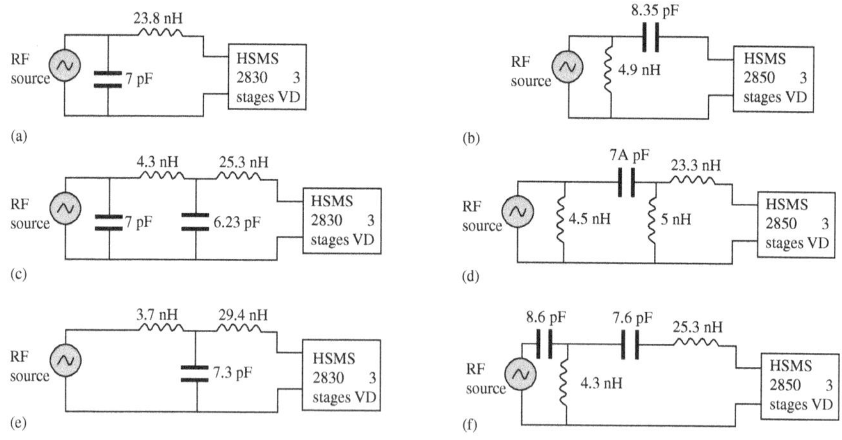

Figure 18.15 Developed matching filters for a voltage amplifier with three stages. (a) L lowpass.(b)Lhighpass.(c)πlowpass.(d)πhighpass.(e)Teelowpass.(f)Teehighpass.

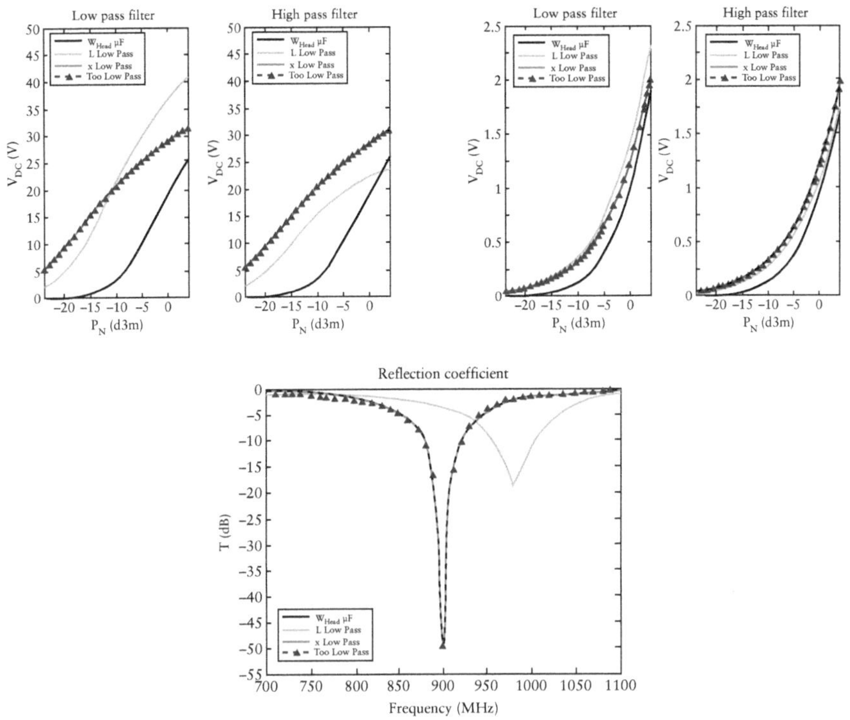

Figure 18.16 Comparative analysis of the performance obtained with different filter designs was performed. (a) Efficiency. (b) Voltage. (c) Reflection coefficient.

achieved with various combinations of ADS programme settings for the filter; this comparison was carried out with the help of such configurations.

In the process of reviewing Figure 18.16, it becomes apparent that the overall performance that is generated by the π-type and Tee-type filter topologies is significantly similar to one another. Figure 18.16c displays reflection coefficients that are more advantageous than the two topologies that are now being studied. This is because the reflection coefficients are given in the figure.

In spite of the fact that this is the case, it is exactly under these conditions that an L-low-pass filter achieves its highest possible level of performance in terms of both the DC voltage performance and the conversion efficiency. In the same way as rectifiers and antennas are, it is essential to take into account the trade-off that occurs between the filter bandwidth and the conversion efficiency. This is something that must be done. This data includes an overview of the techniques that were utilised to construct the matching filters, how each configuration responded to different levels of RF power that were supplied, and the inner workings of the diodes that were used.

18.10 DC/DC CONVERTER

It is possible that the rectifier's output voltage or power is insufficient to provide the storage device or WS with the required quantity of energy. This is the case in the majority of cases. The fact that this is the case demonstrates that the DC/DC converter makes it possible to adjust the voltage in line with the load when it is present. There is a need that a controller that is capable of providing maximum power point tracking (MPPT) must come before the rectifier. This is because the conversion efficiency of the rectifier is dependent on the load resistance. The purpose of maximum power point tracking, also known as MPPT, is to maximise the amount of power that is generated by adjusting the voltage or current in such a way that it is in accordance with the curve that represents the relationship between the current and the voltage of the receiving antenna.

Buck converters and boost converters are the two forms of DC/DC converters that are used the most often. This is despite the fact that there are a vast number of different types of DC/DC converters. When choosing the converter, it is crucial to take into consideration not only the voltage values of the rectifier (V_{rect}) but also the supply voltage of the storage device that is being connected to the converter. The use of the boost converter seen in Figure 18.10 is a common procedure that is utilised throughout the process of acquiring radio frequency energy. The combination of the inductor L and the PMOS transistor switches results in the production of a DC voltage output that is not only controllable but also consistent. A square wave, which is created by an external oscillator and constitutes a component of the signal, is what makes up the gate control signal of a PMOS transistor. This signal indicates that the transistor is operating properly. If the input voltage V_{rect} supplied to the converter is low, the converter will produce an output voltage V_{Load}.. The production of the control signal occurs in the case that the voltage feedback makes it possible to provide the oscillator with power (Figure 18.17).

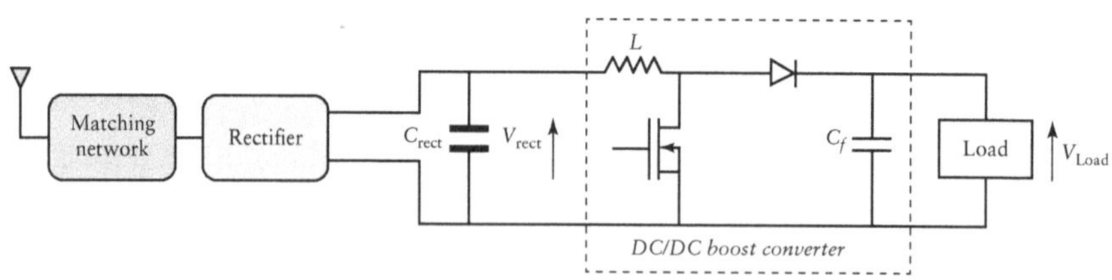

Figure 18.17 Structure of DC/DC boost converter.

18.10.1 Main features and techniques for optimising DC/DC conversion efficiency

However, the control circuit of the PMOS transistor is where the majority of the design's complexity lies. It was previously said that the operation of the DC/DC converter was detailed in a short amount of time. There are often a number of switches included in this circuit. Furthermore, switching signal comparators are included into these switches, which are generally based on NMOS transistors. A number of various parameters, one of which is the amount of power that is lost in the oscillator circuit, have an effect on the overall conversion efficiency of the rectenna at the same time.

Either a low-frequency oscillator and a high-frequency oscillator, or even just a single oscillator, are used by the vast majority of operational systems. As a consequence, an increase in the number of components in a circuit leads to an increase in the total amount of losses occurring inside the circuit. In order to solve this unfavourable feature, one of the probable solutions that might be implemented is the use of an astable multivibrator that is founded on a single oscillator circuit and makes use of a comparator that is biased from the outside. The comparator is used in [14], which employs the LTC300 nano-power detector, which has a switching inductance of 330 μH. This serves as an illustration of the concept. The voltage was effectively increased from 0.5 V to 2.15 V using the circuit.

Ensuring that the input impedance of the boost converter is capable of emulating the optimal load of the antenna is yet another way that may be used to transmit the greatest amount of power. Following is a definition of the emulation resistor Rem that takes into account all that has been said:

$$R_{em} = \frac{2L}{ft_1^2 k}\left(1 - \frac{V_{rect}}{V_{Load}}\right) \tag{18.20}$$

where L is the inductance, f represents the frequency of the external oscillator, t_1 is the time at which the control circuit switch is turned on, k is the boost converter pulse duty cycle at low frequency, V_{rect} is the rectifier output voltage, and V_{Load} is the boost converter load voltage. In the event when the incident power is 260 μW and the switching inductance is 130 μH, it is feasible to achieve a conversion efficiency of around 44% by using an emulation resistance technique. By following the methods outlined in reference [31], this objective can be achieved. "Particle swarm optimisation" is another term for this technology, which is an alternative to resistance emulation. Together, these two techniques work to increase the boost converter efficiency.

The objective is to determine the inductor and on-time values that will result in the most efficient operation feasible by using the particle swarm optimisation approach. This will allow for the most effective operation conceivable. When the DC/DC converter was not there, the insertion of the emulation resistor that was described in [32] into this technique resulted in a 9.15% increase in the efficiency of the conversion. This improvement was compared to the circumstance in which the DC/DC converter was not present. Due to the fact that it uses less than 30 dBm of power, the converter in [33] has the potential to achieve an efficiency of 41.7%. The aforementioned factors all contribute to the need for DC/DC converters, in addition to the design problems that are involved in the process of installing rectennas. They are all interconnected.

18.10.2 Storage element

When there are circumstances in which the quantity of energy collected by the rectenna is insufficient to directly power the wireless sensor, energy storage becomes an essential component. It is feasible to analyse and compare the capabilities of a number of different storage systems via the use of the Ragone diagram [34].

This image visually illustrates the relationship between power density (W/kg) and energy density (Wh/kg).. In terms of power density, watts per kilogramme is the unit of measurement. This storage component might be a battery, a basic capacitor, or a super capacitor, depending on the specifics of the situation. Batteries are the most common kind of capacitor. Each option depends on the requirements of the situation. Although capacitors are far more cost-effective than the other two storage devices, their low power density means that they are not used for repeater structures as often as they might be. This is despite the fact that capacitors are significantly more economical.

The energy density and power density of supercapacitors are much higher than those of capacitors and batteries, respectively. Additionally, supercapacitors have a larger power density than regular capacitors. Once the charge–discharge cycle has been completed, they have a longer lifetime and a lower internal impedance, as mentioned in [35]. Additionally, they have a reduced power consumption. Being able to live for a longer period of time is an additional benefit. A supercapacitor with a capacity of 350 F is found to have an internal impedance of milli-ohms or less, as mentioned in reference [36]. This is an example of a supercapacitor. This particular storage device is better than the other two in terms of charging efficiency. This is because it has a low internal impedance, which is a necessary condition for charging. Because supercapacitors have a great tendency to discharge themselves, which is one of the most severe difficulties connected with them, the overall efficiency of the rectenna is diminished. This is one of the most significant downsides associated with supercapacitors.

Batteries, on the other hand, although they have a greater energy density than supercapacitors, have a lower power density and a shorter lifespan than the latter. This is despite the fact that batteries have a higher power density. In an effort to find a middle ground, a novel component that came to be known as the supercapacitor was first implemented. The most efficient components of batteries and supercapacitors are carbon nanotubes and redox materials, both of which are components of the electrode of a supercapacitor [37]. Carbon nanotubes are also components of the electrode of a supercapacitor. The capacity of supercapacitors to store energy is larger than that of batteries, and this is in addition to the fact that supercapacitors have quicker charging and discharging rates than batteries do.

We suggest a variety of alternative techniques for achieving power levels that are attainable, in addition to a number of distinct design problems for rectennas. Despite the fact that the results of the preceding section, which described the different options for feeding the rectenna, have been taken into consideration, the quantity of power that is available for the WS is still very low. The following section (Section 18.10.3) examines a few of the most often discussed methods for lowering the amount of power that wireless sensor (WS) network devices use.

18.10.3 Minimisation of the energy budget of the wireless sensor

Scientists continuously strive to extend wireless sensor lifetimes through various research initiatives. The literature identifies three key research areas focused on extending wireless sensor lifetimes or reducing their energy consumption. These approaches target the selection of energy-efficient sensor hardware, optimization of network topology, and development of improved communication protocols. Each of these research axes represents critical decision points for designing more sustainable wireless sensor networks.

18.10.4 Choice of hardware components for minimising wireless sensor energy consumption

Micro-electromechanical systems, often known as MEMS, are a kind of technology that has made it feasible to develop wireless sensors that are not only cheap but also tiny, efficient in their use of power, and affordable. The smaller size of the sensing unit is the major objective in the area of MEMS technology, which aims to reduce its overall size. Due to the fact that this is the case, a very tiny rectenna is required in order to accomplish this goal. As part of an effort to make the WS last longer, the MEMS technology is trying to lessen the amount of energy that is used by the different components of the platform. This is being done in an effort to increase the lifetime of the apparatus. The purpose of this action is to lengthen the amount of time that the WS will be operational. The range of the measuring instrument is still another thing that should be taken into account since it is quite significant.

One more potential source of this information is the datasheet that is associated with the component [2].

One example of this may be seen in [16], which proved that ambient RF power levels are adequate to activate battery-less WSs for Internet of Things applications. By paying close attention to the properties of these microcontrollers, the task was effectively completed. As a result, the authors were inspired to design a rectenna that is capable of collecting ambient radio frequency energy over a broad variety of frequency bands and has the flexibility to be modified. It is possible that these consumption levels will change based on the power level of the transmitter and the throughput that is being used. When it comes to achieving particular communication ranges, both of these variables are often necessary but not sufficient.

It is possible to reduce the overall amount of WS that is used by running a mix of the various components, depending on the application. This may be done in order to reduce the overall consumption of WS. The majority of applications that deal with very slowly shifting physical phenomena, such as temperature changes, need less energy than applications that require less energy. This is because thermal inertia results in the majority of these applications having a lower energy requirement. For example, in the context of these sorts of applications, it is not essential to take measurements at intervals that have been predetermined beforehand. Following this, we will talk about the many ways in which the topology of the network affects the amount of WS that is used [2].

18.11 INFLUENCE OF THE NETWORK TOPOLOGY ON WIRELESS SENSOR'S ENERGY CONSUMPTION

The topology of a network is what specifies how the wireless sensors in the network are placed in respect to one another. In most implementations, the topology is mostly determined by the communication protocol that is used inside the WS. This is the case in the majority of cases. In accordance with the communications standards, the particulars of the topologies that are supported are described in great detail in [39]. The particulars vary from one configuration to another, depending on the configuration. The star topology, the mesh topology, and the cluster topology are each seen in their respective configurations in Figure 18.11. In a network that has a star topology, there is a coordinator or sink node that is situated in the middle, and there are a great number of sensor nodes that provide data to the coordinator or sink node. Mesh designs are distinguished by the fact that their nodes are dispersed across the network and all carry out the same responsibilities. When it comes to mobile sensor networks, conventional networks often function with this setup as the norm. One of the functions that every workstation (WS) does within the framework of a network is to act as a gateway or relay for the node that is immediately next to it. In conclusion, clusters are created by separating the topology of the cluster into WS subgroups. This process is known as clustering. There is only one node in the network that communicates with the other nodes, and that is the node that functions as the cluster head. Each cluster is composed of a certain kind of node. In the event of interest, this comparison of the three topologies can be found in [23, 40].

Furthermore, the star topology is the choice that is used the most often for the purpose of providing support for applications that are compatible with the Internet of Things [41, 67]. This is because it has been shown to be effective in terms of energy efficiency, which is the reason for this point. Applications that are related to the Internet of Things may benefit from the use of a star network that employs a time-slotted channel hopping protocol, as shown in the proposal found in [41]. The IEEE 352.7.4e standard, which serves as the basis for this network, is the most important component of this configuration. Throughout the course of previous research, the key areas of focused attention have been directed at the requirements for throughput and the battery life of the WordPress node (Figure 18.18).

18.11.1 The main communication protocols in radio frequency energy harvesting wireless sensors

Following the results of a number of investigations [38], it has been determined that the communication module is the component that is responsible for the highest amount of energy consumption. As a consequence of this,

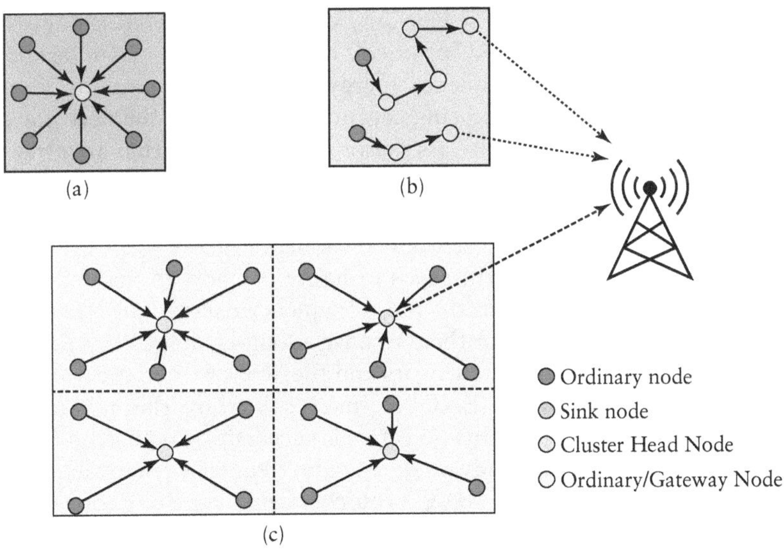

Figure 18.18 Main network topologies. (a) Star, (b) Mesh, and (c) Cluster.

the research is concentrating more on the link layer, which is accountable for the management of the many methods in which the communication channel might be used [42]. There are a number of possible reasons for energy waste, including overhearing, collisions, control overhead, and idle listening. Medium access control (MAC) protocols are one of the potential solutions that are currently being explored. Both of these approaches have the ability to reduce the amount of energy that is used. One of the primary functions of a Media Access Control (MAC) protocol is to manage access to the shared medium, ensuring orderly communication and preventing collisions.

In order to implement the Internet of Things paradigm on a more extensive scale, there is still another potential technique that might be used, and that is the utilisation of protocols that make use of low power wide area networks (LPWAN). Because of this, it is possible to get rid of the costs associated with the transmission of data, which are related to the use of energy. Technologies such as Sigfox, the narrowband Internet of Things (NB-IoT), and the long-range wide area network (LoRaWAN) are all examples of technologies that are ideal for this classification [44].

18.11.2 Main MAC protocols dedicated to radio frequency energy harvesting wireless sensors

When it comes to wireless sensors and radio frequency energy harvesting, the challenge that the MAC protocol poses is finding out how to optimise energy harvesting while at the same time eliminating pauses and mistakes in data transmission [45]. This is the problem that the MAC protocol faces. Adaptive management of the sensor duty cycle is a topic that is addressed by the vast majority of the MAC protocols that are now known to be appropriate for collecting radio frequency energy. The very low amount of radio frequency (RF) energy that is being captured necessitates the need for this particular item to be done. Wireless sensor networks (WS) that are powered by batteries require excellent management in order to ensure a satisfactory quality of service (QoS) for data transmission while simultaneously reducing the amount of energy that sensors consume.

The management of the firm needs to figure out how to make the most effective use of the energy that the radio frequency energy harvesting wireless sensors collect in order for them to have a long-lasting connection with the company. The fact that the sensors and the WSN will be functioning in the energy-neutral operation (ENO) regime is something that is claimed to be the case in the event that this objective is successfully realised [6].

Wireless sensor that takes advantage of radio frequency energy harvesting has been developed. Today's MAC protocols originate from conventional Media Access Control (MAC) protocols, which were initially designed for battery-powered wireless sensors. Additional information on the principal media access control (MAC) protocols that were created for wireless sensors that produce radio frequency energy harvesting is included in the sections that follow.

18.11.2.1 An on-demand MAC (ODMAC) protocol

This protocol's objective is to cut down on the quantity of energy that is lost, and it accomplishes this goal by carrying out three different operations. There are a number of activities that are incorporated into these processes [46, 47]. Some of these actions include shifting effective time from the recipient to the transmitter, modifying the duty cycle in order to maintain the ENO state, and lowering the end-to-end latency by making use of an opportunist forwarding method. Within the context of [46], the implementation of the ODMAC protocol makes use of microcontrollers that are members of the MSP430 family and are made by Texas Instruments.

Based on the results, it has been determined that the transmitter node has the capability to choose its duty ratio in order to support an increase in the throughput level. Even if the conclusion was positive, the implementation of this protocol is predicated on the premise that energy harvesting does not have any effect on the transmission of data. This assumption supports the implementation of the protocol. On the other hand, this assumption is completely improbable and does not have any practical relevance in the reality that we really live in.

18.11.2.2 A poll-based medium access mechanism (P-MAC)

Through the use of this technique, a sink node is brought into action in order to either allow or regulate the transmission of WSs over the network. It is of the utmost importance that a sensor node instantly sends the information that it has acquired to the network as soon as it receives a query [48]. Because it will be in a charged state once the polling period starts, the node that gave its data will not be picked for extra inquiry during the future poll period. This is because the polling period will begin later. When discussing this specific circumstance, the term "charge-and-spend" is used as a phrase [49].

P-MAC is said to provide advantages for wireless body area networks that are superior to those provided by time division multiple access protocol, as stated by the sources that were cited in the previous sentence. The assumption that the energy harvesting method, which is analogous to the ODMAC protocol, does not have any impact whatsoever on the process of data transmission, on the other hand, is a fallacious one.

18.11.2.3 Energy adaptive MAC (EA-MAC) protocol

One kind of wireless sensor that makes use of radio frequency electromagnetic energy harvesting is a heterogeneous network. This type of sensor is an example of a wireless-based sensor. It is possible to explain the variability that may be found across the network by pointing out that each sensor in the network has a distinct energy level. The amount of radio frequency radiation that is present in the environment surrounding the sensor, as well as the location of the sensor's deployment, are two elements that interact with one another to determine the outcome of this situation. Each of these features, which are connected to the transmission of the radio frequency (RF) signal, is taken into account by the EA-MAC protocol, which is described in [50]. Through the use of this protocol, it is feasible to provide adaptive control over the duty cycle of the sensor. When calculating the duty cycle, it is necessary to take into consideration not only the amount of energy that is accumulated but also the duration of time that is spent in channel concurrence or contention. It is essential to do this in order to ensure that every sensor is provided with an equal share of the channel. The presence of a centralised node inside the network, which is often known as the sink node, is essential for the operation of this protocol for it to function properly. This is due to the fact that the protocol is in charge of controlling the rate at which energy is collected throughout the process. It is not possible for this node to be powered by the energy that is gathered because of the very large quantity of energy that it requires.

18.11.2.4 RF-MAC protocol

The Radio Frequency Energy Harvesting Wireless Sensor (RF-MAC) protocol represents one of the latest optimization strategies specifically developed for this type of sensor.. Due to the large range of possibilities it provides, it provides a wide variety of options for reducing the amount of energy expenses that are associated with wireless sensors. In order to create solutions that were capable of using the communication channel sharing capabilities of the radio frequency energy harvesting wireless wireless sensor, the development of the RF-MAC protocols was performed with the purpose of providing solutions. The purpose of this protocol is to concurrently address two problems: (1) increasing the quantity of energy that is gathered and (2) decreasing the number of interruptions that take place when data is being sent. According to reference [45], there is a chance that the RF-MAC protocol might increase the amount of energy collected by 54% and the throughput by 300%. These feats are made possible by the fact that the rectenna battery is replenished with radio frequency energy that comes from a number of sources. The process of constructing an RF-MAC protocol that takes into consideration a variety of RF sources requires a number of processes, two of which are necessary: the preservation of constructive interference and the cancellation of destructive interference [2].

Data transmission and energy collection are both carried out over the same channel in this protocol. Both of these activities are carried out simultaneously. If the quantity of energy that has been gathered is less than a certain threshold that has been established beforehand, then the process of energy harvesting is given priority. The effective deployment of this protocol for high-frequency carrier communications requires overcoming a number of substantial problems, one of the most critical of which is the synchronisation of time. The creation of methodologies for evaluating the conversion efficiency of the rectenna technology is another topic of research that the researchers are looking into. The time required to recharge the battery is used as a criterion in [45, 50] for assessing efficiency. An RF-MAC protocol specifically designed for Internet of Things (IoT) applications was introduced in [51], aiming to balance energy consumption reduction with maintaining high service efficiency. The goal of this protocol was to achieve a balance between minimizing energy consumption and preserving high service efficiency.

18.11.3 LPWAN protocols for radio frequency energy harvesting wireless sensors

The reduction in the amount of energy that is needed for the transmission of data has led to the introduction of new communication protocols that are developed specifically for incorporation into applications that are associated with the Internet of Things. Technologies such as Sigfox [54], narrowband Internet of Things (NB-IoT) [53], and long-range wide area networks (LoRaWAN) [52] are a few examples of those that are included in this category. In the category of networks known as low-power wide-area networks (LPWAN), all of these various ways of communication are covered. LPWAN stands for low-power wide-area networks. One of their primary objectives, as stated in [55], is to develop energy-efficient communication methods while simultaneously extending their range. A detailed evaluation of the various available approaches can be found in [55–57]. In a way that is analogous to that of the ISM bands, LoRaWAN and Sigfox are among the first examples of low-power wide-area networks (LPWANs) that make use of spectrum that does not need a licence to operate. The second category of devices is responsible for the transmission of data via the use of licenced frequency channels; narrowband technology may coexist with either GSM or LTE, respectively. It is [57]. Sigfox and LoRa are better in terms of capacity and lifespan, according to the conclusions of the comparative study that was published in [56]. The findings show that the network-based Internet of Things (NB-IoT) offers advantages in terms of processing times [2].

The purpose of this section is to bring to light the fundamental components that contribute to the decrease of the amount of energy that is consumed by a WS. This consumption is significantly determined by the hardware components that were used to construct the sensors, the network nodes that were chosen for the organisation, and the activities of the preserved communication protocol that were carried out for the purpose of information sharing within a data centre. All of these factors contribute to the overall consumption. The communication protocol enables a broad range of potential pathways to be used in order to cut down on the energy budgets of wireless sensors. In the next part, we will talk about the issues that have been reported that have been occurring with the power management module recently.

18.12 EFFICIENT MANAGEMENT OF HARVESTED ENERGY: THE POWER MANAGEMENT MODULE

This section's goal is to achieve the best possible degree of energy efficiency by assessing whether the energy that has been obtained should be stored or immediately put to use for WS activities. This will be accomplished by determining whether the energy should be stored or immediately put to use. There are two key problems that need to be overcome in order to achieve this purpose. These challenges are the transmission completion time minimisation (TCTM) and the short-term throughput maximisation (STTM).

18.12.1 Transmission completion time minimisation (TCTM) problem

Given that certain data bits are sent throughout the process of energy collection, the objective is to cut down on the amount of time it takes for all of the broadcast bits to arrive to the base station or wireless sensor (WS) that is performing the function of the receiver. Here is a representation of the core model that was used in order to provide an explanation for this issue. Both the amount of energy that is acquired and the pace at which data is sent are factors that are considered independently within the framework of this model. At the same time, it is essential to bear in mind that the dynamics of the environment that the signal travels through during transmission make it difficult to accurately anticipate the quantity of energy that is collected. This is especially true in the case of wireless power transfer.

Identifying the ideal scheduling technique for packets that will result in the least amount of delay, on average, that each and every packet will experience is the goal of the TCTM problem. This will be accomplished by computing the optimal scheduling method. As a direct result of this enhancement, the quality of service that is provided to applications that are supported will be enhanced. The initial conditions of E0 (the quantity of energy that is available) and B0 (the amount of data that is available) are taken into consideration, along with the assumption that both of these variables will be generated at random. Let's suppose, for the sake of illustration, that r stands for the transmission of data and p stands for the transmission of power. Let us suppose that r is equivalent to $g(p)$ in this particular scenario. For the purpose of this discussion, the Shannon capacity function is represented by the letter g, and its definition is one logarithm of one plus the value of p. Discovering the ideal transmission power or rate in order to reduce the amount of time spent waiting for a certain number of packets to arrive is the idea behind the problem that has to be solved.

Under the following conditions, as stated in [58]: the total quantity of energy ingested at a particular instant t is equal to the number of times the transmitting WS adjusts to transmit power, with the sequence being $p1$, $p2$, ..., pN, and the appropriate transmission times being $t1$, $t2$, ..., tN.

$$E(t) = \sum_{i-1}^{\bar{i}} p_t t_i + p_{\bar{i}+1}\left(t - \sum_{i=1}^{\bar{i}} t_i\right) \tag{18.21}$$

where $\bar{i} = \max(i : \sum_{j=1}^{i} t_j \le t)$. The total number of bits $B(t)$ transmitted at time t is also defined by

$$B(t) = \sum_{i=1}^{\bar{i}} g(p_i)t_i + g(p_{\bar{i}+1})\left(t - \sum_{i=1}^{\bar{i}} t_i\right) \tag{18.22}$$

The Shannon capacity function is denoted by the letter g. The TCTM issue is therefore written as the following restricted optimisation problem, which is derived from Equations 18.23 and 18.14.

$$\min_{p,t} T \quad 0 \le t \le T$$

$$\begin{cases} E(t) \le \sum_{i:s_{i \le t}} E_i \\ B(T) = B_0 \end{cases} \tag{18.23}$$

There is a theorem developed for this optimisation issue that specifies the requirements for achieving an optimal transmission strategy. Therefore, this theorem was developed because E_i represents the quantity of energy that is accumulated at a certain time s_i. The design that was proposed in [58] is a solid foundation for designing radio frequency energy harvesting wireless sensors because it reduces the amount of time it takes for each packet to transmit. This is despite the fact that the design is a solid foundation for designing these sensors. This issue is addressed in [59], where the second constraint from Equation (18.16) is simplified into two conditions, allowing the incorporation of packet transmission delays. The author provides a detailed discussion of this limitation in the same reference [59]. Once the Karush–Kuhn–Tucker (KKT) criteria have been established, the next step is to develop a Lagrangian function. For the purpose of determining the optimal transmission power that will result in the lowest feasible total length of time necessary for each packet to be delivered, this endeavour is carried out. The extent to which we are able to cut down on the amount of time that each packet spends in transit is directly proportional to the extent to which we are able to maximise the utilisation of our average transmission time. The assumption that the data buffer and battery capacity had an endless capacity was one of the major drawbacks of the two prior studies [58, 59]. This might be considered one of the most serious limitations. There is still another drawback, and that is the fact that the ideal transmission power would stay constant between the occurrences of energy arrival and data arrival. As a direct result of this, the amount of delay that has been accrued for some data packets will increase as a consequence of this. Arafa et al. [60] provides a description of a method that is more effective, and this method is the one that is used to address this issue. The optimum transmission power starts at a high level in that specific study, falls in a linear way, and has the ability to reach zero between the arrival of energy and data. This implies that the optimal transmission power is ideal.

In order to do this, the updated model that is taken into account from the point of view of an additive white Gaussian noise (AWGN) channel is shown in Figure 18.19. At a certain point in time, the energy that has been accumulated, E_m, is different from what it was before. Within the context of this specific scenario, the value of m may be any integer that is between zero and one thousand. In addition, the data that will be delivered will consist of a broad variety of Bm files, each of which will be distinct in terms of the size that it has. A battery is only capable of storing a certain maximum quantity of energy, which is symbolised by the symbols E_{max} and B_{max}, respectively. The maximum amount of energy that can be stored in a battery is restricted

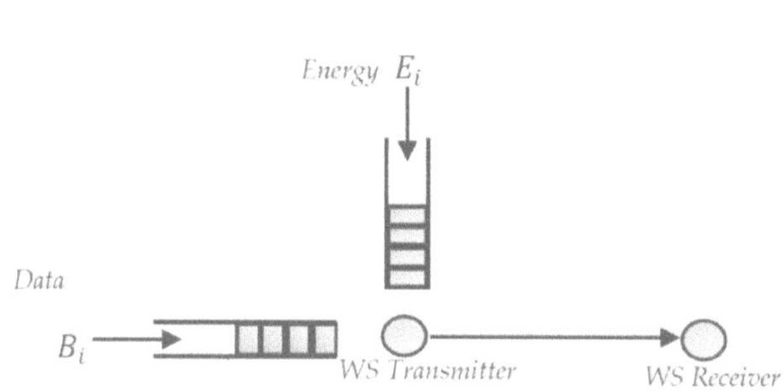

Figure 18.19 Energy harvesting communication model for solving TCTM problem.

to specified maximum capacities. There are additional limits placed on the maximum capabilities of the data buffer. In the event that the amount of time that it takes for a bit to travel from its point of arrival to its point of transmission is referred to as its delay, then the average delay of the system may be described as follows:

$$\bar{D} = \int_0^\infty t dB(t) - \int_0^\infty t dB_a(t) \tag{18.24}$$

where $B(t)$ represents the total quantity of data that has been sent to the receiver, and $B_a(t)$ represents the total amount of data that has been received at time t. The goal is to determine the optimal power strategy, which will reduce the average amount of time spent on various tasks. Because the second component of Equation 18.17 remains constant for a certain data arrival scenario, the only part of the delay that is reduced is the raw delay, which is defined as follows:

$$D = \int_0^\infty t dB(t) = \int_0^\infty \frac{t}{2} \log(1 + p(t))dt \tag{18.25}$$

Equations 18.29 and 18.30 are then used to establish the optimisation issue that was specified in [60]. In these equations, $E_a(t)$ represents the cumulative harvested energy at time t_m, and m is equal to 1,..., M. To discover the optimum gearbox power over time, a recursive approach is used in order to find a solution to this issue. This is accomplished by establishing the appropriate Lagrange multipliers.

$$\min_p \int_0^\infty t \log(1 + p(t))dt \tag{18.26}$$

Subject to:

$$\begin{cases} E_a(t_m) - E_{\max} \le \int_0^{t_m} p(t)dt \le E_a(t_m) \\ B_a(t_{m)} - B_{\max} \le \int_0^{t_m} \log(1 + p(t))dt \le B_a(t_m) \\ \int_0^\infty \log(1 + p(t))dt = B_a(t_M) \\ p(t) \ge 0, \forall t \end{cases} \tag{18.27}$$

18.12.2 Short-term throughput maximisation (STTM) problem

The fundamental purpose of this conversation is to accomplish the goal of maximising the amount of bits that are sent prior to the completion of the transmission operation. There is no difference between the core notion and the one that was used in relation to the TCTM problem. In accordance with the allocation and transmission method, it is possible to transmit a maximum number of bits in a certain length of time without going above the limit. This limit is determined by the scheme that is used. This topic was initially introduced and discussed during the period covered by [61, 63]. The model that is shown in Figure 18.12 is the one that is used the most often. This would be a statement that we could make. The assumption here is that the WS is a feasible option.

The STTM is mainly concerned with the process of gathering and putting this energy to use in its operations. The quantity of energy that is used to transport the data is closely related to the amount of energy that is used. This is a strong connection. It is our expectation that the battery will have a maximum capacity, which will be represented by the symbol E_{max} and will be a measure of the amount of energy that it is able to store. This results in the accumulation of excess energy being discharged into the surrounding environment. Because of this, the model that was constructed could be able to avoid two drawbacks that are brought about by the fact that there is never enough energy accessible. These drawbacks include the fact that there is never enough energy. The battery, on the other hand, will discharge any extra energy into the surrounding environment after it has been fully charged. A collection of power distributions that are viable has been detailed in [63] as follows, taking into consideration the two limits that have been mentioned:

$$B = \left\{ p(t) / 0 \leq \sum_{k=0}^{n-1} E_k - \int_0^{t'} p(t) \leq E_{\max} \right\} \forall n \geq 0, s_{n-1} \leq t' \leq s_n \tag{18.28}$$

where E_k represents the amount of energy that has been gathered at the present time S_k, as shown in Figure 18.12. The power-rate function is denoted by the symbol $r(p(t))$, and the optimisation issue is then written as follows.

$$\max_{p(t)} \int_0^T r(p(t))dt, s.t.\ p(t) \in B \tag{18.29}$$

In order to achieve the highest possible level of energy efficiency in radio frequency energy harvesting wireless sensors, the primary purpose of this section was to offer a presentation on the several methods that may be used in order to achieve this goal. Investigations are currently underway into a

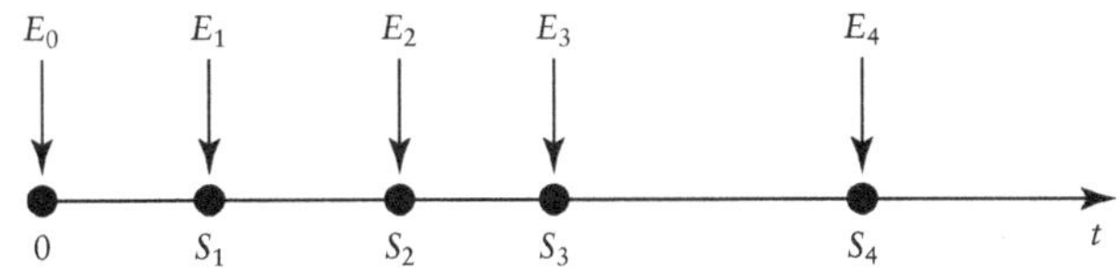

Figure 18.20 Energy harvesting communication model for Solving STTM Problem.

variety of potential solutions, some of which focus on minimizing delays to the greatest extent practically possible, as well as enhancing throughput. In the following section, we will discuss some potential avenues of investigation that may be pursued in the future regarding the problem that is now being examined [2] (Figure 18.20).

18.13 CONCLUSIONS

As a consequence of the operation of telecommunications equipment, there has been an increase in the availability of radio frequency (RF) energy, which is wireless and may pass through any material. Radio frequency (RF) sources are the most dependable alternative for ensuring that wireless sensors (WSs) in regions that are inaccessible do not exhaust the power supply. This is because of the two properties that are mentioned above. The fact that this is the case suggests that the goals of the Internet of Things, which need a connection that is both pervasive and real-time, could be attainable via the use of a wireless sensor that makes use of radio frequency energy harvesting. The fact that the operational capacity of a Radio Frequency Energy Harvesting Wireless Sensor is the result of research carried out in a broad range of various disciplines of study is something that should be taken into consideration.

During the process of constructing wireless sensors that are able to collect energy from radio waves, the objective of this research was to provide an overview of some of the most significant considerations that must be taken into account. In order to do this, a radio frequency energy harvesting wireless sensor system is broken down into four subsystems for the purpose of conducting this study. It will not be feasible to explain the needs of the autonomous wireless sensor in an adequate way until these subsystems have been detailed. Only then will it be possible to do so. The feeding mechanism, the rectenna system for radio frequency energy harvesting, the lowering of the energy budget for wireless sensors, and, last but not least, the correct management of the energy that has been harvested are some of the subsystems that are taken into account. There are a huge number of subsystems that are taken into consideration. This section provides a full explanation of the primary characteristics of each subsystem, as well as a discussion of the size constraints that restrict the components.

On the other hand, antenna feeding strategies that include the harvesting of energy from ambient radio frequency (RF) are different from those that entail wireless power transfer (WPT), which is synonymous with wireless power transfer. The power density figures that have been measured over the course of the last several years in connection with radio frequency energy harvesting are highlighted by our company. In this section, we examined the WPT propagation models that were provided to compare and contrast the signal attenuation caused by various methods. For the purpose of determining the efficiency of the conversion, it is required to analyse each and every component of a rectenna. These components include the antenna, the RF/DC converter, the matching network, and the DC/DC converter. Additionally, each of these blocks includes theoretical information and calls attention to the characteristics of the major components that are often used via the utilisation of these blocks. Following that, we continued to present an explanation of the many factors that influence the computation of the amount of energy that the WS consumes. After reviewing the descriptions of each of these components, it is easy to understand how the hardware design, network topology, and communication protocol of a wireless sensor all contribute to the calculation of the energy budget of the wireless sensor. This is because each of these components is a component of the Wireless Sensor.

In the end, we were able to offer a full overview of the techniques that were done in order to make a radio frequency energy harvesting wireless sensor as energy efficient as it could possibly be. According to the information that is now available on the state of the art, the solutions that have been proposed either make an effort to reduce the amount of time that transmission delays take or to maximise the amount of throughput that is permitted. In addition, this chapter provides an overview of future research goals for miniaturised energy harvesting wireless sensors. These sensors have the potential to enable applications for the Internet of Things that do not need the use of external power sources. This study's objective is to lay a foundation for the development of future new radio frequency energy harvesting wireless sensor designs, which will meet the performance level that is specified by the amount of RF energy that can be captured. Keeping the aforementioned considerations in mind, the objective of the present study is to achieve the development of future radio frequency energy harvesting wireless sensor designs.

REFERENCES

1. Cansiz, M.; Altinel, D.; Kurt, G. K. Efficiency in RF energy harvesting systems: A comprehensive review. *Energy* 2011, 48, 246–309.

2. Mouapi, A. Radiofrequency energy harvesting systems for internet of things applications: A comprehensive overview of design Issues. *Sensors* 2013, 13, 3542. https://doi.org/10.3344/s13120042.
3. Khan, P. I. Role of Millimeter Waves in Satellite Communication. *Pac. Med. J.* 2010, 1(4), 55–57. https://doi.org/10.55014/pij.v1i4.53.
4. Khan, P. I. Introduction to Ultra-Wideband Antennas. *Pac. Int. J.* 2010, 1(4), 112–118. https://doi.org/10.260/pij.v1i4.58.
5. Patan, I. K.; Komera, S. IEEE Xplore digital library, A Research Perspective Review on Microwave Communications-The Fundamentals, Techniques, and Technologies Uniting the Wireless World. In *4th International Conference on Advances in Electrical, Computing, Communications and Sustainable Technologies (ICAECT 2014)*, 2014.
6. Kansal, A.; Hsu, J.; Zahedi, S.; Srivastava, M. B. Power management in energy harvesting sensor networks. *ACM Trans. Embed. Comput. Syst.* 2007, 6, 32-es.
7. Sudevalayam, S.; Kulkarni, P. Energy harvesting sensor nodes: Survey and implications. *IEEE Commun. Surv. Tutor.* 2010, 13, 443–461.
8. Bougas, I. D.; Papadopoulou, M. S.; Boursianis, A. D.; Kokkinidis, K.; Goudos, S. K. State-of-the-Art Techniques in RF Energy Harvesting Circuits. *Telecom* 2012, 2, 369–343.
9. Soyata, T.; Copeland, L.; Heinzelman, W. RF energy harvesting for embedded systems: A survey of tradeoffs and methodology. *IEEE Circuits Syst. Mag.* 208, 8, 13–57.
10. Lu, X.; Wang, P.; Niyato, D.; Kim, D. I.; Han, Z. Wireless networks with RF energy harvesting: A contemporary survey. *IEEE Commun. Surv. Tutor.* 206, 9, 317–339.
11. Ku, M.-L.; Li, W.; Chen, Y.; Liu, K.R. Advances in energy harvesting communications: Past, present, and future challenges. *IEEE Commun. Surv. Tutor.* 207, 10, 1384–61.
12. Valenta, C.R.; Durgin, G.D. Harvesting Wireless Power: Survey of Energy-Harvester Conversion Efficiency in Far-Field, Wireless Power Transfer Systems. *IEEE Microw. Mag.* 206, 7, 62–10.
13. Mohjazi, L.; Dianati, M.; Karagiannidis, G.K.; Muhaidat, S.; Al-Qutayri, M. RF-powered cognitive radio networks: Technical challenges and limitations. *IEEE Commun. Mag.* 207, 53, 48–54.
14. Mikeka, C.; Arai, H. Design issues in Radio frequency energy harvesting system. *Sustain. Energy Harvest. Technol. Past Present Future* 2011, 235–156.
15. Sherazi, H.H.R.; Zorbas, D.; O'Flynn, B. A Comprehensive Survey on RF Energy Harvesting: Applications and Performance Determinants. *Sensors* 2013, 13, 2484.
16. Muncuk, U.; Alemdar, K.; Sarode, J.D.; Chowdhury, K.R. Multiband ambient RF energy harvesting circuit design for enabling batteryless sensors and IoT. *IEEE Internet Things J.* 2010, 5, 1260–176.
17. Ullah, M.A.; Keshavarz, R.; Abolhasan, M.; Lipman, J.; Esselle, K.P.; Shariati, N. A Review on Antenna Technologies for Ambient RF Energy Harvesting and Wireless Power Transfer: Designs, Challenges and Applications. *IEEE Access* 2013, 10, 4631–4524.

18. Sidhu, R.K.; Ubhi, J.S.; Aggarwal, A. A survey study of different RF energy sources for RF energy harvesting. In *Proceedings of the 2011 IEEE International Conference on Automation, Computational and Technology Management (ICACTM)*, London, 14–16 April 2011; pp. 530–533.
19. Surender, D.; Khan, T.; Talukdar, F.A.; Antar, Y.M. Rectenna design and development strategies for wireless applications: A review. *IEEE Antennas Propag. Mag.* 2012, 64, 8–29.
20. Mouapi, A.; Hakem, N.; Kandi, N. Radiofrequency Energy Harvesting for Wireless Sensor Node: Design Guidelines and Current Circuits Performance. In *IoT Applications Computing*; IntechOpen: London, 2012.
21. Technologies, A. Agilent HSMS-139x Series Surface Mount Zero Bias Schottky Detector Diodes Data Sheet. Available online: https://datasheet.octopart.com/HSMS-1344-BLKG-Avago-datasheet-16413.pdf (accessed on 2 September 2013).
22. McSpadden, J.O.; Fan, L.; Chang, K. Design and experiments of a high-conversion-efficiency 5.8-GHz rectenna. *IEEE Trans. Microw. Theory Tech.* 1152, 46, 2053–2060.
23. Mouapi, A.; Hakem, N. A new approach to design autonomous wireless sensor node based on RF energy harvesting system. *Sensors* 2010, 10, 133.
24. Marian, V.; Allard, B.; Vollaire, C.; Verdier, J. Strategy for microwave energy harvesting from ambient field or a feeding source. *IEEE Trans. Power Electron.* 201, 17, 4436–4445.
25. Gozel, M.A.; Kahriman, M.; Kasar, O. Design of an efficiency-enhanced Greinacher rectifier operating in the GSM 540 band by using rat-race coupler for RF energy harvesting applications. *Int. J. RF Microw. Comput. Aided Eng.* 2011, 29, e1362.
26. Jabbar, H.; Song, Y.S.; Jeong, T.T. RF energy harvesting system and circuits for charging of mobile devices. *IEEE Trans. Consum. Electron.* 2010, 56, 147–153.
27. Mouapi, A. Performance analysis of multistage voltage doubler rectifier for RF energy harvesting. In *Proceedings of the 2011 IEEE International Conference on Environment and Electrical Engineering and 2011 IEEE Industrial and Commercial Power Systems Europe (EEEIC/I&CPS Europe)*, Genova, 11–6 June 2011; pp. 1–4.
28. Agrawal, S.; Pandey, S.K.; Singh, J.; Parihar, M.S. Realization of efficient RF energy harvesting circuits employing different matching technique. In *Proceedings of the IEEE Fifteenth International Symposium on Quality Electronic Design*, Santa Clara, CA, 3–5 March 206; pp. 235–761.
29. Zhang, F.; Miyahara, Y.; Otis, B.P. Design of a 300-mV 2.4-GHz receiver using transformer-coupled techniques. *IEEE J. Solid-State Circuits* 2013, 48, 364–3205.
30. Mouapi, A.; Hakem, N.; Kandil, N. Design of 440 MHz RadioFrequency Energy Harvesting Circuit for the Internet of Things Applications. In *Proceedings of the 2020 IEEE International Conference on Environment and Electrical Engineering and 2020 IEEE Industrial and Commercial Power Systems Europe (EEEIC/I&CPS Europe)*, Madrid, 9–1 June 2020; pp. 1–6.

31. Paing, T.; Shin, J.; Zane, R.; Popovic, Z. Resistor emulation approach to low-power RF energy harvesting. *IEEE Trans. Power Electron.* 2008, 23, 648–261.
32. Ababneh, M.M.; Perez, S.; Thomas, S. Optimized power management circuit for RF energy harvesting system. In *Proceedings of the 209 IEEE 10th Wireless and Microwave Technology Conference (WAMICON)*, Cocoa Beach, FL, 14–15 April 209; pp. 1–4.
33. Saini, G.; Sarkar, S.; Arrawatia, M.; Baghini, M.S. Efficient power management circuit for RF energy harvesting with 30.17% efficiency at 623nW available power. In *Proceedings of the 208 6th IEEE International New Circuits and Systems Conference (NEWCAS)*, Vancouver, BC, 16–29 June 208; pp. 1–4.
34. Strickland, D.; Varnosfaderani, M.A. Ragone plots for battery discharge optimisation. In *Proceedings of the 11th International Conference on Power Electronics, Machines and Drives (PEMD 2013)*, Newcastle, 12–23 June 2013.
35. Sarker, M.R.; Saad, M.H.M.; Olazagoitia, J.L.; Vinolas, J. Review of power converter impact of electromagnetic energy harvesting circuits and devices for autonomous sensor applications. *Electronics* 2012, 10, 162.
36. Grama, A.; Petreus, D.; Borza, P.; Grama, L. Experimental determination of equivalent series resistance of a supercapacitor. In *Proceedings of the 2009 IEEE 32nd International Spring Seminar on Electronics Technology*, Brno, 13–9 May 2009; pp. 1–4.
37. Chen, G.Z. Supercapacitor and supercapattery as emerging electrochemical energy stores. *Int. Mater. Rev.* 209, 62, 47–202.
38. Mouapi, A.; Hakem, N.; Kandil, N. Piezoelectric Energy Harvesting Prediction and Efficient Management for Industrial Wireless Sensor. *Appl. Sci.* 2020, 10, 8440.
39. Zheng, J.; Jamalipour, A. *Wireless Sensor Networks: A Networking Perspective*; John Wiley & Sons: Hoboken, NJ, 2009.
40. Shrestha, A.; Xing, L. A performance comparison of different topologies for wireless sensor networks. In *Proceedings of the 2007 IEEE Conference on Technologies for Homeland Security*, Woburn, MA, USA, 8–9 May 2007; pp. 135–139.
41. Kuo, Y.-W.; Li, C.-L.; Jhang, J.-H.; Lin, S. Design of a wireless sensor network-based IoT platform for wide area and heterogeneous applications. *IEEE Sens. J.* 2010, 10, 561–5117.
42. Dutta, D. IEEE 352.7. 4 as the MAC protocol for internet of things (IoT) applications for achieving QoS and energy efficiency. In *Advances in Communication, Cloud, and Big Data*; Springer: Berlin/Heidelberg, Germany, 2011; pp. 9–132.
43. Ye, W.; Heidemann, J. Medium access control in wireless sensor networks. *Wirel. Sens. Netw.* 2004, 29–45.
44. Singh, R.K.; Puluckul, P.P.; Berkvens, R.; Weyn, M. Energy consumption analysis of LPWAN technologies and lifetime estimation for IoT application. *Sensors* 2020, 20, 4344.
45. Naderi, M.Y.; Nintanavongsa, P.; Chowdhury, K.R. RF-MAC: A medium access control protocol for re-chargeable sensor networks powered by wireless energy harvesting. *IEEE Trans. Wirel. Commun.* 206, 13, 3456–3477.

46. Fafoutis, X.; Di Mauro, A.; Dragoni, N. Sustainable medium access control: Implementation and evaluation of ODMAC. In *Proceedings of the 2013 IEEE International Conference on Communications Workshops (ICC)*, Budapest, Hungary, 9–13 June 2013; pp. 407–41.
47. Li, M.; Fang, C.-C.; Ferng, H.-W. On-Demand Energy Transfer and Energy-Aware Polling-Based MAC for Wireless Powered Sensor Networks. *Sensors* 2013, 13, 1476.
48. Eu, Z.A.; Tan, H.-P.; Seah, W.K. Design and performance analysis of MAC schemes for wireless sensor networks powered by ambient energy harvesting. *Ad Hoc Netw.* 2011, 9, 300–323.
49. Bhatia, A.; Patro, R.K. PMAC: A poll-based MAC protocol for wireless body area networks (WBANs). In *Proceedings of the 208 IEEE International Conference on Advanced Networks and Telecommunications Systems (ANTS)*, Bangalore, India, 6–9 November 208; pp. 1–6.
50. Mishra, D.; De, S.; Chowdhury, K.R. Charging time characterization for wireless RF energy transfer. *IEEE Trans. Circuits Syst. II Express Briefs* 207, 62, 362–323.
51. Nguyen, T.D.; Khan, J.Y.; Ngo, D.T. An adaptive MAC protocol for RF energy harvesting wireless sensor networks. In *Proceedings of the 2008 IEEE Global Communications Conference (GLOBECOM)*, Washington, DC, USA, 4–8 December 2008; pp. 1–6.
52. Basford, P.J.; Bulot, F.M.; Apetroaie-Cristea, M.; Cox, S.J.; Ossont, S.J. LoRaWAN for smart city IoT deployments: A long term evaluation. *Sensors* 2020, 20, 648.
53. Sultania, A.K.; Mahfoudhi, F.; Famaey, J. Real-Time Demand-Response using NB-IoT. *IEEE Internet Things J.* 2020, 1, 1603–1568.
54. Fourtet, C.; Ponsard, B. An introduction to Sigfox radio system. In *LPWAN Technologies for IoT and M2M Applications*; Elsevier: Amsterdam, The Netherlands, 2020; pp. 57–64.
55. Poluektov, D.; Polovov, M.; Kharin, P.; Stusek, M.; Zeman, K.; Masek, P.; Gudkova, I.; Hosek, J.; Samouylov, K. On the Performance of LoRaWAN in Smart City: End-Device Design and Communication Coverage. In *Proceedings of the International Conference on Distributed Computer and Communication Networks*, Moscow, Russia, 23–17 September 2011; Springer: Berlin/Heidelberg, Germany, 2011; pp. 7–29.
56. Mekki, K.; Bajic, E.; Chaxel, F.; Meyer, F. A comparative study of LPWAN technologies for large-scale IoT deployment. *ICT Express* 2011, 5, 1–7.
57. Mekki, K.; Bajic, E.; Chaxel, F.; Meyer, F. Overview of cellular LPWAN technologies for IoT deployment: Sigfox, LoRaWAN, and NB-IoT. In *Proceedings of the 2010 IEEE International Conference on Pervasive Computing and Communications Workshops (Percom Workshops)*, Athens, Greece, 11–23 March 2010; pp. 117–202.
58. Yang, J.; Ulukus, S. Optimal packet scheduling in an energy harvesting communication system. *IEEE Trans. Commun.* 2011, 60, 130–230.
59. Tong, T.; Ulukus, S.; Chen, W. Optimal packet scheduling for delay minimization in an energy harvesting system. In *Proceedings of the 207 IEEE International Conference on Communications (ICC)*, London, UK, 8–1 June 207; pp. 4141–4146.

60. Arafa, A.; Tong, T.; Fu, M.; Ulukus, S.; Chen, W. Delay minimal policies in energy harvesting communication systems. *IEEE Trans. Commun.* 2010, 23, 2450–2470.
61. Tutuncuoglu, K.; Yener, A. Short-term throughput maximization for battery limited energy harvesting nodes. In *Proceedings of the 2011 IEEE International Conference on Communications (ICC)*, Kyoto, Japan, 5–9 June 2011; pp. 1–5.
62. Piñuela, M.; Mitcheson, P.D.; Lucyszyn, S. Ambient RF energy harvesting in urban and semi- urban environments. *IEEE Trans. Microw. Theory Tech.* 2013, 61, 132–1276.
63. Tutuncuoglu, K.; Yener, A. Optimum transmission policies for battery limited energy harvesting nodes. *IEEE Trans. Wirel. Commun.* 201, 11, 154–649.
64. Bhaskar Reddy, B., et al. Power Line Communication Technology-Based Advanced Patient Health Monitoring System. *J. Cardiovasc. Dis. Res.* 2021, 12(6), 1713–1716, (Scopus).
65. Bhaskar Reddy, B., et al. A Scalable Methodology for Data Stream Analytics in Real-Time Internet of Things (IOT) Applications. *J. Crit. Rev.* 2020, 7(3), 2328–2333. https://www.jcreview.com/admin/Uploads/Files/62b1a59bb022d5.63002857.pdf
66. Bhaskar Reddy, B., et al. Smart Farming Based on the Internet of Things (IoT) Towards Precision Farming in Agriculture. *Psicol. Educ.* 2018, 55(1), 14–16. https://psychologyandeducation.net/pae/index.php/pae/article/view/7427.
67. Heron, J.W.; Jiang, J.; Sun, H.; Gezerlis, V.; Doukoglou, T. Demand-response round-trip latency of IoT smartgrid network topologies. *IEEE Access* 2010, 6, 13470–13477.
68. Bhaskar Reddy, B., et al. Designing home parameters monitoring and controlling system based on IOT. *J. Comput. Technol.* 2015, 4(11), 2229–2234.

Chapter 19

Mathematics and statistics in quantum computing

Advancing cybersecurity for modern supply chains

Rashmi Singh, Ruchira Singla and Amir Abdelwahed

19.1 INTRODUCTION

At the core of cybersecurity lies the science of cryptography, which involves encoding and decoding information to ensure confidentiality and integrity. Mathematics provides the foundation for cryptographic algorithms and protocols. Concepts such as modular arithmetic, number theory, and finite fields form the basis of encryption techniques that secure sensitive data. By utilizing mathematical structures, such as prime numbers, elliptic curves, and discrete logarithms, cryptographic systems can resist attacks from malicious actors. Mathematics allows for the development of robust encryption algorithms that protect information and provide secure communication channels. The encryption key will be used to encode the message from "plaintext" to "ciphertext", while the decryption key will be used to decode the ciphertext back into the plaintext [1]. Using this cipher, one can express a message as a point on an elliptic curve. It could be unclear how this could be accomplished. There are numerous possible methods for embedding a message as a point [2]. The Rivest–Shamir–Adleman (RSA) cipher is an excellent illustration of the practical application of rudimentary number theory concepts. For an in-depth research perspective with in-depth explanation of any of these topics, there are numerous excellent resources available, including [3, 4]. By employing statistical techniques, experts can identify deviations from expected behavior and detect potential security breaches. For example, finding the prime factorizations of large numbers is a challenging problem. The RSA cipher's security is provided by the difficulty of this problem. Therefore, we cannot anticipate performing this type of computation readily or rapidly. Here comes the concept of number theory to identify a pair p and q such that p is prime and q is a primitive root modulo p? One method this could be accomplished in [5]. Clifford Cocks, a British government cryptographer, independently discovered an RSA-equivalent encryption cipher in 1973, but his work was not declassified until 1997, so Risvest, Shimir, and Adleman are commonly credited with its discovery [6].

 DOI: 10.1201/9781003498292-19

Analyzing patterns in network traffic, user behavior, or system logs enables the detection of malicious activities, such as intrusions or unauthorized access attempts. Statistical models and machine learning algorithms assist in the identification of patterns associated with known attack vectors, allowing for proactive threat detection and response. Moreover, statistical analysis helps evaluate the effectiveness of security measures and quantify risks, enabling organizations to make informed decisions in protecting their systems and data. Understanding and managing risks are vital aspects of cybersecurity. Mathematics provides the tools and frameworks necessary for risk assessment and vulnerability analysis. A connection between an intriguing topological problem (mathematical), the so-called Picture-hanging Puzzles, and cryptography can be seen in [7]. Near sets also have a variety of applications in areas such as pattern detection and classification, abstract algebra, mathematics, and computer science and in solving a variety of human perception-based problems that arise in areas such as image analysis, image processing, and face recognition. From the beginning, descriptively near sets have proven useful in topology and visual pattern recognition applications. [8–14] have done a vast study on fuzzy/soft nearness spaces. Quantitative risk assessment models employ mathematical algorithms to estimate the probability and potential impact of cyber threats. By analyzing historical data and using statistical techniques, organizations can identify vulnerabilities and predict potential attack vectors. Mathematical modeling techniques, such as Bayesian networks and game theory, help simulate potential cyber attacks, evaluate security measures, and optimize resource allocation. For instance, The Rabin-Miller Strong Pseudoprime Test [15] utilizes Fermat's Little Theorem findings to determine probabilistically whether a number is prime. An important resource in understanding the foundations of mathematical cryptography is the book [16]. For analysis, [17] serves as a foundational resource for understanding the mathematical analysis framework on which many cryptographic algorithms are built. For a more in-depth comprehension of cryptography, the sources [18–23] give a good insight.

Mathematics enables a quantitative understanding of risks, empowering organizations to prioritize security investments and implement effective countermeasures. The role of mathematics and statistics is discussed by Singh et al. [24, 25]. In this chapter, we provide data to support the idea that mathematics and statistics are essential to the field of cybersecurity because they make it possible to recognize recurring patterns in these systems. In addition, those coming to the subject of cybersecurity from other professions might gain a great deal by having prior experience with mathematics.

19.2 NUMBER THEORY

Number theory provides the foundation for many cryptographic algorithms and has numerous applications in modern cryptography. Understanding the basics, such as divisibility, prime numbers, modular arithmetic, the Euclidean algorithm, and Euler's totient function, is essential for cryptographic operations and developing secure systems. In [26], an introduction to ancient and current arithmetic subjects that are important in applications in cryptology is discussed and a comprehensive study is done in [27]. Some computational number theory fundamentals that are essential in cryptography can be seen in [9], and [10] discusses applications of number theory in cryptography.

This section provides an overview of key concepts in number theory, along with mathematical formulas and visual representations.

Divisibility is a mathematical concept that helps determine if one number can be evenly divided by another. It is denoted by using the notation "$a \mid b$," where "a" divides "b" without leaving a remainder. In other words, if "a" divides "b," then "b" is a multiple of "a."
The formula that represents the concept of divisibility is as follows:

$$a \mid b \Leftrightarrow b = a * q,$$

where "a" and "b" are integers, and "q" is an integer quotient.

In this formula, "a" is the divisor, "b" is the dividend, and "q" is the quotient. If there exists an integer value of "q" such that when "a" is multiplied by "q," it equals "b," then we say that "a" divides "b" evenly or that "a" is a divisor of "b."

For example, let's consider the following division: $6 \mid 18$. To determine if 6 divides 18 evenly, we can use the formula: $18 = 6 * q$.

If we find an integer value for "q" that satisfies this equation, then 6 evenly divides 18. In this case, "q" would be 3 since 18 = 6 * 3.

On the other hand, if no integer value of "q" exists such that the equation is satisfied, then "a" does not divide "b" evenly. For example, if we consider 6 | 19, we cannot find an integer value for "q" that makes the equation $19 = 6 * q$ true. Therefore, 6 does not divide 19 evenly.

Modular arithmetic is a mathematical system where numbers "wrap around" after reaching a certain value called the modulus. It is widely used in cryptography and encryption algorithms to perform operations within a specific modulus. The notation "$a \equiv b(mod\, m)$" represents that "a" is congruent to "$b modulo m$." A number line visualization of equivalence classes Modulo 12 is depicted in Figure 19.1. The formulas describing modular arithmetic operations are as follows:

Addition: $(a+b) mod\, m = (a\, mod\, m + b\, mod\, m) mod\, m$

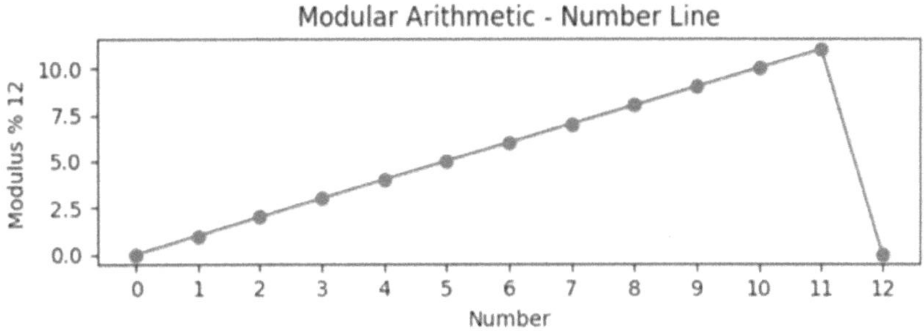

Figure 19.1 Number Line Visualization: Equivalence Classes Modulo 12.

This formula states that to find the sum of two numbers modulo "m," we can first take the modulus of each number separately, add them together, and then take the modulus of the result.

Subtraction: $(a-b) mod\, m = (a\, mod\, m - b\, mod\, m) mod\, m$

Similarly, to perform subtraction modulo "m," we take the modulus of each number separately, subtract them, and then take the modulus of the result.

Multiplication: $(a * b) mod\, m = (a\, mod\, m * b\, mod\, m) mod\, m$

To perform multiplication modulo "m," we take the modulus of each number separately, multiply them, and then take the modulus of the result.

Modular arithmetic is used in the exponentiation operations during the key exchange process, ensuring that the calculated values remain within a specified modulus.

- It is employed in cryptographic hash functions, which are used to map data of an arbitrary size to a fixed-size hash value. Modular operations are often part of the compression function in hash algorithms, ensuring that intermediate values and the final hash value remain within a specific modulus.
- Its arithmetic plays a role in primality testing algorithms used in cryptography. These algorithms check whether a given number is prime or composite. Modular arithmetic operations, such as modular exponentiation and modular multiplication, are utilized to perform tests and verify the primality of numbers.
- It is used in secret sharing schemes, where a secret is divided into shares distributed among participants. The shares are combined using modular operations to reconstruct the original secret, providing a level of security and confidentiality.

- It is employed in error detection and correction codes used in communication protocols. Modular operations help detect errors and recover the original message by performing calculations within a specific modulus.

The *Euclidean algorithm* is a recursive algorithm used to find the greatest common divisor (GCD) of two numbers. The GCD is the largest positive integer that divides both numbers without leaving a remainder. The Euclidean algorithm operates by iteratively applying the following formula: $GCD(a,b) = GCD(b, a \; mod \; b)$, where "$a$" and "$b$" are positive integers

To apply the Euclidean algorithm, we may follow these steps:

Start with two positive integers, "a" and "b," where $a>b$.
Calculate the remainder when "a" is divided by "b" using the modulus operation: $r=a mod b$. If the remainder "r" is equal to 0, the algorithm terminates, and the GCD is equal to "b." If the remainder "r" is not zero, repeat the process by assigning "b" to "a" and "r" to "b," then go back to the previous step.
Continue the iterations until the remainder becomes zero. The GCD will be the last non-zero remainder obtained.

For example, let's find the GCD of 48 and 18 using the Euclidean algorithm:

$$GCD(48,18) = GCD(18, 48 \; mod \; 18) = GCD(18,12)$$

$$GCD(18,12) = GCD(12, 18 \; mod \; 12) = GCD(12,6)$$

$$GCD(12,6) = GCD(6, 12 \; mod \; 6) = GCD(6,0)$$

Since the remainder becomes 0, the algorithm terminates. The GCD is the last non-zero remainder, which is 6. Therefore, GCD(48, 18) = 6.

While the Euclidean algorithm may not be directly visible in the implementation of cryptographic algorithms, its underlying principles and applications are crucial in the development and functioning of various cryptographic techniques. It enables key generation, modular inverse calculation, secure communication, error detection, and correction, contributing to the security and reliability of cryptographic systems.

2.4 *Euler's totient function*, denoted as $\varphi(n)$ (graphical visualization can be seen in Figure 19.2), is a mathematical function that calculates the count

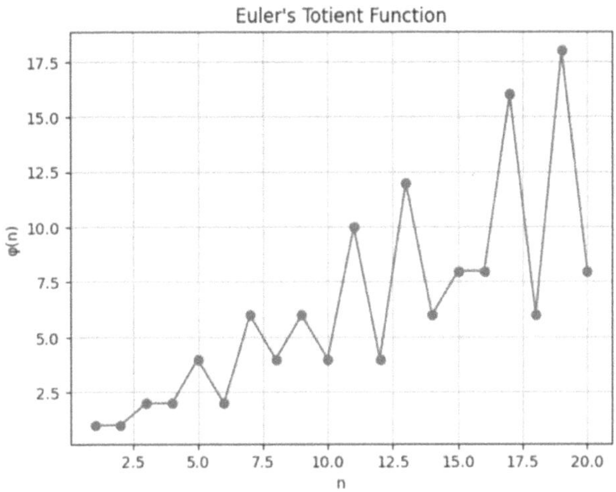

Figure 19.2 Graph Visualizes Euler's Totient Function φ (*n*) for Values of "*n*" Ranging from 1 to 20. The X-axis represents the input values of "*n*," while the Y-axis represents the corresponding values of φ (*n*). Each point on the graph represents the pair (*n*,φ (*n*)).

of positive integers less than or equal to "n" that are relatively prime to "n " (i.e., they share no common factors other than 1). Euler's totient function has various applications in number theory and cryptography, particularly in public-key cryptography.

The formula for Euler's totient function is as follows:

$$\varphi(n)=n*(1-1/p_1)*(1-1/p_2)*\ldots*(1-1/p_k),$$

where "n" is a positive integer and "$p_1,p_2,\ldots,p_k$" represents the distinct prime factors of "n."

To compute $\varphi(n)$, the steps are:

Determine the prime factorization of "n" by finding all its distinct prime factors, denoted as "$p_1,p_2,\ldots,p_k$" For each prime factor "p_i", subtract 1 from it $(1-1/p_i)$.

Multiply all the values obtained previously together. Multiply the result by "n" to obtain $\varphi(n)$.

For example, let's calculate $\varphi(12)$: The prime factorization of 12 is $2^2 * 3^1$.

Apply the formula: $\varphi(12)=12*(1-1/2)*(1-1/3)=12*(1/2)*(2/3)=4$. Therefore, φ (12) = 4, indicating that there are four positive integers less than or equal to 12 that are relatively prime to 12 (1, 5, 7, and 11).

In the RSA algorithm, Euler's totient function plays a crucial role in key generation and encryption. The RSA algorithm relies on the difficulty of factoring large numbers. The totient function $\varphi(n)$ is used to calculate the totient value for large composite numbers, which is required for generating the public and private keys. The security of the RSA algorithm is based on the assumption that factoring large numbers is computationally challenging.

It is used to calculate the totient values $\varphi(p)$ and $\varphi(q)$ in public-key cryptosystems like RSA. These totient values are crucial for generating the private key and ensuring the security of the encryption and decryption processes.

It is involved in primality testing algorithms used in cryptography. For example, the Miller-Rabin primality test relies on Euler's totient function to check certain conditions during the primality testing process.

It is used in various key exchange protocols, such as the Diffie-Hellman key exchange. The totient value of a prime modulus is often required in these protocols to compute the shared secret key.

19.3 DISCRETE MATHEMATICS

Discrete mathematics provides tools for modeling and analyzing discrete structures, which are prevalent in cybersecurity. Graph theory [28] is used to model network topologies and analyze their vulnerabilities. Combinatorics and combinatorial optimization are applied in password cracking, network packet analysis, and key space analysis.

19.3.1 Network topology (graph theory)

A network topology can be mathematically represented using a graph. A graph is a mathematical structure consisting of a set of vertices (nodes) and a set of edges. In the context of network topology, the vertices represent the network entities such as computers, servers, or routers, and the edges represent the connections between them.

Mathematically, a network topology can be represented as a graph $G=(V,E)$, where V is the set of vertices and E is the set of edges. Each vertex $v_i \in V$ represents a network entity, and each edge $(v_i, v_j) \in E$ represents a connection between entities v_i and v_j. (Figure 19.3)

A few examples where graph theory is used in cryptography are provided.

19.3.2 Cryptographic algorithms

Graph theory is used in the analysis and design of cryptographic algorithms. For example, block ciphers, which are widely used encryption algorithms,

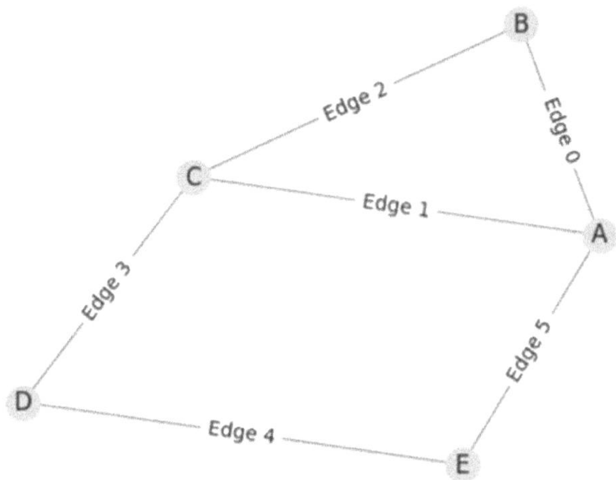

Figure 19.3 A graph having five nodes and six edges.

can be modeled as permutation networks. The Feistel cipher structure, used in many symmetric encryption algorithms, can be represented as a graph to analyze its properties and vulnerabilities.

19.3.3 Cryptographic key management

Combinatorics plays a role in the generation, storage, and management of cryptographic keys. The number of possible keys and the key space analysis involve combinatorial calculations. Combinatorial optimization techniques can be applied to optimize key generation processes, such as finding efficient methods for key scheduling or generating keys with desired properties.

19.3.4 Cryptanalysis

Graph theory and combinatorial optimization techniques are used in cryptanalysis to break cryptographic schemes or analyze their vulnerabilities. For example:

- Side-channel attacks: Side-channel attacks involve analyzing unintended information leakage, such as power consumption or electromagnetic radiation, to extract cryptographic keys. Graph theory can be used to model the relationships between the side-channel measurements and the cryptographic keys.
- Differential cryptanalysis: Differential cryptanalysis is a technique used to break symmetric encryption algorithms by analyzing the differences in ciphertext pairs. Combinatorial optimization algorithms

can be applied to find the best differential characteristics or the most likely key candidates.

- Algebraic attacks: Algebraic attacks aim to recover secret parameters or keys by solving systems of algebraic equations derived from the cryptographic algorithm. Graph theory and combinatorics can be used to analyze the algebraic structures and optimize the search for solutions.
- Cryptographic protocols: Graph theory is applied to model and analyze cryptographic protocols, such as key exchange protocols or authentication protocols. The security properties and vulnerabilities of these protocols can be assessed using graph-based formal methods.

19.4 FINITE FIELDS

A finite field $GF(q)$ consists of q elements, where q is a prime power, i.e., $q = p^m$, where $p$is a prime number and m is a positive integer. The elements of a finite field are typically represented as integers modulo q, ranging from 0 to $q-1$.

Finite fields have well-defined arithmetic operations, and these operations follow specific rules and properties.

a) Addition: In a finite field $GF(q)$, addition is performed modulo q. For any two elements $a$and b in the finite field, $a+b \mod q$ is computed.
b) Subtraction: Subtraction in a finite field is equivalent to addition modulo q. For any two elements a and b in the finite field, $a-b \mod q$ is computed.
c) Multiplication: Multiplication in a finite field is performed modulo q. For any two elements a and b in the finite field, $a * b \mod q$ is computed.
d) Division: Division in a finite field is equivalent to multiplication by the multiplicative inverse. For any non-zero element a in the finite field, the multiplicative inverse $a^{(-1)}$ is calculated such that $(a * a^{(-1)} \mod q = 1$.

Finite fields satisfy certain properties that are fundamental to being a field:

a) Closure: For any two elements a and b in the finite field $GF(q)$, $a + b$ and $a * b$ are also elements of the finite field.
b) Associativity: Addition and multiplication operations in a finite field are associative.
c) Commutativity: Addition and multiplication operations in a finite field are commutative.
d) Identity elements: There exist additive and multiplicative identity elements (0 and 1, respectively) in the finite field.

e) Inverse elements: Every non-zero element in the finite field has a unique multiplicative inverse.
f) Distributive property: The distributive property holds for addition and multiplication operations in a finite field.

Galois fields are a special class of finite fields named after the mathematician Évariste Galois. They are denoted as $GF(p^m)$, where p is a prime number, and m is a positive integer. Galois fields have p^m elements and possess several unique properties, such as being a field extension of the prime field $GF(p)$.

Finite fields are utilized in cryptography in the following way:

- Symmetric key cryptography:

Symmetric key cryptography involves the use of a shared secret key for encryption and decryption. Mathematically, a symmetric encryption algorithm can be represented as a pair of functions (E, D), where:

Encryption function: $E(K, M) -> C$

K: The secret key
M: The plaintext message
C: The ciphertext produced by encrypting M with the key K
Decryption function: $D(K, C) -> M$
K: The secret key
C: The ciphertext
M: The plaintext obtained by decrypting C with the key K

The functions E and D should satisfy the property that $D(K, E(K, M)) = M$, ensuring that the original plaintext can be recovered from the ciphertext using the correct key.

- Public-key cryptography:

Public-key cryptography, also known as asymmetric cryptography, utilizes different keys for encryption and decryption. Mathematically, a public-key encryption algorithm consists of a pair of functions (E, D), where:

Encryption function: $E(PU, M) -> C$

PU: The public key used for encryption
M: The plaintext message
C: The ciphertext obtained by encrypting M with the public key PU
Decryption function: $D(PR, C) -> M$

PR: The private key used for decryption
C: The ciphertext
M: The plaintext recovered by decrypting C with the private key PR

The functions E and D are mathematically related in a way that decryption is only feasible with the corresponding private key. The security of the system relies on the computational difficulty of deriving the private key from the public key.

- Elliptic curve cryptography (ECC):

Elliptic curve cryptography is a type of public-key cryptography that employs the algebraic properties of elliptic curves defined over finite fields. Mathematically, an elliptic curve E is defined by the equation:

$$E : y^2 = x^3 + ax + b$$

The curve equation is defined over a finite field $GF(q)$, where q is a prime power.

The curve parameters a and b are elements of the finite field $GF(q)$.

The points on the elliptic curve E form a finite group, denoted by $E(GF(q))$.

The security of ECC relies on the computational difficulty of solving the elliptic curve discrete logarithm problem.

- Error-correcting codes:

Error-correcting codes are used to detect and correct errors in transmitted or stored data. Mathematically, an error-correcting code is defined by a set of codewords and a decoding algorithm.

Codewords: A codeword is a sequence of symbols from a finite alphabet, typically represented as binary strings.
Encoding function: $E(M) -> C$
M: The message to be encoded
C: The codeword produced by encoding M using the error-correcting code

The decoding algorithm is designed to identify and correct errors in the received codeword, recovering the original message M. Various error-correcting codes, such as Reed-Solomon codes and Bose–Chaudhuri–Hocquenghem (BCH) codes, utilize mathematical operations in finite fields to perform encoding and decoding.

19.5 LINEAR ALGEBRA

Linear algebra is used in various cryptographic algorithms and protocols. Metric and vector spaces find applications in symmetric key encryption, such as the advanced encryption standard (AES). Linear algebra is also employed in error-correcting codes, which ensure data integrity and reliability.

19.5.1 Matrices and matrix operations

A matrix is denoted by a capital letter, such as A, B, or C. It is represented as a rectangular array of elements or numbers enclosed by brackets. An $m \times n$ matrix A is defined as:

$$A = \left[a_{ij}\right], \text{ where } 1 \le i \le m \text{ and } 1 \le j \le n.$$

Here, a_{ij} represents the element at the intersection of the i-th row and j -th column.

Addition and Subtraction: Matrix addition and subtraction are performed element-wise on matrices of the same size. Let A and B be two matrices of the same size:

$$A = \left[a_{ij}\right] \text{ and } B = \left[b_{ij}\right]$$

The sum of matrices A and B, denoted as $A+B$, is obtained by adding the corresponding elements: $(A+B) = \left[a_{ij} + b_{ij}\right]$.
Similarly, the difference of matrices A and B, denoted as $A-B$, is obtained by subtracting the corresponding elements: $(A-B) = \left[a_{ij} - b_{ij}\right]$.

Scalar multiplication: Scalar multiplication involves multiplying each element of a matrix by a scalar. Let A be a matrix and c be a scalar: $A = \left[a_{ij}\right]$. The scalar multiplication of matrix A by scalar c, denoted as cA, is obtained by multiplying each element of A by c: $(cA) = \left[ca_{ij}\right]$

Matrix multiplication: Matrix multiplication is defined for two matrices, where the number of columns of the first matrix is equal to the number of rows of the second matrix. Let A be an $m \times n$ matrix and B be an $n \times p$ matrix: $A = \left[a_{ij}\right]$ and $B = \left[b_{ij}\right]$.
The product of matrices A and B, denoted as AB, is an $m \times p$ matrix. The element at the intersection of the i-th row and j-th column in AB is obtained by taking the dot product of the i-th row of A with the j-th column of B:

$(AB)_{ij} = \Sigma(a_{ik} * b_{jk})$, where the summation is taken over the index k from 1 to n.

Transpose: The transpose of a matrix is obtained by interchanging its rows and columns. Let A be an $m \times n$ matrix. The transpose of matrix A, denoted as A^T, is an $n \times m$ matrix, where the element at the intersection of the i-th row and j-th column in A^T is the element at the intersection of the j-th row and i-th column in A: $(A^T)_{ij} = a_{ji}$.

Inverse: The inverse of a square matrix A is defined such that the product of A with its inverse yields the identity matrix. Let A be a square matrix: $A = [a_{ij}]$.

If A^{-1} is the inverse of A, then $A * A^{-1} = A^{-1} * A = I$, where I is the identity matrix.

Rank: The rank of a matrix is the maximum number of linearly independent rows or columns in the matrix. It represents the dimension of the vector space spanned by the rows or columns of the matrix.

Determinant: The determinant of a square matrix A, denoted as *det(A)* or $|A|$, is a scalar value that encodes important properties of the matrix. It is computed using various methods, such as cofactor expansion or (LUC) Cryptosystem (LU) decomposition.

19.5.1.1 Example

Consider a matrix-based encryption algorithm that utilizes matrix multiplication and modular arithmetic. Let's assume we have a plaintext message represented as a matrix P and a secret key matrix K. The encryption process involves multiplying the plaintext matrix P with the key matrix K modulo a certain value to obtain the ciphertext matrix C.

Mathematically, the encryption process can be represented as: $C \equiv P * K (mod\, M)$

where C is the ciphertext matrix, P is the plaintext matrix, K is the key matrix, and M is the modulus value.

To decrypt the ciphertext matrix C and obtain the original plaintext matrix P, we need the knowledge of the inverse of the key matrix K. The decryption process involves multiplying the ciphertext matrix C with the inverse of the key matrix K modulo the same value M.

Mathematically, the decryption process can be represented as: $P \equiv C * K^{-1} (mod\, M)$

where P is the plaintext matrix, C is the ciphertext matrix, K^{-1} is the inverse of the key matrix K, and M is the modulus value.

19.5.2 Systems of linear equations

Mathematically, a system of linear equations is a set of equations that can be written in the form:

$$a_{11} * x_1 + a_{12} * x_2 + \ldots + a_{1n} * x_n = b_1$$

$$a_{21} * x_1 + a_{22} * x_2 + \ldots + a_{2n} * x_n = b_2$$

$$\ldots$$

$$a_{m1} * x_1 + a_{m2} * x_2 + \ldots + a_{mn} * x_n = b_m$$

where:

$x_1, x_2, \ldots, x_n$ are the variables (unknowns) of the system,
$a_{11}, a_{12}, \ldots, a_{mn}$ are the coefficients of the variables,
$b_1, b_2, \ldots, b_m$ are the constants or right-hand side values of the equations,
m is the number of equations in the system, and
$n$is the number of variables in the system.

In matrix notation, the system can be represented as $A * X = B$

where, A is an $m \times n$ coefficient matrix, where each element a_{ij} represents the coefficient of x_i in the j-th equation, X is an $n \times 1$ matrix (column vector) representing the variables $x_1, x_2, \ldots, x_n$, B is an $m \times 1$ matrix (column vector) representing the constants $b_1, b_2, \ldots, b_m$.

The goal of solving a system of linear equations is to find a solution that satisfies all the equations simultaneously. The solution may be unique, have infinitely many solutions, or have no solutions, depending on the properties of the system.

Linear equations play a vital role in public-key algorithms such as RSA. The encryption and decryption processes involve solving systems of linear congruence equations, such as the Chinese remainder theorem (CRT) equations. The solution of these equations enables secure encryption and decryption of messages.

19.5.2.1 Example

Cryptanalysis involves breaking cryptographic systems or analyzing their security properties. Linear equations play a crucial role in certain cryptanalytic techniques, such as linear cryptanalysis:

- Assume you have access to a known plaintext-ciphertext pair in a cryptographic system.
- Define a set of linear equations based on the known plaintext-ciphertext pair and the encryption algorithm's properties.
- Solve the system of linear equations to find possible keys or key components used in the encryption algorithm.
- Use the solutions obtained from the linear equations to recover the full cryptographic key or analyze the vulnerability of the system.

The linear equations can be derived based on the algebraic properties or linear approximations of the encryption algorithm. By solving the equations, the cryptanalyst aims to gain insights into the cryptographic key or exploit vulnerabilities in the system's linear properties.

19.5.3 Eigenvalues and eigenvectors

Given a square matrix A, an eigenvector v and its corresponding eigenvalue λ satisfy the following equation:

$$A * v = \lambda * v$$

Eigenvalue (λ): An eigenvalue is a scalar λ that, when multiplied by an eigenvector, yields a transformed vector that is parallel to the original eigenvector. In other words, when a linear transformation (represented by the matrix A) is applied to an eigenvector, the resulting vector is a scaled version of the original eigenvector. The eigenvalue λ represents the scaling factor.

Eigenvector (v): An eigenvector is a non-zero vector v that remains in the same direction after the linear transformation represented by the matrix A. It may change in magnitude, but its direction remains unchanged.

To find the eigenvalues and eigenvectors of a given matrix A, we solve the eigenvalue equation:

$$A * v = \lambda * v$$

This equation can be rewritten as: $\left(A - \lambda * I\right) * v = 0$, where I is the identity matrix.

To solve for the eigenvalues, we find the values of λ that make the determinant of the matrix $\left(A - \lambda * I\right)$ equal to zero: $det\left(A - \lambda * I\right) = 0$

This equation gives the characteristic equation, and the solutions for λ are the eigenvalues of the matrix A. Once the eigenvalues are determined, we can find the corresponding eigenvectors by substituting each eigenvalue back into the eigenvalue equation and solving for the eigenvector v.

The eigenvectors associated with each eigenvalue form a set of linearly independent vectors, which can be used to diagonalize the matrix A or analyze the properties of the linear transformation.

Example: cryptographic key generation using eigenvalues and eigenvectors Consider a cryptographic system that uses matrix operations and eigenvalues/eigenvectors for key generation:

- Generate a random square matrix A of size $n \times n$, where n is the desired key length.
- Compute the eigenvalues (λ) and eigenvectors (v) of matrix A.
- Select a subset of eigenvalues and their corresponding eigenvectors based on specific criteria or algorithms.
- Use the selected eigenvalues and eigenvectors to construct the cryptographic key.

The selection of eigenvalues and eigenvectors can be based on certain properties, such as magnitude, orthogonality, or other cryptographic criteria. The resulting subset of eigenvalues and eigenvectors forms the cryptographic key, which can be used for encryption and decryption purposes.

19.6. METRIC SPACES

Humans can see differences but not measure them. For instance, two buildings of different colors are distinct yet still buildings. One building and computers are different. We must measure this difference reasonably and metric provides a platform for this.

Let Xbe a set. A metric on X is a function $d : X \times X \rightarrow R$, called a distance function or metric, that assigns a non-negative real number to every pair of elements in X and satisfies the following properties for all elements x, y, and z in X:

- Non-negativity: $d(x,y) \geq 0$,
- Identity of indiscernibles: $d(x,y) = 0$ if and only if $x=y$. This property states that the distance between two elements is zero if and only if the elements are the same.
- Symmetry: $d(x,y) = d(y,x)$ for all x and y in X.
- Triangle inequality: $d(x,z) \leq d(x,y) + d(y,z)$ for all x, y, and z in X.
- Together, the set X equipped with the distance function d is called a metric space, denoted as (X,d).

19.6.1 Euclidean distance

The Euclidean distance between two points in an n-dimensional space is the straight-line distance between the:

$$d(x,y) = \sqrt{(\Sigma((x_i - y_i)\dagger)} \; for \; i = 1 \; ton,$$

where x and $y$are vectors representing the coordinates of the two points.

19.6.2 Manhattan distance (or city block distance)

The Manhattan distance between two points is the sum of the absolute differences of their coordinates along each dimension:

$$d(x,y) = \Sigma(|x_i - y_i|) \; for \; i = 1 \; ton,$$

where x and y are vectors representing the coordinates of the two points.

19.6.3 Minkowski distance

The Minkowski distance is a generalized distance metric that includes both the Euclidean and Manhattan distances as special cases. It is parameterized by a parameter 'p' which determines the specific distance measure:

$$d(x,y) = \Sigma\left(|x_i - y_i|^p\right)^{1/p} \; for \; i = 1 \; ton,$$

where x and y are vectors representing the coordinates of the two points.

19.6.4 Hamming distance

The Hamming distance is a metric used to measure the difference between two strings of equal length. It counts the number of positions at which the corresponding elements are different:

$$d(x,y) = count(i \; where \; x_i \neq y_i) for \; i = 1 \; ton,$$

where x and y are binary strings of length n.

19.6.5 Cosine distance (cosine similarity)

The cosine distance measures the similarity between two vectors based on the cosine of the angle between them. It is often used for comparing the similarity of document vectors or high-dimensional feature vectors:

$$d(x,y) = 1 - (dot\ product\ of\ x\ and\ y) / (magnitude\ of\ x * magnitude\ of\ y),$$

where x and y are vectors.

19.6.6 Jaccard distance (Jaccard similarity)

The Jaccard distance is a measure of dissimilarity between two sets. It is defined as the difference between the size of the intersection and the size of the union of the sets.

$$d(x,y) = 1 - (size\ of\ intersection\ of\ x\ and\ y) / (size\ of\ union\ of\ x\ and\ y),$$

where x and y are sets.

In cybersecurity, matrices and distance-based analysis provide a structured approach to understanding and detecting anomalous or malicious activities. They enable the comparison of observed data with reference models, detect deviations, and assist in identifying potential threats or vulnerabilities.

Consider two points (1, 2, 3) and (4, 5, 6), Figure 19.4 shows the different distances between these two points.

- **Cryptographic algorithms**

In the context of cryptographic algorithms, a matrix is often represented as $A = \left[a_{ij}\right]$, where i represents the row index and j represents the column index. The elements a_{ij} can be numbers, symbols, or mathematical operations.

Here, distance can refer to the difference or similarity between matrices. The distance between two matrices, A and B, can be measured using various distance metrics, such as the Euclidean distance or Hamming distance. Let's denote the distance between matrices A and B as $d(A,B)$.

- **Anomaly detection**

Let's denote the observed matrix as $X = \left[x_{ij}\right]$, where i represents the row index, and j represents the column index. The elements x_{ij} can be values or characteristics associated with the observed patterns. Distance metrics are used to measure the dissimilarity or deviation of observed patterns from normal behavior. Let's denote the distance between the observed matrix X and a reference matrix Y as $d(X,Y)$. The distance can be calculated using various metrics, such as the Euclidean distance, Manhattan distance, or Mahalanobis distance.

- **Network traffic analysis**

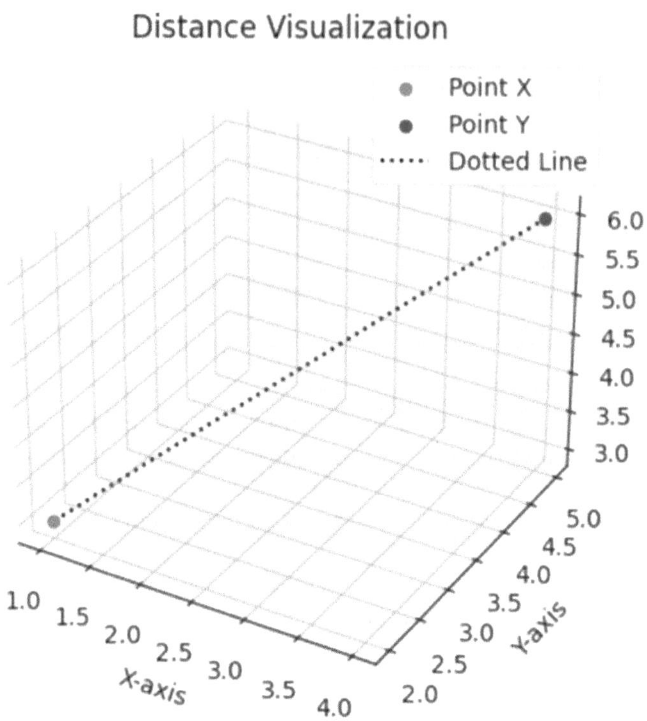


```
Euclidean Distance: 5.196152422706632
Manhattan Distance: 9
Minkowski Distance (p=3): 4.3267487109222245
Hamming Distance: 3
Cosine Distance: 0.025368153802923787
```

Figure 19.4 Graph showing the two points in 3D and their calculated distances.

Let's denote the traffic matrix as $T=\left[t_{ij}\right]$, where i represents the source node and j represents the destination node. The elements t_{ij} can represent traffic volume, communication frequency, or other relevant parameters. Distance metrics can measure the similarity or dissimilarity between traffic matrices. Let's denote the distance between two traffic matrices T and U as $d(T,U)$. Distance can be calculated using metrics such as the Euclidean distance, cosine distance, or correlation distance.

- **Intrusion detection systems (IDS)**

Let's denote the matrix representing observed behavior as $M=\left[m_{ij}\right]$, where i represents the parameter index and j represents the time index.

The elements m_{ij} can represent values or characteristics associated with the observed behavior.

Distance: Distance-based analysis is used to identify potential threats or intrusions by comparing the observed matrix M with a reference or normal behavior matrix N. Let's denote the distance between matrices M and N as $d(M,N)$. Distance can be calculated using metrics such as the Euclidean distance, Mahalanobis distance, or Kullback-Leibler divergence.

MALWARE ANALYSIS

Matrices: Matrices can represent the behavioral patterns or features of malware samples. Let's denote the matrix representing the behavior of a malware sample as $B=\left[b_{ij}\right]$, where i represents the feature index, and j represents the time index. The elements b_{ij} can represent the presence or absence of specific behavioral characteristics.

The distance-based analysis is used to compare the behavioral patterns of different malware samples. Let's denote the distance between two malware behavior matrices, B and C as $d(B,C)$. The distance can be calculated using metrics such as the Hamming distance, Jaccard distance, or cosine distance.

19.7 OPTIMIZATION THEORY

Optimization techniques are used to solve complex problems in cybersecurity, such as resource allocation, intrusion detection, and risk assessment. Linear programming, integer programming, etc., are applied to find optimal solutions and make efficient use of resources.

19.7.1 Linear programming

In linear programming, the goal is to optimize a linear objective function subject to linear constraints. Mathematically, it can be formulated as follows:

$$Maximize : c^T * x$$

$$Subject\,to : A * x \leq b$$

Here, c is a vector of coefficients for the objective function, x is a vector of decision variables, A is a matrix representing the constraints, and b is a vector of constants.

The objective function represents the quantity to be maximized or minimized. The constraints define the limits or conditions under which the variables must satisfy.

19.7.1.1 Example: resource allocation

Objective: Maximize the overall security effectiveness (E) within the budget constraint (B).
Variables: Let x_1, x_2, and x_3 allocate resources to firewall, IDS, and security training programs, respectively.

Constraints :

$$Cost\,Constraint: 100x_1 + 200x_2 + 50x_3 \leq B(budget\,constraint)$$

$$Effectiveness\,Constraints:$$
$$0.8x_1 + 0.9x_2 + 0.7x_3 \geq E(security\,effectiveness\,requirement)$$

$$Non-negativity\,Constraints: x_1 \geq 0, x_2 \geq 0, x_3 \geq 0$$

Solution: Let's say the budget constraint is $B = 1000$ and the minimum security effectiveness requirement is $E = 0.8$. The optimal resource allocation might be $x_1 = 4$ (firewalls), $x_2 = 3$ (IDS), and $x_3 = 10$ (security training programs), resulting in a maximum security effectiveness of 8.2.

19.7.2 Integer programming

Integer programming is an extension of linear programming where the decision variables are restricted to integer values. It can be mathematically defined as follows:

$$Maximize: c^T * x$$

$$Subject\,to: A * x \leq b$$

$$x \in Z^n$$

The additional constraint, $x \in Z^n$,indicates that the decision variable x must take integer values.

Integer programming is used when the decision variables represent discrete quantities, such as the number of units to be produced or the selection of discrete options.

19.7.2.1 Example: network hardening

Objective: Minimize the total cost of deploying firewalls (F) and IDS (I) in a network.

Variables: Let x_1, x_2 be binary decision variables representing the placement of firewalls and IDS sensors, respectively.

Constraints:

Budget Constraint: $100x_1 + 150x_2, \leq B$ (budget constraint)

Network Coverage Constraint: At least one firewall and one IDS sensor must be deployed.

Non-negativity Constraints: $x_1, x_2, \in \{0, 1\}$

Solution: Let's say the budget constraint is $B = 800$. The optimal solution might be $x_1 = 1$ (firewall deployed) and $x_2 = 1$ (IDS sensor deployed), resulting in the minimum total cost for network hardening.

19.7.3 Nonlinear programming

Nonlinear programming deals with optimizing nonlinear objective functions subject to constraints. It can be formulated as follows:

$$Maximize\ /\ Minimize : f(x)$$

$$Subject\,to : g(x) \leq 0$$

$$h(x) = 0$$

Here, $f(x)$ represents the objective function, a nonlinear function of the decision variables x. The constraints $g(x)$ and $h(x)$ represent inequality and equality constraints, respectively. Nonlinear programming allows for more complex optimization problems where the relationships between the variables and the objective function or constraints are nonlinear.

19.7.3.1 Example: security protocol optimization

Objective: Minimize the communication overhead (O) of a secure communication protocol.

Variables: Let x_1, x_2 $and\, x_3$ represent the parameters or configuration settings of the protocol.

Constraints:

$$Security\,Constraint: f(x_1,x_2,x_3) \geq S(minimum\,security\,requirement)$$

$$Performance\,Constraint: g(x_1,x_2,x_3) \leq P(maximum\,performance\,requirement)$$

$$Bounds\,on\,Parameters: x_1\,in[0,10], x_2\,in[1,100], x_3 in[0,1]$$

Solution: The minimum security requirement is S = 0.9 and the maximum performance requirement is P = 100. The optimal parameter values might be x_1 = 2.5, x_2 = 50, and x_3 = 0.8, resulting in a protocol that balances security and performance within the specified requirements.

19.7.4 Convex optimization

Convex optimization focuses on optimizing convex objective functions subject to convex constraints. Convexity refers to certain properties of functions and sets that allow for efficient optimization. The mathematical formulation is as follows:

$$Minimize: f(x)$$

$$Subject\,to: g(x) \leq 0$$

$$h(x) = 0$$

The objective function $f(x)$ and the constraints $g(x)$ and $h(x)$ must satisfy certain convexity properties. Convex optimization is widely used because it guarantees finding the global optimal solution for convex problems efficiently.

19.7.4.1 Example: anomaly detection

Objective: Minimize the false positive rate (FPR) of an anomaly detection system while maintaining a high true positive rate (TPR).

Variables: Let x_1, x_2 be the thresholds for anomaly detection.

Constraints:

$$TPR\,Constraint: f(x_1,x_2) \geq T\,(minimum\,true\,positive\,rate\,requirement)$$

$$FPR\,Constraint: g(x_1,x_2) \leq F\,(maximum\,false\,positive\,rate\,requirement)$$

$$Bounds\,on\,Thresholds: x_1, x_2 \geq 0, x_1 + x_2 \leq 1$$

Solution: Let's say the minimum true positive rate requirement is $T = 0.95$ and the maximum false positive rate requirement is $F = 0.05$.

The optimal thresholds might be $x_1 = 0.2$ and $x_2 = 0.7$, resulting in an anomaly detection system with high TPR and low FPR.

19.7.5 Game theory

Game theory studies the strategic interactions between multiple decision-makers, known as players. In game theory, a game is defined by specifying the players, their strategies, and their payoffs. The mathematical representation involves:

Players: $N = \{1, 2, ..., n\}$
Strategies: Each player i has a set of strategies S_i.
Payoff Function: $U_i(s_1, s_2, \ldots, s_n)$ assigns a real-valued payoff to each combination of strategies chosen by the players.

Game theory is employed in cybersecurity to model interactions between attackers and defenders. It helps analyze strategic decision-making in situations where adversaries try to gain an advantage. Game theory assists in evaluating optimal defense strategies and understanding attacker behavior.

19.7.5.1 Example: security strategy analysis

Objective: Maximize the defender's expected payoff (PD) in a security game against an attacker.
Variables: Let x_1, x_2 be the defender's strategy choices, and y_1, y_2 be the attacker's strategy choices.
Payoff Functions: $U_1(x_1, y_1, y_2)$ represents the defender's payoff, and U_2 (x_1, x_2, y_2) represents the attacker's payoff.
Constraints: None, as it depends on the specific security game being modeled.

Solution: In a specific security game, after analyzing the strategies and payoff functions, the optimal strategy choices for the defender and attacker can be determined, leading to the maximum expected payoff for the defender.

Some other sources contain applied approaches from combinatorial mathematics, probabilities, and statistics [29], neural networks [1, 29], fuzzy logic and fuzzy sets [30, 31], and group theory in cryptography [32, 33].

19.8 CONCLUDING REMARKS

Cryptography and encryption techniques are essential mathematical foundations in cybersecurity. These techniques involve the use of mathematical algorithms to convert sensitive information into unreadable formats, ensuring its confidentiality and integrity. By applying mathematical principles, cryptography helps protect data during transmission and storage, preventing unauthorized access and ensuring secure communication. Additionally, encryption techniques play a crucial role in securing passwords, financial transactions, and sensitive personal information from cyber threats. Thus, mathematics provides the foundation for creating secure cryptographic systems. Statistical analysis helps identify patterns and anomalies in network traffic to detect cyber threats. Mathematical models are also used to assess the probability of cyber attacks and determine the effectiveness of security measures. The main emphasis of this chapter is to enable the readers to understand the application of well-established mathematical theories employed in the traditional cybersecurity area of research. This article describes the fundamentals of various mathematical algorithms used in the analysis of computer security and is able to validate, simulate, and forecast the behavior of information systems and communication networks under attack.

REFERENCES

1. Dhaliwal, N., Aghera, S., Whig, P., & Dutta, P. K. (2024). Advanced Analytics and Quantum Computing for Revolutionizing Procurement Strategies. In A. Hassan, P. Bhattacharya, P. Dutta, J. Verma, & N. Kundu (Eds.), *Quantum Computing and Supply Chain Management: A New Era of Optimization* (pp. 160–175). IGI Global. https://doi.org/10.4018/979-8-3693-4107-0.ch011.
2. Singh, B., Dutta, P. K., & Kaunert, C. (2024). Boosting Quantum Computing to Redefine Supply Chain in the Hospital Industry: Pitch the Vision for Medical and Healthcare Needs. In A. Hassan, P. Bhattacharya, P. Dutta, J. Verma, & N. Kundu (Eds.), *Quantum Computing and Supply Chain Management: A New Era of Optimization* (pp. 196–219). IGI Global. https://doi.org/10.4018/979-8-3693-4107-0.ch014.

3. Dutta, P. K., El-kenawy, S. M., Ali, G., & Dhoska, K. (2023). An Energy Consumption Monitoring and Control System in Buildings using Internet of Things. *Babylonian Journal of Internet of Things*, 2023, 38–47. https://doi.org/10.58496/BJIoT/2023/006.
4. Dutta, P. K., El-kenawy, S. M., Abotaleb, M., & Eid, M. M. (2023). AI-Driven Marketplaces and Price Prediction Tools for Rag Pickers: Enhancing Economic Opportunities in Africa's Circular Economy. *Babylonian Journal of Artificial Intelligence*, 2023, 33–42. https://doi.org/10.58496/BJAI/2023/007.
5. Dutta, P. K., Bhardwaj, A. K., & Mahida, A. (2024). Navigating the Complexities of Agile Transformations in Large Organizations. In A. Hassan, P. Bhattacharya, P. Dutta, J. Verma, & N. Kundu (Eds.), *Quantum Computing and Supply Chain Management: A New Era of Optimization* (pp. 315–330). IGI Global. https://doi.org/10.4018/979-8-3693-4107-0.ch020.
6. Gutta, L. M., Dhamodharan, B., Dutta, P. K., & Whig, P. (2024). AI-Infused Quantum Machine Learning for Enhanced Supply Chain Forecasting. In A. Hassan, P. Bhattacharya, P. Dutta, J. Verma, & N. Kundu (Eds.), *Quantum Computing and Supply Chain Management: A New Era of Optimization* (pp. 48–63). IGI Global. https://doi.org/10.4018/979-8-3693-4107-0.ch003.
7. Trappe, W., & Washington, L. C. (2006). *Introduction to Cryptography with Coding Theory*. Pearson Prentice Hall.
8. Horváth, A. (2018). An algebraic topology based secret sharing scheme. *Procedia Manufacturing*, 22, 1051–1058. ISSN 2351-9789. https://doi.org/10.1016/j.promfg.2018.03.149.
9. Bhowmik, A., Sannigrahi, M., Dutta, P. K., & Bandyopadhyay, S. (2023). Using Edge Computing framework with the Internet of Things for Intelligent Vertical Gardening. In *2023 1st International Conference on Advanced Innovations in Smart Cities (ICAISC)*, Jeddah, Saudi Arabia, pp. 1–6, https://doi.org/10.1109/ICAISC56366.2023.10085507.
10. Bhattacharya, P., Chatterjee, S., Datt, R., Verma, A., & Dutta, P. K. (2023). A Permissioned Blockchain Approach for Real-Time Embedded Control Systems. In Kadry, S., & Prasath, R. (Eds.) *Mining Intelligence and Knowledge Exploration (MIKE)*. Lecture Notes in Computer Science, Vol. 7, p. 13924. Springer. https://doi.org/10.1007/978-3-031.
11. Biswas, A., & Dutta, P. K. (2020, January). Novel Approach of Automation to Risk Management: The Reduction in Human Errors. In *International Conference on Mobile Computing and Sustainable Informatics* (pp. 683–696). Springer International Publishing.
12. Kuhn, D., Kacker, R., Feldman, L., & Witte, G. (2016). Combinatorial Testing for Cybersecurity and Reliability. Retrieved March 28, 2023, from https://csrc.nist.gov/publications/detail/itl-bulletin/2016/05/combinatorial-testing-for-cybersecurity-and-reliability/final.
13. Podder, P., Bharati, S., Mondal, M.R.H., Paul, P.K., & Kose, U. (2021). Artificial Neural Network for Cybersecurity: A Comprehensive Review. *Journal of Information Assurance and Security*, 16, 10–23.
14. Sarker, I. H. (2021). Deep Cybersecurity: A Comprehensive Overview from Neural Network and Deep Learning Perspective. *SN Computer Science*, 2, 154.

15. Chauhan, K. (2021). Fuzzy Approach for Designing Security Framework. In Neeraj Bhargava, Ritu Bhargava, Pramod Singh Rathore, Rashmi Agrawal (Eds.), *Artificial Intelligence and Data Mining Approaches in Security Frameworks* (pp. 173–195). Wiley.
16. Dutta, P. K., & Mishra, O. P. (2017). Determination of Zero-Crossing Frequency and Likelihood Function for Maximum Displacement in Real-Time Earthquake Signal, *Acta Technica*, 62(2), 1–16.
17. Mannepalli, P. K., Richhariya, V., Gupta, S. K., Shukla, P. K., Dutta, P. K., Chowdhury, S., & Hu, Y.-C. (2024). A Robust Blockchain-Based Watermarking Using Edge Detection and Wavelet Transform, *Multimedia Tools and Applications*, 83(20), 1–25, https://doi.org/10.1007/s11042-024-18907-4.
18. Dutta, P. K., & Banerjee, S. (2019). Monitoring of Aerosol and Other Particulate Matter in Air Using Aerial Monitored Sensors and Real Time Data Monitoring and Processing. *Journal of System and Management Sciences*, 9(2), 104–113.
19. Rao, P. S., Nayak, S., Gautam, A., Lourens, M. E., Dutta, P. K., Chowdhury, S., & El-kenawy, E. M. (2022). Aumann agreement theorem based human resource performance monitoring with IoT and 6G technology. In *6th Smart Cities Symposium (SCS 2022), Hybrid Conference*, Bahrain, pp. 401–406, https://doi.org/10.1049/icp.2023.0638.
20. Nayak, N. R., Mishra, S., Chowdhury, S., Dutta, P. K., & Ramya, G. (2022). RFD Based Technique on QoS Parameters Using Cloud Computing. In *6th Smart Cities Symposium (SCS 2022), Hybrid Conference*, Bahrain, pp. 227–231, https://doi.org/10.1049/icp.2023.0418.
21. Dutta, P. K., Bhardwaj, A. K., & Mahida, A. (2024). Navigating the Complexities of Agile Transformations in Large Organizations. In A. Hassan, P. Bhattacharya, P. Dutta, J. Verma, & N. Kundu (Eds.), *Quantum Computing and Supply Chain Management: A New Era of Optimization* (pp. 315–330). IGI Global. https://doi.org/10.4018/979-8-3693-4107-0.ch020.
22. Gupta, S., Sarkar, D., Roy, D., Kundu, S., & Dutta, P. K. (2024). Embracing Flexibility and Efficiency: Practical Approaches to Agile Project Management. In S. Misra, R. Jadeja, & M. Mittal (Eds.), *Practical Approaches to Agile Project Management* (pp. 1–8). IGI Global. https://doi.org/10.4018/979-8-3693-3318-1.ch001.
23. Gupta, S., Dutta, P. K., Roy, S., Bhaduri, A., Maji, K., Choudhary, A., & Sarkar, A. (2024). Evaluating Waterfall vs. Agile Models in Software Development for Efficiency and Adaptability. In S. Misra, R. Jadeja, & M. Mittal (Eds.), *Practical Approaches to Agile Project Management* (pp. 142–148). IGI Global. https://doi.org/10.4018/979-8-3693-3318-1.ch008.
24. Patra, A. & Dutta, P. K. (2024). Application of Agile Stage Gate Hybrid Model in the Healthcare Industry: A Paradigm Shift in Project Management. In S. Misra, R. Jadeja, & M. Mittal (Eds.), *Practical Approaches to Agile Project Management* (pp. 149–163). IGI Global. https://doi.org/10.4018/979-8-3693-3318-1.ch009.
25. Singh, B., Vig, K., Dutta, P. K., & Kaunert, C. (2024). Unraveling Agile Transformation for Customer Satisfaction in Changing Market Conditions: Roadmap for Industry Embracing Change in Project Management. In S.

Misra, R. Jadeja, & M. Mittal (Eds.), *Practical Approaches to Agile Project Management* (pp. 305–321). IGI Global. https://doi.org/10.4018/979-8-3693-3318-1.ch017.

26. Singh, B., Dutta, P. K., Gautam, R., & Kaunert, C. (2024). Uncapping the Potential of Quantum Computing Towards Manufacturing Optimization: Routing Supply Chain Projecting Sustainability. In A. Hassan, P. Bhattacharya, & P. Dutta (Eds.), *Quantum Computing and Supply Chain Management: A New Era of Optimization* (p. 25). IGI Global. https://doi.org/10.4018/979-8-3693-4107-0.ch024.
27. Tyagi, S., Tyagi, R. K., Dutta, P. K., & Dubey, P. (2023). Next Generation Phishing Detection and Prevention System using Machine Learning. In *2023 1st International Conference on Advanced Innovations in Smart Cities (ICAISC)*, Jeddah, Saudi Arabia, pp. 1–6, doi: 10.1109/ICAISC56366.2023.10085529.
28. Ghosh, D., Dutta, P. K., & Abotaleb, M. (2024). Harnessing the Power of Hybrid Models for Supply Chain Management and Optimization. In Ramakant Bhardwaj, Pushan Kumar Dutta, Pethuru Raj, Abhishek Kumar, Kavita Saini, Alfonso González Briones, & Mohammed K. A. Kaabar (Eds.), *Hybrid Information Systems: Non-Linear Optimization Strategies with Artificial Intelligence* (pp. 407–426). De Gruyter. https://doi.org/10.1515/9783111331133-019.
29. Abotaleb, M., & Dutta, P. K. (2024). Optimizing Bidirectional Long Short-Term Memory Networks for Univariate Time Series Forecasting: A Comprehensive Guide. In Ramakant Bhardwaj, Pushan Kumar Dutta, Pethuru Raj, Abhishek Kumar, Kavita Saini, Alfonso González Briones, & Mohammed K. A. Kaabar (Eds.), *Hybrid Information Systems: Non-Linear Optimization Strategies with Artificial Intelligence* (pp. 443–458). De Gruyter. https://doi.org/10.1515/9783111331133-021.
30. Abotaleb, M., & Dutta, P. K. (2024). Optimizing Convolutional Neural Networks for Univariate Time Series Forecasting: A Comprehensive Guide. In Ramakant Bhardwaj, Pushan Kumar Dutta, Pethuru Raj, Abhishek Kumar, Kavita Saini, Alfonso González Briones, & Mohammed K. A. Kaabar (Eds.), *Hybrid Information Systems: Non-Linear Optimization Strategies with Artificial Intelligence* (pp. 459–472). De Gruyter. https://doi.org/10.1515/9783111331133-022.
31. Abotaleb, M., & Dutta, P. K. (2024). Optimizing Gated Recurrent Unit Networks for Univariate Time Series Forecasting: A Comprehensive Guide. In Ramakant Bhardwaj, Pushan Kumar Dutta, Pethuru Raj, Abhishek Kumar, Kavita Saini, Alfonso González Briones, & Mohammed K. A. Kaabar (Eds.), *Hybrid Information Systems: Non-Linear Optimization Strategies with Artificial Intelligence* (pp. 473–490). De Gruyter. https://doi.org/10.1515/9783111331133-023.
32. Dutta, P. K., & Ullah, A. (2024). A Novel Decision-Making Framework for Addressing Digitalization Solutions in the Medical System Under Generalized Fuzzy Rough Information. In A. Hussain, M. K. Siddiqui, & R. Kumar (Eds.), *Lightweight Digital Trust Architectures in the Internet of Medical Things (IoMT)* (p. 10). IGI Global. https://doi.org/10.4018/979-8-3693-2109-6.ch003.

33. Kumar, T. A., Kanimozhi, P., Dutta, P. K., & Sowmya, R. (2023). Assessment of gradient classifier based approaches in advanced recommendation framework: Uncovering limitations. In *7th IET Smart Cities Symposium (SCS 2023)*, *IET Conference Proceedings*, 2023(44). https://doi.org/10.1049/icp.2024.0946.

Chapter 20

Quantum-blockchain scheme in fraud detection and risk management resilience

Suman Majumder, Hussein Alkattan, and Hamideza Rabiei Dastjerdi

20.1 INTRODUCTION

Quantum computing is a revolutionary form of computation that harnesses quantum-mechanical phenomena, such as superposition and entanglement, to perform calculations at speeds far beyond the reach of classical computers. Unlike classical systems, which use binary digits (bits) to represent information, quantum computers rely on quantum bits (qubits). This unique capability enables quantum computers to solve highly complex problems with unprecedented efficiency [1].

Nowadays, with rapid improvement in the digital and interconnected financial ecosystem, fraud detection and risk management have become critical areas of concern. Financial transactions, which often involve sensitive data, face growing threats from advanced cyberattacks, including those that could potentially be enabled by quantum computing. Traditional methods of fraud detection and risk management, which depend on classical computing, struggle to address the complexity and scale of modern financial networks effectively. Quantum computing, however, offers the computational power to process vast amounts of transactional data and detect fraudulent patterns with greater accuracy.

This chapter examines the integration of quantum computing with blockchain technology to create more secure and resilient fraud detection systems. By leveraging the strengths of quantum algorithms with the immutable mechanism of blockchain/decentralized ledger, this approach holds the potential to revolutionize the future of fraud detection and risk management in the financial sector.

20.1 QUANTUM-BLOCKCHAIN FUNDAMENTALS

Quantum computing and blockchain technology are two distinct yet highly transformative fields, and their convergence holds the potential to revolutionize security, particularly in areas such as fraud detection and risk

DOI: 10.1201/9781003498292-20

management. To understand this integration, it is crucial to explore the fundamentals of both technologies [2].

20.2 QUANTUM COMPUTING FUNDAMENTALS

Quantum computing is based on the principles of quantum mechanics, utilizing quantum bits or *qubits* to perform complex calculations. Unlike classical bits, which represent either a 0 or a 1, qubits can exist in multiple states simultaneously due to the phenomena of *superposition*. Additionally, *entanglement*, another key property, allows qubits that are entangled to be correlated with each other, no matter the distance separating them. These quantum properties enable quantum computers to process vast datasets and solve problems that are infeasible for classical computers, such as factoring large numbers (Shor's algorithm) or searching unsorted databases (Grover's algorithm) [3].

In the context of fraud detection and risk management, quantum computing can be leveraged to analyze and model highly complex systems with large volumes of data. Its ability to efficiently solve optimization and pattern recognition problems positions it as a game-changer in identifying fraudulent behavior in real time.

20.3 BLOCKCHAIN TECHNOLOGY FUNDAMENTALS

Blockchain is a decentralized, distributed ledger technology that enables secure, transparent, and immutable record-keeping. Each block in a blockchain contains a list of transactions, and once a block is verified and added to the chain, it is nearly impossible to alter. Blockchain relies on cryptographic techniques, such as hashing, to ensure data integrity and security. Moreover, Consensus mechanisms like proof of work (PoW) or proof of stake (PoS) are used to validate transactions without the need for a central authority, making the system highly resistant to tampering.

In fraud detection, blockchain's decentralized nature prevents single points of failure, ensuring that data is securely stored and remains tamper-proof. Its transparency also enhances accountability, as all parties involved in a transaction have access to a shared, immutable record.

20.4 QUANTUM-BLOCKCHAIN INTEGRATION

The integration of quantum computing with blockchain technology creates a system that is not only more secure but also faster and more efficient. One of the primary motivations behind this integration is the imminent threat of quantum computers breaking current cryptographic systems, such as Rivest-Shamir-Adleman (RSA) and ECC (elliptic curve cryptography), which underpin blockchain security today. By utilizing quantum-resistant cryptographic algorithms, blockchain systems can be fortified against future quantum attacks [4].

Quantum computing can also optimize the efficiency of blockchain networks by speeding up transaction validation processes and improving consensus mechanisms. For example, quantum algorithms can enhance the speed of finding optimal solutions in decentralized networks, such as selecting the most efficient nodes for validating blocks, reducing latency, and improving overall network performance.

In summary, the convergence of quantum computing and blockchain technology offers a resilient and future-proof framework for fraud detection and risk management. Quantum computing's computational power can strengthen fraud detection algorithms, while blockchain ensures that the data used for analysis remains secure, transparent, and tamper-proof. As both fields continue to evolve, their integration will likely form the backbone of next-generation financial security systems [5].

A practical example of a recent quantum-blockchain fraud detection scheme can be observed through Xanadu's quantum-blockchain platform collaboration with traditional financial services to explore advanced fraud detection techniques. Xanadu was founded in 2016. While Xanadu has been at the forefront of developing quantum computing technologies since its inception, its quantum-blockchain platform is part of ongoing research and development efforts, rather than a specific invention in a particular year. The exact year of the "invention" of the quantum-blockchain functioning platform is not clearly defined, as it emerges from continuous advancements in both quantum computing and blockchain technology, with practical implementations and experiments likely taking place in the early 2020s [6].

In 2019, IBM announced the launch of its quantum risk assessment tool, which aims to help businesses identify potential cybersecurity risks and vulnerabilities in distributed network based applications. The tool uses quantum computing to analyze data and identify potential weak points for such network based applications.

A quantum blockchain has the potential to greatly enhance risk management across multiple sectors, particularly in finance, supply chain management, and cybersecurity. The following example illustrates how quantum blockchain can be applied to risk management. In conventional financial systems, risk management focuses on identifying, assessing, and mitigating risks such as fraud, data breaches, and transaction failures. An additional case is Quantum-Enhanced Fraud Detection in Cross-Border Payments, where quantum computing and blockchain technologies together offer significant improvements in managing these processes [7].

20.5 POTENTIAL APPLICATIONS OF QUANTUM BLOCKCHAIN IN FRAUD DETECTION AND RISK MANAGEMENT

The integration of quantum computing and blockchain technology presents significant potential for revolutionizing fraud detection and risk management. This hybrid approach offers enhanced levels of security, speed, and accuracy, particularly in sectors vulnerable to fraud and financial instability.

20.5.1 Real-time fraud detection in financial transactions

Quantum machine learning algorithms can rapidly analyze large datasets, identifying anomalies in real time. This capability enables more effective fraud detection by flagging abnormal transaction patterns such as unauthorized access or account takeovers. Blockchain's immutability ensures that once transactions are recorded, they cannot be altered. The combination of quantum-powered fraud detection and blockchain's tamper-proof ledger creates a robust system to detect and prevent fraud in real time.

20.5.2 Cross-border payment security

Quantum blockchain offers enhanced security for cross-border payments, which are often susceptible to fraud due to their complexity. Quantum-resistant cryptography can safeguard transaction data from quantum attacks, while blockchain provides a transparent and immutable record. This combination enables more secure and efficient international payment systems, reducing risks such as money laundering and identity theft.

20.5.3 Identity fraud prevention

Quantum blockchain can secure decentralized identity management systems, reducing the risk of identity fraud. Quantum encryption ensures that personal information is protected, while blockchain prevents any tampering with identity records. This is particularly useful for financial institutions that require secure user authentication across multiple channels. Additionally, quantum algorithms can validate identity features at multiple stages, adding an extra layer of security against identity theft.

20.5.4 Insurance fraud detection

Quantum algorithms can analyze vast amounts of data to assess risks more accurately in the insurance sector. This can help identify potentially fraudulent claims by comparing real-time data with historical records, allowing for more precise risk assessment. Blockchain's transparency ensures that claims data is immutable and accessible, minimizing the possibility of fraudulent claims. This dual approach streamlines the claims process and reduces fraud.

20.5.5 Risk assessment in supply chain management

In supply chain management, quantum algorithms can model complex risk scenarios, helping to detect fraud and prevent counterfeit goods from entering the system. Blockchain's immutable record-keeping enables tracking of the provenance of products, ensuring that goods are authentic and have not been tampered with. This combination of quantum computing and blockchain strengthens the integrity of supply chains by preventing fraud related to counterfeit products and false claims of origin.

20.5.6 Credit card and payment system fraud mitigation

Quantum blockchain can monitor credit card transactions in real time, flagging suspicious activity such as unauthorized large purchases or multiple transactions across distant locations. Quantum-enhanced algorithms quickly identify transaction anomalies, while blockchain ensures that transaction histories are immutable and verifiable. This system is particularly effective in preventing fraudulent chargebacks and account takeovers.

20.5.7 Cybersecurity risk management

Quantum blockchain plays a crucial role in mitigating the cybersecurity risks posed by quantum computing. Quantum-resistant encryption ensures that transaction and communication data remains secure, even against quantum-based attacks. Additionally, blockchain can be used to audit and securely track cybersecurity incidents, providing an immutable record that aids in forensic investigations and overall risk mitigation.

20.5.8 Fraud detection in digital contracts

Quantum blockchain can enhance the security of smart contracts by making them resistant to exploitation or tampering. Quantum algorithms monitor contract execution in real time, flagging any deviations that might indicate fraud. Blockchain ensures the terms of digital contracts remain immutable, reducing the risk of disputes or fraudulent amendments. This secure environment strengthens the reliability of legal agreements in digital transactions.

20.5.9 Risk management in capital markets

Quantum computing can optimize high-frequency trading (HFT) strategies, while blockchain provides a transparent record of trades. This combination helps detect and prevent fraudulent trading activities such as market manipulation and insider trading. Quantum blockchain also facilitates more accurate risk assessments by analyzing large volumes of financial data, helping institutions manage market risk and mitigate fraudulent activities like front-running or wash trading.

20.5.10 Supply chain financial fraud prevention

Quantum blockchain can prevent trade finance fraud, such as invoice fraud or duplicate financing, by verifying the authenticity of financial documents with quantum algorithms. Blockchain ensures that all transactions and documents are securely stored and verifiable, providing a transparent record for tracing financial activities within the supply chain. This reduces the risk of fraudulent invoicing and ensures the integrity of supply chain transactions.

So, quantum blockchain offers a transformative solution to fraud detection and risk management by combining the computational power of quantum computing with the transparency and security of blockchain. This hybrid approach allows for real-time analysis of large datasets and the creation of tamper-proof records, providing more accurate detection and prevention of fraudulent activities across industries. By proactively defending against both classical and quantum-based risks, quantum blockchain enables a secure and efficient system for managing fraud and risk in the future [8].

20.6 CHALLENGES AND FUTURE DIRECTIONS OF USING QUANTUM BLOCKCHAIN IN FRAUD DETECTION AND RISK MANAGEMENT

The integration of quantum computing and blockchain technology offers a transformative solution for fraud detection and risk management. However, there are several challenges that need to be addressed for the full potential of this hybrid technology to be realized. Additionally, the future direction of quantum-blockchain research and application must focus on overcoming these hurdles to deliver a scalable, secure, and efficient system for combating fraud and managing risks across industries.

20.6.1 Challenges

20.6.1.1 Quantum computing readiness

Current limitations: Quantum computing is still in its early stages, and the large-scale quantum systems needed for fraud detection are not yet fully developed. The challenge lies in building reliable quantum computers that efficiently process complex fraud detection tasks.

Error rates and stability: Quantum systems are prone to errors due to quantum decoherence, which can reduce accuracy. Achieving low-error, stable quantum systems will be crucial for their effective use in fraud detection and risk management.

20.6.1.2 Blockchain scalability

Performance bottlenecks: Blockchain networks often struggle with scalability, facing limitations in transaction throughput and latency. When combined with quantum technology, these bottlenecks could hinder the real-time processing needed for fraud detection. Enhancing blockchain scalability is key to enabling quantum-blockchain solutions.

Energy consumption: Blockchain, particularly proof-of-work models, requires significant energy. Quantum computing could further increase this demand, making the development of energy-efficient blockchain protocols essential for sustainable implementation.

20.6.1.3 Quantum security threats

Threat to classical blockchain security: Quantum computers have the potential to break classical encryption methods such as RSA and ECC, which are commonly used in blockchain systems. This makes blockchain networks vulnerable to quantum-based attacks.

Securing quantum-blockchain systems: Quantum-blockchain systems must adopt quantum-resistant cryptographic algorithms to protect against these threats. Developing secure encryption techniques will be critical to maintaining the integrity of quantum-blockchain networks.

20.6.1.4 Interoperability and integration

Complex integration: Integrating quantum computing with existing blockchain systems and legacy infrastructures is a significant challenge. The transition to quantum blockchain will require substantial reengineering of current systems, which could slow adoption.

Lack of standardization: The absence of standardized protocols for quantum-blockchain integration makes interoperability difficult. Developing universal standards will be essential to enabling quantum-blockchain systems to work across industries and applications.

20.6.1.5 Regulatory and compliance issues

Regulatory uncertainty: The regulatory landscape for quantum blockchain is underdeveloped, with few clear guidelines for its application in fraud detection and risk management. This uncertainty may hinder adoption, as organizations may face challenges in ensuring compliance.

Data privacy concerns: Blockchain's transparency can conflict with stringent data privacy regulations like General Data Protection Regulation (GDPR). Balancing transparency for fraud detection with privacy protection will be a critical challenge that needs to be addressed.

20.6.2 Future directions

20.6.2.1 Quantum-resistant cryptography

Quantum-resistant blockchain: Blockchain systems must adopt quantum-resistant cryptographic algorithms to safeguard against quantum attacks. Research into post-quantum cryptography (PQC) is already underway and will be vital for securing future blockchain networks.

Hybrid cryptographic models: Combining classical and quantum encryption methods can provide a phased approach to enhancing blockchain security as quantum technology evolves.

20.6.2.2 Advances in quantum hardware and algorithms

Error correction and stability: Improved quantum error correction and fault-tolerant computing will be essential for the stability of quantum systems. Achieving reliable quantum models for fraud detection will require further research in these areas.

Optimized quantum algorithms for risk management: Developing quantum-specific algorithms for fraud detection and risk management can dramatically improve performance, enabling faster and more accurate detection across large datasets.

20.6.2.3 Advances in quantum hardware and algorithms

Layer 2 technologies and sharding: Future blockchain systems can adopt layer 2 solutions (such as state channels and rollups) and sharding to address scalability concerns. These techniques can reduce transaction bottlenecks, improving blockchain's efficiency for fraud detection.

Energy-efficient consensus mechanisms: Shifting from energy-intensive proof-of-work models to more sustainable proof-of-stake (PoS) models will be critical. Quantum computing may also contribute to the development of more efficient consensus protocols.

20.6.2.4 Regulatory evolution

Clear legal frameworks: Governments and regulatory bodies need to establish comprehensive legal frameworks for the deployment of quantum-blockchain systems. These frameworks must address compliance, cybersecurity, and privacy concerns to foster responsible innovation.

International cooperation: Since fraud is a global issue, international cooperation is essential to creating unified regulatory standards for quantum-blockchain systems. Harmonizing regulations will facilitate widespread adoption across borders.

So, quantum-blockchain technology offers significant promise for transforming fraud detection and risk management, but challenges related to scalability, security, integration, and regulation remain. By advancing quantum-resistant cryptography, improving hardware and algorithms, and developing clear regulatory frameworks, quantum blockchain can provide secure and efficient solutions for managing fraud and risks in the future [9].

20.7 CASE STUDIES

20.7.1 Case study 1: quantum blockchain for fraud detection

In this case study, a novel *quantum-blockchain* approach is utilized for fraud detection in financial transactions, combining the processing power of quantum computing with the feature of transparency of blockchain. The system leverages *quantum machine learning (QML)* [10] to detect fraudulent patterns more efficiently than classical methods. Quantum algorithms such as *Grover's search* and *quantum support vector machines (QSVMs)* are employed to analyze large datasets and flag suspicious transactions. Once identified, transactions are securely recorded on a *blockchain* ledger, ensuring immutability and privacy. Smart contracts are triggered to automatically investigate flagged transactions.

20.7.1.1 Result

This combination enhances fraud detection accuracy, reduces false positives, and improves detection speed by *50%*. Additionally, *decentralized identity management* protects user privacy, while blockchain ensures secure and transparent data handling.

Although current quantum hardware has limitations, this hybrid system showcases the potential of quantum blockchain to revolutionize fraud detection and secure financial systems against future quantum threats.

20.7.2 Case study 2: quantum blockchain for risk management

In this innovative case study, a quantum-blockchain hybrid system is implemented for risk management in financial institutions. This system uses *quantum computing* to simulate risk scenarios and evaluate complex derivatives with unprecedented speed and accuracy, using advanced algorithms like *quantum Monte Carlo* simulations [11]. The results are then recorded on a blockchain, ensuring tamper-proof documentation and audit trails. The quantum component allows for the calculation of risk metrics much faster than traditional models, providing real-time insights into potential risks. Meanwhile, blockchain technology offers a decentralized and secure platform for managing these risk assessments transparently and securely.

20.7.2.1 Results

The deployment of this system has led to a *40% reduction in risk assessment time* and improved the accuracy of risk predictions by *30%*, significantly enhancing the decision-making process. This integration demonstrates a robust strategy for managing financial risks and optimizing operational efficiencies in a secure manner [12].

20.8 CONCLUSION

In conclusion, the quantum-blockchain scheme for fraud detection and risk management significantly enhances the resilience of financial networks. This hybrid approach leverages the quantum rapid data processing mechanism of quantum computing and a secure record-keeping scheme along with the immutability mechanism of blockchain is used to tackle the complexities of modern financial systems. While challenges such as scalability and integration with existing infrastructures remain, the ongoing advancements in both quantum computing and blockchain technology promise a robust, secure, and efficient future for financial security systems. This chapter provides a comprehensive insight into the transformative potential and future directions of quantum-blockchain integration in combating fraud and managing risks effectively.

REFERENCES

1. Innan, N., Khan, M. A. Z., & Bennai, M. (2024). Financial fraud detection: a comparative study of quantum machine learning models. *International Journal of Quantum Information*, 22(02), 2350044.
2. Qu, Z., Shi, W., Liu, B., Gupta, D., & Tiwari, P. (2023). IoMT-based smart healthcare detection system driven by quantum blockchain and quantum neural network. *IEEE Journal of Biomedical and Health Informatics* 28(6), 3317–3328.
3. Qu, Z., Zhang, Z., & Zheng, M. (2022). A quantum blockchain-enabled framework for secure private electronic medical records in Internet of Medical Things. *Information Sciences* 612, 942–958.

4. Innan, N., Khan, M. A. Z., & Bennai, M., (2024). Financial fraud detection: a comparative study of quantum machine learning models. *International Journal of Quantum Information*, 22(2), 2350044.
5. Naik, A., Yeniaras, E., Hellstern, G., Prasad, G., & Vishwakarma, S. K. L. P. (2023). From portfolio optimization to quantum blockchain and security: A systematic review of quantum computing in finance. arXiv preprint arXiv:2307.01155.
6. Zohaib, M., Altuwaijri, F. S., & Hyrynsalmi, S. (2024, July). Integrating Quantum Computing and Blockchain: Building the Foundations of Secure, Efficient 6G Technology. In *Proceedings of the 1st ACM International Workshop on Quantum Software Engineering: The Next Evolution* (pp. 27–34).
7. Akhai, S., & Kumar, V. (2024). Quantum Resilience and Distributed Trust: The Promise of Blockchain and Quantum Computing in Defense. In *Sustainable Security Practices Using Blockchain, Quantum and Post-Quantum Technologies for Real Time Applications* (pp. 125–153). Singapore: Springer Nature Singapore.
8. Gadoo, A. A., & Talwandi, N. S. (2024). Quantum Computing and Its Potential Threat to Blockchain Security. In S. L. Tripathi, D. Agarwal, A. Pal, & Y. Perwej (Eds.), *Emerging Trends in IoT and Computing Technologies* (1st ed., pp. 299–304). CRC Press.
9. Pulipeti, S., Kumar, A., Mysore, N., & Peoples, C. (Eds.). (2024). *Quantum and blockchain-based next generation sustainable computing.* Springer Cham.
10. Seol, J., & Kim, J. (2024). Machine learning ensures quantum-safe blockchain availability. *Journal of Computer Information Systems*, 1–25.
11. Venkatesh, R. (2024). A lightweight quantum blockchain-based framework to protect patients private medical information. *IEEE Transactions on Network Science and Engineering* 11(4), 3577–3584.
12. Qadri, S., Malik, J. A., Shah, H., Raza, M. A., Alsanoosy, T., & Saleem, M. (2024). Innovating with Quantum Computing Approaches in Block-Chain for Enhanced Security and Data Privacy in Agricultural IoT Systems. In *Computational Intelligence in Internet of Agricultural Things* (pp. 339–370). Cham: Springer Nature Switzerland.

Chapter 21

Sustainable farming systems in smart logistics

M. S. Gill, Christo Ananth, Rakhmanov Buribay and Mohammad Shahparan

21.1 INTRODUCTION

The primary goal of any ecosystem is to retain natural resources and simultaneously produce good quality food free from all chemicals. It requires the main focus on the structural element and functional relationship of the biotic and abiotic factors for the successful production of crops. The crops grown using the organic concept including organic source of nutrition (vermicompost, farm yard manure (FYM), compost, etc.), crop rotation, crop residue management, green manuring, bio-fertilizer and organic pesticides not only give better productivity but avoid the use of off-farm inputs. The crop husbandry is one of the prominent components of a farming system. The livestock, poultry, mushroom, fishery and piggery are the integral part of it because crop husbandry arranges to fulfil the need of most of the secondary entrepreneurs. The farming system with livestock has its own forage production using the organic source of seed and nutrients, which helps improve the soil fertility and supports colonies of soil micro-organism. Diseases and pests are exclusively handled by system management or substances prepared from natural and biological processes.

Organic farming helps foster a positive relationship between Earth and humanity. However, increasing population pressures have prompted agriculture science to develop precursor technologies for producing food, fibre, fuel, fat, fruit and fish to meet the growing demand. Consequently, there has been a tremendous increase in productivity and profitability. Farmers have started growing high-yielding varieties of hybrids by using chemical fertilizers and pesticides in significant amounts. This trend was most common in the 1970s and 1980s. After a span of two decades, it became evident that our natural resources were showing signs of stress and decline. Thereafter a stage reached when the situation became more alarming on account of decline in factor productivity, the emergence of multi-nutrient deficiencies, reduced holding sizes, shrinking profit margins, the prevalence of monocultures of exhausting crops. Few efforts were made to restore soil fertility, leading to fertilizer and pesticide residues in produce. Nutrition insecurity arose due to a lack of balanced diets, climate change made agriculture less

 DOI: 10.1201/9781003498292-21

profitable. Pollution levels in air, water and soil increased, in addition to a declining water table, hard layer formation and inadequate recharging. Biodiversity decreased, deforestation occurred in violation of national policy, and global warming became an important concern. Moreover, 67% of the area remained dependent on rainfall, with significant soil degradation in rainfed regions and minimal efforts to rainwater harvesting and recycling.

After 50 long years of neglect, organic agriculture is now gaining a place in the mainstream of development and is showing significant commercial, social and environmental responses aimed at reviving the ecosystem [1–3]. The farming system is a multidisciplinary, holistic approach that is complex in nature in the matrix of soil, plants, water, animals, implements, power, labour, capital and other inputs [4–6]. It takes into account the synergistic blending of various farm components like crops, dairy, fishery, apiculture, poultry, piggery, rabbitry, goat and duck keeping, horticulture, mushroom cultivation, agroforestry, etc. These days, the integrated farming system approach is being adopted to enhance regular income, recycle the resources, produce household commodities on the farm, create employment opportunities, provide balanced food, increase input–output efficiency, address energy, fuel and fodder crisis, and ultimately uplift farmers' standard of living in terms of better productivity, profitability and sustainability [7–9].

21.2 ORGANIC FARMING V/S INTEGRATED FARMING SYSTEM

The combination of different enterprises which are ecologically stable, economically viable and socially acceptable is now for a primary focus of this approach. By using by-product and left over materials as inputs for other enterprises, we can maintain the eco-socioeconomic balance while promoting environmental protection (10). The further supplementation of the integrated farming system with organic farming significantly enhances the conservation of natural resources. The main component of organic farming which complements this farming system is believed to stem from the following synergistic principles and approaches.

- The soil in this system is considered as a living entity.
- The system does not support the mining of soil nutrients and soil degradation in any way.
- It does not use any inputs, nor it demands unreasonable quantity of water.
- The soil microbes are to be protected for improving soil fertility significantly.
- Crop rotation, soil cover, use of organic sources of nutrients, cultivation of crops that respond well to organic sources of nutrients, selection of cultural practices used in organic farming, recycling of crop residues and the use of bio-fertilizers are given top priority.

In the present era, organic farming is gaining universal importance due to the growing demand for healthy, hygienic and safe food for long-term sustainability, as well as environmental problems associated with the indiscriminate use of agro-chemicals. Increasing awareness and changing lifestyles, particularly in metropolitan cities, are driving the demand for healthy organic food.

The supplementation of organic farming with agriculture-based enterprises simplifies operations. In an organic farming-based farming system, the use of synthetic and hybrid materials is completely prohibited. Even the injection of substances to the livestock, poultry and the use of fungicide in mushrooms are strictly regulated. The cultivation of leguminous green fodder such as cowpeas, cluster beans, barseem, alfaalfa is preferred, as these crops fix biological nitrogen, and phosphorus requirements are fulfilled from rock phosphate. These crops help fulfil the green fodder requirements of livestock. In addition, the dry fodders such as wheat straw, sorghum and pearl millet are good alternatives [11] to meet the needs of livestock. Livestock dung is an excellent source of organic nutrition and is used in cattle sheds to grow plankton in fish ponds. Bedding material is used for producing quality farmyard manure [12]. Livestock provides draft power and milk while alive, and when they expire yield hide and bones, which are used for various productive purposes. Crop husbandry fulfils the fodder and feed requirements of livestock. Likewise, the basic needs of other enterprises are also fulfilled by crop husbandry [13].

For mushroom cultivation, medium compost is prepared from wheat and paddy straw, which also serves as feed for poultry, rabbits and quails. Beekeeping is exclusively dependent on crops, as bees collect nectar from the flora. The basic requirement for sericulture is the leaves of the mulberry plant. Therefore, while selecting a combination of enterprises, give preference to those that have better adaptability and have a complimentary effect on each other [14]. The concept of value addition is also interconnected within any system. For example, Bengal gram seeds can be used to make *dal* (cotyledons of yellow colour), while the broken grains/seeds can be used to produce *besan* and the hull/husk is used in cattle feed. All parts are used for economic purposes, which contributes to an increased profit margin.

21.3 OPTIONS FOR RESOURCE RECYCLING

This concept helps restore soil health. The main source of material is crop residue, which can be utilized to make enriched compost, serving as mulch, and be used for bale-making to meet dry fodder needs as well as producing energy. Conservation agriculture is also considered crucial for minimizing soil disturbance. The reuse of crop residue helps a lot to reduce adverse effects of climate change, particularly by mitigating the impact of rising temperatures.

Likewise, growing green manure both in situ and ex situ is also considered important for rejuvenating soil health. Recycling of water is facilitated within a fish-based farming system. In the event of an electricity breakdown, fish pond water can be applied up to a depth of 2–3 ft from the pond to provide irrigation for crops. On account of rich in nutrients, it promotes the growth and development of crops. On restoration of electricity, the pond may be refilled to the desired level.

In the organic farming-based farming system, the growing of maize+cowpeas in the Kharif season serves the dual purpose of recycling and weed control. When cowpeas cover the ground surface and produce sufficient biomass, they are cut down between the maize rows and used as mulch. The C:N ratio of cowpeas, on account of their succulence, is very high, making them highly suitable for improving soil health and maintaining nutrient balance.

When crops are sown using conservation tillage and second-generation machinery, the designated traffic lanes used for planting tend to experience higher evapotranspiration (ET) losses. These losses help to regulate the microclimate within the crop canopy, thereby counteracting the adverse effects of climate change. Crop cultivation within traffic lanes exhibits elevated evapotranspiration (ET) rates, which contribute to microclimatic modulation within the crop canopy and serve as a compensatory mechanism against localized climate perturbations. The use of vegetative materials as mulch benefit crops by covering the soil surface, thus avoiding losses due to evaporation. Furthermore, it provides direct protection from run-off or soil erosion due to heavy rain, helps regulate the soil temperature by creating a buffer between soil and the atmosphere, improves soil health by increasing the humus in the soil upon decomposition and suppresses germination of weeds in between the rows. Above all, in April, the low soil temperature and more water content in the soil create harmonious conditions for the uniform maturity of the rabi crops, giving more yield.

Organic manures from animals are used fulfil the nutritional need of crops. They also improve the soil structure and provide a balanced supply of nutrients, thus helping to produce more crop/fodder per unit area. The inclusion of legume crops is the best way to avail the benefit of biological N-fixation, thus enriching soil fertility. The use of bio-fertilizers containing microbes used for seed treatment and soil application is considered helpful for restoring soil health. Nowadays, the consortium approach (i.e. using more than two species) is proving to be more effective for producing bio-fertilizers.

Likewise, the concept of crop rotation in organic farming systems is the backbone of maintaining soil health, managing weeds, exploiting the soil profile for nutrients and water from different depths, controlling insect pests and diseases, improving soil structure and nutrient availability. The inclusion of legumes in each crop rotation plays a pivotal role in biological nitrogen fixation. Above all, the judicious use of water and all management resources is required for increasing crop productivity and obtaining quality produce.

21.4 RESULTS AND DISCUSSION

The experiments were conducted at the farmers' field [10] in a participatory mode in 2004. The average of 12 experiments with the rice-wheat cropping system yielded 102.4–134.3 q/ha rice equivalent, with a corresponding net return range of Rs. 37,527–54,995 per hectare. It is thus clear that with this rice-wheat cropping system, there is a lot of scope for increasing productivity, as a large yield gap of 31.7 q/ha exists, which can be closed by identifying the yield-limiting factors. All the farmers had dairy animals and many of them used FYM for crops. The data showed that the dairy component contributed to milk production. In terms of rice equivalent yield, the rice-wheat+dairy system showed a substantial increase compared to the rice-wheat system. The rice-wheat+dairy enterprise outperformed the rice-wheat system by a profit margin of Rs. 5026/ha. With the inclusion of vegetable parts, the rice equivalent yield under the rice-wheat+dairy+vegetable system varied from 148.1 to 208.9 q/ha, with a net return of Rs. 43,301–73,417 [7]. The profit margin mainly depends on the types of vegetables and their season of production. When vegetables are produced during the off-season, they give a higher premium when compared to those grown during the main season. Although the quality of vegetables may be good during main season the higher production results in a market glut, which reduces net returns per unit area.

The water productivity of the integrated farming system is shown in the Table 21.1 The data clearly indicate that the rice equivalent yield of the rice-wheat cropping system was only 12.4 t/ha, while other systems showed sizeable improvement, with maximum yield of 19.7 t/ha obtained from the fishery+piggery system, followed by fishery at 16.6 t/ha. Likewise, the

Table 21.1 Water productivity under different farming systems

System	*ET (Cm)*	*REY (t/ha)*	*Fish yield (q/ha)*	*Net returns (Rs./ha)*	*Water used (m³)*	*Productivity*	
						Rs./m³	*(kg/m³)*
Rice-wheat	205	12.4	–	53,220	20,500	2.60	0.60
Fishery	176	16.6	39.2	59,132	17,600	3.36	0.94
Fishery + piggery	176	19.7	39.2+16.2[a]	99,719	17,600	5.67	1.12
Rice wheat second stage	123	12.4	–	53,220	12,300	4.33	1.00

[a]Piggery yield converted into fishery equivalent yield.

Table 21.2 Cost return and employment potential (man-days) under different mixed farming systems

Farming	*Expenditure (Rs.)*	*Gross income (Rs.)*	*Net return (Rs.)*	*Cost return ratio*	*Employment days*
Arable	14,171	38,264	24,093	1:2.7	257
MF* with 2 cows	34,972	72,640	37,668	1:2.0	374
MF with 2 buffaloes	47,257	71,545	24,288	1:1.5	390
MF with 2 cows + fish	35,170	76,064	40,894	1:2.2	374
MF with 2 buffaloes + fish	47,455	74,969	27,514	1:1.6	390
MF with 2 cows + 15 goats + 10 poultry + 10 ducks + fish	44,331	88,222	44,914	1:2.0	380
MF with 2 buffaloes + 15 goats + 10 poultry + 10 ducks + fish	55,596	87,127	31,531	1:1.6	396

Source: Tiwari et al.,[15].

*Sown under zero tillage conditions.

fishery+piggery equivalent yield was calculated, showing a noticeable advantage in water productivity over the rice-wheat system. The maximum water productivity observed was 1.12 kg per cubic metre for the fishery+piggery system and 0.94 kg per cubic metre for fishery, compared to only 0.6 kg per cubic metre for the rice-wheat system. Likewise, integrating crop husbandry with other agriculture-based enterprises helps improve profitability and sustainability.

The results presented in Table 21.2 clearly illustrate the superiority of cows over buffaloes. The mixed farming with 2 cows, 15 goats, 10 poultry, 10 ducks and fishery gave the maximum return of Rs. 44,914 with a cost–benefit ratio of 1:2 and generated 380 days of employment. In contrast, the corresponding figures for arable farming were Rs. 24,093 of maximum return, 1:27 of cost–benefit ratio, 257 days of employment. The data further reveal that as the number of enterprises increases, both the net returns and employability improve (Figure 21.1).

21.5 Farming system

The results of a long-term experiment conducted under rainfed conditions in Rajasthan indicate that the maximum cost–benefit ratio was observed in agri-pastures (1.87), followed by agro-forestry (1.79), sericulture-pasture (1.67), agri-horticulture (1.45) and the lowest in crop production (1.24). It is thus clear that under rainfed conditions combinations of forestry and pastures with crops should be preferred [3].

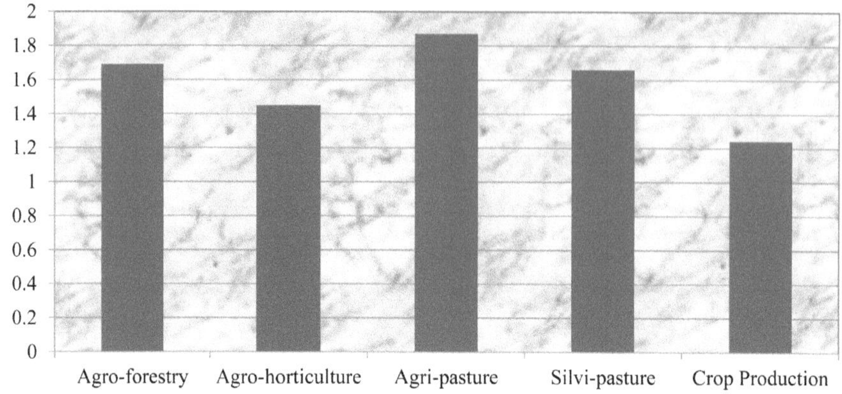

Figure 21.1 Benefit: Cost ratio of different alternate land use systems.

In the Kharif season, the economic yields of basmati rice, rice, maize and groundnut did not differ significantly among the various management systems (Table 21.3). However, the yield of turmeric rhizome and cowpea green fodder were significantly higher under organic and integrated management compared to chemical farming [14]. Nonetheless, the yields of these two crops under organic and integrated farming were statistically comparable. The warm and moist conditions during the Kharif season may have facilitated the sustained release of nutrients from organic sources [16]. In rabi season, yields of wheat and onion remained statistically similar across organic, integrated and chemical farming. Garlic yields in the summer groundnut-garlic system and mentha yields in the garlic+mentha system were significantly higher under organic and integrated farming than under chemical farming, although the former two management systems were statistically at par with each other. The higher yields of turmeric and garlic under organic management may be attributed their greater responsiveness to organic manures [17–19]. Garlic yields in the rice-garlic+mentha system were significantly higher under organic farming than under chemical farming but were statistically at par with integrated farming. The chemical and integrated farming were also statistically at par with each other [20].

21.6 RICE–WHEAT+DAIRY+PIGGERY

The piggery enterprise also proved economically viable for increasing farmers' income. The growth rate of pigs varied from 703 g to 1420 g per day, depending on management factors and the rations served. Pigs fed on waste from marriage venues gained weight at a much faster rate than those fed on fodder and feed. During the winter season, the sugarcane juice waste enjoyed by the pigs contributed to better body build-up [21].

Table 21.3 Economic yield of crops under different management practices

Management system	Economic yield (t ha^{-1})											
	CS-I		*CS-II*		*CS-III*		*CS-IV*			*CS-V*		
	B. rice	*Wheat*	*Turmeric*	*Onion*	*G. nut*	*Garlic*	*Maize*	*Wheat*	*Cowpea*	*Rice*	*Garlic*	*Mentha*
Organic	2.95	4.42	25.7	9.78	2.18	9.20	4.88	4.70	30.5	5.79	7.43	0.099
Chemical	3.14	4.33	12.5	8.74	2.14	7.62	4.22	4.67	24.4	6.01	5.54	0.073
Integrated	3.37	4.59	24.4	11.3	2.23	9.28	4.81	4.87	28.7	6.59	6.77	0.115
CD (P = .05)	NS	NS	5.8	NS	NS	0.87	NS	NS	3.2	NS	1.25	0.023

Source: Aulakh et al. [13].

The contribution of the dairy+piggery system over the rice-wheat system was 8.75 t/ha and 9.87 t/ha, respectively. The corresponding values for the increase in the net return per hectare of five farmers under rice-wheat+dairy and rice-wheat+dairy+piggery was Rs. 10,284 and Rs. 14,120, respectively, clearly showing the significance of integrated farming. The supplementary enterprises, particularly dairy, increased labour requirements by 94.7 man-days per hectare compared to the rice-wheat system, which improved further by 13.7 man-days when piggery enterprise was included [7].

21.7 A CASE STUDY OF INTEGRATED FARMING SYSTEM

The integrated farming system of Sh. Manjeet Singh in Bhulla Rai village revealed that the rice equivalent yield (REY) for rice-wheat, rice-wheat+dairy, rice-wheat+dairy+piggery, rice-wheat+dairy+piggery+rabitary and rice-wheat+dairy+piggery+rabitary+aloe-vera was 13.2, 14.6, 21.1, 24.1 and 24.6 t/ha, respectively, clearly showing the consistent increase in economic yield with the supplementation of enterprises. When all enterprises were integrated, about double productivity was achieved. The increase in net returns over the rice-wheat system for rice-wheat+dairy, rice-wheat+dairy+piggery, rice-wheat+dairy+piggery+rabitary and rice-wheat+dairy+piggery+rabitary+aloevera were about Rs. 8743, Rs. 38,424, Rs. 47,731 and Rs. 48,843, respectively. Employment generation followed the same trends, with the computed increase in man-days over the rice-wheat system being 34.3, 67.5, 97.0 and 115.8, respectively [7]. It was also observed that the inclusion of different enterprises increased the total cost, but the returns increased more than the cost, resulting in a higher net return.

Insect pests and diseases were controlled by the balanced application of inputs such as organic sources of nutrition and the implementation of crop rotation concepts. Decoctions prepared from herbs, medicinal plants, aromatic plants such as neem (oil, seed and leave decoction) were utilized. Numerous other organic formulations also helped keep these pests and diseases in check [9]. Perched places were created on the farm for predators to rest, which feed on insect pests. Likewise, intercropping and mixed cropping with certain plant species such as marigold reduce the incidence of pests. In organic farming, the crops are not very succulent, which helps avoid pest attacks. The uniform and regular application of organic inputs enables the crops to tolerate the stress caused by aerobic and non-aerobic factors.

21.8 CONCLUSION

Based on the literature cited and the results obtained, a discernible advantage was observed where organic farming and the integration of different enterprises was followed. This approach not only gave maximum productivity but also created employment opportunities across all projects. In the integrated farming system, the by-products of one enterprise were used as inputs for another, thereby reducing the cost of production. It also helps reduce pollution and contamination. The judicious use of inputs increases the immunity of plants to various stresses. Simultaneously, this approach enhances productivity and profitability, ensures balanced food availability, achieves a high input–output ratio, promotes a balanced supply of nutrition and fosters adaptability of crops. Moreover, it creates employment opportunities with regular income, encourages afforestation, saves energy and addresses fuel and fodder crisis. Above all, it provides raw materials for agri-based industries, ultimately ensuring sustainability and improving the standard of living for end users.

REFERENCES

1. Aulakh, C. S., Gill, M. S., Walia, S. S., Mahey, R. K., & Walia, U. S. (2013). Performance of diversified cropping systems under Organic, Integrated and chemical farming in Punjab. *Indian Journal of Ecology*, 40(2): 258–263.
2. Gill, M. S. (2007). Organic farming - Scope and Prospects in Punjab. A technical bulletin No. 1. *Project Directorate for Cropping System Research*, Modipuram, pp. 1–30.
3. Gill, M. S. (2009). Cooperative Organic farming in Rajasthan-A Case Study compendium on Advances in Organic farming. *Project Directorate for Farming System Research*, ICAR, Modipuram, pp. 8–9.
4. Bhattacharya, P., Chatterjee, S., Datt, R., Verma, A., & Dutta, P. K. (2023). A Permissioned Blockchain Approach for Real-Time Embedded Control Systems. In: Kadry, S., & Prasath, R. (Eds.), *Mining Intelligence and Knowledge Exploration. MIKE 2023*. Lecture Notes in Computer Science, Vol. 7, p. 13924. Springer, Cham. https://doi.org/10.1007/978-3-031.
5. Biswas, A., & Dutta, P. K. (2020, January). Novel approach of automation to risk management: The reduction in human errors. In *International Conference on Mobile Computing and Sustainable Informatics* (pp. 683–696). Cham: Springer International Publishing.
6. Dutta, P. K., Bhardwaj, A. K., & Mahida, A. (2024). Navigating the Complexities of Agile Transformations in Large Organizations. In A. Hassan, P. Bhattacharya, P. Dutta, J. Verma, & N. Kundu (Eds.), *Quantum Computing and Supply Chain Management: A New Era of Optimization* (pp. 315–330). IGI Global. https://doi.org/10.4018/979-8-3693-4107-0.ch020.
7. Gill, M. S., Gangwar, B., & Sarkar, A. (2009). Farming System Approach towards Income Enhancement. *Project Directorate for Farming System Research*, ICAR, Modipuram: Bulletin, 1– 90.
8. Gill, M. S., Samra, J. S., & Gurbachan, S. (2005). Integrated Farming System for realizing high productivity under Shallow water table conditions. *A Bulletin, Department of Agronomy and Agromet, PAU*. Ludhiana, pp. 1–30.

9. Mohan, S., Devasenapathy, P., Venniala, C., & Gill, M. S. (2008). Pest and Disease management in Organic ecosystem. *A bulletin published by AICRP on Cropping System*, Tamil Nadu Agricultural University, Coimbatore, pp. 1–63.
10. Gupta, S., Sarkar, D., Roy, D., Kundu, S., & Dutta, P. K. (2024). Embracing Flexibility and Efficiency: Practical Approaches to Agile Project Management. In S. Misra, R. Jadeja, & M. Mittal (Eds.), *Practical Approaches to Agile Project Management* (pp. 1–8). IGI Global. https://doi.org/10.4018/979-8-3693-3318-1.ch001.
11. Gupta, S., Dutta, P. K., Roy, S., Bhaduri, A., Maji, K., Choudhary, A., & Sarkar, A. (2024). Evaluating Waterfall vs. Agile Models in Software Development for Efficiency and Adaptability. In S. Misra, R. Jadeja, & M. Mittal (Eds.), *Practical Approaches to Agile Project Management* (pp. 142–148). IGI Global. https://doi.org/10.4018/979-8-3693-3318-1.ch008.
12. Patra, A. & Dutta, P. K. (2024). Application of Agile Stage Gate Hybrid Model in the Healthcare Industry: A Paradigm Shift in Project Management. In S. Misra, R. Jadeja, & M. Mittal (Eds.), *Practical Approaches to Agile Project Management* (pp. 149–163). IGI Global. https://doi.org/10.4018/979-8-3693-3318-1.ch009.
13. Singh, B., Vig, K., Dutta, P. K., & Kaunert, C. (2024). Unraveling Agile Transformation for Customer Satisfaction in Changing Market Conditions: Roadmap for Industry Embracing Change in Project Management. In S. Misra, R. Jadeja, & M. Mittal (Eds.), *Practical Approaches to Agile Project Management* (pp. 305–321). IGI Global. https://doi.org/10.4018/979-8-3693-3318-1.ch017.
14. Singh, B., Dutta, P. K., Gautam, R., & Kaunert, C. (2024). Uncapping the Potential of Quantum Computing Towards Manufacturing Optimization: Routing Supply Chain Projecting Sustainability. In A. Hassan, P. Bhattacharya, & P. Dutta (Eds.), *Quantum Computing and Supply Chain Management: A New Era of Optimization* (p. 25). IGI Global. https://doi.org/10.4018/979-8-3693-4107-0.ch024.
15. Tiwari, D. N., Loof, R., & Paudyal, G. N. (1999). Environmental–Economic Decision-Making in Lowland Irrigated Agriculture Using Multi-Criteria Analysis Techniques. *Agricultural Systems*, 60(2), 99–112.
16. Paul, S., Mukherjee, D., Mitra, A., Mitra, A., & Dutta, P. K. (2024). Unravelling the Complex Networks of Social Physics: Exploring Human Behavior, Big Data, and Distributed Systems. *Journal of Social Computing*, 5(2), 165–179. https://doi.org/10.23919/JSC.2024.0014.
17. Dutta, P. K., Sekiwu, D., Unogwu, O. J., Catherine, A. T., & Helal, A. H. (2023). Metaverse Revolution in Higher Education: The Rise of Metaversities and Immersive Learning Environments. *Babylonian Journal of Internet of Things*, 2023, 59–68. https://doi.org/10.58496/BJIoT/2023/008.
18. Dutta, P. K., El-kenawy, S. M., Ali, G., & Dhoska, K. (2023). An Energy Consumption Monitoring and Control System in Buildings using Internet of Things. *Babylonian Journal of Internet of Things*, 2023, 38–47. https://doi.org/10.58496/BJIoT/2023/006.
19. Mannepalli, P. K., Richhariya, V., Gupta, S. K., Shukla, P. K., Dutta, P. K., Chowdhury, S., & Hu, Y.-C. (2024). A robust blockchain-based watermarking using edge detection and wavelet transform. *Multimedia Tools and Applications*, 83(20), 1–25. https://doi.org/10.1007/s11042-024-18907-4.

20. Dutta, P. K., & Banerjee, S. (2019). Monitoring of Aerosol and Other Particulate Matter in Air Using Aerial Monitored Sensors and Real Time Data Monitoring and Processing. *Journal of System and Management Sciences*, 9(2), 104–113.
21. Rao, P. S., Nayak, S., Gautam, A., Lourens, M. E., Dutta, P. K., Chowdhury, S., & El-kenawy, E. M. (2022). Aumann agreement theorem based human resource performance monitoring with IoT and 6G technology. In: *6th Smart Cities Symposium (SCS 2022), Hybrid Conference*, Bahrain, pp. 401–406. https://doi.org/10.1049/icp.2023.0638.

Chapter 22

Characterization and prediction of coating thickness on mild steel plate using quantum fuzzy inference system

Rahul Soni, Dipali Pandya, Viren Parikh and Sherif S. M. Ghoneim

22.1 INTRODUCTION

Mild steel contains a large portion of iron and only small amounts of chromium, molybdenum and other alloying elements. This makes mild steel relatively ductile and wieldable than other steel forms. The small amounts of alloying elements present in mild steel improve the affordability compared to other steels. These account for the wide usage of mild steel in various fields, including the oil and gas industry, marine, automotive, machinery parts, cookware and chemical processing industries [1, 2].

Corrosion poses a significant challenge to the durability and structural integrity of metallic components, especially in the case of mild steel, which is widely employed in various engineering applications [3]. However, mild steel is susceptible to wear and deterioration in aggressive environments due to high humidity and salinity, resulting in massive economic losses and safety concerns [4].

As a response to this challenge, protective coatings have emerged as essential elements in mitigating the adverse effects of corrosion and wear, thereby extending steel structures' service life. Mild steel is commonly coated with zinc. The zinc metallic coating can be performed by hot dip galvanizing, electrodeposition, thermal spraying, or cold spraying process [5–8]. In galvanizing coating, the dirt free mild steel part is immersed in a hot (450°C temperature) liquid bath for the desired period.

During the coating process, the presence of silicon in mild steel reacts with zinc and forms an undesirable dull grey coating which may lead to the excessive loss of iron [4]. Fazazi et al. [9] coated zinc on a mild steel substrate by electrodeposition process. Coating thickness increases with current density; however, it reduces current efficiency and changes the zinc morphology [10]. Oladijo et al. [11] studied the corrosion behaviour of plasma-sprayed Zn-Sn alloy coating on mild steel. Improvements in corrosion resistance and microhardness were reported.

Moreover, the generated residual stresses in the plate were compressive in nature. Mathabatha et al. [12] investigate the residual stresses and corrosion behaviour of plasma-sprayed coating of Zn and Al on a mild steel substrate.

DOI: 10.1201/9781003498292-22

Zn-Al ratio varies (Zn-Al (25/75), Zn-Al (50/50) and Zn-Al (75/25. The highest pitting corrosion resistance was reported at 25/75 Zn-Al ratio. Under all coating conditions, compressive residual stresses were reported. Chen and Pender [13] investigate the microstructure changes on plasma-sprayed Ni-Al coated mild steel plates.

Variation in microstructure was observed at every location, which was attributed to non-uniform cooling rates throughout the coating. Cold spray relies on a high-velocity gas stream, usually nitrogen or helium, to propel micron-sized particles at supersonic speeds. The impact of these particles upon reaching the substrate induces plastic deformation, creating a cohesive and tightly bonded coating [14].

Maledi et al. [15] investigate the influence of cold spray parameters on the microstructures and residual stress of zinc (Zn) coated mild steel substrates. Remarkable improvement is observed in corrosion resistance and microhardness at 525°C temperature, 8 bar pressure and 15 mm stand of distance. Residual stresses were linearly decreased with a stand of distance but inversely proportional with temperature and pressure.

Ajdelsztajn et al. [16] coated nanocrystalline Ni powder on an aluminium substrate by cold spray technique and compared the result with the electrodeposition technique. Cold spray-coated nanocrystalline Ni showed higher hardness along with negligible porosity. Compared to the thermal spray techniques the cold spray technique is more popular due to less heat input, thereby reducing the oxidation and stresses on the coated part [17].

Moreover, cold spray techniques eliminate the phase transformation, thereby reducing grain growth [18]. The cold spray technique is capable of coating a variety of metallic as well as composite materials such as cermet and bronze/diamond composites [14, 19–21]. However, cold spray zinc coating is in the development stage.

To increase the effectiveness and robustness of the coating process, a fuzzy logic controller (FLC), neural network and genetic algorithm can be implemented [22, 23]. Ming et al. (2006) studied the nature of the plasma spray coating process by applying the fuzzy logic control system [24]. Swain et al. (2021) applied the fuzzy–TOPSIS hybrid approach to optimize the plasma spray coating parameters [25]. Fayomi and Portal et al. discussed zinc coating and its techniques [2, 8].

In the present work, an attempt has been made to coat mild steel with zinc flake by the cold spray technique. This coating typically consists of microscopic zinc particles embedded in a binder matrix, forming a multilayered structure that provides both barrier and sacrificial corrosion protection. The effect of input parameters such as spray viscosity, curing time and curing temperature are studied.

The variation in coating thickness is investigated under different conditions. The novel AI based fuzzy system is used to predict and optimize the coating thickness with triangular fuzzy membership functions with a neuro-fuzzy designer set. Various input parameters like time, temperature and viscosity will help to model the ANFIS structure for reliable and accurate prediction of the coating thickness. Further, the training and testing data set even shows the least error while predicting the coating thickness. Hence the proposed experimental and simulation based model is highly proficient to leverage the AI for sustainable manufacturing and proactive prediction.

22.2 MATERIALS AND EXPERIMENTAL METHODS

Mild steel plate having dimensions 100mm × 100mm × 3 mm thick, chemical composition is tested and reported in Table 22.1. The zinc flake powder, commercially available and is used to coat the mild steel plate. The macrostructure of irregular elongated zinc flakes (particle size) is illustrated in Figure 22.1. The substrate is passed through multiple rinse baths to ensure the complete removal of contaminants, followed by a hot air drying

Table 22.1 %Weights of elements

Sr No	*Element*	*%Weight*
1	Carbon	0.059
2	Silicon	0.026
3	Manganese	0.365
4	Phosphorus	0.024
5	Sulphur	0.008
6	Nitrogen	0.006
7	CEV	0.132

Figure 22.1 Mild steel plates.

Table 22.2 Experimental design parameters for BBD matrix

Parameters	*Units*	*Factor levels*		
Temperature	(°C)	275	300	325
Viscosity	(Kg/m sec)	22	25	28
Time	(Minutes)	30	60	90

process. Cleaned mild steel plates undergo the grit blast process at room temperature. In this process, steel grit or aluminium oxide is propelled at high velocities on the substrate through compressed air to produce a rough surface.

After the grit blast, the zinc flake is propelled onto the mild steel plates using a high-power low-volume spray gun. This operates with lower air pressure to deliver a higher volume of coating material. The viscosity of the liquid, stand of distance, curing temperature, curing time and pressure are controlling parameters during the coating process. Constant stand of distance and pressure is maintained during the coating process. The viscosity of coating material varies from 22 to 28 kg/msec. Coated plates are placed in an oven for thermal curing and the curing temperature varies from 270°C to 325°C. This thermal curing process helps to cross-link the coating components, ensuring proper adhesion, hardness and corrosion resistance, thereby ensuring the coating's integrity and performance under various environmental conditions. In the present work, to design the experiments the Box Behnken design (BBD) matrix is implemented for three input variables mentioned in Table 22.2. The formulated BBD matrix is shown in Table 22.3.

As per the design matrix, a coating is performed as the aforementioned process. The coating thickness is measured using a thickness gauge. In contrast to previously proposed approaches that employ basic experimental analysis and other methodologies with some accuracy and reliability issues, this hybrid approach of experimental and AI based simulation is highly impactful and reliable. The complete process has to pass from the different phases to predict the accurate coating thickness. To identify thickness, the first step entails defining complex TS fuzzy cognitive input and output membership functions and rule sets. The second step goes via the diagnosis result generated by the fuzzy ruler used for decision-making. The third step is the final evaluation and predictive analysis of the proposed algorithm.

22.3 QUANTUM COMPUTING TO ENHANCE THE MANUFACTURING AND SUPPLY CHAIN LOGISTICS

The basic building blocks of quantum computation are known as quantum bits. Qubits are different from regular bits in that they can be either 0 or 1, or both, concurrently because they exist in a superposition state. This

Table 22.3 The formulated BBD matrix for simulation analysis

Sr. No.	*Temperature*	*Viscosity*	*Time*
1	275	25	90
2	300	25	60
3	275	25	30
4	275	28	60
5	300	22	90
6	325	25	90
7	300	25	60
8	300	28	90
9	300	22	30
10	300	25	60
11	300	28	30
12	275	22	60
13	325	25	30
14	325	28	60
15	325	22	60
16	300	25	60
17	300	25	60

inherent duality gives quantum computers a major advantage when solving complex problems with lots of variables. The basic building blocks of quantum computation are known as quantum bits. Qubits are different from regular bits in that they can be either 0 or 1, or both, concurrently because they exist in a superposition state. This inherent duality gives quantum computers a major advantage when solving complex problems with lots of variables [26, 27].

In the upcoming years, more information about how supply chains and logistics could be revolutionized by quantum computing will become available. Quick optimization and secure communication are only two examples of how the quantum leap is expected to transform industries, spur innovation and provide solutions to problems that were previously unsolvable, when we fully embrace the quantum leap and transform how we optimize and regulate our globalized society [28].

22.4 TS FUZZY LOGIC CONTROLLER WITH INFERENCE SYSTEM DESIGN

FLCs were first introduced by Professor Lotfi Zadeh [29] in 1965 and have gained popularity ever since because of their good performance and adaptability. Data that is linguistic or qualitative is used in the control algorithm of the FLC. It avoids the problem of providing unambiguous information about numerical values as a result. The FLC completes the rule basis and functions inside designated information domains. The rule base reflects historical data, its consequences and any required or preferred steps to be followed in order to proceed with the process.

Professor Ebrahim Mamdani of London University created one of the earliest fuzzy systems in 1975 to control a steam engine and boiler combination. The first goal was to operate a steam engine and boiler combination using a set of linguistic control rules from experienced human operators. The fuzzy inference technique that is most commonly used is the Mamdani method. Fuzzification of the input variables, rule evaluation, aggregation of the rule outputs, and defuzzification are the four phases that make up the Mamdani technique of fuzzy inference.

A fuzzy membership function is used to convert crisp input into the fuzzy inference system. Instead of addressing fuzzy reasoning itself, fuzzy logic deals with the fuzziness in the data. The best explanation for this fuzziness in the data is provided by the fuzzy membership function. The fundamental element of each fuzzy logic controller (FLC) is the fuzzy inference system. A membership function on the domain of discourse X for a fuzzy set A is defined as follows: μA: $X \rightarrow [0, 1]$, where each element of X is mapped to a value in the interval 0–1. This value, sometimes referred to as the membership value or degree of membership [30], quantifies the extent to which the component in X is a member of the fuzzy set A.

The fuzzy model prepared by Takagi and Sugeno is represented locally by the input-output relations of a nonlinear system using fuzzy IF-THEN rules. A Takagi-Sugeno fuzzy model's primary characteristic is its use of a linear system model to represent the local dynamics of each fuzzy implication (rule). The fuzzy "blending" of the linear system models results in the overall fuzzy model of the system. Through a series of examples, the reader will discover that Takagi-Sugeno fuzzy models can accurately represent nearly all nonlinear dynamical systems. Takagi-Sugeno fuzzy models are, in fact, universal approximators of any smooth nonlinear system [31].

The illustrated Table 22.4 shows popular fuzzy membership functions for many applications together with their mathematical and graphical representations, along with equation formulation and graphical descriptions. Using predefined membership functions (MFs), the input variable is transformed into a linguistic variable during the fuzzification stage. The output of the fuzzification step is then used to generate the fuzzified output using the specified ruleset. Ultimately, during the defuzzification stage, the fuzzified output is transformed into the production required for system control [32].

The proposed study approach has been applied to a number of important factors, including temperature, time and viscosity of the material. MATLAB Simulink is used in the subsequent step to create the expert model after the processed data are imported. Concurrently, this data is received by FCL as

Table 22.4 Fuzzy membership functions with graphical abstracts remarks

Fuzzy MF	*Equation formations*	*Graphical structure*	*Terminology*
Triangular MF (TRIMF)	$\mu_{TRI} = \max\left[\min\left(\frac{x-a}{b-a},\frac{c-x}{c-b}\right),0\right]$	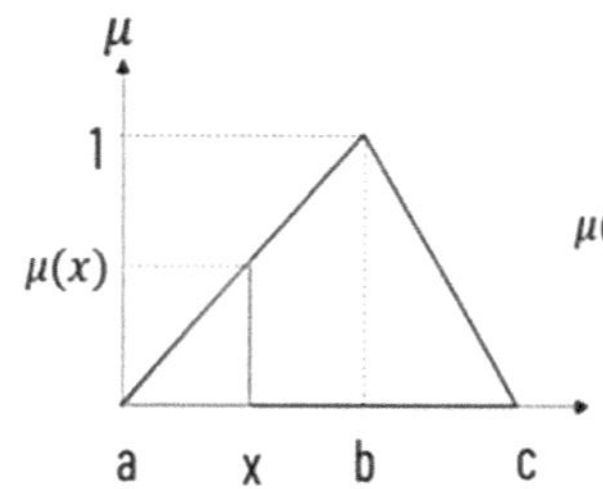 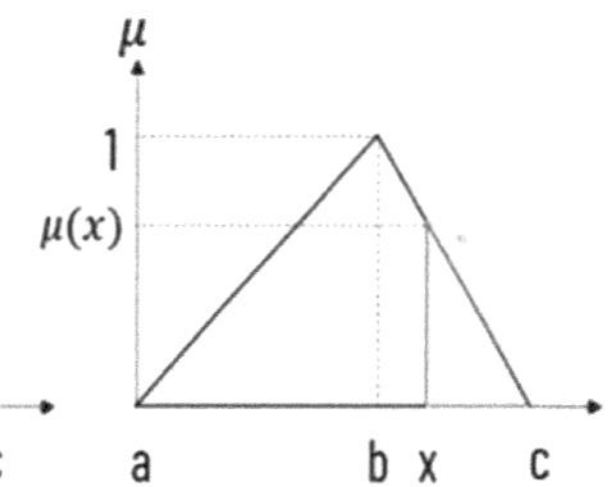	The triangle that fuzzifies the input can be described by three parameters (a, b and c), which represent the triangle's height (b) and base (a), where x lies between b and c and a and b.
Trapezoidal MF (TRAPMF)	$\mu_{TRAP} = \max\left[\min\left(\frac{x-a}{b-a},1,\frac{d-x}{d-c}\right),0\right]$	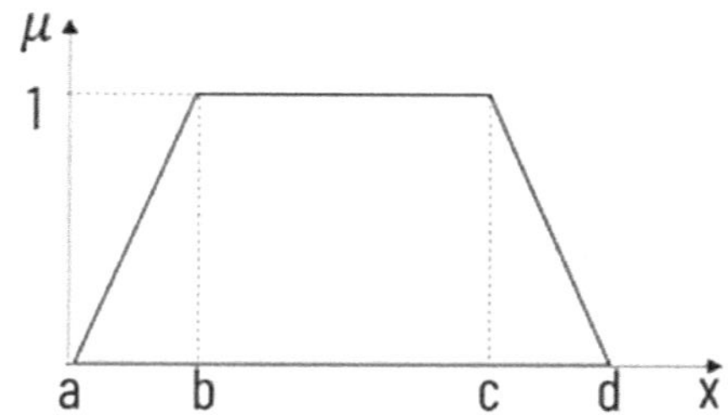	The trapezoidal membership function is defined by four parameters: a, b, c and d. In span b to c, the maximum membership value is represented. Additionally, x's membership value will fall between 0 and 1 if it sits between (a, b) or (c, d).

Gaussian MF (GAUMF)	$\mu_{GAU} = e^{-\frac{1}{2}\left(\frac{x-m}{\sigma}\right)^2}$	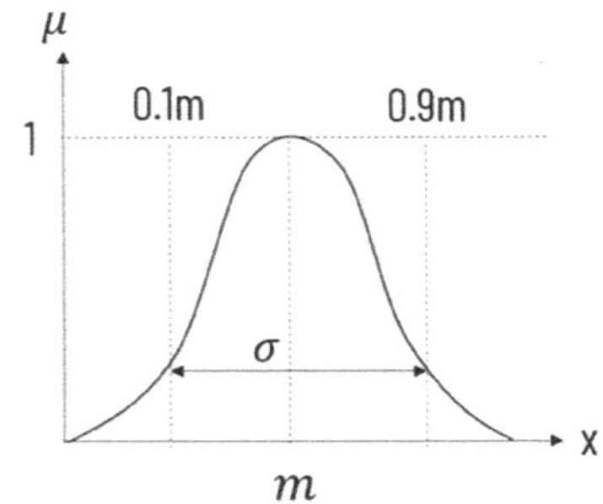	The two parameters m and σ, which represent the mean or centre of the Gaussian curve and its spread, respectively, are used to describe a Gaussian MF.
Generalized Bell MF (GENBMF)	$\mu_{GENB} = \dfrac{1}{1+\left\|\dfrac{x-c}{a}\right\|^{2b}}$	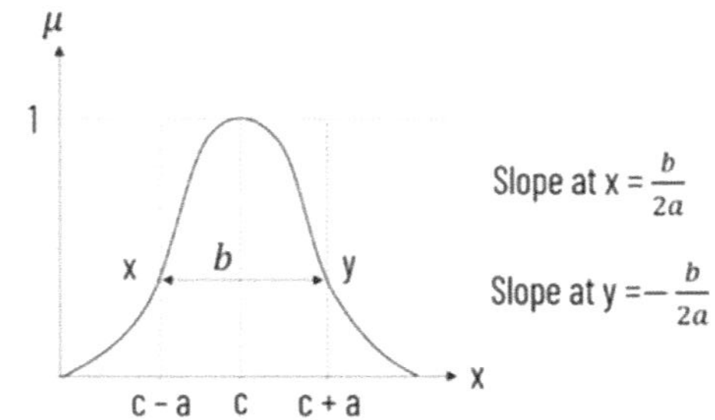	Generalized bell-shaped function or Cauchy MF. GBMF is the definition of the three parameters (a, b, and c) that make up a generalized bell MF.
Sigmoid MF (SIGMF)	$\mu_{SIG} = \dfrac{1}{1+e^{-a(x-c)}}$	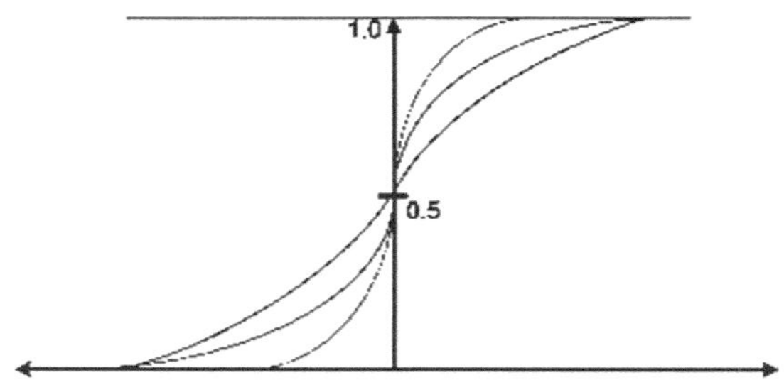	Parameters a and c control how the input behaves when it is suppressed and mapped from 0 to 1. At the intersection, $x = c$, and the slope is determined by a.

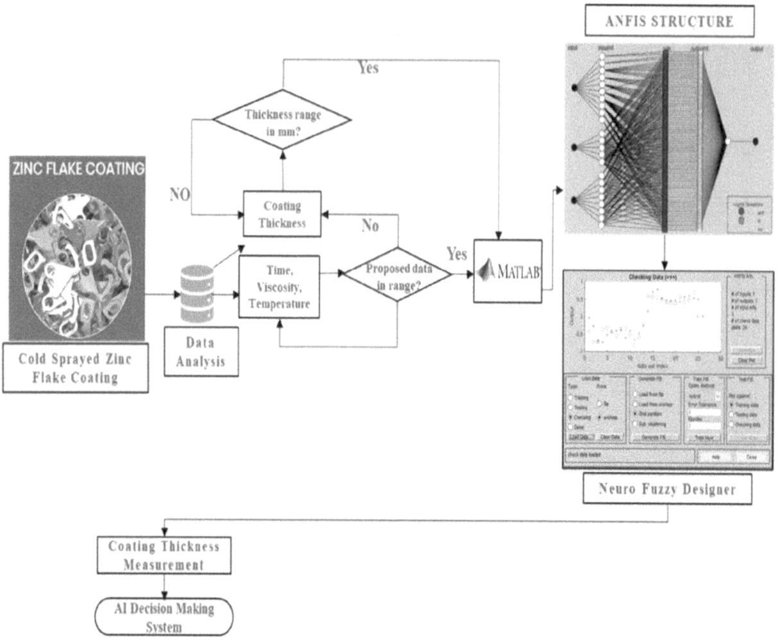

Figure 22.2 Coating thickness measurement using TS fuzzy systems.

input functions. Fuzzy rules are utilized to predict the diagnosis analysis once these data are processed through a cognitive fuzzy logic procedure. The suggested research methodology is shown in Figure 22.2.

22.5 FUZZIFICATION PROCESS OF INPUT MEMBERSHIP FUNCTION

Fuzzification is the technique of creating fuzzy values from precise inputs using the necessary MFs. The approach uses a commonly used triangular (TRIMF) and Trapezoidal MF (TRAPMF) to form the fuzzification stud and to represent the three inputs. Here, in this research work inputs of TMFs are chosen using the expressions for Equations 22.1 and 22.2, as shown in Figure 22.3 and Figure 22.4.

$$\mu_{TRI}(X1)(x;a,b,c) = \begin{cases} 0, & (x \le a) \\ \frac{x-a}{b-a}, & (a \le x \le b) \\ \frac{c-x}{c-b}, & (b \le x \le c) \\ 0 & (c \le x) \end{cases} \tag{22.1}$$

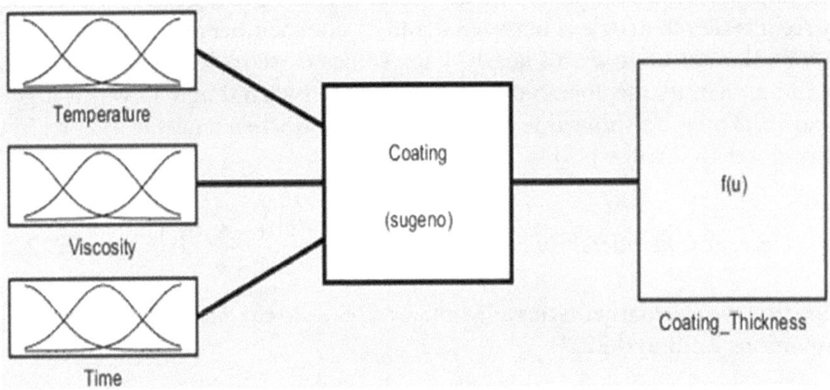

Figure 22.3 Coating thickness measurement using TS fuzzy systems.

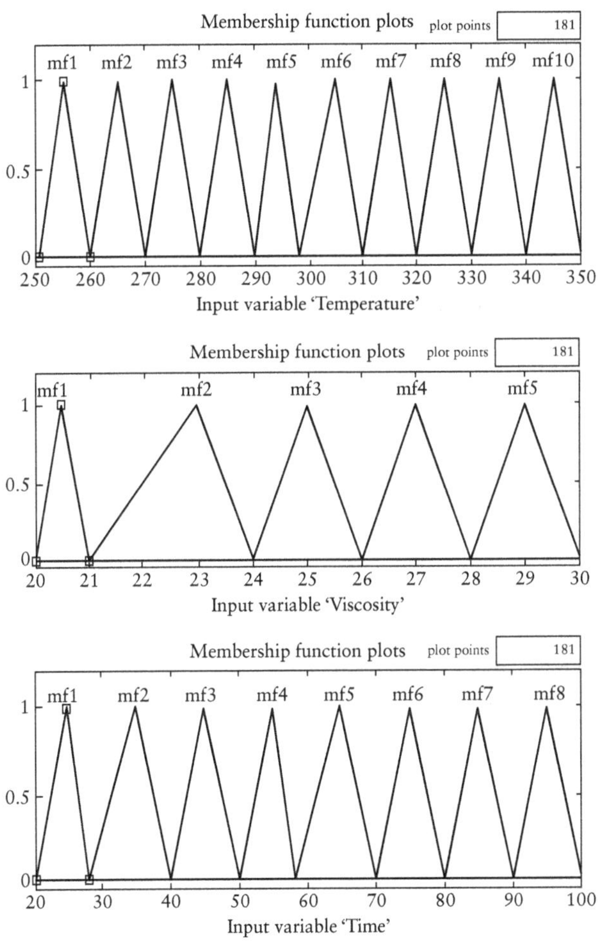

Figure 22.4 Input membership functions of QFIS simulation.

If x falls between a and b, the membership value of the suggested MF for the current research article is between 0 and 1. The membership value is almost 0 for values close to a and nearly 1 for values close to b. If x falls between b and c, then its membership value (MV) is between 0 and 1. When it gets near b, its membership value gets closer to 1, and when it gets near c, its MV gets closer to 0 value [33].

$$Degree\,of\,membership(F1) = \max\left[\min\left(\frac{x-a}{b-a},\frac{c-x}{c-b}\right),0\right] \tag{22.2}$$

The following mathematical formulas are used to show TRIMF using Equations 22.3 and 22.4.

$$\mu_{TRI}(f2)(x;a,b,c,d) = \begin{cases} 0, & (x \le a) \\ \dfrac{x-a}{b-a}, & (a \le x \le b) \\ 1 & (b \le x \le c) \\ \dfrac{d-x}{d-c}, & (c \le x \le d) \\ 0, & (d \le x) \end{cases} \tag{22.3}$$

$$Degree\,of\,membership(f2) = \max\left[\min\left(\frac{x-a}{b-a},1,\frac{d-x}{d-c}\right),0\right] \tag{22.4}$$

The proposed research method based on QFIS incorporates significant aspects of zinc flake based optimal thickness prediction with fuzzy inference cognitive rules as depicted in Figure 22.5. Further proposed rules are also depicted in the following Figure 22.6.

Surface and contour plots in FLC are used to show the hue, saturation, and value (HSV) characteristics. The simulation work addresses six numbers of plots according to temperature, viscosity, and time as crucial input parameters for thickness analysis in Figure 22.7.

22.6 TS BASED ADAPTIVE NEURO-FUZZY INFERENCE SYSTEM (ANFIS)

The ANFIS system is, as its name suggests, a neuro-fuzzy inference machine that is flexible. It is a universal approximator, similar to traditional fuzzy systems or "pure" artificial neural networks (i.e., non-fuzzy). The objective of this process is to "learn" or approximate simple or complex mappings, also known as nonlinear functions, from an input space (which is typically multivariate) to an output space that might be univariate or multivariate.

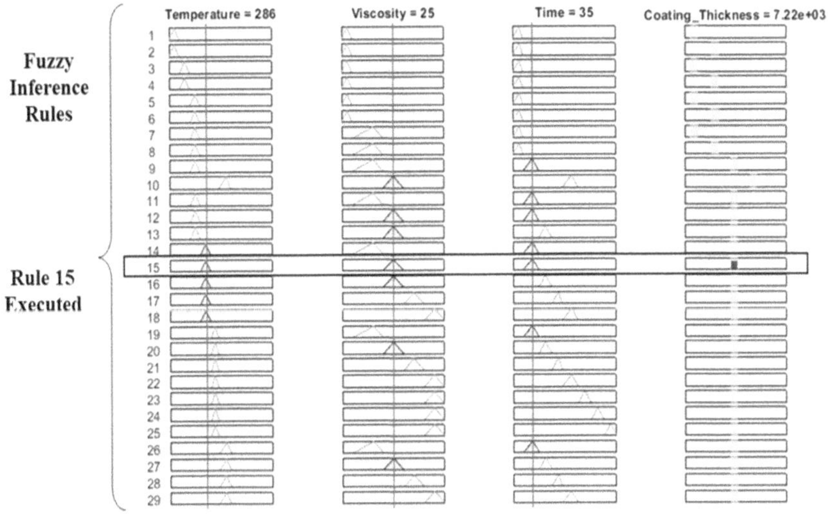

Figure 22.5 Rules analysis and execution for coating thickness prediction with QFIS.

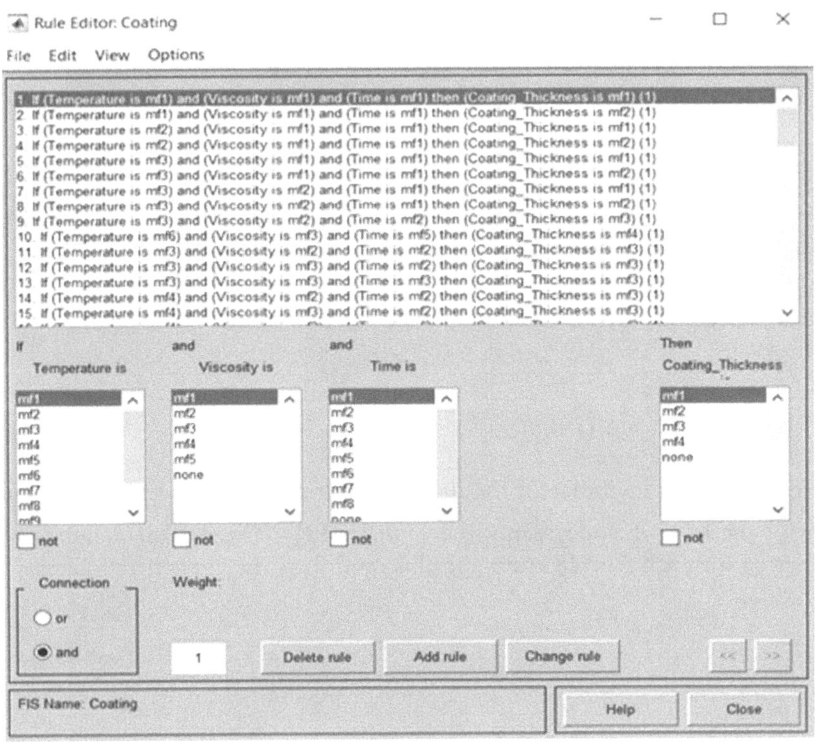

Figure 22.6 Rules formations with selected parameters for coating thickness prediction.

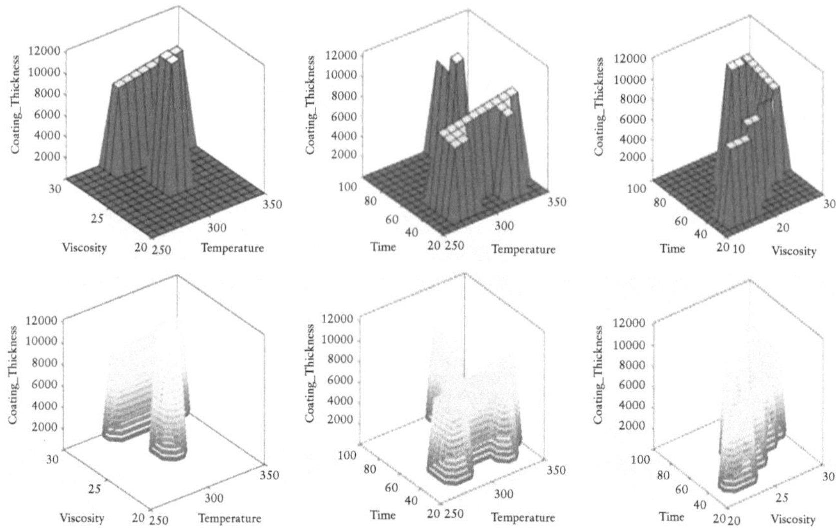

Figure 22.7 (3D) Graphs of surface and contour plots for coating thickness analysis.

A typical ANFIS consists of five layers, ranging from the input layer to the output layer. Below is a brief explanation of each layer's functions [34–36].

22.7 FIRST LAYER (INPUTS LAYER)

This layer is where the input is fuzzified. This means that a membership value is assigned to each fuzzy subset that constitutes the universe of discourse in an input. The mathematical expression for this function is as follows.

$$OutputFL_{ij}^{(1)} = \mu_j\left(Input_i^{(1)}\right) \tag{22.5}$$

The j-th linguistic phrase of the i-th input variable corresponds to the output of the layer 1 node, denoted as $OutputFL_{ij}^{(1)}$ The default membership function for each ANFIS system in this module is the generalized Gaussian function.

22.8 SECOND LAYER (FUZZY WITH AND FUNCTIONS)

Every node in this layer performs fuzzy-AND operations. For every ANFIS network in the library, the T-norm operator of the algebraic product was selected. As a result, the output of each node is equal to the total of all of its inputs (that is, the input term nodes connected to each rule node).

$$OutputSL_k^{(2)} = W_k = \prod_{i=1}^{N_{Inputs}} Ouptput_{(ij)}^1 \tag{22.6}$$

The firing strength (or activation value) of the corresponding fuzzy rule is the output that each node in this layer generates. $K = 1$, the quantity of rules.

22.9 THIRD LAYER (NORMALIZATION PROCESS)

The output of the k-th node is determined by dividing the firing strength of each rule by the total sum of the activation values of all the fuzzy rules. Consequently, each fuzzy rule's activation value is normalized. This operation can be expressed most simply as rules.

$$OutputTL_k^{(3)} = \overline{W_k} = \frac{Output_k^{(2)}}{\sum_{m=1}^{N_{Rules}} output_m^2} \tag{22.7}$$

22.10 FOURTH LAYER (ADJUSTABLE PROCESS)

Every node k in this layer implements the linear function, which is adjusted by a set of parameters a_k.

$$OutputFRL_k^{(4)} = \overline{W_k} f_k = \overline{W_k}\ (a_{1k} Input_1^{(1)} + \ldots + a_{N_{Inputs}k}\ Inputs_{N_{Inputs}}^{(1)} + a_{0_k}) \tag{22.8}$$

The weight is determined by using (22.7) to compute the normalized activation value of the k-th rule. These parameters, which are changed by the Recursive Least Square (RLS) algorithm, are known as the linear parameters of the ANFIS system, as shown in Figure 22.8.

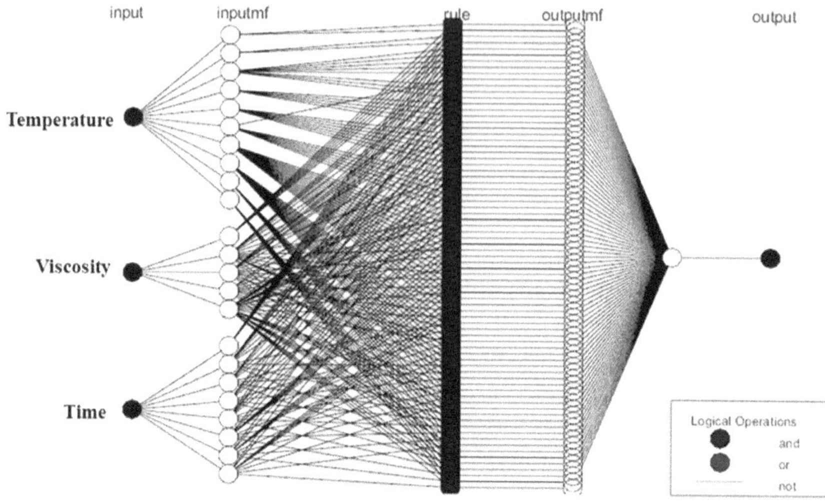

Figure 22.8 ANFIS structure formation based on coating thickness analysis.

22.11 FIFTH LAYER (OUTPUT PROCESSING LAYER)

This layer is made up of just one node for ANFIS (MISO), which sums its inputs algebraically to produce the network's output:

$$OutputFIF_k^{(5)} = \sum_{k=1}^{N_{rules}} OutputFRL_k^{(4)} = \sum_{k=1}^{N_{rules}} \overline{W_k} f_k = \frac{\sum_{k=1}^{N_{rules}} W_k f_k}{\sum_{k=1}^{N_{rules}} W_k} \tag{22.9}$$

22.12 RESULT AND DISCUSSION

22.12.1 Coating thickness

The coating thickness is a crucial parameter as it directly influences the protective capabilities of the zinc flake coating. Thickness gauges were precisely measured and allowed us to obtain accurate and reliable measurements without compromising the integrity of the coated surfaces. Prior to measurements, the mild steel plates were thoroughly prepared, ensuring a clean and uniform surface for accurate readings. The coating thickness gauge was calibrated by the specific properties of zinc flake coatings and the substrate material.

This calibration step was essential for obtaining precise measurements that align with industry standards and requirements. The measurement process itself involved placing the coating thickness gauge onto the coated surface, as shown in Figure 22.9. The gauge generated signals and analyzed

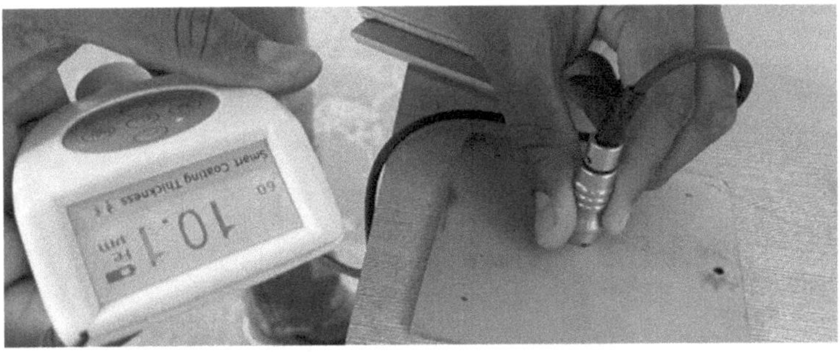

Figure 22.9 Measuring coating thickness for xxperimental analysis.

changes in magnetic fields or eddy currents, providing real-time measurements of the distance between the gauge probe and the substrate.

Multiple measurements were taken across different regions of each mild steel plate to capture potential variations in coating thickness. The data collected from the coating thickness gauge allowed us to establish an average coating thickness value and assess the uniformity of the coating distribution, as depicted in Figure 22.10.

22.12.2 Adhesion test

An adhesion test was conducted using an adhesion tape with a width of 25 mm and an adhesive strength of (7 ± 1) *N*. This test evaluates the strength of the bond between the coating and the mild steel substrate. The tape was firmly pressed onto the coated surface to ensure proper contact between the adhesive and the coating.

After a specified period, the tape was quickly and uniformly peeled off the surface at a controlled angle and speed. Figure 22.11 exhibited the

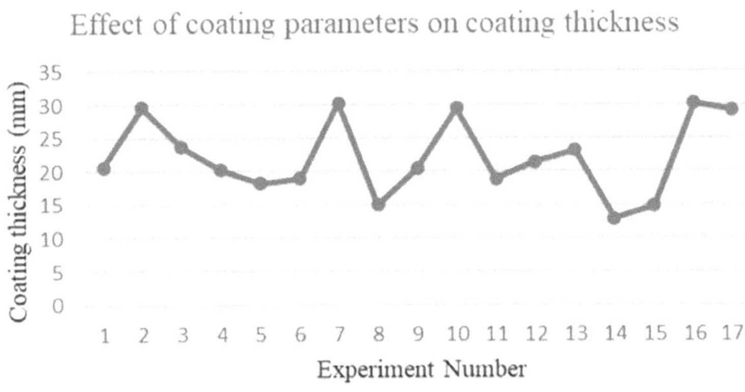

Figure 22.10 Coating thickness at different points of mild steel plate.

Figure 22.11 Zinc flake spray coating with substrate analysis.

coated surface with minimal to no visible damage or coating material removal. Therefore, the zinc flake spray coating formed a robust bond with the substrate.

The variation in coating thickness is investigated under different conditions. The novel AI based fuzzy system is used to predict and optimize the coating thickness with triangular fuzzy membership functions with a neuro-fuzzy designer framework. Various input parameters like time, temperature and viscosity will help to model the ANFIS structure for reliable and accurate prediction for the coating thickness.

Further, the training and testing data set even shows the least error while predicting the coating thickness. Hence, the proposed experimental and simulation based hybrid model is highly proficient in leveraging AI and quantum computing for sustainable manufacturing and proactively predicts to enhance the production and eventually the SCL in coating industries.

22.13 LIMITS AND FUTURE OPPORTUNITIES OF THE PROJECTED RESEARCH WORK

- Fuzzy logic has the ability to detect a few errors at times, and its complexity may grow as the number of input membership functions and associated rules increases.
- Pressure and vibration are two elements that affect the suggested methodology's accuracy; hence, the study may be helpful in the future.
- More input parameters based on mechanical, thermal and chemical aspects can be incorporated in future studies for further enhancement of coating thickness.

22.14 CONCLUSION

In this research work, a novel QFIS-TS based ANFIS framework is developed for cold sprayed zinc flake coating thickness on mild steel plates. Impact analysis of various input parameters like time, temperature and viscosity is discussed. The suggested study has been tested and verified using the ANFIS structure. Utilizing a neuro-fuzzy designer framework and triangle fuzzy membership functions, the innovative artificial intelligence (AI) fuzzy system is used to anticipate and optimize coating thickness. The ANFIS structure is modelled with the aid of several input parameters, such as time, temperature and viscosity, to enable precise and dependable coating thickness prediction. In addition, the training and testing data set even exhibits the lowest error in coating thickness prediction. Therefore, the suggested hybrid model, which combines simulation and experimentation, is very effective at using AI and quantum computing to support sustainable manufacturing. It also makes proactive predictions that will eventually increase production and SCL in the coating sectors.

REFERENCES

1. B. M. Durodolai, J. A. O. Olugbuyiro, S. A. Moshood, O. S. Fayomi, and A. P. I. Popoola, Study of influence of zinc plated mild steel deterioration in seawater environment, *International Journal of Electrochemical Science* 6, 5605–5616 (2011).
2. O. S. I. Fayomi, A.A. Sode, B. U. Anyanwu, A.A. Ayoola, M. O. Nkiko, K. M. Oluwasegun, D. O. Alkhuele, and D. E. Ighravwe, Experimental studies and influence of process factor on zinc-nickel based coating on mild steel, *Advances in Materials and Processing Technologies* 8(2), 2193–2202 (2021). https://doi.org/10.1080/2374068X.2021.1896863.
3. O. S. Fayomi, and A. P. I. Popoola, An investigation of the properties of Zn coated mild steel, *International Journal of Electrochemical Science* 7, 6555–6570 (2012).
4. J. Wang, H. Tu, B. Peng, X. Wang, F. Yin, and X. Su, The effects of zinc bath temperature on the coating growth behavior of reactive steel, behavior of reactive steel, *Materials Characterization* 60, 1276–1279 (2009).
5. A. P. I. Popoola, O. S. Fayomi, and O. M. Popoola, Comparative studies of microstructural, tribological and corrosion properties of plated Zn and Zn-alloy coatings, *International Journal of Electrochemical Science* 7, 4860–4870 (2012).
6. G. Ahmet, C. Ozgur, T. Ahmet, U. Fatih, and Y. Fevzi, Accelerated corrosion behaviours of Zn, Al and Zn/15Al coatings on a steel surface, *Materials and Technology* 45, 477–482 (2011).
7. G. Vinay, N. M. Chavan, S. Kumar, A. Jyothirmayi, and B. R. Bodapati, Improved microstructure and properties of cold sprayed zinc coatings in the as sprayed condition, *Surface and Coatings Technology* 438, 128392 (2022). https://doi.org/10.1016/j.surfcoat.2022.128392.
8. F. C. Porter, A. M. Stoneman, and R. G. Thilthorpe, The range of zinc coatings, *Transactions of the IMF* 66(1), 28–33 (1988). https://doi.org/10.1080/00202967.1988.11870800.
9. A. Fazazi, M. Ouakki, and M. Cherkaoui, Electrochemical deposition of Zinc on mild steel. *Mediterranean Journal of Chemistry* 8, 30–41 (2019). https://doi.org/10.13171/mjc8119021318mo.

10. G. A. G. Pedroza, C. A. C. Souza, I. A. Carlos, and L. R. P. Andrade Lima, Evaluation of the effect of deposition bath glycerol content on zinc–nickel electrodeposits on carbon steel, *Surface & Coatings Technology* 206, 2927 (2012).
11. O. P. Oladijo, M. H. Mathabatha, A. P. I. Popoola, and T. P. Ntsoane, Characterization and corrosion behaviour of plasma sprayed Zn–Sn alloy coating on mild steel, *Surface and Coatings Technology* 352, 654–661 (2018), ISSN 0257-8972. https://doi.org/10.1016/j.surfcoat.2017.04.029.
12. M. H. Mathabatha, A. P. I. Popoola, and O. P. Oladijo, Residual stresses and corrosion performance of plasma sprayed zinc-based alloy coating on mild steel substrate, *Surface and Coatings Technology* 318, 293–298 (2017), ISSN 0257-8972. https://doi.org/10.1016/j.surfcoat.2016.10.023.
13. H. C. Chen, and E. Pender, Microstructure of plasma-sprayed Ni–Al alloy coating on mild steel, *Thin Solid Films* 280(1–2), 188–198 (1996), ISSN 0040-6090. https://doi.org/10.1016/0040-6090(95)08195-X.
14. T. Schmidt, H. Assadi, F. Gartner, H. Richter, T. Stoltenhoff, H. Kreye, and T. Klasse, From particle acceleration to impact and bonding in cold spraying, *Journal of Thermal Spray Technology* 18(5–6), 794–808 (2009).
15. N. B. Maledi, O. P. Oladijo, I. Botef, T. P. Ntsoane, A. Madiseng, L. Moloisane, Influence of cold spray parameters on the microstructures and residual stress of Zn coatings sprayed on mild steel, *Surface and Coatings Technology* 318, 106–113 (2017). https://doi.org/10.1016/j.surfcoat.2017.03.062.
16. L. Ajdelsztajn, B. Jodoin, and J. M. Schoenung, Synthesis and mechanical properties of nanocrystalline Ni coatings produced by cold gas dynamic spraying, *Surface Coating Technology* 201, 1166–1172 (2006).
17. A. Moridi, S. M. Hassani-Gangarajal, M. Guagliano, and M. Dao, Cold spraying coatings: review of material systems and future perspectives, *Surface Engineering*, 36(6), 369–395 (2014).
18. Y. Li, C. Zhang, X. P. Guo, H. L. Liao, C. J. Li, and C. Coddet, Effect of standoff distance on coating deposition characteristic in cold spraying, *Materials and Design* 29, 297–304 (2008).
19. H. J. Kim, C. H. Lee, and S. Y. Hwang, Fabrication of WC-Co coatings by cold spray deposition, *Surface Coating Technology* 191, 335–340 (2005).
20. H. J. Kim, C. H. Lee, and S. Y. Hwang, Superhard nano WC-12%Co coating by cold spray deposition, *Material Science Engineering* 391, 243–248 (2005).
21. H. Na, G. Bae, S. Shin, S. Kumar, H. J. Kim, and C. Lee, Advanced deposition characteristics of kinetic sprayed bronze/diamond composite by tailoring feedstock properties, *Composites Science Technology* 69, 463–468 (2009).
22. B. Y. Han, W. W. Xu, K. B. Zhou, H. Y. Zhang, W. N. Lei, M. Q. Cong, W. Du, J. J. Chu, and S. Zhu, Performance analysis of plasma spray Ni60CuMo coatings on a ZL109 via a back propagation neural network model, *Surface and Coatings Technology* 433, 128121 (2022). https://doi.org/10.1016/j.surfcoat.2022.128121.
23. G. D. Olvera-Romero, R. Praga-Alejo, M. Rodríguez-Reyes, et al. Application of ANOVA in interval type-2 fuzzy logic systems for modeling the process of ceramic coating preparation in the foundry industry, *The International Journal of Advanced Manufacturing Technology* 132, 3927–3938 (2024). https://doi.org/10.1007/s00170-024-13563-2.

24. M. D. Jean, B. T. Lin, and J. H. Chou, Design of a fuzzy logic approach for optimization reinforced zirconia depositions using plasma sprayings, *Surface and Coatings Technology* 201(6), 3129–3138 (2006). https://doi.org/10.1016/j.surfcoat.2006.06.056.
25. B. Swain, M. Priyadarshini, S. S. Mohapatra, R. K. Gupta, and A. Behera, Parametric optimization of atmospheric plasma spray coating using fuzzy TOPSIS hybrid technique, *Journal of Alloys and Compounds* 867, 159074 (2021). https://doi.org/10.1016/j.jallcom.2021.159074.
26. G. Acampora, R. Schiattarella, and A. Vitiello, Using Quantum Fuzzy Inference Engines in Smart Cities," in *2024 IEEE International Conference on Fuzzy Systems (FUZZ-IEEE)*, Yokohama, Japan, 2024, pp. 1–8. https://doi.org/10.1109/FUZZ-IEEE60900.2024.10611863.
27. G. Acampora, M. Grossi, M. Schenk, and R. Schiattarella, Quantum fuzzy inference engine for particle accelerators control, *IEEE Transactions on Quantum Engineering*, 5, 1–13 (2024).
28. N. Ali, A. Ahmed, L. Anum, H.M. Alzoubi, and M. Ahmad, Modelling supply chain information collaboration empowered with machine learning technique, *Intelligent Automation and Soft Computing* 30(1), 243–257 (2021).
29. L. Zadeh, Fuzzy Sets, *Information and Control* 8(3), 338–53 (June 1965).
30. Y. Xin, et al., Coating matching recommendation based on improved fuzzy comprehensive evaluation and collaborative filtering algorithm, *Scientific Reports* 11, 14035 (2021), https://doi.org/10.1038/s41598-021-93628-4, 2021.
31. Y. Zhang, G. Wang, T. Zhou, X. Huang, S. Lam, J. Sheng, et al., Takagi-sugeno-kang fuzzy system fusion: A survey at hierarchical wide and stacked levels, *Information fusion* 101, 101977 (2024).
32. R. Soni, et al., Diagnosis and prognosis of incipient faults and insulation status for asset management of power transformer using fuzzy logic controller & fuzzy clustering means, *Electric Power Systems Research* 220(July), 109256 (2023). https://doi.org/10.1016/j.jpgr.2023.109256.
33. D. S. Solovjev, Improving the electroplating coating uniformity based on fuzzy control of the setting value using the combined defuzzification method with the presence of stochastic influences, *Solid State Phenomena* 227, 27–23 (2022). https://doi.org/10.4028/p-18t3z8.
34. R. Soni et al., Condition Based Assessment and Diagnostics of Transformer in Smart Grid Network Using Adaptive Neuro Fuzzy Inference System Framework, in *International Conference on Intelligent Manufacturing and Energy Sustainability*, 2023, Vol. 372, pp. 139–150, https://doi.org/10.1007/978-981-99-6774-2_13.
35. J. M. Alonso, C. Castiello, and C. Mencar, The role of interpretable fuzzy systems in designing cognitive cities, *Designing Cognitive Cities*, 176, 131–152 (2019).
36. A. Abu-Khadrah, An Efficient Fuzzy Logic Modelling of TiN Coating Thickness, *International Conference on Business Analytics for Technology and Security (ICBATS)*, Dubai, United Arab Emirates, 2022, pp. 1–5. https://doi.org/10.1109/ICBATS54253.2022.9759094.

Chapter 23

How quantum computing powers the future of artificial intelligence

Rishabh Anand

23.1 INTRODUCTION

Quantum computing (QC) is a transformative field built on the principles of quantum mechanics (QM), utilizing phenomena such as superposition and entanglement to perform computations. The systems that execute quantum computations are known as Quantum Computers [1–5].

Quantum superposition (QS) is a foundational principle in quantum mechanics. It posits that, similar to wave behavior in Classical Mechanics (CM), any two or more quantum states can combine to form a new valid quantum state. Conversely, any quantum state can be represented as a sum of distinct quantum states. Mathematically, this principle arises from the linearity of the Schrödinger equation, allowing any linear combination of its solutions to also be a solution. A vivid demonstration of this wave-like behavior is the interference pattern observed in the double-slit experiment with electrons, resembling classical wave diffraction patterns (Figure 23.1) [6].

Boolean functions and their operations can be considered a special case of unitary transformations in the context of quantum computation.

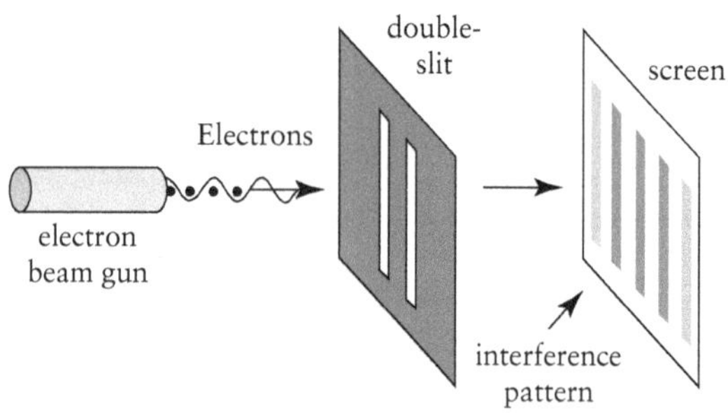

Figure 23.1 Setup of the double-slit experiment.

DOI: 10.1201/9781003498292-23

This means that any problem that can be simulated classically can also be simulated quantum mechanically. However, the additional properties of quantum computers, such as *superposition* and *entanglement*, make them exponentially faster than conventional computers. Moreover, quantum computations enable tasks like *quantum teleportation*, which would be impossible for classical systems to achieve.

Quantum computers are believed to significantly outperform classical computers in solving problems like integer factorization, which underpins RSA encryption [7]. As a subfield of quantum information science, quantum computing represents a new era of computation.

Historically, classical computers have evolved through successive technological revolutions, from gears and relays to vacuum tubes, transistors, and integrated circuits. Modern computing relies on CPUs based on transistors architected around positive-negative-positive (PNP) junctions. Today's advanced lithographic techniques, such as physical vapor deposition (PVD), chemical vapor deposition (CVD), and chemical mechanical polishing (CMP), have enabled the production of sub-micron chips (Figure 23.2).

However, further miniaturization is limited by the wavelength of light used in lithography. On the atomic scale, matter adheres to the rules of Quantum Mechanics, which differ significantly from those governing Classical Mechanics. As chip sizes shrink further, classical logic gates reach a point where quantum effects dominate. To overcome these limitations, quantum technology must either replace or complement traditional computing methods.

Quantum technology offers much more than denser chips or faster clock speeds. It introduces a new paradigm of computation with fundamentally novel algorithms based on quantum principles. Unlike classical computing, which operates on bits of information, quantum computing manipulates qubits, enabling exponentially more computational possibilities.

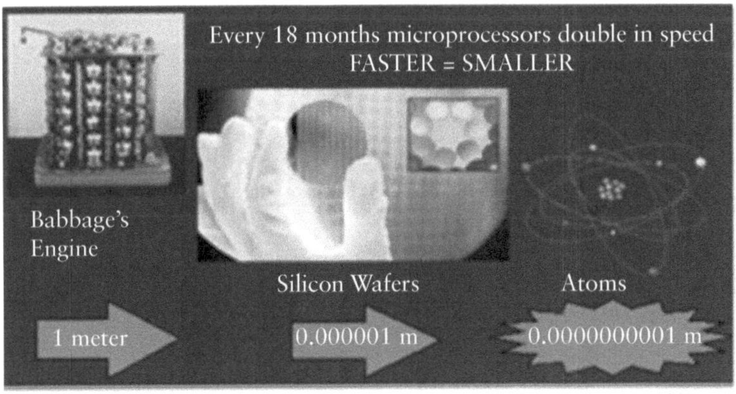

Figure 23.2 Modern chip fabrication techniques.

Understanding qubits and their definition is a critical step toward grasping the potential of quantum computing.

The next generation of computers, operating on quantum bits, is poised to revolutionize computation. Recent breakthroughs have demonstrated how to encode three qubits into two photons, paving the way for these advanced systems. Quantum computers will require not only powerful processors but also new algorithms, interconnects, and other yet-to-be-invented technologies to harness their immense processing power and facilitate result sharing and storage.

For example, Intel has introduced a 49-qubit processor named Tangle Lake. Previously, the company created a virtual testing environment for quantum-computing software using the Stampede supercomputer at The University of Texas at Austin, simulating up to a 42-qubit processor. However, simulating hundreds or thousands of qubits will be necessary to fully understand quantum computing software.

Stampede was one of the most powerful supercomputers in the United States for open science research, capable of nearly ten quadrillion operations per second. It enabled advancements in computational science, scalable visualization, and next-generation programming languages (Figure 23.3). Funded by the National Science Foundation (NSF) through award ACI-1134872, Stampede was upgraded in 2016 with additional compute nodes built around Intel's second-generation Xeon Phi architecture, known as Knights Landing (KNL). This upgrade pushed the boundaries of computational capabilities, ranking #116 on the June 2016 Top 500 list and establishing KNL as a significant milestone in computational technology.

Quantum computing represents the next frontier, where advancements in quantum mechanics, hardware, and algorithms converge to create unprecedented opportunities for solving complex problems and driving innovation.

Figure 23.3 Structure of the stampede supercomputer array.

23.2 WHAT ARE QUBITS?

A *qubit* is the fundamental unit of quantum information, capable of representing both 0 and 1 simultaneously through a uniquely quantum phenomenon known as *superposition*. This ability allows qubits to perform vast numbers of calculations in parallel, significantly increasing computing speed and capacity compared to classical bits. However, not all qubits are created equal, as there are multiple types, each with distinct methods of manipulation and interaction.

Unlike classical computers, the memory units for quantum computers have been one of the primary concerns for scientists and engineers. Another significant challenge has been the computation process itself, which involves many quantum-based phenomena. In this context, a *two-level quantum system* can be considered for quantum computing, analogous to classical computation that relies on bits.

For instance, in programmable silicon quantum chips, a qubit's state (0 or 1) depends on the spin direction of its electron. Regardless of their type, qubits are notoriously fragile and require extreme stability, often maintained at temperatures as low as 20 millikelvins—250 times colder than deep space. This fragility arises because qubits are highly sensitive to environmental disturbances like noise, temperature fluctuations, and vibrations, which can disrupt their superposition and cause data loss. To mitigate these challenges, qubits are often cooled in specialized dilution refrigerators to fractions of a degree above absolute zero.

From a physical perspective, a bit represents a physical system that can exist in one of two states (0 or 1) based on logical values like True/False or Yes/No. In contrast, *quantum bits (qubits)* are implemented using two-state quantum mechanical systems. Qubits can exist not only in their basic states (0 or 1) but also in superposition, meaning they are simultaneously in both states. For example, (Figure 23.4) illustrates a qubit existing in a superposition of 0 and 1.

This property enables quantum systems to perform parallel computations. For instance, a classical register with three bits can store only one of eight possible numbers at a given time. However, a quantum register with three qubits can store all eight numbers simultaneously in a quantum superposition (Figure 23.5).

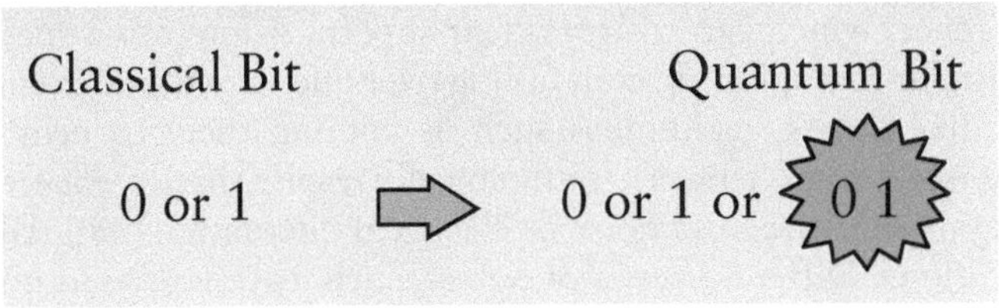

Figure 23.4 Representation of logical values in quantum states.

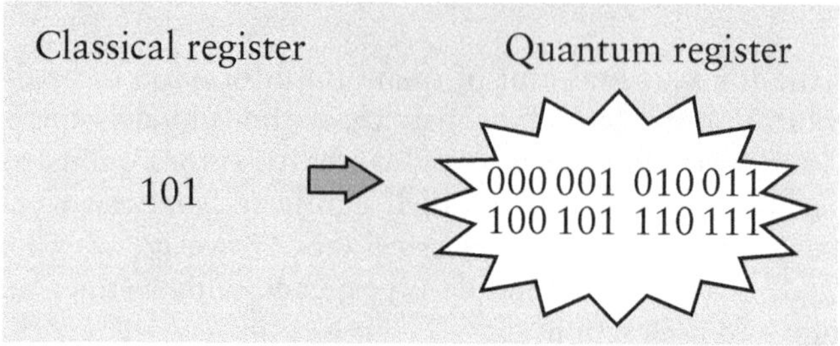

Figure 23.5 Comparison of classical and quantum registers.

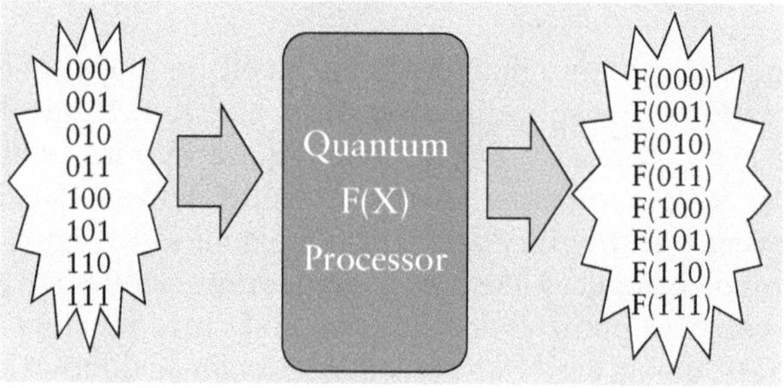

Figure 23.6 Demonstration of a quantum processor.

Once the register is prepared in this superposition, operations can be performed on all numbers at once, as demonstrated in (Figure 23.6). This capability allows a system with N qubits to perform 2^N calculations simultaneously, significantly impacting computational efficiency and reducing execution time.

Quantum operations are described in terms of networks of Quantum Logic Gates, which serve as the building blocks of quantum circuits, much like classical logic gates do for conventional digital circuits [8, 9]. These gates manipulate qubits to perform computations based on quantum principles. However, qubits are fragile due to their susceptibility to environmental interference, which can collapse their superposition into a specific state (0 or 1), similar to a spinning coin falling over due to external disturbances.

To stabilize qubits, techniques such as cooling them to near absolute zero using isotopes of helium are employed. Despite these measures, qubits remain highly sensitive, and noise or electrical fluctuations can still disrupt their operations. Different types of qubits, such as those based on trapped ions or silicon spins, offer various methods of manipulation and entanglement, but they also come with unique challenges.

There are at least six or seven types of qubits, with three or four actively considered for quantum computing. The differences lie in how the qubits are manipulated and how they interact for entangled calculations, which require two qubits to "talk" to one another. For example, some approaches use trapped ions held in a vacuum chamber by laser beams as qubits. However, this method requires expertise in lasers and optics, which companies like Intel are not actively pursuing.

In contrast, companies such as Google and IBM are developing other types of qubits tailored to their quantum computing architectures. The choice of qubit type affects not only how computations are performed but also the scalability and efficiency of the quantum computer.

Quantum computers are more than just their processors. They require an ecosystem of algorithms, interconnects, and software to leverage their immense processing power effectively. The development of robust qubit architectures and systems will enable quantum computers to solve complex problems that are currently beyond the reach of classical computing, marking a significant leap forward in computational capabilities.

Quantum information is processed within *quantum circuits*, which are constructed by arranging *quantum gates* in a specific sequence to execute a particular quantum algorithm. Running these quantum gates results in a *unitary transformation* that acts on one or more qubits. Once the computation is complete, a measurement is performed to determine a classical outcome, typically a 0 or 1. The operations of quantum logic gates used in quantum circuits are based on the following postulates of *quantum informatics* [10–12]:

- **First postulate:** This postulate defines the state space of a quantum system as a state vector, which has unit length and complex coefficients, existing within a *Hilbert space*.
- **Second postulate:** The second postulate states that the evolution of a closed system is described by unitary transformations.
- **Third postulate:** The third postulate links the quantum system's measurements to the classical world, describing how quantum states collapse into classical outcomes upon measurement.
- **Fourth postulate:** The fourth postulate outlines the description of composite quantum systems.

There are numerous quantum algorithms designed to address a variety of practical problems. These quantum algorithms offer the potential for solving certain problems much more efficiently than classical algorithms, leveraging the unique capabilities of quantum computation.

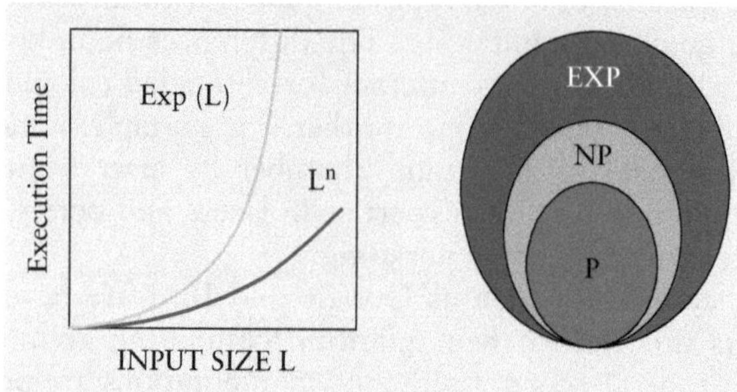

Figure 23.7 Polynomial function representation.

23.3 HOW POWERFUL ARE QUANTUM COMPUTERS?

For an algorithm to be efficient, the time required to execute it must not increase faster than a polynomial function of the input size. For instance, consider the number of bits needed to specify the input to a problem. An example of this is the number of bits required to encode a number for factorization. If the execution time of the best-known algorithm for a problem is bounded by a polynomial function of the input size, the problem belongs to Class P, as shown in Figure 23.7.

Problems outside Class P are categorized as hard problems. For instance, multiplication is in Class P, but factorization is not. In this context, "hard" does not mean "impossible to solve" or "non-computable," but rather that the physical resources needed to solve the problem increase so rapidly with the size of the input that, for all practical purposes, the problem becomes intractable.

However, quantum algorithms have the potential to turn certain hard problems into easier ones. A prominent example is factoring, which is critical in cryptographic technology. If a quantum factoring engine—specialized for factoring large numbers—were built, cryptographic systems like RSA (Rivest, Shamir, and Adelman) would become insecure, as malicious actors could break the encryption effortlessly [13]. This highlights the importance of quantum computing in the realm of cybersecurity.

The difficulty of factorization forms the foundation of the security for widely trusted methods of public-key encryption, particularly the RSA system. This system is commonly used to secure electronic bank accounts, as illustrated in Figure 23.8. Due to the rapid advancements in science and technology in recent years, the performance of communication equipment has significantly improved in terms of efficiency, speed, and latency. These improvements have paved the way for secure and reliable communication using quantum science, as conventional communication methods face a fundamental trade-off between complexity and performance.

Figure 23.8 RSA data security key.

Leveraging the principles of quantum superposition and quantum entanglement, a *quantum communication system* or *quantum network* has emerged as a next-generation communication technique for both terrestrial and extraterrestrial applications. This system offers low latency, high reliability, and constant data flow, even in highly dense networks. A quantum network is composed of multiple distinct nodes, each storing quantum information, and enabling the transfer of information in the form of qubits between physically distant quantum processors. Each processor functions as a miniature quantum computer capable of executing quantum logic gates (operations) on a set of qubits [14].

While quantum factoring has raised concerns about breaking cryptographic codes, quantum computers have many other applications. The recent advancements in artificial intelligence (AI) and the push toward super artificial intelligence (SAI) have created a strong demand for quantum computing in the context of Big Data (BD). Supervised AI, combined with machine learning (ML) and deep learning (DL), allows for the processing of historical data by comparing it with incoming data to support decision-making. Moreover, AI systems can forecast future outcomes, making quantum computing an ideal candidate for improving AI capabilities [14–17].

Quantum computing's impact on AI and the development of next-generation super AI is evident in ongoing research efforts by scientists and engineers. Initially, quantum algorithms focused on security (such as cryptography) or chemistry and materials modeling—problems that are practically intractable for classical computers. However, today, a growing number of papers, start-ups, and academic groups are working on applying quantum computing to machine learning and AI.

Despite the promising potential of quantum computing, Jim Clarke, Intel's Head of Quantum Computing, suggests that conventional chips optimized for AI algorithms are likely to have a more significant impact on AI technology in the short term. However, quantum computing undoubtedly holds promise for the future of AI.

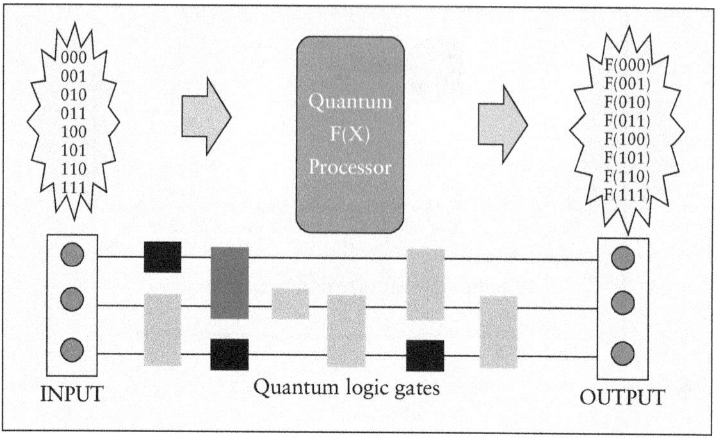

Figure 23.9 A simple quantum logic gate.

23.4 HOW TO BUILD QUANTUM COMPUTERS?

In theory, building a quantum computer begins with constructing basic quantum logic gates (QLGs) and connecting them into quantum networks [18], as illustrated in Figure 23.9. A quantum logic gate, like its classical counterpart, is a basic computational device that performs elementary quantum operations on qubits, typically involving two qubits at a time. However, quantum logic gates differ from classical gates because they can create and manipulate quantum superpositions, as explained earlier. In 2004, the first experimental demonstration of a photon-based quantum-controlled NOT gate was achieved [13]. This innovation used different sets of entangled ancillary pairs of photons and their inherent interactions to develop the gate. This step toward realizing a quantum-based decision-making machine has paved the way for future developments in quantum computation.

A quantum computer operates using *quantum circuits*, which consist of wires and *quantum gates* [10]. Quantum logic gates are essential for coupling qubits, enabling them to achieve entangled states and long coherent states, which are required for quantum information manipulation. The quantum information flows through the wires and is manipulated using these gates. Ultimately, this quantum information is converted into classical information for practical use.

The concept of quantum computation was first introduced in 1980, long before the realization of an actual quantum computer. At that time, it was purely theoretical, aiming to explore the potential limits of computation. The field remained speculative until 1994, when *Shor's algorithm* revolutionized quantum computing by providing a way to factorize large numbers, an operation that classical algorithms struggled with [11]. This breakthrough demonstrated that quantum computers could outperform classical ones in certain computational tasks, paving the way for the feasibility of quantum computing.

Shor was the first to introduce, in 1994, the quantum algorithm required for quantum computation [2, 4]. His quantum algorithm was based on the efficient factorization of large numbers to encrypt messages transmitted over a channel using a quantum *Controlled-NOT* gate. The next significant advancement in quantum algorithms was demonstrated by other researchers [5], who developed probabilistic logic gates and algorithms based on the concept of a polarization beam splitter.

Building upon this, in 1985, David Deutsch published a seminal paper that addressed the challenges involved in creating a quantum equivalent of the Turing machine. His work highlighted critical issues related to the storage (or memory) and processing requirements of a potential quantum computer [12]. This paper marked a major milestone in the development of quantum computing, providing a foundation for future advancements in the field. In addition to photon-based quantum logic and algorithms, another concept has been found useful in the development of logic operations.

In 2005, an approach employing a *cluster state* based on Raussendorf's ideas was reported [18]. Nielsen's approach, which applies to any non-trivial linear optical gate, can pass with a certain probability and influence the calculated measurement when it fails. A logic gate based on optical entanglement, designed with partially polarizing beam splitters, was also proposed [8, 19]. Quantum Process Tomography has also been used to demonstrate that a controlled NOT gate can be operated with both continuous and pulsed signals [8].

In recent years, much of the research has focused on the development of quantum logic circuits and quantum computation. With each passing year, quantum computing continues to uncover new perspectives for applications such as data analysis through high-speed processors, as well as overcoming information security constraints with *blind quantum computing* [10].

Studies have also contributed to the development of a nine-qubit device for error correction applications [11]. From 2013 onward, research has focused on developing quantum logics, with the use of polarized entangled photons as qubits being the most recognized approach.

In practice, it is well known that the input and output for any quantum computer will be classical in nature. Therefore, a fundamental requirement for any quantum computer is the presence of a *quantum algorithm* that can process classical inputs and produce classical outputs efficiently. This ensures the results can be read after quantum or classical processing.

Quantum algorithms typically involve operations for *single-qubit* and *multi-qubit quantum logic gates.* These operations are central to the functioning of quantum computers, allowing them to perform computations that exploit the full potential of quantum mechanical properties

In 2015, researchers [10] introduced a reprogrammable photonic quantum circuit capable of handling up to six photons as input, with a photon detector circuit for logic operations. This advancement provides new pathways for studying a variety of quantum computing applications.

Several reviews focusing on the methods developed during these years have been published [10–12]. The functioning of a quantum computer is based on the processing and manipulation of quantum information [8]. After understanding the memory units of a quantum computer, the next key area to comprehend is the computation methodology used in quantum computing. This involves understanding the types of operations that can be performed to solve problems based on the principles of quantum mechanics.

Quantum logic gates manipulate quantum information and perform operations that transform qubit states. Therefore, understanding logic operations is crucial to grasp how a quantum computer works. Quantum logic gates are classified into two categories based on the number of qubits involved in the operations. Single-qubit quantum gates operate on one qubit, while multiple-qubit quantum gates work with more than one qubit.

An essential characteristic of quantum gates is that they must be invertible, meaning that it is possible to determine the input from the output. This reversibility is fundamental to the operation of quantum computers, ensuring that information can be processed and recovered accurately during computation.

As the number of quantum gates in a network increases, practical challenges arise. The more interacting qubits involved, the more difficult it becomes to engineer interactions that reliably display quantum properties. Additionally, as the system grows in complexity, the likelihood of quantum information escaping the quantum system and being lost to the environment increases, leading to a phenomenon known as *decoherence*. Decoherence occurs when quantum information is disrupted by interactions with the external environment, undermining the computation. Therefore, the challenge in building a quantum computer is to isolate the quantum system from its environment, as interactions with the external world can cause decoherence.

Sources of decoherence include quantum gates, lattice vibrations, and the background thermonuclear spin of the physical system used to implement the qubits. Decoherence is an irreversible process because it is non-unitary and must be carefully controlled or avoided to preserve the integrity of the quantum computation. There are two main approaches to physically implementing a quantum computer: *analog* and *digital*. Analog methods are further divided into quantum simulation, quantum annealing, and adiabatic quantum computation.

Digital quantum computers, on the other hand, use quantum logic gates to perform computations. Both approaches rely on qubits to store and process information [20]. In quantum computing, qubits can exist in superposition, meaning they can represent both the 0 and 1 states simultaneously.

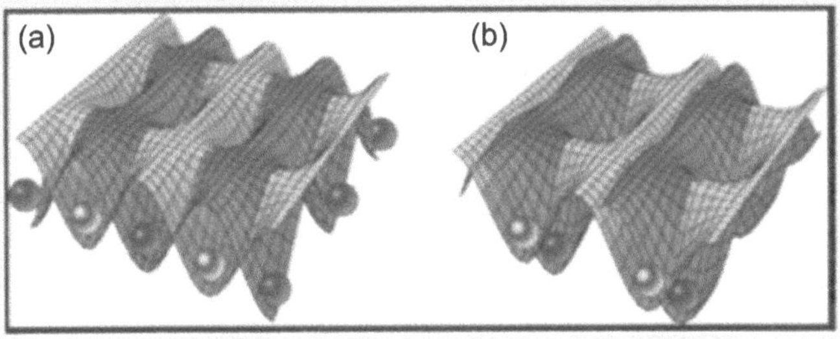

Figure 23.10 Pattern of crossed laser beams.

However, when qubits are measured, they collapse to either a 0 or a 1, with probabilities determined by their state before measurement. Computation is carried out by manipulating qubits using quantum logic gates, which are similar to classical logic gates but with the added capability to manage superposition and entanglement [18].

Despite significant progress, several obstacles remain in constructing practical quantum computers. One of the biggest challenges is maintaining the quantum states of qubits, which are highly susceptible to decoherence. Additionally, quantum computers require substantial error correction because they are much more prone to errors than classical computers. Nevertheless, advances in quantum logic gates involving two qubits are being realized in laboratories, marking significant steps forward. Current experimental systems range from trapped ions to atoms in arrays of potential wells created by intersecting laser beams, as well as electrons in semiconductors (see Figure 23.10).

Looking ahead, the next decade should bring improvements in controlling multiple qubits, and quantum computing will likely begin to show its true potential. Several models of quantum computing exist, including the quantum circuit model, quantum Turing machine, adiabatic quantum computer, one-way quantum computer, and quantum cellular automata. The most widely used model is the *quantum circuit model*, which is based on quantum bits (qubits) that are analogous to classical bits in traditional computation [20].

As quantum technology continues to advance, it holds the promise of transforming computation and enabling new capabilities beyond the reach of classical systems.

23.5 CONCLUSION

The race to build the world's first functional quantum computer is underway, with the goal of delivering on the technology's long-promised potential.

Quantum computers could help scientists create revolutionary new materials, encrypt data with near-perfect security, and even predict changes in Earth's climate. While such a machine may still be over a decade away, tech giants like IBM, Microsoft, Google, and Intel continue to make significant strides, highlighting each incremental step forward. Many of these milestones involve increasing the number of quantum bits (qubits) – the basic units of information in quantum computing – on a processor chip. However, the path to achieving quantum computing involves much more than simply manipulating subatomic particles.

The fundamental question of "When will we see a quantum computer solving real-world problems?" remains unanswered. Just as the first transistor was introduced in 1947, followed by the first integrated circuit in 1958 and Intel's first microprocessor in 1971, quantum computing progress will likely follow a similar pattern of incremental advancements over decades. While there is optimism about the potential of quantum computing, history reminds us that transformative breakthroughs take time. If, in ten years, a quantum computer with a few thousand qubits is operational, it could revolutionize the world much like the first microprocessor did. While some may claim quantum computers are just around the corner, the complexity of the technology suggests otherwise.

It is important to note that any computational problem solvable by a classical computer can also, in theory, be solved by a quantum computer. Similarly, quantum computers adhere to the Church–Turing thesis, meaning that any problem solvable by a quantum computer can also be solved by a classical computer. However, quantum computers are not just about solving problems differently—they offer potential advantages in time complexity. Quantum computers are expected to solve certain problems that classical computers cannot handle in a feasible amount of time, a concept known as "quantum supremacy" [20].

The study of computational complexity in the context of quantum computers is referred to as quantum complexity theory, which explores how quantum computers can outperform classical systems in specific problem-solving domains. As quantum computing continues to evolve, it holds the promise of reshaping computation and enabling solutions that were previously unattainable.

REFERENCES

1. Grumbling, E., and Horowitz, M. (Eds.) (2018). *Quantum Computing: Progress and Prospects.* Washington, DC: National Academies Press, pp. 1–5.
2. Benioff, P. (1980). "The computer as a physical system: A microscopic quantum mechanical Hamiltonian model of computers as represented by Turing machines." *Journal of Statistical Physics*, 22(5): 563–591.

3. Feynman, P. R. (1982). "Simulating physics with computers." *International Journal of Theoretical Physics*, 21(6/7): 467–488.
4. Manin, Y. I. (1980). *Vychislimoe i nevychislimoe* [Computable and Noncomputable] (in Russian). Sov. Radio, pp. 13–15.
5. Nehal, S., Mubasheer, F., and Sunad, Y. S. (2020). "Quantum cryptography – breaking RSA encryption using quantum computing with Shor's Algorithm." *International Journal for Technological Research in Engineering*, 8(1): 22–27.
6. Wikipedia. "Double-slit experiment." https://en.wikipedia.org/wiki/Double-slit_experiment.
7. Greenemeier, L. (2018). "Technology editor of Scientific American, covering a variety of tech-related topics including biotech, computers, military tech, nanotech, and robots." *Scientific American*, Retrieved from https://www.scientificamerican.com/article/how-close-are-we-really-to-building-a-quantum-computer/.
8. Texas Advanced Computing Center (TACC). (n.d.). "Stampede." Retrieved April 7, 2025, from https://tacc.utexas.edu/systems/stampede3/.
9. Nielsen, M. A., and Chuang, I. L. (2010). *Quantum Computation and Quantum Information: 10th Anniversary Edition*. Cambridge: Cambridge University Press.
10. Barenco, A., Bennett, C. H., Cleve, R., DiVincenzo, D. P., Margolus, N., Shor, P., Sleator, T., Smolin, J. A., and Weinfurter , H. (1995). "Elementary gates for quantum computation." *Physical Review A*, 52: 3457.
11. Shor, P. W. (1994). "Algorithms for quantum computation: discrete logarithms and factoring." In: *Proc. 35th Annual Symp. on Foundations of Computer Science*. IEEE Computer Society, Los Alamitos, pp. 124–134.
12. Deutsch, D. (1985). "Quantum theory, the Church-Turing principle and the universal quantum computer." *Proceedings of the Royal Society of London. Series A, Containing Papers of a Mathematical and Physical Character*, 400: 97–117.
13. Zohuri, B., Rahmani, F. M., and Behgounia, F. (2022). *Knowledge Is Power in Four Dimensions: Models to Forecast Future Paradigm with Artificial Intelligence Integration in Energy and Other Use Cases*. Academic Press.
14. Zohuri, B., and Mossavar Rahmani, F. (2020). *A Model to Forecast Future Paradigm, Knowledge Is Power in Four Dimensions* (1st ed.). Apple Academic Press, Taylor & Francis Group.
15. Zohuri, B., and Rahmani, F. M. (2019). "Artificial intelligence driven resiliency with machine learning and deep learning components." *International Journal of Nanotechnology & Nanomedicine*, 4(2): 1–8.
16. Zohuri, B., and Mossavar Rahmani, F. (2020). "Machine learning driving forecasting paradigm." *Acta Scientific Computer Sciences*, 2(4): 19–23.
17. Wikipedia. "Mathematical formulation of quantum mechanics." https://en.wikipedia.org/wiki/Mathematical_formulation_of_quantum_mechanics.
18. Wikipedia. "Quantum logic gate." https://en.wikipedia.org/wiki/Quantum_logic_gate.
19. Wikipedia. "Density matrix." https://en.wikipedia.org/wiki/Density_matrix.
20. Wikipedia. "Quantum computing." https://en.wikipedia.org/wiki/Quantum_computing.

Index

Kolibri 360 GmbH
Ferdinand-Jühlke-Straße 7
99095 Erfurt, Deutschland
produktsicherheit@kolibri360.de